CRE**A**TIVE
HOMEOWNER®

HOME BOOK

THE ULTIMATE GUIDE TO REPAIRS, IMPROVEMENTS & MAINTENANCE

3,300 color photos & illustrations
Over 300 step-by-step projects

CREATIVE HOMEOWNER, 24 Park Way, Upper Saddle River, New Jersey 07458

Editorial Director: Timothy O. Bakke
Art Director: W. David Houser
Production Managers: Ann Bernstein, Stan Podufalski

Senior Editor: Mike McClintock
Associate Editor: Paul Rieder
Assistant Editor: Craig Clark
Contributing Editors: Roy Barnhardt, Joseph Gonzalez, Michael Morris, Ken Textor, Laura Tringali, Bruce Wetterau
Photo Researchers: Craig Clark, Dan Lane, Amla Sanghvi
Editorial Assistants: Laura DeFerrari, Dan Lane, Stanley Sudol
Photo Assistants: Craig Clark, Melisa DelSordo, Christine Elasigue, Dan Lane, Montree Puangsawdi, Keith Zackowitz
Thanks to: Mark Arduino, Juan Calle, Richard L. DeJean, Craig Fahan, Joseph L. Fucci, David Geer, Rafael Lian, Felix Nieves, Andrew Parsekian, Ann Parsekian, James Parsekian, Neil Soderstrom
Indexer: Sandi Schroeder/Schroeder Indexing Services

Senior Designer: Glee Barre
Design Assistants: Virginia Wells Blaker, Susan Hallinan
Senior Photographer: John Parsekian
Staff Photographer: Brian C. Nieves
Staff Illustrators: Vincent Alessi, Clarke Barre
Contributing Illustrators: Tony Davis, Ron Hildebrand, Greg Maxson, Thomas Moore, Ian Worpole
Chapter Paintings: Eileen O'Connell
Cover Design: W. David Houser

Technical Consultants:
Association of the Wall and Ceiling Industries, Intl., Lee Jones
Brick Industry Association, Brian E. Trimble, CDT, Director, Technical Services Engineering and Research
California Redwood Association, Charles Jourdain
Carpet and Rug Institute, R. Carroll Turner
Carrier Corp.
Concrete Foundation Association, J. Edward Sauter, Executive Director
Merillat Industries
National Association of Homebuilders, David DeLorenzo
National Association of the Remodeling Industry, Brett S. Martin
National Concrete Masonry Association, Dennis W. Graber, P.E., Director of Technical Publications
National Oak Flooring Manufacturers Association, Mickey Moore
North American Insulation Manufacturers Association, Charles Cottrell
Plumbing Manufactures Institute, David W. Viola, Technical Director
Plumbing, Heating, Cooling Contractors National Association, Robert Shepherd
Roofing Industry Education Institute, Richard L. Fricklas, Founder
Ross Electrical Assessments, Joseph A. Ross, former Chief Editor of the NFPA-NEC Handbook
Scotts Training Institute, John Marshall, Instructor
Southern Forests Products Association, Richard Wallace
Tile Council of America, Duncan English
Western Wood Products Association, Frank Stewart, Director, Technical & Product Support
Window and Door Manufacturers Association, Alan J. Campbell, President

Printed in the United States of America

Current Printing (last digit)
10 9 8 7 6 5 4 3 2 1

Home Book, the Ultimate Guide to Repairs, Improvements & Maintenance
Library of Congress Catalog Card Number: 00-100566
ISBN: 1-58011-069-X

CREATIVE HOMEOWNER®
A Division of Federal Marketing Corp.
24 Park Way, Upper Saddle River, NJ 07458
Web site: www.creativehomeowner.com

RRD-100M-70#JS-8/00

safety

Though all the designs and methods in this book have been reviewed for safety, it is not possible to overstate the importance of using the safest construction methods you can. What follows are reminders—some do's and don'ts of work safety. They are not substitutes for your own common sense.

◆ Always use caution, care, and good judgment when following the procedures described in this book.

◆ Always be sure that the electrical setup is safe, that no circuit is overloaded, and that all power tools and outlets are properly grounded. Do not use power tools in wet locations.

◆ Always read container labels on paints, solvents, and other products; provide ventilation; and observe all other warnings.

◆ Always read the manufacturer's instructions for using a tool, especially the warnings.

◆ Use hold-downs and push sticks whenever possible when working on a table saw. Avoid working short pieces if you can.

◆ Always remove the key from any drill chuck (portable or press) before starting the drill.

◆ Always pay deliberate attention to how a tool works so that you can avoid being injured.

◆ Always know the limitations of your tools. Do not try to force them to do what they were not designed to do.

◆ Always make sure that any adjustment is locked before proceeding. For example, always check the rip fence on a table saw or the bevel adjustment on a portable saw before starting to work.

◆ Always clamp small pieces to a bench or other work surface when using a power tool on them.

◆ Always wear the appropriate rubber or work gloves when handling chemicals, moving or stacking lumber, or doing heavy construction.

◆ Always wear a disposable face mask when you create dust by sawing or sanding. Use a special filtering respirator when working with toxic substances and solvents.

◆ Always wear eye protection, especially when using power tools or striking metal on metal or concrete; a chip can fly off, for example, when chiseling concrete.

◆ Never work while wearing loose clothing, hanging hair, open cuffs, or jewelry.

◆ Always be aware that there is seldom enough time for your body's reflexes to save you from injury from a power tool in a dangerous situation; everything happens too fast. Be alert!

◆ Always keep your hands away from the business ends of blades, cutters, and bits.

◆ Always hold a circular saw firmly, usually with both hands so that you know where they are.

◆ Always use a drill with an auxiliary handle to control the torque when large-size bits are used.

◆ Always check your local building codes when planning new construction. The codes are intended to protect public safety and should be observed to the letter.

◆ Never work with power tools when you are tired or under the influence of alcohol or drugs.

◆ Never cut tiny pieces of wood or pipe using a power saw. Always cut small pieces off larger pieces.

◆ Never change a saw blade or a drill or router bit unless the power cord is unplugged. Do not depend on the switch being off; you might accidentally hit it.

◆ Never work in insufficient lighting.

◆ Never work with dull tools. Have them sharpened, or learn how to sharpen them yourself.

◆ Never use a power tool on a workpiece—large or small—that is not firmly supported.

◆ Never saw a workpiece that spans a large distance between sawhorses without close support on each side of the cut; the piece can bend, closing on and jamming the blade, causing saw kickback.

◆ Never support a workpiece from underneath with your leg or other part of your body when sawing.

◆ Never carry sharp or pointed tools, such as utility knives, awls, or chisels, in your pocket. If you want to carry such tools, use a special-purpose tool belt with leather pockets and holders.

table of contents

FUNDAMENTALS

INTERIORS

MECHANICALS

See complete Projects listing on pages 6–7.

EXTERIORS

*To find over 300
how-to projects,
turn the page.*

table of projects

inside the Home Book

INTRODUCTION

Welcome to the Creative Homeowner *Home Book*. Think of it as the ultimate owner's manual for your house, a comprehensive guide that you can turn to any time to help you in day-to-day homeownership. After all, you have owner's manuals for other possessions, like your car, so why not your house—your family's shelter from the elements and the biggest investment you're likely to make in your life? You'll find that you can use this book not only to make repairs when things go wrong in the house but to maintain it so that it doesn't lose its value. In fact, you can *improve* your house's value using the right projects in this book.

But your house is much more than a mere shelter and investment. It's your *home*. The heart and hearth of family . . . the place you raise your children . . . the place in which you greet each new morning . . . the place you come to at the end of the day . . . the gathering place for friends and relatives. You want it to be comfortable. You want it to be attractive. You want it to be sound. You want it to run smoothly and efficiently. That's where the *Home Book* comes in. It will help you do all that and more.

Inside, you'll find over 600 pages of helpful information that covers your house from top to bottom, inside and out. We've laid out the full spectrum of home repair and improvement in 28 chapters that cover tools and materials, home remodeling, your yard, and every part of the building, including the foundation, the framing, the mechanical systems—the works.

Home improvement is a big subject, and experienced do-it-yourselfers know it can sometimes be complicated. The *Home Book* helps seasoned homeowners make sense of the subject and further their skills, but you don't need to be an accomplished do-it-yourselfer to use it. You'll find the information you need in sensible text that takes the time to cover the basics. It also offers money- and time-saving tips, explains your options, and shows you what to do using over 3,300 photographs and illustrations.

There are 324 step-by-step projects that run the gamut from simple repairs, such as fixing a stuck window, to major improvements, such as installing replacement windows. In addition, you'll find help with plumbing, heating, cooling, and electrical systems with how-to photo sequences that focus in on the information you need.

The *Home Book* also offers a few special sections that you won't find in most home how-to books, but which cover important aspects of owning a home. One is the Remodeling Guide (page 132), a special photo-illustrated section that covers the ins and outs of contracts, contractors, building codes, payment schedules—everything you need to know to successfully manage your own remodeling project.

And when you come across a special tool or unusual building material in one of the *Home Book's* projects, you can find out more about it in the Resource Guide (page 578), a photo-illustrated index of innovative products, services, and consumer information sources. Of course, we've also provided a glossary (page 590), if you need help with construction terms, and a comprehensive index (page 594) so that you can easily pinpoint the subject you're interested in.

Throughout the *Home Book,* you'll also find reminders on working safely—a key part of any project—and tips that will help you get the best results.

All in all, the *Home Book* is your ultimate guide to how a house works, what you can do to improve it, what can go wrong, and what you can do about fixing it. You're sure to find yourself turning to it again and again as you make your house a home.

Best of luck with your projects.

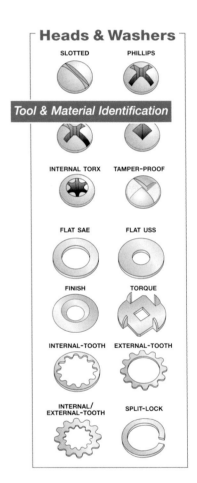

1 *Use a small flat bar* to pry quarter-round trim away from the baseboard. Work slowly from one end to avoid splitting.

main features and other elements

Remodeling Guide

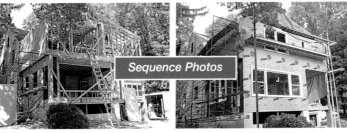

It looks much too big from the outside.

From the inside the rooms seem too small.

Have to pick paint colors by next week.

Sequence Photos

Drain Leaks

To find out whether the sink's drainpipe or drain flange is leaking, pour water into the drain. If water leaks below, the [...] j. If not, [...] ange seal. Unscrew the flange, clean it off, install fresh caulk, and retighten it. Leaks in the drainpipes usually occur in the trap. Some traps have a cleanout nut that makes it easier to clean.

Information Boxes

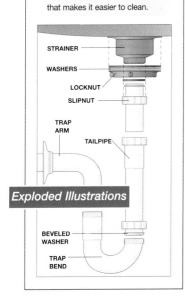

- STRAINER
- WASHERS
- LOCKNUT
- SLIPNUT
- TRAP ARM
- TAILPIPE
- BEVELED WASHER
- TRAP BEND

Exploded Illustrations

Planting & Fertilizing

Color Photos

Diagnosing Surface Problems

Tip Boxes

◆ **BLISTERING:** Blistering can form when paint is applied to a wet surface or in direct sunlight. Moisture migrating outward from inside the wall or in the house itself can also cause paint to blister.

◆ **PEELING:** Peeling can occur when paint is applied in one very thick layer. But the problem is most commonly due to interior moisture working through the exterior wall.

Window Wells

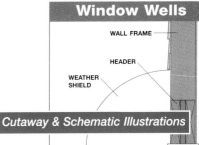

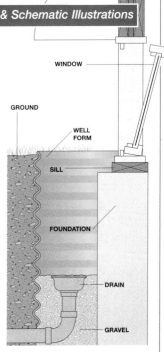

- WALL FRAME
- HEADER
- WEATHER SHIELD
- WINDOW
- GROUND
- WELL FORM
- SILL
- FOUNDATION
- DRAIN
- GRAVEL

Cutaway & Schematic Illustrations

---

marker ▶ thin scrap wood • masking tape

2 *Use the same procedure* to separate top molding from the base. You may need a chisel or second bar for leverage.

3 *Set a thin piece of wood,* such as a shingle, behind the baseboard to avoid marring the wall as you pry.

4 *Some baseboards* may pop off the wall. To remove stubborn nails, set a metal bar between the nailhead and the wall.

5 *With the metal bar in place,* tap the baseboard (on scrap wood) to force out the nailheads so you can pull them.

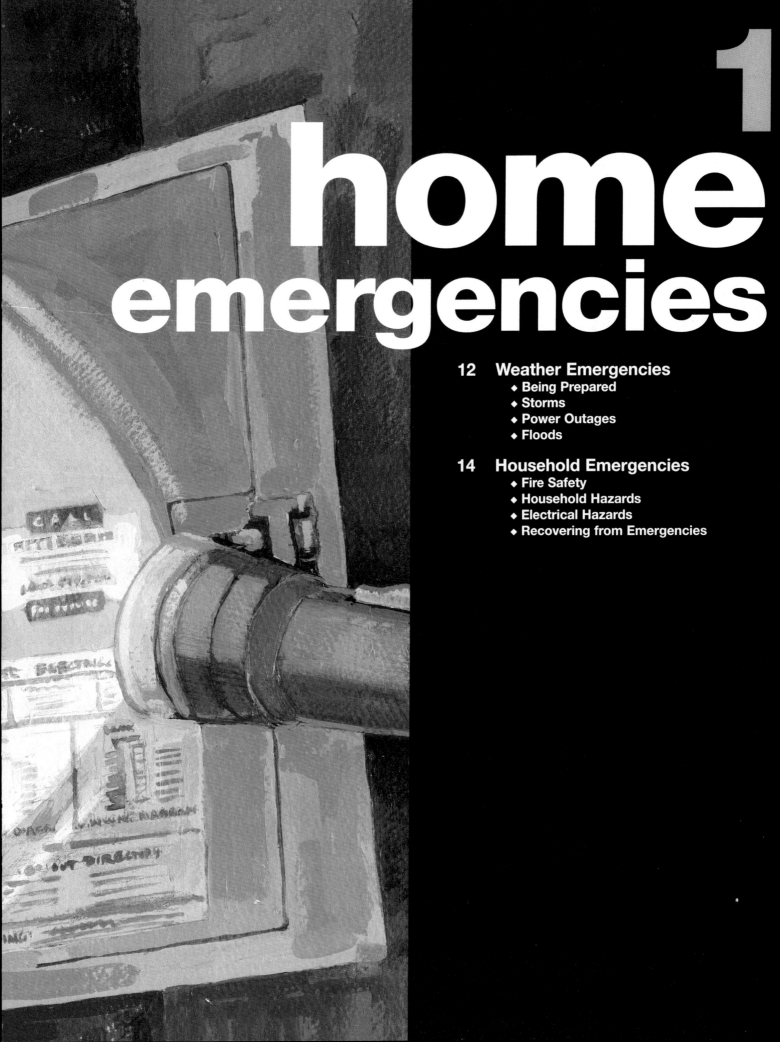

home
emergencies

home emergencies

Being Prepared

Not every emergency can be prepared for, but if you live in an area prone to hurricanes, floods, earthquakes, or tornadoes, you should have basic emergency supplies on hand, and your family should be aware of what steps to take when disaster strikes.

Hurricanes. The National Hurricane Center recommends that those living in low-lying areas have an evacuation plan. Find out about the best routes from your local police or Red Cross chapter. Also plan for emergency communication, such as contacting a friend out of the storm area, in case family members are separated. Listen to the radio or TV for warnings, check your emergency supplies, and fuel the car. Bring in outdoor objects such as lawn furniture, and close shutters or install plywood before the storm arrives. Unplug appliances, cut off the main circuit breaker, and turn off the main water-

supply valve. If time permits, elevate furniture to protect it against flooding.

Tornadoes. Have a place ready where you can take shelter—if you don't have a basement, find a windowless spot on the ground floor, such as a bathroom or a closet under stairs. As tornadoes usually happen with little warning, each family member should know the danger signs, where your emergency supplies are, and what to do in case of a power outage or gas leak.

Earthquakes. If you live in an earthquake zone, have all shelves fastened securely to your walls, and store heavy or breakable items close to the floor. During an earthquake, the safest place in your home (according to FEMA) is under a piece of heavy furniture or against an inside wall, away from windows or furniture that may topple.

Survival Tips. If you plan to ride out a storm, have basic emergency supplies on hand, including flashlights and extra

batteries, a battery-operated radio, first-aid kit, extra nonperishable food and water, and essential medicines. Turn the refrigerator to its coldest setting, and open and close it only when absolutely necessary. Store drinking water in jugs and bottles—and in clean bathtubs.

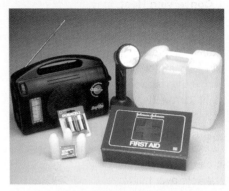

Your basic emergency kit *should include a first-aid kit, flashlights and extra batteries, bottled water, and a portable radio.*

Storms

Severe storms are quantified by their power and the damage they do—like the Richter scale for the force of an earthquake. Hurricanes, for example, are measured according to the Saffir-Simpson scale, which predicts five levels of damage you can expect as storm winds rise from 74 miles per hour (when hurricane warnings are issued) to over 155 mph. Often, it's a combination of wind and rain that causes damage, particularly to roofs.

Temporary Roof Repairs. It's natural to try to patch an active leak but unwise to work on a wet roof in bad weather. There are exceptions: mainly, if the house has a low-sloped or flat roof that you wouldn't roll off even if you slipped. When you can work safely, temporarily stem roof leaks with roof cement (not roof coating). On standard shingles, flashing, roll roofing, and even built-up flat roofs, pry apart the

leaking seam, and fill the opening with the thick tar. Then, push the shingle seam or flashing edge back in place, and add another thick layer of tar on top. If a shingle tab (the exposed section) has blown off, cover the area with tar, particularly exposed nailheads on the shingle layers below, and weave in a cover layer—if you don't have spare shingles, a piece of tarpaper or even a plastic bag will work—to maintain the system of overlapping edges that shed water.

Clearing Bottlenecks. To help prevent damage, it pays to regularly check and clear gutters and downspouts, particularly the S-shaped offset fitting that directs water from roof overhangs back toward the building leader board. These fittings typically are held in place with sheet-metal screws, which you need to remove to gain access for cleaning.

De-icing. To prevent gutters and drains from becoming laden with ice during a winter

storm, you can install UL-approved electric heat cables equipped with built-in thermostats that trigger a power flow when temperatures drop to the freezing point. Once the drainage system freezes, ice dams can form on the roof edge.

An early storm warning *can allow time to pack up essentials and batten down the house with plywood or boards.*

Power Outages

The best way to know what you'll need is to remember what you most missed last time there was an outage. For example, in a house with a well and only a small holding tank, you might miss water more than lights, which can be replaced temporarily with candles.

Conserving Heat. In winter, conserve heat during an outage by making only the quickest entries and exits through exterior doors and opening drapes and blinds to winter sun for solar heat gain during the day. If power goes out at night, drape blankets over windows to provide more insulation. Stay in the warmest room, normally on the south side of the house, and insulate the space from colder areas by hanging blankets over hallways.

Automatic Lighting. To avoid a maddening search for a flashlight with good batteries, use a recharging flashlight. Leave it plugged into an outlet, and when the power goes off, the light will turn on automatically so that you can see where it is. Remove the unit, and use it as a portable flashlight.

Portable Generators. A home generator is handy for an area with frequent power outages or for anyone who relies on electricity for their water or heat. To prepare a generator to run your lights and outlets, have an electrician install a transfer panel at your main service panel (the main circuit-breaker box where electricity enters the house). With this kind of hookup, you can supply limited power through your normal house wiring. Without a transfer panel, you need to string extension cords from the generator and plug the refrigerator, well pump, and a few lights directly into the unit. Remember, never run a gas-powered generator in the house or garage. Its exhaust fumes can be lethal.

Restarts. Before you resume the normal operation of appliances after a power outage has ended, check the manufacturer's restart instructions. Some, particularly older furnaces and water heaters, may require a specific sequence in order to restart safely.

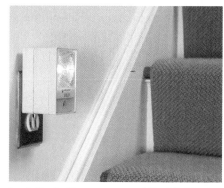

Install a battery-powered flashlight at stairwells. It charges when power is on and lights automatically when power fails.

Floods

The natural impulse after your house is flooded is to remove as much water as quickly as you can. But after a major flood, you should resist the impulse, and drain the water slowly.

Pumping Out Water. The hidden danger is that the ground outside the foundation wall is saturated and pressing against the masonry with the potential force of a mudslide. In extreme cases, several feet of water inside the wall pressing in the opposite direction may be the only thing preventing a collapse. According to the Federal Emergency Management Agency (FEMA), you should wait until water on the ground outside begins to drain away before pumping out the basement. Even then, you should reduce the level only 2 or 3 feet the first day. Remember, don't use a gasoline-powered generator or pump inside the house because it releases deadly carbon monoxide fumes.

Sump Pumps. Check your sump pump; it can prevent major damage from flooding. Many models turn on when a float rises along a wire as water rises in the sump hole. If the sump hasn't kicked in recently, the float can seize in place. Run it up and down a few times to make sure that the sump, and everything else in the basement, won't wind up submerged.

Foundation Repairs. Interior surface patches won't work on foundations because leaks have a wall of water behind them—sometimes massive hydrostatic pressure from a yard of compacted dirt that has turned to mud. But there is one material, hydraulic cement, that has the potential to stem an active leak through masonry. The dense cement mix should be forced into wet cracks, packed in layer after layer, and held in place with a cover board. Even if water continues to flow, the mix will harden and swell as it sets up. If you pack the crack tightly, the swelling mix fills nooks and crannies and can stop the leak.

On many building sites, flood waters from heavy rains can fill basements and rise close to window height.

home emergencies

Fire Safety

The most important fire protection is a working smoke detector. Next is a fully charged ABC-rated extinguisher you can use against any type of home fire. For fireplaces and stoves, use a special chimney extinguisher. Most look like a road flare. You remove a striking cap, ignite the stick, and toss it into the fireplace or wood stove. It can suppress a fire in the chimney by displacing oxygen needed for combustion with a large volume of noncombustible gas.

Smoke Detectors. If your smoke detectors are battery-powered, change the batteries on a set schedule. There are also hard-wired smoke detectors that run off house current (with battery back-ups). Install at least one smoke detector on every level of the home, and one in an open area near bedrooms.

Chimneys. Have a chimney sweep inspect chimneys, even if you use a fireplace only occasionally. Sweeps have the tools to dislodge hardened creosote, a by-product of incomplete combustion that can reignite and start fires. You can make an unlined flue safer with one of the proprietary masonry mix systems that forms a fire-safe shell inside the flue or by running code-approved stainless steel exhaust duct through the chimney.

Extinguishers. Mount extinguishers near points where fires may start—say, one in the kitchen and one at the entrance to the utility room that houses a gas-fired furnace, water heater, and clothes dryer. Check the pressure dials to make sure extinguishers are fully charged.

Escape Routes. For maximum safety, particularly with children in the house, make sure you establish an evacuation plan with two ways out of every room, and walk children through the routes so they know what to do in an emergency.

Emergency Numbers. Post telephone numbers of local fire, police, and emergency services. Use an extinguisher against small, spot fires, but don't try to fight large, developing fires; leave the house, and call the fire department.

Your best protection against property loss and injury from fire is a smoke detector. Push the test button to check it.

Household Hazards

Every year, 27,000 people are killed by poisonings, falls, and other common household accidents. More than 7 million others are seriously injured at home in preventable accidents. "Preventable" means that you can correct the conditions that lead to accidents—for instance, by storing chemicals, medicines, and other potentially hazardous products in locked cabinets where children can't reach them. One million children under five years old are injured by unintentional poisoning every year. You can also prevent the most dire consequences of threats that you can't eliminate—for example, reducing the possibility of being injured in one of the 400,000 reportable home fires every year by installing smoke alarms.

Falling Hazards. Reduce the chance of falling by improving visibility at night with low-wattage night lights near bedrooms, baths, and stairs. Eliminate dark paths to exterior lights with fixtures triggered by timers or motion sensors. Install nonslip mats or tack strips in bathtubs to provide better footing; also install grab bars and handrails. Sand-finish polyurethanes are available for traction on wooden stairs. Brush-finishing concrete improves traction on exterior walks.

Safety Glazing. Be sure that shower doors and all large glass panels in the home are made of safety glass, which pebbles when broken. A safety-glass mark is permanently etched into the lower corner of every panel.

Cutoff Valves. Locate and check the operation of the cutoff valves that control the flow of natural gas or propane to appliances such as furnaces and stoves.

Gas and CO Detectors. As a backup to regular maintenance, install both natural gas and carbon monoxide detectors that can detect leaks of methane and propane. If you smell gas, the safest course is to leave the house immediately and report the leak. All gas utilities provide a 24-hour emergency number.

One easy way to ensure a supply of clean indoor air is to periodically clean heating and cooling equipment.

Electrical Hazards

There are two basic ways to reduce risks when you work on wiring. First, make a circuit map and post it at the main service panel so that you know which breaker to trip. Second, double-check wires and outlets with a neon tester. If the power is off, the tester bulb won't light.

Built-in Shock Protection. Safety is provided from the point where electricity enters the house and through the network of wiring to appliances it powers. At the service panel, there is a main cutoff, usually a double toggle at the top of the box, that shuts off all power. Next in line are individual circuit breakers in rows beneath the main cut-off. Each controls a loop of wiring that services a specific part of the house. Some circuits feed several lights and outlets, while others only a single appliance that uses a lot of electricity like a kitchen range.

GFCIs. More protection against electrical shock is provided by ground-fault circuit interrupters (GFCIs) at electrical outlets that are most likely to produce a shock because they are close to sources of water. GFCI outlets are more sensitive than standard circuit breakers and trip instantaneously. GFCIs are required by the National Electrical Code in all new baths, kitchens, laundries, and exterior outlets. Some electrical appliances, including hair dryers manufactured since 1991, are equipped with appliance leakage current interrupters (ALCIs) or immersion detection circuit interrupters (IDCIs), which give extra protection against shock when an appliance is accidentally dropped in water.

Extension Cords. Permanent wiring systems have many built-in safety features, but extension cords, which are widely used, do not. Check the UL label, and you'll find that there are different types (for inside versus outside use) and different wattage ratings. A standard cord is fine for a lamp with a 100-watt bulb. But plug in a room heater, and the cord can heat up and start a fire. To be safe, the extension cord wattage rating should be 1.25 times the rating of the appliance.

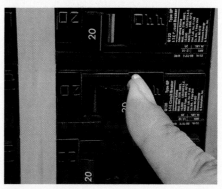

Circuit breakers trip automatically when there is a problem. Reset them once, but if they trip again, call in an electrician.

Recovering from Emergencies

When a severe storm causes damage to your house, you may have to make many temporary fixes, such as covering a leaking roof with a tarp, before the weather improves and you or your contractor can work safely to make permanent repairs.

Temporary Roof Repairs. When you can work safely, use roof cement to stem leaks. It has a thick consistency and won't run on sloped roofs. Use it to fill punctures from tree limbs and to cover nailheads and exposed courses where shingle tabs have been damaged or blown away.

Releasing Leak Reservoirs. To safely release leak reservoirs in a ceiling, put a big basin under the area, and pop the bulge with one small hole away from the center of the bulge. As that hole drains, make another hole closer to the center to release the water gradually.

Clearing Iced Gutters. A propane torch or a heat gun will melt small blockages in frozen gutters. The most drastic solution is to pull frozen downspouts off the wall. Remember, if gutters and leaders are filled with ice, they will be extremely heavy. Once you pry them loose, stand clear, and let them fall like a tree. That way, water trapped on the roof and in the gutter can begin to drain without waiting for the giant icicle in the downspout to melt.

After a Storm. If you return to a damaged home after a storm, enter with caution; beware of animals that were driven to higher ground by flooding. If you smell gas, open a window, leave immediately, and report the leak. If you see sparks or broken electrical wires in a flooded house, do not enter; have the problems fixed by an electrician. Be wary picking through a structurally damaged building. FEMA reports that after one of the most devastating hurricanes of the 1990s (Hurricane Andrew), 18 of the 54 deaths attributed to the storm occurred after the weather cleared, when some people fell in unsafe buildings or were struck by falling debris.

Sometimes a simple job such as heating a frozen water pipe is all you need to do to restore essential services.

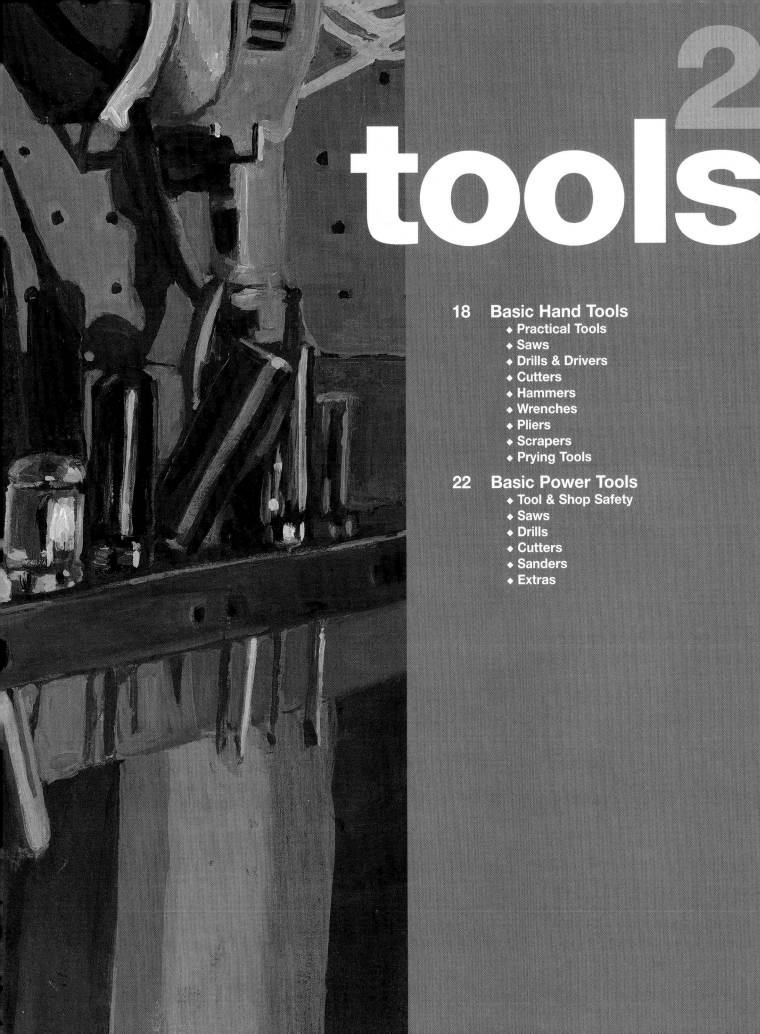

tools²

tools

Practical Tools

Some DIYers need a basement full of tools, while others get by with the basics. It depends not only on the work you want to do but also on how often you use tools, how expert you are at handling them, and how much you want to spend. Here are some of the key points to consider if you're starting or adding to a collection.

Durability. It's nice to buy the best, but the high-priced, long-lasting version often isn't necessary. One example: the throw-away brush, which is fine for slapping some stain on a fence post. Generally, it's wise to buy better quality in tools you'll use often—basics like a hammer and saw, a set of screwdrivers with comfortable handles, or chisels with steel-capped instead of plastic heads. Don't pay top dollar for a tool you rarely use or a very specialized tool that you can rent.

Precision. The truth is that inexperienced do-it-yourselfers don't get professional results by using professional tools. Skill comes from the hand that holds them, not from the tools themselves. Most DIYers should stick with DIY tools instead of the super-heavy-duty professional model designed to run for hours every day.

Strength. Look for hammers, wrenches, and pry bars that are drop-forged instead of cast metal. Casting traps air bubbles in molten metal, creating weak spots that can break under stress. (Cast tools often are painted.) Drop-forging removes more bubbles and makes the metal stronger and safer. When manufacturers take the time and money to drop-forge a tool and machine-grind its surface, they generally leave the metal unpainted.

Feel. Try the tool in the store to see if it feels controllable, too heavy, or too light. It can be difficult to compare tools you can't normally test on the spot, such as power saws—but some tools you can test, such as levels. Check three or four on the store floor or counter, and stack them on top of each other to catch the one whose bubble is out of line with the others. If a tool feels bulky or clumsy in the store, it's likely to feel even worse plugged in and running.

Price. The best bet is to avoid the most and least expensive models. The top end often has more capacity than you need, and the bottom end often has fundamental flaws that make work difficult even for an expert.

Saws

There are specialized trim saws and rip saws, but crosscut saws with 7 or 8 teeth per in. are the most versatile.

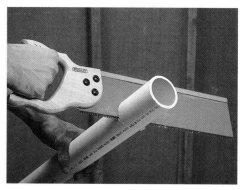

Short, stiff backsaws have fine teeth for detail and trim work. The teeth are not splayed, so the saw kerf is very narrow.

Drills & Drivers

In the basic screwdriver collection, you need a flat tip and a Phillips tip. Two sizes of each will handle most screws.

The nut driver, a pint-sized alternative to a full set of socket wrenches, will handle nuts and boltheads for most appliances.

Cutters

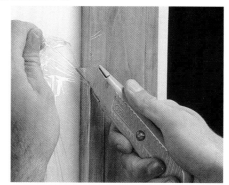

A utility knife handles everything from cutting drywall and batts of insulation to trimming the edges of a door mortise.

You'll need metal-cutting shears to cut the materials a utility knife can't handle, including flashing, downspouts, and more.

The keyhole saw's narrow, pointed blade is handy for making small cutouts. Drywallers use a stubby version to cut openings.

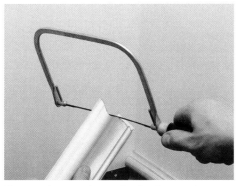

Once a home shop staple, the coping saw now is used mainly to join curved-profile moldings. Modern saber saws do the rest.

The fine teeth of the hacksaw will handle bricks, nails, old pipes, and other materials too tough for wood saws.

Consider two hand-powered alternatives or additions to your ¼-in. drill. The first is a versatile, old-fashioned hand drill.

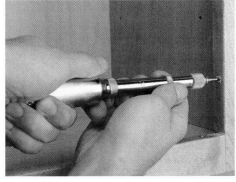

The second, a self-ratcheting drill, turns the bit as you push the handle. It's handy for drilling small pilot holes in wood trim.

A staple gun will come in handy for jobs such as installing insulation and tacking telephone wires.

Handle most woodworking jobs with a ¼-in. chisel and a larger ¾- or 1-in. model. Steel caps stand up under pounding.

A hardened cold chisel can score and cut concrete blocks and bricks. Always wear eye protection when you use one.

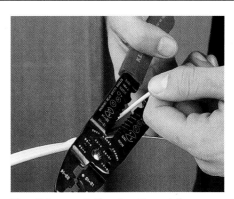

Use this specialized cutter-stripper instead of a utility knife to cut wire and safely strip its insulating sheath.

tools

The Basics

Saws. The most practical handsaw is a crosscut model with a tapered blade about 24 inches long that ends in a big wooden handle. Crosscut saws have 7 or 8 teeth per inch. More teeth make a finer cut but work more slowly; fewer teeth move faster but leave rougher edges. You may also want a backsaw with 12 or 13 teeth per inch to make smooth-edged cuts on trim.

If you prefer power, try a 7½-inch model circular saw. (Size goes by blade diameter.) Look for one with good balance that is easy to adjust for angle and depth, and make sure it has a comfortable handle position that lets you push instead of drag through the work.

Drills. A portable power drill has long been a DIY staple. Now, most are cordless, and some pack 18 volts of power. Among a slew of features and a wide range of power capacities, you will not be disappointed with a ⅜-inch model that reverses, has variable speed (which makes the drill more versatile), and has a keyless chuck. A torque limiter is handy but not essential; it keeps you from ruining screwheads and surrounding wood. It's nice to have one charger and two battery packs so that one is always ready to go, but it's not necessary if you remember to store the pack in the charger instead of the drill. Most DIYers can handle projects and repairs with a 12-volt model, while 14–18 and higher voltages are good for big projects.

Hammers. The most versatile is a curved-claw nail hammer. Many stores offer at least three sizes, determined by weight: 13, 16, and 20 ounces. The governing principle is to use the heaviest hammer you can while maintaining control. More weight drives nails with fewer blows; too much weight causes muscle fatigue and makes it harder to hit nails on the head.

As to handles, ten carpenters will give you ten different reasons why one type is better than another. Wood is durable, absorbs shock, and transmits a good feel for the work. Fiberglass is supposed to be stronger than wood but may provide less feedback. Rubber-covered steel tends to have more rebound than other types—and sometimes transmits the zing of metal on metal. They also can become slippery. If a wood handle gets slippery, try the carpenter's trick of scuffing up the sides of the handle with rough sandpaper or a finishing saw.

Hammers

The basic claw hammer *is the most versatile model for DIY repairs and home improvement projects.*

Use a drop-forged 2-lb. hammer *for heavy-duty jobs such as splitting brick pavers and concrete blocks.*

A sledgehammer, *generally 10 lbs. or heavier for demolition work, is known in the trade as a persuader.*

Wrenches

Use ¼- or ⅜-in.-drive ratchets *for household and automotive jobs. Larger, ½-in. drives are truck tools.*

There are dozens of adjustable *wrench designs, but the classic crescent will handle small and large jobs.*

For heavy-duty plumbing work, *a Stilson wrench with serrated jaws provides the most turning power.*

Pliers

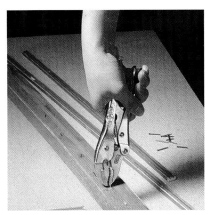

Use locking pliers (such as Vise-Grip or Robo-Grip brands) to securely grab what you're turning.

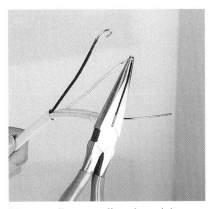

The needlenose pliers is mainly an electrician's tool but is handy for detail work in tight places.

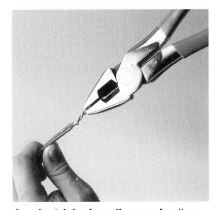

An electrician's or lineman's pliers is the most useful for wiring work. It can twist wires and cut through cable.

Scrapers

Use a scraper to remove paint and old caulk from siding and to prep old surfaces for refinishing.

A sharp block plane is the right tool when you need to trim wood just a little but not enough to use a saw.

For shaping and trimming, use a wood rasp and a metal file. Use a mill bastard file to touch up saw blades.

Prying Tools

Use a pry bar to pry off old moldings and move materials more efficiently than you can with a hammer claw.

One step up from a pry bar is a crowbar, with more leverage for heavy-duty moving and demolition work.

Need to pull out a nail? Drive a cat's paw under the head, and pry it up with minimal damage to the wood.

tools

Tool & Shop Safety

The how-to tools of a first-time homeowner may fit in a kitchen drawer, but the collection of hammer, screwdrivers, and duct tape is bound to grow. Wherever you keep them and use them, consider these measures that can help make your workplace safe.

Hazardous materials. You can read label cautions and safely use hazardous materials, but unless your shop is a separate, locked room, don't assume that everyone else will, particularly children. Protect them by designating one cabinet for dangerous materials. Lock it, and hang the key out of sight high up where only an adult can reach it.

Secured power tools. Most manufacturers build in safeguards, including key-lock start-stop switches. But the best bet is to unplug power tools when you're not using them. Also be sure that your shop wiring is up to code.

Operating power tools. Owner's manuals contain such a long, legal-sounding list, including a few ridiculous warnings, that people don't take the cautions seriously. But there are a few guidelines worth noting. Don't remove built-in and sometimes cumbersome safety features such as a blade guard on a saw. You could wind up hurting yourself, damaging the tool, and voiding the warranty. Make a quick check of high-speed power tools before you turn them on to be sure there is nothing in the cutter path and that adjustment wrenches or chuck keys have been removed. Don't use excessively dull blades, bits, and cutters. They can make wood and other materials chatter and jump unexpectedly—and won't produce clean cuts.

Personal protection. Use appropriate personal protection—for example, safety glasses when cutting hard or splintering materials and a respirator mask when you're doing a lot of power sanding. Don't wear anything loose like a tie (or loose sleeves or jewelry) that can become tangled and pull you into machinery. Include a well-stocked first aid kit as standard shop equipment. And if your shop has stationary power tools and a stock of wood, also install a smoke alarm and an ABC-rated extinguisher that can be used against any type of fire.

Abundant lighting. Install lighting that is more than adequate. It will make your work safer and help you produce better results.

Saws

A 7½-in. circular saw with a combination blade is the most practical model for most DIY building projects.

A reciprocating saw is valuable mainly for demolition work such as removing an old stud wall. It makes rough cuts.

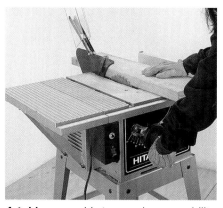

A table saw adds tremendous capability to a home shop because you can rip sheets of plywood and boards to suit.

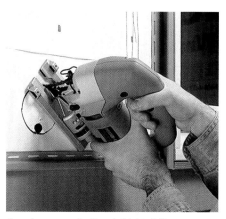

A saber saw is the right tool for many furniture and hobby projects where you need to cut curved shapes in wood.

A power miter saw can be the right choice to increase production if you don't have space for a table or radial-arm saw.

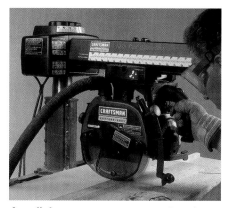

A radial-arm saw can crosscut and, with the cutter rotated, can work as a rip saw to size lumber.

Drills

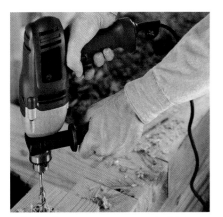

A ¼- or ⅜-in. drill will handle DIY projects, and a cord will save you the trouble of recharging batteries.

Cordless drills are convenient in tight spots. Also consider a keyless chuck that makes bit changing easier.

Cutters

A router can cut dadoes and create decorative edges on your woodworking and furniture projects.

A cutout tool can save a lot of time making holes in drywall or paneling, such as for outlets and lighting fixtures.

Sanders

Depending on the grit of the sanding belt, you can use the sander to remove wood or finish a surface.

A random-orbit pod sander is probably the most practical tool overall for finishing wood surfaces.

Extras

You can't have too many clamps. Among the most versatile are quick-clamps; you just squeeze the handle.

For paint and touch-up work, keep a brush, roller and pan, a pair of drywall knives, and a caulking gun.

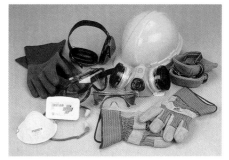

Basic safety equipment is a must, including work gloves, safety glasses, and a respirator mask.

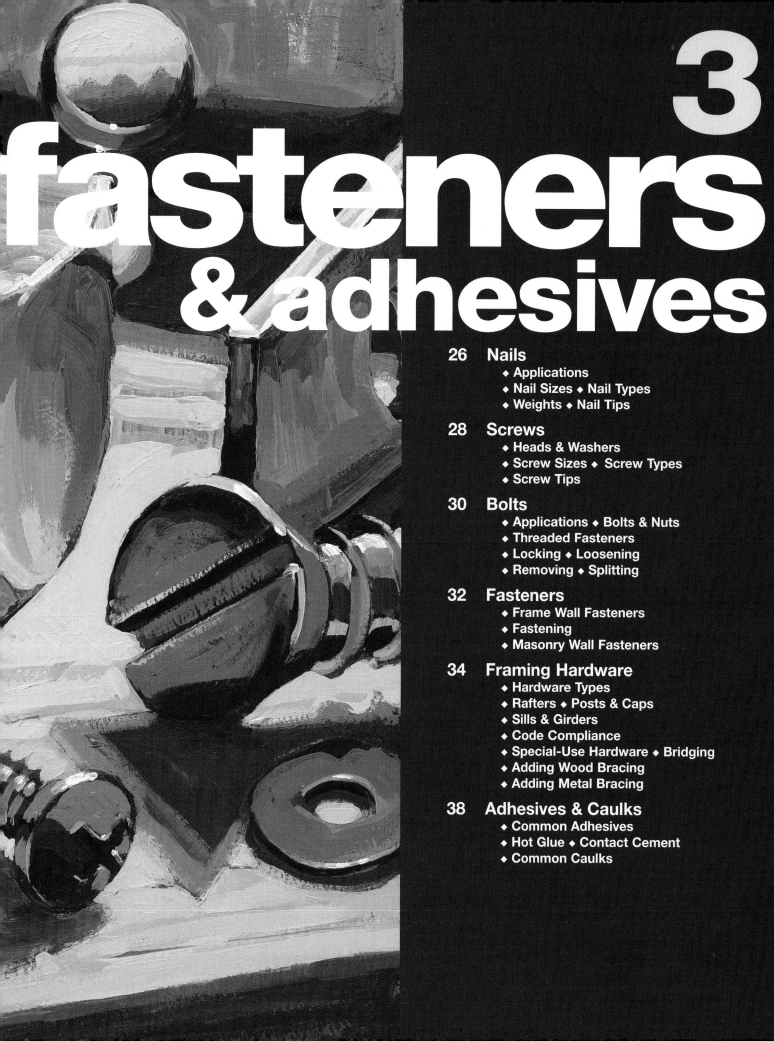

fasteners

& adhesives

3

fasteners & adhesives

Applications

Pound for pound, nails are probably the least expensive, most available, and easiest fasteners to use for all manner of construction. There are many different shapes and sizes, and more than one way to use most of them. Spend some time on a few different construction sites, and you'll find that one carpenter will toenail a stud with an 8d (eight-penny) nail, while another will start a little higher on the stud and use a 10d nail. In general, of course, there are finishing nails for trim, common nails with large heads and increased holding power for framing, and several other types for specialized purposes, such as concrete nails for when you need to connect wood to masonry.

For DIYers working on home repairs and improvements, the best bet is to keep a small supply of several types on hand. You can buy a handful of the most common types or choose a prepackaged kit. If you need to buy nails in quantity for a project, be prepared for the slightly confusing practice of ordering nails by pennyweight (notated by the small letter d) instead of by length. For example, if you want 3-inch common nails for framing, standard procedure is to order 10d nails by weight. The chart on p. 27 gives a general guide as to how many nails you get per pound.

Nailing Specs

As a rule, it's wise to use the largest possible nail. The larger the nail, the more holding power you get. But using too large a nail can cause two problems. First is splitting, particularly where the thick shank of a nail is driven close to the end of a board. The other problem is that sharp points may protrude through boards. That won't decrease the strength of the connection but could cause an accident during construction. For example, if you are spiking together two 2x10s to make a header, the sharp points of 10d (3-inch) nails could poke through because the header is just 3 inches thick. You could angle the nails slightly, or use 8d (2½-inch) nails instead. But if you are building the header with a ½-inch plywood spacer between boards, 10d nails will suit. Nailing specs are rarely listed on plans or blueprints, but a building inspector is likely to spot inadequate nailing on site.

Nail Sizes

Nail Types

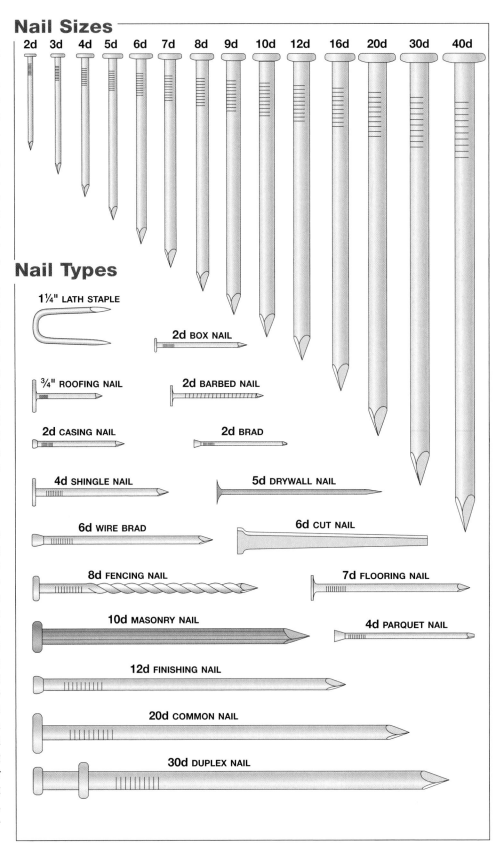

2d — 3d — 4d — 5d — 6d — 7d — 8d — 9d — 10d — 12d — 16d — 20d — 30d — 40d

1¼" LATH STAPLE

2d BOX NAIL

¾" ROOFING NAIL

2d BARBED NAIL

2d CASING NAIL

2d BRAD

4d SHINGLE NAIL

5d DRYWALL NAIL

6d WIRE BRAD

6d CUT NAIL

8d FENCING NAIL

7d FLOORING NAIL

10d MASONRY NAIL

4d PARQUET NAIL

12d FINISHING NAIL

20d COMMON NAIL

30d DUPLEX NAIL

Weights

Type of nail	Nails/lb.
3d box (1¼")	635
6d box (2")	236
10d box (3")	94
4d casing (1½")	473
8d casing (2½")	145
2d common (1")	876
4d common (1½")	316
6d common (2")	181
8d common (2½")	106
10d common (3")	69
12d common (3¼")	63
16d common (3½")	49
2d roofing (1")	255
6d roofing (2")	138

SAFETY

Pneumatic tools used by DIYers and professionals have built-in safety features. The most important is a lock-out device that won't let you fire the tool unless the head is firmly against a board. Still, these tools require maximum caution.

Air-powered nailers have a clip of banded nails that feed into the gun and fire with a trigger squeeze.

Nail Tips

Toenailing

Start your nail at an angle, up an inch or so from the joint. As the tip goes in, steepen the angle slightly.

In some cases, driving a toenail may be the only fastening option—it's also a good way to move a nailed board over slightly.

One-Hand Nailing

When you don't have the helper or the extra clamps you need, try this carpenter's trick of one-hand nailing.

Hold the head squarely against the side of your hammer to set the point; then grab the handle and drive the nail home.

Cat's Paw Pulling

Remove nails with minimal damage to surrounding wood by driving the forked end of a cat's paw under the nailhead.

Rotate the cat's paw handle to raise the nailhead, and finish pulling it out with the claw of your hammer.

fasteners & adhesives

Heads & Washers

SLOTTED

PHILLIPS

COMBINATION

SQUARE

FREARSON

TAMPER-PROOF

INTERNAL TORX

CLUTCH

FLAT SAE

FLAT USS

FINISH

TORQUE

INTERNAL-TOOTH

EXTERNAL-TOOTH

INTERNAL/
EXTERNAL-TOOTH

SPLIT-LOCK

Screw Sizes

2 3 4 5 6 8 10 12 14 16

The numbers for screws, unlike penny numbers for nails, refer not to length but to the thickness of the shank; #10 screws can have different lengths but will have the same shank thickness.

Screw Types

FLATHEAD WOOD SCREW

MACHINE SCREW

HANGER BOLT

ROUNDHEAD WOOD SCREW

SHEET-METAL SCREW

OVALHEAD WOOD SCREW

DOWEL SCREW

DRYWALL SCREW

PARTICLEBOARD SCREW

LAG SCREW

SCREW EYE

SCREW HOOK

CUP HOOK

SWAG HOOK

GATE HOOK & EYE

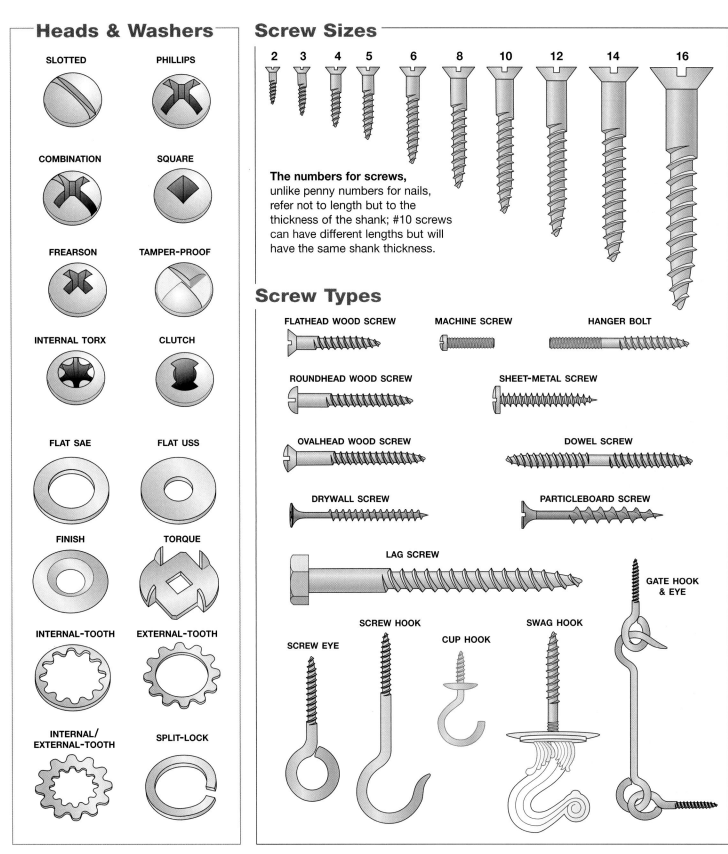

Screw Tips

Holders

Cordless electric drill/drivers have become a standard DIY tool. They're good for drilling but sometimes hard to control driving screws. That's where an extension holder will help. These tube-shaped attachments fit into the drill chuck and can be fitted with different driving tips. To keep the tip engaged and drive screws in a straight line, the tube extends over the screw head and along its shank. The tube withdraws as you seat the screws.

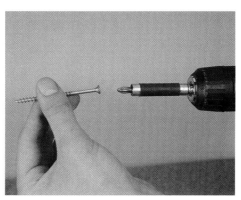

Tighten the driver attachment in the drill chuck, and fit one of the interchangeable driving tips onto the screwhead.

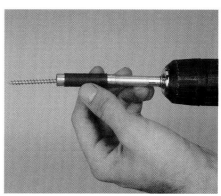

You can let go of the screw because the driver head is magnetized; then, slide the guide tube over the shank.

Countersink

A countersink is a shallow, conical hole that allows a screwhead to sit flush in the wood surface. This is a standard feature of screwed connections, and typically requires two bits—and a time-consuming bit change every time you drive a screw. First, you need a pilot hole for the screw shank. Second, you need a countersink for the screw-head. Countersink bits do both jobs in one pass. You can adjust drilling depth with a collar on the bit.

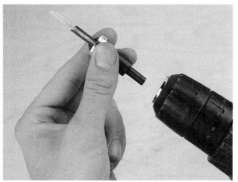

A combination bit has a blade tip that carves a hole for the screw and a secondary cutter to make a countersink.

Most countersink bits have an adjustable collar so that you can control the depth and size of the recess.

Extract

When you need to remove a screw and the turning slot is damaged or stripped bare, most DIYers resort to a pliers. Sometimes you can grab just enough metal to start backing out a screw. When you can't, use a screw extractor bit. The idea is to bore a small hole in the screwhead, and turn in a specially spiraled extractor bit that tightens when you turn it to the left instead of to the right. Once it seats, continue turning to back out a stuck screw.

To extract a screw with a damaged head, drill a pilot hole in the head. Its diameter should match the extractor bit's diameter.

You can turn the extractor bit with a drill or by hand. When its reverse threads take hold, the damaged screw backs out.

fasteners & adhesives

Applications

On most DIY repairs and improvements around the house, you'll use nails and screws instead of bolts and nuts. But there are a few places where the extra strength of bolts is valuable. One is along the foundation where there is a critical change in materials from masonry to wood. The great weight of the building should be enough to keep the sill, typically a 2x6, in position. But to prevent any shifting on top of the concrete or blocks, it is standard practice to attach the sill with long, J-shaped anchor bolts instead of nails, screws, or other kinds of fasteners. The bottom of each bolt is embedded in solid concrete, and the threaded end is attached to the sill with a washer and nut.

Also consider bolted connections on decks to secure posts and railings—another location where you can't afford to have loose screws or nails that might give way. You can use roundheaded carriage bolts with large washers to permanently pin 2x4 or 4x4 posts to the solid framing of the deck platform. Recess the nuts and washers for improved appearance.

Fine Threads

The difference between standard threads and fine threads is significant in some applications—for example, where you need maximum holding power between metal components in cars. If you want the highest possible strength on critical projects, fine threads provide it by creating more interlocked surfaces between male and female threads.

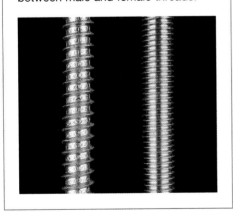

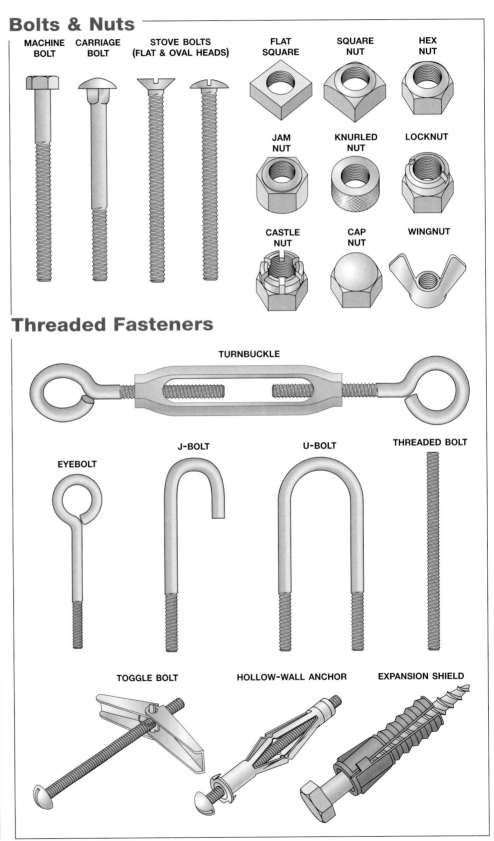

Bolts & Nuts

MACHINE BOLT CARRIAGE BOLT STOVE BOLTS (FLAT & OVAL HEADS) FLAT SQUARE SQUARE NUT HEX NUT

JAM NUT KNURLED NUT LOCKNUT

CASTLE NUT CAP NUT WINGNUT

Threaded Fasteners

TURNBUCKLE

EYEBOLT J-BOLT U-BOLT THREADED BOLT

TOGGLE BOLT HOLLOW-WALL ANCHOR EXPANSION SHIELD

Locking

In most cases you can tighten nuts enough with a wrench or ratchet. But on installations subject to regular use and vibration, such as garage door tracks, there are two ways to add security. One: coat bolt threads with an adhesive agent such as Locktite. (You can untighten the nut later if need be.) Two: coat the nut with silicone caulk, which also helps prevent corrosion.

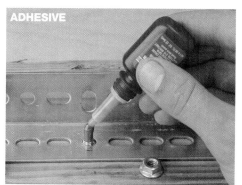

ADHESIVE

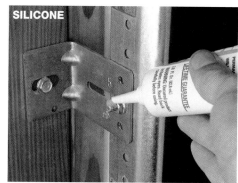

SILICONE

Loosening

Some nuts and bolts won't come apart no matter how much leverage you apply, particularly if the connection is rusted. In those cases, try breaking the corrosion with a penetrating lubricant. Another option is to break the rust bond by impact, with one hammer below the nut so the bolt won't bend, and another striking from above.

OIL

TWO HAMMERS

Removing

When lubricants and hammering won't budge the nut off a bolt, remove it with a hacksaw. Instead of trying to saw through the bolt shank (and possibly damage the surface underneath), cut through one of the facets on the nut. This weakens the nut enough so that you can twist off the remaining section with a wrench.

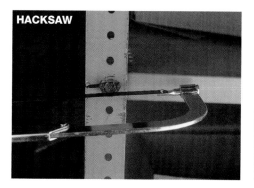

HACKSAW

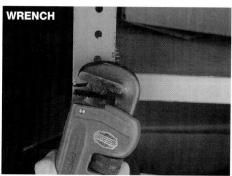

WRENCH

Splitting

As a last resort, you can free a frozen nut—the kind you might find on a rusted bracket or license plate—with a nut splitter. First, fit the head of this hardened tool over the nut and tighten down its splitting wedge by hand. Then, use a wrench or ratchet to drive the wedge into the side of the nut. This pressure will crack the nut.

SPLITTER

CUT

fasteners & adhesives

Frame Wall Fasteners

TOGGLE BOLT

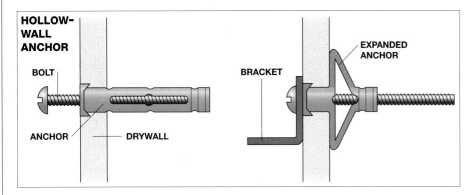

PREDRILLED HOLE
EXPANDED TOGGLES
TOGGLES
BOLT
BRACKET
DRYWALL

HOLLOW-WALL ANCHOR

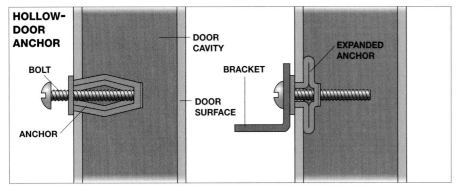

BOLT
EXPANDED ANCHOR
BRACKET
ANCHOR
DRYWALL

HOLLOW-DOOR ANCHOR

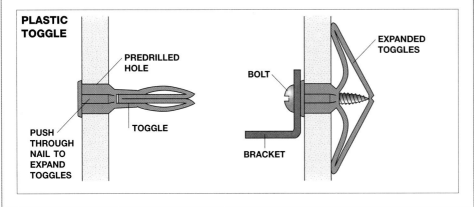

DOOR CAVITY
EXPANDED ANCHOR
BOLT
BRACKET
DOOR SURFACE
ANCHOR

PLASTIC TOGGLE

PREDRILLED HOLE
EXPANDED TOGGLES
BOLT
TOGGLE
BRACKET
PUSH THROUGH NAIL TO EXPAND TOGGLES

Fastening

Your standard ¼-in. drill will handle most drilling and fastening jobs. But for wood, an old fashioned brace and bit provides good control on slow-speed drilling, and a hand-cranked rotary drill does the same on smaller holes. A compact, ratchet-action pin drill is handy for drilling pilot holes in moldings. There are many options when it comes to drilling holes for fasteners in masonry.

AUGER

ROTARY DRILL

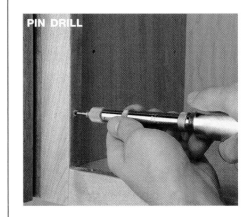

PIN DRILL

For drilling by hand, use a star drill and hammer, rotating the tip of the tool with each blow. With a drill, use masonry bits that have a wide carbide tip to do most of the cutting. For maximum production, use a hammer drill. It has a cam that drives the bit back and forth into the masonry with a hammering action as it rotates. It's important to wear eye protection, particularly when drilling in masonry.

STAR

BIT

HAMMER DRILL

Masonry Wall Fasteners

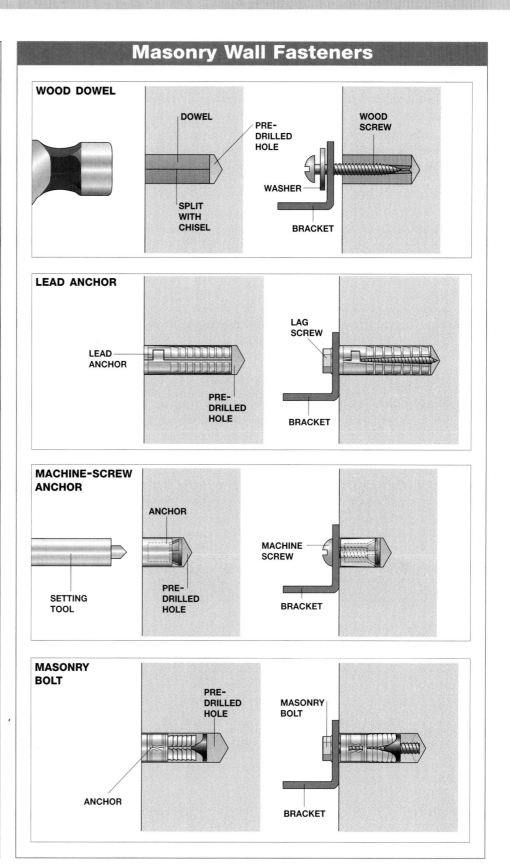

WOOD DOWEL

DOWEL
PRE-DRILLED HOLE
WOOD SCREW
SPLIT WITH CHISEL
WASHER
BRACKET

LEAD ANCHOR

LAG SCREW
LEAD ANCHOR
PRE-DRILLED HOLE
BRACKET

MACHINE-SCREW ANCHOR

ANCHOR
MACHINE SCREW
SETTING TOOL
PRE-DRILLED HOLE
BRACKET

MASONRY BOLT

PRE-DRILLED HOLE
MASONRY BOLT
ANCHOR
BRACKET

fasteners & adhesives

Hardware Types

How much strength does your house really need, and how much protection does it pay to build in against storms? In a theoretical design for a nuclear power plant off the coast of New Jersey, the U.S. Army Corps of Engineers built in protection against the worst storm that could be anticipated in 1,000 years—a double hurricane producing 50-foot waves. It's not economically practical for homeowners to anticipate such freak events. But there are ways to make a building more storm-resistant, particularly in regions where hurricanes and tornadoes are common.

Corner Bracing

After corner posts are plumbed, add let-in bracing. A 1x4 runs from the top of the corner down at approximately a 45-degree angle across several studs to the bottom of the wall frame. Cut a series of pockets (¾ inch deep) so the brace will sit flush with the outside of the wall. Installing two let-in braces angled away from each corner will tie walls together and strengthen the corner.

Rafter Bracing

Use a similar system to strengthen the outermost rafters in a roof. Diagonal bracing, or 2x4 blocking (wide side down), can be set at approximately 45 degrees between the outside rafter near the top and bottom of the rafter run. These braces provide more resistance to move-ment and may keep high winds from raising the roof edge and getting into the attic where it can push up at the entire frame.

Tie-Down Strapping

Most buildings are not designed to deal with an uplift force. They rely on gravity and the weight of construction materials, pinned together with nails, to hold them down, which is more than enough in most areas most of the time. But you can easily build in extra protection by adding tie-down straps at critical connections: where rafters join the walls and where walls join the foundation.

Several manufacturers offer metal hardware preformed to fit around different framing combinations—for instance, a wing-shaped piece called a ridge strap, which fits across the top of a ridgeboard with two extensions that fasten along the rafters on either side. The hardware is prepunched. You just set it in place, and then nail through the holes.

Stirrups

The most common construction hardware is a U-shaped bracket, often called a joist hanger, or stirrup. It makes framing connections stronger, for instance, where deck framing joins a ledger along the house wall. Hardware also speeds construction. You can nail up all the hangers, drop joists into the U-shaped pockets, and nail through the prepunched holes to secure them.

Rafters

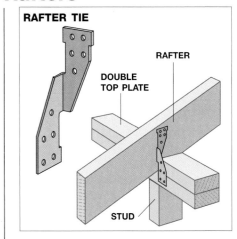

RAFTER TIE

RAFTER

DOUBLE TOP PLATE

STUD

Posts & Caps

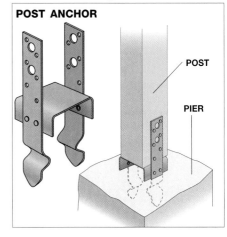

POST ANCHOR

POST

PIER

Sills & Girders

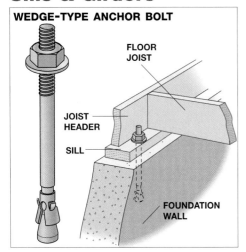

WEDGE-TYPE ANCHOR BOLT

FLOOR JOIST

JOIST HEADER

SILL

FOUNDATION WALL

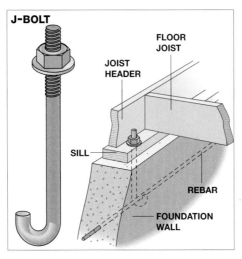

J-BOLT

FLOOR JOIST

JOIST HEADER

SILL

REBAR

FOUNDATION WALL

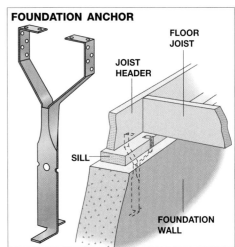

FOUNDATION ANCHOR

FLOOR JOIST

JOIST HEADER

SILL

FOUNDATION WALL

HURRICANE TIE

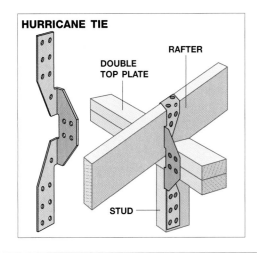

DOUBLE TOP PLATE

RAFTER

STUD

RAFTER CLIP

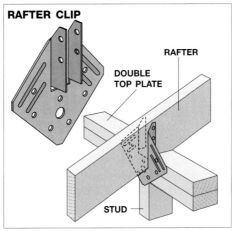

RAFTER

DOUBLE TOP PLATE

STUD

RIDGE STRAP

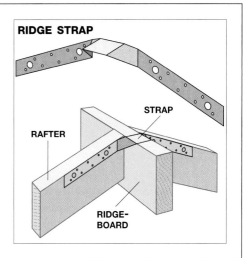

STRAP

RAFTER

RIDGE-BOARD

POST ANCHOR WITH BOLT

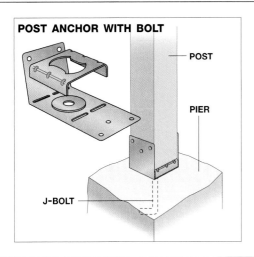

POST

PIER

J-BOLT

POST BEAM CAP

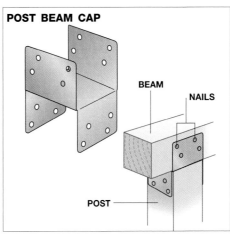

BEAM

NAILS

POST

POST BOLT CAP

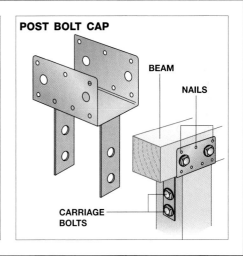

BEAM

NAILS

CARRIAGE BOLTS

FOUNDATION STRAP

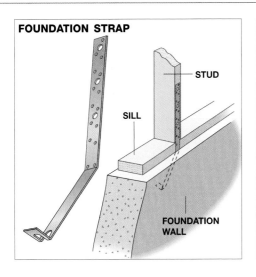

STUD

SILL

FOUNDATION WALL

TOP-MOUNT HANGER

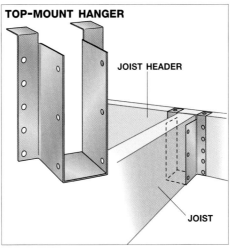

JOIST HEADER

JOIST

TOP-MOUNT MASONRY HANGER

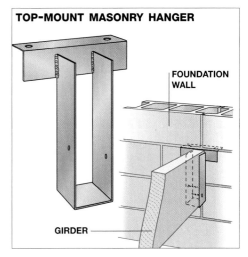

FOUNDATION WALL

GIRDER

Code Compliance

The building inspector is unlike other housing professionals on a major remodeling or construction project. He can come and go at will, call a halt to work if he sees something wrong, and make you or your contractor peel off siding or drywall that may have been installed prematurely without his okay.

There are cases where inspectors seem to go overboard and insist on details, such as the number of nails in a sheet of drywall, that do not impact on safety. But overall, the inspection process provides a valuable double-check of your plans, and oversight of your contractor.

You might not be on site when the walls are clad with drywall and the details of framing and insulation vanish from sight. But at key stages of the project, an inspector will get a look before important components such as the foundation, framing, and insulation are hidden. It's important to remember that you have to schedule these inspections and give the inspector some advance warning. In the middle of a busy building season, it may take a few days to get the inspector on site. In some regions, you may also deal with more than one inspector, even though one person handles most of the oversight work. For example, you may deal with one inspector who specializes in septic systems, and another who handles wiring.

If you build without a permit or manage to conceal features such as an extra lavatory during construction, you could save on permit fees and reduce increases in your real estate assessment. But you could be in for trouble later on. A future inspection could uncover the non-permit work and make you liable to fines. Your home insurance might not cover damages to work found to be done illegally. And you could have problems when it comes time to sell your house and the current footprint doesn't match the one on record at the town tax office.

Special-Use Hardware

NAIL PLATE

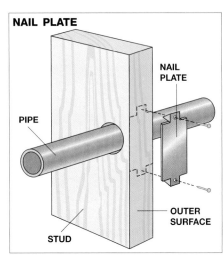

NAIL PLATE

PIPE

OUTER SURFACE

STUD

TRUSS PLATE

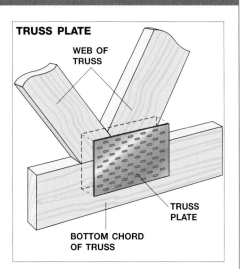

WEB OF TRUSS

TRUSS PLATE

BOTTOM CHORD OF TRUSS

DECK NAILER

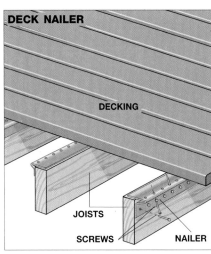

DECKING

JOISTS

SCREWS   NAILER

GAZEBO ROOF TIE

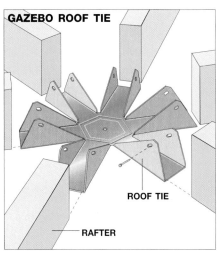

ROOF TIE

RAFTER

Adding Wood Bracing

USE: ▶ circular saw • wood chisel • hammer

Tack a 1x4 at an angle across the studs near the corner. Mark along the edges of the brace where it crosses the studs.

Adding Metal Bracing

USE: ▶ chalk-line box • circular saw • hammer

Many DIYers will find metal bracing easier to install than wood bracing. Start by snapping a chalk-line guide at the corner.

Bridging

Bridging is a standard feature of most floor construction. There is some controversy about how much it actually helps to stiffen the structure. But even a floor with large joists and plywood decking seems a little more secure when the joists are secured to each other with bridging. The traditional braces are short pieces of the joist material set at midspan. But you can use other systems instead. The most common is an X-pattern of wooden 1x3 or metal strapping nailed to the tops and bottoms of each joist. Connectors called Z-clips are used to anchor braces between I-joists.

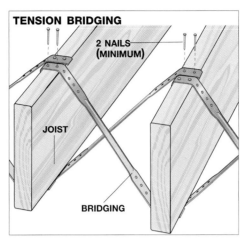

TENSION BRIDGING

2 NAILS (MINIMUM)

JOIST

BRIDGING

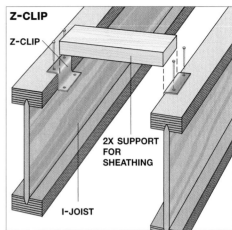

Z-CLIP

Z-CLIP

2X SUPPORT FOR SHEATHING

I-JOIST

• pencil • eye protection ▶ 1x4 bracing • nails

Set your saw to cut ¾-in. deep *(the thickness of the brace), and cut along the two sets of pencil marks.*

Use a hammer and chisel *to remove the wood between cuts and form a recess for the brace. Extra sawcuts make the job easier.*

Set the 1x4 brace *back in position, this time nailed into the recesses of each stud, to stiffen and strengthen corners.*

• eye protection ▶ metal bracing • nails

As you do with wood bracing, *set your saw to cut only as deep as the brace, and make one cut along the chalk-line guide.*

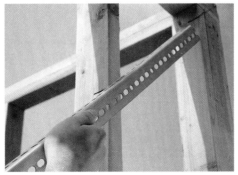

Metal let-in bracing *is L-shaped. You simply set one edge into the straight line of cuts angled from the corner to the sill.*

The metal bracing is perforated, *so it's easy to nail it in place at each stud. Installing two braces strengthens corners.*

Common Adhesives

White Glue Also known as PVA or polyvinyl acetate, and perhaps best known by the brand name Elmer's Glue-All, white glue is the one kind of adhesive most people keep around the house. It's useful for making quick repairs to furniture, woodwork, ceramics, and paper. Because it's water-soluble, never use it in a place that might get wet.

- ◆ **Solvent:** soap and warm water
- ◆ **Curing:** sets in 1 hour, cures in 3–8 hours

Yellow Glue Often called carpenter's glue or aliphatic resin, yellow glue is a good general-purpose woodworking glue. Like white glue, it dries clear and is often used to repair furniture and indoor woodwork. It sets more quickly than white glue, usually within an hour. Also like white glue, it isn't waterproof and shouldn't be used outside.

- ◆ **Solvent:** warm water
- ◆ **Curing:** sets in 1 hour, cures in 3-8 hours

Acrylic Acrylic adhesives come in two parts—either powder and liquid, which must be mixed before use, or liquid and paste, which must be separately applied to the opposing surfaces being joined. Acrylic is used for quick-bonding adhesion of metal, glass, and wood. It is waterproof and dries to a light brown color.

- ◆ **Solvent:** acetone
- ◆ **Curing:** sets in 5 minutes, cures overnight

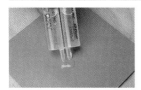

Epoxy Epoxy is particularly good for joining together dissimilar materials, such as glass to metal. It's also useful for bonding ceramics, wood, and many other materials. Epoxies come in tubes, in syringes, or as a mixable putty. It provides a very strong bond, is waterproof, and dries clear to brownish.

- ◆ **Solvent:** acetone
- ◆ **Curing:** set times vary widely, cures 3–72 hours

Hide Glue Hot hide glue is prepared from granules (made from animal hides) and water. You can adjust its curing time, making it useful for complex projects such as kit furniture. It has superior strength, a powerful grip when setting (handy for gluing veneer). Joints won't "creep" once they dry, and dry glue can also be "reactivated" with steam. Premixed hide glues are also available.

- ◆ **Solvent:** warm water
- ◆ **Curing:** set time varies with formula, cures in 24 hours

Resorcinol Resorcinol is an extra-strong adhesive particularly adaptable to laminating wood, making outdoor furniture, and boatbuilding. It will cure at 70°F and up, but no lower. It is available in a liquid with a separate (usually powdered) catalyst—just mix up the amount that you need. It is waterproof, very durable, and dries to a dark red.

- ◆ **Solvent:** cool water
- ◆ **Curing:** sets and cures in 10 hours at 70°F, 6 hours at 80°F

Cyanoacrylate Most commonly known as super glue (or by the brand name Krazy Glue), this is a powerful, fast-curing adhesive that can be used to bond most metals, plastics, ceramics, vinyl, and rubber; the gel form of the glue can be used on wood. It is water-resistant and dries clear. Always use extra caution not to get any on your skin.

- ◆ **Solvent:** acetone
- ◆ **Curing:** sets in 10–30 seconds, cures ½–12 hours

Construction Adhesive Sometimes called mastic adhesive, this is used to bond wood and concrete. Many brands also can be used on acoustic tile and other materials. While not a substitute for thorough nailing, it can improve the overall strength and rigidity of face-to-face connections—for example, where you sister one joist onto an existing joist. It can be spread with a notched trowel but is commonly applied with a caulking gun from a tube.

- ◆ **Solvent:** usually mineral spirits
- ◆ **Curing:** sets in 15 minutes to 1 hour, cures in 4–24 hours

Hot Glue

Glue guns are excellent for home-improvement projects because they dispense a versatile range of adhesives that bond quickly. The solid glue or caulk cartridges are heated and melted in the gun. Once dispensed, the glue usually sets within one minute.

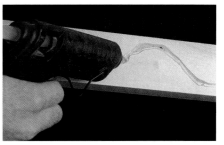

Contact Cement

To bond plastic laminate and wood—on a countertop, for example—use contact cement. A full coat is spread on each piece and allowed to dry until it feels dry but tacky. Use wood strips to keep the components from bonding until they are in position.

Common Caulks

Acrylic Latex Acrylic latex caulk (slightly longer-lasting than similar, cheaper vinyl latex) is inexpensive and easy to apply, but degrades in direct sunlight and adheres poorly to porous surfaces.
- ◆ **Drying skin:** ½ hour ◆ **Curing:** 1 week
- ◆ **Life:** 5–10 years

Butyl Also called butyl rubber, this caulk has better adhesion and stretching ability than acrylic, but costs more and takes longer to cure. It also degrades in sunlight.
- ◆ **Drying skin:** 24 hours ◆ **Curing:** 6 months
- ◆ **Life:** 5–10 years

Use a utility knife to trim an angled opening in the cartridge tip.

Polyurethane Polyurethane caulks are expensive and more difficult to apply than latex and butyl, but they last longer, can cover a wider gap (up to ¾ inch), and will stretch further.
- ◆ **Drying skin:** 24 hours ◆ **Curing:** 1 month
- ◆ **Life:** 20+ years

Silicone Silicone—not to be confused with paintable siliconized acrylic—has good stretching ability and can cover a 1-inch gap, but it can't be painted and adheres poorly to plastic and wood.
- ◆ **Drying skin:** 1 hour ◆ **Curing:** 1 week
- ◆ **Life:** 20+ years

To keep adhesive from hardening in the tip between jobs, insert a common nail.

masonry 4

masonry

Handling Materials

A rustic-looking rock wall for the garden, a flagstone patio, curving brick walkway, or much-needed retaining wall can do wonders for the appearance of your yard. When used as part of an overall landscape design, masonry adds a touch of permanence and solidity. Ditto for more down-to-earth uses, such as foundations and floors, except here it's truly essential. Laid properly, concrete and block foundations will last for a lifetime—and more—with little or no maintenance.

The reason masonry looks so solid is that it really is. If you've never picked up a concrete block or mixed an 80-pound bag of cement before, you're in for a surprise. The stuff is heavy—and the larger the project, the more weight you have to deal with. The bending and lifting that always come with masonry projects can easily get to your back and shoulders if you are not careful, so break the job up into manageable chunks. Wear a lower-back support if you need to, and always lift with your legs, not your back. Remember that cement is caustic and will burn your skin after prolonged contact. Wear sturdy work gloves, a long-sleeved shirt, and rubber boots (because you may have to stand in the wet mix to spread it).

Excavation

Moving dirt is the one part of improvement projects that just about everyone underestimates. The work is messier, more expensive, and more time-consuming than it seems beforehand. On big jobs, such as excavating a foundation for a patio, you will probably need to hire a backhoe.

Save your energy on small jobs by loosening dirt with a pick before removing it with a shovel. If you're digging a hole for concrete footings, try to leave the bottom undisturbed. If the soil seems soft, compact it with a metal tamper or by pounding it with the end of a 2x4. A concrete footing poured over soft, uncompacted fill will settle, and so will anything resting on it, such as a foundation wall.

Moving Dirt

Unless you're looking for exercise, it's wise to move the dirt as little as possible. Before you dig, decide where the leftover dirt will go in the end—into a flower bed or a low spot that puddles in heavy rain. You could load dirt straight from the hole into a wheelbarrow, and take breaks from digging with the comparatively easy work of carting each load away.

After the concrete is poured and it's time to backfill your excavation, add dirt in stages, tamping to compress the loose fill as you go. Though it's always tempting to bury construction debris in the backfill, have it carted away instead. It's okay to fold in rocks or chunks of concrete, but not wood, paper, and other biodegradable job scraps, for two reasons. First, wood and paper make excellent termite food, and you don't want to be spreading appetizers around the house. Second, as the material biodegrades, the dirt above gradually compresses and fills in the space, creating a water-catching trench around the foundation or pier.

Handling Heavy Loads

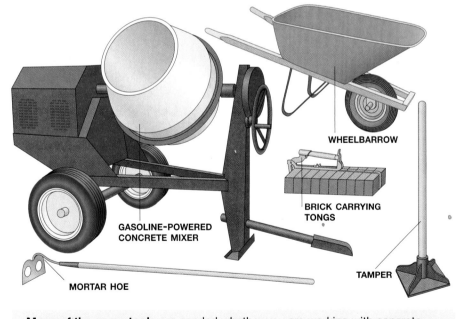

WHEELBARROW

BRICK CARRYING TONGS

GASOLINE-POWERED CONCRETE MIXER

MORTAR HOE

TAMPER

Many of the same tools are needed whether you are working with concrete, brick, or stone. Often you can rent tools such as these, so check before buying a tool you may not use that often. Some tools—such as wheelbarrows, shovels, and hoes—you probably already own.

Weights

◆ **Concrete**
  Plain: 90-144 lbs./cu. ft.
  Lightweight: 35-105 lbs./cu.ft.
  Reinforced: 111-150 lbs./cu. ft.
  1-inch slab: 6-12 lbs./sq. ft.
  Ready-mix: 50-96 lbs./bag. An 80-lb. bag + water weighs near 100 lbs.

◆ **Brickwork**
  4-inch-thick wall: 40 lbs./sq. ft.
  Mortar: 116 lbs./cu. ft.
  Bricks: about 3–5 lbs. each

◆ **Concrete Block**
  8-inch-thick wall: 55 lbs./sq. ft.
  8-inch-thick wall (lightweight): 35 lbs./sq. ft.

◆ **Stone (ashlar)**
  Granite: 165 lbs./cu. ft.
  Limestone: 135 lbs./cu.ft.
  Marble: 173 lbs./cu.ft.
  Sandstone/bluestone: 144 lbs./cu. ft.
  Slate: 172 lbs./cu. ft.

Safety Gear

GLOVES **GOGGLES**

DUST MASK

Always wear a dust mask, gloves, and protective eyewear when mixing masonry products or cutting bricks, blocks, or concrete. Prolonged contact with caustic cementitious materials can also cause irritation, so protect skin with gloves and rubber boots.

Special Tools

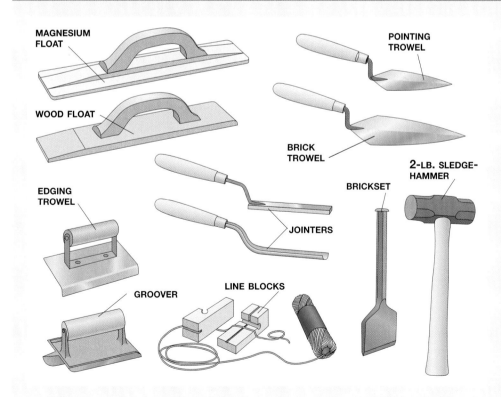

MAGNESIUM FLOAT

WOOD FLOAT

EDGING TROWEL

GROOVER

LINE BLOCKS

POINTING TROWEL

BRICK TROWEL

JOINTERS

BRICKSET

2-LB. SLEDGE-HAMMER

Important tools for concrete-block construction include a line level and line blocks. Mason's twine is strung between line blocks and checked with the line level to help you keep a structure straight, level, and plumb.

Concrete finishing tools include a bull float to level and smooth the surface of wet concrete, an edging trowel to separate concrete from its forms, a wood or magnesium float to apply a smooth finish, and a steel finishing trowel for a final pass. An edging trowel also creates a rounded edge that is safe and durable. A jointing or grooving trowel is used to form control joints.

In brickwork, a brick hammer and brick set are used to split bricks, while various other tools are used to make different profiles in brick mortar joints. (See page 55.)

masonry

Concrete Basics

Fresh concrete is a semifluid mixture of portland cement, sand (fine aggregate), gravel or crushed stone (coarse aggregate), and water. As the cement chemically reacts with water (a process called hydration), the mix hardens to stonelike consistency. Properly mixed and cured concrete creates strong structures that will weather the extremes of summer heat and winter cold with little maintenance.

Formwork and steel reinforcement are needed to build concrete structures. Formwork is generally made from wood, and may be a simple square or complex shape. Reinforcing steel (most often reinforcing bar, or rebar) can be light or heavy, depending on size and strength requirements. Welded or woven wire mesh is also used to reinforce concrete slabs on grade.

Mixing Concrete

For large-scale projects such as a patio, concrete is sold by the cubic yard and delivered in a ready-mix truck ready to pour. For smaller jobs—say, steps for the patio—you can mix your own, by purchasing dry ingredients in bags and adding water. But don't get too ambitious: One wheelbarrow-sized batch is less than 3 cubic feet. You would need about nine batches to make just one cubic yard. For mid-sized jobs, it makes sense to rent a portable power mixer.

You may be tempted to adjust the mix proportions—say, by adding more water to make the concrete easier to mix and pour. However, as water content can drastically affect strength, the best policy is to order concrete ready-mixed or follow directions on the dry ingredient bags.

The standard proportion of water to cement produces concrete with a compressive strength of about 3,000–4,000 pounds per square inch (psi). Adding less water makes mixing more difficult but increases concrete strength. Concrete that dries too quickly can be a problem, however.

Even the best mix may dehydrate in hot weather, robbing the concrete of the water it needs to harden. In extreme cases, a steady hot, dry breeze can even accelerate evaporation so that the masonry surface begins to set before it can be smoothed. Concrete begins to harden as soon as it is mixed, and can support your weight within a few hours. Most of the curing takes place in the first two weeks, but it takes a month to reach maximum hardness.

There are some solutions for extreme cases, such as adding flaked ice or cooling down the aggregates with a sprinkler before adding them to the mix. To eliminate the risk of wasting your efforts on a job that doesn't last, don't pour in temperatures over 90°F; if you must, start very early in the morning to beat the heat.

It's also important to remember that hot surfaces contacting the mix can burn off moisture. For instance, it's wise to spray some cool water on forms that are sitting in the sun, as well as on the reinforcing bar, which can get quite hot to the touch.

Pouring a Patio

USE: ▶ broom • compactor • darby • edging trowel • float trowel • jointing trowel • line level • mason's hoe • mason's string • measuring tape • rebar chairs • screed

1 *Your crew may not bring one this big,* but most jobs begin with a bulldozer that cuts away the sod and levels the ground.

2 *Once the perimeter is established* and the forms are in place, the ground should be compacted.

3 *To strengthen the concrete,* welded wire is laid near the bottom of the slab, generally on short supports called chairs.

44 **masonry**/concrete

Testing Concrete

- **A typical mix** is 11% portland cement, 26% sand, and 41% crushed stone, plus 16% water and 6% air.

- **If concrete is too wet,** ridges made in the mix with a trowel won't hold their shape.

- **If concrete is too dry,** you won't be able to make ridges, and it will be difficult to work.

- **When mixed correctly,** the ridges will hold most of their shape; only a little water will be visible.

Ready-Mix

There are several advantages to ordering ready-mixed cement, aside from the fact that you don't have to mix yards of the stuff by hand. The chute can extend and swivel to pour concrete where it's needed. Ready-mix trucks can deliver concrete at temperatures that make it possible to pour during a heat wave. Also, ready-mix concrete is available with an additive that produces microscopic air bubbles in the mix—air-entrained concrete that is more resistant to cracking than the concrete you can mix on site.

Estimating

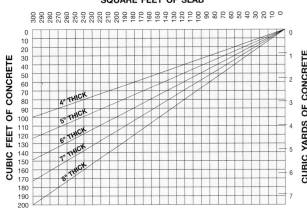

CONCRETE COVERAGE CHART

SQUARE FEET OF SLAB

CUBIC FEET OF CONCRETE

CUBIC YARDS OF CONCRETE

4" THICK
5" THICK
6" THICK
7" THICK
8" THICK

To figure out how much concrete to mix or order, use the chart at left; or, total up the volume inside the forms in cubic feet (length x height x width); then, divide this figure by 27 to convert into the ordering standard of cubic yards. Some contractors build in a reasonable excess factor of about 8% by changing the conversion factor to 25.

• shovel • sledgehammer • wheelbarrow ▶ concrete mix • double-headed nails • formboards • gravel • stakes • welded or woven-wire mesh

4 **As concrete pours** from the ready-mix truck, a straightedge guided by a screed board on each side levels the mix.

5 **The rough surface left by screeding** can be smoothed with a float or textured with a broom finish for better traction.

6 **Control joints** that prevent cracking can be formed into the pour, although some crews cut them after the mix hardens.

masonry

Placing Concrete

Steel reinforcement helps control the cracking associated with the natural shrinkage of concrete as it dries. The two basic types are rebar (reinforcing bar) and welded or woven wire mesh. Rebar ranges in size from ¼ to 1 inch in diameter, and is ridged for a better bond with the concrete or smooth for nonbonding control joints. Rebar is stronger than wire mesh; use it for concrete that will carry a heavy load, such as footings and piers. Wire mesh is made from steel wire in a grid of squares and is sold in rolls and mats. Use it in flat slabs on grade, such as patios and walks. Cut wire mesh with fencing pliers, and flatten it out before use. Fill large areas by overlapping sections of mesh by at least 3 inches and tying them with wire.

Avoiding Problems

Pouring the concrete is a simple matter; the crucial stage begins as the mix sets and begins to cure. Curing is a long-term process during which concrete continues to gain strength. If raw concrete is left exposed to the wind and sun, it may dry too quickly and may not attain half its potential strength. You could still walk on it, but the slab would be likely to crack.

Tooling control joints into the surface of concrete slabs helps make settling cracks break at planned locations. Control joints weaken the concrete surface, causing cracks to occur at the bottom of the joints, where they are inconspicuous and will not spread.

Edging & Jointing

Edging is tooled into fresh concrete as soon as the water sheen disappears after the first floating. Run an edging trowel along the entire perimeter of a slab. Control joints can be hand-tooled into fresh concrete with a jointing trowel, cut into cured concrete with a circular saw fitted with a masonry blade, or (usually with isolation joints) preformed with fixed divider strips of hardboard, cork, rubber, plastic, or felt paper.

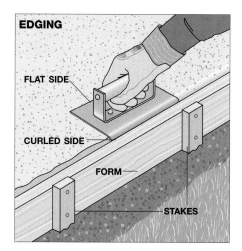

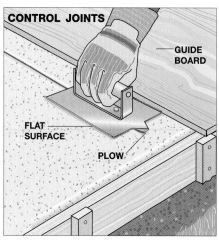

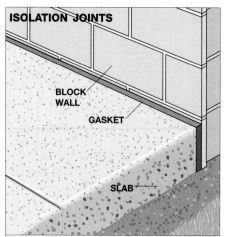

Forming a Curved Corner

USE: ▶ C-clamps • hammer • saw • screw gun or drill driver • small sledgehammer ▶ common nails • 1x4 or 1x6 boards • ¼-inch plywood • screws • 2x4 stakes

1 *To make a curved form,* use a flexible material, such as thin hardboard, that you can bend in a large radius.

2 *Center the hardboard in the corner,* clamp the ends in position, and secure them to the forms with screws.

3 *A flexible form* needs at least one supporting stake to prevent the radius from distorting when concrete is poured.

Reinforcing

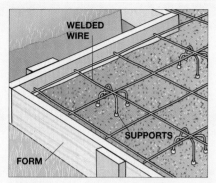

Welded wire mesh must be fully embedded in concrete for maximum strength. Supports called chairs hold it off the ground.

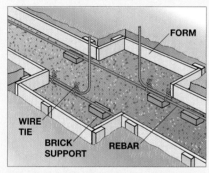

Short sections of reinforcing bar turned up into the foundation at each corner will add support to pilasters on a brick or masonry wall.

Diagnosing Problems

Crazing—many minute, shallow cracks—is caused by over-floating. The surface should be cleaned and sealed to stop further crazing, or entirely resurfaced for a permanent fix. Spalling is also the result of overfloating, and indicates faults in the concrete—requiring resurfacing. Oxidizing iron causes rust-colored stains; these can be cleaned with a solution of oxalic acid crystals, water, and ammonium bifluoride. Always wear a mask when mixing an acid solution.

CRAZING

OXIDATION

SPALLING

Repairing Cracks

USE: ▶ broom • bucket • cold chisel • garden hose • putty knife • masonry trowels • small sledgehammer • wire brush ▶ concrete patch • polyethylene sheet

1 To make the most secure patch in concrete, use a cold chisel to undercut the surface on each side of the crack.

2 To ensure that your patch material bonds with the old concrete, wire-brush and dust out the crack.

3 Use a trowel to force cement into the undercut areas; then, fill the remaining gaps, trying to match the surrounding surface.

masonry

Building with Block

Concrete block, like lumber, is not really the size it's labeled. A standard 8x8x16-inch block is actually $7\frac{5}{8}$ x $7\frac{5}{8}$ x $15\frac{5}{8}$ inches, allowing for the $\frac{3}{8}$-inch-thick mortar joints. Blocks consist of an outside shell with a hollow center that is divided by two or three vertical webs. The ends of a unit have flanges that accept mortar and join with the adjacent block (except blocks intended for corners and the ends of walls). There are many types of blocks, such as solid, load-bearing, and non-load-bearing. Heavier blocks are made with sand, gravel, and crushed stone mixed with cement; lighter blocks have lighter aggregates, such as coal cinders.

Building with masonry block can be taxing. Standard concrete blocks weigh more than 40 pounds each. It's difficult enough to sling one of the rough-surfaced blocks up into position, but it's even tougher when you have to lower it gingerly onto a bed of mortar.

Ties, Flashing & Reinforcement

Most structures are single-wythe—the thickness of a single row of blocks. Multiple wythes of masonry must be tied together with header bricks, cap blocks, and metal ties. Masonry flashing (made of metal, rubberized asphalt, or other material) is used to control moisture by keeping the top of the wall dry. To laterally reinforce joints between wythes, place wire wall ties in the mortar beds at 16 inches on center vertically; foundations and pilasters require rebar to strengthen them.

Cutting Block

Usually you can get by with store-bought, preformed half-sized blocks, but there may be times when you need to cut a slightly smaller or larger partial block. Concrete block, like all other types of masonry, often does not break smoothly. Scoring the block, as shown here, helps improve the odds of getting an even break when using a hammer and brickset. But if you plan to cut even a few, order extra.

You can cut through concrete block with a circular saw, but only if it has a special masonry blade.

To cut a block by hand, score each face with a brickset, making several passes with light pressure along each cut line.

You can keep scoring until a piece breaks free, or turn the block on edge and apply more force to the brickset.

Laying Block

USE: ▶ bricklayer's hammer • brick trowel • brickset • jointing trowel • line level • mason's twine • pointing trowel • spirit level • work gloves ▶ concrete block

1 *To embed the first course* of concrete blocks, trowel on a liberal amount of mortar in two rows under the block edges.

2 *Carefully level the block,* particularly on the first few courses. Use the end of your trowel to make small adjustments.

3 *You may want to build* from one end of your wall to the other; masons often build up a few courses at the corners first.

Estimating

For standard 8x8x16-in. concrete block, calculate 113 blocks per 100 sq. ft. of wall area and add 10% for breakage. For mortar, figure 8.5 cu. ft. per 100 sq. ft. of wall area. A contractor would order the components separately and make the mix on site, but to keep your proportions accurate, buying mortar premixed makes more sense.

Mortar Types

Type M—A high-strength mortar for masonry walls below grade and walls subject to high lateral or compressive loads or severe frost heaving.

Type S— A medium-high-strength mortar for walls requiring strength to resist high lateral loads.

Type N—A medium-strength mortar for most masonry work above grade.

Type O—A low-strength mortar for interior nonbearing partitions.

Type K—Low-strength lime-sand mortar used for tuck pointing.

Concrete Blocks

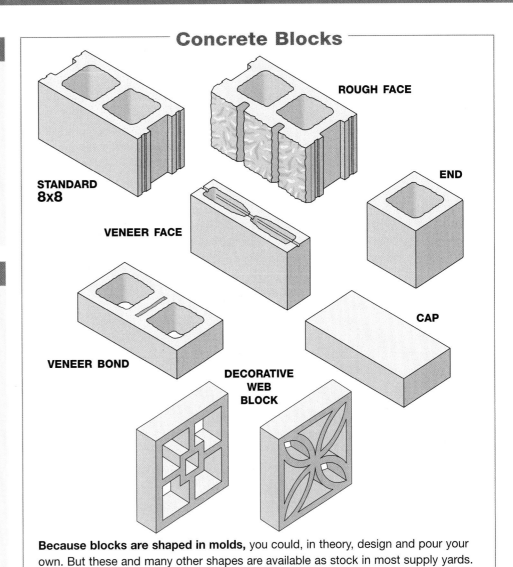

STANDARD 8x8

ROUGH FACE

VENEER FACE

END

VENEER BOND

DECORATIVE WEB BLOCK

CAP

Because blocks are shaped in molds, you could, in theory, design and pour your own. But these and many other shapes are available as stock in most supply yards.

• mortar mix • steel reinforcing bars • truss-type horizontal joint reinforcement

4 **Masons** can toss the right amount of mortar in the right place; you may want to form the mortar bed one small bit at a time.

5 **After spreading mortar** on the final course of full-size blocks, finish the wall with cap blocks.

6 **Use a jointing tool** to smooth the mortar into a water-shedding, slightly concave shape.

masonry

Repairing Block Walls

Usually, the first repair you'll need to make to a block structure will be repointing—using fresh mortar to replace mortar joints that have failed. (This process is the same for brick; see "Maintaining Mortar" on page 54.) Other simple cosmetic repairs to a block structure involve reinforcing a damaged area with a patch of repair compound, or coating the block with paint, stucco, or mortar.

Foundation Wall Repairs

If a block or brick foundation has cracked and chipped on the surface but is still structurally sound, there are several repair options, including repointing the mortar joints, replacing badly chipped units, and covering with stucco. (See "Patching Stucco" on pages 58–59.) If the bricks or blocks don't wobble in and out of line too much, you can use ½-inch pressure-treated plywood or foamboard to bridge the nooks and crannies that let in water and moisture. Even small openings can eventually ruin the foundation's appearance and sap its strength.

To make a complete seal and create a neat line near the ground, clear away enough dirt so the bottom few inches of the new covering can be buried, and tuck the upper edge into a liberal bed of caulking below the house siding. Although pressure-treated wood will resist rot, you might refill the small trench with gravel to encourage drainage before replacing the top layer of sod. The only tricky part of this simple operation is nailing the covering panels into the brick. Get an assist by lacing the backs of the covering panels with construction adhesive, then use several hardened masonry or cut nails to lock each sheet in place. Nailing into the mortar between bricks is easiest, if you can gauge the courses of brick.

For a neutral, masonry-like finish, coat the covering material with heavy-bodied grey exterior stain. From a few feet away, it will look like stucco. While you're at it, consider adding a layer of rigid foam insulating board behind the plywood to insulate the exposed portion of the foundation.

Painting Block

If you plan to finish masonry basement walls, there are special waterproofing paints that roll or brush on thickly, like wet plaster. First, you should patch any open or leaking cracks with a cement-based patching compound or hydraulic cement. Even on rough walls, surface applications look better and last longer over sound, uncracked surfaces.

For painting, opt for a heavy-napped roller, called a "bulldozer" by professional painters because it can be loaded with thick paint and it will push the excess along the wall just as a bulldozer pushes dirt. The thick, ragged nap is essential when working on rough masonry. It helps to work the viscous paint into surface crevices and the joints between courses of concrete foundation block.

Patching Block

USE: ▶ cold chisel • hawk • pointing trowel • small

1 *To make your patch* material bond securely to the block, chip away cracked edges with a cold chisel.

Control Joints

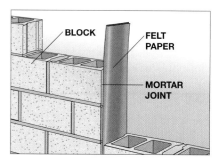

Control joints, made by setting felt paper in continuous seams, isolate wall sections from each other.

Buttering Blocks

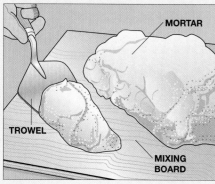

1 **Using a trowel,** slice a wedge of mortar from your mixing board or hawk.

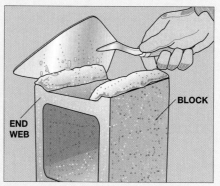

2 **Tap the trowel** against the raised edge of the block to lay the mortar.

Replacing Block

USE: ▶ brickset • jointing trowel • mason's hoe

1 *For many repairs,* you don't have to remove the entire block, only the face. To start, drill a series of holes.

sledgehammer • wire brush • work gloves ▶ cement patch • water

2 Because dust and loose particles *prevent the patch from adhering, sweep the damaged area with a wire brush.*

3 Hold a board or trowel *loaded with cement at the base of patch area, and force the material into the hole.*

4 To smooth out small patches, *use the side of a mason's trowel with each end riding on the undamaged surface.*

Garden Block

Garden block, or screen block, is used to create walls with open patterns. Walls can be made entirely of garden block, or a few courses can top a solid wall or be worked into the middle. Build them as you would a regular concrete block wall. The joints are smaller, so you will have to be a little neater, but you won't need to mix as much mortar and the work goes faster because the units are spaced far apart.

• mortar box • pointing trowel • power drill with masonry bit • safety goggles • small sledgehammer • work gloves ▶ mortar mix • replacement block • water

2 Use a brickset *to chip away the interior webs of the block. Always wear gloves and eye protection when chiseling block.*

3 Split a replacement block, *butter the edges with mortar, and then set the new block face in position.*

4 Because there isn't room *to place mortar above and below the block, force mortar deeply into joints before tooling.*

masonry

Brick Basics

Brick is made from clay fired at high temperatures. Brick textures vary, depending on the molding process. Most bricks made today are dense, hard, and durable. But it is important to choose the right brick for the project.

Types of Brick

Face brick is used where a consistent appearance is required. Face brick (FB) is produced in three varieties. FBX (select) brick have the tightest limits on size variation and flaws. Sharp edges and crisp outlines give them a contemporary look. FBS (standard) has wide color ranges but only slight variations in size. FBA (architectural) has no limits on either size variations or the cracks or chips that are permitted, because it is intended to look like historic brick. **Building bricks** (or common bricks) are rough in appearance but structurally sound. The chips, cracks, color variations, and slight deformations in building brick create a rustic look. **Paving brick** (always solid,

Don't feel too bad if your concrete patio is sinking. The S.S. Atlantus is an entire concrete ship that's sinking, off the coast of Cape May Point, NJ. Built as an experiment during World War I, it was, as the onshore marker reads, "proven impractical because of weight."

unlike other types, because the widest faces will be visible) are pressed into molds, and a longer baking time reduces how much water they absorb—critical for bricks placed on the ground, which will have to withstand freeze-thaw cycles and heavy traffic. Paving brick classes are similar to face brick: PS (standard), PA (architectural), and PX (select). **Firebrick** are a dull yellow, highly heat-resistant type used for fireplaces and ovens.

Brick Grading

There are three grades each for face brick and building brick; the grades are based on how well a brick resists damage from freezing and thawing. Grade MW (moderate weathering) can be used when bricks will be exposed to moisture but not saturated. Grade SW (severe weathering) should be used when bricks will be frozen when saturated. Grade NW (no weathering), available only in building brick, is for indoors only. Paving brick is divided into similar grades: SX (for highest freeze-thaw resistance), MX, and NX.

Cutting Brick

To cut bricks, score all around the brick with a brickset and a bricklayer's hammer. A firm blow on the score line will split the brick. To cut pavers, use a circular saw equipped with a masonry blade. Cut several half-bricks before starting a project.

To cut bricks, score all four sides with a brickset and hammer.

Deepen the score line with repeated blows until the brick splits.

Mortaring Bricks

Mortar is the glue that holds all brick walls together. There are different mortar mixtures to suit different conditions, but every mortar mix should be prepared keeping the same three pointers in mind. First, don't add excess water to make mixing easier; it will weaken the mortar. Second, follow proportions in every small batch to maintain a uniform mix throughout the wall. Third, keep the mix clean, which means periodically cleaning your mixing board of hardened particles from past batches.

USE: ▶ brick trowel • brickset • hammer • hawk • jointing trowel • mason's hoe • mortar box • pointing

1 *Mix just enough mortar* to use before the material sets up, cutting off one trowel's worth at a time.

2 *Carry the mortar* on one side of the trowel, and set it in place by sharply striking the clean side against the masonry

Mortars

Much like block mortar, brick mortars are mixes of portland cement, lime, sand, and water. You can mix your own or purchase factory-blended dry mortars, which you then combine with sand and water.

Mortar Proportions by Volume

Type	Portland Cement	Hydrated Lime	Mason's Sand
Portland cement & lime mortar:			
N	1	1	6
S	1	½	4½
Factory-blended masonry cement mortar:			
N	1	n/a	3
S	1	n/a	3

Materials

Modular brick styles are simpler to work with than non-modular ones because they make for easier planning and estimates. For example, with mortar joints, one modular brick's length is the same as two bricks laid widthwise or three bricks stacked. This makes it easier to turn corners or vary brick patterns in a double-wythe wall.

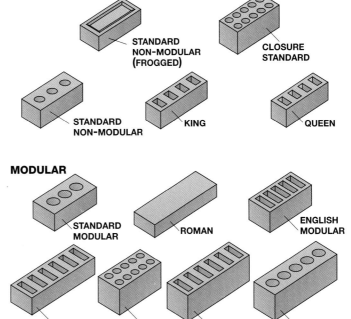

NONMODULAR

STANDARD NON-MODULAR (FROGGED)

CLOSURE STANDARD

STANDARD NON-MODULAR

KING

QUEEN

MODULAR

STANDARD MODULAR

ROMAN

ENGLISH MODULAR

NORMAN

CLOSURE MODULAR

ENGLISH NORMAN

UTILITY

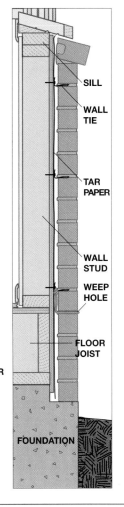

SILL

WALL TIE

TAR PAPER

WALL STUD

WEEP HOLE

FLOOR JOIST

FOUNDATION

---

trowel ▶ metal ties • mortar mix • truss-type horizontal joint reinforcement • water

3 *Turn the trowel over,* face side in, to form the outer edge of the mortar bed. You may need several passes to make it even.

4 *To make sure the bricks* are fully supported along their edges, make a shallow furrow along the center of the mortar bed.

5 *If furrowing* pushes mortar off the bricks, slice away excess with a trowel. Don't reuse mortar from the ground.

masonry

Brick Maintenance

To evaluate a brick wall, each component must be considered. Large cracks, called faults, in the overall structure are usually the most obvious problems and the most costly to repair. Most faults can be traced to uneven settling: When soil under one section compacts more than at another, the foundation and the wall above it can crack under the strain.

Cracking & Curving Walls

The signs of fundamental structural problems are staircase-pattern cracking along many courses of brick, and either large-scale convex or concave cupping of the walls. You can check for this curving, which can be difficult to detect over a large surface, by using line blocks and string.

Don't write off a wall's soundness just because it has some cracks. They may be only cosmetic or from settling that occurred long ago. Old, stable cracks (which usually are somewhat weathered, dirty, and may contain bits of leaves, dirt and debris, or spider webs) can be patched and sealed against the weather. New, unstable cracks (which are usually clean, with the masonry a lighter color than that on the surrounding wall) indicate that the building is still in motion. Such a wall will have to be watched carefully because if it is moving quickly, the foundation is unstable, and it may be in danger of collapse. The only fix for a wall with a poor foundation is to either prop it up with braces (an unsightly, temporary, and potentially dangerous solution) or demolish it and begin again from the foundation.

Maintaining Mortar

The maintenance program for your brick wall should also include a careful check of the mortar joints, the source of the most potential danger next to the foundation. Any mortar that is loose, spongy, and easily scraped away needs to be repointed. This process includes excavating the mortar to a depth of approximately two times the width of the joint, cleaning away all loose dust and debris, and then refilling the joints with mortar. Without repointing, the process of deterioration accelerates, particularly in winter (due to freezing and thawing). You can expect to repoint brick homes built before 1900, but not because of age alone. The mortar commonly used at that time was lime-based, softer, and very porous.

Bricks are generally more durable than the surrounding mortar, although leaks and condensation can sometimes harm them unexpectedly. Water absorption through the brick can lead to fragmentation and flaking of the exterior brick face. This splitting off of the exterior face of bricks—a condition called spalling—can result in the need for expensive repairwork. To avoid the potential problems associated with spalling, keep water out of your masonry walls, and repair leak-prone brick and mortar joints as soon as possible.

Cleaning Brick

Cleaning old brick walls by sand- or water-blasting might do more harm than good. Stresses from high-pressure cleaning could seriously erode if not shatter 19th-century brick, which may not tolerate more than 100 psi. While sand hits the brick with uniform pressure, old brick isn't uniform; this can lead to pitting and channeling. Chemical cleaning may produce good results with less damage.

Laying Brick

USE: ▶ chalk-line box • brick trowel • bricklayer's hammer • brickset • hawk • jointing trowel • line level • mason's hoe • mason's line • measuring tape

1 *Snap a chalk line* to establish the outer boundary of the wall; then trowel on the embedding layer of mortar.

2 *Professionals can tap the brick* into proper position by eye; you may want to check the first few courses with a level.

3 *String a line* from corner to corner, and use it as guide to keep the wall flat. Make fine adjustments by tapping with the trowel.

Tooled Joints

Proper tooling seals masonry joints, but only some types are weather-resistant. Horizontal joints should be tooled first, then move on to the vertical.

WEATHER RESISTANT	NON-WEATHER RESISTANT
CONCAVE 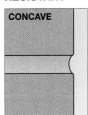	FLUSH
V-SHAPED 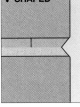	RAKED
WEATHERED 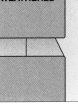	STRUCK

Diagnosing Brick Problems

Eroded mortar joints, caused by old or poorly made mortar, are fixed by repointing. Staircase-pattern cracking is a sign of major structural problems, resolved only by removing the structure and improving its subbase. Spalling occurs when freezing water has caused a brick to fracture—usually the face of the brick cracks off. The entire brick should be replaced, and if possible, water should be redirected away from this area.

ERODED MORTAR JOINTS

STAIRCASE CRACKING

SPALLING

• mortar box • pointing trowel • spirit level ▶ mortar mix • water

4 *When you've set the brick* in proper position, use your trowel to scoop away excess mortar that oozes from the joint.

5 *Regularly check your wall* for level. Every few courses, take a measurement from the footing at several points on the wall.

6 *Unlike rough block joints,* which often are concealed by stucco, brick mortar requires more uniform tooling.

masonry

Working With Stone

Although many types of stone are available throughout the country, only a few can be used for building. Suitable stones must satisfy the requirements of strength, hardness, workability, durability, and density.

Stone can be described by its shape or the form in which it is used (such as rubble, ashlar, or flagstone), by its class or mineral composition (such as granite, limestone, sandstone, or slate), or by the way in which it is obtained (fieldstone or quarry stone). Rubble stone is irregular in size and shape; fieldstone is a type of rubble, naturally rough and angular. Ashlar is stone that has been cut at the quarry to produce relatively smooth, flat bedding surfaces that stack easily. Flagstone is designed to be used for paving and has been cut into flat slabs. Flagstone ranges from ½ to 2 inches thick and may be irregularly shaped or cut into geometric patterns.

Buying Stone

Stone is sold by the cubic yard at quarries and stone suppliers. Cut stone is more expensive than fieldstone or rubble because of the labor involved. To estimate how many cubic yards you will need, multiply the length times the height times the width of your wall in feet, and then divide by 27. For ashlar stone, add about 10% to your order for breakage and waste; if using rubble, add at least 25%.

Dry-Stacking a Stone Wall

Dry-stacked stone walls are built without mortar: Friction, gravity, and the interlocking stones hold the wall together. The wall is flexible enough to absorb some frost heave and is usually built without footings when less than 3 feet tall. Taller dry-stacked walls are not recommended because of the lifting involved and code restrictions. Stone may require cutting and shaping for a good fit. If you are gathering fieldstone, look for angular shapes rather than round stones; larger stones should be kept for the base course. A dry-stacked wall consists of two wythes, with a space between filled with small rubble. The wythes are tied together with bond stones that span the width of the wall. A 3-foot-high wall should have a base about 2 feet wide that tapers at the top.

Stone Wall Patterns

RANDOM RUBBLE

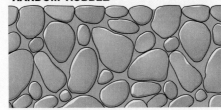

COURSED RUBBLE

MOSAIC

RANDOM ASHLAR

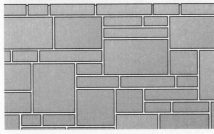

COURSED ASHLAR

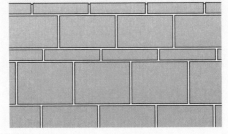

Rubble wall construction uses stones that are irregular in size and shape. Fieldstone is a type of rubble; quarried rubble comes from fragments left over after stonecutting. Random rubble walls are usually dry-laid but can also be mortared. Use this pattern for an informal garden wall or short dry-laid boundary walls.

Coursed rubble walls have a neater appearance than random rubble walls but are more difficult to construct, and require a large selection of stone. Rubble stones can also be roughly squared with a brick hammer to fit into place more easily. Coursed rubble walls can be used for foundations and structural walls as well as garden and retaining walls.

Mosaic, also called web, is a tighter version of a random rubble wall. Large and smaller stones are fit together much more tightly than with a random rubble wall. To ensure that all of the pieces fit together without large gaps, the stones are first laid out on the ground, face down, and test-fitted in the order in which they will be installed.

Ashlar has been cut at the quarry to produce smooth, flat bedding surfaces that stack easily. It is generally cut into small rectangles and has sawed or dressed faces that can be either smooth or slightly rough. Ashlar patterns are not really random; as with brick, a variety of bond patterns are used alone or combined for different effects.

Coursed ashlar has a more formal appearance than random ashlar, and it requires more precisely cut stone. Ashlar mortar joints are sometimes used as a decorative element. They may be a color that complements the stone, raked concave like block joints, or filled and dressed to have an extruded appearance that stands out from the stone.

Laying Face Stone

USE: ▶ brick trowel • bricklayer's hammer • brickset • jointing trowel • line level • mason's line • pointing trowel • spirit level • work gloves ▶ mortar mix • water

1 *Manufactured face stone* (thinner and lighter than full stone) is applied like brick, using a string line to keep the wall flat.

2 *Because the stones* are slightly irregular to create a less manufactured look, periodically check the tops for level.

3 *After the stone* is embedded on the wall, fill the joints between courses, and tool the joints to suit.

Shaping Stone

SCORE LINE

You will often have to cut and shape stones to make them fit—especially when dry-laying a wall. Place the stone on flat, solid ground rather than a hard surface such as concrete. Use a heavy hammer and cold chisel to score the cut line. The stone may break at the line before you finish scoring. If not, strike one sharp blow with the hammer. You can also split flagstone after scoring by placing it over a section of pipe and striking it. Always wear heavy gloves and goggles when cutting stone.

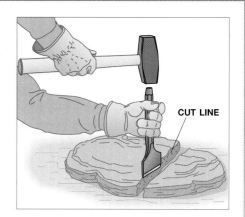

CUT LINE

Laying Full Stone

USE: ▶ brickset • hawk • hoe • line level • mason's line • mortar box • small sledgehammer • trowels • work gloves ▶ mortar mix • rubble • stone • water

1 *The rocks you use* help design the wall you build. But try to use square-edge rocks at corners and flat-faced rocks on the sides.

2 *To build a rock wall* in manageable pieces, use modest-sized stones with flat faces, and fill the hollow core with rubble.

3 *Bind the rocks together in stages,* first with an embedding coat on the foundation, then by filling the rubble core.

masonry

Cleaning Masonry

There are four ways to clean concrete and stone: with chemicals, water, or steam, or by sandblasting. Sandblasting takes away surface and embedded dirt—and often some of the masonry, too. Chemical- and steam-cleaning contractors can tailor their mix of chemicals to the job at hand—for example, removing algae. Always be careful when working with acid cleaners. Water cleaning is a job you can do yourself, either with bucket and brush or with a pressurized sprayer (power washing).

Plant life can be destructive to stone walls. When ivy roots start growing into cracks in mortar joints, you should cut the roots as close to the wall as possible and treat the ends with ammonium phosphate paste to kill the plant. Mold and mildew also may take hold on stone not exposed to enough sunlight. To test discoloration, drop a small amount of bleach on the area. It will whiten mildew and have no effect on dirt. To clear the mildew, scrub the area with a solution of one part bleach to one part warm water, and then rinse.

Stains from iron can be removed with a solution of oxalic acid. Mix about 1 pound of the crystals in a gallon of water with ½ pound ammonium bifluoride, brush the mix over the stained area, then rinse. Stone may also become stained with asphalt and tar from a roof. Remove as much tar as possible. The remaining stain can be cleaned with a solvent such as benzene.

Patching Steps

USE: ▶ chisel • formboards • goggles • sledgehammer • trowel • work gloves ▶ mortar mix

1 *Wire brush the damaged area* to remove all loose debris, and then build a plywood form to square the step repair.

2 *To help a patch adhere,* coat the area with a bonding agent or set a few concrete nails to reinforce the repair.

3 *Nails driven halfway into* the old step are covered by fresh concrete, smoothed out to be level with the form.

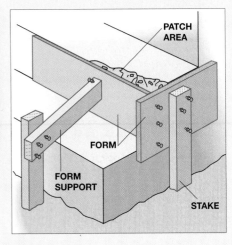

Patching Stucco

USE: ▶ metal snips • brick trowel • hawk • pointing trowel • sponge trowel • spray mister • wire brush • work gloves ▶ 15-lb. felt paper • galvanized-wire lath

1 *To check for damage* beneath cracked and broken stucco, cut away bent reinforcing mesh and tar paper.

2 *Install new lath* over the damaged area, and trowel on a base coat of patch material that nearly fills the hole.

3 *Rake the surface* of the base coat before it hardens. Even a homemade tool (nails through a board) will do the job.

Removing Stains

For stubborn spot stains, *mix cleaners into a paste with flour or talc, which keeps the cleaner on the wall.*

Stain	Solution
Oil	For brick, emulsifying agent; for concrete/ block, automotive degreaser
Iron	1 lb. oxalic acid crystals, I gal. water, ½ lb. ammonium bifluoride
Paint	2 lbs. TSP to 1 gal. water
Smoke	Scouring powder with bleach; or poultice of trichlorethylene and talc; or alkali detergents and emulsifying agents

Efflorescence

Efflorescence is a white powdery deposit of soluble salts leached to the surface of masonry or mortar by moisture from within. Residue is left when the moisture evaporates. For a quick fix, dry brush the deposit using a stiff fiber brush; then saturate the masonry with water. For stubborn deposits, use a 1-to-10 solution of muriatic acid and water, following label cautions, and then rinse thoroughly. Of course, the best solution is to find the source of the leak and stop it.

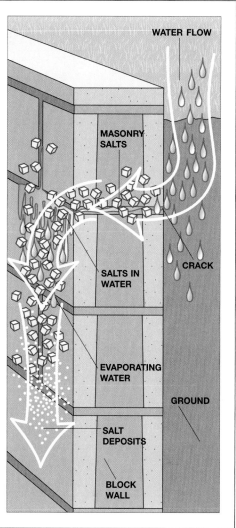

• masking tape • 1¼-inch roofing nails

4 **Keep the finish coat flush** with the surrounding wall by using the stable edges of the damaged area as a guide.

5 **Texture the thin top coat** (about ⅛-in. thick) with a trowel, sponge, broom, or anything that helps the patch blend in.

6 **To harden and cure the stucco,** *moisten the patch at least twice a day for the first two days.*

foundations

5

foundations

Foundation Design

A well-designed foundation is the key to the safety and durability of any structure, whether it's a house or a deck. The foundation supports the building and anchors it to the ground. It also protects the building from frost heave and settling soil. And as long as the foundation is waterproofed and drained, it plays a critical role in keeping water out of a house.

Types of Foundations

There are three basic types of foundations. A **slab-on-grade** is a poured concrete floor slab with a thickened edge, reinforced with steel bars. The slab is laid directly on the ground or over a layer of gravel. This type of foundation is an economical way to support a single-story structure in areas where the ground doesn't freeze in the winter—and as long as you don't need a basement or crawl space.

A **wall foundation** consists of a bearing perimeter wall that encloses a full basement or a crawl space. It is made of poured concrete, concrete blocks, or (less often) pressure-treated wood, and rests on an enlarged base, called a footing, that helps distribute the building's load. Usually made of poured concrete with steel reinforcement, footings are set on firm soil or a gravel bed, below the depth of the frost line. In general, a footing should be as high as the thickness of the wall it supports and twice as wide.

Also built on concrete footings, **pier** or **post foundations** are often used to support lightweight structures, such as decks and porches, as well as many houses in the South and Southwest. Piers are short columns made of concrete blocks or poured concrete. Posts are longer columns made of steel, pressure-treated wood, or concrete poured into tube forms.

Site Conditions

Footings and foundations are only as good as the soil they are built on. If you are designing and building your own foundations—usually jobs best left to professionals—have an engineer analyze the soil on your property to determine its bearing capacity. Consult your local building department to find out what the average frost depth is in your area and all the regulations on foundations that apply to your locality and specific site conditions.

Site Access

When the work area isn't easily accessible from the street, you need to plan a protected route to the job site to accommodate material deliveries and the daily traffic of contractors. Be sure to identify and clearly mark underground utility lines so that they will not be damaged by heavy equipment. To protect a stretch of lawn from the tracks of a wheelbarrow, lay a track of scaffold planks and scrap sheets of plywood.

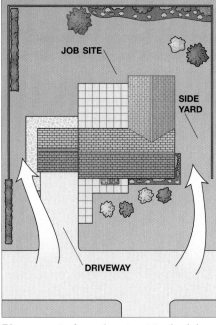

Plan a route from the street to the job-site area. Protect shrubs and trees along the way, and mark underground utilities.

Special Tools

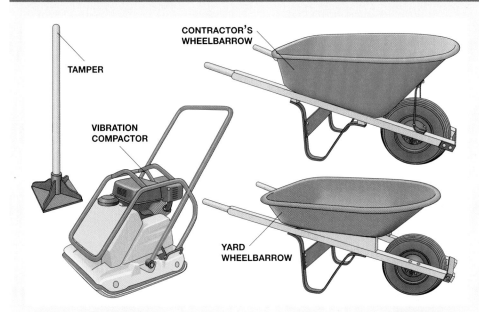

Foundation work requires specialized tools. You'll need a tamper to compact fill or a vibration compactor, which can make the job much easier. Wheelbarrows come in handy for moving such heavy materials as sand, gravel, cement, and concrete.

Sinking & Heaving

The freezing and thawing of soil in cold climates can cause the ground to heave and settle, resulting in cracks in concrete slabs and foundation walls. To prevent cracking, foundation footings must be set below the frost line, the depth to which soil freezes in winter. Because freezing patterns can vary even within the same town, consult the local building department to determine frost-line depth and footing regulations.

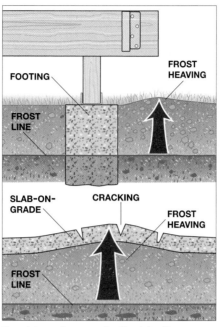

Frost heaving won't affect footings below the frost line but can easily lift and crack a slab-on-grade.

Steel Forms

Steel forms may be used by specialized foundation contractors on large excavations. The strong, interlocked sections can be assembled faster and require less bracing than wood forms. Unlike site-built wood forms, they are reusable.

Average Frost Depth

The map at right shows average frost depths throughout the United States. In the unzoned western and far northern parts of the country, as well as in Canada, ground freezing patterns vary so much within relatively small areas that zoning is all but impossible. But even within zones, frost-line depths can vary widely, depending on local weather patterns, altitude, and soil composition. Well-drained gravelly and sandy soils, for example, have less frost action than poorly drained silts and clays.

Local building codes strictly regulate foundation depth and construction. Always consult your local building inspector before starting a foundation project. And bear in mind that the footing and foundation depths shown in this chapter are not meant to serve as a model for any particular locality.

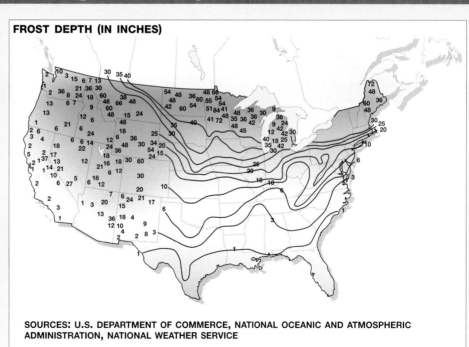

FROST DEPTH (IN INCHES)

SOURCES: U.S. DEPARTMENT OF COMMERCE, NATIONAL OCEANIC AND ATMOSPHERIC ADMINISTRATION, NATIONAL WEATHER SERVICE

foundations

The Job Site

Before turning over the first shovelful of dirt for any foundation work, you should draw (or have drawn) a site plan, showing the exact location of the new foundation relative to other buildings and property lines. Detailed site and building plans are required to get permits from your local building department before you start work. (Build without them, and you risk having to tear the work down.)

With permits in hand, the first step in laying out a foundation is to locate the corners. Using property boundaries or existing structures on your site map, measure out and stake the new foundation corners, or have a surveyor do it for you. About 2 feet outside each corner, set a pair of batter boards at right angles. The boards provide anchoring points for string guidelines that mark the exact outline of the foundation. Because batter boards are set outside the area to be excavated, you do not lose the crucial reference lines once you begin to dig. You just set the strings back up whenever you need to.

Getting the strings to cross at right angles over the corner stakes takes some adjusting of the nails anchoring the strings to the boards. To create true right angles at each corner of the string outline, use the 3:4:5 triangulation method. (See "Squaring Corners" on the facing page.) Once all four lines are in place and the corners have been squared, double-check squareness by measuring the diagonals between opposite corners. If the diagonals are not within 1 inch, readjust the string guidelines until they are.

Excavation

Concrete slabs and footings must rest on either undisturbed virgin soil or compacted soil that is uniformly graded and well-drained. An unsuitable or badly prepared subgrade can cause uneven settling and cracking. In areas with poor drainage, you need to excavate deeply enough to accommodate a 4-inch layer of tamped gravel under the concrete.

Excavating a foundation is difficult work; depending on the size of the project, it is usually better left to a contractor with the necessary heavy equipment. If you decide to undertake a small project yourself, have the utility company inspect your site and locate and mark all the utility lines you'll need to avoid.

Building Batter Boards

USE: ▶ circular saw • hammer • pipe clamps • power drill/driver • short sledgehammer • spirit level

1 Cut pointed 2x4 stakes to support the batter boards (2-ft.-long 1x4s) that will be used to establish the building lines.

2 Offset pairs of stakes at right angles to each other, about 2 ft. outside the rough corners and in line with the building foundation.

Removing Sod

USE: ▶ flat-tipped spade • work gloves

To store healthy sod for reuse after excavating, start by cutting the sod 6 inches outside the guidelines for forms. Cut through the sod with a spade, and pry underneath to dislodge the roots. When it's free, you can begin to roll up sections to replant elsewhere once your foundation or drain work is complete. Dig down deep enough for the foundation and base material, such as a layer of gravel.

1 To remove a section of healthy lawn, first cut down along a guideline using a sharp, flat-tipped spade.

2 Slide your spade under the sod to undercut the roots, working from both sides of the strip, if possible.

3 Roll up the loose sod, keep the roll damp, and store it where it won't be disturbed during construction.

• mason's twine • measuring tape ▶ 2x4 stakes • 1x4 batter boards • nails or screws

3 *Nail or screw predrilled batter boards* to the stakes, using clamps to hold the boards in position.

4 *Check the batter boards* for level and plumb, and make sure they are at 90-degree angles to each other.

5 *Fasten the string guidelines* to nails in the batter boards to establish the exact building corners and overall outline.

Squaring Corners

To create a perfectly square building layout, use the 3:4:5 method of triangulation. Starting at corner A, measure 3 feet along one guideline and mark point B. Starting again from corner A, measure 4 feet along the guideline perpendicular to the first one and mark point C. Adjust the AC line until the distance BC is exactly 5 feet. Angle BAC is now a true 90-degree angle. You can double-check squareness by measuring the diagonals between opposite corners. The distances should be within 1 inch.

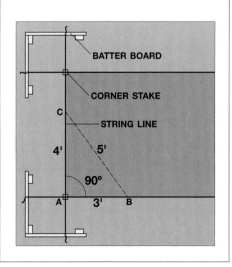

Measuring & Leveling

Accurate measurement is one key to the success of any building project. It is important to be accurate right from the start and eliminate as many small errors as possible, even though foundation work is often rough and on a grand scale.

Professional contractors generally use an electronic level or an old-fashioned surveyor's transit to establish level points on uneven ground. The terrain around your site may be full of small hills and valleys, but forms for the foundation must still be dead level. Modern electronic equipment is accurate to small fractions of an inch.

It's also important to be sure that foundation walls are straight. One of the best ways to ensure straightness is to use strings and blocks. Mount two blocks of equal thickness at the ends of the wall, and stretch a string tightly between them. Then use a third block of the same size to check the margin between the string and the form (or block or brick veneer). You also can use a line level—particularly to check courses of block, brick, or stone—and a 4-foot carpenter's level at corners.

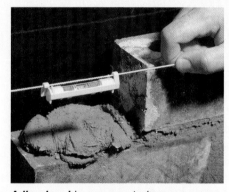

A line level is one way to keep masonry courses in alignment. The small bubble vial hooks onto a tightly stretched string.

An electronic beam level uses a light beam for leveling. The instrument rotates 360° to check any location.

foundations

Formwork Basics

Wet concrete is poured into molds called forms, which hold and shape the concrete until it hardens. Usually made of lumber and (in the case of wall forms) plywood sheathing, forms must be level, plumb, and strong enough to withstand the weight of the concrete pushing against them. Forms for edges of slabs and continuous wall footings are typically made of 2x4, 2x6, or 2x8 lumber, depending on the thickness of the slab or footing.

Form boards should be free of holes, cracks, loose knots, and other flaws that might weaken them or mar the concrete's surface. The boards are set on edge, perpendicular to the subgrade, and are braced every 3 to 4 feet with wood stakes driven firmly into the ground. To make the forms easier to remove, use double-headed nails to fasten the form boards to the stakes. Wherever two boards butt together, screw a plywood gusset across the outside of each joint.

Forms for footings and slabs are usually built on site. The more complicated forms for perimeter wall foundations are either site-built or constructed using prefabricated panels rented from concrete form suppliers.

Continuous Footing Forms

Foundation walls rest on concrete footings set below the frost line to avoid frost-heave damage. The footing height should be the same as the thickness of the wall, or a minimum of 8 inches. The footing width should be twice that of the wall, or a minimum of 16 inches. The batter boards set up to establish the building's outline are also used to establish and mark the width of the footings.

If the soil you're building on can hold an edge without crumbling, an earth trench can serve as the form. However, concrete for wall footings is usually poured into wooden forms anchored by 1x4 stakes driven into the ground and braced with 1x4 spreaders nailed across board tops every 4 to 6 feet. A chamfered 2x4 suspended from the spreaders down the center of the form creates a depression, or keyway, in the footing that will help secure a poured concrete wall.

Wall Foundation Forms

Install basement wall formwork after the footings have cured. The forms are usually made of smooth, knot-free plywood sheathing supported by 2x4 studs, horizontal members, called rangers or wales, and braces. Wire ties hold the plywood walls together; wood spreaders keep them a fixed distance apart.

Pier Forms

Square or cylindrical concrete piers support structures ranging from decks to houses. To make forms for piers, use either a simple wooden box constructed on site or a prefabricated fiberboard hollow tube. The simplest type of pier form is a hole in the ground with or without an above-grade box form.

Form Types

Formwork for a wall can be a simple stud form, consisting of stud wall frames sheathed with plywood on their inside faces. Wire ties hold facing walls together, while 2x4 spreaders keep them a fixed distance apart. A stud-and-ranger form has the added support of horizontal members, called rangers, and braces. You can also rent prefabricated, reusable box formwork from concrete form suppliers. In this type of formwork, both the inside and outside faces of the stud walls are sheathed with plywood.

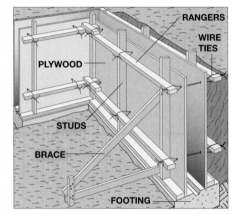

Stud-and-ranger forms are reinforced with horizontal rangers, or wales.

Building Formless Piers

USE: ▶ posthole digger • measuring tape • shovel • wheelbarrow • spirit level • hammer ▶ concrete • steel reinforcement • post • post base or steel dowel

1 *Use a posthole digger* to excavate a hole for a formless pier. The earthen walls of the hole serve as the formwork.

2 *Measure the hole's depth carefully* to make sure that the base of the pier will rest on soil below the frost line for your region.

3 *Fill the hole* with the required concrete mix and steel reinforcing. The bottom of the hole should be undisturbed soil.

Box forms for rectangular piers are easy to construct on site. Cut and assemble four boards to make a box with inside dimensions equal to those of the pier. To keep the box form from sticking and make it easier to remove after the concrete sets, coat its interior with motor oil or form oil, a release agent. To make removal even easier, nail a pair of 2x4 handles to the form above grade level. Lower the box into the excavated hole. Use wire ties to suspend an anchor bolt in the center of the pier, and then pour the concrete.

Stay-in-place tube forms are usually made of high-quality, moisture-resistant fiber that is spiral-wound and laminated with heavy-duty adhesives. Other types of permanent tube forms are made of molded fiberglass, clay tile, or concrete pipe. Also available are fiberboard tube forms that can be peeled off after the concrete has cured. To form a concrete pier, simply lower the tube form into the hole, suspend an anchor bolt in the center of the form with wire ties, and then pour the concrete into the form.

A surface form is a short box form placed over a hole; it serves as the main formwork for a concrete pier. The surface form simply gives a clean-edged finish to the above-ground portion of the pier. After the hole is dug, the box form is installed over it. Temporary stakes driven into the ground and nailed to the form hold it in place. Use wire ties to suspend a steel pin or anchor bolt in the center of the form. Pour the concrete mix into the hole up to the top of the surface form.

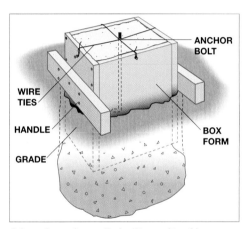

A box form is easily built on-site. Above-grade handles make it easier to remove.

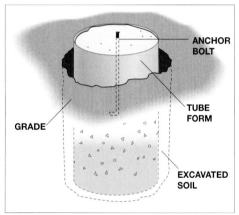

Tube forms, designed to stay in place, need only be positioned and filled with concrete.

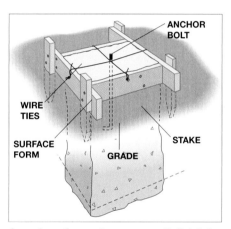

A surface form gives a smooth finish to the exposed part of a formless pier.

4 Insert a metal post base or steel anchor into the concrete when the mix is firm enough to hold it but not yet hardened.

5 Adjust the post base so that it is level, plumb, and properly oriented to support the structural post to be installed later.

6 Install the structural post by nailing it into the metal post base after the concrete pier has hardened.

Building Wall Forms

Wet concrete exerts a great deal of pressure on any form, but especially on tall wall forms. A simple stud form consisting of plywood sheathing over stud walls held together by wire ties might be sufficient for a small garden wall. But a crawl space or basement wall requires a more securely braced stud-and-ranger form.

Assembling the Forms

After the footings have set and their forms have been removed, build 2x4 stud wall frames using 16d nails and spacing the studs 16 inches on center. Drill holes in the plywood panels for wire or snap ties. The spacing of studs and ties depends on the size of the wall and the pour rate, the speed at which concrete is poured. In a typical scenario, ties are spaced 16 inches on center between studs and in horizontal rows 12 inches from the top and bottom of the form and every 2 feet in between.

Nail the plywood to the studs with 8d nails. Snap chalk lines on the footings to mark the edges of the finished wall. Raise the outer walls first, nailing adjacent panels to butting studs. Shore up panels with braces running from panel studs to stakes driven in the ground. Insert snap ties into the predrilled holes. The outer stems of the ties are sandwiched between two horizontal rangers held together by U-shaped brackets that attach to the ties. Overlapping rangers nailed together at outside corners provide added support.

When the outer walls are up, make sure they are level and square, and fasten the bottom plates to the footings with masonry nails. Spray the inside plywood faces of both inner and outer walls with form oil to prevent sticking.

Raise the inner walls, threading the free ends of the snap ties through the predrilled holes in the plywood panels. Install and secure wales and braces. Fasten bottom plates to footings.

Wall Openings

Once the forms are built, you'll need to install blockouts to accommodate pipes, electrical and cable lines, windows, and doors after the concrete is poured. A blockout can be a short length of plastic pipe or a plywood box. You may also have to excavate and build formwork for a well around a basement window.

Rebar & Anchors

To keep cracks from spreading in the finished wall, place steel reinforcing bars (#4 rebar) horizontally 1 foot from the top and bottom of the wall and at intervals in between (depending on the wall's height). Rebar is fastened with wire ties to the snap ties holding the form walls together and to vertical rebar set in the footing.

After pouring the concrete into the forms and smoothing and leveling it, set anchor bolts into the concrete 1 foot from the ends of each wall and 6 feet on center. The bolts will be used to secure the sill plate that anchors the wood house frame to the foundation.

MATERIALS

Formwork for concrete foundation walls is generally constructed with the following materials:

◆ **Lumber**
Formwork studs, rangers (horizontal supports), diagonal braces, and stakes are made of relatively lightweight 2x4s that resist splitting when nailed.

◆ **Plywood**
For formwork sheathing, use smooth, water-resistant ¾-inch exterior plywood. To keep the plywood from sticking to the hardened concrete, spray it with motor oil or form oil.

◆ **Form ties**
Wire ties hold form walls together while wood spreaders keep them a fixed distance apart. Snap ties perform both functions. A snap tie is a steel wire with a bolt head and bracket on each end to grab the outsides of facing form walls and hold them together. Two plastic cones on the wire press against the inside of form walls, keeping them a fixed distance apart.

Building Formed Footings

USE: ▶ power drill/driver • mason's twine • shovel • 4-ft. level • tape measure • hammer • short sledgehammer ▶ concrete • gravel • 2x formwork boards

1 *Set up batter boards,* and string lines to locate the footing excavation. On this wall project, the footing is near grade.

2 *Begin excavating the soil* within your string lines. Remember, your footings should rest below the frost line.

3 *Drive in the stakes* that will support the outside form boards. You can build them from 2x4s with an angled tip.

Pipe-Sleeve Blockouts

Before pouring concrete into foundation wall forms, you need to install blockouts, or barriers, to accommodate electrical conduits and gas and water pipes. The simplest way to create this type of blockout is to drill holes into the formwork and slide a piece of PVC pipe through the openings. You can leave the pipe sleeves long, and trim them flush with the concrete once the mix is set and the forms are stripped. Pipe diameters should be slightly greater than whatever has to pass through them.

Use a drill (or a drill and a saber saw) *to cut holes matching the pipe diameter through the faces of the formwork.*

Insert a sleeve of plastic pipe *through the holes in the formwork to provide access for utility lines.*

Window & Door Blockouts

Openings for doors, windows, and crawl-space vents must also be blocked out inside formwork before any concrete is poured. These rough-opening forms are plywood boxes nailed to the inside of the wall forms. If you are placing a window in a basement wall, you'll also need to excavate a well outside the window and build forms for the walls of the well (as shown at far right).

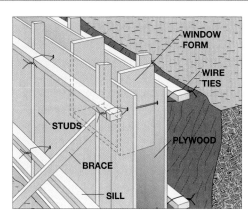

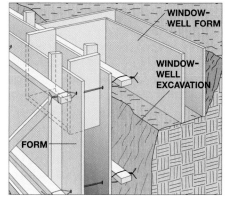

• 2x4 batter boards • 1x4 stakes • double-headed nails • galvanized screws • plywood gussets

4 ***Use a clamp*** *to fasten boards to the stakes temporarily. Check for level, adjust the boards, and then nail or screw them in place.*

5 ***Secure butt joints*** *in the formwork with plywood gussets screwed in place across the exterior face of each joint.*

6 ***Use 1x2 spreaders*** *to bridge the forms so that the weight of the concrete pour will not cause the forms to bulge.*

Mixing Concrete

Once you've built the forms and installed the necessary reinforcing bars, it's time to mix the concrete. For large jobs requiring a cubic yard or more of concrete, you'll save time and labor, and perhaps money as well, by ordering ready-mix concrete delivered to the site by truck. If the job requires less than a cubic yard, you can buy the dry ingredients—gravel, sand, and cement—separately, and mix them yourself with water, either by hand or with a power mixer. For very small jobs, such as anchoring a post or making repairs, use a prepackaged concrete mix and just add water.

Concrete Ingredients

Concrete is a mixture of portland cement, gravel or crushed stone (coarse aggregate), sand (fine aggregate), and water. Easily worked when wet, concrete hardens into one of the strongest of building materials. The workability and strength of concrete depend on the quality of the ingredients, their relative proportions, and how they are mixed.

The key ingredient of concrete is portland cement, a mix of lime, iron, silica, and alumina that is fired in a kiln and ground into a fine powder. When mixed with water, cement forms a paste that binds sand and gravel into a rocklike material. There are five basic types of portland cement, suitable for different types of construction. Type I is the general-purpose cement most often used for residential construction.

Portland cement comes in gray, white, and buff varieties, and is usually sold in 94-pound bags (1 cubic foot). Materials called admixtures are added to cement to modify its properties. Air-entraining agents, for example, improve the resistance of concrete to frost action, weathering, and the effects of salt deposits. (Type I, II, and III cements are available with air-entrainers already mixed in and are designated with the letter A after the type number.) Other admixtures include accelerators, which speed up the hardening process; retarders, which slow it down; plasticizers, which improve concrete flow; and pigments, which add color to white cement.

If cement is allowed to get wet during storage, it will begin to harden. Always store cement bags off the ground—on wooden skids, for example—and cover them with plastic.

The second ingredient of concrete is a combination of coarse and fine aggregates. Coarse aggregate is gravel or crushed stone sold by the cubic foot or yard. The mix should include particles ranging from ¼ inch to 1½ inches in diameter. The particles should not be larger than one-quarter of the concrete's thickness.

Fine aggregate consists of sand particles measuring less than ¼ inch in diameter. Concrete sand should be "bank-run" sand, which is free of silt and contaminants. Never use beach sand or mason's sand for concrete work.

The final ingredient in concrete is water, which triggers the chemical reaction that results in hardened concrete. Water for mixing concrete should be clean and free of organic matter, oil, acid, and other impurities.

Estimating Concrete Quantities

One of the first things you need to do when planning a concrete project is to determine the amount of concrete you'll need. To calculate the volume of a rectangular footing, wall, or slab, multiply length by width by thickness (all in feet or fractions of a foot) and divide by 27 to obtain the total volume in cubic yards, which is how ready-mix is usually sold. To figure the volume of a cylinder, multiply the square of its radius in feet by pi (3.14), multiply the result by the cylinder's height, and then divide by 27. Break down irregular shapes into rectangles and portions of circles, figure the volume of each section, and add them up. To allow for waste and irregularities in concrete thickness, add 5 or 10% to your order.

Reinforcing Concrete Footings

USE: ▶ pliers • hacksaw • wire cutters ▶ rebar • wire ties • wire • bricks, blocks, or wire chairs

Steel reinforcement bar (rebar, for short) is used to strengthen concrete, such as footings and foundations that will carry a heavy load. The bars come in 20-foot lengths and in diameters ranging from ¼ to 1 inch. A 16-inch-wide footing for a house may call for two continuous ½-inch bars set about 8 inches apart down the center of the form. (Check local codes for details.) It's important to elevate the rebar slightly so that it rests in the concrete instead of on the ground. You can support it with bricks or small fittings called chairs.

1 *Support rebar* at the proper height, generally at least an inch or two off the ground, with pieces of brick or block.

2 *Secure rebar* to masonry or special supports, called chairs, with wire ties to keep them from moving during the pour.

3 *Lap adjoining rebar* at least 12 in. around corners to provide unbroken support, and secure them with wire ties.

Proportions

The right mix is the key to making strong and durable concrete. Proportions vary, though, depending on the intended use of the concrete and the conditions it will be exposed to. Especially important is the water-to-cement ratio. Too much water will weaken the concrete; too little will make it unworkable.

Concrete for site-mixed residential projects is typically 1 part cement, 2½ parts sand, and 3 parts coarse aggregate, and requires about 5 gallons of water per bag of concrete. But there are exceptions to the rule; for example, adding more water on hot, dry days to prevent the wet mix from drying out prematurely, which can significantly weaken concrete.

With ready-mix concrete, you don't have to worry about proportions. But when you place an order, you do need to specify the volume of concrete needed, its intended use, its compressive strength (load-bearing capacity) after 28 days, minimum cement content, maximum aggregate size, and any required admixtures.

If you're mixing concrete yourself, measure out the dry ingredients carefully on a clean plywood sheet, and mix them thoroughly with a mason's hoe. Make a well in the middle of the dry ingredients. Slowly add water to the well, and pull the dry ingredients from the sides of the well into the water. Keep adding water and mixing until ridges cut in the concrete with the hoe hold their shape. Hand-mixing concrete is hard work. You can spare yourself some of the effort by renting a small power mixer.

Soil Compaction

A 4x4 post, powered by a good deal of elbow grease, makes an effective, if rudimentary, hand tamper.

Concrete is so heavy that in time it compresses loose soil underneath it. Uneven soil settling creates stresses in concrete that can lead to cracking. The best way to avoid the problem is to leave the subgrade undisturbed when you excavate a footing trench. Remove sod and topsoil, but leave a solid, untouched bed of soil on which the footing will rest. Because this isn't always possible, any soil that has been removed and replaced must be tamped solid with either a hand tamper or a vibration compactor.

Rent a vibration compactor for large jobs or to avoid the effort of hand-tamping smaller ones.

Reinforcing Slabs

USE: ▶ wire cutters • pliers ▶ wire mesh • bricks, blocks, or wire chairs • metal ties

Reinforcing mesh, made of steel wires woven or welded into a grid of squares, is used primarily to minimize any cracks that might form in concrete slabs. Like rebar, welded wire should be elevated so that it rests in the slab instead of on the ground. You can use special fittings (chairs) or pieces of brick, block, or stone. If you need to reinforce an irregularly shaped slab, overlap sections of mesh at least 6 inches and bind them together with wire ties. As with rebar, check your local building codes for welded-wire requirements.

1 Welded or woven wire mesh comes in rolls or sheets. You need to thoroughly flatten the mesh inside forms.

2 Cut back mesh reinforcement so that it is separated from form boards by about 2 in. on all sides.

3 Use brick or block sections or metal chairs to support wire mesh at the height required by code.

foundations

Handling Concrete

Whether you mix your own concrete or have ready-mix delivered to the site, it's important to work quickly when placing concrete in forms. Have on hand all the equipment and helpers you'll need, and try to mix the concrete or have the ready-mix truck park as close as possible to the job site. If you must transport concrete to the forms in wheelbarrows, lay 2x12s across your lawn to create a protected path, and build ramps over the forms so that you don't disturb them. Before placing the concrete, wet the forms and the soil or gravel base with a garden hose to keep them from drawing water from the concrete mix. This is especially important on warm and windy days.

Placing the Concrete

Start placing concrete in the farthest corner of the form, dumping it in piles slightly higher than the form. Place each successive load against the previous one, using a shovel or a hoe to spread the concrete evenly. If the form contains wire mesh, periodically lift it with a hammer claw so that it stays in the middle of the slab.

During the pour, keep tamping out air bubbles by jabbing a shovel or hoe in and out of the concrete. Use a trowel to fill corners, and tamp concrete near the edges of the form. Don't overwork concrete, however. If you do, water will separate and rise to the top, weakening the surface. To further settle the concrete, tap the outside of the form with a hammer.

Screeding & Floating

Once the form is completely filled and tamped, use a screed—a straight 2x4 slightly longer than the form is wide—to level and compact the concrete. Drag the screed along the top of the form while moving it back and forth sideways in a sawing motion. As you drag the screed, keep both ends pressed down on top of the form to force aggregate into the concrete. Fill hollow spots with a shovelful of concrete, and screed the filled areas again.

Right after screeding, use a bull float (for larger pours) or a darby (for smaller ones) to smooth the concrete and further embed large aggregates. Run the bull float back and forth on the concrete, slightly raising the leading edge

Pouring Forms

USE: ▶ mason's hoe • wheelbarrow • shovel • trowel • 2x4 screed ▶ plywood • concrete • anchor bolts

1 *Mix only as much concrete* as you can place in about 45 min. After that, concrete may become too stiff to work.

2 *Transport the concrete* to the formwork using a wheelbarrow, bucket, or other container, and pour it into place.

3 *Fill the forms* completely, tamping the concrete as you go to eliminate voids and air bubbles.

4 *To ensure a smooth edge,* use a trowel to fill corners, and tamp concrete at the perimeter of the form.

5 *Use a 2x4 screed,* cut longer than the width of the footing, to strike off excess concrete above the level of the formwork.

6 *Embed steel anchor bolts* in the screeded concrete at 4 ft. on center and within 12 in. of each corner or opening.

to avoid gouging the surface. Move a darby in sweeping arcs across the concrete surface.

Floating causes water to rise to the surface. When a water sheen appears, don't do anything more to the concrete until the sheen disappears. How long this takes depends on the temperature, wind, humidity, and type of concrete. If you start finishing the concrete with the sheen still visible, you risk weakening the surface.

Finishing & Curing

As soon as the water sheen disappears, start the finishing process. The first step is to give the concrete smooth, rounded, crack-resistant edges by running an edger back and forth around its entire perimeter.

The final smoothing of the concrete surface is done with a hand float. For a rougher texture, use a wood float; for a smoother finish, or if the concrete is air-entrained, use a magnesium float. Hold the float nearly flat on the concrete, and sweep it back and forth in wide arcs, keeping the leading edge slightly raised so you don't gouge the surface. For an even smoother finish, run a steel trowel over the floated concrete. Touch up edges with the edger after floating and again after troweling.

To cure and harden properly, concrete must be kept moist and warm (above 50°F) for about five days after finishing. Moisture levels and curing time will depend on air temperature and humidity. To keep concrete wet enough to cure

properly, you either have to apply water periodically or prevent water loss by covering the concrete with plastic sheets or by applying a curing compound. In cold weather, protect concrete with straw covered by plastic sheeting.

Stripping Forms

After the concrete has cured for a day, remove formwork carefully so as to minimize damage to the concrete and the forms. The concrete won't fully harden for about a month, so don't pry or hammer against it. Remove or cut flush all wires and nails protruding from the forms. Scrape and wash the forms, and then lay them out to dry. Remove snap tie ends protruding from the concrete, and fill any voids.

Anchor Bolts

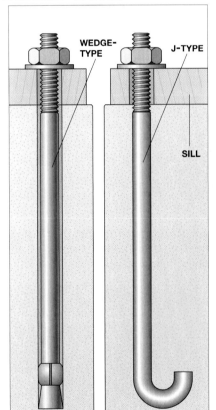

To secure sills, embed anchor bolts (⅝ inch in diameter and 18 inches long) in concrete foundation walls. Place the bolts after screeding, before the concrete sets. Space them 4 feet apart and 1 foot from each corner.

Curing Concrete

USE: ▶ garden hose • paint roller (optional) ▶ sheeting • bricks • curing compound (optional)

There are several ways to keep concrete moist during the curing process. Moisten the concrete with a garden hose, and then cover it with large plastic sheets or waterproof paper to prevent evaporation. (Weigh down the coverings with bricks.) Applying a curing compound to the damp surface is another way to lock in moisture. You can also cover the concrete with water-saturated burlap or canvas, and keep the coverings wet during the curing period. Or apply water periodically with a lawn sprinkler or soaking hose.

1 *Spray the surface* of finished concrete lightly but thoroughly with water from a garden hose.

2 *A curing compound,* applied to concrete with a paint roller is one way to prevent water loss during curing.

3 *Another way to prevent concrete* from drying prematurely is to cover the slab with plastic sheeting.

foundations

Masonry Walls

Unlike concrete walls, which are poured into forms, masonry walls are built up of individual units—clay bricks, concrete blocks, glass blocks, or stone—usually held together with mortar and often reinforced with steel. The main advantages of masonry construction are that it does not require formwork, and the units, especially bricks, are relatively lightweight and easy to handle. The main disadvantage of masonry is that even a reinforced concrete block wall won't be as strong as a reinforced poured-concrete wall.

Like concrete walls, masonry walls must rest on reinforced footings placed below the frost line. (For recommended footing dimensions, see "Continuous Footing Forms," p. 66.) In addition to vertical and horizontal steel reinforcement, brick and block walls may also require expansion joints (for brick walls) and control joints (for concrete block walls) to control cracking caused by the natural expansion and contraction of masonry units. Before building a masonry wall, always consult your local building department for footing, reinforcement, and other code requirements.

The 66 million tons of concrete in Hoover Dam could have taken 100 years to harden; cold water flushed through pipes placed every 5 feet in the forms cooled it in 20 months.

Bricks

An ancient building material, bricks are made of fired clay in a great variety of sizes, shapes, colors, and textures. Strong, decorative, and versatile, bricks are used for many different purposes, from building walls to paving walkways and lining fireplaces.

Brick walls may be solid structural walls, freestanding decorative walls (such as a garden wall), cavity walls, and veneer walls. Structural and freestanding decorative walls are usually double wythe, or two bricks thick. (A vertical tier of bricks in a wall is called a wythe.) In this type of wall, the wythes are bound with mortar and tied together with metal ties or alternating rows of header bricks. (Headers are bricks laid perpendicular to the length of the wall so that they overlap both wythes and create what is known as a pattern bond.) A cavity wall consists of two brick wythes, or a concrete-block backing wythe and a brick facing wythe, separated by a 2- to 4½-inch air space and held together by corrugated metal ties. A veneer wall is a single-wythe, non-bearing brick wall separated by a 1-inch air space from a structural wall to which it is anchored with metal ties.

Concrete Blocks

Economical and versatile, concrete blocks also come in a variety of shapes and types for different uses, such as foundations, interior and exterior walls, retaining walls, and garden walls. A standard hollow-core block consists of an outer shell with a hollow center divided into two or three cells by vertical partitions, called webs. Cells can be filled with insulation or grouted and reinforced. Block ends are flanged, to accept mortar, or smooth, for corners and wall ends.

Mortar

The mortar that binds bricks or concrete blocks together is a mixture of portland cement, hydrated lime, sand, and enough water to produce a smooth, workable consistency. Mortar is mixed much like concrete, and it's applied to bricks and blocks with a trowel. The techniques involved, however—loading the trowel, throwing a line of mortar on a row of bricks, "buttering" (applying mortar to) the end of a brick or block before placing it, and finishing mortar joints with a jointer—all require some practice.

Block Foundations

Concrete-block foundation walls are built without formwork on reinforced-concrete footings. The blocks are laid in a running bond, in which each row of blocks is offset by a half block so that vertical joints are staggered. The walls are reinforced with vertical rebar extending from the footing through the blocks' cells and anchored with a cement grout. Horizontal truss-type reinforcing wire is embedded in mortar under every other course. Anchor bolts and, if needed, horizontal rebar are grouted into the top course.

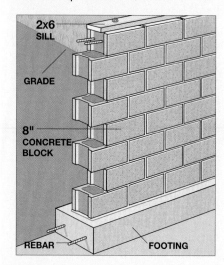

Reinforcing Block

USE: ▶ trowel • work gloves ▶ rebar • grout

1 *Cells will align* *even though blocks are staggered, leaving a clear vertical space for rebar. Cells with rebar must be grouted solid.*

Brick Veneer Walls

USE: ▶ mason's trowel • hammer • mason's twine • level • masonry bit • work gloves ▶ bricks • mortar • flashing • metal ties • galvanized nails

A brick veneer wall is built 1 inch out from the house sheathing, either on existing footings or steel angles bolted to the foundation. It is secured to the structural wall with metal ties nailed to house framing and embedded between courses every 16 inches vertically and 32 inches horizontally. Flashing installed over the first above-grade course directs any moisture behind it to weep holes opened in the second above-grade course of bricks.

1 Lay the first above-grade course of bricks so that there's a 1 in. space between the veneer wall and the house sheathing.

2 Flashing installed over the first brick course and weep holes in the second course drain water from behind the wall.

3 Nail corrugated ties to house framing so that the free end will be in the middle of the mortar joint, not below it.

4 Apply mortar carefully between brick courses to make sure that metal ties are properly embedded within the mortar joint.

5 Check bricks for level, plumb, and alignment as you fill in a course. Tap a brick into place with a trowel handle.

• reinforcing wire

2 Vertical rebar (placed every 4 ft. on center for a foundation wall) should extend from the footing to the top of the wall.

3 Spread a bed of mortar across the entire webbed surface of a concrete block to support horizontal joint reinforcement.

4 Embed truss-type horizontal masonry reinforcing wire in mortar under every other course and under the top two courses.

Site Drainage

Unless rainwater runoff is directed away from a building, the excess water can undermine a foundation. Hydrostatic pressure against the walls and erosion of the soil under the footings can cause serious cracking and uneven settlement. The water can also leak through cracks in the foundation or seep through basement walls and floors, resulting in a damp, musty basement.

Keeping a foundation dry requires a drainage system made up of several elements. Footing drains collect and carry off excess groundwater at the base of the structure. Gutters and downspouts channel rainwater off the roof, often into surface drains that carry runoff away from the building. A key feature of a drainage system is the ground (or grade) itself, which should slope away from the building a minimum of 1 inch per foot for about 6 feet to divert surface water away from the foundation.

Water from downspouts and drains typically runs through pipes to storm sewers or dry wells. A dry well is essentially a large hole in the ground filled with crushed rocks and gravel. Burlap or other filter fabric is laid over the gravel and then covered with sod. Surface and groundwater that would have flowed against the foundation drop instead into the very porous well and slowly filter back into the surrounding soil. (See "Building Dry Wells," p. 569.)

Footing Drains

A footing drainage system consists of 4-inch-diameter perforated drainpipe placed around the foundation either right on top of the footing or alongside it. The drainpipes connect to a leader pipe that either surfaces farther downhill or drains into a storm sewer or dry well.

The footing drains are embedded in gravel with their perforations facing down so that rising water will flow into the pipe and be carried off. Filter fabric covers the gravel bed to keep fine particles from clogging the drain pipe. Gravel backfill (placed against the foundation up to a foot below grade), drainage mats, or boards conduct water down to the footing drains. That way, water can be carried away from the foundation before it has a chance to build up and begin to seep through cracks in the foundation.

Roof Runoff

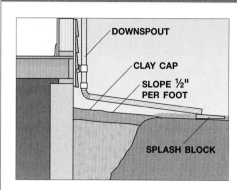
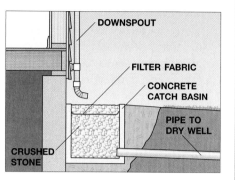

Your roof may be capable of shedding torrents of rain, and your gutter and leader system may be capable of carrying the flow down to the ground. But on many houses, that's where controlled drainage ends. Downspouts deposit the deluge of water beside the foundation, where it can leak into the basement, erode joints in masonry, and eventually undermine the foundation footing. There are several ways to reduce these problems. One is to regrade around the foundation to create a slope away from the building. Even a gradual slope extending a few feet will do. Second, carry water away from the building by extending the downspout. Placing a splash block under the downspout also helps. Where this isn't practical, direct water to a buried drainpipe or dry well.

Surface Drain Systems

USE: ▶ circular saw with masonry blade • cold chisel • hacksaw ▶ pipe • surface drain • pipe collars

Foundation drains set underground carry off subterranean water. But many walls are rimmed by concrete walks that need drainage as well. To give rainwater a place to go, form a channel in the surface concrete, and insert segmented drain fittings. Water enters through a grille and drains through a pipe to a dry well or outlet away from the house.

1 *Set prefabricated surface drains in a formed channel in walkways and patios that butt against foundations.*

2 *Slots in the top grid of the drain filter water running down the foundation and channel it into a pipe built into the unit.*

3 *At the end of the drain channel, connect a pipe collar to the fitting and direct the water into a standard drainpipe.*

Drains at Grade

A surface drainage system may consist of unperforated plastic pipe connected to downspouts and area drains, perforated poly sheeting under a layer of crushed stone, or unit pavers that divert surface water away from the foundation wall.

To keep perforated drain pipes *from clogging, slip on a filter fabric sleeve that lets water through but keeps out dirt.*

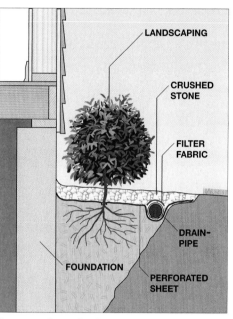

Layers of crushed stone and perforated polyethylene sheeting conduct excess surface water to drain tiles.

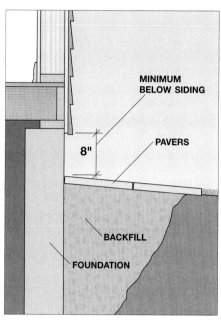

Unit pavers sloped away from a house divert runoff, reducing the amount of water that reaches foundation walls.

Footing Drains

Footing drains are set in different locations depending on the type of pipe used and drainage requirements on site. Flexible plastic pipe is generally placed on top of footings. Rigid pipe sections (below) are placed alongside them. In order to conduct groundwater away from foundations, footing drains need to be sloped at least ⅛ inch per foot.

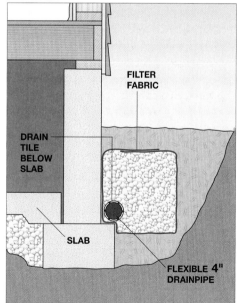

Flexible drainpipe is usually placed on top of footings to keep it from caving in as the ground below it settles and shifts.

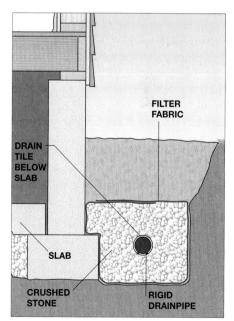

Rigid drainpipe is embedded in crushed stone alongside footings and below the level of the floor slab.

foundations

Drying Out Basements

Poor drainage in the ground around your house can lead to a wet basement (and, at worst, foundation failure). The excess water either leaks through cracks, holes, or mortar joints in the foundation walls or floor slab, or it seeps through pores in the masonry or concrete itself. But there is another, less serious cause of basement moisture: condensation, which occurs when water vapor in warm air hits the cool foundation walls and turns to liquid.

The sources of leaks can usually be identified by sight and repaired by plugging them with hydraulic cement or epoxy. (See "Patching Holes & Joints," p. 80.) To tell whether moisture on basement walls or floors is due to seepage or condensation, perform the test described at right.

Condensation problems can be solved by improving ventilation and using air conditioners and dehumidifiers. Eliminating seepage, however, is another matter. If seepage occurs only during heavy rains, the solution could be as simple as extending a downspout so that runoff is directed farther away from foundation walls, or regrading the soil so that it slopes away from the foundation. Minor seepage can often be corrected from the inside, by coating interior foundation walls with a masonry sealer (either a cement- or tar-based product or a waterproof silicone sealer). As a last (and very expensive) resort, you may have to re-excavate the foundation down to the footings to install perimeter drains and apply new waterproofing.

Testing for Leaks

USE: ▶ hair dryer or heat gun ▶ aluminum foil • electrical tape

Water leaking through a crack in a foundation is usually easy to detect. But basement walls also can become wet due to excessive moisture in the air that condenses on the masonry, particularly in the summer. To determine whether you have a leak (which may require joint repairs and more extensive grading and drainage work outside the building), or simply a moisture problem that requires a dehumidifier, conduct this simple DIY test using a piece of aluminum foil and some tape.

1 *Dry a wet area* on the wall using a hair dryer, and tape a square of aluminum foil over the spot, sealing it well with tape.

2 *Check for moisture* after 48 hrs. If the foil surface is wet but the wall below it is dry, the problem is condensation.

3 *If the foil surface* is dry but the wall beneath it is wet, then the problem is water seeping through the wall.

Exterior Waterproofing

USE: ▶ broom or wire brush • power drill/driver • caulking gun • work gloves ▶ cement patch • hot tar & felt paper or bituminous asphalt • waterproof caulk

1 *Foundations need waterproofing* below grade. This contractor starts by clearing debris from the footing joint.

2 *The next step on this house* is to patch holes in the concrete left by wire ties that keep the forms together during the pour.

3 *The most basic damp-proofing* is simply a layer of hot tar mopped in place. This is only the first step on some modern systems.

Waterproofing Foundations

Keeping water out of a basement requires both adequate foundation drainage and the application of an appropriate moisture barrier to the exterior of foundation walls. Such barriers should be applied at the time of construction. Retrofitting to moisture-proof a foundation is an expensive and difficult job best left to professional contractors.

There are two types of moisture barriers. Damp-proof barriers resist the seepage of moisture through foundation walls but don't keep out water under pressure. More expensive waterproof barriers prevent water under pressure from penetrating foundation walls. Damp-proofing may be sufficient for crawl spaces and for full basements in well-drained soil, as long as the basements are not meant to be used as living space. Waterproofing is recommended for all finished basements.

Damp-proofing usually consists of one or two coats of water-based asphalt emulsions applied to the exterior of foundation walls with a roller or brush. Waterproofing systems are often applied by professionals and include laminated asphalt (layers of hot- or cold-applied asphalt emulsion alternating with fiberglass or asphalt-saturated cotton fabric), liquid-applied elastomers, and self-sticking asphalt membranes. Waterproofing must be applied to clean walls and protected from backfill, either with roofing felt or with boards or mats that provide drainage and insulation as well.

Adding Basement Drains

USE: ▶ circular saw & masonry blade • trowel • hammer drill • gloves ▶ drainpipes • gravel • concrete

If a basement floods often and exterior waterproofing is not feasible, the only solution may be to install an interior trench drainage system. There are several ways to install drains. One is to chisel a channel at the perimeter of the floor slab, digging down 12 inches or more, and placing drainpipes pitched to a sump pit installed below the basement floor to collect water with a sump pump and pipe to direct water out of the house.

1 *To make a neat channel,* score the surface along both edges of the trench with a masonry blade.

2 *Drill a series of holes* along the cut lines to make it easier to break out the concrete channel.

3 *Insert drainpipes* within the channel on a bed of gravel. You can cover the pipe with gravel as well.

• drainage mats (optional)

4 *A layer of foamboard* provides insulation to keep the basement more comfortable and protects the wall coating.

5 *A thick bead of waterproof caulk* is applied along the top of the foamboard. This area will be above the final grade.

6 *The foundation is ready* for backfilling. Some waterproofing systems use drainage mats in addition to asphalt and foam.

Basement Repairs

To keep small basement moisture problems from turning into larger ones—such as a chronically wet basement—inspect basement walls and floors for seepage and leaks on a regular basis, especially after heavy rains or a spring thaw. In addition to checking for cracks and holes, look for moisture penetration through the mortar joints between concrete blocks and through floor-to-wall joints.

Repair holes and cracks as soon as you discover them, but bear in mind that filling a crack takes care of the symptom, not the underlying cause. A large amount of water entering a basement is a sign of a groundwater or surface water drainage problem that will have to be dealt with sooner or later. As part of a periodic basement inspection, also look for gaps around windows, doors, and vents (such as dryer vents)—all of which can let in water. Weatherstrip these openings completely, and seal them with silicone caulk.

Detecting Problem Cracks

Small to moderate-sized cracks that are stable (not expanding) are easy to repair and usually do not indicate a major structural problem. Larger or expanding cracks could signal a structural flaw in the foundation wall or a site drainage problem that is undermining the foundation. Either way, the result could be serious damage to your house if the problem goes unchecked. Be on the lookout for new cracks (or old ones that reopen after being repaired),
and monitor them carefully to determine whether they are active or expanding. (See "Monitoring Cracks," facing page.) Have a professional architect or engineer examine any active cracks in foundation walls or floors, and take care of the underlying problem.

Filling Cracks & Holes

To patch a small crack, apply an asphalt-based sealer to the crack, cover it with a fiberglass patch, and brush on a final layer of sealer.

Moderate-sized cracks can be filled with hydraulic cement, two-part epoxy filler, or a combination of the two. (Two-part epoxy is more permanent, but it's also more expensive than hydraulic cement and harder to work with.)

Cracks in walls and floors are filled the same way. The crack is first enlarged and undercut with a hammer and cold chisel. (Undercutting creates a key that holds the filler in place.) Then brush the crack clean and moisten it. Use a trowel to apply hydraulic cement or epoxy to within ½ inch of the crack's surface. Allow the filler to dry; then finish with hydraulic cement.

To fill a hole, shape a handful of hydraulic cement into a cone, squeeze the point into the hole, and hold it in place for several minutes until the cement hardens.

Repairing larger, more severe, or active cracks may require the use of flexible joint-fillers and sealants. Refinish an extensively repaired wall with masonry sealer.

Patching Holes & Joints

USE: ▶ mason's trowel • hammer • cold chisel • wire brush • jointing tool • caulking gun • work gloves

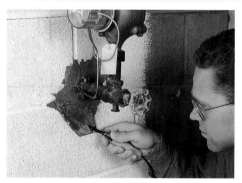

1 *Seal holes* where pipes extend through the foundation by using a trowel to fill the broken-out area with cement.

2 *To repair a leaking joint* in concrete block walls, start by chipping out any loose mortar and sweeping away debris.

Finishing Rough Walls

USE: ▶ sledgehammer • cold chisel • wire brush • wet-dry vacuum • sponge-faced trowel • bucket • mason's trowel • paint roller • work gloves • rubber gloves

1 *Use a heavy hammer* and cold chisel to chip off excess mortar. Wear gloves and eye protection when chipping masonry.

2 *Brush off dirt* from the interior surface of the masonry with a stiff wire brush, and sweep away any loose debris.

3 *To get the best adhesion* from a masonry surfacer, take the time to wash down the wall first.

Monitoring Cracks

Minor stable cracks in concrete walls are usually nothing to worry about (although they should be repaired). Larger cracks that appear suddenly or keep expanding could signal a serious structural flaw. If you notice a new crack, track its progress. Tape gridded tracing paper over the crack, and trace its outline. Measure the length of the crack and its widest parts. Mark the corners of the tracing paper on the wall so that you can reposition it exactly in order to see if the crack changes over time.

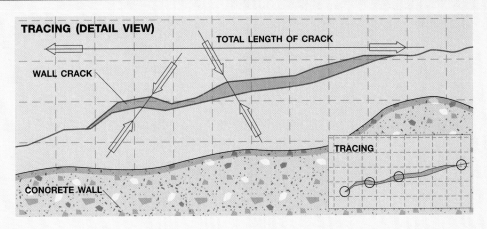

TRACING (DETAIL VIEW)

TOTAL LENGTH OF CRACK

WALL CRACK

TRACING

CONCRETE WALL

(optional) ▶ cement • hydraulic cement • elastomeric joint sealant

3 Once the joint is dry, *fill the seam with fresh mortar. To fill an active leak, use hydraulic cement, which hardens when wet.*

4 Before the fresh cement hardens, *use a jointing tool (or any curved tool) to smooth out the joint.*

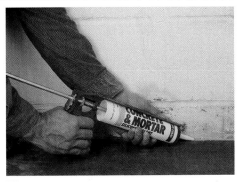

5 Small cracks at the floor seam *can be sealed with an elastomeric joint sealant or hydraulic cement patch.*

• eye protection ▶ hydraulic cement (or two-part epoxy filler) • masonry sealer

4 Use a trowel to fill joints and holes *with cement. The seams on block walls often are left rough by builders.*

5 Use a stiff brush *to apply a prime coat of masonry surfacer (the consistency of a very thick paint) to patch areas and seams.*

6 Use a roller and heavy-napped sleeve *to roll on the masonry surfacer. The highly textured surface partially conceals seams.*

wood

6

Wood Basics

If there were only one kind of tree in the world, and all the lumber companies cut them up into one size, ordering a piece of lumber would be as easy as ordering a glass of water. But forests are more diverse and complicated than that, and so is the language of lumber.

There are hundreds of wood species, from Abura (an acid-resistant wood used to make battery boxes and oil vats) to Zebrano (a West African wood with a striped, zebra-like pattern). But it's more likely that for your project you'll need a less exotic variety, such as fir, pine, redwood, spruce, or hemlock.

Lumber Sizes

Construction lumber, such as 2x4s and 2x6s, is sold by length, generally in 2-foot multiples from 6 feet up to about 24 feet. Long lengths are more likely to be available at large lumberyards, while smaller yards may not stock lumber over 16 feet long.

Boards such as 1x6 pine shelving may also be specified by length. But you may encounter a confusing measurement system based on board feet (the one used for pricing finish and common lumber in most yards). Unlike a square foot measurement of surface area, board feet takes thickness into account. This makes the overall measurement of 1-inch-thick wood completely different from the measurement of lumber that is the same length and width with a different thickness.

Technically, one board foot is a 12-inch length of 12-inch-wide, 1-inch-thick material. A 1-foot length of 1x12 pine shelving would be one board foot, for example. But a 1-foot length of 2x6 lumber would also measure one board foot. It's only half as wide but twice as thick. In neat multiples, this system is not too difficult to keep track of. Once you get into 2x10s, and mixed orders of 1-inch and 2-inch thick materials, hold on to your hat.

The kicker to all this number crunching is that a 2x4 isn't really a 2x4; it's a 1½x3½. This difference between what the wood products industry calls the nominal and actual dimensions is due to a lumber trimming and finishing process called dressing, even though "undressing" would be a more accurate description. A lot of wood disappears in the process.

Lumber Rejects

Although most of the keys to picking good lumber are visual, one of the most important is evident only in handling. As you heft several 2x4s of the same length, they should feel about the same weight. But it's possible that you will come across a few that quite obviously weigh more. That's because they are loaded with water. Avoid this lumber because it is likely to warp and twist dramatically after your project is built and the excess water gradually leaves the wood fibers.

To check lumber, simply pick up one end, check its weight, and then sight down the length of the board, putting aside those having obvious twists and turns. Although most lumber is not perfectly straight, it's easier to work with straight lengths. This avoids the problem of nail-popping stresses in curves that you straightened out in nailing. Besides, the non-waterlogged, straight-as-an-arrow 2x4s are the same price as those clunkers better left behind.

The legendary lumbermaker himself, Paul Bunyan, embodied the harvesting of a continent's wood bounty for homes and industry across the U.S. and Canada.

Lumber from Logs

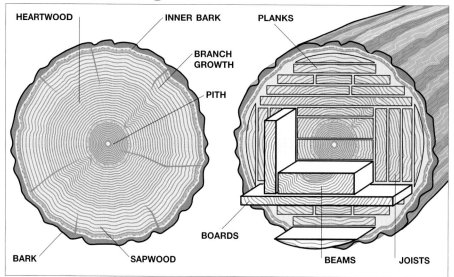

HEARTWOOD INNER BARK PLANKS
BRANCH GROWTH
PITH
BARK SAPWOOD BOARDS BEAMS JOISTS

Two types of wood grow within all trees: sapwood and heartwood. Sapwood is located at the outer perimeter of the tree and carries sap to the branches. Heartwood comes from the center of the tree and is denser than sapwood. All trees have this characteristic, and lumber taken from either the sapwood or heartwood region is graded accordingly. Studs are typically sawed from the sapwood area, large-dimension and higher-grade boards and planks come from the inner area, and beams come from the heartwood area.

Lumber Language

- **Softwood.** A fast-growing species of conifer, such as spruce, fir, or pine, whose wood is used primarily in home construction.
- **Hardwood.** A slow-growing deciduous tree, such as cherry or maple, with dense, heavy wood that is usually used for furniture, flooring, and trim.
- **Quartersawn.** Whole logs are split into quarters, and the wood is sliced across the grain to produce richly figured boards and dimensionally stable lumber.

- **Plainsawn.** Plainsawn lumber often has arched sections of growth rings on its faces, and may be less stable than quartersawn lumber.
- **Construction Lumber.** Cut from softwood trees, this easily worked wood is ideally suited for building projects. Wall studs, joists, and rafters are examples.
- **Finish Lumber.** Typically taken from the heart-wood section, free of knots and defects, used in making furniture or in construction spaces where wood is visible.

Board-Foot Formula
Multiply the thickness (inches) by the width (inches), by length (feet) and divide by 12.
Example: for an 8-foot 2x4: 2x4x8 = 64; 64/12 = 5.3 board feet of lumber in every full-size stud.

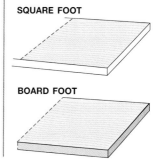

SQUARE FOOT

BOARD FOOT

Size Conventions

NOMINAL	ACTUAL
1x4	¾ x 3½
2x4	1½ x 3½

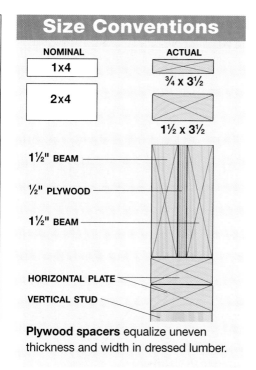

- 1½" BEAM
- ½" PLYWOOD
- 1½" BEAM
- HORIZONTAL PLATE
- VERTICAL STUD

Plywood spacers equalize uneven thickness and width in dressed lumber.

Building with Logs

Log buildings *are fast and easy to construct. Some precut kits use only logs small enough to be handled into place, while other structures require a crane to lift large, heavy logs or timber sections.*

Your idea of a log home may be Lincoln's log cabin, or a 5,000-square-foot castle with solid, 12-inch-thick walls. Either way, you can build one yourself from a kit or hire a log-home company. Hand-craft companies use traditional tools and techniques (plus a chain saw), sculpting one log to fit precisely onto another. In these homes, the solid logs make up the entire exterior and interior walls, siding, structure, insulation, and paneling. Hand-crafters cut the house at their remote log yards, truck the pieces to your foundation, and assemble it in one or two days. Precut companies, on the other hand, mill their logs to make them uniform, and cut the logs to form interlocking joints and corners. Some rip their logs in half and back what looks on the outside like a full-size timber with an air-infiltration barrier and 6 inches of insulation. Precuts may not be for purists, but they can cost one-third less than a standard, stick-built house of the same size. You can even assemble one yourself if you're handy and have experience with tools.

wood

Wood Strength

Different species of wood not only look different, they have different strengths and weaknesses as well. Even two pieces of the same type of wood can behave so differently that they are better suited for vastly different purposes. Their characteristics depend on what section of the tree they are cut from, how many knots they contain, and other factors.

Architects and engineers quantify the different strengths of wood species (and different cuts of the same species) in mathematical tables that must be consulted to find out if a certain size beam of a certain type of wood can adequately carry its load. At this level of detail, calculations might show, for example, that changing from one wood species to another or paying more for a better, stronger grade of the same species could allow an increased floor-joist span and eliminate the need for a central support girder.

But in most cases, you don't have to get this technical. For instance, if you want to replace a rotted 2x4 wall stud, you can simply ask for a 2x4 and expect to get a strong type of wood such as fir, which is commonly used for structural timbers. Lumber companies wouldn't manufacture 2x4s out of a softwood such as balsa, which is great for model carving but inadequate for holding up houses.

However, if a standard 2x4 rotted the first time, you should consider replacing it with redwood or cedar, which is more resistant to rot, or a pressure-treated 2x4 infused with rot-resistant chemicals. So instead of simply asking for a 2x4, ask the lumber dealer what type and grade of 2x4 would be best suited to your project. Most, if not all, of the wood you buy for home projects will be graded as either finish or common lumber.

Appearance Grade

Whatever wood you need is probably available in several grades. Finish lumber (such as pine boards used for shelving) is graded by letter, from A (the best) to E (the worst, which many lumberyards don't stock).

As a rule, Grade A denotes completely clear, knot-free wood. Such pristine lumber is extremely costly and may be available only on special order. Grade B—often called "clear" although it has a few, small imperfections—should be more than equal to any piece of fine woodworking you have in mind. In fact, some boards from Grades A and B may look just about the same; the slight differences may never show up on your project, particularly under a few coats of stain.

Grade C finish lumber has more visible blemishes but is still suitable for exposed moldings and woodwork. Grade D has visible knots and imperfections that cannot be completely hidden under a coat of paint. Of course, this grading system assumes that clearer, which is rarer and more expensive, is better. So if you like the look of knotty pine paneling, which is less clear and less expensive, you're in luck.

If in doubt, ask to see a sample. If the pine is for bookshelves, you might buy two nearly clear boards for the end panels and save money by using a knotty grade for the shelves. If your wood will have a clear finish such as polyurethane that enhances natural variations in the grain, clearer grades may look more subdued, uniform, and elegant. But if you plan to stain the boards, the appearance of knots and blemishes may be reduced instead of highlighted.

Grades for Common Lumber

Common lumber, such as 2x4s that generally are covered by other materials, is graded by number, from 1 (the best) to 3 (the worst). Wood graded Number 1 has blemishes and knots, but it is sound and watertight. As a practical matter, almost every stick of lumber used for do-it-yourself projects will be whatever the local lumberyard or home center has on hand—you can't always request a grade.

Typical Grades

Number 1: *Construction lumber, free of defects. Used in exposed beams.*

Number 2: *Construction-grade Douglas fir. Unseasoned wood.*

Span rating: *A measure of the elasticity and strength of wood (machine rated).*

Standard studs: *Douglas fir species. Kiln-dried, top; unseasoned, bottom.*

Vertical stud: *With glued finger joints. Not for horizontal spans.*

Select decking: *Free of defects, with moisture content (MC) at 15%.*

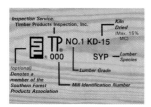

Number 1: *With moisture content, species, mill identification, and grade.*

Number 2, top; Number 1, bottom: *With grades and mill identification.*

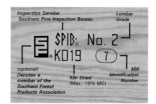

Number 2: *With inspection bureau stamp and moisture content.*

Composite Lumber

There are now a number of engineered lumber products available to the consumer. Some of these products were created in response to declining wood quality and rising costs, some to respond to the changing span requirements of house design.

A glue-laminated beam is built up from smaller pieces of wood finger-jointed and glued with waterproof glue. Six 2x4s, for example, will create a 9x3½-inch beam. These beams can be as long as you like—25 feet or more. Laminated-veneer lumber (LVL) is made from wood plies laminated together to a thickness of 1¾ inches thick. Parallel-strand lumber (PSL) is an engineered beam between 1¾ and 7 inches thick, made of matchstick-like strands of Douglas fir and/or southern yellow pine glued together parallel to one another. Wood I-beams and I-joists consist of a web made from ⅜-inch plywood or oriented-strand board (OSB), with 2-inch LVL or high-grade lumber flanges at the top and bottom. Wood I-beams come between 9½ and 16 inches deep and are lighter and easier to work with than the other types of composite lumber.

The lumber used in many new houses is manufactured using chips or strips of wood that make straight, strong beams.

Wood I-joists, which have a plywood center (web) glued to 2x4 rails (flanges), are lighter and stronger than solid lumber.

Metal stirrups, or hangers, are used to fasten composite joists and rafters, such as wood I-beams, to support beams.

Engineered wood framing often needs special fasteners, but this system offers benefits over conventional framing.

Building Loads

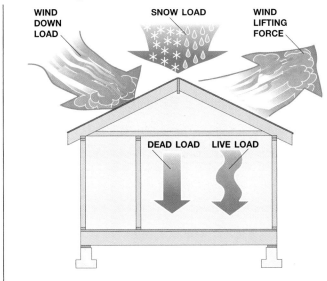

WIND DOWN LOAD · SNOW LOAD · WIND LIFTING FORCE · DEAD LOAD · LIVE LOAD

Your house must withstand many forces that engineers call loads. When a storm hits and high winds push at one side of the roof and pull on the other, the rafters must be strong enough to stay put. And when you invite a crowd over to barbecue on the deck, the joists must be strong enough to support the extra weight. There are two basic types of loads, called dead loads and live loads. Dead loads include the weight of building materials and other components that can be calculated from tables. Live loads include wind, piles of snow on the roof, furniture, people, and other changeable forces. The local building department will want your plans to account for all loads—for example, floor joists large enough to carry 40 pounds per square foot. A substantial safety margin is built into the codes so the floor won't collapse under 41 pounds.

wood

Wood Diseases

Framing lumber, even when sheltered by siding and drywall, can weaken and rot from attack by a variety of wood-destroying organisms. Here are some of the signs of decay and steps you can take to stop the deterioration.

Fungi

Wood-decaying fungi, including varieties of mold, mildew, and rot, flourish in temperatures between 50° and 95° F, invading wood that has at least a 20% moisture content. That covers a lot of the wood in a house, particularly any lumber that is damp from leaks, spills, or condensation. **Slime mold** can look as though someone has spread an egg white over the wood, and it can sprout surface growths. **Mildew** shows as powdery, gray-green or dark gray dots. You're likely to pick up a noxious, stale-bread odor from flourishing deposits, which stain wood instead of weakening it.

Because the growth is on the surface, you can brush the spots away and sand the wood to remove discoloration. If stains remain visible, apply a 50% bleach solution to lighten the grain; then sand and refinish. In damp areas, you can apply a fungicide paint, but reducing the moisture is a better solution.

Rot

Brown rot, named for the damage it does (not its appearance), creates a lacy white mat on damp lumber. It eventually cracks the timber into a grid of elongated, almost cork-like, dark brown cubes. Once you spot it, picking into the wood reveals substantial structural damage. Remove brown-rot damaged wood, and stop the moisture source to help preserve the replacement timber.

Dry rot can attack dry wood. It creates long tubes that can carry water for yards along a dry beam, and allow fungus to spread decay. Dry rot also shows a lacy surface mat, but it tends to be fan-shaped with tubular tendrils.

White rot bleaches the wood surface and creates a spongy timber with weak, stringy fibers. When the damage is widespread, the wood must be replaced. Soft rot occurs commonly on timbers in contact with damp ground, such as building sills, or posts with exposed end grain that soaks up water like a sponge.

Termite Risk Map

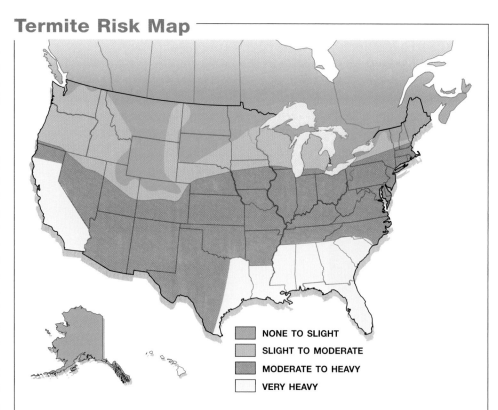

- NONE TO SLIGHT
- SLIGHT TO MODERATE
- MODERATE TO HEAVY
- VERY HEAVY

Identifying Problems

◆ **Surface signs.** Wood is a natural food source for many organisms, including mold, mildew, and insects such as those described on the next page. Wood is also susceptible to dampness and decay if left unprotected. Obvious signs of external attack include discoloration, dampness or slime, softening, dryness or powdery appearance, and sawdust or debris piled at the base of the wood. Some of this damage can weaken a structure beyond repair.

◆ **Hidden damage.** If surface signs indicate a problem not otherwise visible, some investigation is necessary to determine the cause and a suitable remedy. A penknife, awl, or other sharp probe can often tell you if structural damage has occurred beneath the surface and if infestation is underway. It's possible to actually hear insects grinding away at wood; today, dogs are sometimes used to find termite and carpenter ant colonies hidden deep within walls.

Wood Pests

◆ **Termites.** These highly destructive insects live in large colonies above or below ground. Their range is spreading, and many areas are now heavily infested. Subterranean termites dislike light, so they burrow into the soil and create mud tubes to reach food sources. Surface-dwelling termites will attack and eat wood wherever they find it.

◆ **Signs.** Look for winged termites swarming in spring and fall. Mud tubes on foundation walls, multiple borings, and waste pellet piles are other indicators of infestation.

◆ **Powder post beetles.** This crawling insect lays its eggs in cracks and crevices of wood; when the eggs hatch, the larva tunnel through the wood as they exit. The holes these pests make are very small, but if ignored, powder post beetles can be very destructive to softwoods, including structural lumber, and occasionally to hardwoods, such as finished flooring.

◆ **Signs.** Look for tiny holes and fine sawdust in piles on floors or gathered at the base of wood columns.

◆ **Carpenter ants.** Big, black, and aggressive, carpenter ants do not eat wood but burrow into it to form large colonies. They prefer damp, water-softened wood, and can create severe structural damage within large posts and beams.

◆ **Signs.** Look for individual scout ants foraging for new food and nest sites. Sawdust, droppings, and insect carcasses indicate a colony nearby.

◆ **Carpenter bees.** These look like large, mostly black bumblebees, and they make unsightly holes in wood siding and trim. Holes can be up to ½ inch in diameter and may tunnel several inches through the wood. Found in small groups with individual burrows, they prefer to bore into the underside of boards and railings.

◆ **Signs.** Bees will hover near nests, which are usually in weather-protected areas under or behind overhangs. As they work, they spew sawdust and yellow droppings.

Wood Defects

Any number of defects can occur in wood as it is milled, dried, and finally shipped to the consumer. Below are some common imperfections.

BOW

Bowed wood is warped along its longest axis—caused by moisture, it doesn't affect strength.

CUP

A cupped board is warped on the narrow axis of its face; these boards tend to pull loose from fasteners.

SPLIT

A crack or split that passes through the board is a serious structural flaw and should be avoided.

KNOT

A knot is the dense spot where a limb joined the trunk; knots should be avoided in load-bearing framing.

WANE

This rounded edge is caused by a board being cut too close to the edge of the log; it has no affect on strength.

wood

Redwood

Considered the Rolls-Royce of woods, it combines qualities of rot and insect resistance with esthetic beauty.

Use/Grade

Available with smooth, embossed, or saw-textured surfaces, redwood is ideal for decks, beams, and paneling.

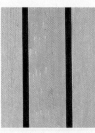

- ◆ **Clear all heart**
  Finest grade heartwood
- ◆ **Heart B**
  Limited knots
- ◆ **Clear (sapwood)**
  Some defects
- ◆ **B grade**
  Limited knots

Cedar

Naturally resistant to bugs and rot, cedar is the choice for siding and roofing as well as closets.

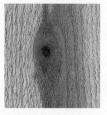

Use/Grade

Used in fences, decks and patios, and roofing shingles. Fresh cedar gives off an aromatic odor that is moth-repellent. Cedar shavings are often sold in pet stores for cage litter.

- ◆ **Clear Heart**
  Exposed wood
- ◆ **Grade A Clear**
  Shingles
- ◆ **Grade B Clear**
  Fencing
- ◆ **Knotty grades**
  Closets

Rot-Resistant Wood

When it comes to withstanding weather, insects, and various forms of decay, few woods can match redwood and its close cousin, cedar. These woods are also among the most attractive—and expensive—species used in and around homes today. Because of this, it pays to know something about the broad variety of grades available. Merchantable grade redwood contains large knots and softer, light-colored sapwood from the outer edges of the tree. This grade is recommended for fencing, trellises, and similar outdoor applications. But a beam of clear all-heart redwood, an extremely dense, knot-free grade, is often specified for critical roof beams in homes situated in high-risk fire areas. The dense beams char slowly in a fire, sometimes retaining enough strength to keep a roof from collapsing.

Protecting Redwood

Left unprotected, redwood loses its reddish hue, darkens, and may turn dark gray with black streaks before it gradually begins to bleach out. The final hue is like driftwood with a touch of silvery tan that some people find very attractive, although it doesn't resemble new redwood. Sealing the wood can reduce or eliminate the unattractive black stain part of the weathering cycle, and it keeps the wood looking newer longer. Two coats of a clear sealer, with one additional coat every year or two, would do a good job, particularly if you use one with an ultraviolet light (UV) inhibitor, which blocks at least some of the sun's rays that fade the wood and take away its color.

Once the color fades, you can renew the wood with a semitransparent, redwood-colored stain or by washing the surface with one of several chemical restorers. But handle the chemicals carefully, and observe restrictions because some can damage nearby plants. Another option, often used on decks, is to wash the wood with a power washer (set at minimum effective pressure) or simply a scrub brush and a solution of half water and half bleach.

Wood Treatments

A variety of treatments can protect wood from the effects of weathering, water, decay, and insects.

◆ **Water repellents.** Paraffin wax, tung or linseed oils, and natural or synthetic resins are used as additives to many types of finishes. These materials retard moisture's ability to enter or be absorbed by wood. Their effectiveness gradually wears away, and they must be reapplied.

◆ **Preservatives.** Chromated copper arsenate (CCA) is the most familiar preservative today, but commercial wood treaters use many other varieties. All wood containing these or other chemicals must be labeled to indicate the type and amount.

◆ **UV inhibitors.** These additives of solid pigments or particles reflect, absorb, or block harmful ultraviolet radiation to retard weathering.

◆ **Stains and bleaches.** Clear, semi-transparent, and solid stains contain pigments that add color (in any shade including white) and some measure of protection. These finishes also may contain water repellents and UV inhibitors. Bleaching stains contain pigments that give wood a gray finish.

Pressure-Treated Lumber

The raw material of pressure-treated (PT) wood comes from softwood varieties such as pine, fir, and hemlock. What makes the wood durable is the extra step of subjecting the lumber to chemicals in a pressure chamber. So much pressure is applied that the chemicals seep throughout the thickness of the lumber, not only on its surface.

A grade stamp on PT wood indicates the retention level of the preservative chemicals expressed in pounds per cubic feet. The numbers range from 0.25 for aboveground applications to 2.50 for saltwater applications. A rating of 0.40 is used for ground contact, and 0.60 for wood foundations.

The grade stamp also includes information on the year of treatment, the preservative used—usually chromated copper arsenate (CCA)—the name of the company that treated it, and the trademarks of various agencies. In addition, it mentions the species of wood and the manufacturer.

Pressure-treated wood foundations *are a recent innovation—only use wood with high PT ratings for in-ground use.*

Durable and weather resistant, *PT lumber is widely used for decks and outdoor structures.*

Special Handling

All wood preservative chemicals are toxic, so always wear eye protection and rubber gloves. Activated carbon respirator masks will protect against some fumes.

When cutting treated wood, work with caution. Wear a dust mask (and goggles, if you're using a power saw), and dispose of scraps and sawdust in plastic bags. Never bury or burn any materials that have chemical preservatives, and after working with the wood, wash before eating, drinking, or smoking.

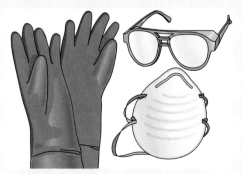

Don't take chances with wood preservative chemicals. Observe hazard warnings and wear protective gear.

Creosote and pentachlorophenol (penta), two well-known preservatives that were widely used for outdoor or ground-contact wood, have been banned from consumer sale and use because they are suspected carcinogens. Considering this, it's wise not to use any type of treated wood that could leach chemicals into the soil to become a component of food. CCA was tested and approved for in-ground use, but some questions remain as to its effects on soil or crops over the long term.

wood

Wood Joinery

Fastening two pieces of wood together can be done in a number of ways. For construction purposes, most joining involves simple cuts and a few fasteners, although in some cases (particularly house framing), special hardware is called for. The tools needed to do the job are most often a handheld circular saw, drill, and hammer, along with nails, screws, or bolts. In furniture-making, on the other hand, special tools and a dedicated wood shop are needed to make the complicated cuts required of fine joinery. (Nails, screws, and adhesives are covered in detail in Chapter 3.)

Types of Joints

The most basic connection is a **butt joint**—two pieces of wood, ends squared and fastened together. There are two tricks to the process. First, because a lot of lumber used in woodworking is only ¾ inch thick, you should predrill nail holes to avoid splitting. Also, because wood swells and shrinks with the seasons, sliding along the nail shanks, you should back up the connection with a layer of glue.

On a common butt joint—a bookshelf butting against an upright, for example—structural stresses do not transfer directly from one board to another. They must be carried across the joint by nails and glue. If appearances allow, butt joints can be strengthened (and locked into a 90-degree angle), by metal supports or glue blocks.

L-shaped metal angle irons (with predrilled holes for screws) will hold the pieces together and actually carry most of the load if they are snugged up into the joint between shelf and upright. Furniture makers frequently use wooden glue blocks instead, when they can be hidden beneath upholstery. On the bookshelf, you would glue the right-angle of a triangular block in place beneath the shelf and against the upright.

Two joints that make two short pieces of wood into one longer piece are **scarf joints** and **finger joints**. Scarf joints offer little structural support and are mainly used to provide continuity or to lengthen a framing member. Glued finger joints, made with precision woodworking machinery, can be stronger than the wood itself.

A **lap joint** is created when two pieces of

Basic Wood Joints

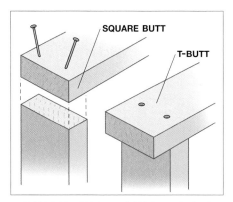
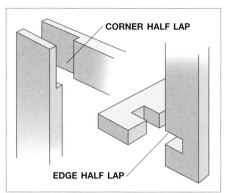

Butt joints are made with the ends of two boards joined at 90-degree right angles. Metal braces are sometimes used to reinforce the corners. **Lap joints** are made by cutting out sections of wood and joining the two pieces together.

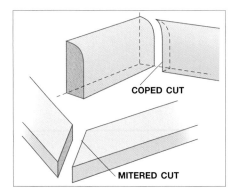
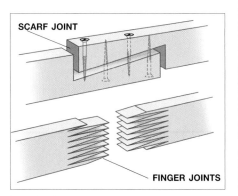

In miter joints, corners are cut at a 45-degree angle and joined to form a 90-degree edge. Miters and coped joints are used in trim and finish work. **Scarf and finger joints** (right) are examples of joints used to splice or extend wood lengths.

Power Miter Saws

Power miter saws, also called cutoff saws or chop saws, are a great time-saver for making angle cuts. These tools are circular saws mounted on a pivot assembly, which enables you to make precise straight, angled, or beveled crosscuts. You can get saws with 8-, 10-, or 15-inch blades, and some that tilt and slide, called compound miter saws. Make sure the saw has a stable base and a convenient source of power. Always wear goggles when cutting.

wood overlap one another. One piece of wood may be notched out, allowing the other piece to fit down into it—this is known as a full-lap joint. Both pieces may also be notched to half their thickness, which is known as a half-lap joint.

A **miter joint** is formed by cutting corresponding angles, usually 45 degrees, on the ends of two pieces of wood and joining them together. A familiar use of the miter joint is in picture frames. A miter joint may be reinforced with pins, dowels, or splines.

A **rabbet joint** is created when you notch the edge of a piece of wood and use that notch to join two boards. Rabbet joints are usually secured by nails or glue. A **dado joint** is formed by cutting a groove (dado) into one piece of wood the exact size of the edge of another piece. This type of joint is commonly found in bookshelves.

Joints seen in work as diverse as furniture-making or post-and-beam construction include mortise-and-tenon joints, dovetail joints, and dowel joints.

Types of Metal Connectors

Some joints in house framing may need hangers, ties, anchors, or other metal supports to reinforce wood joints. This is especially true in earthquake- or hurricane-prone areas, where local codes generally require connectors.

Hangers and ties are available for a wide range of applications, for nearly every type of framing joint—for example, **rafter ties** for the joint between rafters and top plates, and joist hangers for joining ceiling or floor joists to headers or rim joists. Other commonly used fasteners include **post anchors**, which attach posts to concrete foundations; **truss plates**, which hold together the elements of prebuilt roof trusses; plywood sheathing **panel clips**, which join adjacent plywood panels; and **nail-stopping plates**, which prevent drywall nails from being driven into pipes, wires, or ductwork.

Most metal hangers have nailing clips or teeth stamped into them, but these have no fastening strength and are used to hold the hanger while you nail it permanently in place. Special nails are available, or you can use common nails. Be sure to nail through each of the holes provided.

Basic Wood Connectors

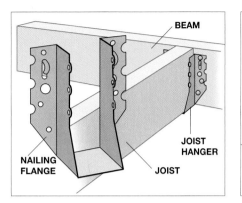

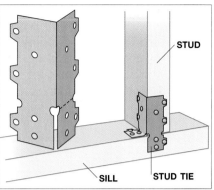

Joist hangers are a secure way to attach lumber to other lumber and are available in shapes to accommodate and reinforce every type of structural connection. Hangers, anchors, ties, and other metal supports are often required by codes.

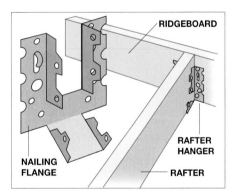

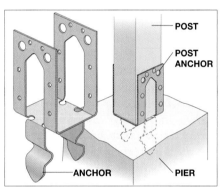

Rafter hangers attach the rafters to ridgeboards at the roof peak and to top plates on the wall. **Post anchors** are mounted in wet concrete piers, allowing posts to be easily attached and raised above wet surfaces.

Miter Boxes

Hand-cut the exact angles for miter joints with a miter box. Steel miter boxes have guides on the front, back, and top to hold the backsaw at any desired angle during the cut. The most basic wooden and plastic miter boxes generally have slots that only allow you to cut 90- and 45-degree angles. If you clamp them securely (and clamp the wood inside to the box), they are useful for rough work. But they are not accurate enough for fine joinery.

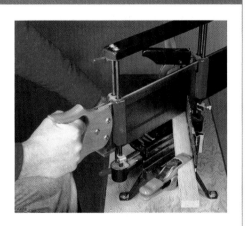

wood

Sheet Goods

Man-made panels, called sheet goods in the woodworking trades, have outstripped solid slabs of the real thing in just about every way lumber can be judged. Unlike solid lumber, which must be run through a thickness planer before use, manufactured panels are uniform. They are also more widely available and come in large 4x8-foot sheets, so you don't have to glue up a series of solid boards to make a wide piece.

Also, solid wood with grain running in one direction is susceptible to swelling, shrinking, and all sorts of twisting. Even wood dried in a kiln and assembled perfectly with glue and screws into a solid bookcase may start to warp in humid weather. But panels are made like a layer cake, some with as many as 13 laminations. Each layer's grain runs in a different direction to add strength and reduce warping.

Types of Panel Products

Among the many trade names for types of panels, there are four basic types: plywood, hardboard, strand board, and particleboard. For woodworking purposes, **plywood** is the category with the most distinct subdivisions. These panels, which generally range from ¼ to ¾ inch thick, can have a surface in any number of wood species from plain, paintable birch to the richest cherry or walnut. Underneath are layers of common wood with alternating grain directions—unless it's composite board (see below). CDX plywood is most commonly used for sheathing house framing.

Besides particleboard, strand board, and hardboard, other common panel types include **orientated-strand board** (OSB), which uses strands of wood glued together and cross-laminated for strength, and **composite board,** a hybrid of plywood and particleboard or fiberboard (commonly called MDF for medium-density fiberboard). These boards have a reconstituted wood center but a face and back of plywood. Both core types are made from different preparations of compressed wood chips and fibers that lumber mills used to throw away. Both these products are used for wall sheathing and floor underlayments, if local building codes allow.

Because there are so many types and grades of plywood, it's smart to talk over your options with a lumber dealer before you buy.

Plywood grade stamps incorporate span ratings, exterior or interior applications, wood-grain orientation, the type of wood, and the name of the manufacturer.

Common Plywood Varieties

◆ **1/4-inch,** the thinnest of the plywood grades, is primarily used for temporary projects, hobbies, and nonstructural applications. It can be bent to create curving surfaces or arches. Also available as interior paneling.

◆ **1/2-inch** is typically used in roof sheathing and siding. It can be pressure-treated, and it comes in several grades from A to D. Economical finish-quality plywood is also sold with one good face and a lower-quality backing.

◆ **3/4-inch** subflooring plywood will provide resistance against loads. If used where moisture is present, specify exterior-grade made with water-resistant glue.

PLYWOOD STRUCTURES

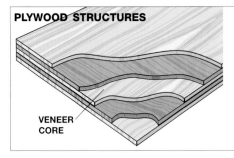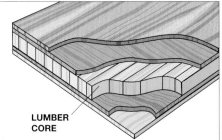

VENEER CORE

LUMBER CORE

Particleboard

Particleboard is made from wood chips, splinters, and sawdust glued together with urea formaldehyde resin and pressed together into 4x8-foot sheets. Along with a similar product, called medium density fiberboard (MDF), it is used for a variety of applications inside the house such as countertop underlayment and core material for cabinets and furniture. Particleboard does not hold nails or screws very well by itself, and tends to chip or flake near the edges unless attached to another material.

Strand Board

The first generation of this structural panel was called waferboard, although panel terms often are mixed at lumberyards and home centers. Waferboard was a step up from particleboard mainly because the particles in the panel were larger and stronger. Where particleboard used mainly sawdust-sized material, waferboard used random strips of wood. The second generation, called oriented-strand board (OSB), use opposingly placed strips for even more strength and serves as subflooring and sheathing.

Hardboard

Hardboard is a versatile manufactured wood product used in a number of nonstructural applications such as door filler, drawer bottoms, cabinets, and tabletops. It's also manufactured with a plastic or melamine laminate or with a series of predrilled holes (a product known as pegboard). It is made by bonding wood chips, sawdust, and fibers with phenol formaldehyde. Hardboard is usually thin (1/8 inch), does not hold screws or nails well, and is typically fastened to wooden frames for support.

Building Nonsqueak Floors

Creaking floors are common in older homes, but new floor systems have been developed to overcome this. If the various components stay tight, they won't squeak. Wood I-joists flex and shrink less than solid-lumber joists, so fasteners don't pull loose. Subflooring with tongue-and-groove edges lock together. They are also glued to the joists and fastened with ring-shanked nails that won't pop out when stresses occur. Bridging or solid blocking between joists is also important. To correct squeaks in an existing floor, check from below to see if bridging is missing. The subflooring also may have pulled loose or warped away from the joists in the area near the squeak. Use wood screws to pull the subfloor in place, or add shims to fill any gaps.

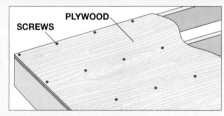

Tongue-and-groove subflooring should be glued to floor joists and fastened with ring-shanked nails. **Wood screws** are used for added strength or where nails may split wood.

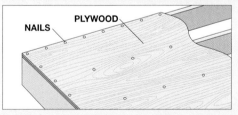

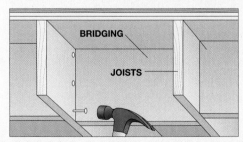

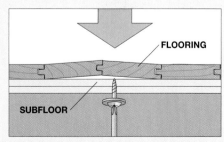

Finished floor joints that prevent squeaking include 1-in. lapped joints and tongue-and-groove joints. Properly glued, subflooring resists vibration, bounce, and loose nails.

wood

Paneling Products

Sheet paneling—of real or simulated wood—is a popular wall surface for do-it-yourselfers. It adds warmth to any room in the house and is particularly desirable in recreation rooms because it holds up under hard use. Paneling goes up quickly, as well, without the time-consuming finishing steps required by drywall.

Building codes regulate whether paneling may be applied directly to studs. Sometimes, a layer of drywall must be installed beneath thin paneling to support it, as well as to add a measure of fire resistance.

As nice as sheet paneling may look, it can't duplicate the richness of a room lined with real wood, however. Boards allow you to create your own pattern, and they may be nailed up directly over studs with no drywall needed, unless fire codes prohibit this. Board paneling is more expensive than sheet paneling and can take more time to install and finish, but the results are worth the effort.

Prefinished Paneling

Among the least expensive paneling is prefinished hardboard. Sometimes referred to by the trade name Masonite, hardboard paneling often has a top layer that is factory-finished with a wood-grain pattern. Hardboard panels usually measure 4x8 feet and range from ⅛ to ¼ inch thick.

Prefinished plywood paneling is available in a wide selection of colors, patterns, and thicknesses. Sheets are most often 4x8, ranging from ⁵⁄₃₂ to ½ inch thick (with ¼ inch being the most common). The face of each panel is printed, embossed, or color-toned with wood grain or other decorative effects. Some are laminated with an overlay that offers even more variety. In addition, some types are grooved to simulate individual wood boards.

Board Paneling

Board paneling can be bought in a variety of hardwoods and softwoods milled especially for this use. It can be from ⅜ to 1 inch thick and comes in various widths up to 12 inches. The boards have either tongue-and-groove or shiplapped edges. In addition, the surface edges of the boards may be beveled for decorative effect.

Installing Sheet Paneling

USE: ▶ saber saw or keyhole saw • 4-ft. level • hammer • measuring tape • straightedge • caulking gun

1 Butt one end of the first sheet into a corner; then adjust the other end against a level so that the sheet is plumb.

2 Measure the height, and width of utility boxes for cutouts. Precut them with a saber saw or keyhole saw.

Sheet-Paneling Options

Type	Application
Standard 303	The name for a variety of APA siding patterns.
T1-11 siding	A widely used APA-303 panel with vertical grooves.
Pine or fir	Usually exterior, must be painted or stained.
Bead-board plywood	Used for porch ceilings or interior wainscoting; paint-grade only.

Installing Plank Paneling

USE: ▶ saber saw or keyhole saw • chalk-line box & plumb bob • scriber • straightedge • 4-ft. level • drill

1 Walls need to be furred out with furring strips to ensure an even nailing surface. Shim any low spots.

2 After the furring is completed, nail the first board into place. Scribe and cut its edge if the adjacent wall is not plumb.

▶ sheet paneling • finishing or ring-shanked nails • prefinished trim as required • caulk

3 *Using a caulking gun,* apply a bead of construction adhesive in a zig-zag pattern along the length of each stud face.

4 *Nail the panel into place* with paneling nails. Special ring-shanked nails are available in colors to match the paneling.

5 *For a coordinated look,* nail prefinished matching molding along the base and around windows and doors.

Plank-Paneling Options

Type	Application
Shiplap	Exterior or interior, vertical or horizontal, edges overlap.
Tongue and groove	Exterior or interior, vertical or horizontal, edges lock in place.
Clapboard	Usually exterior horizontal siding, edges overlap.
Hardboard	Exterior or interior, needs painting or staining.
Board and batten	Usually exterior, rough-sawn vertical, battens overlap edges.

Concealing Nails

An easy and effective way to fill nailholes and repair surface dings is with a crayon-like colored wax pencil.

• hammer • measuring tape • pencil ▶ plank paneling • finishing nails • furring strips • wood trim as required

3 *Boards will have lapped edges* or tongue-and-groove slot fittings. Attach boards to the furring with finishing nails.

4 *Measure for cutouts as they occur.* Mark the cutout on the board, drill a starter hole, and finish cutting with a saber saw.

5 *Fit sections together* over the cutout. If necessary, use an electrical junction box extender for the outlets.

wood

Finish Work

Trim is both practical and decorative. It covers rough edges and seams between different building materials inside and out, and it adds a distinctive touch that gives a house architectural detail and character. Installing trim can be a rewarding job if you master the art of making various kinds of simple miter cuts and getting a tight fit. To cut miters, you need a good miter box and a backsaw with a sufficient number of teeth per inch to make fine cuts without splintering the molding. Power miter saws make quick work of cutting even difficult angles.

Trim is sold by the foot, in lengths ranging from 6 to 14 feet. Try to get lengths that will span each wall, corner to corner, to avoid unsightly splices. Keep in mind that many softwood varieties of trim can be either finger-jointed or clear. Finger-jointed is less expensive because it has splices and must be covered with paint. Clear trim can be stained.

Types of Molding

Home centers carry pine, oak, and poplar moldings in a great variety of shapes that are designed for specific locations and uses. The first trimwork to be installed are the casings that go around doorways and windows. Next are base and shoe moldings, which trim the wall at the floor. Cove or crown molding is used along the wall at the ceiling, and corner molding for both inside and outside corners is used to hide seams and protect corners.

Because techniques for milling are not perfectly standardized, it's best to buy all the pieces of trim from the same milling lot to avoid fractional differences in size.

Biscuit Joinery

USE: ▶ biscuit joiner • bar clamps • measuring tape • pencil ▶ biscuit wafers • yellow wood glue

1 *Before cutting,* position the pieces of wood as you will join them, and mark reference lines for the biscuits.

2 *Biscuit slots* are cut with a biscuit joiner, a tool that cuts to a specific depth and width sized for the biscuit you will use.

Common Molding Profiles

BASE MOLDINGS

Base moldings can be as simple as plain square stock (S4S) or more elaborate with built-up components like shoe and base cap. Colonial base (top) is a more traditional style, while Ranch base (center) is common in today's homes. Contemporary base (bottom) is a stock item or easily made with a router or saw.

CHAIR RAILS

These moldings do what their name implies— protect walls from damage caused by chair backs bumping up against them. They have evolved into purely decorative trim that visually divides open wall space or creates a demarcation between paint, wallpaper, or paneling. There are many styles available that range from simple to sublime.

Back-Cutting Joints

To make tight miter joints, use a sharp saw blade and a miter box or miter cutter to produce a clean angle cut. Test-fit the joint, and if it doesn't close tightly, use a block plane to shave a thin amount of wood from the bottom part of the cut. Be careful not to plane along the cut line on the face of the joint. This back-cutting ensures that the two cut faces will touch.

Use a plane to back-cut miter edges, shaving with the grain of the wood.

For exact 45-degree joints, sharp saw and plane blades are a necessity.

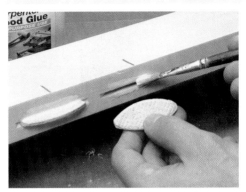

3 *Either white or yellow wood glue* can be used in biscuit joinery. Test-fit biscuits to be sure the slot is free of sawdust.

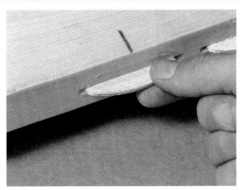

4 *Biscuit wafers,* made from compressed beech wood, expand when glued to fit the slot. The result is a tight, concealed joint.

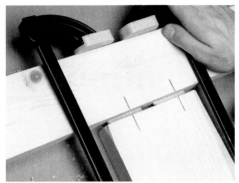

5 *After filling the slots with glue,* the biscuits are inserted into both slots and the wood sections are clamped.

CROWNS

Aptly named, crown moldings are often the most elaborate and costly moldings in a room; they can add a crowning touch to almost any space. Styles range from simple coves ⅞ inch wide to custom-made crowns up to a foot or more edge to edge. They may be used alone or layered with other moldings for dramatic effect.

CASINGS

Perhaps the most utilitarian molding style, casings serve mainly to cover openings or joints between walls and window or door jambs. Because they must be miter-cut at corners and other intersections, always use pieces from the same stock run to ensure that the molding profiles will match up when installed.

BUILT-UPS

Although there are many ready-made molding profiles, "trimming out" can be a carpentry art form. By combining different types of molding and square stock, you can create unique built-up trim profiles to suit your taste or your home's décor. The illustration at right is just one example, using four basic molding styles.

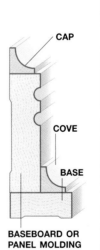

CAP

COVE

BASE

BASEBOARD OR PANEL MOLDING

Coping Joints

For inside corners, coped joints allow you to match two intricate molding faces. Cut the first piece square, and butt it into the corner. Cut the other piece on a 45-degree angle, leaving the face exposed. Use a pencil to outline the cut edge, and follow this when you make the second cut with a coping saw, back-cutting it slightly so the cut face mates tightly with the corner piece.

Cut a 45-degree face onto the intersecting trim piece; then, scribe the cutout.

Use a coping saw to back-cut along the scribed line; file the edge if necessary.

framing

7

framing

Framing Basics

Only a few DIYers ever tackle the job of framing a house, but an understanding of framing can help you with many less daunting home-improvement projects, such as adding or removing interior walls, finishing a basement, building a tool shed, or adding a new room to a house. Even if you don't intend to do the work yourself, having a firm grasp of what is involved in framing will make working with architects and contractors that much easier.

Understanding Loads

To understand how a framing system works, think of it as a network of streams along which structural loads flow from the roof, through the building and foundation, and into the ground. The network directs loads the way a stream gathers water drained from the surrounding terrain. Like water, loads tend to take the path of least resistance to the lowest point in accordance with the law of gravity. Just as water won't run uphill, structural loads from a rafter won't jump out into the attic to appear in the middle of the floor: they flow down the rafter to the support framing below.

Loads must be carried from the top of the structure to the foundation without interruption. If there is a break in the system, for example, if you fail to install an adequate header over a door, weight from above will cause binding and the door will stick. Structural weaknesses also can pop nails in drywall, crack trim, and create other problems.

Floors, posts, columns, roof framing, and all exterior walls are load-bearing. They carry the weight of the structure and everything in it (such as people) or on it (such as shingles). Many interior walls are not load-bearing. These partition walls simply divide up space. You can cut through a partition to create a doorway or remove the wall altogether. But wherever you cut into a bearing wall, you need to account for the load it carries—for example, by installing a header over a door. Consult the local building department about changing a load-bearing wall.

Types of Loads

Structural loads consist of dead loads, such as the weight of the building materials and mechanical equipment, and live loads, such as the weight of people, furnishings, stored materials, and snow on the roof. Other loads include such natural forces as high winds and earthquakes. A structure's design should also account for point loading, which is the downward force exerted by a single heavy object inside or on top of the structure, such as a fireplace, water heater, or roofing equipment. The architect's or engineer's job is to anticipate all conditions that could reasonably be expected at the site.

Designing for Loads

In house design, potential loads and stresses are typically provided by local building codes. (In a fire or earthquake zone, special engineering is required.) For example, floor systems are generally designed to support 40 pounds of live loads per square foot. (Loads are uniformly distributed across the joists and flooring, so that a person weighing a lot more than 40 pounds can be standing on one square foot of floor.) The system won't collapse under 41 pounds, but the beams might start to bend (or deflect, the engineers' term). Because wood is resilient, the frame can absorb the extra strain as you jump around or do calisthenics. The standard limit of bending (called deflection in a building beam) is 1/360th of the span. Statistically, that means if the floor joists were 360 feet long they would have to be strong enough to bend no more than 1 foot when loaded with people and furniture.

Framing Loads

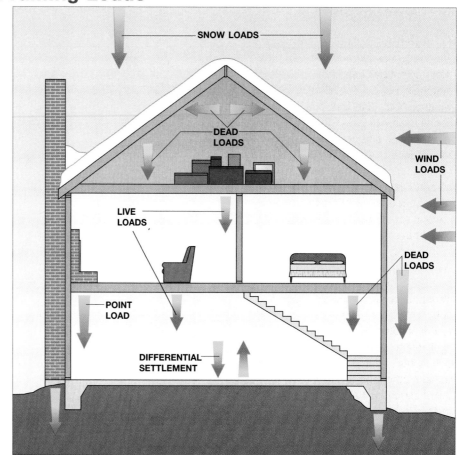

SNOW LOADS

DEAD LOADS

WIND LOADS

LIVE LOADS

DEAD LOADS

POINT LOAD

DIFFERENTIAL SETTLEMENT

The total load on an existing structure can be substantial and must be accounted for using proper design standards and beam and lumber sizing.

Blueprints

Blueprints lay out your job in measured detail. On large jobs, you need at least two sets for the building inspector, one for yourself, and several for contractors. A complete set includes a plot plan locating your house on its site according to surveyed boundaries; a floor plan for each level; elevations or building sections; and door, window, and finish schedules. Key components are drawn to scale, and their sizes are noted to avoid confusion.

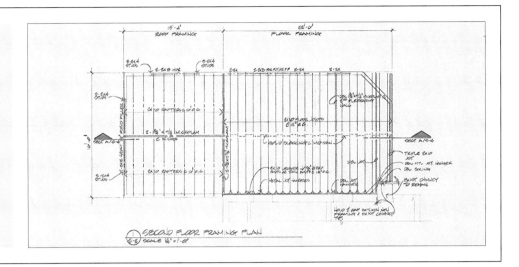

Special Loads

In some parts of the country, your house can be expected to bear more than the normal loads from building materials, people, furnishings, and the weather. You'll find that local building codes in areas subject to hurricanes, earthquakes, and other extreme forces may require special materials and construction details. In addition to those safeguards, plans for additions and other structural alterations in these regions should be checked with a structural engineer or architect.

In hurricane-prone areas, where high winds can peel roofs from houses, cause severe water damage, and lead to structural collapse, hurricane and seismic ties are used to secure the roof to the building. Frame connectors are available to reinforce every structural connection, tying framing components to each other and to the foundation. Local codes may also require specific installations, such as nailing instead of stapling roof sheathing to rafters. In the wake of 1992's Hurricane Andrew in Florida (with winds of up to 160 mph), the most wind-resistant combination turned out to be low-slope hip roofs covered in clay or cement tiles.

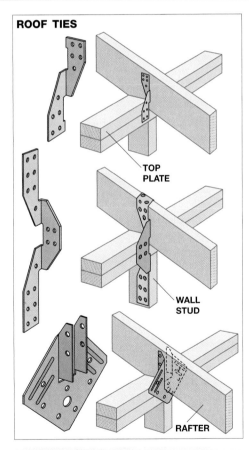

ROOF TIES

TOP PLATE

WALL STUD

RAFTER

Local codes may require that you install rafters or roof trusses with nails, and lock the joints with connectors.

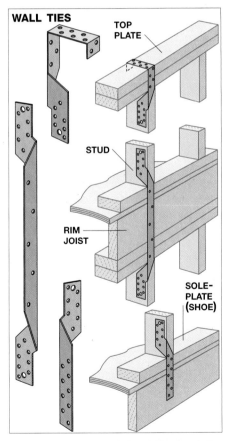

WALL TIES

TOP PLATE

STUD

RIM JOIST

SOLE-PLATE (SHOE)

Framing ties are made of steel bent to fit typical frame connections and perforated for nailing.

Framing—Old & New

A common complaint of homeowners is the amount of repair work required on their new homes. Too often the smooth, freshly painted surfaces deteriorate after only one or two heating seasons; the wood framework beneath those surfaces dries out, twists, pops nailheads out of the wall, and opens seams between drywall panels. Decades ago, when labor and materials were relatively inexpensive, these problems were overcome by following a simple principle: if in doubt, overbuild. Now, the expense of using 2x12 joists instead of 2x8s makes this principle unrealistic. Even though wood is a renewable resource, the emphasis in current construction is to engineer systems that use less wood without sacrificing strength and durability.

This is not a new idea. Just consider the evolution from log cabins to timber-frame structures, and the change from beams on the scale of 8x8 inches and larger to conventional modern framing (aptly called stick-built construction). Now, highly engineered wood-framing systems have been developed that deliver more strength from less wood and decrease construction time as well as cost.

Modern Framing Methods

The vast majority of houses built today are stick-built using a system called platform framing. Platform framing breaks the job into discrete components that are easier to work on than a whole building at once, and it allows you to use shorter pieces of lumber. It's the easiest way to build a multistory structure because you work from framed platforms for each story.

Alternative methods of framing a house are used in varying degrees, however. The old-fashioned techniques of building a home from rough-hewn logs, or framing with full-size timbers, are popular enough to have magazines devoted to them. These days in the Southwest, you might even see a house built out of straw bales, a technique first used by settlers in Nebraska in the 1880s. It's not unknown for houses to have a framework of used automobile tires, rammed earth, lightweight concrete blocks, or steel framing members, which were once seen only in commercial buildings.

Framing Systems

Balloon framing, with long wall studs that run from foundation to roof, was widely used in multistory wood frame houses through the mid-twentieth century. The system took advantage of mass-produced lumber and enabled people to build with 2x4s and 2x6s instead of heavy posts and beams. Declining lumber quality, floor-to-floor fire code regulations, and the use of drywall instead of plaster led to the layer-cake approach called platform framing.

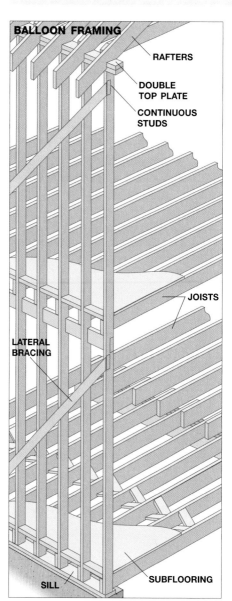

BALLOON FRAMING

RAFTERS
DOUBLE TOP PLATE
CONTINUOUS STUDS
JOISTS
LATERAL BRACING
SILL
SUBFLOORING

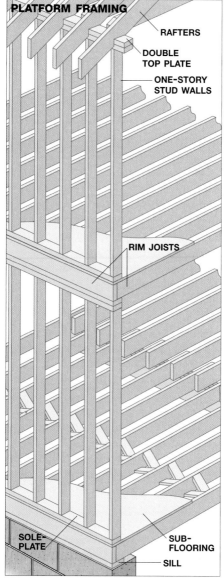

PLATFORM FRAMING

RAFTERS
DOUBLE TOP PLATE
ONE-STORY STUD WALLS
RIM JOISTS
SOLE-PLATE
SUB-FLOORING
SILL

Most houses today are stick-built with 2x4 or 2x6 walls using platform framing, where each story is built separately. Walls are framed on the decks and raised into place. Many roofs are now built with trusses instead of separate rafters.

Alternative Systems

Log buildings don't have a frame in the same sense as other buildings—as with a stone wall, the whole structure is built from one self-supporting material. Even without framing, a rectangle built of solid logs is exceptionally strong. The right-angle, interlocked corners take some time to build, but they are nearly impossible to rip apart. Log buildings do need a sturdy footing system, however, because of their great weight. Today, the majority of log homes are kit structures, which have logs that are cut to the correct size and shape by the manufacturer before they are shipped to your site.

Post-and-beam timber frames require high-quality carpentry work, involving classic skills such as making mortise-and-tenon joints that fit without play—as well as the trouble of moving huge treelike timbers to your property or milling them on-site. But timber framing is much stronger and more durable than stick-building, and the huge posts and beams can be left unfinished in the interior of the house and clad with prefinished, insulated roof panels. Unlike conventional stick-built homes, a complete post-and-beam frame may consist of only a hundred or so individual pieces. As a result, the frame can be erected quickly.

Pole framing is similar in many ways to structural steel framing. A pole-framed structure doesn't rest on the ground with a full foundation but sticks into the ground in selected locations, much like the poles sunk to build a dock. The poles are set in a grid, and timbers that support the floor and roof are tied into them. All the structural loads travel down the poles, which may be the size of telephone poles or larger. Pole framing is an economical system that has long been used for barns. It allows large, open rooms and high ceilings, and is a good way to build on a steeply sloped site.

Rammed Earth & Cordwood

Rammed-earth walls are constructed by compacting a mix of screened soil and cement inside extremely sturdy forms.

There are several building systems that don't rely mainly on dimensional lumber or concrete. Rammed-earth building (left), a variation on one of the oldest forms of construction, has walls made from compacted layers of soil and cement. Cordwood masonry (right) has thick insulating walls made from split logs set in mortar. Many alternative systems have proven track records, but your local building department may need some convincing to give you a permit.

This cordwood masonry house near the Canadian border is heated with wood stoves and only 4 cords of firewood a year.

Framing Tools

Framing for a project of any size, from a closet to an entire house, requires accurate layout, marking, and cutting. Because even a ¼-inch error may lead to unsatisfactory results in framing, it's a good idea to invest in quality tools that, when used properly, will give you the advantage of accuracy.

The past 15 years have seen an explosion of tools for builders, from laser-guided power miter boxes and levels to computer-driven drills and high-tech moisture meters. However, many such tools and gadgets are expensive. Some of them can make your job easier and more enjoyable, but there's a core group of standard—and inexpensive—hand and power tools that allows you to do the job of framing adequately.

The most familiar, and most often used, framing hand tools include the framing hammer, saw, framing square, chalk-line box, measuring tape, and spirit level. The basic designs of these tools date back to antiquity, and although improvements have been made over time, they really have changed little.

Some improvements have created specialized tools that make framing easier and faster. Straight-claw ripping hammers are useful for prying and wedging, and even do double duty as a hatchet when needed. Measuring tapes have stud and joist layout marks imprinted on their blades. Framing squares have rafter tables that allow you to compute angles and board lengths.

SAFETY

▶ **Wear safety glasses** whenever you work with power tools. This is important during any operation that produces flying chips of wood or masonry. Wear a dust mask when cutting pressure-treated lumber.

▶ **Ladders and scaffolding** should all be OSHA-approved. A personal fall-arrest system, consisting of a body harness that clips to the framing, can prevent a dangerous fall from a second story or roof.

Measure

A reel-type measuring tape, 50 or 100 ft. long, helps you avoid errors when marking long framing runs.

A 25-ft. retractable tape is useful for measuring and marking most wall, floor, and roof framing.

Folding wooden rulers have a slide-out extension that makes it easy to accurately measure between framing.

Cut

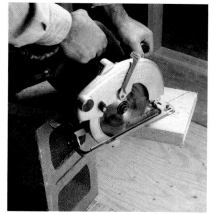

A 7½-in. circular saw is the best model for most DIYers. Smaller models can cut through two-by lumber.

Power miter saws are handy for cutting many timbers to the same size and for trim work.

Reciprocating saws are rough-cutting tools used for demolition and for working in tight places.

Nail

Framing hammers have straight claws, heavier heads, and can drive 16d nails into wood with a few blows.

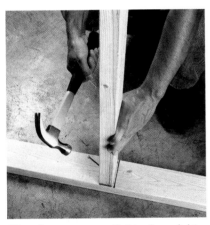

Claw hammers are lighter in weight but are easier to control for jobs such as toenailing studs.

A gunpowder-actuated fastening tool makes attaching lumber to concrete easier than just hammering nails.

Square

A framing square is a useful tool for checking stud layout, aligning cabinets, and marking long cuts.

A combination square has a sliding blade. It's the best all-around marking tool for framing work.

A bevel square has an adjustable pivot point between the blade and handle so you can mark angle cuts.

Plumb & Level

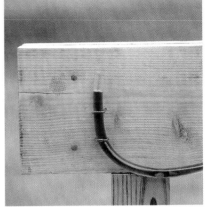

Water levels use colored water in a tube—it can weave up and down, but the water at each end is level.

Spirit levels come in many lengths, but a 4-ft. model is best for accurate work on joists and studs.

Extend the useful range of a construction level by resting it on a long, straight 2x4.

Choosing Fasteners

By far the most common fastener used in framing is the 16d nail. But lumberyards, home centers, and hardware stores carry a wide variety of other hardware for reinforcing joints between most sizes of framing timbers. For example, a joist hanger is a U-shaped bracket that supports a joist or rafter and connects it to an adjoining timber with perforated flanges you nail through.

Do-it-yourselfers often don't drive nails correctly, or they use the wrong sizes; using this hardware provides a welcome safety net, particularly on old work where there isn't enough room to end-nail and you have to toenail connections. On new work, check with your local building department to comply with codes requiring joist hardware.

Choosing the right nail size and type is not a matter of guesswork. Fasteners are engineered for specific tasks, and your lumber or hardware dealer has reference books that are exact in their recommendations. You'll make every wood-to-wood framing connection using a specific size and number of nails. If you plan on doing any wood construction, it will pay to study a framing manual to learn the right way to make these connections. Roofing materials also have very particular fastening requirements. The length of the nails, their head shape, and even the amount you'll need to apply roofing to areas of any size can be determined from the specification sheets for those materials.

Fasteners

Most framing connections are fastened with hot-dipped galvanized common nails. They have the most holding power driven through the face of one timber into the end grain of another. Toenails, driven at an angle, are weaker. Lag screws and carriage bolts are commonly used on large timber connections instead of nails—for example, where the 2x10 ledger of a deck joins the house framing.

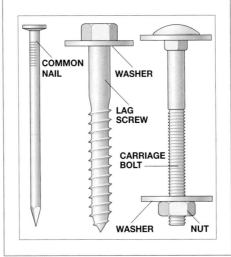

COMMON NAIL
WASHER
LAG SCREW
CARRIAGE BOLT
WASHER — NUT

Connectors

Framing connectors are generally required on floor joists, but you can use them at other locations, too, to reinforce nailed connections. If you need to add studs between an existing double plate and sole plate, for example, you will have to fasten them by toenailing, which can be difficult for DIYers to do. For additional security, use wrap-around, galvanized connectors nailed to both boards.

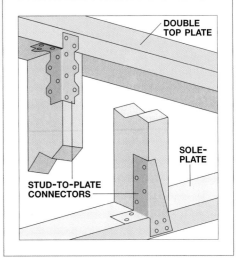

DOUBLE TOP PLATE
SOLE-PLATE
STUD-TO-PLATE CONNECTORS

Dimensional Lumber

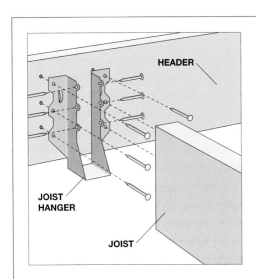

HEADER
JOIST HANGER
JOIST

Experienced carpenters are so sure of their layouts that they can nail up a series of hangers and drop joists into place for final nailing. DIYers are generally better off installing the joists first (and some carpenters do, too). This allows you to make small adjustments and be sure that each joist is flush with the ledger or header against which it butts. You may need to add a toenail here and there to move a joist. Then you can slip on the hangers and secure the connections.

Nails through perforated flanges hold the boards to the hanger, and the hanger holds the boards to each other.

Special Grades

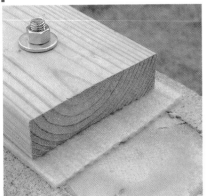

Pressure-treated wood is a good choice for sills, bolted to the foundation over an insulated sealer.

Unusual grades and sizes, such as this huge heart-redwood beam, have to be special-ordered at most yards.

Lumber Quality

When you pick up two 2x4s of the same length, they should be about the same weight. Watch out for the one that clearly weighs more: it's loaded with water, even though the grade stamp says S-DRY. Framing lumber should have a moisture content below 20%. Any more than that and even a stud that's straight when you nail it in place will twist as the excess water gradually leaves the wood fibers.

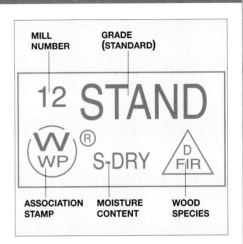

MILL NUMBER
GRADE (STANDARD)
12 STAND
W WP ® S-DRY D FIR
ASSOCIATION STAMP
MOISTURE CONTENT
WOOD SPECIES

Pick through the supply whenever possible to remove exceptionally heavy, warped lumber with obvious defects.

The best framing tends to be lighter—which means drier—and straighter so it will stay in place where you nail it.

Engineered Lumber

Consider engineered lumber on large jobs where you buy lumber in quantity or when plans call for long spans that would require large and expensive conventional timbers. The most common engineered lumber is a truss-type construction with solid wood top and bottom and a plywood center. Glue-laminated lumber also is available in long lengths—for example, 32-foot joists that are strong enough to meet codes when set 24 inches on center with one central girder support.

BEAM OR HEADER
TRUSSED JOIST
JOIST HANGER
STIFFENER

If you use engineered lumber, you have to plan the job carefully and order special framing connectors to fit.

When to Brace

Because a good framing contractor uses dozens of braces during construction, it's natural to wonder whether some of the temporary support they provide should be included in the frame permanently. However, permanent braces serve a different purpose from that of temporary building braces.

In general, temporary braces are used to maintain vertical and horizontal alignment in parts of the frame before the entire structure is tied together and covered with sheathing. It's easy to dislodge a carefully plumbed corner of one wall while tipping and nailing the adjacent wall frame into place. To avoid constant re-plumbing and realigning once a wall has been set correctly, the idea is to lock in the position with temporary bracing.

Permanent Bracing

When those temporary supports come down, there are a few spots that can still use extra, built-in strengthening. One is the closing side of a sliding-door frame. Large 3- or 4-foot wide panels of insulated glass are so heavy that unless they are closed gently, they can slam into the frame. While the doors may be solid enough to take repeated bumping, it could eventually loosen nails in trim, drywall, and the adjoining frame, and cause maintenance headaches from popping drywall nails to a misaligned door lock.

To build in extra strength, add short, horizontal lengths of 2x4 (or 2x6, whichever matches the framing material) between the double studs next to the door frame and the next two single studs in the wall. You might use two horizontal braces in each framing bay, splitting the vertical space into thirds. This ties together about 32 inches of wall frame, which masses its collective strength and stiffness against the door.

It's also wise to anticipate special loads or mounting conditions with built-in braces (although a carpenter might call them nailers instead). These can include short sections of 2x4 installed horizontally between studs for mounting a bathroom medicine chest or a length of 2x4 used to support the edge of a drywall sheet.

Bracing Corners

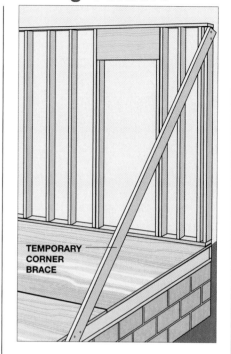

TEMPORARY CORNER BRACE

Once you take the time and trouble to plumb a corner or an entire wall, lock the position in place with a solid 2x4 brace. Then, leave the brace in place until the framing is finished. You can nail the brace outside the frame so it won't be in the way.

Temporary Support

To prevent ceiling joists or rafters above a new opening in the wall from sagging during the job, build a temporary support wall before you remove any framing. Frame the temporary wall with timbers at least as big as those in the building walls, and set them with the same frequency (generally 16 inches on center). If in doubt, overbuild, using 2x6 studs set a foot apart. Also remember to pick up these loads beneath the first floor where they are not supported by the foundation.

To minimize surface damage where the temporary structure bears on the ceiling and floor, place the temporary studs directly under the ceiling joists and over floor joists where possible. Even then, you should spread the load by toenailing them to wide boards (2x6s or 2x8s) on the top and bottom.

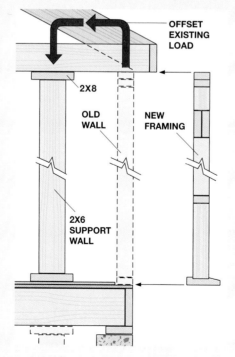

OFFSET EXISTING LOAD

2X8

OLD WALL

NEW FRAMING

2X6 SUPPORT WALL

Straightening Frames

USE: ▶ come-along (with steel cables and hooks)

1 *A come-along* is a winch between two cables. You can anchor the cables anywhere on or near the frame you need to straighten.

Bracing Walls

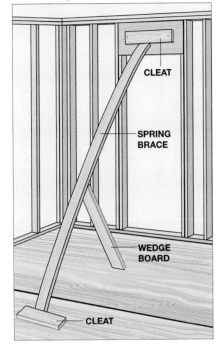

A spring brace is one way to apply enough pressure to straighten out a bow in a framed wall. Nail a flat two-by brace (at least 8 feet long) to cleats on the subfloor and on the wall, and force the wall into plumb by wedging a 2x4 underneath.

Racking

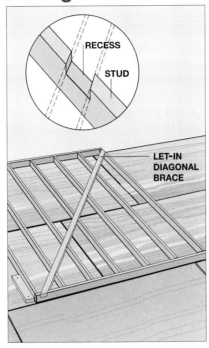

A diagonal brace helps to keep studs in line and stiffens the wall until you apply sheathing. Let-in braces make this extra stiffness permanent. Typically made of 1x4s (or L-shaped lengths of metal), they run flush with the stud faces in recesses.

Spacing

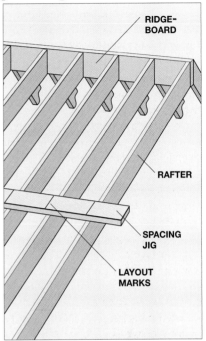

To keep long runs of rafters or joists evenly spaced during framing, copy your 16-inch on-center layout onto a spare 2x4, and then tack it at mid-span to bring each timber into alignment. You can remove this jig when you have sheathing nailed down.

• safety goggles • work gloves ▶ wood blocking

2 *Attach the hook and cable* on the other end of the come-along to the corner of the frame you need to pull into plumb position.

3 *Come-alongs* can connect to cables with hooks. Take up most of the slack before you start cranking the handle.

4 *Cranking the handle* turns a ratchet-type gear in the come-along and tightens the cables enough to pull a stud wall into plumb.

On the Foundation

Most houses have a poured-concrete or concrete-block foundation. The floor framing doesn't sit right on top of the foundation but instead lies on a sill of pressure-treated 2x4 or 2x6 lumber. The sill is attached to the foundation using either ½-inch anchor bolts placed every 4 to 6 feet in the concrete slab (or grouted into the fill in the webs of the foundation block), or by using a double-strap anchor, which holds the sill in place like a joist hanger on its side.

A sill makes the transition between the foundation and the framing; it is your last opportunity to straighten out a crooked foundation. A sill sealer must be installed in between the sill and the foundation—usually a gasket of caulk or a strip of fiberglass insulation. In regions prone to termite damage, install a termite shield on top of the foundation before you install the sill sealer.

When you set the sill over the anchor bolts, the outside edge of the sill should align with the outside edge of the slab or foundation wall—unless the foundation is out of square. In this case, some variation between the foundation and sill is acceptable because it's more important to make the sill plates perfectly square and true. Also make sure they are level, shimming them where necessary. Any misalignment of the sill can come back to haunt you when you frame the floors, walls, and even the roof.

Girders

If you want a wide-open basement with no walls or columns to break up the space, then the entire floor load must be transferred to the perimeter walls. Install a beam beneath the floor joists to carry the weight across the center of the span. Each end of this beam sits in a pocket in the foundation wall. Steel I-beams are the strongest and can span greater distances. Wood girders—whether glue-laminated, made from two-bys, or manufactured wood I-beams—are less expensive.

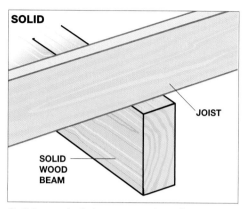

Solid wood girders measuring 3½ in. wide are generally used where the beam is exposed under the floor framing.

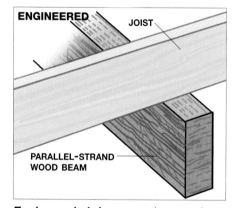

Engineered girders come in several forms, including glued-up wood strips that carry more weight than solid wood.

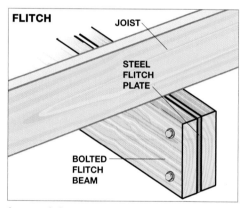

In special cases with exceptional loads, you can use a flitch design—a piece of steel bolted into a wood-beam sandwich.

Installing Sills

USE: ▶ circular saw • combination square • measuring tape • pencil • drill • wire brush • socket wrench ▶ pressure-treated two-by sill plate • sill sealer

1 *Set the sill,* typically a 2x6, on the foundation, and use a combination square to mark the locations of anchor bolts.

2 *Measure along the mark* to duplicate the distance of the bolt from the outside of the foundation, and drill a hole.

3 *Thin foam sheeting,* called sill sealer, fills the slightly irregular space between the foundation and the sill.

BUILT-UP

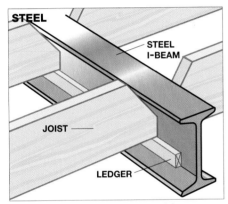

JOIST

BUILT-UP WOOD BEAM

Most girders are made of two or even three two-by timbers spiked together. The greater the depth, the greater the span.

STEEL

STEEL I-BEAM

JOIST

LEDGER

Steel I-beams are rarely used in residential construction but can be combined with standard floor joists.

End Support

Girders are often supported in pockets cut or formed into opposite ends of the foundation. Most codes require beam pockets to be a minimum of 4 inches deep to bear the load. You also need to guard against wood rot by setting the girder on a piece of steel base plate. Allow ½ inch of space on both sides of the beam for ventilation. If pockets won't provide enough support for your design, you can raise girders to the sill (which also raises the floor) or set them on pilasters built onto the foundation.

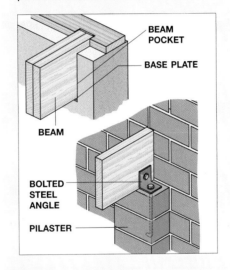

BEAM POCKET

BASE PLATE

BEAM

BOLTED STEEL ANGLE

PILASTER

Columns

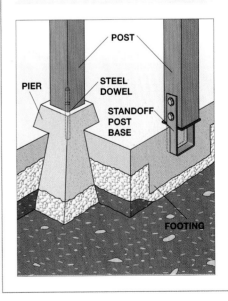

BEAM

STEEL PIPE

STEEL TOP PLATE

BEAM

POST CAP

WOOD POST

On many girder designs, there is a point of diminishing returns. You can keep adding boards to the girder to increase their depth so that the beam can create an unsupported span. But once you get to the point of using three 2x10s, it's generally more economical to install a post. You can use wood or steel, securely fastened at each end. Some steel columns have an adjustable cap, so you can raise the girder slightly should it sag.

POST

PIER

STEEL DOWEL

STANDOFF POST BASE

FOOTING

• anchor bolts & washers

4 *The threads of anchor bolts* often become clogged with concrete and need to be wire brushed before you install a nut.

5 *Set the sill* onto the foam sealer with the anchor bolts protruding. Slip a large washer on each one, and then tighten the nuts.

Floor Joists

After installing the sill and girders, the next step is to install the floor framing, a box-like arrangement of joists and headers (called rim joists) set on their edges. The 4x8 sheets of plywood subflooring are then nailed directly to the floor framing. Before placing joists on the sill, measure and mark your joist layout, spacing the joists 16 inches on center—all except for the second joist. Because the subfloor sheets are nailed flush with the outer edge of the floor deck, the distance from the first joist to the second will actually be only 15¼ inches on center. (To be flush with the floor's outside edge, the sheet must be an extra ¾ inch beyond the center of the outside joist. So one joist, the second, is set ¾ inch closer to compensate.)

When determining joist length, deduct the thickness of the headers (rim joists)—boards nailed across the ends of the floor joists. Rim joists secure floor joists upright on their edges. They also provide a clean edge for attaching subflooring. Consult a floor joist span table, available from your local building department, to be sure of the allowable length and depth of floor joists for a given load. You may need to add supporting columns or use a different grade of wood than you planned in order to meet your local codes.

Rough Openings

Most joist-framed floors have openings in them for such things as stairways and chimneys. The framing members used to make the rough openings are called trimmers when installed parallel to the floor joists and headers when they run perpendicular to the joists. These pieces are the same dimension as the floor joists, but they are doubled to provide the strength needed to reinforce the floor and transfer the load around the openings. Attaching joists with metal hangers ensures that the opening framework is solidly secured.

The spaces between joists form natural conduits for ductwork, plumbing, and electrical runs, but openings often have to be cut through the joists to allow for wiring and pipe. Building code rules determine when, where, and how large a hole you can make. "Cutouts" on p. 117 gives some general guidelines on how these holes should be cut.

Solid Floor Framing

The most common connection in framing is between one board and another that butts against it at a right angle. This basic T-shape occurs where studs join bottom sills and top plates, and where floor joists meet headers. To nail these boards together, you use the most common type of carpentry, called face-nailing. First, make sure that the stud or joist makes a square connection. (You may want to draw a square layout line with a combination square as a guide.) Then, drive nails through the face of one board into the center of the other.

Solid, oversized timbers in floor framing call for heavy-duty bolts and post caps to prevent shifting.

Engineered Floor Framing

The design of most engineered joists uses an I-beam shape; the top and bottom of the beam is substantial, but the center is thin. That center section, typically ½-in.-thick plywood, is so thin that it would split even if you could nail accurately enough to find its center. You can tack these beams top and bottom where there is more wood, but to make secure connections, you need to use metal hangers. Check your local codes whether you use solid or engineered lumber: they may require hangers.

Engineered joists have less material than solid lumber but are just as strong when you make connections with hardware.

Installing Bridging

There is some controversy about how much stronger a floor is with bridging than without it. But most people can feel the solid difference when bridging is added between joists. It connects the joists to each other and can prevent twisting where the bottom edges are left exposed—for example, over a crawl space. There are three types. Solid bridging is made of the joist lumber. Old-fashioned angled bridging is made of ⁵⁄₄x3s that are cut at an angle. Metal bridging uses two strips of steel in an X-pattern.

USE: ▶ circular saw or handsaw • framing hammer

1 *Solid bridging* fits between joists in a staggered pattern. This allows you to end nail through each joist.

PERPENDICULAR TO FOUNDATION WALL

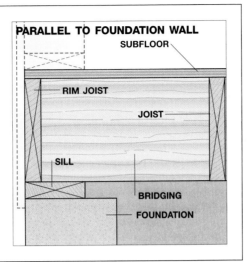

SUBFLOOR

RIM JOIST

JOIST

SILL

FOUNDATION

PARALLEL TO FOUNDATION WALL

SUBFLOOR

RIM JOIST

JOIST

SILL

BRIDGING

FOUNDATION

TO SOLID BEAM

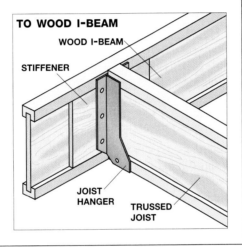

BUILT-UP WOOD BEAM

JOIST HANGER

TRUSSED JOIST

TO WOOD I-BEAM

WOOD I-BEAM

STIFFENER

JOIST HANGER

TRUSSED JOIST

Metal Bridging

Nailing flanges at each end of metal bridging strips rest on top of one joist and underneath the next one in line.

The X-pattern locks the joists in place. It's wise to brace the joists with a 1x4 to maintain correct spacing.

• combination square • measuring tape • pencil • safety goggles ▶ metal or wood cross-bridging • common nails

2 Snap a chalk line to use as a center mark on each joist. Then, square up the mark, and make an X on one side.

3 Cut each piece of bridging to fit snugly between the joists. If you cut bridging too long, it will bow the joists.

4 If the bottom of the floor will be covered, make sure that the bridging is flush with the joists before nailing.

Subflooring

With the floor joists in place, it's time to put down subflooring, or floor decking. The subflooring forms the base for floor coverings such as carpet or finished wood. For finished flooring such as tile or vinyl, which require an absolutely smooth and level base, you'll need to add another layer of material, called underlayment, on top of the subfloor. Of course, you could leave the subfloor unfinished if you're going to use the room as a workshop.

Generally, subflooring is ⅝- or ¾-inch plywood. Use the thinner plywood if you're going to install underlayment and the thicker if you're going to install carpet or wood floors. Choose lumber-core plywood for floor decking because much of the nailing is along the edges.

Other panel materials you can use as subflooring (if local codes permit) include waferboard and OSB (oriented-strand board). Building codes generally only allow these materials if they've been made with exterior-grade phenolic resin.

Installing Subflooring

Use a caulking gun to apply a bead of construction adhesive to the tops of the joists. Adhesive creates a strong bond between joists and plywood and cuts down on squeaky floors. Lay down the subflooring by staggering panel edges so that the seams don't line up across the floor. If you start the first row with a full panel, start the second with a half-panel to keep the seams staggered. Leave a ¹⁄₁₆-inch gap between end joints and a ⅛-inch gap between the long edge joints, to prevent the panels from buckling when they expand. Attach the panels with either 6d ring-shank nails (8d for panels thicker than ⅞ inch) or 2-inch deck screws.

Nail or screw the subflooring every 12 inches along the edges and in the field of the plywood. If you don't use adhesive, nail or screw every 6 inches on the outside edges and 10 inches in the field.

Gaps between subflooring and joists can cause the floor to feel spongy. To avoid this problem, follow the fastening schedules above, use adhesive, and don't use warped panels. If a subfloor feels spongy as you walk across it, add more fasteners until it feels secure.

Framing Openings

The most efficient framing plans try to minimize labor time and lumber use and create short headers instead of long ones. But wherever all or part of several joists have to be removed or left out, you must add extra lumber to pick up the loads they carried. There are two parts to this basic framing operation. First, install a double header at the head and foot of the opening. These beams carry the joist loads to the sides of the opening. Second, double the full joists along the sides of the opening to carry the extra load from the headers.

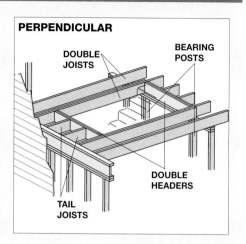

PERPENDICULAR

DOUBLE JOISTS — BEARING POSTS — DOUBLE HEADERS — TAIL JOISTS

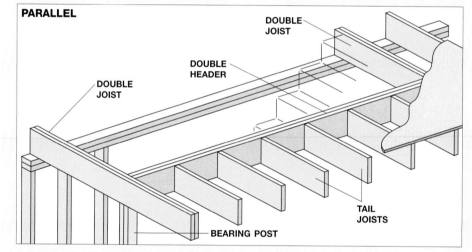

PARALLEL

DOUBLE JOIST — DOUBLE JOIST — DOUBLE HEADER — TAIL JOISTS — BEARING POST

Strengthening Floors

USE: ▶ hydraulic jack • circular saw • clamps • drill • caulking gun • 4-ft. level • measuring tape

1 *Pinpoint a weak, sagging floor joist by* checking several joists with a level, which will rock over the lowest joist.

2 *Wedge 2x4 or 4x4 posts* under joists to raise them slightly. Use hydraulic jacks with posts to raise very low joists gradually.

Cantilevers

Cantilevers—either parallel or perpendicular to floor joists—extend beyond the foundation to support a load-bearing exterior wall. (The same kind of framing can extend deck joists beyond a supporting girder.) Like other framing sizes and spans, cantilever design is controlled by building codes. But the general rule of thumb is that you need to support two-thirds of the frame to safely extend one-third without support. A 2-foot extension needs at least 4 feet supported.

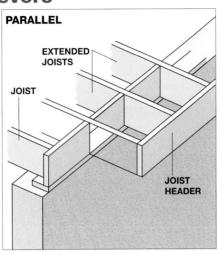

PARALLEL

EXTENDED JOISTS
JOIST
JOIST HEADER

PERPENDICULAR

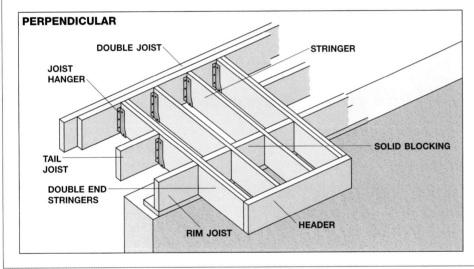

DOUBLE JOIST
JOIST HANGER
STRINGER
TAIL JOIST
DOUBLE END STRINGERS
RIM JOIST
HEADER
SOLID BLOCKING

Cutouts

Some ducts, pipes, and wires can run between joists. But where mechanical lines have to cross joists, you need to drill access holes. To drill without overly weakening joists, try to follow these general guidelines.

- Don't cut a hole in a joist closer than 2 inches to the edge.
- Don't cut a hole bigger than ⅓ the depth of the joist.
- Don't make a notch in the middle third of a joist's length.
- Don't make notches deeper than ⅙ of the joist's depth.

To drill joists *in place, it's handy to use a cordless drill and a hole saw attachment to cut large access holes.*

• pencil • safety goggles ▶ 2x4 or 4x4 bearing posts • common nails or wood screws • construction adhesive

3 ***Help a second,*** *or sistered, joist adhere to the weak joist by spreading a thick bead of construction adhesive along the side.*

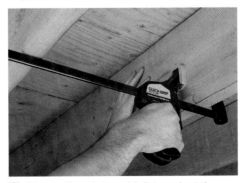

4 ***Clamp the sistered joist*** *against the weak joist as you maneuver it into position. Set the crown, or natural bow, up.*

5 ***You can nail the sistered joist*** *in place, but screws have more holding power and are easier to set in tight spots.*

Wall Studs

Before you can lay out a wall for framing, you need to know how typical wood-frame walls are constructed. All walls have a bottom or soleplate, a top plate (doubled in bearing walls), and vertical supports called studs. There are three kinds of studs: king studs, jack (or trimmer) studs, and cripple studs. King studs run from the soleplate all the way to the top plate. Jack studs run from the soleplate up alongside a rough opening to the underside of its header. Cripple studs can run from either the soleplate to the underside of a rough opening's sill or from the top of the opening's header to the top plate.

Most load-bearing walls are framed with 2x4s or 2x6s, depending on structural or insulation demands. A 2x6 wall is proportionately stronger; although each stud costs more than a comparable 2x4, the overall cost is only marginally different because fewer 2x6s are needed. (Building codes usually allow them to be placed 24 inches on center, while 2x4s must be spaced every 16 inches on center.) Wider studs also allow more space for insulation. A 2x4 wall can accommodate a 3½-inch-thick batt of fiberglass insulation, while a 2x6 wall accepts batts up to 5½ inches. Federal guidelines call for higher insulation values in exterior walls; this is one of the easiest ways to attain it. For any other framing jobs you may tackle, such as sheds, dormers, and garages, 2x4 studs are recommended; they are the most economical.

Step-Ahead Layout

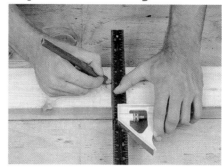

Avoid layout confusion by marking studs the same way all the time. First, draw your square line on the layout.

Once the square line is drawn, step ahead of the line to mark the location of the stud with an X.

2x4s vs. 2x6s

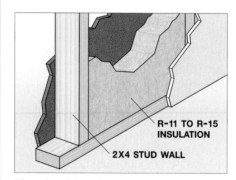

R-11 TO R-15 INSULATION

2X4 STUD WALL

Most load-bearing walls are framed with 2x4s. They are strong enough, the most economical, and space-saving.

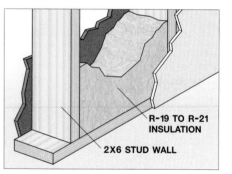

R-19 TO R-21 INSULATION

2X6 STUD WALL

Using 2x6s allows more room for insulation and mechanicals in the wall, but you rarely need the extra strength.

Framing Walls

USE: ▶ circular saw • combination square • 4-ft. level • hammer • measuring tape • pencil • safety goggles ▶ 2x4 or 2x6 lumber • common nails

1 ***Start by marking the layout*** on both the soleplate and one of the two top plates at the same time so studs will line up.

2 ***Work on the subfloor*** to assemble the frame. Position each stud, stand on it to prevent shifting, and nail through the soleplate.

3 ***When the soleplate is nailed on,*** shift to the top of the wall, and follow the same procedure to nail on one of the top plates.

Partitions

CROSSING JOISTS

DOUBLE TOP PLATE

CEILING JOIST

PARTITION WALL

SUBFLOOR

SOLEPLATE

FLOOR JOIST

BETWEEN JOISTS

CEILING JOISTS

2X4 BLOCKING

NAILER

PARTITION WALL

FLOOR JOISTS

Corners

Corners are key to a building because they do three important jobs: support a lot of weight, form a plumb connection between two walls, and provide nailing for siding outside and drywall inside. There are many types of corners. DIYers may want to build the most substantial, a stud-and-block corner that provides maximum support and nailing surfaces. Using three studs without blocking is almost as good. Some builders looking for maximum economy use the two-stud corner. Interior drywall has no nailing on one side and relies on clips for support.

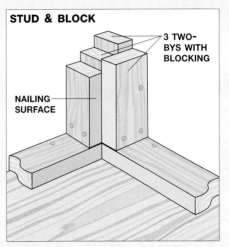

STUD & BLOCK

3 TWO-BYS WITH BLOCKING

NAILING SURFACE

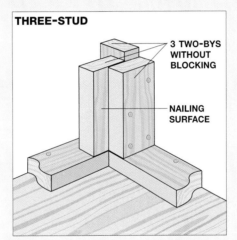

THREE-STUD

3 TWO-BYS WITHOUT BLOCKING

NAILING SURFACE

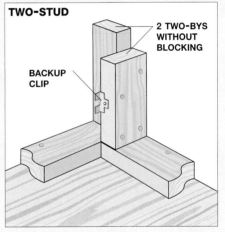

TWO-STUD

2 TWO-BYS WITHOUT BLOCKING

BACKUP CLIP

4 Check the frame alignment by comparing diagonal measurements. If the wall is square, the diagonals should be equal.

5 Use a 4-ft. level to check several studs for plumb. It's easiest to assemble corner posts on the deck and add them later.

6 With corner posts in place, install the second layer of top plate. Stagger the joints over the corner to tie one wall to another.

framing

Wall Openings

A house without windows and doors would be structurally sound but of little use to anyone wanting to live there. Making room for these openings means cutting into load-bearing studs, but framing supports called headers, or lintels, let you do that without sacrificing the walls' structural integrity.

Headers (sometimes called lintels) are short horizontal beams that bear loads for ceiling-to-floor studs that have been cut to make room for a window, door, or passageway. They transfer the load from cut studs to jack studs that run down either side of the opening. While local codes always supersede general rules, you can use these guidelines to produce safe, strong headers. For openings up to 3½ feet, the header should be two 2x6s nailed together; for 5-foot openings, two 2x8s; for 6½-foot openings, two 2x10s; and for 8-foot openings, two 2x12s.

Typical Window Openings

To frame in a window, determine the rough opening—generally the complete frame unit plus ½-inch space for adjustment within the opening. Nail a full-height, floor-to-ceiling stud 2¼ inches on center outside the limits of the opening. Next, set the jack studs in place against the full studs. Finally, nail together two 2x4s to form the sill—the horizontal support for the window—and nail it between the jack studs. Assemble the header, and nail it between the full-height studs over the jack studs.

Headers

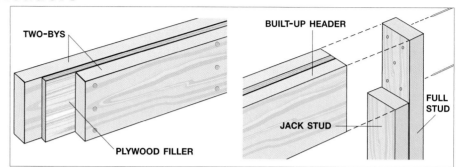

Although solid headers are used in some regions, the most common assembly is 2 two-bys packed out with a sheet of ½-inch-thick plywood. Two pieces of dimensional lumber plus the plywood equals 3½ inches, the thickness of the wall frame.

Nailers

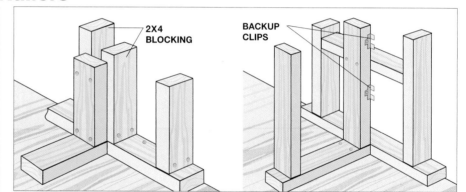

Where partition walls join exterior walls, you need to make provision for nailing drywall and reinforcing the taped corner. You can add a stud on each side of the partition (left) or add horizontal ladder studs and use drywall clips (right).

Building Openings

USE: ▶ circular saw • combination square • hammer • 4-ft. level • measuring tape • pencil • safety goggles ▶ 2x4 or 2x6 studs • 2x headers • common nails

1 *At each side of the opening,* install a short stud called a jack stud. It helps to support the sill under the opening.

2 *A small window* doesn't weigh enough to need a double sill, but it's wise to spike two 2x4s to jack studs and side studs.

3 *Continue jack stud sections* along both sides of the window opening. These pieces will help support the header.

Fire Stops

Horizontal plates and blocking between studs are designed to stop the spread of fire through framing cavities. Be sure to add blocking where required. During new construction and remodeling work, also look for potential fire paths between floors. One that's often overlooked is the open space above kitchen cabinets. If these soffits are built before drywall is added to the room, there may be an unobstructed connection to the floor above.

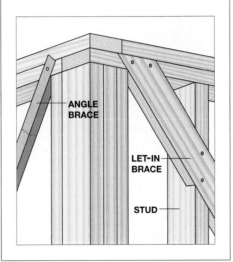

Bracing

The traditional method of adding diagonal corner braces generally is not now required by codes. Many builders don't bother to install them. But this extra feature is worth considering because it reinforces the building. There are two ways to add the bracing. Old-fashioned let-in bracing is recessed into the studs. You need to make two cuts across the studs and chisel out the wood between them so that the bracing lies flush with the studs. The modern version uses an L-shaped piece of metal that fits into a single sawcut.

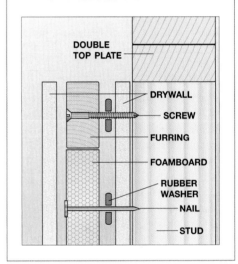

Noise Control

To reduce noise transmission between rooms, you can build thicker walls of 2x6 studs packed with insulation. It also helps to add sound-deadening layers to the wall surface. One way is to add furring strips to the existing drywall using screws and rubber washers as spacers. They break the solid link of materials that transmits sound. Fill the furring with foamboard (or special sound-absorbing material), and cover with new drywall.

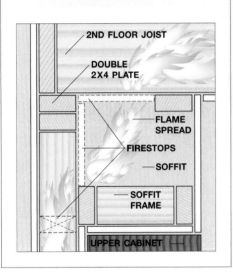

4 *Two 2x6s* with ½-in. plywood generally are more than enough to span small openings. Spike them through side studs.

5 *To maintain the modular layout,* add short studs, called cripples, above the header. You need them for nailing surfaces.

6 *Also add cripples* below. You can avoid toenailing by end-nailing the cripple before adding the second 2x4 sill.

Ceiling Joists

The second floor, or the ceiling of the first floor in a one-story house, is framed with joists supported by the exterior and interior load-bearing walls. Ceiling joists are usually spaced 16 inches on center. If there's no second floor, the joists can be dimensionally smaller than floor joists because they bear a load of only about 30 pounds per square foot (10 if not used for storage), compared with 50–55 pounds per square foot for floors. The loads they will carry and the length of the unsupported span determine the size of joists you must use. (If the house will have a truss-built roof, the bottom chord of the truss will substitute for the ceiling joists.)

Placement of Joists

Most often, ceiling joists will run parallel to the shorter side of the building, although there are some cases where they are parallel to the longer side. Ceiling joists are toenailed to the tops of exterior and interior load-bearing walls. When the roof is framed, the roof rafters will be face-nailed to the ends of the ceiling joists.

If a room's dimensions are too large for the length of normal ceiling joists, frame the ceiling with a built-up beam at the centerline, and then secure the joists to it with joist hangers. A more typical situation is to design the ceiling joists to meet at some point on top of a load-bearing stud wall, thereby reducing the span. Of course, the stud wall itself must be supported from below by a girder or other load-bearing member.

Second-Floor Details

With modern platform framing, the second floor rests mainly on the exterior walls of the first floor. Where joists run perpendicular to the exterior wall, cut them 1½ inches short at each end and cover the cut ends with a header, also called a belt or rim joist. Joists that run parallel to the wall need a nailer along the wall edge to provide nailing for ceiling drywall. To provide nailing and minimize temperature loss, you can sandwich foamboard between two rim joists.

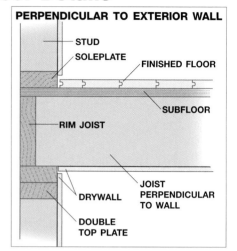

PERPENDICULAR TO EXTERIOR WALL
STUD
SOLEPLATE
FINISHED FLOOR
SUBFLOOR
RIM JOIST
JOIST PERPENDICULAR TO WALL
DRYWALL
DOUBLE TOP PLATE

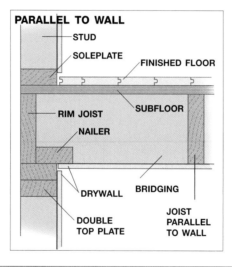

PARALLEL TO WALL
STUD
SOLEPLATE
FINISHED FLOOR
SUBFLOOR
RIM JOIST
NAILER
DRYWALL
BRIDGING
DOUBLE TOP PLATE
JOIST PARALLEL TO WALL

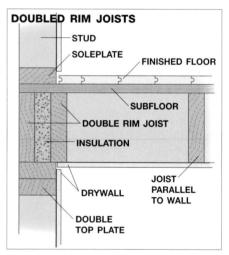

DOUBLED RIM JOISTS
STUD
SOLEPLATE
FINISHED FLOOR
SUBFLOOR
DOUBLE RIM JOIST
INSULATION
JOIST PARALLEL TO WALL
DRYWALL
DOUBLE TOP PLATE

Strengthening Sagging Ceilings

Once a ceiling sags, there are several steps you can take to raise it. However, if the sagging is widespread you probably should have the framing inspected by a contractor, architect, or structural engineer. The framing could be inadequate, which is often the case when an unfinished attic is remodeled and the old joists were not sized to carry increased loads of furniture and people in a finished living space. To take the sag out of one or two joists, try the following sequence and add a strongback.

USE: ▶ circular saw • drill • hammer • caulking gun • chalk-line box • measuring tape • safety goggles

1 *Use a wide board* to protect the ceiling (and floor) and distribute the force of a post wedged or jacked into place to raise the sag.

2 *Snap a chalk line* across the joists down the center of the sagging area. Use it as a guide to fasten part of the strongback.

Ceiling Details

Once the exterior walls are built and topped with double plates, you can add any type of roof. To carry roof loads most efficiently, the rafters should align with the studs. On gable roofs you can nail the ceiling joists next to the rafters, running in the same direction, and trim the upper corners to match the roof line. On hip roofs you can run the ceiling joists either way, with the rafters or perpendicular to them. Most low-slope roofs today are framed with trusses. With minimal lumber in a triangular shape, they provide rafters for roofing and ceiling joists for interior drywall.

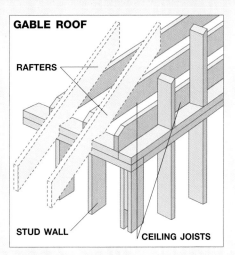

GABLE ROOF

RAFTERS

STUD WALL

CEILING JOISTS

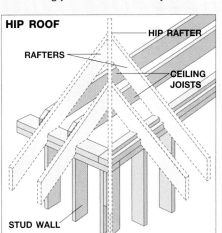

HIP ROOF

HIP RAFTER

RAFTERS

CEILING JOISTS

STUD WALL

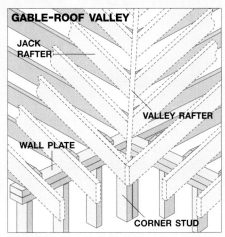

GABLE-ROOF VALLEY

JACK RAFTER

VALLEY RAFTER

WALL PLATE

CORNER STUD

Joint Types

Overlapping ceiling joists staggers the layout room to room but provides full bearing over the bearing wall.

To align ceiling joists room to room, which can be helpful when drywalling, add a back-up block to the joint.

• pencil • floor jack (optional) ▶ 2x6 strongback • 2x4 crossbracing • 2x4 or 4x4 post • 2x10 or 2x12 scrap board • construction adhesive • wood screws or nails

3 *Fasten a 2x4* across the sagging joists. Add a bead of construction adhesive at the laps, and fasten the board with screws.

4 *To prepare the strongback connection,* add more construction adhesive along the entire length of the crossing 2x4.

5 *Set a 2x6 with a natural crown* (upward bow) against the 2x4. Fasten it with screws to the 2x4 and to each joist.

Roof-Framing Basics

Laying out and framing a roof might seem like an intimidating task. Calculating rafter length and the angles at the ridge and rafter tail is more complex than framing walls, but it requires only high-school-level math and geometry skills and the ability to break down a complex task into smaller steps.

Rafter Spans

Like floor joists, rafters must be selected to span distances: the beefier the piece of lumber, the greater the distance it can bridge without support. Unlike floor joists, rafters are set in position at an angle. A low angle puts more strain on a rafter than a high angle, so the allowable span is affected by the roof's pitch.

Spacing also affects allowable rafter span. Rafters on 16-inch centers bear less load than those on 24-inch centers and can therefore be smaller. Lumber species is yet another factor. (See "Using Span Tables" on page 131.)

Longhouses were built by a confederacy of American Indian tribes in the Northeast. The bark-sheathed, elm-timber frames were up to 200 ft. long. This re-creation is at Ganondagan State Historic Site in Victor, NY.

The grade of the lumber also affects the permitted span. For example, No. 1 Douglas fir can have a greater span than No. 2 Douglas fir. Calculate spans with the species and grade of wood you're using. If you change the species or grade, be sure the lumber is adequate for the span. Even though a rafter is rated to carry the required load, it still may not meet code requirements that limit how much a rafter can bend.

Cutting Rafters

Because all common rafters in a simple gable roof are the same, the easiest thing to do is to mark one, cut it to fit, and use it as a template. There are three cuts to be made in most rafters: the ridge cut (where it rests against the ridgeboard or beam), the tail cut (which makes the shape of the bottom end), and the bird's-mouth cut (the notch that lets the rafter sit on the cap plate). The tail cut also establishes the rafter's outer edge, where it forms the eaves and may create an overhang.

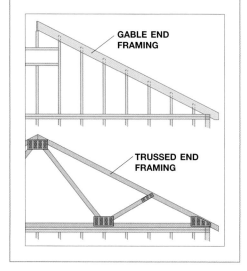

GABLE END FRAMING

TRUSSED END FRAMING

Setting Ridges & Rafters

USE: ▶ circular saw • handsaw • bevel square • framing square • 4-ft. level • C-clamps • hammer • measuring tape • pencil • safety goggles ▶ 2x ridgeboards

1 For maximum safety, *build a plumb post, securely braced, with a short 2x4 cleat to temporarily support the ridgeboard.*

2 Set the ridgeboard *on the braced post, lean it temporarily against the 2x4 cleat, and clamp it in position.*

3 Use a bevel square *to measure the rafter cut. DIYers are wise to get one rafter perfect and use it as a template for others.*

Gable Frame

The gable roof is perhaps the most common roof profile: two sloping sides that meet at a center ridge, much like two shed roofs spliced together. End gables form triangular walls that allow for window or vent openings for extra ventilation. If the roof pitch isn't too low, gable attics can be spacious enough to provide comfortable living space with or without dormers. Steep-pitched gables are ideal in areas with heavy winter snows. The basic gable shape also stands up better than most in areas with high winds.

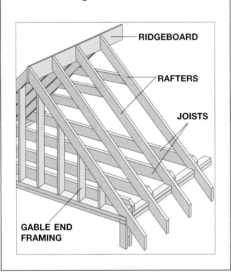

Hip Frame

Hip roofs get their name from the shape of the corner where the planes of the roof meet. The design advantage of hip roofs is that they provide a more interesting roof shape, not just two flat planes like a gable roof. But these roofs are more difficult to frame due to the many angle cuts on the rafters. Jack rafters, which run from the hip to the roof edge, require compound miter cuts—a combination of one angle to account for the upward slope of the roof and another to account for the inward angle of the hip.

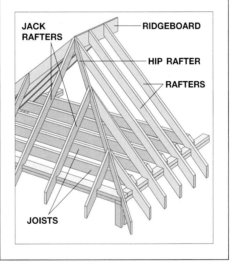

Flat Frame

Most flat roofs aren't really flat. Even with modern roofing systems that can withstand water over seams, some slope is needed to encourage drainage. An imperceptible slope can be built into the joists or created by adding wedge-shaped nailing strips above the joists. The design advantage of flat roofs is that they form both roof support and ceiling support at the same time. The main disadvantage is drainage. Drain outlets can easily clog with debris from surrounding trees and, without constant maintenance, lead to leaks.

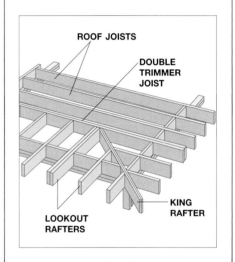

• 2x4 post • 2x4 bracing • common nails

4 **The tail ends** of roof rafters nestle onto the double plate of exterior walls with a notch called a bird's mouth.

5 **Use your bevel square** to mark the ridge angle at the overhang. Most designs call for two cuts: one vertical, one horizontal.

6 **Use a framing square or level** to mark the horizontal cut. When one rafter is complete (and fits) use it to mark the others.

framing

Framing Roof Details

Roof framing would be much easier if all roofs were the simple gable type. Except for the flat shed roof, all the others require complicated framing. These designs may also involve cutting rafters for roofs that have inside corners (valleys), framing openings for chimneys and skylights, and building frames for dormers.

Dormers can be included in new construction or added to an existing roof. They do a good job of breaking up an otherwise bland-looking expanse of roof, and provide light, ventilation, and headroom for rooms in the upper story. Depending on roof style, they can be easy or hard to frame. Flat, shed-roofed dormers are easy because dormer rafters run parallel to the main roof rafters. Cutting rafters for the peaked gable dormers gets fairly complicated.

Sheathing

Roof sheathing begins after all the rafters are in place. Sheathing stabilizes the roof and provides a nailing base for roofing materials. Plywood is the choice for sheathing material, but many building codes allow non-veneer sheathing such as oriented-strand board. Roof sheathing can be a minimum thickness of ⅜-inch for rafters spaced 16 inches on center, or ½-inch at 24-inch spacing. Sheet material joints should be staggered on the rafters as they are installed. You can use the pieces cut off from one end of the roof to fill out the gaps on the other end.

Valleys

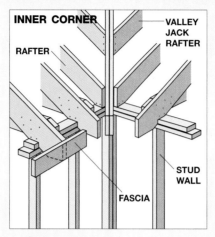

INNER CORNER — RAFTER, VALLEY JACK RAFTER, STUD WALL, FASCIA

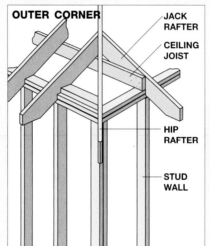

OUTER CORNER — JACK RAFTER, CEILING JOIST, HIP RAFTER, STUD WALL

Eaves

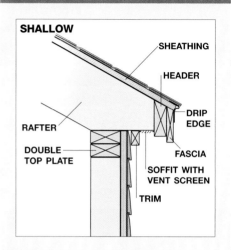

SHALLOW — SHEATHING, HEADER, DRIP EDGE, RAFTER, DOUBLE TOP PLATE, FASCIA, SOFFIT WITH VENT SCREEN, TRIM

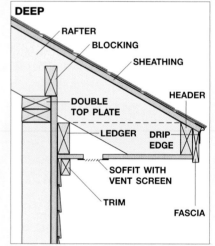

DEEP — RAFTER, BLOCKING, SHEATHING, HEADER, DOUBLE TOP PLATE, LEDGER, DRIP EDGE, SOFFIT WITH VENT SCREEN, TRIM, FASCIA

Framing Openings

USE: ▶ circular saw • hammer • pry bar • caulking gun • C-clamps • measuring tape • pencil • safety goggles ▶ two-by framing lumber • framing connectors

1 *Before cutting a rafter,* build secure braces to support that portion of the roof. After stripping shingles, work from inside.

2 *To make the rough opening,* allow for the opening unit, such as a skylight, plus 3 in. at each end for the double headers.

3 *Also double up the full-length rafters* on each side of the opening. Use construction adhesive to improve the connection.

Overhangs

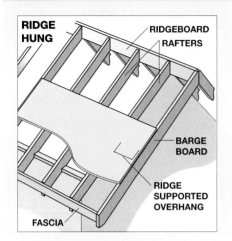

RIDGE HUNG
- RIDGEBOARD
- RAFTERS
- BARGE BOARD
- RIDGE SUPPORTED OVERHANG
- FASCIA

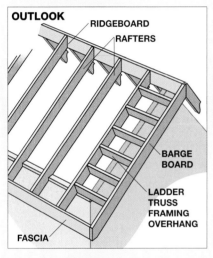

OUTLOOK
- RIDGEBOARD
- RAFTERS
- BARGE BOARD
- LADDER TRUSS FRAMING OVERHANG
- FASCIA

Dormers & Bays

There are many ways to increase living space and light in rooms with dormers and bay window extensions. The two main types of dormers are gable dormers, often used in converted attics, and shed dormers, which raise a larger roof area under a single slope. Bay extensions also need careful calculations on the rafter cuts and may need a cantilevered extension of the floor joists. In all cases, you need to provide flashing to seal seams where the main roof is interrupted.

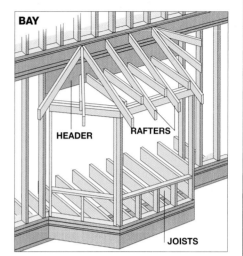

BAY
- HEADER
- RAFTERS
- JOISTS

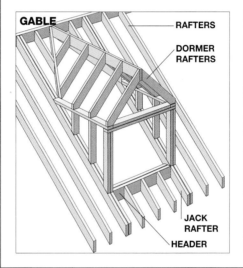

GABLE
- RAFTERS
- DORMER RAFTERS
- JACK RAFTER
- HEADER

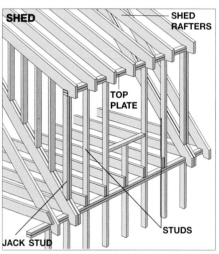

SHED
- SHED RAFTERS
- TOP PLATE
- JACK STUD
- STUDS

• 2x4 bracing • construction adhesive • common nails or wood screws

4 *Clamp the doubled rafter* over the adhesive. Fasten it permanently with nails, or use screws for more holding power.

5 *Fasten half of the header* to your doubled side rafters, and face-nail through the center into the end of the cut rafter.

6 *After nailing on the second half* of the header, secure the connections with framing hardware (often required by code).

The Steel Advantage

Unlike wood, steel stud framing doesn't warp, shrink, or split. Termites and carpenter ants can't chew through it. It's much lighter than masonry, and it's easier and faster to assemble the pieces. It also won't rot, crumble, or add fuel to a fire. Because of all this, and its strength and durability (during a fire it can extend the time of possible escape before the walls collapse), steel framing is now the standard for commercial construction.

If steel offers so many advantages, why is it used in only 3 to 5 percent of residential building frames? For one thing, steel is a lot less accommodating than wood, which can often be coaxed and nudged into proper position. Steel construction also requires tools and skills quite different (though not necessarily more complicated) than wood framing, which is a disadvantage for do-it-yourselfers.

Steel Framing Members

The basic steel framing member is three-sided; a 2x4 stud, for example, has two narrow 1¼- or 1½-inch edges (front and back) connected by only a single 3½- or 4-inch side, creating a shallow C-shape. Connectors are available in many shapes to join the three-sided framing members. Light-gauge steel thickness ranges from 12 to 25 gauge, with the lower numbers being thicker. In a typical right-angle framing joint, one side of an L-shaped bracket is screwed to each steel member to make the connection.

HANDLING

▶ **The edges of steel framing** are rolled over during manufacturing to provide a smooth edge. But when you cut studs with a saw or snip them with shears, you should protect yourself with gloves against the sharp edges.

▶ **A water-based lubricant** is often used to protect steel studs. A few days out in the weather should take care of removing it—but wear gloves when handling slippery studs.

Using Screw Guns

A typical house framed with steel studs may take as many as 20,000 screws to hold it together. Even figuring only 20 seconds per screw, that's 111 hours. Pros who do this full time use quick-loading screw guns, some with bandoliers of screws that feed in line one after another. DIYers who don't want to invest in this kind of dedicated equipment can speed the job along by using a simple attachment on their ¼-in. drills.

A screw attachment with a screw-driving tip (sometimes called drill-and-drive) fits into the drill chuck.

A magnetic tip holds the screw, and a sleeve slides down the driver shaft to keep the screw running straight.

Run the screw into the framing, and the sleeve retracts. Drills with a torque clutch release when the screw sets.

Assembling Wall Frames

USE: ▶ metal snips • drill/driver or screw gun • hacksaw • chalk-line box with plumb bob • clamps

1 *To begin the installation,* snap a chalk line that is plumb with the soleplate, and screw a stud section to the framing above.

2 *Nestle a stud* into the channels of the soleplate and top plate, and clamp it in position before driving your screws.

Power Nailers

Power nailers *use the same kind of charge that propels a 22-caliber bullet to drive special nails in concrete.*

Use extreme caution *(and complete protection including safety glasses) when power-driving nails.*

Headers

In steel framing systems, you have to pick up loads where studs are removed to make openings the same way you do with wood framing. The most basic openings—for example, framing around a doorway or small window—normally require only a single piece of metal. Large framing members are available to carry exceptional loads. You will also need the equivalent of wooden jack studs along the sides. Because steel studs are hollow and formed in a U-shape, you need to add an extra piece with the solid side facing the opening.

Building sites *can be piled with wood or metal. But metal may provide a better fire rating and cheaper home insurance.*

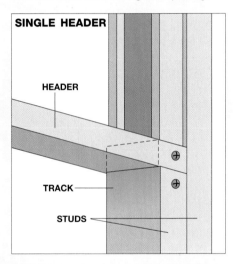

SINGLE HEADER

HEADER
TRACK
STUDS

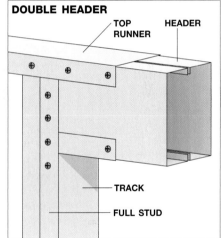

DOUBLE HEADER

TOP RUNNER
HEADER
TRACK
FULL STUD

• caulking gun • 4-ft. level • work gloves ▶ steel studs • sheet metal screws • silicone caulk

3 ***To fit a header between studs,*** *snip each edge at a 45° angle. Pros can work barehanded; you may want gloves.*

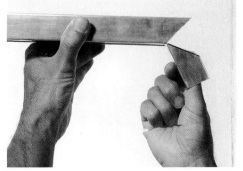

4 ***One way to make a connecting flange*** *for the header: bend the overage of the header down to a 90° angle.*

5 ***Fit the straight section*** *of the header in position, tuck the overage flange around the stud, and screw it in place.*

framing

Old & New Wood

The lumber industry has an unusual word for the process of trimming rough-cut boards into standard sizes of dimensional timbers. They call it dressing, even though undressing would be more accurate. You could forgive them this misleading term, except every decade or so the dressing process eats away just a little bit more of the usable lumber in studs, joists, and rafters.

If you check the framing of a house built 50 or 60 years ago, you may find that a 2x4 stud actually measures 2 by 4 inches. Next to the original building in an addition built in the 1970s, the studs are likely to be smaller: 1⅝ x 3⅝ inches. For a while now, most studs have been shipped from the mill at 1½ x 3½ inches.

None of this is a problem, of course, if you are building one complete structure with one load of lumber. But mismatches can cause extra work in remodeling—for example, where a wall framed with small 2x4s joins a wall made from older, full-size versions.

As a general rule, the best you can do in those cases is make one side flush and pack out the other. By taking very careful measurements ahead of time, you may find that using lattice strips or thicker drywall can make up the difference.

Although the most obvious discrepancies between old and new lumber show up in framing, they can also cause delays and require special finishing in flooring and trim materials.

Old to New

Trying to join a new partition to an older wall? Be prepared for a difference in the depth of the studs.

Permanent Wood Foundations

Prefabricated sections of pressure-treated lumber and sheathing are lowered onto a sill board set on gravel.

Treated wood sections can be installed even in subfreezing temperatures so that upper-floor framing can continue.

Most permanent wood foundations call for a poured concrete floor, although you can use pressure-treated joists.

Manufactured Housing

Manufactured houses account for more than one in five new homes. Construction is controlled in the factory.

Large sections—completely insulated, plumbed, and wired inside—are trucked to your prepared building site.

A crane lowers single-wide sections onto the foundation, which makes these so-called mobile homes very permanent.

Using Span Tables

The allowable spans for joists, rafters, beams, and other elements are all subject to local building codes. Codes will specify the loads that framing members in each location must bear—for example, a live load of 40 pounds per square foot for floor joists in living space. They will also set the deflection limits for wood in different parts of the house; this figure is given as span in inches (L) over a given number. An L/360 limit for floor joists means that a 10-foot joist can bend a maximum of 120"/360, or ⅓ inch under the designated load.

Some span tables, like the one at top right, are organized by wood species and grade. Different sizes for each grade are given different maximum span lengths in feet and inches for the most common on-center spacings. For example, looking at this table, if you wanted to span 13 feet with Southern pine, you'd need to use at least No. 1 grade at 16 inches on center; with No. 2, they'd have to be spaced 12 inches on center.

Other municipalities use two tables: one gives design values for each grade of wood, and one gives different span lengths according to these values. To use these tables, you'd have to check two values for the type of wood you're using—measurements of strength (F_b) and elasticity (E-value). The span table will give you the minimum for these values for particular spans, and the design value table will give the rating for types of wood by species and grade.

Finished manufactured homes can be assembled in sections that make the final product look completely site-built.

Floor Joist Span Ratings (feet & inches)

Strength: For 40 psf live load, 10 psf dead load
Deflection: Limited in span in inches divided by 360 for live load only.

Species Group	Grade	2x8 Spacing on center			
		12	16	19.2	24
Spruce/ pine/fir (Southern)	Sel. Struc.	15-0	13-7	12-10	11-11
	No. 1 & Btr.	14-8	13-4	12-7	11-8
	No. 1	14-5	13-1	12-4	11-0
	No. 2	14-2	12-9	11-8	10-5
	No. 3	11-3	9-9	8-11	8-0

Excerpted from Western Wood Products Association, Western Lumber Span Tables.

Design Values for Joists & Rafters

Species & Grade	Size	Design Value in Bending (F_b)		E-Value (million psi)
		Normal	Snow Loading	
Hemlock/Fir	**2x10**			
Select Structural		1700	2035	1.6
No. 1 & better		1330	1525	1.5
No. 1		1200	1380	1.5
No. 2		1075	1235	1.3
No. 3		635	725	1.2

Excerpted from CABO's One- and Two-Family Dwelling Code.

Floor Joist Span Ratings (feet & inches)

With L/360 deflection limits. For 40 psf live load.

Joist Size (in.)	Spacing	E-Value (in million psi)			
		0.8	0.9	1.0	1.1
2x6	12	8-6	8-10	9-2	9-6
	16	7-9	8-0	8-4	8-7
	24	7-3	7-7	7-10	8-1
2x8	12	11-3	11-8	12-1	12-6
	16	10-2	10-7	11-0	11-4
	24	11-8	9-3	9-7	9-11
2x10	12	14-4	14-11	15-5	15-11
	16	13-0	13-6	14-0	14-6
	24	11-4	11-10	12-3	12-8
Minimum F_b (all sizes)	12	718	777	833	888
	16	790	855	917	977
	24	905	979	1050	1119

Excerpted from CABO's One- and Two-Family Dwelling Code.

remodeling guide

8

remodeling guide

BEFORE

Every home is different, but most successful remodeling jobs follow a similar course. Here is the process from a winter start to a fall finish, with pictures from a major overhaul.

Planning a Remodeling Job

When you're lounging in the new family room, finally free of whining saws and paint fumes, it may seem incredible that such a complicated remodeling project began on the back of a napkin. But that's the way many jobs start—with a simple sketch. The question is how to develop the idea into a plan that balances what you want, what you need, and what you can afford.

Not every homeowner is up to the task of developing home-improvement dreams into working blueprints. But the more information you gather and the more details you give a remodeling contractor, the more likely you are to get a reasonable version of what you want at a reasonable price. And that's the final measure of a successful project. The work may cost more and take longer than you imagined. But if you can transform the heart of your first sketch into long-awaited extra living space, you'll find that the hassles tend to fade.

There are some nightmare jobs. But talk to friends and neighbors who have lived through a major project, and you'll find that most report their own take of the same basic experience. They may grumble about the delays and disruptions—and the money, of course—but then they'll want to take you on a guided tour

through the new addition. To reach that position, your ideas must be on paper in the form of measured drawings. You need them to get realistic estimates, to get a building permit, and to pin down construction details for your contractor. Although there are many variations, you have three basic options: hire a design professional, work with a design-build construction firm, or draw your own.

Design Professionals

Both interior designers and architects must meet standards and follow guidelines set by professional societies. They work for you and can represent your interests with workers and suppliers. They can come up with a plan, help you analyze estimates, select a contractor, and follow through with regular checkups on materials, schedules, payments, and job quality.

Although there are exceptions, interior designers, true to their title, are likely to give more attention to the surface than the structure, while architects take it in reverse. This built-in bias is reflected in their drawings: full-color perspectives from interior designers and measured blueprints from architects. That means an interior designer may be the best choice if you need a lot of ideas about remodeling an existing space, and an architect may be a better choice if you need to reshape the building.

Despite some controversy about who can legally use the word "design" to describe their services, design-build firms are an attractive option because they offer a complete package. On a kitchen remodeling job, you may be able to view dozens of designs on a computer screen and get detailed plans, plus cabinets and installation. Some firms have an architect or engineer on staff for more comprehensive jobs, while others work with code-approved plans that can be modified to suit your needs. Whatever the circumstance, you deal with one company instead of an array of design professionals and independent contractors. That's good, because one party is responsible for every phase of the job. But if problems develop, there is no intermediary to sort things out.

Do-It-Yourself Plans

It's a good idea to develop your ideas in detail, even if you turn to an architect or design-build firm to complete the final version. This preliminary planning will refine your best ideas and weed out the worst variations. You can work from stock designs in plan books and, in some areas, use pre-approved plans supplied by the building department for basic projects such as decks. Steal ideas from the pages of shelter magazines that show materials and designs you like, and survey displays in local home centers. It helps to see materials firsthand instead of in a catalog where the scale can be deceiving.

Sketch out a basic floor to scale on graph paper, and use models to approximate furniture—or use home-design computer software to work up your plans. Even basic programs allow you to try different furniture arrangement and change materials with the click of a mouse. But it pays to test your plan at full scale—for example, by laying out the lines of a new deck with stakes and strings. Seeing even the barest outline helps to guard against a chronic planning problem that can occur no matter who draws the plans—the underwhelming moment when the new area fills with people and furniture and seems smaller than the ample space you drew months ago on the back of a napkin.

When to Call for Help

Once you have plans for a remodeling project, you need to find contractors to carry them out—or maybe not. You can save money by handling part of the work yourself—maybe 30% of the job price if you act as the general contractor and manage the project. But you can run into pitfalls, too, mainly when you get in over your head on jobs that require skills you

Your contractor doesn't want to hear...

> **" *But you're going to the landfill anyway.* "**
>
> This is one of the many twists to the as-long-as-you're-there idea in which a client stretches the boundaries of the project to include all kinds of little favors and accommodations that amount to freebies, and acts wounded if the contractor doesn't oblige.

don't have. You may start with the best intentions but wind up getting in the way of pros who are accustomed to the daily regimen—and work weekdays when you're at that other job.

There are no set rules about which jobs to tackle and which to leave to the pros. Do-it-yourself skills, interests, and budgets vary so widely that you might do an excellent job on part of the project your neighbor wouldn't touch. But there are sensible guidelines you can apply. Number one is if in doubt, don't. Don't plunge into a project unless you have a realistic idea of the tools, skills, time, and money involved. Then you can make common-sense decisions, including the most important one: whether or not you can do the work safely.

So when you consider the array of jobs on a major remodeling project—from foundation work to roofing—the best approach is to avoid work that is inherently dangerous. Naturally, that depends to some extent on your idea of danger. For one do-it-yourselfer, laying shingles on a low-slope roof may be a snap. But if you start sweating halfway up a ladder, even the simplest roof improvement can be hazardous. You don't need construction expertise to sort this out. There is a good reason painting

is at the top of the do-it-yourself list and wiring is at the bottom: Paint can't kill you.

You can't rule out everyday accidents. Some scrapes and bruises are inevitable when you handle a lot of tools and building materials. But it's wise to steer clear of jobs where problems due to lack of experience could result in structural defects or serious injury.

As to structure, that means in most cases you should leave foundations, framing, and similar work to the pros, and concentrate on finishing trades such as drywalling, trimming, and painting that use the structural systems for support. Foul up on the surface and you may make a mess, but nothing is likely to collapse.

As to injury, that means in most cases you should let pros handle mechanical systems and equipment—heating and cooling, electrical, and plumbing. Don't take a shot at installing a new furnace that could burn down the house if it's installed incorrectly. Plumbing is a bit of a gray area because on some pipes, the worst you'll get from a mistake is a leak, and you can fix leaks—or call a plumber. But making the wrong kind of connection on other piping, such as gas lines and sewer lines, can have serious consequences.

A surprise extra: removing an old oil tank.

Blocks delivered for the foundation.

The hole in the ground takes shape.

remodeling guide

Blocks rise, and the floor is ready to pour.

The truck only crushed a few bushes.

First-floor framing—and the new porch.

If you don't know enough about a project to have a reasonable idea about its potential dangers and the crucial installation steps that prevent them, leave it alone. Also rule out installation work that could void a warranty and jobs that require special licenses or inspec-

tions. Removing asbestos is one good example; wiring a new addition is another. With the proper permits, you can pour a bump-out foundation and nail up framing on your own house, although a building inspector may pick your work apart. But in many areas there are jobs, such as installing a septic system and wiring, that won't be approved unless you are licensed to do the work.

Management Options

If you decide to have others do most of the work, you may want to consider hiring a remodeling manager to monitor the job. They have no standardized qualifications and no professional society, so finding one is often a matter of word of mouth. Some provide supervision on the job site; others help you select materials and deal on your behalf with architects, designers, contractors, and even mortgage bankers. You may pay a flat fee or a percentage of the job price for what amounts to a hand-holding service provided by a manager

who may be very helpful but doesn't design or build anything. But some homeowners need a friendly voice on the other end of the phone who will do some of their negotiating—someone who doesn't have a stake in the design or a hand in the construction.

" You're not eating dinner, are you? "

It's aggravating to be constantly on call, and hand-holding a client day and night, Saturdays and Sundays, even though the questions can wait a few hours and both of you are done with work for the day and at home with other things to do.

The next rung up from hiring a remodeling manager is managing—acting as your own general contractor. On the plus side, you can save at least some of the contractor's markup buying materials in bulk. However, you probably won't get the best price that suppliers reserve for repeat customers (year-round contractors), and you may not save anything on a small, one-time order.

The most taxing part of being a general contractor is hiring and managing several subcontractors. To start with, you probably won't get their best price, either. They might trim down a bid for the general contractor who keeps them working job to job—and who knows where the excess is—but not for you. You will save the general contractor's salary, of course, but only if you have the time to spend on site and figure your time is free. Don't try to run a remodeling job from your other job over the phone unless you're clairvoyant. You need to be there to see what's happening and have enough general construction knowledge to understand what you're

seeing. You don't have to know as much about electricity as the electrician. But you will need to be familiar with the basics of every trade so you aren't taken advantage of, or simply stumped by conversations about the project.

The best jobs to manage yourself are short in duration, relatively inexpensive, straightforward, and self-contained—like adding new siding. Whole-house remodeling that involves plumbing, electrical, heating, cooling, and structural systems throughout the building are more difficult, particularly kitchen and bathroom jobs that cram a lot of mechanical and finishing work into a small space. As you hire more subs with different expertise, interests, and schedules, the job becomes exponentially more difficult to control.

You may save money when you're the boss, but you'll be shouldering a lot of responsibility. It can be a difficult spot to be in—when the buck stops with you, and it's your own buck.

Hiring a Contractor

If every homeowner with a remodeling job gets a top contractor who comes highly recommended, puts in 10-hour days, and always finishes on time, then who hires all the other guys? And when the economy is strong, loan rates are low, and a lot of homeowners are remodeling, how can you snag these top contractors? The search can be time-consuming and frustrating, and many contractors you call may be unavailable.

Locating the right contractor takes legwork: developing leads, tracking down referrals, verifying recommendations, conducting face-to-face interviews, and keeping track of the one who seemed so forthcoming and the one who rubbed you the wrong way.

The ideal shortcut is to hire a contractor recommended by a trusted friend or neighbor who has just finished a project like the one you have in mind—a situation where you'll be able to find out about costs, schedules, attitudes, and see the results firsthand. Short of that ideal, the best bet is to leave a lot of time for the search and to start with the biggest possible pool of qualified contractors. You can get names from many sources that generally fall into two categories: referrals and recommendations. Referrals come from advertisements—for instance, the side of a truck or a card posted at the lumberyard. There is no screening involved; they are just names.

Recommendations carry more weight than referrals because they include an evaluation— say, from a friend or neighbor, your homeowners' insurance agent, mortgage banker, real estate agent, or someone else in the housing business who knows what you want.

Before you start weeding out candidates, also consider the Internet. In a typical Web search, you'll get lost in lists of contracting firms halfway across the country. But keep looking and eventually you will hit trade associations, such as the National Association of the Remodeling Industry (NARI, at www.remodeltoday.com), and a growing number of Internet-based contractor-referral services. Several on-line referral services are dead ends; either too new or too disorganized to use. You scroll through snappy-looking option screens (and ads to click on, of course), but when you finally start to zero in, it turns

out that only a few states and counties can be searched—and yours is not among them.

But fully operational sites, such as www.improvenet.com, one of the largest referral services with a national database of 600,000 contractors, help to make a match. You submit the particulars of your job and receive a list of screened contractors that omits anyone who has been in business less than three years and does not have a clean legal and credit record.

The service is free to consumers; contractors pay for the referrals. It's a good way for them to get leads and screen out homeowners who aren't really serious about starting a project in the near future and are just shopping for ideas. A typical response, via E-mail, may give you four local names within 48 hours. But there is no guarantee that these contractors will be agreeable, work for the price you have in mind,

Finally, the contractor must be available to do the job—but not immediately without a good explanation. You can't be the only one to find the guy. If he's good, a lot of people want him, and you may have to get in line.

Watching the Budget

Soliciting bids from remodeling contractors is like shopping for any consumer service—just more drawn out and confusing. The main mystery is that even though the product—your project—is painstakingly defined with plans and specifications, everyone who looks at it sees a different price tag. Few will be as low as the one you envision, and some will be so far from others that it will be hard to imagine the contractors are estimating the same job.

Your contractor doesn't want to hear...

“*So what do you think about these nine kinds of tile?*”

This syndrome occurs when clients in the thrall of a major remodeling project come to believe that their house is endlessly fascinating and fail to realize that rehashing every possible feature is like showing their most recent 200 baby pictures to a pediatrician.

or produce high-quality results. All that is for you to discover.

By whatever method, gather as many names as you can, and make the basic checks with local consumer protection agencies and the Better Business Bureau to find out if the contractor has a license, plus a record that is free of consumer complaints.

Variation can stem from basics like the law of supply and demand, of course. When loan rates are low, the weather is warm, and a lot of homeowners are looking for estimates, availability falls and prices rise. If you solicit a highly sought-after contractor who doesn't really need the work, the estimate may soar. But if your job involves a lot of demolition

It looks like the drawings—sort of.

At last: some big windows and a view.

There used to be a really nice lawn here.

remodeling guide

It looks much too big from the outside.

From the inside the rooms seem small.

Have to pick paint colors by next week.

work, and no one can know ahead of time how much rebuilding will be required, the bid may rise to cover the worst scenario. Bids also can increase if you impose extra conditions on the work such as a tight schedule, if your house is full of custom details and odd angles—and if you come off as difficult as your house.

After a few meetings to check the site and talk about the plans, an experienced contractor can tell the accommodating client from the one who will check for paint blemishes with a magnifying glass—and adjust the bid accordingly. But don't dismiss a bid just because it's high. Find out why it's higher and if the increased labor and material estimate is for features that offer durability or convenience others don't provide.

Checking Estimates

This part of the project involves a continuation of the sorting and sifting, first through references and recommendations of many contractors to find the bidders, and then through the sometimes complex estimates of your short list of candidates. But if you take the time to solicit and analyze bids thoroughly, you can discover a lot more than price. A detailed breakdown can reflect the contractor's professionalism, attention to detail and overall attitude, and help you make the final selection.

The first key is to be sure that you are getting real prices, which means that you should be prepared to hire any of the bidders. You can try to get a bid or two purely for comparison. But when a contractor gets the idea that you want an estimate only for negotiations with another contractor who basically has the job, the bottom line may not be realistic.

The second key is to make sure that every contractor bids on the same job, based on a complete description of the project. If three contractors have different ideas about your deck, ask them to price the same basic platform, and list their plans for floating stairs or built-in benches separately. If you're not sure yet about some of the materials in your project—say, exactly what type and brand of window—pick one for the bids so you won't be stuck comparing apples and oranges. Whenever possible, and particularly on big projects, submit plans that show the job pictorially, as well as specifications, which list every door and floor tile and appliance by type, size, and model.

Because labor often costs more than materials and has the greatest effect on overall job quality, it's also crucial to know whose labor you'll be getting for the money: who will be the main job supervisor on-site every day. Occasionally, firms send an estimator to lock

Your contractor doesn't want to hear...

66 *How could it possibly cost so much?* 99

No one likes a whiner, and this is whining.
Every remodeling product and service has a cost, and before
a client orders a top-of-the-line commercial stove or triple-glazed
windows, it's easy enough to find out what the bill would be.

up the bid—someone you never see again who may forget to tell the contracting crew all the things you were promised.

Some firms start off with a general contractor who seems to be the supervisor but only visits the site from time to time and leaves most of the work to employees with less expe-

rience and subcontractors who only know about their part of the project. You ask why the door will swing one way instead of the other, and no one knows for sure except the general contractor, who may respond to his pager in the next few minutes—or not until the end of the day when the door is already installed. The worst scenario is paying for the reputation of a particular contractor or crew and getting the second team stocked with apprentices.

To help you analyze and compare bids, ask for an itemized estimate. Bottom lines and square-foot prices will give you an overall view. But itemized bills allow you to decide between differently priced materials, isolate parts of the job you might do yourself, and find key steps one bid includes and another leaves out or glosses over. Even on modest remodeling jobs, it's helpful to have bids broken down by labor and materials for four major operations: foundation and framing, closing in (installing windows, doors, siding, and roof-

ing), mechanicals (heating, cooling, plumbing, and electrical), and interior finishing.

To be practical, every bid should predict true and complete costs, which means the best bids may contain some bad news—mainly, charges for remodeling related jobs, including fees; permits; inspections; preliminary demolition;

carting, which can loom large if several rooms are gutted; relandscaping to cover the tracks of heavy equipment or a new sewer line; and upgrading piping and wiring in the old part of the house to meet the demands of modern systems in remodeled rooms. Leaving them out can make a bid look enticingly low—until you start paying for all the extras.

Contracts

No legal language can make dishonest people honest or change slow, sloppy carpenters into expert woodworkers. But on the up side, contracts put the job into words that describe its components in enough detail that you don't have to rely on memory or good will.

A good contract also allows for misunderstandings with a provision for third-party arbitration—a last-chance to maintain job progress on-site where work is done instead of in court. Nobody installs roof flashing in court. On commercial projects with millions of dollars at stake, it may pay to pursue a settlement. On many residential remodeling jobs, even when you're sure that you're right and the contractor is wrong, it rarely pays to sue. It takes too much time, too much money, and prolongs the life-disrupting overload of aggravation.

To guard against problems, use a contract that begins with basic provisions, the who's-who and what's-what: details of names, addresses, the contractor's license and insurance, starting and completion dates, and a detailed description of what the job entails. To simplify the contract, it can refer to blueprints instead of listing every design feature, and to a separate document called the specifications, which lists wood types, appliances, paint colors, and everything else in enough detail to avoid substitutions and misunderstandings. Here is a look at some key provisions.

Starting & Completion Dates

To have any teeth, dates should be described as "of the essence of the contract." That phrase will give more weight to your case in court. But on the job what helps most is a detailed schedule you and your contractor agree to before work begins. It should include target dates for acquiring permits, ordering a dumpster for debris, initial demolition, and the first material deliveries.

The more detailed your schedule, the better your chance of avoiding serious trouble—of almost any kind and at any stage of the project. Track progress in small, detailed steps that can be corrected before they mushroom into complex problems that can seem insurmountable. Delays don't count if they are generally beyond the contractor's control—including weather and your decision to change to windows that don't arrive for two extra weeks.

To coerce a projected completion date into reality, some contracts contain a bonus clause for finishing early and a penalty clause for finishing late—bad ideas for three reasons. First, many older homes ripe for remodeling contain too many unknowns to pick a reliable date months in advance. Second, you don't want anyone to cut corners in search of a bonus. Third, end-of-job penalties intended to encourage completion can have the opposite effect as the final payment erodes to the point where the contractor will be financially better off starting another project than finishing yours.

Payments

The best course with remodeling work is to pay for services as you receive them, typically in stages tied to job progress—with two exceptions: a down payment that gives the contractor a financial head start, and a final payment that gives you some leverage with the checklist. Percentages vary (and they're negotiable), but should be large enough to count—say, 15–20% of the total at each end of the job.

The rest can be split into four equal payments: for the structure, for closing in, for mechanicals (plumbing, heating, cooling, and electrical work), and for finishing work. No reputable contractor needs 40–50% up front to cover costs. They have credit at lumberyards,

> *Your contractor doesn't want to hear...*
>
> ## "*Lend me a saw; I'll help.*"
>
> It sounds so cooperative—like we'll all pitch in and raise the barn frame together—but it can strain the relationship, slow up the job, and raise hackles when a client doesn't have enough sense to know that you shouldn't inflict a part-time hobby on a full-time professional.

White trim but natural wood railings.

Saws run all day, inside and outside.

In place of the wobbly old steps.

Inside now, it sounds like a train wreck.

The antique appliances leave for good.

The kitchen: like camping out inside.

and don't pay their subcontractors in advance. A contract also should direct suppliers and subcontractors on the project to provide a release called a Waiver of Mechanic's Lien Rights. Once signed, the plumber can't sue you for payments you provided to the general contractor that were not passed on.

Following Codes

With a plan in hand and a contractor in the wings, there is a moment of calm before the remodeling storm when you can clear out rooms, prepare for material deliveries, allocate parking space, and arrange the details of a subject that's rarely mentioned in contracts: bathroom facilities for a crew of contractors. Most of the pre-job jobs are organizational chores that contractors will eventually tend to if you don't. But there are two subjects that won't tolerate a haphazard or last-minute approach: building codes and zoning ordinances.

Building codes are unlike everything else about remodeling because you can't change them. There is no fussing or fudging the way there is with paint colors. The building inspector says your foundation trench is 2 inches too shallow; you start digging. Inspectors have the final say on the size of girders, the locations of electrical outlets, the thickness of drywall, and just about everything else. And they can show up unannounced to tour the job and set you straight. It's not that you want to be bowing and scraping when the inspector pulls up, but it pays to be accommodating.

To start the relationship on a positive note, it's a good idea to visit the building department with your preliminary plans, particularly on small jobs where you sketch the drawings yourself. Ask questions, including the most obvious one: Do I need a permit? Generally, you do if the project involves structural work such as extending a foundation or breaking through bearing walls. But you also need a permit to change the use of a structure—say, to convert an attached garage or storage attic into living space.

The most common problems stem from incomplete plans—failures of omission such as showing joists in the right places but failing to specify their sizes, and showing a new second story without accounting for the extra load on the old foundation. But details that aren't caught in planning probably will be on site, where you can expect at least four inspections: one to verify the depth of footings, one to examine framing, one to check mechanical systems, and one to make a final check before granting a Certificate of Occupancy.

Some homeowners try to avoid the supervision and do the job without a permit, generally to keep the value of the job from increasing their real estate taxes. But this omission leaves you vulnerable to substandard work, unsound materials—and a disgruntled neighbor who doesn't like the construction noise. One call to the building department and you could be

liable for fines on top of the costs and hassles of rebuilding to code.

You have to observe building codes that govern the details of construction and zoning regulations that control what you can do with your site. The main zoning categories are commercial and residential, but there are many subcategories. For instance, in one area you can remodel a large house into a two-family, but a few blocks away in a different zone you can't. Single-family houses on one street may need 2 acres of land but only ¼ acre on another. In historic districts, your plans may have to be altered to include certain styles of windows, siding, and even paint colors.

But the main stumbling blocks for remodelers expanding the building footprint are two restrictions on property: the percentage of land that can be covered by buildings and how the uncovered property can be distributed among front, side, and backyards. For example, the

"I changed my mind."

Your contractor doesn't want to hear...

This is fine in the planning stage. It would be okay at any stage if the client were willing to pay the full tab of extra time and materials for switching in midstream from, for example, casements to double-hungs —and didn't grumble later about delays caused by the indecision.

code may specify at least 100 feet of side yards, with a distribution percentage no greater than 80-20. That means the narrowest yard must be at least 20% of 100 feet—in theory, to prevent next-door neighbors from building nearly on top of each other. The rules can box you in, but there may be a way out. It's called getting a variance, and each jurisdiction has its own, generally time-consuming procedure for granting variances.

Typically, you submit copies of your blueprints (including a detailed plot plan) to an appeals board, and present your case at a hearing after posting notices of the hearing up and down your street so your neighbors have a chance to object. You can present the case yourself—relying as much as possible on facts and figures instead of what you want—or hire a real estate attorney to present a complex case where you anticipate objections from adjacent property owners.

Supervising a Project

How do you keep track of a complicated process undertaken by people you don't know who use techniques that may be unfamiliar and report their progress in terms you may not understand? You could turn over every detail of job management to the general contractor. But that's too much like falling asleep in the

may be time-consuming, expensive, or even impossible to correct.

The best way to safeguard your investment is to establish a schedule for meetings on job progress where you can divide the project into manageable pieces, watch for signs of trouble and plot the progress of work done and money paid. End-of-week meetings are best, even if everyone stops work a half-hour early to attend. A slight dip in productivity is a good trade for up-to-date information. Include the general contractor and any major subcontractors, such as a kitchen firm hired by the G.C., as well as the architect, designer, or decorator. Review the previous week's work (mainly things on the schedule that didn't get done); the upcoming week, including materials in hand or on order; and an update of payments made and due.

The idea is to uncover potential problems and small delays, although you may have to probe for the bad news because many contractors tend to minimize trouble. They know you don't want to hear it and may honestly think that they can

demolition or cutoffs—for instance, periods when the power or water supply will be shut down and inevitable disruptions, such as when you'll have to vacate rooms while two coats of polyurethane take two days to dry. The meetings are likely to expose a few surprises. Three of the most troublesome are subcontractor scheduling, material and design changes, and debates about work that you think is part of the contract and the contractor thinks is an extra.

On many projects, even with a supervising general contractor who seems to take part in every operation, most of the work is handled by subcontractors such as roofers and plumbers.

The main stumbling block with them is coordination—a logical sequence that prepares foundations for framers and framing for drywallers. If the electrician disappears before the rough wiring is complete, the general contractor may not be able to call for an inspection, which means a delay for drywallers, finish carpenters, painters, and other trades.

To make sure that there aren't any gaps—and to avoid a few days of Keystone Kops where everyone shows up at the same time—you should know whom to expect next on the job, roughly what they are supposed to do, and how long it will take them to do it.

Your contractor doesn't want to hear...

" *What do you mean it's not in the contract?* "

It may seem reasonable for a contractor who hangs drywall in the new garage to tape and finish the seams—but not for free. Experienced contractors specify in the contract for all to see exactly what work will be done and tag any steps or finishing touches that won't be with the initials N.I.C (not in contract).

barber's chair. If there aren't any problems, you can wake up to a happy ending. But if there are—and you can count on more than a few glitches on most projects—the problems

fix the wound before it begins to fester.

To minimize the disruption that a major remodeling job can inflict on a household, also solicit advance warnings of any significant

Changes & Extras

Another potential monkey wrench, changes in the plan, can occur because materials weren't available or because someone forget to order the windows; it happens. And sometimes the change is an improvement everyone wants and no one foresaw. Whatever the reason, any sig-

Didn't even scratch the paint; amazing.

It's almost there; ready for finishing.

Another three days with no furniture.

The new family room.

The new kitchen.

One of the new bedrooms.

nificant deviation from the blueprints needs a little last-minute planning because it wasn't scheduled initially.

On big jobs, these alterations are committed to paper with a change order. You can use an official form, or at least note what's being changed and whether it effects the job price. That's raises one of the touchiest subjects: extras. It's often contentious because contractors tend to see most changes as extra work,

includes things that are inescapably part of an explicitly detailed job, such as hardware for doors—unless they are marked N.I.C. (not in contract) in the contract. Be prepared to negotiate the cost of unexpected work, such as installing a beam to beef up joists that turned out to be undersized only when the job was underway and the fault was exposed.

You could argue, and some homeowners do, that a contractor should be liable for any unex-

work. Some problems can be settled by compromises and negotiations. But when it comes to major differences about materials, time, and money, discussions too often deteriorate into ugly disputes that can bring the job to a halt.

Material Substitutions

Effective contracts include an "or equal" clause to deal with situations where you can't get what you planned. It means that a substitute window must be similar to the one already planned—not much more expensive, which wouldn't be fair to the contractor, or a bargain model, which wouldn't be fair to you.

If you disagree about what's equal, get together with the contractor and a copy of the material specifications (or blueprints or contract) that list the windows by manufacturer and model number. Price one, and only agree to a replacement that matches the cost and basic characteristics of the original.

This process does not require specialized construction knowledge. If the plan calls for a window with low-E glazing—the central feature of the window—don't accept a less efficient glazing system in a substitute. Most building materials are nearly duplicated by several manufacturers. Even when they aren't, for instance, when no local lumberyard has the Clear Heart redwood decking you wanted, you can switch to a top-end variety of cedar that has a similar description and price. If you upgrade, except an extra charge. If you downgrade, insist on a refund of the reduced cost.

Your contractor doesn't want to hear...

> ❝ *I'm a little strapped right now; how about a check next week?* ❞
>
> **How about some interest on the loan would be more like it, because guess who may be strapped, too—and have subcontractors to pay for work already done on the client's house and a bill at the lumberyard for materials already installed?**

particularly toward the end of a job when payments for materials and subs leave a smaller than expected share of the job price as profit.

Across the table, homeowners tend to see most changes as part of the contract—simple replacements. There are obvious points of agreement at both ends of the spectrum. If the basic cooktop you specified is out of stock, and you want to substitute a six-burner restaurant stove, that's an extra. If the contractor can't locate the off-white paint you wanted, substituting a slightly whiter white is a non-issue. But there is so much gray in between, and there's not much you can do about it except talk out your differences. Be firm on any material or work that is either written into the job specs or drawn in the blueprints. That

pected conditions. But no G.C. or architect has X-ray vision. The only other option is to draw a contract that includes charges for every foreseeable extra, which will prove to be a bad deal when most don't materialize. The goal is to keep the job moving, and that won't happen if you try to take advantage of a miscalculation. You need to find a middle ground on extras—and try to balance them with a give-back on jobs or materials you can live without.

Settling Disputes

A few parts of your remodeling job will be different than the picture you had in mind. Some problems can't be helped—for instance, a week of rain that bogs down the excavating

Time Problems

The number-one consumer complaint about building and remodeling projects—that they don't finish on time—is unlike most other job problems, such as unpainted walls or leaking roofs, which are obviously right or wrong. Time problems are rarely that clear-cut. They fester like a bad case of poison ivy, and generally begin with an itch here and there you hardly notice.

Bathroom windows won't arrive for a few days, so the tile contractor is going to another job: only a few days and he'll be back. Add on some porch trim that has to be special-ordered, a holdup with appliance installations because the new electrical circuit isn't in yet, a few long weekends, a plumber with the flu (the possibilities are almost endless), and you have a full-blown delay.

That's when you notice the rash. The job schedule is so disrupted that other contractors can't be on site when you need them. Materials delivered in a timely fashion pile up and have to be moved again and again because they're in the way. Everyone spends more and more time doing things to work around the delay, which keeps the job moving but makes it take even longer. Then the landscaper finally gives up on you and sells the plantings you reserved to someone else. That's when the problem gets so bad that it infects the entire job and undercuts overall job quality because there isn't enough time to do things correctly.

To catch time problems at an early stage, start by asking the contractor who delivers the bad news about a hard date for returning to schedule. Even if the delay is an unexpected deluge that floods the new foundation, it's up to the contractor to make an adjustment.

Don't leave a delay up in the air or leave yourself at the mercy of someone who doesn't work for you such as a material supplier. Insist that the contractor use another supplier, or hire another roofer to fill in for the one who is ill—and give you a deadline for resolving the delay.

Resolving Disputes

Standard practice is to draw up a checklist (or punch list) at the end of the job to cover work not done or done incorrectly. But this collection of molehills can seem like a mountain with only a week to go. It's more sensible to check details in stages—for framing, mechanical systems, windows, and doors—and leave the final list for finishing touches. This also helps to keep one problem from creating a negative chain reaction and exposes problems that require extra money to fix. If a problem develops that can't be sorted out in discussions on site, document the difficulty in a registered letter to the contractor. Explain why you are entitled to a solution (listing a provision of the contract, for example), and offer a reasonable time frame for a response to the letter and the problem. Also include your ideas about a solution. A dispassionate letter may bring a positive response by offering a way to make right what is wrong without financial penalty. If it doesn't, an arbitration service or attorney will probably want to see some record of your attempt to solve the dispute before they get involved.

If you do wind up in front of a third party, the best policy is to present facts, not a hand-wringing case of what you wanted and how terrible it is that you didn't get it. Use records of estimates, payments, meetings, and material orders to corroborate your complaint.

You could join the many consumers who complain about home contractors to the Better Business Bureau—like the American Arbitration Association, it offers dispute resolution services. You can even start the process on line at www.bbb.org by clicking on-line dispute-resolution forms. The best bet is to include in your contract a provision for binding arbitration that can prevent serious job problems from becoming disastrous.

Before: the old house in the snow; and after, finally, the new addition.

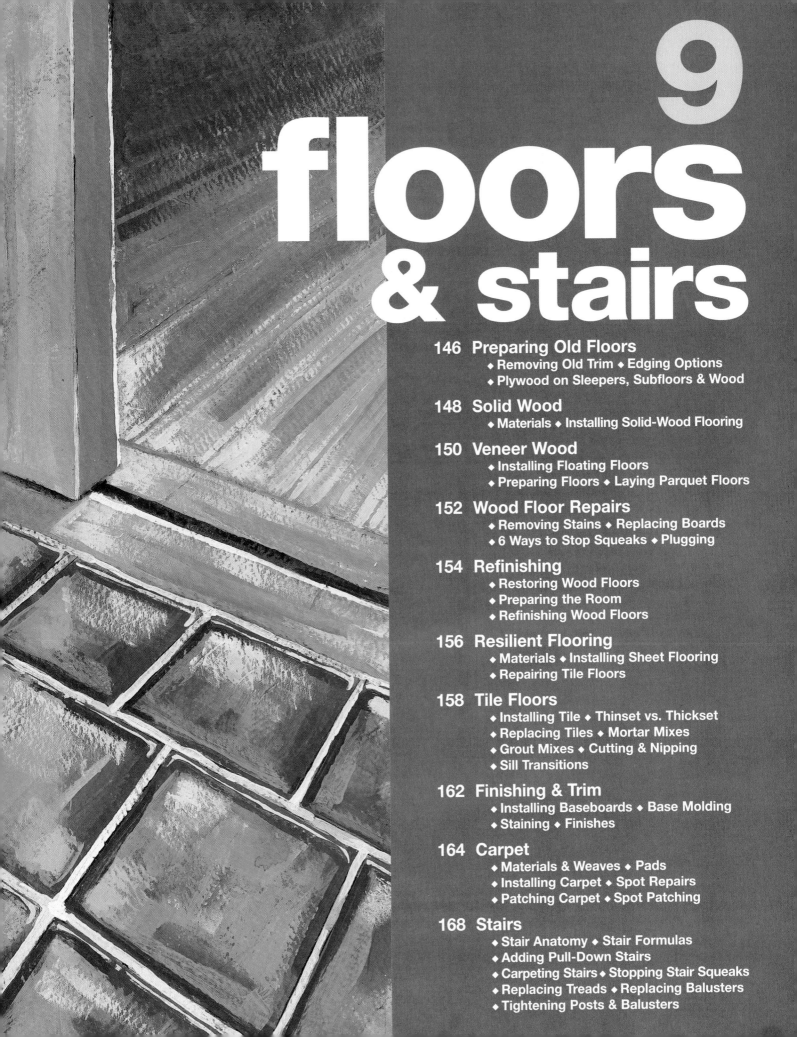

9

floors
& stairs

Saving the Old Floor

We expect a lot of floors: we walk all over them; grind in spilled food, dirt, and grease; and park tons of furniture on them. And that's not even counting the special abuse small children and pets can inflict. Little wonder floors sag, squeak, and become a bit dingy after a while.

Sure, floors are functional—so much so that it's easy to overlook their importance as a design element in any room. Painting walls and ceilings or adding new furniture by themselves can do a lot to perk up a room. But if the floors need work because they are stained, scraped, cracked, or just plain dull-looking, then the redecorating job is only half done, and it will show. Laying the new floor covering does require more skill than a simple paint job, but fortunately the work is well within the range of most do-it-yourselfers.

A Stable Base

That new floor covering won't last very long if the supporting structure underneath it isn't in good shape. For example, floor joists—the floor's underlying framework—have to be straight, solid, and level. You can feel low spots where joists have sagged or settled as you walk across a floor. Don't expect new flooring to hide the peaks and valleys though; in the long run the unevenness will damage it.

Subflooring is another important part of the floor structure. Nailed to the floor joists, the subfloor is made of plywood sheets or wood planks. Sometimes another layer of plywood, called the underlayment, is also nailed down over the subflooring to provide a more stable base for the floor covering. The problem with both subflooring and underlayment is that nails can work loose, causing the floor to lift slightly and creak as you walk over it. The noise is a nuisance, but for vinyl, ceramic tile, and even wood, that slight flexing can crack the flooring.

When laying new flooring, you don't always have to rip out the old floor covering (unless it is carpeting). For example, you can lay carpet directly over old solid-wood flooring, but you'll have to install an underlayment over it for new ceramic or vinyl flooring (after refastening loose boards). If old vinyl or ceramic tile flooring is in bad shape, it probably will have to be removed, or at least covered with a new underlayment. But usually you can lay new flooring over either one after repairing and smoothing over damaged spots. Remove floating floors (p. 150) before laying new flooring.

If you've torn up the old flooring, check the underlayment. If it's level, smooth enough, and thick enough, you can probably reuse it after covering chips and dips with leveling compound. If necessary, replace it with ¼ to ½-inch-thick, exterior-grade AC plywood for vinyl and wood floors. Ceramic and stone tiles are heavier, so they need a heavier underlayment. Cement backer board is best for ceramic tile, especially in kitchens and bathrooms.

Edging Options

To mark cuts around complicated molding, use a contour gauge. It duplicates even intricate shapes.

To recess new flooring, cut the trim short with a saw resting on a sample of the flooring and subflooring.

Removing Old Trim

USE: ▶ flat pry bar • chisel • hammer • permanent marker ▶ thin scrap wood • masking tape

1 Use a small flat bar to pry quarter-round trim away from the baseboard. Work slowly from one end to avoid splitting.

2 Use the same procedure to separate top molding from the base. You may need a chisel or second bar for leverage.

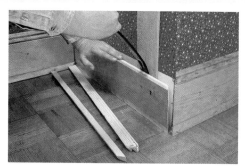

3 Set a thin piece of wood, such as a shingle, behind the baseboard to avoid marring the wall as you pry.

Plywood on Sleepers

If a floor is dry and level, you can install solid-wood strip flooring on pressure-treated 1x4 or 2x4 sleepers glued to the floor. Seal the concrete, and then apply adhesive made for bonding concrete to wood in ribbons about ⅛ inch thick and 4 inches wide. Do the perimeter first; then fill in the floor with sleepers cut 18 to 48 inches long. Overlap any short sleepers 4 to 6 inches, and secure each with two concrete nails. Allow about 10 to 12 inches between rows.

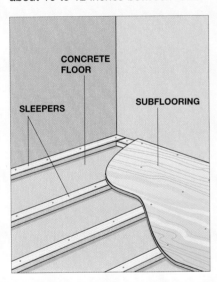

Plywood on Subfloors

Resilient flooring, parquet, and laminated wood all can be installed on dry, sealed concrete. But in damp basements (and for better insulation) lay flooring over a built-up subfloor. A built-up subfloor also is needed when using solid wood flooring wider than 4 inches. Over an old subfloor—for example, plywood or old boards uncovered when you removed wall-to-wall carpeting—run new sheets of plywood subflooring perpendicular to the old sheets.

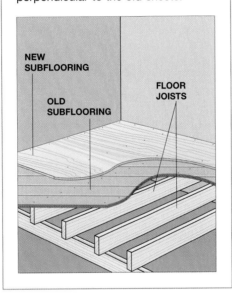

Plywood on Wood

A sound wood floor makes a good base for plywood underlayment. Lay the first panel across the floorboards. If the end of the panel falls over a seam, cut the panel to fall in the middle of a board. Use ring-shank nails every 6 inches along panel edges (keep them ⅜ inch in from the edges) and every 8 inches in the field. Nails should penetrate the flooring but not the framing. Leave 1/16 inch between the ends of sheets of plywood.

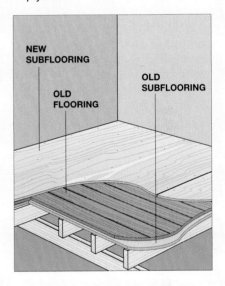

4 *Some baseboards* may pop off the wall. *To remove stubborn nails, set a metal bar between the nailhead and the wall.*

5 *With the metal bar in place,* tap the *baseboard (on scrap wood) to force out the nailheads so you can pull them.*

6 *Label the location of each piece* as *you remove it. On a room with many corners, this will make reinstallation easier.*

Solid-Wood Flooring

Solid wood floors offer a richness that's hard to beat, but properly installing the flooring requires some expertise with tools and wood. You can choose from strip or plank flooring, either prefinished or unfinished, in a variety of woods. Strip flooring generally measures between 1½ and 3¼ inches wide, with 2¼-inch strips being a popular size. Planks are at least 3 inches wide, and are often secured with countersunk screws topped with wooden plugs in a matching color. Manufactured wood-veneer products designed for do-it-yourself installation (as shown on pp. 150–51) look like solid wood, but there are limits to the repairs that can be made.

Ordering & Storage

Most solid-wood flooring is graded according to color, grain, and imperfections, as shown at right. You will have to weigh the cost against the wood quality. When ordering 2¼-inch-wide flooring, multiply the number of square feet in the room by 1.383 to find the amount of board feet needed, including the waste. For flooring of other sizes, ask your dealer how to compute the quantity.

When the wood is delivered, stack it in the room where the floor will be installed for several days—this allows it to acclimate to the moisture content of the room. Never store wood flooring in a poorly ventilated, damp place, because the wood may warp or twist as it picks up moisture. In addition, damp wood will shrink as it dries after installation, leaving behind unsightly gaps between boards and perhaps even cracks.

Installation Tips

Solid-wood flooring is generally installed parallel to the long dimension of the room. To allow room for the wood to expand and contract with seasonal changes in humidity, leave a gap around the perimeter of the room equal to the thickness of the boards. This gap will be covered by the baseboard trim. Finally, don't nail down the flooring without a dry run. Take the time to lay out the pieces of the floor, arranging them so that long boards alternate with shorter pieces, and end-to-end joints are evenly distributed over the floor.

Materials

GRADES OF OAK FLOORING

Type	Description
Clear	Mostly heartwood, uniform appearance, minimum number of character marks such as burls and small tight checks.
Select	May contain sound sapwood and slight imperfections.
No. 1 Common	Contains prominent variation in color and characteristics; checks and knotholes permitted.
No. 2 Common	Contains natural variations as well as minor defects and a limited number of pieces without tongues.

Hardwoods are most durable but most expensive; oak is most common.

Softwoods are less durable and less expensive; pine is most common.

Stain an oak floor with a pale tone, or apply a clear sealer for the lightest finish.

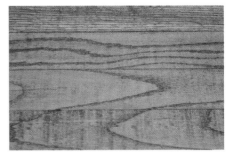

Stain the same oak floor with a dark tone for a completely different look.

Flooring can come prestained and prefinished, and in thin parquet patterns.

Flooring can come in slabs of cedar or redwood for porches and decks.

Installing Solid-Wood Flooring

USE: ▶ floor nailer • flat pry bar • backsaw • chalk-line box • framing square • hammer • permanent marker ▶ flooring • flooring nails • masking tape • wedge

1 *Use a flat pry bar* to pry molding and baseboard off the wall. Label it to make installation easier when the floor is laid.

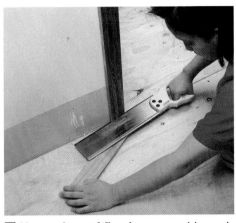

2 *Use a piece of flooring* as a guide, and shorten vertical trim where necessary to make room for the new floor.

3 *Check the room for square,* and snap a chalk line to help you set the first piece. Bury uneven margins under baseboard trim.

4 *Set the first board* on your line, slightly away from the wall to allow for expansion. Predrill and nail this board, setting the nails.

5 *Take the time* to lay out several rows before nailing. It helps you plan staggered seams and match wood grains and tones.

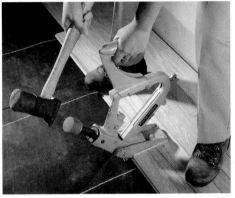

6 *Rent a floor nailer* to edge-nail boards. You load it with nails and pound with a heavy hammer on the driving arm.

7 *Some boards have a crook* and won't fit easily. Apply pressure by driving a wedge between the board and a nailed block.

8 *To finish rows,* measure the required length on a full board next to the end gap. Remember to leave wall clearance.

9 *To close up joints on the last row,* use a pry bar against a wood block on the wall to tighten the joint, and face-nail the board.

floors & stairs

Manufactured Flooring

You have two basic choices when buying manufactured flooring: a hardwood veneer glued to a plywood base or a synthetic, wood-like laminate over a fiberboard base. Both offer the look and feel of solid wood but are quicker and easier to install. Manufactured wood flooring is surfaced with various types of hardwood and comes prefinished with a factory-applied top coat. That cuts out a lot of work, letting you wrap up the job that much sooner.

Another important advantage of manufactured flooring is that it's more stable than solid wood. Because it isn't as prone to swelling and buckling, use it over concrete floors in basements and places that would be too damp for solid wood. But manufactured flooring does have one big drawback—the wood veneer is thin. You can't just sand and refinish the flooring when it has been damaged or worn down.

Installation

Plywood-backed veneered flooring can be glued directly to an underlayment or installed as a floating floor. But laminate-over-fiberboard flooring should only be installed as a floating floor. Be sure to leave a ½-inch gap around the edges of the floor for expansion.

Floating floors are not nailed or glued directly to the underlayment or floor below. Instead, you glue the tongue-and-groove edges of the boards together as you lay the boards over a ⅛-inch-thick pad of high-density foam.

Preparing Floors

You can install a manufactured wood floor over either an existing solid-wood floor or new plywood underlayment. To get the best results when installing a new veneer floor over plywood, lay the new plywood panels at a 90-degree angle to the seams of the existing floor. (With a floating floor, orientation of the new floor panels doesn't matter.) Plan the subfloor layout to maximize the use of full sheets and minimize seams. Before you nail down the sheets, check the old floor for high spots, which should be planed or chiseled flat.

1 *Instead of piecing plywood* at door openings, make a cutout with a saber saw; a full sheet provides more stability.

3 *To provide a completely smooth* surface for the new finished floor, cover the screwheads with putty.

4 *Drive screws about 6 in. apart* along joints between sheets. Use a drywall knife to fill the joints with putty.

Installing Floating Floors

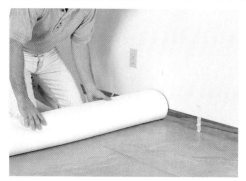

1 *Manufacturers' installation directions* will vary, but they generally include laying a foam-backed pad on which the floor floats.

2 *Pieces of finished flooring* are locked to each other with glue in the mating seams but not fastened to the subfloor.

3 *Use scrap wood* or an extra piece of flooring to seat one panel of flooring against another. Hammer blows damage the joints.

• power drill/driver ▶ plywood • screws • putty

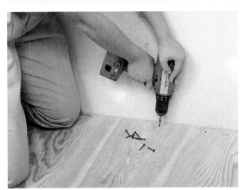

2 *Use screws instead of nails,* set about 6 in. apart, along the edges of the plywood. Drive them flush or just below the surface.

5 *Finish the subfloor preparation* by sanding the dried putty. Even small ridges of putty can disrupt a veneer floor.

Laying Parquet Floors

USE: ▶ notched trowel • saber saw • hammer • framing square ▶ parquet flooring • adhesive

1 *Typical parquet floors* (solid or veneer) rest in a bed of adhesive. Apply them with a notched trowel that leaves ridges.

3 *To fit a stubborn piece,* use a scrap section of flooring with its tongue or groove aligned to avoid damage.

2 *Make layout lines* to square the flooring in the space. Try to leave partial pieces of equal size around the edges.

4 *Make small cutouts* so full tiles turn the corners of obstructions. Use a saber saw with a fine-toothed blade.

4 *When you apply too much glue* and it oozes onto the finished surface, wipe the excess away with a damp rag.

5 *You can remove base trim,* install the new floor, and reinstall the old trim to cover the expansion gaps.

6 *On multipart base molding,* you may want to pull only the base quarter-round and reset it over the finished floor.

floors & stairs

Fixing Floors

Because people will naturally take the quickest route from one room to another, wood floors remain pristine in corners while taking abuse in the heavily traveled areas.

Sometimes you will have to replace floorboards, but as most hardwood flooring is interlocked with tongue-and-groove joints, you can't pry up just one or two boards without damaging others. When you do install a piece of new flooring, lightly sand it along the grain, and then match the surrounding finish by applying stain in light coats. Obviously, it also helps if you use a replacement board with a grain pattern that blends in—not a clear board in a grainy section or a boldly streaked board in a nearly clear section of the floor.

Dents & Cracks

If the damage is in one spot, such as a deep dent that can't be erased with surface sanding, a plug offers the easiest solution. Select a drill bit with a diameter slightly larger than the damaged spot; then, drill until you hit undamaged wood. Insert a plug as described at right.

You can fill deep cracks and splits in hardwood floors with wood fillers. Some fillers may be stronger than the wood itself—dense mixtures that resist scratches but also don't take wood stain. A few may leave a yellowish streak even more noticeable than the original crack, however. To prevent this, test the filler to see how it accepts stain, or opt for a softer,

more porous, powdered filler that can be sanded, stained, and sealed like natural wood.

Stains

If you have an area that has been stained by a pet, you can remove both the stain and odor with wood bleach or household bleach after sanding the area down to bare wood. Soak the sanded area with full-strength bleach, let the wood dry, sand again, and soak the wood a second time. Because bleach kills odors but also lightens the wood, stain the patch before resealing the surface. Apply several coats of polyurethane to seal any odors in the wood, and blend the surface with coats of wax.

Removing Stains

There are dozens of recipes for removing stains, but one of the oldest and most reliable is household bleach.

Replacing Boards

USE: ▶ power drill • wood chisel • hammer • putty knife ▶ replacement board • finishing nails • putty

1 **When a board is beyond repair,** remove the bad section. Start by drilling a row of holes just past the damaged area.

2 **Use a sharp chisel** to square up the edges of the holes. Create a slight undercut so the new piece fits tightly.

6 Ways to Stop Squeaks

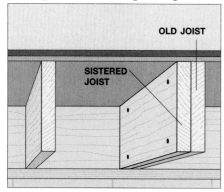

Double up a weak joist using lumber of the same size. Secure it with construction adhesive and screws.

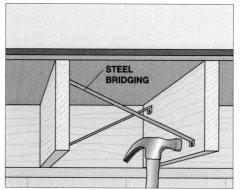

Attach steel X-bracing or a solid piece of framing between joists. This stabilizes the flooring and provides more support.

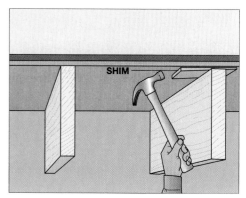

If floor joists aren't tight against the subfloor in the squeaking area, wedge shims in the gap, and tap them into place.

Once a dark stain is lightened, sand lightly (or use steel wool), and then blend the repair with stain and paste wax.

Plugging

To repair deep stains—such as a burn—or to conceal small gouges, drill out the damage, and insert a plug.

You can use dowels or cut your own plugs. Use the same wood if you have extra, and finish the new plug to match.

• scrap wood

3 To fit a new piece into the interlocking system of tongues and grooves, you have to remove the bottom lip of the replacement.

4 Angle the replacement into position by hand, and use a block of scrap wood or flooring to seat the trimmed edge.

5 Predrill the replacement board to prevent splitting, drive finishing nails, putty the holes, and finish to match.

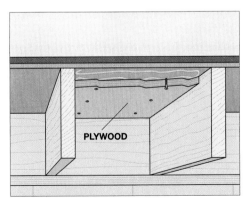

PLYWOOD

Glue and screw a section of ¾-in. plywood between joists just under the squeak, and screw through it into the floor.

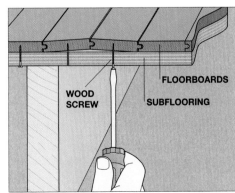

WOOD SCREW **FLOORBOARDS** **SUBFLOORING**

Pull down loose or bulging boards with screws driven from below. The screws should stop ¼ in. below the finish floor.

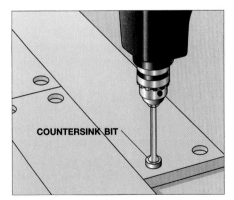

COUNTERSINK BIT

If all else fails and you can't anchor squeaking boards from below, drill surface countersinks, drive screws, and add plugs.

floors & stairs

Restoring Wood Floors

When a wood floor is so worn that wax does little to improve it, it's time for refinishing. Instead of hiring a pro for the job, you can save quite a bit of money by refinishing the floor yourself. You'll have to sand off the old finish (making more dust than you ever thought possible), apply a sealer, and then finish with two coats of polyurethane or floor varnish.

With a rented floor sander you can sand about 200 to 250 square feet of flooring in a day. If you use a water-based acrylic sealer and water-based urethane floor finish, you could seal and top coat the floor in one day. (The floor still must cure for about a week, however, before it can stand up to heavy traffic.)

If your floors haven't been refinished for some time, don't automatically assume that they must be sanded down. Varnished or polyurethaned floors that are in reasonably good condition sometimes can be restored by cleaning with a good paint cleaner. Rub out any heel marks with steel wool or fine sandpaper, smooth out rough spots with fine sandpaper, vacuum away all dust, and apply two coats of varnish or polyurethane.

Sanding Wood Floors

If your floors do need sanding, you'll have to clear all furniture and objects from the room; everything must go because you need to get at the entire floor, and you have to remove the dust between sandings. You must also clean all room surfaces before refinishing, and any extraneous objects will just collect dust that could contaminate the final finish.

Mask doors, heat registers, and any outlets to other rooms to prevent the spread of dust, even if your sander comes equipped with a dust bag. Check the floor for exposed nailheads or raised boards, which can easily rip a sanding belt, and clean the floor of waxy materials, which will clog the belt. Fill holes, nicks, or dents with putty to match the finish. Because sanding creates so much dust, it's best to wear a dust mask. You also should wear goggles or safety glasses.

Using Power Sanders

For most do-it-yourselfers, stopping and starting a power sander are the hardest operations.

Once the big drum of a floor sander gets going, it's fairly easy to keep the machine moving ahead at a steady pace. You can slow down over stained or dirty areas, but not too much because the belt keeps chewing through the wood at the same quick pace.

As soon as the belt starts turning, the sander should be moving across the floor. With most drum sanders, when you get to the end of the room and the belt is still turning, you have to tip the machine up quickly. Otherwise, the belt will cut a noticeable furrow in the wood that's difficult to blend out with the edger. If you can rent a lever-action type of floor sander (the kind most professionals use), you will not have to tip up the machine at the end of a pass. Instead, a lever on the handle raises the sanding drum inside the housing.

With edgers, which spin sanding discs instead of rotating belts in a loop, you have to supply the off-and-on touch by hand. You use a medium-grit sandpaper to clean the outermost edges of the floor, and then blend the straight-line drum pattern with the rotary edger pattern using fine-grit paper. If you like, after you return the rented equipment, you can use a random-orbit electric sander to get a better blend and to touch up hard-to-reach areas missed by the larger machines.

The first step-type escalator made for public use was invented by Charles D. Seeberger, and introduced by Otis Elevator at the Paris Exhibition of 1900, where this ornate beauty won first prize.

Preparing the Room

Before sanding a floor, strip the room of anything removable. Take down drapes, or pin them up from the floor and wrap them in plastic bags. Seal up switches, outlets, and heat registers with plastic and masking tape. Because sanding creates inflammable dust, turn off any pilot lights in the area.

To protect yourself *from the dust generated by sanding, use a dust-mist respirator or a disposable dust mask.*

Cover up switches*, outlets, heat registers, and any other opening with heavy plastic sheeting and masking tape.*

To seal a doorway, *you can buy commercial barriers with zippers, or just fasten plastic sheets or tarps around the trim.*

Refinishing Wood Floors

USE: ▶ drum sander • edger • rotary buffer • orbital sander • scraper or wood chisel • vacuum • sponge mop ▶ sandpaper for all equipment • sealer

1 *Use a scraper or chisel* to reduce raised edges. Also check for splinters or nailheads that can tear sanding belts.

2 *You can use medium-grit* paper to sand most floors. On very rough surfaces, make initial passes on the diagonal.

3 *Make your first pass* with the edger, blending its circular sanding traces with the linear traces of the drum.

4 *Use a hand scraper* to clean into corners and against baseboard trim. (Another option is to remove the trim.)

5 *After vacuuming*, make a second pass using fine sandpaper. Most residential floors need only two passes.

6 *Finish the second pass* with your edger, and then vacuum again to remove dust, which can mar the finish.

7 *Apply the first coat of sealer* or stain to product instructions. Work slowly to avoid trapping air bubbles.

8 *Many sealers require* a light sanding or steel-wooling between coats. Handle this step with a rotary buffer.

9 *Make sure the surface is clean* (you may want to use a tack rag) before applying at least one more coat.

floors & stairs

Sheets & Tiles

Not all resilient flooring is the same—the most obvious difference is between the type laid in large sheets up to 12 feet wide, and the familiar 9-inch or 12-inch square tiles. But there are other important considerations. The more vinyl the flooring contains, for instance, the more durable and costly it tends to be. Solid vinyl is best, followed by vinyl composition. Printed vinyl is inexpensive, but only a thin layer protects the floor from wear.

Both tile and sheet vinyl flooring come in a mind-boggling array of solid colors and patterns. The big plus with tiles is that you can get creative by laying out patterns using contrasting colors, including light or dark borders, diagonals, a checkerboard layout, and so on. And individual tiles can be removed and replaced, making repairs on the flooring easy.

You lay out vinyl tile floors in much the same way as ceramic tiles. (See pp. 158–59.) A sturdy flat underlayment is important for both tiles and sheet vinyl; it's usually plywood sheets laid over the subfloor. The tiles can be either self-stick or dry back (with adhesive applied separately).

The main advantage of sheet vinyl, on the other hand, is that there are few seams. That's better for kitchens and other rooms where spills and splashes are common. For rooms wider than the 12-foot sheets, you have to decide where the seam will fall.

Materials

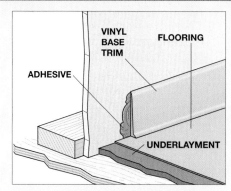

You can run flooring near the wall, and add either wood trim or molded vinyl base secured with adhesive.

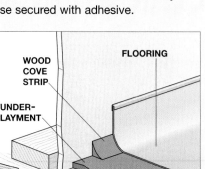

Another trim option is to install an angled block of wood to reinforce the curve and run the flooring up the wall.

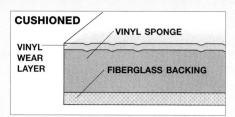

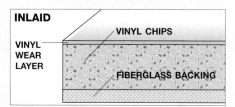

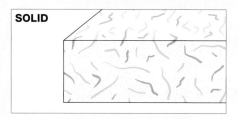

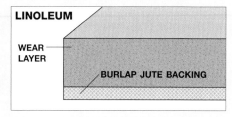

Installing Sheet Flooring

USE: ▶ scissors (for paper template) • utility knife • hook knife (optional) • trowel • rolling pin or commercial floor roller ▶ sheet flooring • paper for template

1 DIYers are wise to take the extra time and effort to make a paper template, particularly on a project with many corners.

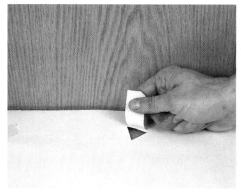

2 To hold the paper template in place while you work, cut out several 1-in. triangles, and tape across them.

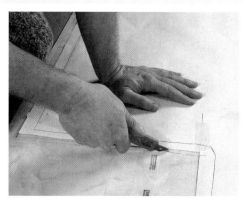

3 Lay the paper template over the sheet vinyl, and tape it down. Use a utility knife or hook knife to trim the vinyl to size.

Repairing Tile Floors

USE: ▶ utility knife • straightedge • putty knife ▶ new vinyl patch • tile adhesive • seam sealer • masking tape

1 *To repair torn vinyl,* cut a square of new vinyl, and tape it over the damaged area. Align the patch so that the patterns match.

2 *Use a straightedge* and sharp utility knife to cut through both layers of vinyl. This ensures a perfect fit for the patch.

3 *With both layers* sliced through cleanly, remove the tape, and lift out the underlying damaged section.

4 *Lift the existing flooring* where possible, and apply a thin layer of flooring adhesive under the edges.

5 *Spread adhesive* across the underlayment, and lay in the vinyl patch piece. Press it firmly in place.

6 *Use a two-part seam sealer* to fuse the edges of the new patch to the old vinyl. Work it in with the applicator tip.

• masking tape • vinyl flooring adhesive • embossing leveler

4 *Before laying vinyl* over existing embossed vinyl, spread embossing leveler over the floor to fill the depressions.

5 *When the leveler sets,* spread flooring adhesive over the floor with a blade or trowel. You may need a notched trowel.

6 *Lay the sheet vinyl* out in the room, and use a rolling pin or commercial roller to smooth and bond it to the floor.

floors & stairs

Setting Ceramic Tile

Ceramic tiles make durable floors, well suited to high-traffic, rough-use, and potentially wet areas such as entry halls, baths, and kitchens. In deciding color and design, remember that floors with busy patterns or several colors tend to look smaller. Similarly, dark colors shrink the floor visually, while light colors expand it. Small tiles give the illusion that the floor is larger. Large tiles make the floor look smaller.

Layout

The key to a good tile job is layout. The standard procedure is to center the pattern in the room, which means drawing diagonals on the floor to locate the center and then snapping a guideline through that point parallel to the longest straight wall. The premise is that stock-sized tiles won't fit without some cuts and that it makes sense to have full tiles in the middle of the room and equal cuts around the edges.

But there are at least two exceptions. The first is when walls aren't square. In this case, you need to adjust the layout so that angled cuts will lie along the least visible wall. The second exception occurs in rooms with many wall jogs. Here, use full tiles starting from a highly visible corner just inside the door, and let the odd sizes fall in hard-to-see areas.

Setting Tile

Adhesive manufacturers' recommendations typically specify a consistently even bed of adhesive, spread with a notched trowel. For tiles smaller than 8 inches square, use a trowel with ¼-inch deep notches. Use a trowel with ⅜-inch deep notches for larger tiles. Spread the adhesive over the area in sections measuring 3 square feet with the flat edge of the trowel. The adhesive should be at least the depth of the trowel's notches. Then, comb the adhesive into parallel ridges with the notched edge, holding the trowel at a 45-degree angle. When you press the tile into the adhesive, the ridges will flatten and completely cover the back of the tile. Slide the tiles perpendicular to the ridges as you press them into place for the best contact. Clean oozed adhesive out of the joints between tiles so that you'll have room for the grout.

For a tiled surface to look good, grout seams have to be the same width and perfectly straight. With large tiles, you can create a nearly perfect grid using tile spacers (although it's time-consuming to set them between each tile); just remove them before applying grout. Small tiles are usually sold on sheets already spaced for grout—you can't get them too close together, but you could install individual sheets of tiles too far apart. You might want to try a dry layout to see whether you will have trouble estimating joint width where full sheets meet. Lay out several, and step back to see whether you can spot the sheet seams. If they stand out, ask the tile supplier for a few spacers that you can use to make sure the sheet-to-sheet joints match the other seams.

Thinset vs. Thickset

Thickset is the time-consuming, old fashioned way to set tile. With this installation, also called a mud set, you trowel out a thick bed of mortar to level the floor and support the tiles. It requires some experience with masonry work but makes a very durable floor. The thinset method is faster and easier for DIYers. You comb ridges of adhesive with a notched trowel onto a smooth underlayment surface (such as cement board) and simply press the tiles in place.

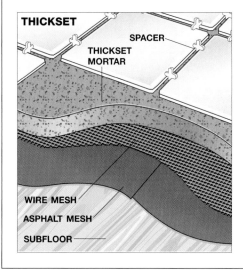

THICKSET
SPACER
THICKSET MORTAR
WIRE MESH
ASPHALT MESH
SUBFLOOR

Installing Tile

USE: ▶ snap cutter • tile nippers • wet saw (optional) • notched trowel • framing square • chalk-line box • measuring tape • rubber float or squeegee

1 *You can lay thinset tile* in adhesive directly on plywood, but cement board makes a more durable underlayment.

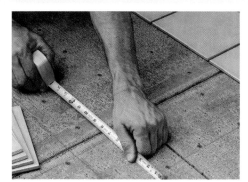

2 *Measure the area,* and snap lines to create a square layout, with full tiles in the main field and equal pieces at the edges.

3 *Spread a layer of adhesive* with a notched trowel that leaves ridges, according to manufacturer's instructions.

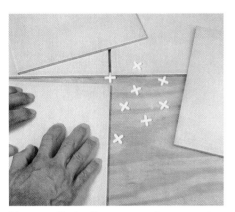

Use small plastic spacers to account for grout joints in your dry-run layout. You can also use them during the job.

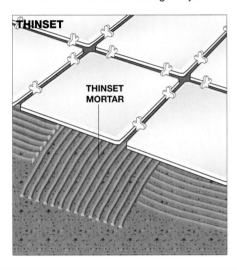

Materials

◆ Ceramic

Ceramic tiles are fired from a bisque of natural clay. Glazed tile is coated with fired-on color; the glaze can be glossy, matte, or textured. Don't use high-gloss glazed tiles on bathroom floors because water will make them slippery.

◆ Quarry Tile

This term applies to any hard, red-bodied clay floor tile of consistent dimensions not less than ⅜ inch thick. The color is usually a deep, brick red, although other colors are available, depending on the clays that are used. Glazed quarry tile comes in a wide range of colors.

◆ Mosaic

Mosaic tile (2 inches square or smaller) comes in many shapes and sizes. The tiles are usually mounted on sheets for easy installation. In porcelain tiles, the color runs through the body of the tile, so scratches are practically invisible.

◆ Stone

Stone tiles are cut from slate, marble, granite, limestone, and other materials, and sawed and ground to a consistent thickness. Granite and marble usually are sold polished and sealed, while slate has a more natural, textured look.

• sponge paintbrush • soft cloth • work gloves ▶ floor tile • joint spacers (optional) • tile adhesive • grout • sealer (optional)

4 *Set the tiles into the adhesive,* leaving room for grout between tiles. You may want to use plastic joint spacers.

5 *Apply grout* over the floor with a rubber float. Work the mix on an angle to force it into seams; then wipe away the excess.

6 *To protect grout joints,* the weak links in a tile floor, you can take the extra step of applying a sealer to the grout only.

floors & stairs

Preventing Tile Trouble

If ceramic tile is such an indestructible building material, why would a tile floor need maintenance and repair? Often, the fault lies not in the tile but in the floor below. Follow a manufacturer's requirements for the supporting floor, and the tile is likely to require only cleaning, not mending.

Wood-frame floors give a little as you walk on them, which makes them more comfortable than concrete. But tile is rigid, which sets up a conflict when it's laid over anything but a masonry base—unless you make the frame almost as rigid as solid concrete. For example, you can double up the existing joists, gluing and nailing a second 2x8 to each one.

In most houses with wood floors, sheets of plywood laid over the joists are ½-inch thick. For tile, it's wise to add an additional layer of ¾-inch-thick plywood to make the floor strong enough to bridge the spaces between joists without flexing. When adding a second layer of plywood, make sure to stagger the new layer so the seams don't line up.

Most tile is designed to have a specific amount of space for grout. Some have protrusions that keep the tiles uniformly separated; some are sold with spacers. In any case, you should follow the instructions for grout seams, even though they may appear to be a little wide. If the grout pattern seems to overshadow the tile, you can increase or decrease its prominence with color.

Mortar Mixes

	Latex Portland Cement Mortar	Dry-Set Mortar	Epoxy Mortar	Organic Mastic Adhesive
Form	Mix at site	Mix at site	Mix at site	Ready-mix
Bed thickness	³⁄₃₂–⅛" 1¼" (thickset floor)	³⁄₃₂–⅛"	³⁄₃₂–⅛"	³⁄₃₂–¹⁄₁₆"
Application	Somewhat difficult	Somewhat difficult	Very difficult	Easy
Pros & cons	Strong, flexible, resistant to freeze/thaw, but more expensive than dry-set	Strong, resists freezing, 3-day wait before grouting	Strong, resists water & chemicals, tricky application	Inexpensive, weaker, not waterproof

Grout Mixes

Uses	Commercial Portland Cement	Sand Portland Cement	Dry-Set	Latex Portland Cement	Epoxy	Silicone or Urethane
Glazed wall tile		x	x	x		x
Ceramic mosaic tile	x	x	x	x	x	x
Quarry, paver & packing-house tile	x	x		x	x	
Dry or limited water exposure	x	x	x	x	x	x
Wet areas	x	x	x	x	x	x
Exteriors	x	x	x	x	x	x

Replacing Tiles

USE: ▶ power drill • hammer • cold chisel • pry bar • small trowel • notched trowel • vacuum • work gloves • rubber gloves ▶ replacement tile • tile adhesive

1 *To remove a damaged tile* without damaging others, drill a row of holes and score a line with a hammer and cold chisel.

2 *Use a pry bar* to work along the chisel line and pry up sections of tile. Once you remove a piece, the rest will come easily.

3 *Clean out loose grout and dust,* and spread a new layer of tile adhesive. Use a notched trowel to make ridges.

Cutting & Nipping

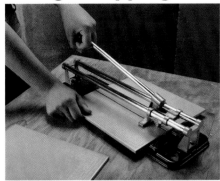

Cut tiles with a snap cutter (for straight cuts) or tile nippers (for curved cuts). You may want to rent a tub saw (also called a wet saw) if you're tiling a large area and have many cuts to make. Snap cutters work by scoring the tile, which weakens it and allows it to snap apart in a straight line. They come in sizes for small and large tiles. Nippers work by nibbling away small pieces of tile one bite at a time. Use them to form small irregular shapes and curves.

Align your cut mark on the cutter bed, apply pressure to the handle, and drag the cutter wheel across the tile.

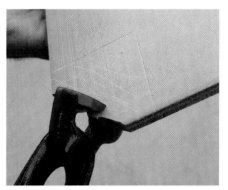

Nippers look like pliers with a sharp edge on the jaws. Make very small cuts to avoid breaking the tile.

Sill Transitions

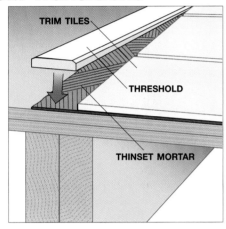

Ease the transition from a tiled room with a threshold, or saddle. You can use wood, marble, or synthetic material. Most are formed with a beveled edge to reduce the chance of tripping where floor levels change, and are thicker than the tiles that butt against them. You may need to trim the bottom of an existing door to fit a new threshold. Attach the threshold with adhesive, leaving a gap for a grout joint between the threshold and the tiles.

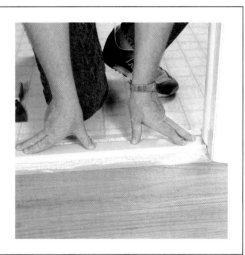

• grout • scrap wood • sealer (optional)

4 *Set a replacement tile* into the bed of adhesive. Center it in the patch area to create even grout joints.

5 *With the tile in position,* use a block of wood to protect the tile surface, and seat the tile evenly with the surrounding floor.

6 *When the tile adhesive sets,* mix a small batch of grout, force it into the seams with a trowel, and wipe off the excess.

Finishing a Wood Floor

Wood finishes come in many varieties, each with its own features. Choose carefully—ease of application is one consideration, but don't forget maintenance. Hard finishes that stay on top of the wood will typically require less maintenance than those that penetrate the wood's pores.

No matter what material you select, follow the manufacturer's instructions to the letter. Many finishes contain toxic or inflammable chemicals. Water-based finishes are less hazardous to work with than solvent types, but even these require precautions.

Some open-pore woods, such as oak, may require filling before the final finish is applied if you want a smooth surface. Floors made of maple, a closed-grain wood, don't need filling. Both neutral and colored fillers are available.

One of the most effective ways to apply filler is to use burlap. Rub against the grain to force the filler into the pores of the wood. Then, rub with the grain to remove any excess before the filler dries on the surface. Before applying the filler, thin it as needed with the recommended solvent.

Baseboard Trim

Baseboard trim provides a decorative look and finishes off a room. The most popular designs are shown at right, but many other styles are available. All base trim runs along the bottom of the wall, covering any horizontal gap between the wall and floor. A shoe molding normally is used with base trim to close any horizontal gap between the base and the floor.

Lumberyards stock both softwood and hardwood trim. Softwoods such as cedar, pine, fir, larch, and hemlock are usually available, but this depends on where you live. Redwood is more plentiful on the West Coast, for example, than in Florida.

You can buy standard, unfinished trim in any length up to 16 feet, with lengths available in 2-foot increments. The miter is the most common joint that is required for joining pieces of base trim, so a good backsaw and miter box or power miter saw are essential to the job. (See also "Back-Cutting Joints" and "Coping Joints" on pp. 98–99.)

Once the base is cut, you can fasten it with finishing nails, brads, and/or glue. If you use glue, use just enough so that the glue will adhere to the material but not so much that it squeezes out when the piece is pressed into place. As a rule of thumb, try to use as few nails as possible to hold the trim in position—the job will look much neater and much more professional.

Sometimes trim must be sanded to remove minor imperfections. Do this very carefully so that you will not change the shape of the trim with the abrasive. Use a fine-grit, closed-coat sandpaper.

Base Molding

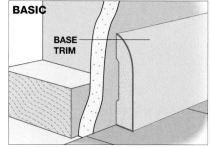

BASIC
BASE TRIM

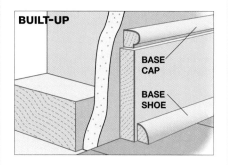

BUILT-UP
BASE CAP
BASE SHOE

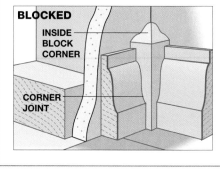

BLOCKED
INSIDE BLOCK CORNER
CORNER JOINT

Installing Baseboards

USE: ▶ power miter saw or backsaw with miter box • power drill/driver • hammer • nail set • measuring tape • pencil ▶ baseboard trim • finishing nails

1 *You can rely on a ruler,* but DIYers are wise to rough-cut boards and set them in position to mark the miter cuts.

2 *For accurate miter cuts* (45° cuts on mating boards), use a power miter saw that swivels or a miter box with fixed stops.

3 *Fasten baseboards* with finishing nails. You may want to predrill pilot holes near the ends to avoid splitting.

Staining

While a clear finish is fine for most wood floors, you can stain the wood first to alter its natural color. Just make sure the stain you choose is compatible with your finish. Before you apply stain, give the wood a final sanding and vacuuming. Test the color on a scrap piece of wood before working on the whole floor. Brush it on (or use a paint pad or clean cloth), let it set, and then wipe off. You need to let most applications dry for 24 hours, and use steel wool to knock down raised grain before sealing.

***Use stain** to darken wood, or unify the appearance of a floor made of boards with a lot of grain variation.*

Finishes

◆ **Polyurethane**
Poly is durable and easy to apply. Water-based poly dries more quickly than oil-based but is not as durable. Use two or three thin coats instead of one thick one.

◆ **Penetrating sealer**
This finish colors and seals in one step. Apply it with a brush or paint pad, let it soak into the wood for several minutes, and then wipe off the excess.

◆ **Varnish**
Varnish creates a hard, durable finish but with a slight yellowing. It comes in high or medium gloss or a flat finish—choose a type formulated for floors.

◆ **Pickling**
Pickling accents the wood grain. Brush on a coat of paint cut about 30% with thinner and, after about 15 minutes, wipe off the excess along the grain.

◆ **Wax**
Applied over a sealer, multiple coats can produce a lustrous patina that poly-urethane cannot. Wax is not as durable, though—but it's good for spot repairs.

***Clear sealers** are normally brushed on, but you can also spray them on to apply several thin coats to intricate shapes.*

***Aside from staining** or clear sealing, you can use other treatments such as pickling to create colored finishes.*

4 ***Drive the nails** almost flush with the wood surface to avoid marring the wood with hammer blows.*

5 ***Use a nail set** to drive nails home. On floors that will be carpeted, it's wise to finish the baseboard in advance.*

6 ***Work around the room** one board to the next. Leave the leading edge rough cut until the joint fits; then, measure for length.*

floors & stairs

Wall-to-Wall Carpeting

Most brand-name wall-to-wall carpeting (such as DuPont's Stainmaster, and Solutia's Wear-Dated Gold Label) combines nylon fibers—which have excellent durability and resistance to abrasion, crushing, and mildew—with improved fibers that are less shiny, antistatic, and have been treated with a stain-resistant coating. Besides the fiber type, you have to take into account pile depth, pile density, and texture when selecting carpeting.

Bear in mind, for example, that increased density (the number of yarn tufts in a given area) usually means a better appearance, feel, and durability. Also, a dense, low-pile, level-loop design, which presents a pebbly, uniform surface, is generally the easiest to vacuum. More irregular surfaces, like twist and shag carpeting, tend to trap the dirt in the pile.

Before ordering carpet, make a scale drawing of the room on graph paper, setting each square equal to one square foot. Include all doors and obstacles—the more accurate the drawing, the easier it will be for the dealer to recommend the amount of carpet you need.

If your carpet must be seamed, place the seam in a low-traffic area. Seams are less noticeable when they run parallel to light rays and should run toward the room's primary source of light (such as a south-facing window). If your carpet has a pattern, you will have to buy additional yardage so that you can match the pattern.

Materials & Weaves

◆ Nylon
The longest-wearing synthetic material, nylon resists stains and is resilient, although not as springy as wool. It's easily cleaned, but the colors tend to fade when exposed to sunlight.

◆ Polypropylene
Polypropylene (or olefin) resists fading because the pigment is built into the fiber, but it is probably the least durable and soil-resistant of the synthetics—don't use it where it will receive heavy wear. It's generally found only in loop-pile designs.

◆ Polyester
This material approximates the softness of wool and has bright, clear, fade-resistant colors and excellent stain-resistance. It is less expensive and less resilient than nylon. It's generally found only in cut-pile constructions.

◆ Wool
Wool is soft, durable, fade-resistant, and rich-looking, but it's expensive and less resistant to stains than synthetics. Of all the carpeting materials, wool is the most resilient—meaning it springs back after you walk on it.

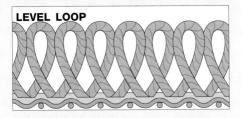
LEVEL LOOP

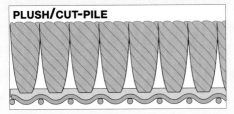
PLUSH/CUT-PILE

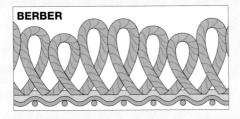
BERBER

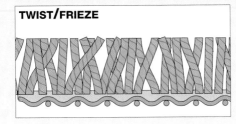
TWIST/FRIEZE

Installing Carpet

USE: ▶ hammer • utility knife • power stretcher & kicker (optional) ▶ carpet • carpet pad • tack strips • double-faced seam tape

1 *Install tack strips* around the room, leaving about a ⅜-in. gap next to the baseboards. The sharp nailheads face up.

2 *Roll out the pad,* and trim the edges just inside the tack strips. Fasten the pad with staples (wood) or adhesive (concrete).

3 *To fit carpet into corners,* make a relief cut with a utility knife, press one side in place, and cut away the overage.

Pad vs. Cushion-Backed

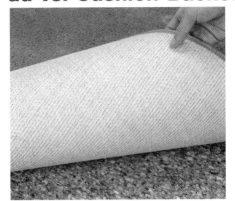

A carpet plus pad makes the most comfortable and durable floor.

There are two types of wall-to-wall carpet. Standard carpet is installed on a pad and secured to tack strips around the room after stretching (such as with a power stretcher). Cushion-backed carpet has the foam backing already attached to its underside. It is laid in latex or fastened to the floor with a special double-faced tape; it is easier to lay because it requires no stretching. It is also less expensive than conventional carpeting but will generally not last as long.

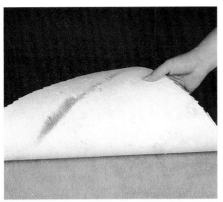

Carpet with a foam backing is easier to install but less durable.

Pads

NATURAL RUBBER

FELT

Carpet padding adds luxury and warmth, helps cut noise, and prevents wear. The least expensive is bonded polyurethane; only dense polyurethane should be used in high-traffic areas. Prime urethane and grafted prime foam shouldn't be used with a stiff-backed carpet such as a berber. (Use a cellular sponge-rubber padding instead.) Other foam pads are graded by thickness and density—choose the best you can afford.

POLYURETHANE

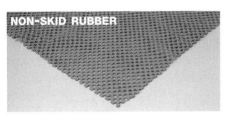

NON-SKID RUBBER

4 *Where you have to join carpeting* (or padding) one of the easiest methods is to use double-faced seam tape.

5 *You can rent special tools* like this kicker, which grips the carpet to work out any wrinkles and get a tight fit.

6 *The last step* is to tuck the edge of the carpet into the gap between the tack strips and the baseboard.

floors & stairs

Spot Repairs

Carpet may seem to be a very durable material, but it's actually one of the less sturdy floor coverings. Stains, burns, snags, and beaten-down pile—especially in heavy-traffic areas—can all ruin the carpet's appearance. With proper care, you can avoid these problems, but when necessary, it's possible to make simple repairs yourself.

Scraps from the original installation are the best material to use for repairs, but you can also make patches for holes by taking bits of carpet from out-of-the-way areas like the backs of closets or underneath furniture you never move. Small areas often can be repaired by pulling out old tufts and setting in new tufts with a tuft setter, a machine that is available from most carpet dealers. It's important to be aware that the repair will probably be quite visible, especially if the carpet is worn or the color has faded. Allow some time for the repaired area to blend in with its new surroundings.

Carpet Repair Basics

The key to a successful carpet repair is to work slowly and patiently. To patch a small rip, first fold back the torn section, and then apply a good-quality latex seam adhesive. Carefully tuck the torn part back into the carpet, and press it down with a smooth rolling action, using a large bottle or rolling pin. If any of the adhesive happens to ooze up, be sure to clean it off immediately with water and detergent. When the adhesive has dried, replace any loose or missing pile.

If the rip is larger, you'll have to release the tension on the carpet using a knee-kicker in the corner nearest the rip. Lift the corner off the tack strip, and roll it back. Using heavy thread that matches the color of the pile, mend the rip by sewing with 1-inch long stitches spaced ¼ inch apart. Depending on the direction of the rip, run the stitches either parallel to rows of pile or perpendicular to them. Check frequently to make sure that you are not stitching any strands of the pile down on the face of the carpet. Then, carefully work a thin, wavy strip of latex adhesive into the stitched backing, and cover the damp surface with a paper towel. Lastly, roll the carpet back to the wall and rehook it back on the tack strip.

Caring for Carpets

Periodic vacuuming is the surest route to long carpet life. Without a once- or twice-weekly vacuuming (whether the carpet looks as if it needs it or not), the grit and dirt that settle on the top layer of the carpet will eventually be ground into the fabric, where it will do damage. You'll probably notice after vacuuming that the carpet looks shaded. That's because the piles of most carpets are directional. Carpets with a pile that is woven in different directions, such as a textured saxony, won't have this problem.

Beyond regular vacuuming, it's a good idea to clean your carpets annually, to rid the fibers of deep grime and to restore the carpet to its original color. You can do this yourself or hire a professional carpet cleaner. Hot water is the most common method of rug cleaning. With any wet cleaning (such as shampooing), there's a danger of overwetting the carpet, though, which can distort it. Try to shampoo the carpet on clear dry days, so that the floor will dry more quickly.

Because most stains sit on top of carpets treated with soil-resistant finishes, you usually have enough time to mop them up, and deep penetration doesn't become the problem it used to be. Commercial spot removers can handle a wide variety of stains, but as a last resort for stubborn stains, you should call in a professional cleaner.

Stretchers & Kickers

To make your carpet fit tightly and lie flat, you'll want to rent one or both types of carpet-stretching tools. A power stretcher grips the carpet and stretches it without tearing. The tool comes with long extensions for bracing against the opposite wall. You crank the handle to increase pressure. A kicker is shorter, and lifts the carpet and hooks it on the tack strip when you bump it with your knee. It's especially useful in tight areas where you can't fit the stretcher.

Patching Carpet

USE: ▶ hammer • utility knife ▶ carpet remnant • carpet tacks • double-faced seam tape

1 To make a large patch, box the area with scrap carpet, and drive tacks to maintain the tension and avoid wrinkling.

2 Cut a patch piece to fit within the box. If the carpet has a pattern, you may want to cut an irregular patch following the design.

Spot Patching

USE: ▶ carpet patch tool ▶ carpet remnant • adhesive • double-faced seam tape

1 *Use a circular carpet patch tool* to remove a cookie-cutter section around a deep stain, burn, or tear.

2 *Peel the cover tape* from a piece of double-faced adhesive patch tape. Cut it larger than the hole, and fold to insert.

3 *Use the circular cutter* to cut a patch piece from a remnant, and press it firmly in place over the adhesive.

Tuft Patching

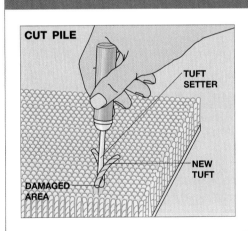

CUT PILE
TUFT SETTER
NEW TUFT
DAMAGED AREA

To patch a small area of cut-pile carpet with replacement tufts, cut the damaged pile down to the backing with scissors, and pick out the pile stubs with tweezers. Apply latex cement to the carpet backing. Set replacement tufts into position using a tuft setter; drive the setter through the carpet backing with a few taps from a hammer. For loop-pile carpeting, poke one end of a long piece of yarn into the backing, and make successive loops, adjusting the length.

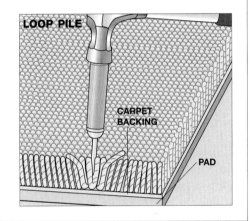

LOOP PILE
CARPET BACKING
PAD

3 *Set the patch* over the damaged area, and cut through the bottom layer of carpet using the patch as a guide.

4 *Remove the damaged section,* lift the edges of the carpet, and install double-faced seam tape on all sides.

5 *Set the patch in position,* and press it firmly onto the tape before pulling the temporary tacks and releasing the tension.

floors & stairs

Stair Building

The easiest staircase to build is a set of straight-run stairs; in most circumstances, a straight-run design will be your first choice. While spiral stairs are space savers and prefabricated models are fairly easy to install, they aren't recommended for a main stairway because they compromise safety and make moving large objects up and down all but impossible. In terms of materials, straight-run stairs require nothing more than a few stringers and the steps.

All the steps must be the same size—the most critical components of stair design are the ratio between unit rise and unit run and their consistency from one step to the next. Local building codes regulate the acceptable dimensions. In "Stair Formulas" at right, the minimum and maximum requirements are listed, but these are not necessarily optimums. For most people, a 7-inch rise and 11-inch run are the most comfortable (the maximum rise generally allowable is 7¾ inches; the minimum run is 9 inches).

Building codes also address landings and the room people will need to get onto and off of the stairs safely. Headroom is another important issue—it's defined as the vertical distance measured from an imaginary line connecting the front edge on all of the treads on up to the overhead. Again, most codes establish a minimum (80 inches) from that line to any object above. This is required to prevent you from knocking your head against the ceiling or other obstruction.

Stair Formulas

1 Maximum riser height is 7¾ inches. Divide total rise of stairs by 7¾ inches; then divide total rise by the number of resulting risers to determine unit rise.

2 Minimum tread depth (run) is 9 inches—10 or 11 inches is safer. Simple formulas to match tread depth to riser height: rise + run = 17 to 18, or alternatively rise x run = 70 to 75.

3 Typical code requirements specify a minimum of 80 inches of headroom in all parts of stairway.

Stair Anatomy

GOOSENECK

BANISTER

BALUSTER

LANDING NEWEL

LANDING

FINIAL

STARTING NEWEL

TREAD

RISER

NOSING

STRINGERS (OR CARRIAGES)

Most stairs are supported by saw-toothed boards called stringers, although there are exceptions, such as circular stairs. Because it is difficult to plan stairs, DIYers (and most contractors) leave this job to stair subcontractors.

Adding Pull-Down Stairs

USE: ▶ reciprocating saw • power drill/driver • saw

1 *Mark the stair opening,* and cut out the drywall ceiling. You need to brace a center joist at both ends, and cut out a section.

5 *To support the stair assembly* in the new opening while you attach it, screw a supporting wood lip to both sides.

Carpeting Stairs

There are several options when carpeting stairs. One is to use the narrow tack strips used for wall-to-wall carpeting. Install the strips with the points facing up, so they bite into the carpet—but not through it—and hold the carpet in place. You could also use tack strips made especially for stairs—like those for wall-to-wall carpet, except they have opposing barbs to hold the carpet in a corner from two directions at a time. If you don't mind seeing the fasteners, use decorative stair rods to retain carpet runners at each turn on the stairs.

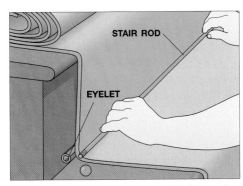

You can pin carpet runners with decorative stair rods, staple them, or wedge them into the step/riser joint with a stair tool.

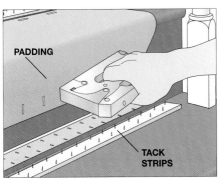

You can pin padding with staples, and secure carpeting with standard tackless strips or special tackless stair clips.

• hammer • socket wrench • framing square • measuring tape ▶ pull-down stairs • 2x lumber (for framing & nailer) • framing connectors • nails • lag screws • shims

2 *Install half of a double header* at each end of the opening. Nail up the end of your cut joist, and then add the second board.

3 *Although some stair manufacturers* don't call for the detail, it's wise to double up full joists on each side of the opening.

4 *To finish framing* the opening, add a short joist between headers to box in the stair opening. Use metal framing hangers.

6 *Following manufacturer's directions,* bolt the stair frame onto the opening. You may need to use wooden shims.

7 *Measure from the fold-down hinge* to the floor in a straight line—first on top of the leg, and then on the bottom.

8 *Transfer the two measurements* to the extended leg, draw a line between them, and cut off the excess portion.

floors & stairs

Common Problems

Squeaking stairs may be one of the better low-tech burglar alarms around, but all that creaking gets to be a nuisance after a while. And when the stair tread finally loosens up enough, it could cause someone to trip and fall. The same is true for loose handrails and balusters, too. You don't want the railing to break just when it's needed most—when someone falls on the stairs.

In most cases, repair is quicker and cheaper than replacement, plus a new part will probably look out of place on a well-worn staircase. For balusters, you may be able to find a suitable replacement at a building-supply store. Or you can commission a woodturner to make a replacement baluster. If several balusters need replacing, the best choice may be to tear them all out and install a new set.

Loose handrails are a common problem. Handrails along the wall side of stairs usually attach to brackets that are screwed to the wall. When tightening a wall-hung handrail, make sure the brackets are screwed into studs or blocking between studs; then, install longer screws or reposition the loose bracket so that you can drive the screws into new holes. Handrails on the open side of stairs usually are attached to a newel post at the bottom and to the balusters along the handrail's length. Repairing one of these handrails usually tends to be just a matter of tightening the connections at the newel post.

Stopping Stair Squeaks

Squeaking is generally caused by a loose joint where your weight makes one piece of wood rub against another, or shift on the nails holding pieces together. It's easy to pinpoint problems by walking on different parts of a squeaking tread. It's also easy to fix the problem on stairs where the construction is exposed underneath. There are several ways to stop squeaks on exposed stairs. Without that access, however, you're forced to make repairs from above, driving a screw and plugging the head.

Replacing Treads

Worn, cracked, or badly warped stair treads should be replaced. Begin by removing molding or nosing and balusters from the tread. Pry the tread loose enough to remove nails. Put a piece of wood under the pry bar to protect risers and skirtboards from damage. If you can't pry out the tread, drill a starter hole at the rear of the tread, and cut it out with a keyhole or reciprocating saw. On landings made from floorboards, you can add a new nosing piece secured with screws.

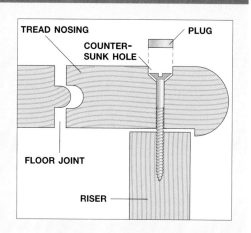

Tightening Posts

Because of their location at the end of the stairway, and because they can't be braced side to side, newel posts are especially prone to loosening. To firm up a loose post you may be able to tighten the bolt holding the post base from beneath the stairs. If the connection to the banister is loose, you can drill through the post and secure the joint with a screw or lag screw. Countersink the hole, and conceal the screwhead with a wood plug.

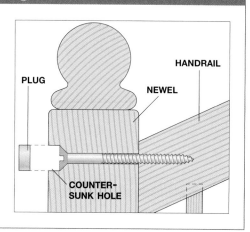

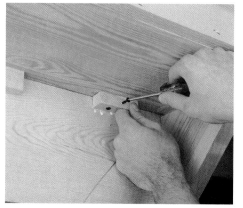

To support the joint between a horizontal tread and a vertical riser, add small blocks fastened with glue and screws.

Screwing on a shelf bracket also reinforces the tread-riser joint. Use screws that won't protrude through the boards.

Tightening Balusters

You can tighten a connection between the baluster and the railing by wedging the joint and pinning it with a screw.

Add glue to the wedge, tap it into the loose joints with a hammer, and cut off the excess with a trim saw.

To secure the connection with a screw, first predrill a pilot hole to avoid splitting the baluster. Countersink the screwhead.

Replacing Balusters

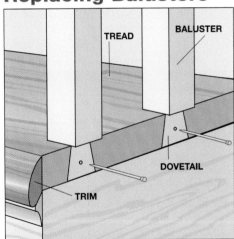

Traditional railings have balusters set into the treads. There are two basic types: dovetails and pins. Because dovetails are cut into the side of the tread, you have to remove a piece of trim to expose and replace them. Pinned balusters are fastened into a hole in the top of the tread. To remove either type, it helps to cut the damaged baluster in half and remove each section. Some modern railings have a molded track top and bottom. Replace these by matching the angle cuts and nailing in place.

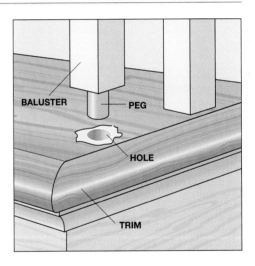

Tighten loose joints by driving a wooden wedge into the seam between treads and risers. You can add glue to the wedge.

You can also use a wedge on the edges of treads and risers where they are recessed into a diagonal stringer.

Drill a pilot hole, and screw the riser to the tread. Measure carefully to center the screw in the tread board.

10

walls
& ceilings

walls & ceilings

Underneath It All

The most common kind of wall in residential construction is the wood-framed wall, or stud wall. The framework of studs provides space for wiring and outlets, plumbing, ducts, and insulation. Studs also support a surface that covers these utilities. Before the 1940s, this surface was generally plaster, but sometimes solid-wood paneling, brick, or stone.

The walls and ceilings of most houses today are covered with drywall. Also known as plasterboard, wallboard, or by the trade name Sheetrock, it provides a solid foundation for interior finishes such as wallpaper, paneling, or tile. But because its paper-covered face can easily be painted, drywall often serves as the finished surface.

Skilled laborers once spent many hours working with wet plaster to lay up new walls, smoothing several layers over a base of wood or metal lath to achieve smooth interior surfaces. Drywall crews today finish off a room in a fraction of the time, using preformed 4x8 (or larger) panels. These sheets are quickly cut and nailed or screwed in place on the wall studs—or even attached directly over an old plaster surface that is beyond repair.

Decorative Options

Besides resurfacing with new drywall, you can change the appearance of existing walls with paneling, which gives a room the warm glow of wood. Sheet paneling is inexpensive and easy to put up; board paneling takes a little more labor and costs more, but many people feel that the depth of real wood tones make the effort worthwhile. Solid wood also has the advantage of installation right over the studs. Wall tile is another fairly expensive and labor-intensive option, but ceramic tiles should last a lifetime. Also, tiling a half-wall or sink surround requires more patience than expertise.

If you're looking for something more ornate than painted walls, wallpaper (more properly, wallcovering, which includes solid or fabric-backed vinyl) is much simpler than it used to be, with adhesive-backed products eliminating messy paste-mixing and brushing. If you'd like to exercise some artistic skill, add decorative touches with a stenciled border or one of the decorative paint techniques on pp. 190–91.

Paneling

Simulated wood boards are available as 4x8-foot sheet paneling, which is easy to install, and a good way to resurface damaged walls. (Local codes may require a layer of fire-resistant drywall underneath.) Solid-wood boards provide a more traditional look. When solid wood is overwhelming in a small room, try paneling just one wall or applying half-height wainscoting.

Wallcoverings

VINYL-COATED   VINYL

Wallpaper isn't as popular today as surface treatments and glaze finishes, but there are many situations where wallpaper is a good choice. Most pre-pasted papers that DIYers use have a thin vinyl coating (left). Many are available with matched border strips. In high-moisture areas, you can use heavy-duty vinyls (right). These wallcoverings have a tougher (advertised as scrubbable) surface.

Drywall

Gypsum drywall (often called by the USG brand name Sheetrock), is made from a slurry of powdered gypsum rock and water that is poured between sheets of paper and dried. Drywall is easier to install than plaster, the material it replaced. The panels can provide stability and fire protection in large spaces. Laminations of thin sheets can even be applied over curving surfaces.

ANAGLYPTA

FIBERGLASS

Some old-style papers such as Anaglypta (left) are available today in reproductions. The paper is much thicker and stiffer than conventional wallcoverings, and typically embossed with a pattern. The material is costly but substantial enough to bridge minor wall imperfections. The modern equivalent is fiberglass wallcovering (right), which also is fire- and moisture-resistant.

Scaffold Setups

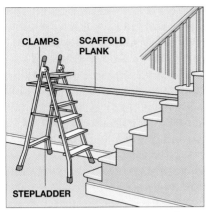

CLAMPS **SCAFFOLD PLANK**

STEPLADDER

In a stairwell, *reach lower areas from a scaffold-grade plank clamped to a stepladder and resting on a stair.*

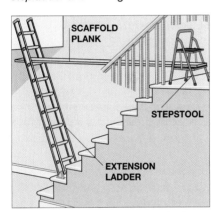

SCAFFOLD PLANK

STEPSTOOL

EXTENSION LADDER

To reach higher, *clamp the plank between an extension ladder and a stepstool on the landing.*

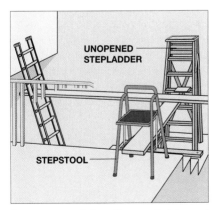

UNOPENED STEPLADDER

STEPSTOOL

In a narrow stairwell, *use a ladder and stepstool to support one plank that in turn helps to support a second plank.*

walls & ceilings

Paneling Options

Paneling may have a slightly bad rap because some low-end products are simply artificial-looking—a poor likeness of wood grain glued to a flimsy backer board. Most paneling is anything but a cheap coverup, though. Solid plank paneling, sheet paneling covered with pre-finished wood veneers, and combinations of plank and veneer paneling can be quite expensive. With plank paneling, you can use hardwoods such as birch, maple, and oak, or softwoods such as pine, cedar, or cypress. Sheet paneling, made from real wood veneers bonded to plywood, can be bought with or without a finish applied. Choose light-colored woods (such as birch or maple) in either plank or sheet to keep a room bright, or go with more traditional, darker woods. All have a subtle patina that can't be duplicated by simulated finishes. (For more information, see "Paneling," p. 96.)

Built-Up Walls

Custom-designed, built-up panel walls give a room a touch of elegance. Start with a base layer of ¼-inch-thick hardwood veneer panels attached to studs or furring strips. Over that base you can apply any number of raised panel designs—say, outlining a large box grid with 1x4s, subdividing them with 1x2s, and trimming with quarter-rounds and other molding profiles. But this kind of paneling project requires a lot more carpentry skill and experience than installing sheet paneling.

Panel Trim

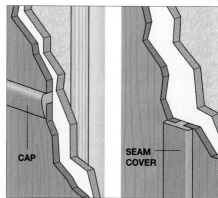

Cap molding is installed at the top of wainscoting or at horizontal seams. Seam cover trim hides vertical joints.

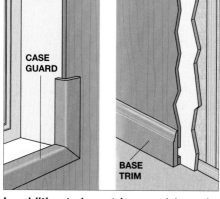

In addition to base trim, special panel trim pieces protect panel ends. Use round-edged case guard at windows.

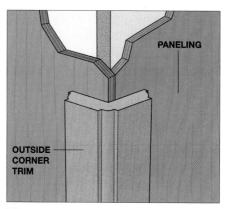

Like corner guard on drywall, this trim covers and protects the seam where two panels meet at a corner.

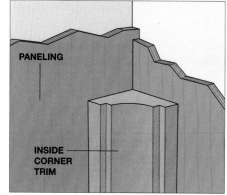

Almost any stock trim, including simple corner round or a beaded molding, will cover seams at inside corners.

Installing Panels

USE: ▶ 4-ft. level • T-square • hammer • table saw, circular saw, saber saw, or handsaw (to cut boards) • saber saw or keyhole saw (to cut holes for electrical

1 **Use a 4-ft. level** or other straightedge to check the walls for level and plumb. Mark low spots—these will need to be shimmed.

2 **Nail up 1x3 or ¾ furring strips** and check them for level; they provide an even nailing surface for the paneling.

3 **The surfaces of the furring strips** should be plumb from top to bottom. Use pairs of shingle shims to fill low spots.

Solid Paneling

You can cover a room quickly and economically with sheet paneling, but it won't have the richness or detail of solid wood. Solid paneling is usually built around a frame of ¾-inch-thick boards that can run up to 12 inches wide. Many combinations of thinner panels and moldings can be used within the frame. Solid paneling also can be applied board to board. There are many styles of interlocking planking.

Knotty-pine planking *is one of the most common applications, often installed over horizontal furring nailed to the stud wall.*

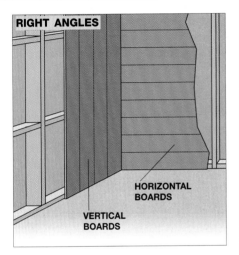

RIGHT ANGLES

HORIZONTAL BOARDS

VERTICAL BOARDS

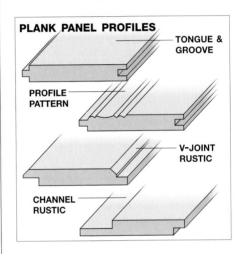

PLANK PANEL PROFILES

TONGUE & GROOVE

PROFILE PATTERN

V-JOINT RUSTIC

CHANNEL RUSTIC

Solid hardwood paneling *with inset frames is probably the most expensive but also the most elegant wallcovering.*

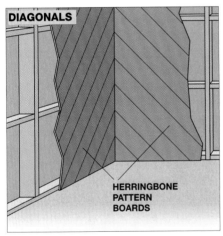

DIAGONALS

HERRINGBONE PATTERN BOARDS

boxes) • clamps • scriber • eye protection • gloves ▶ sheet paneling • furring strips • panel adhesive • common nails • finishing nails • shims

4 **Install filler strips** *to provide support for the panels and seams. Leave small gaps at the ends of the strips to prevent buckling.*

5 **Set the glued panel** *with the bottom shimmed off the floor. Pull the panel away from the wall until the glue gets tacky.*

6 **Remove the blocks,** *reset the panel, and nail it in place. Color-matched panel nails in the grooves won't be noticeable.*

walls & ceilings

Brighten a Dark Lair

For a cavelike room with small windows and dark paneling, there are three basic options for bringing light to the gloom: replacing, painting, or restaining. In many cases, replacing is the easiest option, because you can usually nail new paneling right over the old.

Printed panels with a synthetic finish can't be stained and painting very easily, so replacement with a lighter-tone paneling is the best option. If the old paneling was nailed up without adhesive, you may also be able to restore the plaster or drywall surface below if you prefer. Pulling off glued paneling will likely rip the drywall or plaster, and may expose problems covered by the paneling. Before deciding, carefully pry away the paneling in a couple of out-of-the-way places and inspect the wall—then you'll know what you're getting into.

If the paneling is either solid wood or a wood veneer, you can scuff-sand and paint it; or, with more effort, you can lighten the wood with bleach and/or power sanding, and then apply a new coat of light-toned stain. If the paneling has a sheen, sand off the finish first so that the bleach will soak into the wood grain. Try commercial wood bleach or a 50:50 solution of household bleach and water. Numerous washings or applications may produce the results you want; if not, the paneling will have to be replaced. After bleaching, sand the surface to remove more color and smooth it—it will be roughened by the bleaching.

Replacing an Interlocked Plank

USE: ▶ circular saw • pry bar • block ▶ replacement plank

1 Cut the damaged plank up the center using a circular saw with the blade set to the thickness of the panel.

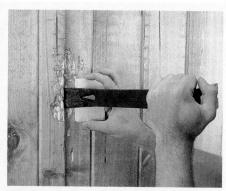
2 Remove the plank in sections with the flat end of a pry bar, using a block of wood to give you leverage.

3 Use a circular saw to cut the bottom groove edge off the new plank so it can be fitted in place next to the old planks.

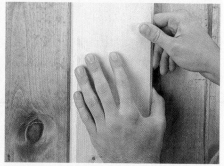
4 Fit the tongue of the new plank into the old groove, and seat the opposite side on top of the tongue next to it.

Patching Paneling

USE: ▶ saw • utility knife • caulking gun • hammer ▶ panel patch piece • furring strips • panel adhesive • masking tape • finishing nails

1 Choose a patch piece of paneling that closely matches the color, grain, and groove pattern of the area that needs replacing.

2 Tape the patch over the damaged area, and use a utility knife to score the patch outline onto the damaged wall panel.

3 Remove the patch, and keep scoring carefully with the utility knife until you cut all the way through the old paneling.

Touch-ups

To conceal skin-deep scars *in either solid plank or sheet paneling, use a color-matched repair stick.*

To patch deeper scars, *cut away loose wood fibers, apply a wood filler, smooth, and touch up with wood stain.*

Scribing Joints

If a panel will butt against a corner that's not straight or against an uneven surface such as a fireplace mantle, you'll have to use a scriber (or a contour gauge) to duplicate the shape and trace it onto the panel. Hold the panel in place plumb on the wall, with the edge an inch away from the corner. Use a compass (or scriber) to transfer a layout line to the panel; then, cut the line with a saber saw. To minimize chipping, fit the saw with a fine-toothed blade or with a special panel-cutting blade that has teeth oriented to cut only on the plunge.

Use a scriber *to transfer the shape of an irregular surface (such as an out-of-plumb wall) onto a piece of paneling.*

A contour gauge *has small, sliding pins that make an accurate impression of a complex contour, such as a countertop.*

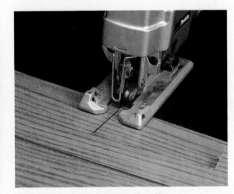

To cut along an irregular line *or complex contour, use a saber saw fitted with a panel-cutting blade.*

4 Glue furring strips *behind the hole to support the patch piece. Clamp the pieces in place, and let the adhesive dry completely.*

5 Apply construction adhesive *to mating surfaces of the furring and the patch piece, and set the patch in position.*

6 Seat the patch piece firmly; *then countersink color-matched paneling nails around the perimeter, and putty the holes.*

walls & ceilings

Drywall Basics

The standard drywall panel for new construction and remodeling is ½-inch thick. Special ½- or ⅝-inch-thick ceiling panels are recommended for ceilings, especially those with 24-inch-on-center framing. Lighter ⅜-inch panels are good for resurfacing work. When a plaster wall is beyond repair, you can nail the thin drywall right over it. Special ¼-inch panels are used for curved surfaces.

Drywall is generally available in 4-foot widths and 8-, 10-, 12-, and 14-foot lengths. It may seem easiest to hang 4x8 sheets vertically, running the long dimension from floor to ceiling. And it's true the 4x8 sheet, which weighs about 60–70 pounds, is easier to maneuver and install than longer sheets—especially on ceilings. But whenever possible, you should install sheets horizontally on walls, and always choose the longest practical length to minimize the number of end joints. You'll need a helper, but horizontal installation saves work during the time-consuming process of taping and finishing joints. Also, vertical joints are harder to tape—you have to stoop to do the lower section and stretch to get the top. The long horizontal seam is easy to reach.

When you handle drywall during installation, remember to treat it gently because it breaks easily if dropped or hit, and you will crush a corner if you put the full weight of a sheet on it. Stack drywall flat to prevent warping if you don't plan on using it right away.

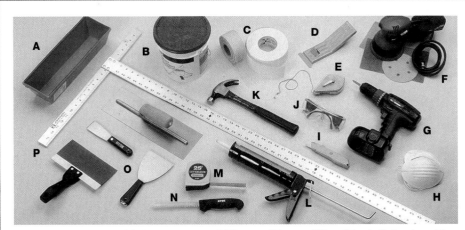

Tools & Materials

Drywall tools: *trough (A); joint compound (B); tape (C); panel lifter (D); chalk-line box (E); power sander (F); drill/driver (G); dust mask (H); utility knife (I); safety glasses (J); hammer (K); caulking gun (L); measuring tape (M); drywall saw (N); taping knives (O); T-square (P).*

You may need a lot more than nails, screws, tape, corner bead, and joint compound to drywall. In addition to the specialized tools above, you have a choice of gypsum materials. The residential range includes ¼-inch panels for resurfacing existing walls to ⅝-inch panels for heavy-duty applications. There are also special board treatments, for example, a fire-code board that makes sense in utility rooms, and a moisture-resistant board for kitchens and baths.

Material	Quantity
Drywall panels	For 4x8 panels: divide room perimeter by 4, deduct about ⅓ sheet for a door, and ¼ sheet for a window
Joint compound	About 1 gal. per 100 sq. ft. of drywall
Joint tape	About 400 ft. per 500 sq. ft. of drywall
Nails or screws	About 1 fastener per sq. ft.

Installing Drywall

USE: ▶ measuring tape • T-square • utility knife • pencil • drywall hammer or power drill/driver • caulking gun • panel lifter • eye protection ▶ drywall panels

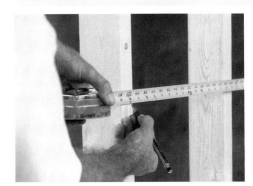

1 *Before cutting panels,* measure along the framed wall to be sure that the drywall edges (every 48 in.) will fall on a stud.

2 *To cut drywall,* score the surface with a utility knife, snap-break the panel along the cut, and slice through the paper backing.

3 *Ceiling panels* are difficult to install without a helper; if you're working solo, use a deadman (p. 183) to hold up the panel.

Hammers vs. Screwdrivers

It's convenient to nail on drywall, but you'll get more holding power and fewer repairs by using pointed, sharply threaded drywall screws, especially on ceilings. The traditional nailing tool (used by some but not all pros) has a wide head on one end and a cutting hatchet on the other. DIYers generally do better with a basic clawhammer. Power screwdrivers need a special screw-setting head.

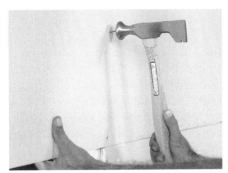

Practical power screwdrivers have a belt clip, a screw-holding head, and a torque clutch to disengage when the screw seats.

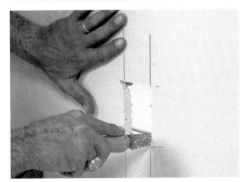

The hatchet end of a traditional drywall hammer is rarely used for cutting. DIYers are better off (and safer) with a utility knife.

Cutting for Outlets

USE: ▶ measuring tape • drywall saw • utility knife • pencil ▶ drywall panel • outlet box

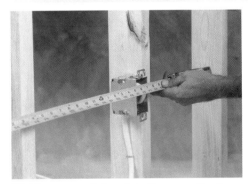

1 *Always mark box locations* on the floor to avoid burying them accidentally. Measure from side wall and floor to mark the panels.

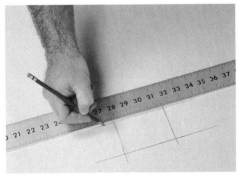

2 *Transfer the measurements* onto the front of the panel using a 4-ft. T-square. You can also trace a spare outlet box.

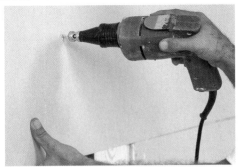

3 *Use a pointed drywall saw* to cut out the hole. Don't push on the panel to fit a miscut; trim the hole with a utility knife.

• construction adhesive • drywall nails or screws

4 *You can apply construction adhesive* to studs to make a stronger, continuous bond that is less likely to pop nails or screws.

5 *Install the top wall panel first,* butting it against the ceiling. If you're working alone, a pair of nails can support the panel for nailing.

6 *Butt the bottom panel* against the top using a panel lifter; the gap near the floor will be covered by baseboard trim.

walls & ceilings

Finishing Drywall

Nailing up drywall doesn't require much skill, but covering the seams to create a smooth, continuous surface does. Pros make finishing drywall look easier than it really is, but with a little practice, and by avoiding common mistakes, do-it-yourselfers can get good results, too.

Don't take shortcuts or rush the job. Taping should be done in three stages. Trying to get by with two thick coats can cause the compound to take too long to dry, shrink excessively, crack, or droop. Failure to allow enough drying can have similar effects.

Gaps at the seams between sheets should never be wider than ⅛ inch. If you try to fill a larger gap, the joint will likely fail. Drywall is cheap—take down the poorly fit piece and install a new one correctly. And don't use dehydrated joint compound or a mix that has been stored in freezing temperatures.

When smoothing out compound, the knife blade must ride smoothly on the drywall surface. When a knife ticks a nail head or other imperfection, a ridge appears in the compound. So before applying the compound, go over the surface with a wide knife to locate any culprits. Give each nail a final, solid thwump—don't break the paper but do leave a dimple—and trim any small tears away with a utility knife.

Taping Drywall Joints

Knife blades must be clean when you start and throughout the process. One hardened speck on the blade will leave a distinctive groove, requiring extra spackling and sanding. Don't allow debris or hardened specks to ruin the mix, and don't dip a dirty knife in the bucket of compound—use a hawk or mud pan to hold a working supply. Scrape the compound off the blade before each smoothing stroke.

Any dry spots under the tape are likely to bubble under successive coats. The key is to watch for a continuous and uniform color change as you smooth the tape. Also avoid running the blade over a seam again and again. You will remove too much compound.

Imperfections not reduced by scraping or sanding will cause problems in successive coats. But don't oversand, or you'll scuff up the paper tape and drywall surface paper. That furry result persists through finishing and painting.

Finishing Panel Seams

USE: ▶ 3-, 6-, and 12-inch drywall taping knives • sanding pole • mud tray or hawk • tape dispenser

1 *Use a drywall taping knife* to apply a first coat of joint compound about 4 in. wide over the seam between panels.

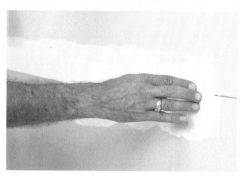

2 *Embed paper drywall tape* in the first coat of compound by smoothing it against the wall with the drywall knife.

Special Tools

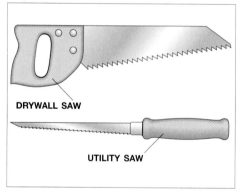

DRYWALL SAW

UTILITY SAW

A **drywall saw** is good for cutting out door and window openings; use a utility saw for cutting out holes for utility boxes and pipes.

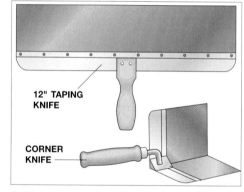

12" TAPING KNIFE

CORNER KNIFE

A **12-in. taping knife** is used to apply wide finish coats; a two-faced corner knife works on both walls of an inside corner.

Finishing Corners

USE: ▶ drywall hammer • 6-inch drywall knife (or outside corner knife) • sanding pole • mud tray or hawk

1 *Nail on corner guard* to strengthen outside corners. Use a drywall nail every 6 in., or set it in place with a corner crimper.

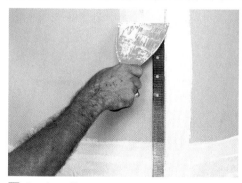

2 *Apply a first coat* of joint compound, and remove the excess; after drying and sanding, apply two more coats.

(optional) • stepladder or scaffolding (as required) ▶ joint compound • drywall tape • sandpaper

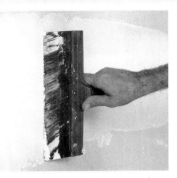

3 *Once the coat dries,* apply a second coat of compound with a wider taping knife. Sand lightly between coats where needed.

4 *Also finish nail- and screw-heads* with three coats; each one should be dry and sanded before you apply the next coat.

5 *Sanding long seams* is much easier with a sanding pole loaded with 120-grit sandpaper or a sanding screen.

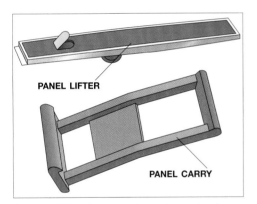

PANEL LIFTER

PANEL CARRY

A panel lifter keeps a drywall panel a few inches off the floor; a panel carry allows one person to move a 4x8-ft. sheet.

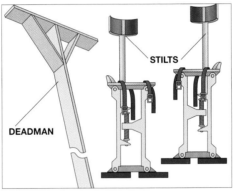

STILTS

DEADMAN

A deadman can prop up a ceiling panel when you're working solo; drywall stilts let you finish seams without moving a ladder.

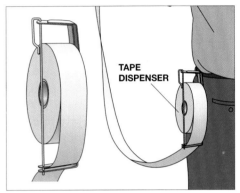

TAPE DISPENSER

A tape dispenser hooks to your belt, giving you a ready supply of drywall tape while you work your way around a room.

• tape dispenser • corner crimping tool (optional) • stepladder or scaffolding (as required) ▶ corner bead • joint compound • drywall tape • sandpaper

3 *Finish inside corners* with paper tape. Make a crease down the center, and set it into the corner over embedding compound.

4 *Finish inside corners* by applying a second coat of compound over the tape, working on one side at a time.

5 *After a light sanding,* apply a finish coat. Try to smooth the fresh compound instead of oversanding after it dries.

walls & ceilings

Drywall Repairs

Drywall is tough, but it can be torn, chipped, cracked, or even punctured accidentally, especially when moving furniture around. Large holes require more time and effort to fix, but you can make minor repairs quickly with only a few simple tools. For example, a deep scrape sometimes tears the surface paper on the wallboard. The first step is to remove any loose or frayed paper facing by neatly trimming the paper to a straight edge with a utility knife. Then fill in the shallow paperless section with compound.

Chronic Cracks

Many house frames move enough seasonally to disrupt drywall joints on a regular basis. If standard taping hasn't held in the past, try another approach. Instead of using fiberglass mesh tape (popular with do-it-yourselfers because it is easier to apply) and conventional all-purpose joint compound, use paper reinforcing tape and setting-type joint compound (powder). Although it's tricky to mix correctly and harder to work with because it dries so fast, you will get a harder and more durable bond, which reduces the chance of the crack reoccurring.

Start by removing any reinforcing tape and scraping out the crack. Fill the crack, and embed the tape with setting compound. Then, if you want, use ready-mix for the next two coats. If cracks like these persist at the ceiling-wall joint, consider installing crown molding.

Fixing Small Holes

USE: ▶ taping knife • sandpaper ▶ patching material • joint compound

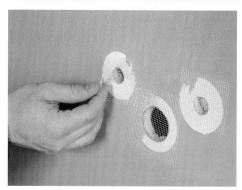

1 You can plug small openings with screening, or apply surface mesh to support and reinforce repair compound.

2 Instead of falling into the hole, joint compound embeds in the mesh. Multiple coats are needed to create a smooth surface.

1 Over larger holes, you can use a self-sticking patch kit that has a reinforcing panel. Just peel off the backing and apply.

2 Once the mesh is fixed to the wall, you can spread joint compound over the entire patch; then sand, prime, and paint.

Fixing Large Holes

USE: ▶ drywall saw or utility knife • caulking gun • power drill/driver or hammer • 6-inch taping knife • sanding sponge ▶ drywall patch • 1x3 scraps or furring

1 Cut out the damaged area, leaving a clean-edged rectangular shape. Cut 1x3 braces to fasten inside the new cutout.

2 Set the braces with construction adhesive and drywall screws. Hold or clamp the brace as you drive the screws.

3 Apply construction adhesive to the side braces before setting the patch. Add top and bottom braces on larger holes.

Fixing Corners

USE: ▶ utility knife • hacksaw • floor scraper • metal snips • power drill/driver • drywall knives ▶ corner bead • drywall screws • joint compound • sandpaper

1 To fix a broken outside corner, first make a rectangular cutout with a utility knife around the damage to prevent tearing.

2 Use a hacksaw to cut through metal corner guard above and below the damage. You also can use metal shears.

3 Use a pry bar and the claw end of a hammer to pull the nails that are driven through the corner guard into the drywall.

4 Use metal shears to cut a replacement piece of corner guard. Clear away torn paper and gypsum in the replacement area.

5 Screw the new piece of guard in place on the corner. Make sure that the new piece aligns with the old guard.

6 Use a taping knife to apply drywall joint compound. Install three coats, allowing each to dry, and sanding lightly in between.

• drywall nails or screws • joint compound • construction adhesive

4 Place the patch piece on the braces, move it back and forth to set in the adhesive, and secure it with drywall screws.

5 Finish the seams of the patch with drywall tape (either paper or fiberglass) and three coats of joint compound.

6 Finish-sand the final coat with a small-celled sanding sponge. Prime the fresh compound before repainting the wall.

walls & ceilings

Paint Basics

Nothing livens up a room like a fresh coat of paint. By taking the time to choose a new color scheme carefully, you can even get a completely new look out of a paint bucket or two. The new colors can be light or dark, warm or cool, depending on the mood you want.

Light colors, for example, create bright, spacious rooms. That's because to your eye, light colors seem to recede, making rooms appear larger and ceilings higher. Dark colors, on the other hand, make for an intimate room. Walls appear closer because dark colors absorb light. Decorating magazines are a good source of ideas for color schemes, and you can usually get help at stores where paint is sold.

Types of Paint

Most paints are either water-based or alkyd-based. (Synthetic alkyd resins have replaced oils.) Water-based paints, which include latex, vinyl, and acrylic paints, are the easiest to work with—they cover well, dry quickly, and tools can be cleaned with soap and water. They also retain color under sunlight and form a flexible film, making them the choice for exterior work. Alkyd paint is more expensive, takes longer to dry, and must be cleaned with paint thinner; it is generally tougher than water-based paint and stands up better to scrubbing. Both paints come in various sheens from flat to gloss and alkyds come in high-gloss. Generally, the more shiny the paint, the easier it will be to clean, but the more imperfections it will show.

Special Tools

A brush spinner (above) whirls dirty brushes through rinse water and dries them quickly, too. A paint mixer (below) attaches to a power drill.

Safety Gear

Always wear a respirator when you paint without adequate ventilation. Use a tight-fitting spray-paint mask or a cartridge-style respirator with replaceable filters. Disposable paper dust masks aren't sufficient to keep you from inhaling paint vapors, which can make you sick. You should also wear a respirator whenever you spray paint from a can or paint sprayer. It's also a good idea to wear goggles to protect your eyes. Also protect yourself by checking product label cautions. Some sealers and cleaners can produce vapors that can be ignited—for example, by a stove pilot light.

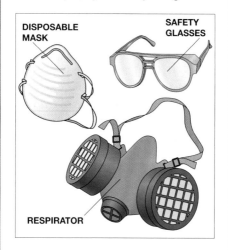

DISPOSABLE MASK
SAFETY GLASSES
RESPIRATOR

Paint Choices

PAINT	APPLICATIONS	PROS/CONS
Latex primer	New plaster or drywall, uncoated wallpaper, finished wood, new brick	Easy clean-up, quick-drying, almost odor-free; doesn't perform well on unfinished wood
Alkyd primer	New plaster or drywall, finished or unfinished wood, any new masonry	Best primer for wood, good for all paints; doesn't perform well on drywall, needs solvents for cleanup
Primer-sealer	Unfinished wood, mildew stains	Quick-drying, good for bleeding knots; needs alcohol for cleanup
Latex paint	Plaster/drywall, primed wood, vinyl trim, steel, aluminum, cast iron	Easy clean-up, quick-drying, inexpensive; not as strong as alkyd, needs primer over wood, adheres poorly to gloss finishes
Alkyd paint	Plaster/drywall, unprimed wood, vinyl trim, steel, aluminum, cast iron	More durable than latex, adheres to all types of paints; slow-drying, cleans up with solvents, needs primer for drywall and plaster

Paint Application Options

Once you pick out your paint, you need to select applicators best suited to the job. Use a synthetic brush (polyester or nylon) for all latex-based paints. Natural fibers (bristle) will absorb the water in latex paint, making the brush heavy and bushy. Use a polyester or natural bristle brush with alkyd paint. A 2½-inch-wide trim brush with a long handle is ideal for most painting projects. The best brushes are flagged and tipped, two extra manufacturing steps that let the brush hold more paint and spread it more evenly.

A paintbrush that will last through many projects has a hardwood handle, a tight metal ferrule at the neck, and thick bristles.

Some DIYers like paint pads. They are not flexible the way a brush is, but can work along trim and in corners.

Rollers & Sleeves

Rollers make short work of large, flat surfaces—and you can attach a long handle to reach ceilings and high walls. A 9-inch-wide roller is standard, but smaller and larger rollers are made for special applications. Roller sleeves (the replaceable part) come in a variety of naps, from very short for smooth surfaces to long for rough surfaces. Generally, it's best to use a ⅜-inch-long nap for walls and ceilings. Longer naps produce a heavier paint stipple; shorter naps produce less surface pattern.

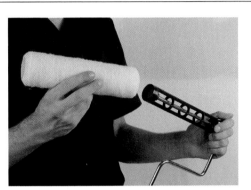

Use a synthetic roller sleeve for water-based paints and a wool, wool/nylon, or mohair cover for alkyd-based paints.

Roller pans should be sturdy to avoid spills and deep enough so you can almost submerge the sleeve.

Painters & Sprayers

Power painters and sprayers get a job done quickly. Power painters allow you to keep rolling without reloading your roller. Sprayers are good for hard-to-brush surfaces and create a very smooth finish. The trick to spraying is to keep the tool moving whenever paint is flowing. You also need to keep the tool parallel to the surface you're painting, even as you swing back and forth across the surface.

A power sprayer uses compressed air to spray a fine mist of paint. You can rent the gun and an electric-powered air compressor.

Power painters pump paint straight through to the applicator under pressure. A trigger allows you to limit the flow.

walls & ceilings

Before You Paint

Painting would be much easier if you could find a contractor to do the prep work, and you handled the painting yourself. Yet you probably wouldn't save much money, even if you could find someone willing to do it. Preparation—the tedious and time-consuming scraping, patching, and sanding—is the worst part of the job, but the most important for a good-looking and long-lasting finish. Poor surface preparation is the number-one cause of paint failures.

Cleaning

Take time to dust and vacuum all surfaces first. Then wash the walls with soap and water, especially in kitchens and bathrooms. If there are little gray-green dots of mold, add up to a quart of bleach to 3 quarts of an ammonia-free detergent solution. Protect nearby floors with newspapers and drop cloths. Allow the bleach solution to remain on the wall for 15 minutes, and then rinse thoroughly.

Smoothing Surfaces

Paint won't hide imperfections—in fact, it accentuates them, making any previously unnoticed bumps or dents stand out. To avoid surprises, shine a bright light at a low angle across the surface to spot problem areas before you begin to paint. Apply joint compound to fill in any depressions, and sand off bumps, ridges, or other raised imperfections.

Priming

Follow the paint manufacturer's recommendations for priming. Some surfaces, such as unpainted wood, require primer with certain paints but not others. Failure to use a primer will reduce paint adhesion and lead to flaking and peeling paint. Previously painted walls and ceilings generally do not require a primer unless you plan a radical color change (such as white over red) or you have stains to cover. But if you've patched with joint compound, the unpainted compound will absorb paint differently than surrounding painted areas, leaving a blotchy finish. Although you can usually apply two topcoats, it's better to use a less-expensive primer, perhaps tinted to a similar color as the top coat, covered by one top coat.

Preparing Walls

USE: ▶ paint scraper • utility knife • taping knives • palm sander • paintbrushes • eye protection

1 *Scrape any cracked or flaking areas* with a paint scraper until you reach paint that is solidly fixed on the wall.

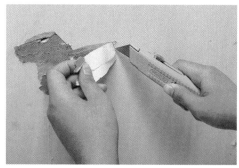

2 *Where the paper surface of drywall is* torn, trim the tear free with a utility knife, and apply joint compound over the damage.

Sealing Over Stains

Remove surface stains as best as you can with a detergent/water solution or an appropriate solvent/spot remover. To prevent remaining discoloration from bleeding through, seal the area with a stain-killing primer, such as pigmented white shellac. These sealers dry fast and won't slow you down. Similarly, coat knots in paneling or trim so that resins won't bleed through.

Pigmented white shellac has tremendous hiding power. It also makes a good primer on metal.

Painting Walls

USE: ▶ angled sash brush • wide paintbrush or paint roller and tray • extension pole for paint roller

1 *Use a trim brush* to cut in a 2- to 3-in. strip of paint around all trim and in areas you can't easily reach with a roller.

2 *Dunk the paint roller* at the deep end of the pan; then roll it over the ribs at the shallow end to distribute the paint evenly.

▶ joint compound • 120-grit paper for palm sander • primer

3 *Use a wide blade* to fill large bare patches with joint compound. Apply several thin coats instead of one thick layer.

4 *Use a power palm sander* or a sanding block to smooth the patches. Oversanding can scuff the drywall surface.

5 *Prime all repaired areas.* This prevents the dry joint compound from sucking water out of the paint, which creates dull spots.

Repainting Trim

To help new paint adhere to old trim, lightly sand glossy surfaces. Also sand away small imperfections, feathering to areas of sound paint so that you don't leave ridges. If need be, take old trim down to raw wood by stripping, sanding, or heating and scraping. If paint was applied before the late 1970s, test for lead before removing the finish. Contact the National Lead Information Center at 800-424-LEAD for handling tips.

Use a heat gun to gradually soften layers of paint. Work on one small area at a time, and keep the gun nozzle moving.

Use a stiff scraper to remove layers of paint heated by the gun. Use a razor-edge scraper to clear grooves in molding.

▶ paint • drop cloths • cleanup rags

3 *One basic and economical approach* to painting is the load-on method. Start by applying thick layers in vertical stripes.

4 *Roll left and right* on the diagonals across the thick stripes. This spreads the paint evenly on the wall.

5 *When the original stripes* have been spread over a section of wall, roll straight up and down to create a uniform stipple finish.

walls & ceilings

Paint Problems

Sometimes you think you have done everything right, down to following all the directions on the paint can, and yet the job still goes wrong. The fresh paint looks nice for a while, but then the trouble starts—flaking, cracking, and other problems appear from a cause or causes unknown. Some problems become evident almost immediately. Wrinkling or sagging, for example, can occur shortly after the paint is applied but before it dries, indicating that the paint was applied too thickly. Apply two thin coats instead of just the thick one to avoid the problem.

Peeling & Blistering

Peeling is a problem more often associated with exterior painting. If peeling occurs indoors, especially in an older home, and you have not painted over a glossy surface, the culprit is often calcimine paint, an old-fashioned mix with a low binder content. If you live in an older home with the original paint in place, wash surfaces with hot water and scrub off the calcimine residue.

First developed in the 1930s as an underlayment for plaster, gypsum drywall soon made plaster obsolete—it went up faster and easier, required no lath, and presented a flat surface without painstaking finish work.

Blistering, a problem that is similar to peeling, can occur if a latex paint is exposed to very high humidity or moisture before the paint has dried sufficiently. Showering after you paint is fine, but not if you've just painted the bathroom.

Dull/Brown Spots

Dull spots are often caused by a failure to prime patched areas. Both joint compound and unfinished drywall absorb paint differently than the surrounding painted areas. Applying too much compound can cause dull spots in these areas even if you have primed them.

Brown spots on a painted surface—sometimes appearing either glossy, soapy, or sticky—occur when ingredients in latex paint leach out to the surface. The culprit is excessive moisture, and brown spots are most likely to form on bathroom ceilings, especially right over the shower. The spots will wash off with soap and water but may occur once or twice again before disappearing.

Mold & Mildew

Mold and mildew spots often occur in bathrooms, but you'll also find them in other rooms by windows where ceilings join exterior walls. Inadequate insulation makes these interior surfaces cold, causing condensation. Mold feeds on the moisture and eventually forms gray-green spots that bleed through paint. Soap or detergent solution won't kill mold. Use a solution of household bleach and water with a non-ammonia detergent. (Never mix ammonia and bleach.) Allow it to soak into the mold for 15 minutes before scrubbing and rinsing.

To clean up severe mold damage such as this, you may need several applications of full-strength bleach.

Special Finishes

You can transform the look of a room with one of many decorative painting techniques. While some require considerable skill and artistry, others (such as those shown at the right) are easily mastered. Before you tackle a real wall, it's wise to experiment with these finishes on a sample piece of drywall. These finishes have become increasingly popular, in part, because there is no single correct way to do them. Feel free to try different applicators and mixing ratios.

Sponging paint on a wall with a natural sea sponge creates a dappled finish, either subtle or bold, depending on the colors.

Ragging involves applying a layer (or layers) of paint over a surface with a bunched-up rag, creating a textured look.

Spot-Painting Patches

To make spot repairs blend in without repainting the entire wall, start with a careful sanding to eliminate any ridges of dried joint compound. Then prime the patched area so the top coat will be evenly absorbed over the patch and surrounding surface. Use a fairly dry roller so the painted area won't dry to a well-defined edge. Also select a sleeve that will produce a finish closely matched to the existing wall stipple. Then coat the patch area with paint, and begin to feather the painted edge. Do this by applying normal pressure as you cross the patch, and lighter pressure, lifting the roller, as you coat the nearby wall.

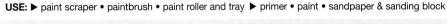

USE: ▶ paint scraper • paintbrush • paint roller and tray ▶ primer • paint • sandpaper & sanding block

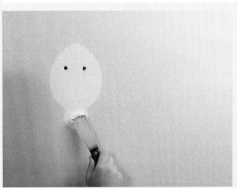

1 *Fill nailholes and small dents* with lightweight joint compound. Leave a slight mound—the compound shrinks as it dries.

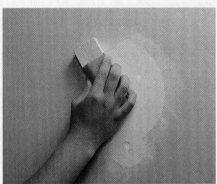

2 *Use 150-grit sandpaper* to sand down the dry joint compound until it is flush with the wall surface.

3 *Because joint compound* absorbs paint differently than drywall, prime the patched area before topcoating.

4 *Roll paint onto the patch,* and work the topcoat across the area. Keep a wet edge on the paint to avoid leaving ridges.

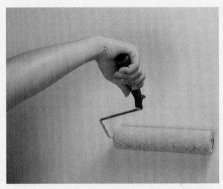

5 *Feather out the edges* of the new paint with light, lifting strokes. To cover, you may need to repeat this process.

Combing paint (also called dragging) involves making narrow lines in a painted surface with a paint comb or other tool.

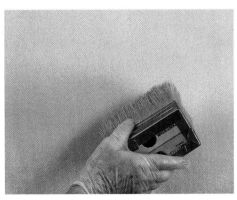

Stippling involves pouncing a special brush straight up and down, creating dots that blend when viewed from a distance.

Spattering is a technique of adding a partial topcoat of a contrasting color or glazing agent. Just tap the brush on the stick.

walls & ceilings

Wallpapering Tips

Wallpaper comes in two basic types, those that are prepasted and those that need pasting. DIYers should use prepasted wallcoverings because the application is straightforward: you dunk it and hang it. Planning, cutting, and measuring is the same for both types, but the alternative to prepasted paper—mixing and brushing on the adhesive—increases the chance for errors, including premature drying, lumps under the surface, and air pockets that are difficult to fix.

Pick an unobtrusive starting point. You can make minor corrections where paper turns a corner, but it's nice to have a finish line that's separated from the starting line—such as a door in the corner, preferably one that's normally left open. On a highly visible wall, misaligned patterns would be glaring, but it would take an eagle eye to spot it behind a door.

After soaking, prepasted papers should be set aside for the time specified by the manufacturer. Keep it consistent from sheet to sheet because the paper may expand or shrink a little while it absorbs the adhesive. If one strip is hung right away next to a sheet that had a long soak, you could get enough of a mismatch to notice. Overworking the paper and stretching it into position can cause the same problem. Instead of tugging on it, which can stretch some materials by ¼ to ½ inch, shift the sheet by pushing on it with your hands.

Making Spot Repairs

USE: ▶ utility knife • square • wallpaper syringe • seam roller ▶ patch • adhesive • masking tape

1 *To patch a damaged area,* align a patch piece over the pattern, tape it down, and cut through both layers.

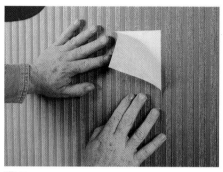

2 *Remove the patch* and the damaged piece from the wall; the cutout part of the patch should fit exactly in the hole.

1 *To fix an air bubble,* first make a small puncture hole in the bubble with a razor knife.

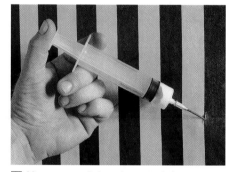

2 *Use a special syringe* to inject adhesive so that the bubble can be rolled flat with a seam roller.

Stripping Old Wallpaper

USE: ▶ wallpaper scarifier • paint roller and tray • paint scraper or drywall taping knife ▶ wallpaper remover

1 *Use a wallpaper scarifying tool* to score the surface of the paper. This will allow the remover to soak in thoroughly.

2 *You can steam off paper,* or apply a chemical stripper. It works through the surface and loosens the glue underneath.

3 *Use a drywall knife* to scrape away pieces of the wallpaper. You may need multiple applications on stubborn spots.

Hanging Wallpaper

USE: ▶ 4-ft. level • chalk-line box • tray • utility knife • scissors • seam roller • paste brush (if needed) ▶ wallpaper • adhesive (if needed)

1 *Use a level or a chalk-line box* to mark lines where the seams will fall. It pays to plan the layout of strips before you paste.

2 *Dunk prepasted wallpaper* in a pan of lukewarm water; unpasted papers need to have adhesive spread on them with a roller.

3 *Fold the soaked roll* onto itself—a process called booking—to make it easy to carry and place the strip on the wall.

4 *Unbook the paper,* and position it on the wall. Align it at the ceiling line and close to your plumb guideline.

5 *Unroll the strip,* and press it in place by hand. Allow enough material to turn the corner, which may not be plumb.

6 *As you hang more strips,* smooth them with a brush, starting at the top corner near the guideline and moving down and across.

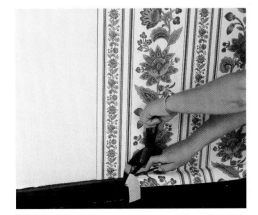

7 *Trim away excess paper,* called the allowance, at the top and bottom with a guide (a drywall knife) and a utility knife.

8 *You can raise the seam* to make small adjustments and match the pattern. You can butt seams or overlap them.

9 *You can overlap seams* by hand-cutting through both strips for a perfect match. Finish edges by using a wallpaper roller.

walls & ceilings

Wall Tile Basics

Ceramic tile is not only attractive, it's a practical solution for bathrooms and kitchens because it's waterproof, durable, and easy to clean. It also works well on floors. (For applying tile to floors, see "Floors & Stairs," p. 158.)

Tile is made from clay that has been fired. Glazed tile, available in matte or shiny finish, has a hard surface that is impervious to stains, but it can be scratched; it is the standard tile around sinks and tubs. Unglazed tile, made only in matte finish, picks up stains from grease and oil but resists scratching; it is often the choice for floors.

Flat tiles are called field tiles; those with finished edges or shaped to fit around corners are trim tiles. Tiles larger than 4x4 inches are sold loose; smaller tiles can be purchased in sheet form, with a few square feet of tile bonded to a thin webbing on the back.

Hanging Backer Board for Tile

The type of material required as backer board for tile depends on the tile's location and the type of adhesive you will use. If you're using organic mastic adhesive and the area will not get consistently wet, standard (or water-resistant) drywall panels are adequate. However, if the area will be subject to regular soakings (such as a shower stall or kitchen-sink area), you should use a cement-based backer board. This material also works well in areas that call for a heavy underlayment, such as a tiled half-wall around a woodstove, where the surface must be fire-resistant.

Cement backer board, which is made from portland cement and fiberglass mesh, comes in ½- and ⅝-inch thicknesses. You can purchase 4x8-foot stock, but the panels typically measure 32 or 36 inches wide by 5 or 8 feet long. Fasteners must be spaced more closely than with ordinary drywall—8 inches apart along the studs. You'll also need special fasteners for cement panels: Use 1½-inch galvanized roofing nails or 1¼-inch galvanized-steel screws. Regular drywall nails or screws will rust through. Cement-panel joints must be taped as well: Use tile-setting mortar or tile adhesive instead of joint compound. Tape the joints with a fiberglass mesh tape that is specially designed for backer board.

Patterns

PAINTED BORDERS

CUT SQUARES

RECTANGLES

MOSAICS

Thinset

In baths and kitchens, as well as other high-moisture areas, you can spread a thinset bed over cement board.

You can also spread a thinset bed over drywall. Use a towel with a notch depth specified by the tile manufacturer.

Grouts

You can grout seams when the tile has set up. (Set-up time depends on the set method and adhesive used.) You can choose a grout based on the type of tile, expected wear and tear, and color. Many manufacturers offer dozens of color choices. Use a shade close to the tile to minimize the grid effect of seams and hide irregular spacing between custom tiles. Generally, lighter grouts highlight the grid, and darker grouts highlight the tile—a good choice on layouts where accent tiles form a pattern.

If you add colorant to a grout mix, set aside a sample, and let it dry to get a true reading of the final color.

Installing Tile

USE: ▶ T-square • drill/driver • taping knife • notched trowel • sponge-faced float • tile cutter • tile nippers • sponge ▶ tile • adhesive • grout • fiberglass tape

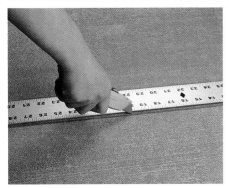

1 *Cut cement backer board* the same way you cut drywall: score it with a utility knife, and snap it along the score line.

2 *Backer boards* can be nailed up with galvanized roofing nails or screwed in place for more stability with galvanized screws.

3 *Finish the backer-board seams* with fiberglass mesh tape and a coat of tile mortar or adhesive.

4 *Mark plumb and level lines* to begin the layout. Your starting point should leave equal-sized partial tiles in corners.

5 *Apply a coat of thinset adhesive* to a section of the wall with a notched trowel. Don't cover your layout lines.

6 *Press each tile firmly in place,* using a slight twisting motion to bed it in the adhesive. Leave equal spaces for grout.

7 *Cut tiles as needed* for corners and the top of the wall. Use tile nippers to make irregular cuts (such as for pipes).

8 *After the adhesive cures,* spread grout with a sponge-faced float or squeegee. Sweep at angles across the tile seams.

9 *After firming the joints,* wipe off the excess with a damp sponge. Allow a dry haze to form; then polish with a cloth.

walls & ceilings

Cleaning Tile

Tile is a durable material and extremely easy to maintain. However, tile and grout joints require periodic cleaning. Also, over time you will occasionally have to repair deteriorating grout and possibly even have to replace cracked or broken tiles.

For day-to-day cleaning, simply wipe the tile down with warm water and a sponge. A baking soda and water solution or a mild solution of white vinegar and water remove light buildups of dirt, grease, and soap scum. For more stubborn cleanups, use a strong solution of all-purpose cleaner or a commercial tile cleaner. Rinse thoroughly with clean water.

Ceramic tiles with metallic glazes should be cleaned and polished with a metal polish. If you need to scour the surface, use a woven-plastic pot scrubber rather than steel wool, which can leave black marks and metal hairs that cause rust stains in grout joints.

If tile cleaner does not seem to be able to remove a stain, try one of the following. For tar, asphalt, and oil stains, use lighter fluid followed by household cleaner. For ink, coffee, tea, blood, or dyes, use a 3% hydrogen peroxide solution or full-strength household bleach. For liquid medicine and shellac, use denatured alcohol. For rust, use a commercial rust remover followed by a household cleaner. For nail polish, use nail polish remover. For chewing gum, chill the gum with an ice cube, and then peel it off the tile surface.

Grout Repairs

Water can puddle on tile all day without leaking, but even a hairline crack in grouted seams lets water seep through. If you catch cracks in time, you can scrape out existing joints (a can opener works well) and regrout. You may have to experiment with grout samples to get a good color match—aging affects the color—even if you use a leftover supply of the original material.

If adjacent tiles are loose, don't expect to secure them by fixing the grout. Grout helps to bind tiles together, but it can't keep them in place. Before you fix the grout, pry off loose tiles, and cut down the ridges of old adhesive on both the tile and on the wall or floor. Let the exposed area dry, and then reset the tile with adhesive and grout the surrounding seams.

Cutting Tile

A tile cutter or diamond-blade wet saw will make straight cuts in tile; special drills are required to make a hole in the middle of a tile. For the curved or irregular cuts needed to fit tiles around supply pipes, sink cutouts, or other contours, use tile nippers. As the name implies, these tools nip away tiny bits of tile. Working with nippers takes a strong wrist and plenty of patience. To use them, hold the tile glazed side up and take small, ⅛-inch bites to break off tiny pieces. If you take too large a bite, the tile is likely to break.

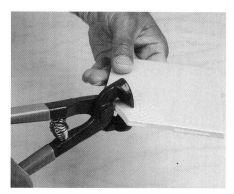

Tile nippers have sharp jaws to crack through a glazed finish. By taking small bites, you can form irregular shapes.

Replacing Tile

USE: ▶ cold chisel or glass cutter • hammer • putty knife • rubber gloves ▶ tile • adhesive • grout

1 Remove a damaged tile by scraping out the grout, scoring the tile with a chisel or glass cutter, and breaking it out.

2 After scraping off the old adhesive, spread new adhesive on the replacement tile and in the empty space.

3 Press the new tile tightly in place. You can use masking tape to keep it centered while the adhesive sets.

4 When the adhesive is dry, regrout the tile, tool the joints, and wipe away the excess. You can seal grout with silicone.

Restoring Bath Tile

USE: ▶ razor knife • bucket • sponge-faced float • sponge • screwdriver • rubber gloves ▶ grout • sealer • caulk

1 *Razor out old grout* with a utility knife or a grout saw; for narrow joints, use an awl or a nail driven into a dowel as a tool.

2 *Old caulk* in the corners and at the tub seams must also be cut out and removed with a razor knife.

3 *Mix a batch of new grout* according to the manufacturer's instructions. You may want to seal the tiles first to prevent staining.

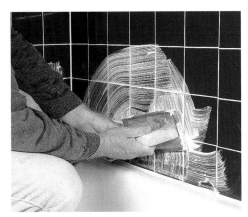

4 *Apply the grout* with a sponge-faced float or a squeegee. Do not spread grout into the corners at the tub-tile seam.

5 *After tooling the grout joints,* wipe off the grout with a damp sponge. Allow a dry haze to form; then polish with a damp cloth.

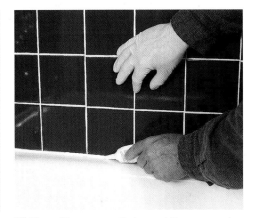

6 *Use silicone caulk* to seal the seam at the tub, the joints at the corners, and wherever the tile meets a different material.

7 *Tool the caulked joints* with your fingertip. Allow grout and caulk to cure before using the shower or bathtub.

8 *To recaulk the escutcheon,* first remove the faucet handle by unscrewing the setscrew in the middle of the handle.

9 *Spread a bead of caulk* around the rim of the escutcheon plate, set it back in place, and reattach the faucet handle.

Walls of Glass

Building walls with blocks of glass may sound like a dumb idea—something like making a child's building set out of bone china. But modern glass blocks are rugged enough to make large exterior walls that let in light and keep out the weather. Interior partitions or half-walls of glass block can create rooms within rooms, defining spaces in a house without isolating them from one another. Glass block is also a popular material for custom shower enclosures and partitions in bathrooms, because it distorts images enough to ensure privacy.

Installation

Glass block is traditionally installed with solid mortar joints like bricks or concrete block. However, good glass block work is a specialized skill, more so than laying concrete block or brick. It is normally a job for a mason; make sure before hiring a contractor that he or she has experience laying glass block.

Some blocks are designed to make installation easier for DIYers. Glass-block kits with clear plastic spacers are stacked and sealed with silicone caulk instead of mortar. Other types include glass blocks that snap into a metal framework and glass-like blocks made of plastic that clip together with interlocking flanges. And if you don't want an entire wall of glass, you can buy prefabricated glass block windows that install in a rough opening the way a regular window does.

Glass Blocks

Glass blocks offer a lot of design options, including finishes that control the amount of light transmitted and different surface textures that blur or completely distort images for privacy. The blocks are made by fusing two sections together to create an airspace that gives glass block an R-value of about 2.0, which is about the same as an insulated glass window and better than the thermal value of a 12-inch-thick concrete wall. Locating glass block on a south-facing wall adds greatly to overall energy efficiency, thanks to the solar energy it transmits during the day.

OPAQUE FINISH

CLEAR FINISH

ICE FINISH

Installing Glass Blocks

USE: ▶ power drill/driver • framing square • measuring tape • utility knife • caulking gun ▶ glass blocks • metal channel • gaskets • caulk

1 Kits are available that make installations easier. A structural channel screwed to the framing conceals the glass blocks' edges.

2 Your framing dimensions need to account for both the width of the glass blocks and the caulked joints.

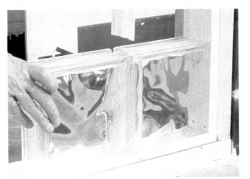

3 Set the blocks into the channels, and use a sample piece of the flexible gasket material to check your spacing.

Mounting Mirrors

Most mirrors are ¼-inch thick and therefore quite heavy. Handling large mirrors safely requires special equipment such as glass suction cups. Whenever you mount a mirror larger than 3 to 4 square feet, use adhesive in addition to any mechanical supports. The best supports are J-clips or J-channels, which also hold the mirror in place until the adhesive cures. The channels also protect edges from damage and prevent water from getting behind the mirror, where it can ruin the silvering on the back. Always use mirror mastic. Other adhesives, such as those containing silicone, may react with the silvering. If you are setting a mirror on a backsplash or similar hard edge and not using a J-channel, place rubber setting blocks under the mirror edge about one-quarter of the distance in from each end. Mirrors that are mounted without frames should have finished edges.

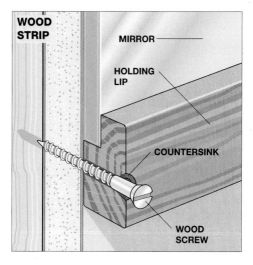

WOOD STRIP

MIRROR

HOLDING LIP

COUNTERSINK

WOOD SCREW

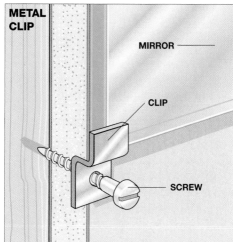

METAL CLIP

MIRROR

CLIP

SCREW

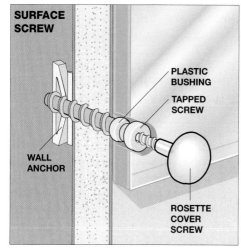

SURFACE SCREW

PLASTIC BUSHING

TAPPED SCREW

WALL ANCHOR

ROSETTE COVER SCREW

4 *When you complete one full course,* set a full length of the gasket. It is molded to fit into ridges along the blocks.

5 *The gaskets are set* in all horizontal and vertical seams. Exposed seams that are normally grouted are caulked instead.

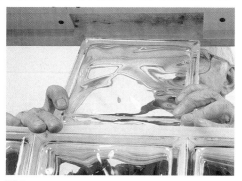

6 *Leave out one block-sized section* of channel on the top course. Insert the last blocks here, and slide them into position.

Decorating With Trim

Trim does have a functional side—it covers gaps, rough edges, and transitions between building materials. But when skillfully laid out, it can do much more. Wide baseboards, wainscoting along walls, picture molding, crown molding, and false beams on ceilings all add architectural detail and a decorative touch that can't be achieved with paint or wallpaper.

The overall design, type of trim used, and variety of wood you choose will have a lot to do with the results you achieve. (For more details on trim stock, see "Wood," pp. 98–99.) Clean, tight mitered joints are also important to the overall effect. For that you'll need a good miter-box saw or a power miter saw like the pros use (even if you have to rent it).

Installation Tips

Mark the locations of studs on the floor before the walls are drywalled so you know where to nail the trim. Note also the locations of any in-wall braces you may need to secure the trim.

Despite good equipment and careful layout, some trim joints still need a little adjusting. To close up a joint, try a trick called back-cutting. Use a sharp block plane to undercut the back edges on both pieces of trim so the boards won't touch until the visible surfaces meet.

You can usually nail through trim without splitting the wood, but predrill if you are nailing near the edge, into oak (or other hardwoods), or nailing very thin or narrow trim.

Molding Details

You can use combinations *of beaded molding and decorative medallion blocks to create distinctive door trim.*

More elaborate door surrounds *are available in precut hardwood kits. Period moldings also are now made from foam.*

Cornice moldings *for ceilings can be built up in stages from stock lumber or ordered in paintable foam sections.*

Elaborate cornice moldings *can be painted, stained, or treated with a variety of faux-finish surface glazes.*

Installing Molded Trim

USE: ▶ power miter saw or backsaw & miter box • pencil • caulking gun • hammer • drywall taping knife • paintbrush ▶ molded trim • construction adhesive •

1 ***Hold a section of the molded trim*** *in place, and mark guidelines along the top and bottom edges with a pencil.*

2 ***Following manufacturer's directions,*** *install a bead of adhesive just inside your lines on the wall and ceiling.*

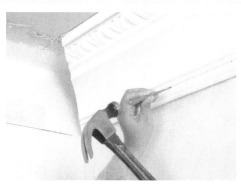

3 ***Press the molding*** *into the beads of adhesive, and fasten the lightweight sections with finishing nails.*

Originally made from plaster, ceiling medallions are now made of light foam glued and joint-compounded in place.

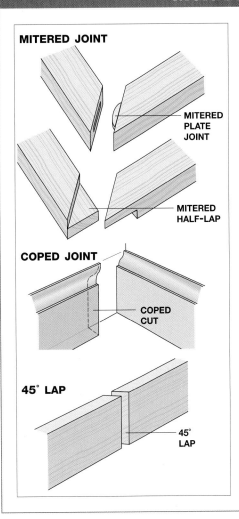

Complex cornices, medallions, mantles, and other special trim pieces also are available in exotic hardwoods.

Molded Cuts

MITERED JOINT

MITERED PLATE JOINT

MITERED HALF-LAP

COPED JOINT

COPED CUT

45° LAP

45° LAP

There are many ways to join wood trim—for example, with miters, half-laps, and biscuits. On some baseboard corners, you may have to make a coped joint. If you have to butt baseboards, cut mating edges at 45 degrees so that if the joint opens slightly, you won't see a gap. With reproduction trim made of rigid polyurethane foam, you can use a utility knife or trim saw to make cuts. Install this trim with adhesive and nails.

Foam moldings are cast from original, carved-wood trim. The cladding accepts paint.

finishing nails • sandpaper • primer & paint

4 **Where molding sections meet,** and along the top and bottom edges, use drywall compound to fill seams and gaps.

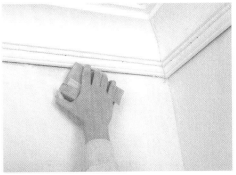

5 **Spread the compound smoothly,** and when it dries, lightly sand the wall and ceiling seams with fine sandpaper.

6 **Wipe away sanding dust,** cover the fresh compound with a prime coat of paint, and finish with a full-strength coat.

walls & ceilings

Controlling Noise

Drywall, insulation, and even air spaces inside walls and ceilings all help dampen sounds that pass from one room to another. Sometimes just adding a rug or stuffed furniture will make a room quieter, but in houses built with thin walls (and no insulation in interior walls), drastic measures may be needed.

An easy first step is to use acoustic sealant or caulk to seal all joints and openings between the noisy area (say, the basement) and the rooms you want to keep quiet. If the framing is exposed on one side of the wall or ceiling (or if you are willing to remove the drywall), install sound attenuation blankets in the wall cavities.

When you install drywall, use ⅝-inch-thick sheets instead of the usual ½-inch. And don't secure it directly to the framing; any vibrations that strike one side of the wall, floor, or ceiling will be transmitted through the framing to the other side. Instead, attach resilient metal channels to the framing, and then attach the drywall to the channels. Depending on the degree of noise and the results you are trying to achieve, you may want to install a sound-deadening board on top of the drywall, and cover it with another layer of drywall.

Instead of the second layer of drywall on the ceiling of a noisy room, try installing an acoustical ceiling below the drywall. Small tiles can be glued on directly, stapled to wood furring strips, or snapped into metal channels; larger panels can be suspended in a metal grid.

Sound Transmission

Sound is carried from room to room by impact, through openings (such as heating ducts), and by vibrations transmitted through the structure. The intensity of a sound is measured in decibels (dB). A jump of 10 dB represents a doubling of perceived sound. The ability of materials to absorb sound is measured by the noise-reduction coefficient (NRC), which is an average of sound reduction for the material across a range of frequencies; the higher the number, the more sound it absorbs. Construction techniques and materials both effect sound levels.

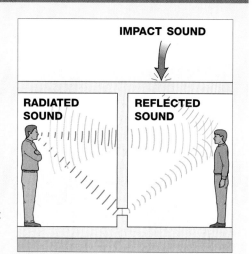

Sound level	Intensity
Threshold of pain	120–130 dB
Train, circular saw	100–110 dB
Factory, traffic noise	80–90 dB
Face-to-face conversation	60–70 dB
Average office	50 dB
Quiet radio	40 dB
Quiet conversation	20–30 dB
Soundproof room	10 dB
Threshold of audibility	0 dB

Material	NRC
Carpet on foam pad	0.55
Carpet on slab	0.29
½" drywall	0.16
Plywood-paneled wall	0.15
Plaster wall	0.09
Bare wood floor	0.09
Painted concrete block wall	0.07
Bare brick wall	0.04
Bare concrete floor	0.02

Making Sound-Absorbing Walls

USE: ▶ hammer • power drill/driver • caulking gun ▶ 2x6 and 2x4 lumber • blanket insulation • drywall screws • construction adhesive • metal hat channel (opt.)

1 *To hold extra insulation* and two rows of studs, build the partition with a 2x6 plate nailed to the subfloor with 16d nails.

2 *Set one row of 2x4 studs* in a conventional 16-in.-on-center layout, flush with one side of the partition wall.

3 *Nail another row* of standard studs between the others, but nail them flush with the other side of the partition wall.

Sound-Resistant Construction Options

You can take several steps during construction to reduce noise transmission. It's important to insulate partition walls, as well as ducts and pipes—this reduces the noises of moving air and water, and saves energy. Wall design is also important. Different configurations rate different sound transmission classes. (See the different STCs at right.) Thicker walls with separated layers break the transmission of sounds and reduce noise room to room.

Reduce plumbing sounds *from drain lines in framing cavities by wrapping the pipes with batts of insulation.*

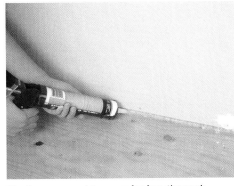

Batts of insulation *also reduce sounds from rushing air in ducts, and reduce temperature loss through duct walls.*

Reduce sound transmission *through partition walls by caulking small gaps, even when they will be covered by trim.*

SOUNDPROOFING WALLS

STC 30
⅝" DRYWALL ON BOTH SIDES OF STUDS SET AT 16" ON CENTER
STC 35
TWO LAYERS ⅝" DRYWALL ON STUDS SET AT 24" ON CENTER
STC 43
⅝" DRYWALL, ONE SIDE ON METAL HAT CHANNEL
STC 46
⅝" DRYWALL ON STAGGERED STUDS 12" ON CENTER OF 2X6 BOTTOM PLATE
STC 50
⅝" DRYWALL, ONE SIDE ON HAT CHANNEL, WITH 3½" INSULATION BETWEEN STUDS

4 Weave blankets of insulation *through the two rows of studs to reduce sound transmission through the wall surfaces.*

5 Install a first layer of drywall *vertically over the studs, using nails or screws. You can leave the seams unfinished.*

6 Install a second layer of drywall *horizontally, and finish the seams. This layer can also be installed on resilient metal channel.*

walls & ceilings

Finishing Ceilings

Nearly anything you can put on a wall—paint, wallpaper, paneling, trim—can also be used effectively on ceilings. The work will be more difficult, though, because everything has to be done over your head. Painting, of course, is the easiest and most common way of finishing off a ceiling, but textured drywall and suspended ceilings offer some special advantages, especially in remodeling situations.

Ceiling Textures

A ceiling texture adds a low-tech, inexpensive design feature to any interior. These textures may appear difficult to achieve, but with the right equipment, they're quite simple—they can even help disguise mistakes made while installing drywall and taping seams.

Blown ceilings require equipment most people will have to rent. A popcorn-like material (polystyrene or vermiculite) is fed from a hopper into an airless spray gun attached to an air compressor. Once blown onto the ceiling, it is usually left to dry without retouching. This texturing takes some practice to apply properly. If you don't have a place to practice, hire a painting or drywall contractor to do the job for you. You can also create a textured ceiling by spraying diluted joint compound through an airless paint sprayer. However, you must add just the right proportion of water, and mastering the spraying technique takes practice.

Wood Planking

There are many places to use wood paneling aside from walls. For example, beaded, tongue-and-groove boards are commonly used on the ceilings of porches. It may seem more difficult to work on a ceiling than on a wall, but that job may go faster once you set up because there are no windows and doors in the way.

Whether you use a softwood (such as pine) or a hardwood (such as oak), you can surface-nail planks in place. It's wise to predrill at the ends of boards, even when the lumber is ¾ in. thick and you are using finishing nails. You can set the nailheads and fill the holes with putty.

One time-saving option is to drive your nails in the seams between planks where they will be concealed. Many planks have a beaded or grooved edge that creates a V-shaped seam. The idea is to set a finishing nail at an angle, placing it deeply into the edge of the leading panel, and driving it home with a nailset. As you continue, the edge of the next board in line will cover the nailhead. It also helps to use a bead of construction adhesive along the supporting wall studs or furring strips.

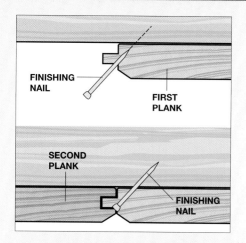

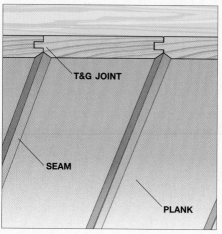

Installing a False Beam

USE: ▶ table saw • measuring tape • hammer • router • paintbrush • power drill/driver • nailset • eye protection ▶ 1x pine boards • scrap wood • nails • wood

1 *You can make an elegant false beam* from three pine boards. Start by cutting 45° miters on the board edges.

2 *Use scrap wood* as a spacer, and clamp the sides of the beam in place. Then add glue and nail on the bottom edge.

3 *You can leave the beam edges* as plain miter cuts, or use a router to create a decorative bead along the exposed edges.

Installing a Suspended Ceiling

USE: ▶ level • hammer • utility knife • straightedge ▶ edge track (molding) • metal channel (main tees and cross tees) • hanger wires • nails • ceiling tiles

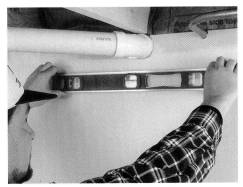

1 *To conceal the pipes,* electrical conduit, and joists above the basement, start by establishing a level line on the walls.

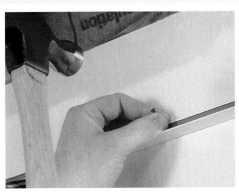

2 *A typical hung-ceiling system* includes edge track that captures the edges of the tiles. Nail it on your level lines.

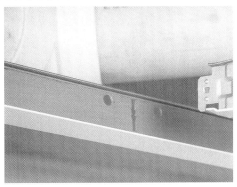

3 *Lightweight, molded aluminum* channels carry the tiles and conceal the edges in the main tile field over the room.

4 *The channels* run from wall to wall, and tie into the edge tracks. Use wire wrapped around nails to support them.

5 *If you have to trim ceiling tiles,* use a sharp utility knife held against a straightedge, such as a framing square.

6 *With the perimeter tiles in place,* finish the ceiling by inserting full tiles into the grid pattern of suspended channels.

glue • wood putty • stain • 1x2 or 1x3 nailer

4 *Finish your false beam* to suit the room decor. After filling nail holes and sanding, you can stain it or paint it.

5 *One easy way to install a false beam* (it will conceal the copper plumbing pipe) is to install a nailer on the ceiling.

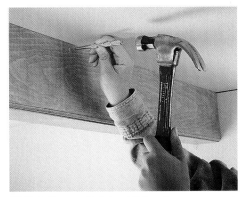

6 *Set the prefinished false beam* around the ceiling nailer, attach it with finishing nails, and set the nails to finish.

unfinished spaces

unfinished spaces

Renovating an Attic

Instead of building an addition from scratch, many homeowners can perform the cost-effective trick of bringing unused space they already have to life. One space that is particularly ripe for renovation is the attic.

Converting unused attic space to habitable space isn't much of a trick in a house with a large area under the roof, especially if it already has plenty of headroom, windows at each end, and a solid floor. The project is more challenging in houses with low-slope roofs over an airless jumble of exposed ceiling joists, electrical wires, and insulation.

Some unused spaces need more revitalization (meaning time and money) than others. But some basic design and construction decisions are similar no matter what shape your attic is in—even on the easiest jobs in which the original builders did a lot of the work for you.

Structural Limits

Some older houses are overbuilt—with extra structural capacity built in. When lumber and labor were inexpensive it was no big deal to make joists in the attic as big as the ones on the first or second floor.

Most houses built in the last 10 or 15 years are not overbuilt. To keep costs down, joists in the attic floor were generally smaller than those in the first and second floor. The discrepancy is allowed by building codes because first- and second-floor joists must be large enough to support dead and live loads, but attic floor joists may be much smaller—designed to support as little as one-third of the loads calculated for the living space downstairs.

Of course, you must comply with state and local building codes. But this can be a challenge when you want to renovate, and an architect or building contractor informs you that new attic floor joists must be added. And if you're adding sizable dormers to the top of the house, some of the posts or load-bearing walls in the existing frame—and even the foundation—may have to be beefed up to carry the new loads.

Trusses & Braces

Here is another case where owners of newer homes may lose out. Trusses are triangular shapes made of small-dimension lumber. The bottom of the truss serves as ceiling to the living space below. The upper sections serve as roof rafters. But to make the truss out of small lumber (such as 2x4s), many cross braces are attached in a maze of zigzags from one side of the house to the other. Unfortunately, you can't pull out some of the braces to make room. Each one adds strength to the overall truss

shape. To add a dormer in a truss-framed roof, trusses would have to be replaced by more substantial floor joists and rafters—a complex job.

Even in large, open attics, you may be hindered by cross beams, called collar ties, that tie opposing rafters together—like the horizontal line in the letter A—to help them resist uplift from high winds and the pressure of the rafters against the outside walls. Often they can be raised enough to provide headroom. However, to be effective, they must be located in the top third of the floor-to-ridge height.

Light & Ventilation

Successful attic conversions must overcome limitations of the space. One such limitation: A window at each end wall might be adequate for one large, uninterrupted storage space, but not for subdivided living space.

Enlarging end wall glazing and installing skylights may be the easiest option. For example, you might exchange one small window for large side-by-side double-hung windows with a spacious, fixed-glass crescent above. That could flood two bedrooms with light, while a central area reserved for closets, stairs, and a bath could be fitted with skylights. Such a plan eliminates the need for dormers—a more complicated and costly structural change in the roof.

Skylights and a half-circle window
provide much-needed light and ventilation for this renovated attic room.

Meeting Codes

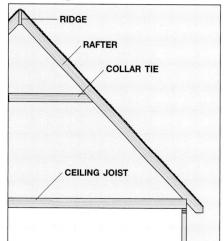

RIDGE
RAFTER
COLLAR TIE
CEILING JOIST

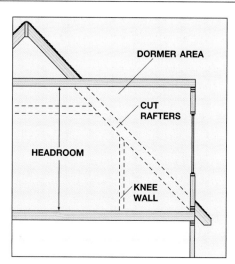

DORMER AREA
CUT RAFTERS
HEADROOM
KNEE WALL

Before you change dead space to living space, check building codes for rules about collar ties, headroom, and knee-wall height above the finished floor.

Dormers

A gable dormer (top) is a good way to create additional space while supplying light and ventilation to an attic room. A continuous shed dormer (bottom) will provide even more space.

Basic Stairway Variations

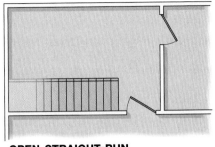

OPEN STRAIGHT-RUN

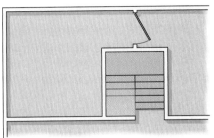

HALF-CLOSED U-SHAPED RETURN

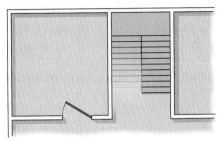

OPEN U-SHAPED RETURN

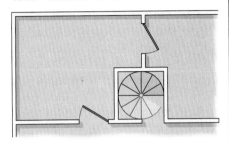

SPIRAL STAIRS

When locating a new stairway, use the option that best fits the space in as well as below the attic. Stairs to any living space must meet building codes.

Obviously, on jobs where dormers must be raised above a low-slope roof to gain headroom, windows can be added in many configurations along the face of the dormer.

The job of renovating unused space in your existing home can be disruptive. The house could be crawling with contractors for weeks. But you'll be saving the time and cost of building foundations and other parts of the building that are already in place.

Access to the Attic

Accessibility is most troublesome in attics reached solely by a trap door or pull-down stairs—local building codes don't allow this for habitable space. There may not be enough room in narrow, second-story halls to install a conventional permanent stairway. Stairs to an attic must be at least 2–6 feet clear between handrails or between a single handrail and the opposite wall. Needed space can frequently be stolen from an existing room or closet. Another option is to gain access with spiral, or library, stairs. If the living space does not exceed 400

square feet, spiral stairs may be permissible. These stairs are available in diameters as small as 4 feet and may fit easily into an alcove or at the end of a hallway.

Installing a Dormer

Dormers serve a number of purposes: They provide light, ventilation, and headroom for renovated attic spaces, and they bring architectural interest to an otherwise nondescript roof. The two main types are gable dormers and shed dormers.

Easiest to build during the initial framing, dormers can, however, be built into existing roofs. The job will be messy, though—involving stripping and cutting out a section of the roof—and will require reshingling at least the roof area around the dormer. Building any kind of dormer requires the application of the same framing principles discussed in chapter 7 (pp. 102–9, 124–27). Gable dormers require some advanced rafter cuts for the valley rafters and valley jack rafters, similar to the cuts used in hip roofs. Shed dormers, with their flat roofs, are easier to frame.

Inspection Checklist

- ◆ **Headroom.** A minimum height of 7 feet, 6 inches, in at least 50% of the floor area, is required.

- ◆ **Living space.** Each habitable space must be at least 80 sq. ft.

- ◆ **Ventilation.** Natural clear ventilation through windows or skylights must equal at least 4% of the floor area of a habitable space.

- ◆ **Rafters.** Sagging rafters must be evaluated by an engineer.

- ◆ **Floor framing.** Attic floor joists must be checked by an engineer to determine whether or not they can carry additional loading.

- ◆ **Water leaks.** Must be eliminated.

- ◆ **Pests.** Have insects and other pests professionally eliminated.

unfinished spaces

Structural Alterations

Structural alterations, as well as improvements and extensions to existing wiring, plumbing, and heating systems, may all be required when you want to make a fundamental change to how a space is used. Below are a few tips on some of the framing changes you may have to make to finish an attic.

Material Access

Instead of trying to haul long, heavy timbers through the finished areas of your home, and inevitably bashing a few 2x4s against the walls, try to deliver joists, studs, and other lumber directly into the attic. New or existing openings for windows or skylights provide a handy entry point for sliding in materials raised up on a scaffold outside the house. If there are no windows or skylights, you might be able to load them through a gable-end vent.

Joist Size vs. Headroom

In some cases, standard joists large enough to span the floor and bring in compliance with local codes for living space may be much deeper than the existing joists—2x12s instead of 2x6s. Sistering these joists would reduce attic headroom by 6 inches—possibly enough to make the attic not legally habitable. To save space and comply with your building code, you may be able to bridge the floor with smaller joists that are supported along their spans by bearing walls or posts in the space below. In extreme cases, you can increase floor strength without increasing joist depth by setting joists closer together than the standard spacing of 16 inches on center—for example, by setting a new 2x6 joist in between old joists spaced at 24 inches on-center, creating a much stronger floor with joists every 12 inches. Always check with a local building inspector beforehand.

Removing Braces

If you have collar ties running across your unfinished attic, they are not there just for you to bang your head—they're an important part of your roof framing. This can be a stumbling block because the collar ties may be the only framing component limiting headroom. If they weren't there, you might be able to save a lot of time and money required to build dormers. It's worth consulting with an an architect or structural engineer, and definitely with the building inspector, about raising them.

The idea is to install shorter collar ties closer to the upper third of the A shape to gain valuable headroom, and only then to remove the existing collar ties. The roof structure will still be rigid and the smaller space above the ties can serve to ventilate the attic, providing a cooling cross flow from one gable-end vent to the other.

Attic Ventilation

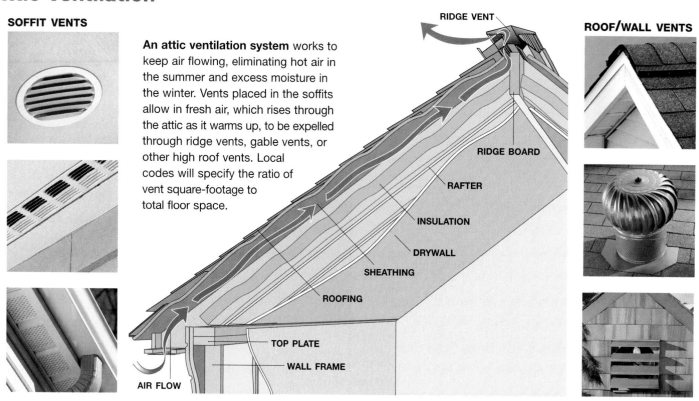

SOFFIT VENTS

An attic ventilation system works to keep air flowing, eliminating hot air in the summer and excess moisture in the winter. Vents placed in the soffits allow in fresh air, which rises through the attic as it warms up, to be expelled through ridge vents, gable vents, or other high roof vents. Local codes will specify the ratio of vent square-footage to total floor space.

RIDGE VENT

ROOF/WALL VENTS

RIDGE BOARD

RAFTER

INSULATION

DRYWALL

SHEATHING

ROOFING

TOP PLATE

WALL FRAME

AIR FLOW

Soffit vents (pictured at left, from top to bottom) include plug vents, strip-grille vents, and perforated vents. **Roof vents** (pictured at right) include ridge vents, turbines, and motorized exhaust fans. **Wall vents** include gable vents and motorized exhaust fans.

Ventilation

Because a minimum headroom of 7 feet, 6 inches is required in an attic, it's tempting to expose the ceiling all the way to the roof peak, creating the most expansive A shape possible. But exchanging the vent area you currently have (the entire attic) for living space may create a prohibitively large cooling load on the new living space in the summer and drive up your utility bills. In a finished space directly under the roof, midday temperatures could soar to 120° F or more and require a massive amount of air conditioning. On top of that, when the temperature dropped at night, you would likely have condensation problems where warm, interior air met the underside of the roof.

That's why the best plan may be a compromise: minimum headroom, but more space for insulation and ventilation. Establish this balance by using the collar ties as the floor of a new mini-attic. This floor, the attic's new ceiling, may be relatively short, but the mini-attic will allow you to vent what remains of the unfinished attic space in two ways. First, air entering the soffit vents in the roof overhangs will vent the eaves, and then it will rise up through the rafter bays to the mini-attic above the newly renovated space. Second, the air flow from the soffit vents will join with the continuous flow of air beneath the roof ridge, running from one gable-end vent to the other.

Collar Ties

Sloped roofs have rafters in an inverted V shape. But to tie rafters together, help them resist uplift in high winds, and reduce the force that rafters exert on walls, cross beams called collar ties are often added to make the inverted V-shape into an A-shape. These collar ties are an integral part of the framing. The roof might not collapse if you removed them, but you could probably get enough movement to pop nails, crack plaster, and stress a window or door frame to the point where it would become difficult to open and close. Worse yet, you might violate building codes.

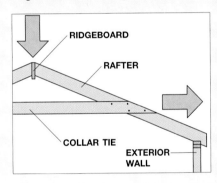

RIDGEBOARD

RAFTER

COLLAR TIE

EXTERIOR WALL

7 Ways to Vent an Attic

1. **Gable-end louvers.** Available in many shapes and styles, screened to keep insects out.

2. **Strip-grille vents.** Long narrow grilles set into soffits.

3. **Plug vents.** Small, circular vents used in the soffits instead of a continuous line of strip grilles.

4. **Perforated soffit vents.** Ventilated panels usually manufactured of aluminum or vinyl.

5. **Ridge vents.** Ideal for attics in which gable cross ventilation is not possible.

6. **Roof turbines.** Designed to improve air flow by turning as warm air rises through the vanes.

7. **Motorized fans.** Normally mounted on an exterior attic wall and used in conjunction with louvers inside the house to draw air up and through the attic.

Strengthening Attic Floor Joists

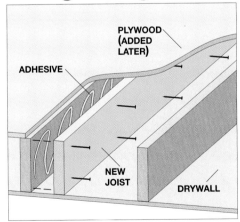

PLYWOOD (ADDED LATER)

ADHESIVE

NEW JOIST

DRYWALL

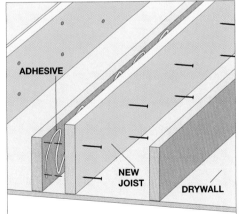

ADHESIVE

NEW JOIST

DRYWALL

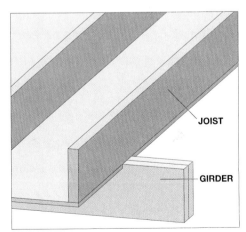

JOIST

GIRDER

Double up joists as needed for additional strength if the existing attic floor is not adequate to carry the live load. Fasten the new joist with adhesive and nails.

Larger joists such as 2x8s and 2x10s can also be glued and screwed to existing joists. The larger boards will decrease headroom, but increase load capacity.

Ceiling joists are supported by beams or girders, usually running along the middle of the house. They may be hidden in the top portion of a load-bearing wall.

unfinished spaces

Finishing a Basement

One of the best bargains you can get is the space gained by converting your basement into habitable space. Homes with full basements already have a floor, walls, and a ceiling, as well as a maze of pipes and wires to supply water and electricity. With these necessities in place, all that is needed is a good plan to turn an unused space into an airy, well-lighted room. Remodeling is often a scaled-down version of doing new construction. Two areas that are critical in remodeling a basement are the concrete floor and masonry walls.

Installing a Floor System

The easiest way to treat concrete floors is with masonry paint. Two coats over a clean, dry floor can make the room much more inviting. If the floor stays dry year-round, a more comfortable solution is carpeting. Even a commercial grade over a foam backing will make the floor softer and warmer; it also absorbs sound that reverberates off hard masonry surfaces.

On floors that are uneven, cracked, or covered with peeling layers of old paint, a sleeper system is often the best solution. Sleepers are treated wood 2x4s laid either flat or on edge on the concrete, usually 16 inches on center in a bed of mastic. A clear waterproof coating over the concrete floor is recommended before installing the sleepers. Rigid insulation is added between the boards, and then a vapor barrier is laid across them. For tile or carpet floor finishes, a ¾-inch plywood subfloor is nailed down. Wood strip flooring may be laid directly over the sleepers, or a second layer of sleepers may be added over the vapor barrier, producing a warm, dry, resilient floor system.

Wall Options

Basement walls are usually unfinished. The simplest alternative is to install a layer of rigid insulation in a mastic bed over the wall and then to nail 1x2 furring strips over this, covered by a layer of wallboard or paneling. Be aware, however, that using masonry nails will create a lot of holes in the wall. Above grade this may not be a problem. But if you have basement walls that don't leak, it makes no sense to puncture them, risking a problem. Nailholes may cause a fault line, inviting stress cracks.

Dancing was the mother of this invention, the Murphy bed. The original Mr. Murphy lived in a small apartment too cluttered to accommodate his afternoon recreation: dancing with his lady friends. Solution? A fold-up bed to make a bigger dance floor.

To avoid this, attach 2x2 furring strips, at 16 inches on center, to a 2x3 sole plate along the floor and a 2x3 top plate along the ceiling. The benefit is that the complete 2x3 frame can be attached to the concrete floor using just a few nails or a bed of construction adhesive, and nailed to the wooden floor joists of the house (the ceiling of the remodeled basement). Individual studs need not be nailed into the masonry wall. Using 2x3s also provides additional room for more insulation than just thin fiberglass batts or rigid polystyrene panels. Cover the assembly with a vapor barrier before applying the new surfacing material. This will keep interior moisture from working through the new wall and condensing on the masonry, where it would come into contact with the frame and the insulation, causing deterioration.

Sealing a Floor

USE: ▶ scrub brush • bucket & sponge mop • pitching chisel or scraper • vacuum cleaner • paintbrush • hand-held sprayer • dust-mist respirator or dust mask

1 *Clean away stains and soiled areas* using a solution of trisodium phosphate or a phosphate-free cleaner.

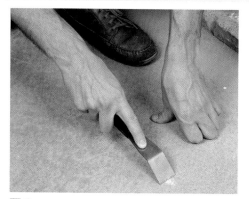

2 *Scrape away rough and uneven spots* in the concrete floor using a pitching chisel or other steel-edged scraping tool.

3 *Vacuum away concrete dust* and other debris in cracks and control joints that could reduce adhesion.

Covering Basement Walls

Masonry paint is an expedient solution for walls, although even a bright color won't disguise the blocks. If the wall was carefully built, a thick coat of masonry paint may just hide the joints, producing a stucco effect. It is more likely that the basement walls were not neatly finished—that's one reason the most common remodeling treatment is nailing furring strips on the wall, covered by a layer of drywall or paneling. The furring strips bridge the little bumps in the wall and the depressions at mortar joints.

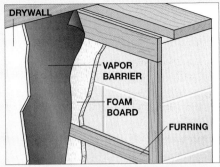

Furring strips can be applied directly onto masonry walls after the walls are painted with waterproofing masonry paint. Nail with 1½-in. masonry nails.

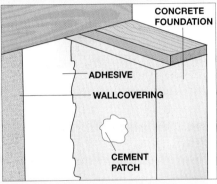

Dry walls can be patched for smoothness and covered with a stiff sisal fiber or fiberglass wallcovering.

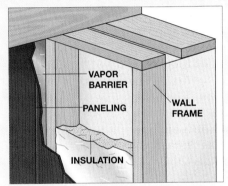

Building 2x4 stud walls is best if you need room to wire for electrical outlets and to insulate your renovated basement.

▶ trisodium phosphate or other cleaner • clear concrete sealer

4 *Using a paintbrush,* coat around the perimeter of the floor with a clear concrete waterproofing sealer.

5 *Spray-apply the sealer* to the remainder of the floor for fast, thorough, and even coverage.

Window Wells

A basement will remain drier if windows are shielded from rain and if drainage is provided by a window well connected to a drainpipe. Waterproof the foundation wall, and then backfill over the drainpipe with gravel.

unfinished spaces

Finishing Touches

Basements usually have a combination of ducts, beams, columns, and pipes that present challenges when it comes to converting the area into living space.

Deciding what kind of ceiling to install in a renovated basement depends in part on the amount of existing headroom you have available, and how many pipes, ducts, and wires cross beneath the joists. One of the best ways to hide all of these is by installing a suspended acoustical tile ceiling.

Suspended ceilings can conceal pipes, ducts, and wiring, yet still leave them accessible. Another advantage is that the ceiling is leveled as you install it—the existing joists need not be level or even straight. A suspended ceiling also makes it easy to install lights: Simply remove an acoustical tile, and replace it with a fluorescent light fixture of the same size.

Concealing a Beam

Concealing a wood beam is a relatively simple task. Concealing a steel beam, on the other hand, is not so easy because fastening material to it is particularly difficult. The proper way to enclose a steel beam is by building a wooden framework around it and then screwing or nailing gypsum wallboard to the framework, enclosing the beam. The beam enclosure can then be finished to match the rest of the room.

Concealing a Duct

Metal ductwork in a house with hot-air heating typically leads from the furnace to every room. If the ductwork reduces headroom, it is possible to move it, but this is a job for a heating and cooling contractor. In an informal space, you can paint ductwork to match the ceiling. Ductwork may also be concealed above a suspended ceiling or boxed into a framed chase covered by drywall or paneling.

Concealing a Column or Post

If a column or post is not ideally placed for your remodeling plans, try revising the plans rather than moving the column. It is often easy to conceal a post within a new partition wall. If not, you can de-emphasize it with a fabric covering, build a bookcase or shelf unit around it, or frame it into a chase (a continuous enclosure) covered with paneling or drywall.

Concealing a Soil Pipe

Typically, the soil stack is the largest pipe in a house. If possible, enclose it within a chase or soffit. To reduce the sound of running water, wrap insulation around the pipe. Be sure to measure carefully along the length of the pipe because it must slope $\frac{1}{8}$- to $\frac{1}{2}$-inch per foot for drainage. If the pipe's cleanout plug will be concealed within an enclosure, build a door for access to the plug.

Boxing In Columns, Beams, Pipes

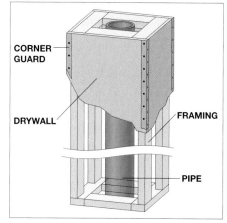

To conceal a column, frame around it using two-by lumber. The frame provides a base for other finishes.

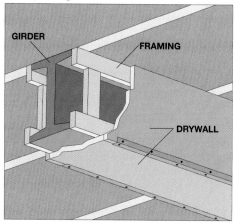

To conceal a steel beam, build and attach a ladder framework to the joists. Cover the framework with drywall or paneling.

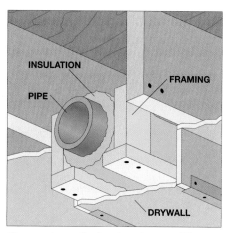

Conceal a soil pipe in a box as if it were a beam. Wrap it in insulation to reduce the sound of running water.

Fixing Water Leaks

USE: ▶ wire brush • vacuum • cold chisel • hammer • trowel ▶ hydraulic cement

1 *Use a wire brush* to remove *loose mortar and dirt from the concrete-block wall; then vacuum the wall to remove dust and debris.*

2 *Chisel out and undercut cracks and small holes to provide a firm anchor for the hydraulic cement. Clean out loose debris.*

3 *Mix hydraulic cement with water, and use a pointing trowel or a jointing tool to apply the cement to the damaged area.*

14 Ways to Eliminate Water

1. Use splash blocks or leader extensions on a functioning gutter system.

2. Grade the area around the house. Grade should drop at least 2½ inches in 10 feet.

3. Repair cracks in masonry walls using hydraulic cement.

4. Seal the space where the house water main and electrical service conduit enter the structure. Use hydraulic cement.

5. Eliminate vegetation close to foundation walls. Plants hold water and reduce evaporation from the soil.

6. Make sure no roof leaks are being carried down to the basement.

7. Keep basement windows closed during rainstorms.

8. Paint concrete floors with two coats of water-locking masonry paint.

9. Insulate pipes and air-conditioning vents to prevent condensation.

10. Install an electric dehumidifier.

11. Install a sump pump to remove water.

12. Hire a contractor to install an interior perimeter drain.

13. Hire a contractor to waterproof the foundation.

14. In extreme cases, hire a contractor to install footing drains around the perimeter of the house, to remove any water that manages to accumulate against the foundation wall.

Sump Pumps

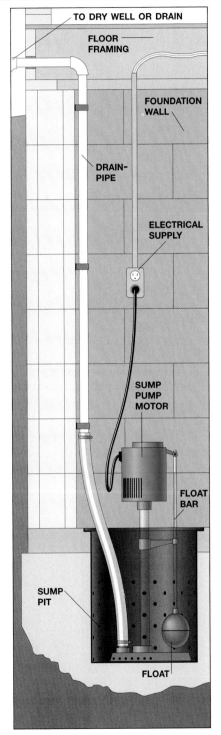

Install a sump pump to keep the basement dry. A check valve will prevent sewer gases from getting in.

unfinished spaces

Converting a Garage

An unused garage is often an ideal place for a home renovation, offering a large space that contains no more than a lally column. What's important is how the garage relates to the rest of the house. If it is off the kitchen, for example, it may be a good place for a family room but not a master bedroom. You may even be able to convert an unattached garage, connecting it to the main house via an enclosed walkway, which itself may become a studio, home office, or child's playroom.

Converting the Floor

Because most garage floors slope toward the garage door opening, you will probably need to level the floor. One way to do this is to pour a new concrete slab over the existing one. If the floor of the house is set slightly higher than the existing garage floor, this may be the easiest and least expensive option.

Another option is to install a sleeper-and-plywood-subfloor system, using shims to create a level surface. Rigid insulation can be placed between the sleepers.

In homes where the garage is one or two steps down from an adjoining area, you may want to build an elevated subfloor. If you choose not to raise the floor of the garage to the height of the adjoining area, you can make the transition a decorative asset by joining the levels with a dramatic stairway. For safety, be sure that the steps are clearly differentiated by using a contrasting material or color on each level, and by providing handrails.

Finishing

In order to make a conversion appear to be an integral part of the original house design, you must finish the outside to look like the rest of the house. If you remove the garage door and enclose the wall, you might consider building a carport over the existing driveway or even tearing out the driveway and landscaping the area to blend in with the rest of the yard.

The first step to enclosing the garage is to remove the existing garage door. You may need to build a concrete knee wall to match the rest of

Installing a Garage Entry Door

USE: ▶ circular saw • hammer • ladder • reciprocating saw (optional) • eye protection ▶ prehung door • door casing • 4-ft. level • 2x4 studs • 2x lumber for header

1 *Frame the rough opening* for a new door in an existing exposed stud wall before cutting the sheathing.

2 *Nail a temporary brace* in the stud wall over the proposed door opening to hold the cripples in place as you cut the studs.

3 *Cut the studs* to make the rough opening for the new door, leaving enough space below the cripples for a new header.

5 *Cut away the existing sill plate,* as well as the sheathing and siding within the new rough opening.

6 *Trim back the siding* to accommodate the exterior casing for the new door, and then test-fit the prehung door assembly.

7 *Run a bead of caulking* around the perimeter of the rough opening; then set the door frame in place and fasten it.

the foundation and to provide support for the new stud wall. This new wall will be a likely place to put a new door or window because a header already exits here. Position the window or door just below the header.

Once you've installed the wall, attach sheathing over the exterior surface, cover it with house wrap or felt paper, and then install siding to match that already on the house. To make a new door opening in one of the existing walls, follow the sequence shown in the photos below.

Before you finish the interior walls, you will want to eliminate any existing moisture problems. You can then use standard methods to finish the walls. Be sure to include electrical outlets, insulation, and a moisture barrier.

Patching & Leveling Floors

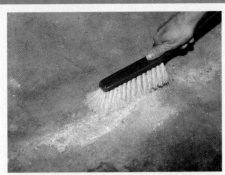

Sweep loose debris and cement dust from the garage floor, and then clean it thoroughly before doing any patchwork.

Dampen cracks, apply a bonding agent, and then trowel patching cement into the crack and smooth it out.

• wood screws or 12d & 16d nails • caulk

4 ***Cut the new header*** for the door, and then nail it in place over the trimmer studs. Toenail the cripples to the header.

8 ***Install the door*** in the frame, and then nail the exterior casing in place. Caulk between the casing and siding.

Interior Finishing System

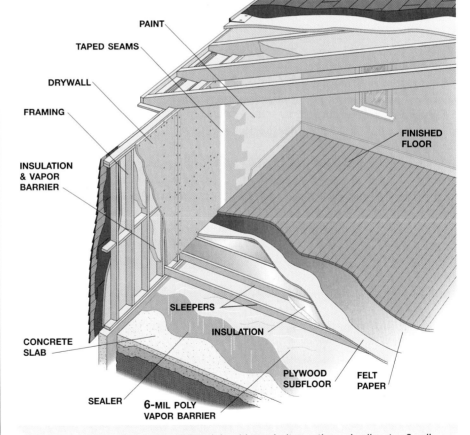

PAINT
TAPED SEAMS
DRYWALL
FRAMING
INSULATION & VAPOR BARRIER
FINISHED FLOOR
SLEEPERS
INSULATION
CONCRETE SLAB
PLYWOOD SUBFLOOR
FELT PAPER
SEALER
6-MIL POLY VAPOR BARRIER

To finish a garage floor, seal the slab with asphalt mastic and roll out a 6-mil polyethylene vapor barrier. Finished wood flooring needs joists or sleepers and a layer of plywood subflooring. Convert open-frame walls by filling the bays with insulation, add a vapor barrier (either foil or plastic), and a layer of ½-in. drywall.

unfinished spaces

Finding More Space

Homeowners with grown children may have the luxury of claiming space that was once a bedroom and converting it into an exercise room, a home office, or the ultimate storage luxury—a walk-in (and walk-around) closet with enough room for bureaus, full-length mirrors, and even a chair so you don't have to balance like a stork to put on your socks.

Yet, even in smaller houses and apartments, you may be able to find more storage space—regardless of whether or not you have a spare room that can be anything you want it to be.

Kitchens

To maximize the use of corner space under kitchen counters—and still be able to get at what's there—store bulk items on multitiered carousels. To better use space in deep but narrow cabinets, install pull-out wire-rack bins.

Many appliance makers offer extensive lines of small appliances and convenience features that can be mounted to the underside of upper kitchen cabinets. These mountings for radios, can openers, recipe and spice racks, coffee makers, and microwave ovens free up counter space. Some companies also offer space-saving larger appliances, such as narrow, 24-inch-wide vertically stacked washers and dryers, which can create additional floor space in your laundry, where it is often badly needed.

Guest Rooms

A time-honored solution for creating a multipurpose room is the Murphy bed. The Murphy Door Bed Co. was founded at the turn of the century by William Murphy, who designed a fold-up bed to gain space in his crowded one-room apartment.

A modern version of the Murphy bed is constructed with a built-in counterbalance mechanism that allows you to tip up the mattress, bedding, and frame into a prefabricated cabinet. Convertible sofas or trundle-bed couches (with a second mattress on a pop-up frame stored beneath the main cushions) are sometimes able to provide twice the bed space within the footprint size of a single bed, allowing more space for furniture. There are even some oversized chairs available that convert into beds, creating even more options.

Closets

Interior shelves in many closets and cabinets are set back and are therefore not as deep as the space behind the door. Even a few inches of such unused space can be reclaimed by mounting one or more ventilated wire-shelving units on the back of the door. (Make sure that the units are a few inches less in width than the door, to allow for closing.)

A split-closet wall can provide a convenient, space-saving plan. Instead of taking dispersed closet space from bedrooms that share a common wall, make the partition wall the depth of a closet, opening half to one room and half to the other. This will reduce noise transmission between the rooms. For even more sound deadening value, insulate the interior closet walls.

Space Savers

A heater/fan-light saves space by combining the comforts of light, warmth, and ventilation.

A lazy Susan rotates inside a corner cabinet, making good use of a difficult-to-reach space.

Garages

The roof framing in garages often includes several cross ties, usually 2x4s or 2x6s, that link the ends of opposing rafters. This platform of framing was probably not designed to support heavy loads, but with a few 1x2s to make a supporting lattice, it's an ideal place to store large but lightweight items such as screens. If you want the space for heavy-duty storage, with a solid floor, you probably will have to install a stronger framework with a ⅝-inch plywood subfloor—roughly similar to the floor framing in a house attic.

Entry Halls

Entry halls, or foyers, may contain a surprising amount of potential storage space. If you have

Kitchen soffits, otherwise empty, can be replaced with high cabinets, useful for storing infrequently used items.

A recessed toe-space heater is especially welcome in a kitchen where available wall space for conventional heating is scarce.

an older home, commonly built with higher ceilings than contemporary homes, you may find several feet of space between the top of an entry door and the ceiling.

Rescue this space by building a platform, 2 to 3 feet deep or more, supported by ledger strips, one on each side wall. In the simplest form, two strips of ¾-inch or larger molding could support a sheet of ½-inch-thick plywood. If you expect to support heavy loads, upgrade the plywood to ¾-inch, and use heavier ledger strips. This construction may be dressed up to simulate a dropped foyer ceiling. Access to the storage is gained through cabinet doors facing the hall. Painted to match the surrounding walls and ceiling, the structure will recede, leaving the entry door as the focus of attention.

In-Wall Hazards

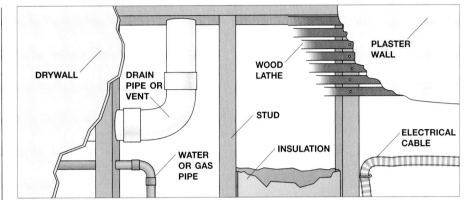

DRYWALL

DRAIN PIPE OR VENT

WOOD LATHE

PLASTER WALL

STUD

ELECTRICAL CABLE

WATER OR GAS PIPE

INSULATION

Do you know what's inside your walls? This illustration shows some of what you might find. Remove drywall or plaster slowly, to avoid hazards or damage.

A Murphy bed can be hidden away into a wall unit. It's a convenient space saver for guest rooms and small apartments.

A pocket door slides between the walls, allowing for furniture to be placed where doors would swing out into the room.

A corner medicine cabinet can make available the use of what would otherwise be wasted space.

A central vacuum system eliminates the need for a free-standing vacuum and helps to remove common allergens from a home.

A pet door in a wall or conventional door can provide your pet with easy passage in time of need, when you don't want to be disturbed, or when you are at work during the day.

An ironing board can fold up onto a door like a Murphy bed, ridding your clothes closets of unnecessary clutter.

unfinished spaces

Concealed Space

Calculating the amount of unused space in a house or apartment is almost as difficult as totaling the interest payments on a 30-year mortgage. The cost of the unused space behind doors, under stairs, and at the back of closets, plus the dead space boxed into kitchen soffits, knee walls, and so on really adds up.

Vanquished parcels of interior real estate may be equal to adding an entire room or moving to a larger apartment, but they can generally ease overcrowding, remove obstacles formed by tight clusters of furniture, even make an unbearably small apartment seem more spacious. And just about everyone can benefit by gaining extra storage space.

Deep Closets

Most clothing hung on hangers is not less than 2 feet wide, yet many closets are only that deep. Roomy closets are luxurious, but they lose their appeal if there is no room for socks and underwear. Without ripping apart walls, you can better use space by resetting the closet pole toward the back of the closet. Gaining even 3 or 4 inches is enough to allow room for wire shelving (plastic-coated steel, like a dish drainer) to be added to the back of the closet door. This narrow shelving is perfect for small items that have a tendency to get lost in bureau drawers. Also consider using coat hooks and small clothes racks on the back of closet doors.

Kitchen Cabinets

Kitchen wall cabinets often do not extend all the way to the ceiling. Because the upper shelves are usually difficult to reach, even with a stepstool, this space is commonly framed into a soffit, covered with wallboard, taped, and then painted. By cutting an opening in the wallboard and adding hinged doors, you can create a substantial storage space for infrequently used items such as turkey platters, large pots and pans, fruit dehydraters, mason jars, and the old toaster your great-grandmother gave you.

Undercounter kitchen cabinets, or base cabinets, sit on a raised framework and project past it to create a kick, or toe, space. Your toes tuck underneath the base cabinets into this space so that you can stand closer to your workspace without leaning. The base may only be only 4 inches high, but the deep, shallow space beneath the base cabinet is a good place to run utilities to other remodeled areas without having to break into the existing stud walls.

It can also be fitted with an electric toe-space heater to warm a chilly kitchen. Electric heat is generally more expensive than heat from a central gas- or oil-fueled furnace, but a toe-space heater may be an economical alternative to new hot-air ducts or hot-water pipes.

The inside face of a cabinet door may also be considered for space-saving devices, such as vinyl-coated wire baskets, cup hooks, towel holders, or even a spice rack.

Eaves

Where dormers will be used to provide light and ventilation for renovated spaces under sloped roofs, there will likely be a lot of dead space created behind the knee walls of the finished room. While not every inch of this triangular space is usable, floor space can be gained by using the space lacking headroom for built-in closets and bureau drawers, leaving more area for living space.

Framing Cavities

You can't use the space within insulation-filled exterior walls for storage, but every interior partition contains a 4-inch deep space that may be used to provide more depth, and therefore more storage capacity, for a built-in fixture such as an extra-deep medicine cabinet.

A large custom cabinet can be recessed into a partition wall near the bathroom lavatory. With a ¾-inch-thick door, it may protrude a couple of inches, yet it might enclose 4- or 5-inch-deep shelves—a medicine chest that actually holds more than tiny medicine bottles. Partition cavities can also free up space, for example, by housing pocket doors that slide into the wall rather than swinging into usable room space. Interior wall spaces can also be used to hide small valuables, such as jewelry, or dangerous articles, such as guns. A painting or a mirror may be readily hung to conceal a shallow, personal storage box or cabinet.

Cabinet Storage

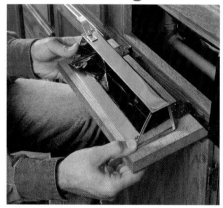

A pull-down false drawer front under a kitchen sink is a handy place to store sponges, steel wool, and scrub brushes.

Roll-out trays are a great back-saving device in base cabinets where easy accessibility to large pots and pans is desirable.

Pull-downs can accommodate anything from appliances to cookbooks, freeing up countertops for clutterless meal preparation.

Underststair Storage

Space beneath a stair is perfect for storing dry goods and other non-flammable household items. For a straight-run stair, consider building a closet or casework under the high side of the stairs, and an access door to a low cabinet on the short side.

Roll-out shelving works well for small-item storage, eliminating the awkward reaching required in a standard cabinet.

The Undiscovered Space

Buried in the maze of joist and studs are many small parcels of unused space. A good eye and a ruler may be the only tools you need to discover hidden space in walls, above closets, beneath stairs, and in many other out of the way places in your house. In older homes, for example, there may be almost a full 4 inches in the wall cavity, enough room for you to recess a large bathroom vanity. In newer houses, high prices per square foot have encouraged builders to use every possible area. And even in locations where some dead space is inevitable—for example, under the eaves of a roof—you can bring some of it back to life by building in bureau drawers and storage closets that free up space in the room.

Crawl Spaces

FLOOR SHEATHING
FELT PAPER
FLOOR FRAMING
FINISHED FLOORING
SILL PLATE
FOUNDATION WALL
BRIDGING
BATT INSULATION
SLAB
6-MIL POLY VAPOR BARRIER
GRAVEL
DRAIN TILE
COMPACTED FILL
FOOTING

Crawl spaces aren't suitable for finishing, but they make a great place for long-term storage. Common problems with a crawl spaces are dampness and limited air circulation. A well-insulated and ventilated space can cut down on moisture.

cabinets & counters

12

cabinets & counters

Cabinetry Basics

Cabinetry projects amount to high-end carpentry—not art exactly, but they tend to be both more complicated and more exacting than other home improvement jobs. After all, it takes a fair amount of skill, and the right tools, to make cabinet drawers that slide effortlessly, doors that swing closed smoothly, and joints between the cabinet's many wood parts that are strong, straight, and tight. Well-crafted cabinetwork can make a room, though, and in kitchens especially, new cabinets and countertops will increase the value of a home.

You can avoid a lot of work by purchasing factory-made cabinets and counters—you just attach the units to the walls and hook up the plumbing and electrical outlets. But whether you go with prefab cabinets or build them yourself, the first step is selecting the materials. On cabinet faces, there is a basic choice between solid wood such as oak and composites such as particleboard covered in plastic laminate.

Counter materials must be resistant to damage from impacts, burning, cutting, and moisture. Granite may be the ideal material, but it's also the most expensive. Modern plastics—both thin laminates and thicker solid forms—are more affordable choices, and by far the most commonly used. Less common are concrete (with many of the positive aspects of granite or marble but without the looks) and solid wood, which makes attractive but high-maintenance countertops.

Special Tools

What tools you'll need for installing cabinets depends upon how you'll be doing it: Cabinets from a kit will require a power drill/driver, clamps, a 4-foot level, and a few other simple tools. If you're making the cabinets yourself, a table saw, router, and electric sander will be indispensible items.

For a custom laminate countertop, you'll also need a saber saw. Laminates should be cut only with very sharp tools. To avoid exposing the dark substrate material under the color surface, countertops and edgings normally are installed with a small overlap and then trimmed using a router equipped with a ball-bearing guide to keep the high-speed bit's friction from scorching the laminate.

Special Tools

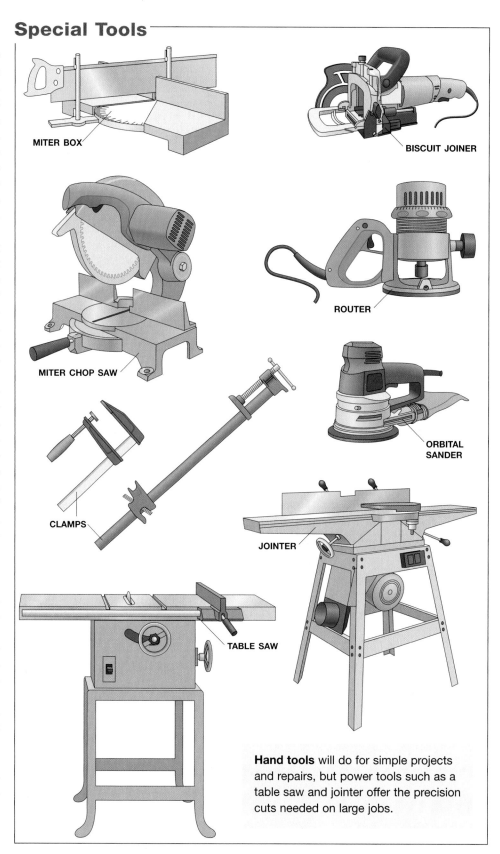

MITER BOX

BISCUIT JOINER

MITER CHOP SAW

ROUTER

ORBITAL SANDER

CLAMPS

JOINTER

TABLE SAW

Hand tools will do for simple projects and repairs, but power tools such as a table saw and jointer offer the precision cuts needed on large jobs.

Table Saw Safety

Turn the saw off when you finish a cut; unplug it before adjusting the blade. Never reach across a moving blade; stand to one side when cutting. Never feed in stock or clear wood scraps freehand; use a push stick and feather boards. Cut knotty or warped wood by hand.

The blade guard is a movable plastic shield that covers the saw blade. Use it whenever you make a through cut—it will keep flying dust and debris out of your face and prevent your hands from accidentally touching the blade.

A feather board is a thin board, the ends of which are cut like a comb. It clamps to a table saw to keep stock under control and moving in one direction. Use one to keep the stock from lifting up and another to keep it against the rip fence.

A push stick has a handle at one end and is notched at the other to fit against the edge of your stock. It should be used to push stock through when cutting, enabling you to keep your hands well away from the blade. If you make one, use solid wood or thin plywood.

Sheet Materials

The easiest way to check whether sheet materials are warped or damaged is to lay them flat on a concrete floor (preferably before you buy them). Remember that these sheets are almost always 4x8 feet—if you don't have a truck or van that can transport them, try to find a lumberyard or home center that will deliver them. (Most will deliver large orders.) Tying them to the roof of your car can be not only nerve-racking but dangerous. Another option may be to have the lumberyard or home center cut the panels for you. Just supply them with your cut list or a set of plans. It's inexpensive, it's great if you don't have a table saw, and you'll be able to fit the stock into a much smaller vehicle.

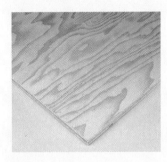

◆ **Plywood**, made from thin layers of wood veneer, is sold in 4x8-foot sheets. It's much cheaper than solid wood and (because of its lightness and flexibility) better suited to cabinetry.

Applications: Construction (softwood) plywood is used to form the carcasses of cabinets and for the undersides of countertops. Thin (1/4-inch) hardwood plywood is used for decorative purposes, much like a veneer— not for frames.

◆ **Particleboard**, waferboard, and oriented-strand board (OSB) are usually cheaper than plywood and are better for making counters than cabinets.

Applications: These boards are often found beneath countertop laminates and furniture veneer. They don't take screws or nails well (tending to split and crumble); it's better to join them with rabbeted joints and glue.

◆ **Hardboard**, also known as fiberboard, is made from wood chips and fibers, held together with phenol-formaldehyde glue.

Applications: Hardboard comes in several types. Standard has one smooth side; prefinished has one painted side. Plastic-laminated has a laminate cemented to one side, making it useful for DIY cabinetmaking.

◆ **Lumber** is used less than manufactured sheet materials as the sole material for cabinets because of the expense. It does, however, make beautiful, extremely sturdy cabinetry.

Applications: Cabinets are often made from a cheap grade of wood covered in veneer: wafer-thin sheets of high-quality hardwood, such as mahogany, walnut, and bird's-eye maple. The solid knotty pine of traditional country cabinets is easy to work with.

cabinets & counters

Cutting & Edging Plywood

USE: ▶ circular saw (with carbide-tipped blade) • straightedge • utility knife ▶ plywood panels • adhesive-backed veneer strip

1 Before you cut plywood with a saw, first score along your cut line with a utility knife to prevent the surface from splintering.

2 When using a power saw, cut plywood with either a carbide-tipped or a fine-toothed plywood-cutting blade.

3 Use adhesive-backed veneer tape (applied with pressure or heat) to cover end grain and create the look of solid wood.

Doweling

USE: ▶ doweling jig • power drill • mallet • bar or pipe clamps ▶ wood dowels • wood glue • glue stick

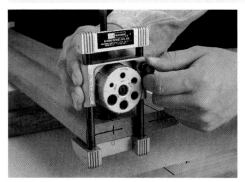

1 To connect edges of panels or boards with dowels, use a doweling jig to bore matching holes in mating edges.

2 Doweling jigs have guide holes in several diameters to guide the right-sized bit into the edge of the board.

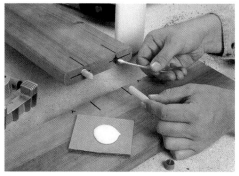

3 Add glue to the dowels, tap them into one set of holes, and then glue the exposed ends and clamp the mating board in place.

Cutting Dadoes

USE: ▶ table saw (optional) • circular saw with rip guide • mallet • wood chisel • C-clamps ▶ wood

1 To cut channels in wood, the best option is a table saw, but you can use a circular saw with a rip guide.

2 Set your blade depth, and adjust the rip guide to cut first along the inner edge, then along the outer edge of the channel.

3 To clear wood from the channel, make several passes with the saw or chisel the scrap. Fasten the board to the worktable.

Making Biscuit Joints

USE: ▶ biscuit joiner • bar or pipe clamps • pencil ▶ biscuits (plate splines) • water-based glue

1 *Biscuit joinery* is the easiest way for DIYers to make professional wood joints. Start by marking centerlines over the joint.

2 *Biscuit cutters* line up with your marks. Adjust the blade depth to cut a groove in the middle of mating edges.

3 *Biscuit wafers* glued in place bridge the clamped joint. The compressed wood wafer expands when glued, so work quickly.

Alternatives for Cutting Rabbets

With a table saw, you can cut dado grooves with a special cutter in one pass or make several passes with a standard blade.

With a circular saw, raise the blade, cut the edge of the dado using a guide, and make repeated passes to clear the groove.

With a router, you can install a bit that's as wide as the groove you need. Test the width on a crosscut before dadoing.

Alternatives for Shaving & Sanding

Electric-powered planers take the effort out of planing boards. You can set the blade for heavy trimming or light smoothing.

The old standard, a hand-powered plane, also will smooth and true up the edge of a board. A sharp blade is essential.

A belt sander also can trim and smooth. Use a coarse-grit belt to remove wood and a fine-grit belt to finish the edge.

cabinets & counters

Cabinet Basics

The basic cabinet component is a carcass—the frame that supports the counter and outlines doors and drawers. These are generally constructed of fir or birch plywood or particleboard, joined together with rabbeted joints and glue. Base cabinets are braced on bottom risers made from 2x4s (which become the toekick).

Doors and drawers fill the carcass openings, and the drawer faces and doors can be built three ways—as overlays (slightly larger than their slots), full overlays (the door and drawer faces nestled against each other), or insets (set flush into the carcass openings).

Designing

If you don't feel comfortable creating your own kitchen layout, there are several options. For an involved project with a big budget, hire an architect or interior designer to draw up your plans. A good contractor can also draft something to your specifications, and he or she will be familiar with local codes. Some home centers provide design services on computers with a CAD program—computer-assisted design software that enables you to play around with different design elements and see realistic pictures of the results.

Stock or Custom?

Stock cabinets are the equivalent of an off-the-rack suit—you won't be getting the highest quality or custom alterations, but you'll save big. The range of frame types is limited, but there are plenty of options available: different styles of doors, sliding shelves, breadboards, wine racks, and the like. Custom-made cabinets, on the other hand, are made to order by a cabinetmaker to fit whatever style and layout you desire. This enables you to have a more unusual design (one to fit an odd layout) or to match your old cabinets or something you see in a magazine. In between these two choices are semicustom cabinets (also known as custom modular), which are mass-produced like stock cabinets but offer more flexibility in terms of materials, layout, and options—you can even alter heights and depths if you want. These cabinets often take longer than both stock and custom cabinets to arrive, though, and must be ordered far in advance.

Cabinet Anatomy

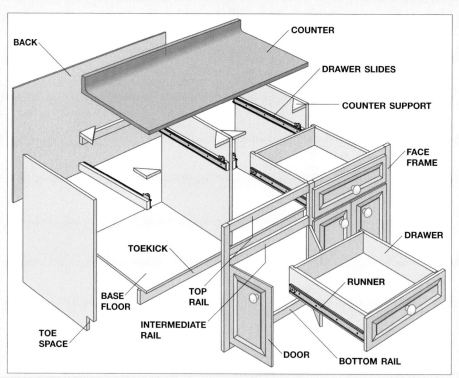

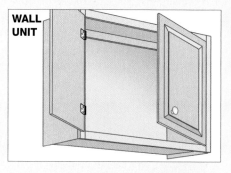

Cabinets are basically empty boxes with interchangeable components. Traditional framed cabinets (shown) have a face frame attached to the front, with doors hinged to this frame and drawer fronts to match. Hardwood is often used for the decorative fronts, while plywood or particleboard is used to construct the boxes.

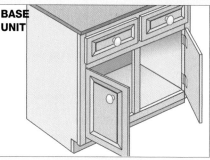

WALL UNIT

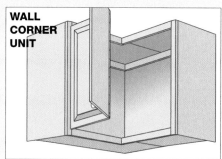

WALL CORNER UNIT

BASE UNIT

DRAWER UNIT

Framed

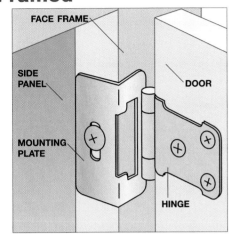

Face-framed base cabinets have a carcass that supports the counter and frames all the openings. The typical way of treating the openings is with overlays: the doors and drawers are larger than the opening. When all the doors and drawers are closed, thin strips of the carcass are visible. This lends itself to contrasting colors or wood tones and decorative hinges. Door and drawer panels also can be set into the openings of the face frame, creating one flush surface.

Frameless

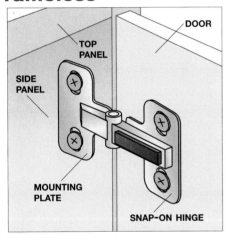

Frameless cabinets (sometimes called "European") are basic boxes that have no face frames—the frames are covered by the doors and drawers. These more expensive, less durable units call for inside hinges (with holes measured in millimeters instead of inches) that can be finicky to adjust and keep aligned. On the plus side, doors can open a full 180 degrees, and overall access is better because there are no face frames in the way, only the walls between sections.

Modular

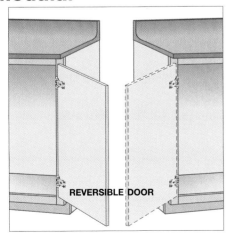

Modular cabinets come in independent units, finished on both sides, that you can fit into your kitchen layout in a number of ways. Of all the types, they're the simplest to install. They can stand alone for use as a vanity or be placed at a counter end without requiring you to order finished sides. They also may be ganged in a continuous lineup by screwing them together through their vertical face stiles. Installers often hide the screwheads beneath the hinge leafs.

cabinets & counters

Preparing Surfaces

Before installing cabinets, make sure the walls are plumb and level. Ideally, you should use a long (more than 4-foot) level. You can also check walls with string and blocks. Cut three blocks of wood to the same width. Nail two of them at the same level on opposite ends of the wall, drive nails partially into them, and run a taut string between the nails flush with the top of the blocks. When you run the third block along the wall under the string, the string will bow out at high spots and gap at low spots. High spots can be shaved down with a rasp or 80-grit sandpaper; low spots should be filled with joint compound applied flush with the rest of the wall. Sand these patches down when dry.

Wall Preparation

USE: ▶ spirit level or straightedge • stud finder • power drill/driver (optional) • measuring tape • pencil

1 *Use a level or straightedge to find low spots on the wall, mark them with a pencil, and fill them flush with joint compound.*

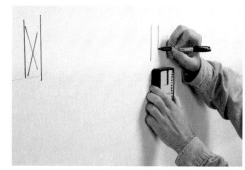

2 *An electronic stud finder can locate the framing members behind the wall. It's wise to drive a nail or two to verify stud location.*

Installing Wall Cabinets

USE: ▶ spirit level • power drill/driver (optional) • handscrew clamps • stepladder • screwdriver • rubber mallet • utility knife • pencil ▶ wall cabinets • filler strips

1 *A glass-door corner cabinet anchors this installation of uppers. Even with the doors off, you may need a helper.*

2 *Plumb the first cabinet carefully (shimming where necessary) so adjoining sections will fit closely and run level.*

3 *Secure the cabinet with screws driven through backing strips (generally at the top and bottom of the cabinet) into wall studs.*

Installing Base Cabinets

USE: ▶ power drill/driver with hole saw or saber saw • handscrew clamps • rubber mallet • spirit level • utility knife • pencil ▶ base cabinets • filler strips • shims

1 *You may need to install a ledger to support the counter, for example, where rounded corner units hold storage carousels.*

2 *Before setting the lower cabinets, use a hole saw (or saber saw) to make access holes for plumbing supply and waste lines.*

3 *Check the base units for square against the wall and each other. The corner cabinet (right) holds revolving storage trays.*

• screwdriver ▶ 1x2 support ledgers • wood screws • joint compound

3 *Locate the highest point on the floor* where you will install the cabinets; this is the base where all measurements originate.

4 *Measure up from the high spot* for the countertop height and down from the ceiling low point to locate the uppers.

5 *Use a 4-ft. level* to install a 1x2 ledger that will help to support the upper cabinets during the installation.

• 1x2 support ledgers • trim • wood screws • shims • stain (to match trim to cabinets)

4 *Set the next cabinet in line* on the support ledger, and clamp its top and bottom to the corner cabinet.

5 *Check each adjoining cabinet* for plumb, clamp it, and drive screws through the reinforced back panel.

5 *Use a power drill* to drill holes for the hardware; if they are predrilled, you just tighten the knobs with a screwdriver.

• 1x2 support ledgers • side trim • toespace trim • wood screws • stain (to match trim to cabinets)

4 *On some installations,* you need to shim the spaces between units. A clamp keeps the face trim joint tight.

5 *Use a level* to maintain uniform support for the counter. Fasten the cabinet with screws through the reinforced back frame.

5 *Glue and nail* long pieces of trim that match the cabinet finish along the toe-space under the lower cabinets.

cabinets & counters

Cabinet Doors

At first glance, making a cabinet door seems like a pretty simple project, but there is more to it than just cutting a slab of wood to fit over the opening. You have to choose hinges, latches, and handles, and determine how the door will fit over—or into—the opening. Then there is the design of the door itself, the materials you will use to make it, and the job of aligning and attaching it all.

Some other larger concerns include planning the layout. Just how will doors swing out from the cabinets, and can any drawers located over them be pulled out when the doors are open? Strength is a factor too, because a door is supported at only two points (the hinges). You have to be sure that both the hinge and the material used to make the door will stand up to the weight of the open door.

Door Construction

Most cabinet doors are not made of a single, solid piece of wood because even slight warping would make closing them almost impossible. (Overlap doors are a little more forgiving than inset types, which will still close but will leave gaps.) Plywood covered with veneer offers more stability than solid wood because it does not warp as easily.

Safety latches on lower cabinet doors will keep contents out of the hands of curious toddlers.

Most high-quality cabinets have doors that are built up from frames and panels. These doors have wooden frames (made from ¾ or one-by stock) with an inside panel of wood, sheet material, or glass.

When they are made correctly, the frames' joints are extremely strong and stable, and the door will stay square. Because the panels are not glued firmly in place but are fitted into grooves, they are free to expand and contract within the frame without affecting how the door sits in its opening. If you can make sturdy joints (using mortises and tenons, dowels, or biscuit joints), you can make a simple frame-and-panel door.

Latches

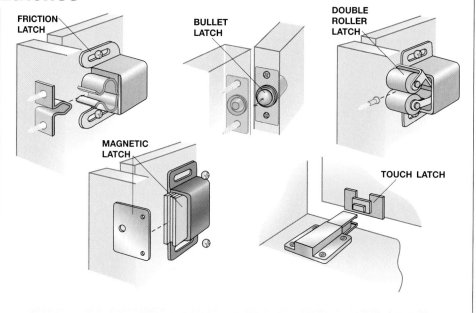

All cabinet latches hold doors closed, but each has a particular advantage. Roller and friction latches are spring-loaded and strong, bullet latches can be inset into narrow edges, and touch latches release when the door is pushed.

Raised-Panel Doors

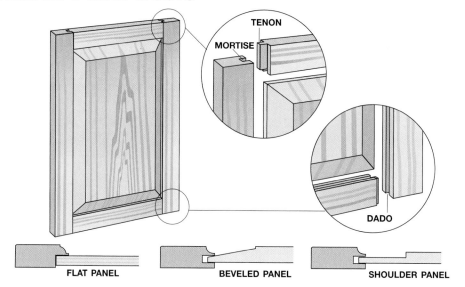

True raised-panel doors have a single panel that floats unglued within a framework. The construction allows it to expand and contract with changes in humidity. **Flat-panel doors** (left) are easier to build but often not as durable.

Flush Doors

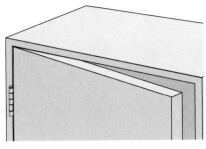

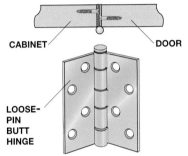

CABINET — DOOR

LOOSE-PIN BUTT HINGE

Butt or leaf hinges are used for flush-fit cabinet doors. Each leaf requires a mortise cut into the frame and door edge.

Flush (or inset) doors are easy to make—they are simple rectangles cut to fit into openings in the cabinet frame. The door faces are flush with the frame surface.

◆ **Style:** In a small kitchen, flush doors help the cabinets appear to recede, while heavy or elaborate surface trim carves up the facade and makes them stand out. But flush doors have drawbacks: misalignment is most noticeable, and light-colored cabinet faces are interrupted by dark joint lines.

◆ **Durability:** Even gradual shifting or slight warping can make a flush door catch on the frame. There is no overlap or margin for error as there is with overlap doors.

Overlap Doors

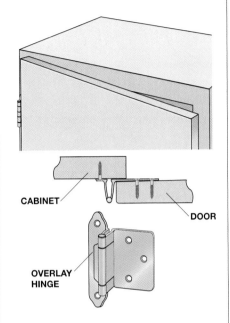

CABINET

DOOR

OVERLAY HINGE

Overlay or surface mount hinges are used for overlap doors. Because the door is not inset, these are the easiest hinges to adjust.

Overlap doors are cut slightly larger than their openings, and they sit on top of the cabinet frame. The overlap takes care of misaligned seams—the seams are all concealed by the doors. But the face frames still show and will need to be finished to match the doors.

◆ **Style:** The door panels—particularly their edges—as well as the hinges, become prominent in this style. If you use plywood or another composite material, you'll have to conceal a lot of rough edge grain with paint or veneer tape.

◆ **Durability:** Problems with the doors are simple to fix: just adjust the hinges or, if necessary, replace them.

Lip Doors

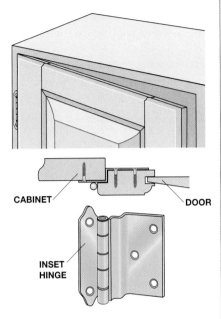

CABINET — DOOR

INSET HINGE

Inset hinges are shaped to fit around a rabbeted edge and are used to hang lip doors. You see only a small slice of the hardware.

Lip doors might be the best compromise among these three styles. With these, half the door thickness sits inside the cabinet opening, and half overlays the cabinet frame. When the exposed edges of solid wood doors are rounded over, the panels blend into the frame. One side of the hinge, a decorative leaf, is exposed on the frame. The other leaf, a wider support, is concealed on the back of the door.

◆ **Style:** These doors look more elegant because they integrate with the face frames.

◆ **Durability:** Lip hinges are easy to install. Both sides of the hinge are surface-mounted, so there is no drilling or chiseling mortises.

cabinets & counters

Drawer Basics

It's easy to tell a well-made drawer from a cheap one. Sturdy drawers are made from solid wood using dovetails, and have full-extension, under-mounted metal guides with ball bearings. Cheaper drawers are made from laminated particleboard, are nailed or epoxied together, and have plastic guides. Drawers for custom-made cabinets are not constructed until after the carcass is built, to ensure a perfect fit.

The best drawer joints are dovetails and other similar joints, which would hold together firmly even without nails (or, worse yet, staples). They make what are called mechanical connections. Next best are connections with a structural bridge from one board to another: for example, doweled joints, or the more modern equivalent, biscuit joints, in which a small wafer is glued into slots aligned in both boards. Simple butt or lap joints won't hold up under repeated use. Joints like these are often rein-

This 1940s-vintage kitchen-of-the-future may not look that different from many kitchens today—except there is no microwave, no dishwasher, and no trash compactor. And that futuristic linoleum that covers the floor is also used on the curvaceous island countertop.

forced with nails or staples, which can eventually work loose. Mechanical connections might not even come apart if you try and force them. (See Chapter 14, pp. 264-65, for more about wood joints.)

Types of Drawers

As with cabinet doors, there are three basic types of drawers: flush, overlap, and lip. Flush drawers have faces that fit into their openings flush with the cabinet's carcass. These drawers require the most precise cuts to fit properly, and even a little swelling can make them stick. Both overlap and lip drawers allow more room for error because part or all of the drawer face covers the surrounding cabinet frame.

Drawer options include pull-out platforms for stacking large items like pots and pans, false drawer fronts that hold slide-out cutting boards, and vertical drawers custom-made to fit into an unusual space—these are great for storing narrow items such as cutting boards and trays.

Installing Metal Guides

USE: ▶ measuring tape • power drill/driver

1 *Modernize older cabinets* by installing metal drawer rollers. Most require a sturdy side rail that fits flush with the face frame.

Cutting Dovetails

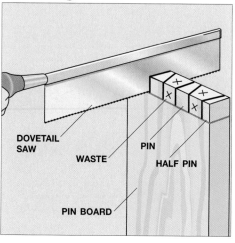

DOVETAIL SAW
WASTE
PIN
HALF PIN
PIN BOARD

Drawer Anatomy

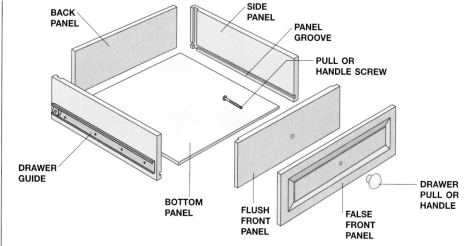

BACK PANEL
SIDE PANEL
PANEL GROOVE
PULL OR HANDLE SCREW
DRAWER GUIDE
BOTTOM PANEL
FLUSH FRONT PANEL
FALSE FRONT PANEL
DRAWER PULL OR HANDLE

Installing Wood Guides

USE: ▶ router • backsaw • miter box • screwdriver

1 *When older wooden drawer glides* wear out, make new ones with a runner strip fastened to a side rail.

(optional) • torpedo level • pencil • screwdriver ▶ drawer • slide hardware • 1x3 or 1x4 side rails • wood screws

2 Mark a level line on the side rail; then use the track as a template to mark screw holes. Drill pilot holes, and attach the guide.

3 Measure depth on drawer sides of the guide placement on side rails; then install mating roller guides on the drawer sides.

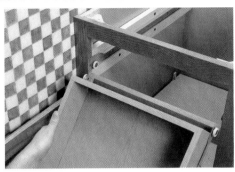

4 Before installing all mounting screws, test-fit the drawer. Tip the drawer into the opening to connect the guide rails.

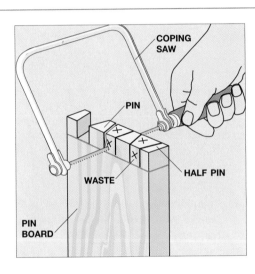

Dovetails are the best joint to use for drawers because they can take a lot of stress in many directions. Each joint has two pieces: The leg piece is cut into keystone-shaped pins, which fit into sockets that are cut into the tail piece. Careful layout and cutting are necessary for a perfect fit that doesn't jam or gap. Mark the layout of the pin piece with a T-bevel set at an angle of 75–80 degrees (use more of an angle for softwoods than hardwoods). The wider part of the pins should be toward the back side. First

make the marks on the end of the piece: three dovetails is typical, and their width is an aesthetic choice. Then lay out their height (the same as the thickness of the wood or slightly larger). Make the vertical cuts for the pins with a dovetail saw (pictured at far left), and then make the horizontal cuts with a coping saw (left). Use this piece as a template to mark the tail. Clean the cuts with a chisel, and test-fit them before you glue and assemble. You can buy special jigs for cutting pins and tails at the same time with a router.

• power drill/driver (optional) • torpedo level ▶ 1x3 or 1x4 side rails • 1x1 wooden runners

2 Install side rails with runner ends flush with drawer opening. Once past the runner, of course, the drawer has no support.

3 Measure and rout new drawer sides to the same dimension as side-rail runners. Rout to final depth in successive passes.

4 Test-fit drawer in the opening. Runners should fit easily in routed grooves. Rub runners with paraffin to smooth operation.

cabinets & counters

Countertop Materials

If there is one place to splurge in kitchens, it's on the counters. The ultimate splurge is granite, the most expensive material available—maybe four or five times more costly than plastic laminates. It's very strong and dense, and resists almost all staining, burns, and scratches from cutting. The entire counter becomes an excellent chopping block and hot plate. Granite is much more durable than marble, another pricey choice. Most grades of marble stain easily, yellow over time, and are a pain to keep clean day by day. Stone countertops also need a strong base to support their weight.

A new group of materials, synthetic solids, may be the next-most expensive and desirable. Seams and joints are epoxy-welded and almost invisible—even backsplashes can be incorporated into what looks like a single, sculptural unit. Synthetic solids also can be routed to create a smooth and safe rounded edge, instead of the typical hard edge of plastic laminate.

Plastic laminates, available in a huge number of colors and finishes, are a popular choice because they are durable, reasonably stain resistant, and relatively inexpensive. The most common problems are chipping and, even more so, burns from a carelessly placed pot. Burns are impossible to repair. Post-form countertops have the laminate preglued to a particleboard platform, complete with backsplash and a curved, front edge. They save you a lot of finishing work, but they might not fit every design; if not, you'll need to make your own countertop and glue the laminate yourself.

Installing Post-Form Counters

USE: ▶ saber saw • straightedge • power drill ▶ wood glue • caulk • drywall screws • veneer strip

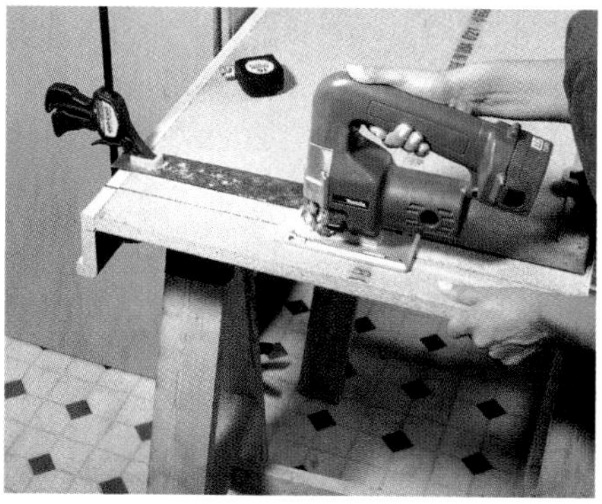

1 ***Use a saber saw*** *to cut the countertop to length; a framing square clamped to the counter can act as a guide.*

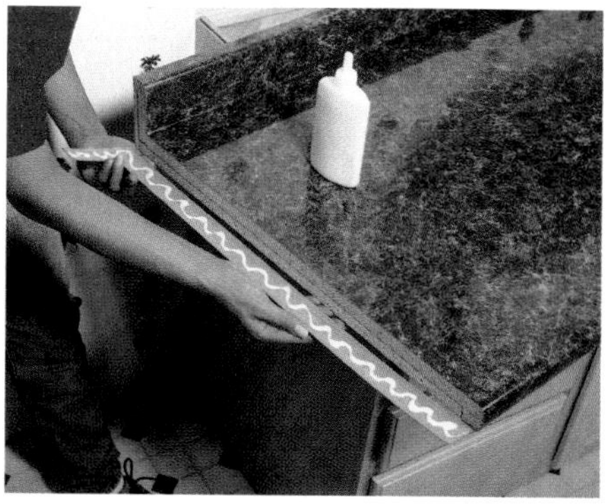

2 ***Exposed ends*** *are covered with end-cap pieces. If they don't have an adhesive, attach them with wood glue.*

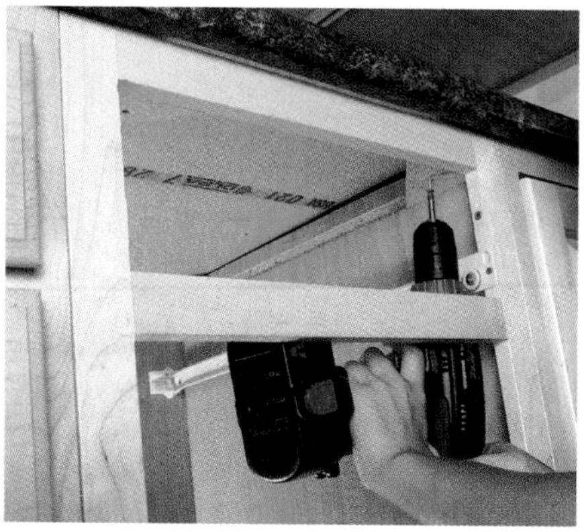

3 ***Position the counter*** *tightly against the wall, and attach it to the cabinets from underneath with drywall screws.*

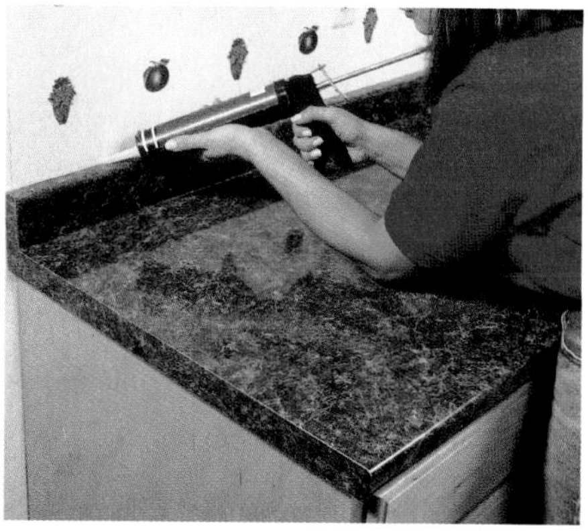

4 ***Apply a bead of silicone caulk*** *in the joint between wall and backsplash and between any joints in the countertop.*

Installing Sinks

USE: ▶ power drill/driver • keyhole saw or saber saw • screwdriver • caulking gun ▶ sink clips and screws • caulk • wood bracing and blocking

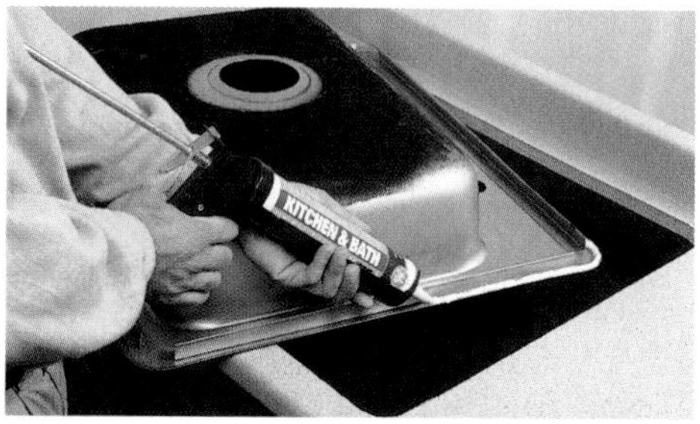

1 ***Before setting a self-rimming sink,*** *turn it upside-down, and apply a thick bead of waterproof caulk under the lip.*

Once the plumbing is roughed in and the counter is ready, you can install the sink. Your choices range from cast iron to stainless or enameled steel. (Be sure to get at least 20-gauge.) Counter-mounted sinks are either frameless/self-rimming (which just need to be fastened down) or framed/rimmed (which require a strip to seal them to the counter). Install the faucets and drain before you install the sink.

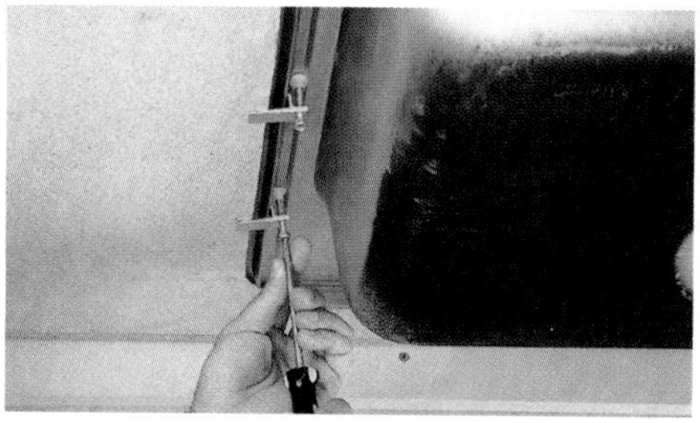

2 ***Center the sink*** *in the countertop opening, set L-shaped sink clips into the perimeter groove, and tighten the screws.*

Laminate

Laminate is the material to use if you're doing the job yourself, and even so it's tricky. The sticking point—literally—is contact cement. This glue is applied to mating surfaces, and when they make a firm connection, they are permanently attached. There is no maneuvering room the way there is with most glues.

Another difficulty with laminate is its hardness. You need this durability on counters, but the brittle sheets chip unless cut with very sharp tools. To avoid exposing the dark substrate material under the color surface, countertops and edgings normally are installed with a small overlap, and then trimmed to a fine joint with a router. But if your bit does not have a ball-bearing guide, friction from the high-speed rotation is likely to scorch the edge. And if you push the router fast enough to avoid scorching, the joint is likely to chip: it takes practice.

The two main advantages to laminates are price (starting at about $1.25 a square foot for $\frac{1}{16}$-inch-thick counter material; $15 to $25 per linear foot installed) and color variation. There are hundreds of options, including different patterns and textures. Color-through laminates cost more but eliminate dark seams. They still chip if you drop a heavy pot, but the damage isn't as noticeable.

Plastic laminate has good resistance to staining, moisture, and abrasion, but a pan hot off the burner will leave a scorch mark that is usually impossible to patch. Also, repeated knife cuts, though small and shallow, eventually discolor and create a cloudy area.

CAUTION

▶ **Contact cement** should be used in a well-ventilated area. Exposure to its fumes can cause irritation to your nose, throat, and lungs, and fumes will explode if ignited. It will also irritate your skin if not washed off with soap and water. Wear eye protection and rubber gloves when handling contact cement. Local codes may require latex-based, VOC-compliant cement.

Installing Laminate

USE: ▶ router • roller • clamps • utility knife • straightedge • paintbrush ▶ lattice • contact cement

1 Trim laminate to size by scoring the rigid material with a utility knife or a special laminate scoring tool.

2 Clamp a straightedge just beyond your score line. Work on a sound, flat surface, and snap off the excess.

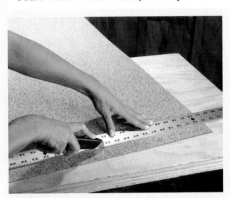

3 Read adhesive label cautions (and check the safety tips below) before rolling on sheets or brushing on edging.

4 Position the edge strip over the double-thick plywood counter edge, and roll the strip firmly to get good adhesion.

5 Set thin lattice strips over the counter while you position the main sheet. Remove the strips in sequence.

6 Use a router to trim laminate edge joints. Use a beveled bit with a ball-bearing guide wheel to avoid scorching.

cabinets & counters

Solid Facts

Solid surfacing for countertops is the same through its full thickness—a blend of resins with mineral fillers. There are more colors and patterns than when it was first introduced, but the selection is still limited. It can be worked like wood; the edges can be molded into elaborate details, and you can make minor repairs by sanding and buffing. Larger gouges can be fixed by bonding in new material—at least on truly solid sheets. So-called solid-surface veneer costs less and has a similar seamless appearance, but does not offer the same, full-thickness advantages. The downside to all solid surfacing is price (installed quotes of $50–$75 and higher per linear foot) and difficulty: creating a multisection counter with invisible seams the first time out is unlikely.

Ceramic tile counters are not just extremely durable—it's no simple thing to smash one of them—but are just as resistant to staining and burning as granite. Unlike granite, tiles are also available in numerous colors and styles. But while the tiles provide durability, all that grout in between them can be trouble. Water discolors grout and can eventually drain through to the base, causing delamination. (The only alternative is to painstakingly paint the grout lines with silicone.) It's also a challenge to get an evenly spaced layout on splashboard, counter, and rounded facing, particularly on wrap-arounds. The cabinet carpentry must be extremely rigid for best results and strong enough to hold up tiles embedded in adhesive over exterior-grade or marine plywood.

Solid Surfacing

Many consumers will recognize this material by one of the best-known brand names, Corian. Unlike plastic laminate, a thin layer that rests on a plywood or particleboard countertop, solid surfacing is one material throughout. Generally, it is installed by contractors who custom-fit counters to your cabinets. Sections can be fastened together with nearly invisible seams, even over wide corner units where sheets of laminate would create a noticeable joint. Also, where solid surfacing is cut or edged—for example, at a sink—the exposed edge needs no extra finishing.

Solid-surface countertops need no edging and show no seams—but you can install decorative inlays and trim.

Installing Tile

USE: ▶ power drill/driver or screwdriver • tile

1 *Typical ¾-in. plywood counters* are reinforced with a second layer to create a 1½-in.-thick edge.

5 *Mark layout lines* for the field tiles, and work one small area at a time, embedding the tiles in adhesive.

Solid Wood

A maple butcher-block countertop is beautiful, but will it last? In its original application—as an actual butcher's block—knife scars were periodically removed by cutting a slice off the thick block. That's impractical on kitchen counters, where the wood will scratch and eventually stain even when sealed with a penetrating oil. Hard-surfaced clear sealers will chip, and pieces can be picked up in food preparation.

Materials

◆ **What you'll need.** You'll need at least a full inch-thick base for the butcher block to withstand typical kitchen chores. Edges can be glued up and routed for decorative overhangs. Special FDA-approved, non-toxic finishing oils are also available.

◆ **Estimating.** Butcher block is sold in 18-, 24-, and 36-inch widths, and in custom sizes.

cutter • tile nippers • notched trowel • rubber float • sponge & bucket • spacing lugs ▶ ceramic tile • thinset adhesive • grout mix

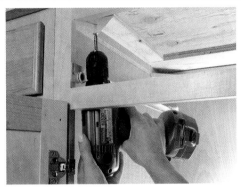

2 *Most cabinets* are sold with triangular brackets at the corners. Mount the counter by screwing up through the brackets.

3 *Make a dry layout* to square up tiles on the counter and plan the installation. Use spacers to allow for grout joints.

4 *Use a notched trowel* or a plastic spreader that leaves ribs of adhesive according to manufacturer's directions.

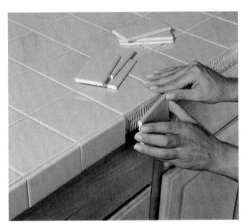

6 *To eliminate a hard corner,* tiles used for counter edging can have a rounded-over top called a bullnose.

7 *To grout tile joints,* spread the soupy grout mix over the entire surface, working mainly at a diagonal to the seams.

8 *When grout hardens,* use a clean, damp sponge to remove the grout haze. You will need to make several passes.

Masonry

Solid masonry counters are among the easiest to clean, the most durable, the most elegant—and the most expensive. Many types of stone can be used, including marble, which requires more maintenance than most, and granite, which resists scratches, heat, and most stains. A contractor can install a jointless, wraparound counter made of concrete. Lower cabinet frames often need to be reinforced to carry the load.

Materials

◆ **What you'll need.** Most stone countertops are ordered and delivered completely finished. Sink cutouts are made with a special blade and a wet saw. For concrete counters, check with local tile or kitchen-cabinet suppliers.

◆ **Estimating.** Precise measurements are required to fabricate masonry counters. Price varies widely by the size, shape, and type of material.

cabinets & counters

Protecting the Wood

Dirt, grease, oils, and even food would quickly stain wood cabinets and counters not protected by some sort of finish. The most basic finishes have only one ingredient. Linseed oil, for instance, adds tone and protects wood at the same time. Other finishes call for several ingredients—for example, a sealer to close the wood grain, stain to add color, and a protective top coating such as varnish.

Types of Finishes

Fast-drying finishes are the most convenient, combining a small amount of solids (the actual coating) and a large amount of thinner. When the thinner evaporates, solids are left in place to protect the wood. But brush strokes may set in the surface as it dries, and lap marks will show if the wet edge dries during application. This is most troublesome on a large surface. You have to move quickly to pick up the wet edge. Fast-drying films are also relatively thin because they have a small proportion of solids.

Slow-drying finishes, such as boiled linseed oil, have more solids and less thinner. These dry to tackiness when they evaporate, and the remaining film hardens gradually—6 to 12 hours is generally needed before the surface can withstand contact without marring. The hardening continues for a much longer period, from a day to a week, depending on the finish.

Finishes on surfaces used for food preparation should be lead-free and free of other metals, such as cobalt or manganese salts, which are used as drying agents.

Finishes

◆ **Sanding sealers** and wood conditioners are applied to wood with large pores (such as pine) before finishing to make stains look even; sometimes sanding sealers are applied to help smooth out rough surfaces. A sealer may also be applied after staining to prevent it from bleeding into the finish. Shellac and oil varnish are common sealers; there's also lacquer sanding sealer, which is used before lacquering.

◆ **Wood stains** add transparent color to wood and bring out subtle grain patterns. Stains contain pigment, a solvent (oil- or water-based), and a binder. Pigmented stains are more opaque and useful for disguising inferior stock. Aniline dyes are sometimes used to impart rich, if artificial, colors—these dyes are more translucent and generally reflect the natural color of the wood.

◆ **Gel stains,** thicker and easier to use than regular wood stains, come in oil-based pigmented and water-based dye formulations. Because of their consistency, they're quite easy to handle and apply without the drips and lap marks of regular stains. The consistency makes them particularly useful if you're refinishing cabinets that are already on the wall.

◆ **Polyurethane,** a synthetic varnish made from plastic resins, provides a clear, hard finish more resistant to yellowing than oil varnishes. Polyurethane dries quickly and is tough enough for floors. Both oil- and water-based varieties are fast-drying, resistant to moisture and heat, and easy to apply. They come in varying glosses, or sheens.

Before Painting

Fill all nicks, depressions, or holes with putty. Cabinet manufacturers sell color-matching putty and paint for touchups.

Before painting, take off doors, drawers, and hardware; wash everything with a mild detergent. Use a liquid deglosser on varnished cabinets to dull the shine. Scrape loose paint off painted cabinets, and sand with 180-grit sandpaper—painted hardware can be soaked in paint remover. Holes should be filled with putty and sanded flush. Prime bare wood before painting.

If you're covering the cabinets with opaque paint, sand filler with 220-grit sandpaper so marks won't show through.

Sanding

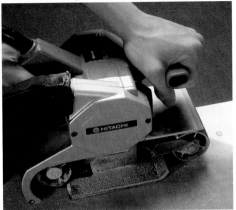

To remove paint traces or surface scars, *use a belt sander with progressively finer grit papers. Don't bear down on veneers.*

A powered pad or orbital sander *will do a good job of finish-sanding large areas without showing directional traces.*

Finish up by hand-sanding *in corners and around intricate detail molding. Start with 80-grit and work up to 220-grit paper.*

Finishing

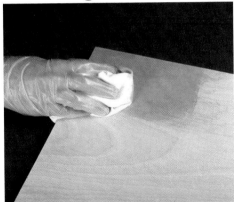

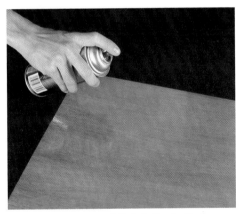

For better control of color absorption, *especially on softwoods, apply stain with a soft, lint-free cloth, and rub it into the wood.*

Use a quality natural-bristle brush *or a foam pad to apply polyurethane finishes. Smooth out brush marks as you work.*

If you use a natural finish *like boiled linseed or tung oil, you can build up shine and keep wood clean with lemon-oil polish.*

Tools

You can finish and refinish most wood surfaces with a simple hand brush, but there are some exceptions, such as a lacquer finish, that must be applied with a sprayer—a brush leaves lap marks. Among many sanding tools that speed up the job, the array of new detail sanders have triangular heads that can dig into corners. One of the most important tools is a tack rag—to make sure the surface is completely clean.

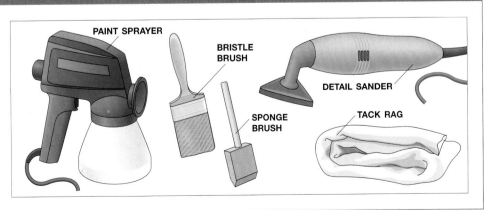

PAINT SPRAYER

BRISTLE BRUSH

DETAIL SANDER

SPONGE BRUSH

TACK RAG

cabinets & counters

Rejuvenating Cabinets

In many kitchens, you'll tire of the appearance of your cabinets long before they wear out. Rather than replace them completely, you can resurface them and make them appear new. The idea is to apply a combination of cabinet doors, drawer fronts, and thin veneers over the visible parts of the old cabinets. You'll need to be familiar with basic woodworking techniques, particularly if you buy stock sizes of solid woods and veneers and custom-cut and fit each piece in place. An alternative is to hire one of the growing number of kitchen cabinet resurfacing firms.

Using a Resurfacing Kit

A resurfacing project can be handled as a considerably less challenging DIY job if you use a kitchen cabinet resurfacing kit. The step-by-step sequence using a kit may vary somewhat from the usual custom resurfacing job. But the basic approach and process is usually the same. If your kitchen is similar to the typical American kitchen (which, according to one resurfacing company, has 15 cabinet doors and 11 drawer fronts), resurfacing with a kit should take from 16 to 24 hours and save up to 70% of the cost of installing all new cabinets. The kits, which you assemble from parts, come in a variety of door sizes and raised panel designs and cost about $600 for an average kitchen.

The overall job can be divided into three basic parts: replacing cabinet doors, adding veneer, and replacing drawer fronts. In brief, here's the sequence for changing laminated particleboard cabinets into oak cabinets: remove all the old cabinet doors and hardware; match the new door fronts to the cabinet openings (or add framing strips to decrease the size of the openings); apply self-sticking wood veneer over the visible frame edges and exposed side panels; then stain, seal, and finish the ¾-inch-thick, solid oak door fronts and oak veneers to suit.

Follow a similar sequence on the drawer fronts: first remove the drawers and hardware; cut the existing drawer fronts flush with the top, bottom, and sides of the drawers; glue, screw, and clamp the new, solid oak fronts over the cut-down drawers; then finish to suit and attach new hardware.

Before...

...and after

Resurfacing systems (available from contractors and in kit form) *save money on a kitchen remodel by saving the underlying cabinet structure and replacing door and drawer fronts.*

Retrimming Bases

USE: ▶ hammer • pry bar • backsaw • wood rasp • coping saw • nail set ▶ nails • wood putty

1 *Use a small pry bar* (or chisel) to pry off old rubber molding. Once an edge is free, pull the strip as you pry.

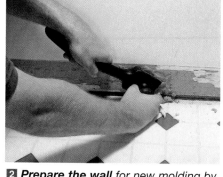

2 *Prepare the wall* for new molding by scraping away old adhesive. Don't use a chemical softener or remover.

3 *Nail new wood molding* into wall studs with finishing nails. Set the nail-heads, and fill holes with putty.

4 *You can use one-piece molding* with a decorative top bead, or build up the base with quarter-round moldings.

Refacing Cabinets

A kitchen resurfacing job can be a major overhaul where every visible piece of wood, including narrow door and drawer edges, is recovered. Sometimes new door and drawer fronts will do. But even a full facelift is easier to manage and less costly than a new set of cabinets. The idea is to save sturdy cabinet frames and clad them in a new skin, which can be a colorful plastic laminate or a light-toned natural wood. The job can include new counters, drawer fronts and drawer liners, trim, hardware, and other details. Here are some of the highlights.

Many older kitchens have solid, well built cabinet frames but a dated or dingy appearance that is ripe for resurfacing.

Once the doors, drawers, and hardware are removed, every visible edge of the frame can be covered with laminate.

Drawer liner kits like this one cover the old bottom and sides with a thin, non-slip, easy-to-clean laminate.

With a new liner installed, you can forget about liner paper or contact paper that inevitablly starts to curl and peel.

New door and drawer fronts generally are available in different woods and laminates with a variety of panel designs.

Finishing Touches

Cover rough plywood edges with self-stick veneer, applied with moderate heat that activates the glue, and pressure.

Resurfacing contractors can replace or conceal every old section of your cabinets. In a typical sequence, cabinets are stripped down to their frames, and exposed surfaces, such as sections of the framework revealed between doors, are sanded and refinished. You get to select new materials, from solid wood to plastic laminate, for the new doors and drawer fronts. Take the opportunity to spray-paint old cabinet interiors.

Install new drawer fronts with glue and screws. Dry-clamp the new wood in position to transfer holes for hardware.

cabinets & counters

Fixing Doors

If a once-perfect door begins to stick, chances are that either the wood has begun to warp or the hinge screws are coming out of the wood. Your first step should be to tighten the screws and see if the door realigns; you might need to remove the door, fill the holes with wood putty, and rescrew them. If it's not the hinges, you'll have to either plane the door, straighten out its warp, or shim the hinges.

Straightening a Warped Door

There are several ways to straighten a warped cabinet door—or at least to try. Some woods have grain with a built-in bias that is almost impossible to straighten out once it has curved. You can try using a combination of water and heat by soaking down the concave side of the warp with wet cloths and drying out the other side with a heat lamp. The door will need to be forced straight and held there—for example, with pieces of 2x4 and clamps.

Another approach is to suspend the door between two supports with the concave-shaped warp turned upside down. The idea is to over-load the warp at its highest point with something heavy, such as a concrete block, and leave it in place until the warp flattens out. In fact, you should let the warp overcorrect because some of the original bend is bound to return once you unload the weight and reinstall the door. It's also a good idea to add a diagonal back brace to stiffen a panel. Use glue and screws to secure the brace.

Unsticking Doors

Half the battle is knowing exactly where the door sticks. Find out by coating the edge with powdered chalk.

Start planing where chalk has rubbed off on the cabinet, and gradually work away from the high spot.

Rehanging Doors

If the door has a gap near the top, remove the hinge screws, and make a cardboard filler to build out the mortise.

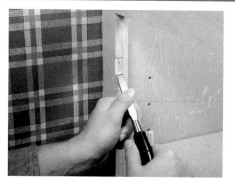

If the door is too tight near the top, remove the door, and use a chisel to slightly deepen the hinge mortise.

Diagnosing Doors

Hinges and catches typically are strong enough to resist even constant opening and closing. The weak links are the hinge screws. When they begin to work loose, the door starts to bind, which applies more stress and causes more binding. Tightening loose screws will help. But you'll get more permanent results by installing longer screws that bite into fresh wood for more holding power.

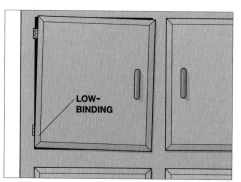

When a cabinet door binds and sticks at the bottom, plane the bottom corners and tighten screws in the upper hinge.

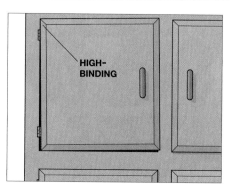

When a cabinet door binds and sticks at the top, plane the top corners and tighten screws in the lower hinge.

Repairing Drawers

A cabinet with drawers that are sticking isn't just a nuisance, it's an eyesore—often the faces of the drawers that are stuck shut will all be at slight angles to one another. Sticking drawers can be blamed on loose or worn runners or cleats or on structural problems with the drawer itself. For minor or occasional sticking, seasonal humidity may be the culprit.

To check an uncooperative drawer, you'll need to empty it and pull it out to examine the hardware. Wooden runners might have shiny spots indicating uneven wear—they can be easily lubricated or planed. Metal or plastic runners and cleats need to be checked for level, for loose or missing fasteners, and for broken parts, which should be replaced. Loose screws should be replaced with larger screws, or the holes should be filled. (See below.) Bearings can be cleaned with ammonia and relubricated if they're not rolling properly.

If a drawer is jamming because its bottom has bowed out (due to being overfilled), you can take out the bottom and reinstall it upside-down. To do this, you may have to carefully knock apart the corner joints to free the bottom. Check for small brads or nails that are often inserted as insurance against glue failure, even in well-made dovetail joints, and pull these first. If the wood splits during this process, remember that it too can be reglued when you reassemble the drawer. The bottom should not be glued into its slot, so it should be easy to remove and reinstall.

Unsticking Drawers

Sometimes lubricating *the cleats and runners does the trick—try running a bar of soap or a candle over them.*

If lubrication doesn't work, *you can plane or sand the runners slightly, test-fitting the drawer as you go.*

Rebuilding Drawers

Remove nails *on bottom or corners. If necessary, separate corner joints, slide out bottom, and reglue sides square.*

Slide drawer bottom *back into its slot, but don't glue in place. Drawers can be cut low in back for bottom repairs.*

Filling Screw Holes

Cabinet hardware is designed to support only limited loads; it can easily be overstressed if doors are ill-fitting. You can improve holding capacity by filling in the existing holes, giving the screw threads solid material to turn through. Use a paste-type wood filler, dowel, or several wooden toothpicks to fill the hole. Trim off the protruding ends, and drive in new screws with wide threads.

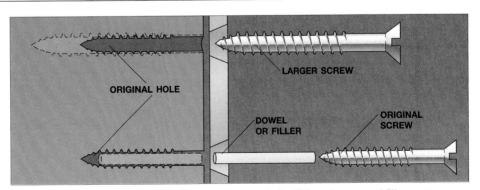

ORIGINAL HOLE
LARGER SCREW
DOWEL OR FILLER
ORIGINAL SCREW

Use a larger screw, if possible, in a worn screw hole. Otherwise, wood filler or a wooden dowel (or a toothpick or two) can be trimmed and dipped in glue to fit snugly into a worn screw hole. The idea is to provide fresh material into which screws can bite.

cabinets & counters

Fold-Down Doors

On wide cabinet doors that are hinged to drop down, making access easier or providing a working tabletop, provide maximum support with a continuous hinge, often called a piano hinge. The hinges need a lot of screws but make a strong connection. To keep the folding door in a level position, also install a folding support bracket on each side. To prevent accidents with doors, consider folding supports that are self-balancing or have adjustable tension springs to slow the door's rate of descent.

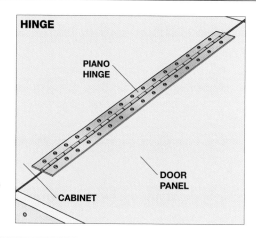

HINGE

PIANO HINGE

DOOR PANEL

CABINET

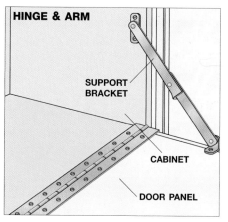

HINGE & ARM

SUPPORT BRACKET

CABINET

DOOR PANEL

Installing a Pull-Out Platform

USE: ▶ power drill/driver or screwdriver • clamps • saw • measuring tape or rule • pencil ▶ pull-out platform kit • screws • shelf lumber

There are some items that you may need to move out of a cabinet without lifting them up and hauling them—a stereo, for instance, or (more typically) a television set. Special hardware (generally sold with a platform) allows a shelf to slide like a drawer on guides that fit into cleats in the cabinet. Many kits include a swivel feature so you can rotate your shelf when it is extended. Or you can add a second, swiveling shelf on top of the pull-out platform. Check to make sure that weight on an extended shelf does not tend to tip the cabinet forward.

1 *Mark the center* of the pull-out kit, and align it with the center of the cabinet opening. Allow room for doors to close.

2 *Extend the pull-out base* to expose the back of the glides, and screw them down to the fixed cabinet shelf.

3 *Extend the pull-out platform,* and check the width of your shelf to be sure that it will rotate in the cabinet opening.

4 *Cut and center your main shelf,* and screw up through the platform into the bottom of the shelf to fasten them together.

5 *From normal viewing height,* even with the shelf extended and swiveled, the hardware can't be seen.

Slide-Away Doors

Special double-acting door hardware can make doors slide back into a cabinet. The hardware is a combination of hinges and glides that are joined together. The hinges allow you to open the doors with a normal swing. If you open them all the way, in line with the sides of the cabinets, a guide panel on which the hinges are mounted can slide on tracks back into the cabinet. These hinges are often used for entertainment centers or anywhere that open doors would be in the way.

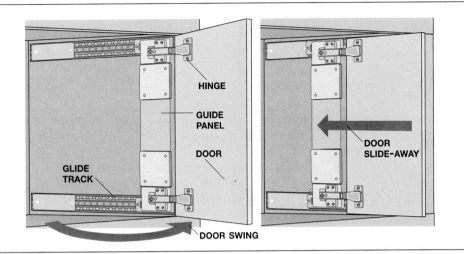

HINGE

GUIDE PANEL

DOOR

GLIDE TRACK

DOOR SWING

DOOR SLIDE-AWAY

Display Details

Cabinets can have a variety of glazing, from plain window glass that will shatter dangerously when broken to elaborate and colorful leaded panels. If you make your own, the safest approach is to use plastic, or tempered glass, the kind required by building codes on patio doors. It breaks into tiny pebbles instead of large shards. It also is safest to have your glass drilled for hinges by the glazier who cuts it. The process requires a special bit turning at slow speed and constant lubrication.

To display the contents of a cabinet, you can use tempered safety glass or clear plastic doors mounted on felt-lined hinges.

In this kitchen, fold-out hoppers edged in wood that matches the cabinets have glass inserts so you can see what's inside.

Knock-Down Hardware

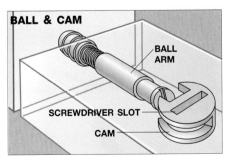

BALL & CAM

BALL ARM

SCREWDRIVER SLOT

CAM

With ball-and-cam hardware, the rounded cam section is turned with a screwdriver to tighten the ball arm.

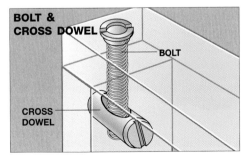

BOLT & CROSS DOWEL

BOLT

CROSS DOWEL

A bolt and cross-dowel fastener copies an old woodworking trick—inserting a nail through a dowel to add holding power.

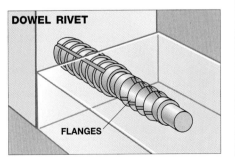

DOWEL RIVET

FLANGES

Dowel rivets are inserted into predrilled holes under pressure. The flanges on the dowel dig into the wood.

13
shelving
& storage

shelving & storage _____

Shelving Types

Shelving is an easy and economical way to add extra storage space in almost any part of your home—along walls, inside closets, and even in the basement or garage. Building shelves doesn't usually require a lot of skill or specialized tools, so this is one project just about any do-it-yourselfer can handle. And unless you decide to use hardwood—which looks great but costs a bundle—it won't cost a lot to install them either.

Solid wood shelving is the way to go when you want to show off the wood or your work. But the cost per board-foot often rules out using classic hardwoods like oak, cherry, or walnut. Softwoods, such as fir or pine, are a better bet; they can be painted or coated with polyurethane to bring out their natural beauty.

Plywood and particleboard offer a couple of advantages when it comes to shelving, though. They cost less than solid wood, and can be bought faced with decorative surfaces. They also come in sheets, which makes them ideal for a really wide shelf. Inexpensive, manufactured storage units ready for assembly often are made from melamine-coated particleboard.

Wood trim will help match your new shelves to the rest of the room or add some interesting detail. Trim is also a handy way to hide seams, gaps, exposed edges of plywood, and other blemishes. You can get trim in either hardwood or softwood. If you plan on finishing a project with stain or sealer, make sure the trim matches the wood you used for the rest of the project.

Materials

PINE

HARDWOOD

PLYWOOD

COMPOSITE

GLASS

Shelf Joinery

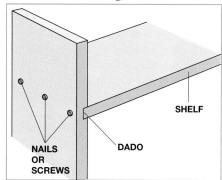

NAILS OR SCREWS · DADO · SHELF

A dado joint is formed when a shelf fits into a channel of the mating piece. The strong joint also keeps the shelf stable.

Reinforcing Shelves

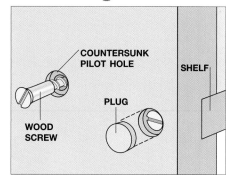

COUNTERSUNK PILOT HOLE · SHELF · PLUG · WOOD SCREW

To reinforce joints with screws, drill pilot holes from the outside, countersink screws, and hide them with wood plugs.

Making Wide Plywood Shelves

USE: ▶ circular saw with rip guide • measuring tape • sawhorses • power drill/driver • hammer • orbital sander ▶ ¾-in.-thick plywood • 1x2 clear pine

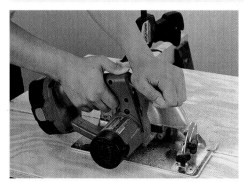

1 *Use a circular saw* to rip sheets of plywood into wide shelves. Stock lumber such as pine normally is no wider than 12 in.

2 *You could conceal* the rough front edge with veneer tape, but a narrow strip of pine is more rugged and adds extra width.

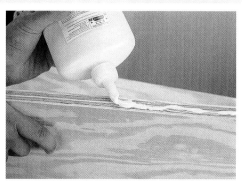

3 *Drill pilot holes* in the leading edge of the pine, and spread carpenter's glue where the other edge will meet the plywood.

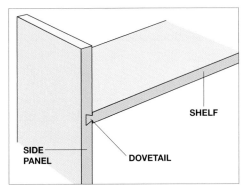

Dovetail dadoes are stronger than standard dadoes, with flared ends on the shelf to prevent withdrawal.

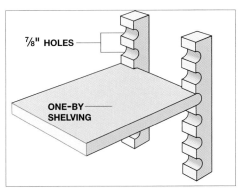

Adjustable shelves can be made in many styles. Here, a shelf with rounded ends fits into supports with rounded grooves.

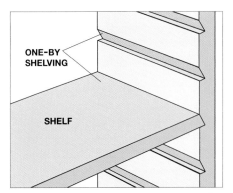

An adjustable shelf with beveled ends slides into 45° kerfs cut at even intervals into the side panels.

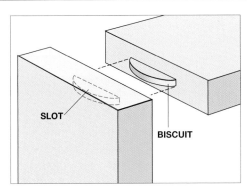

Biscuits are flat, elliptical wood wafers used to reinforce joints. They're glued into slots cut into mating pieces with a biscuit joiner.

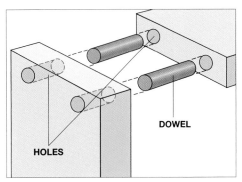

Joints reinforced with dowel pegs and glue are strong but more difficult to make and center than biscuit joints.

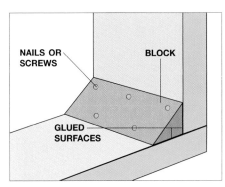

Glue blocks are glued and fastened to the inside surfaces of shelf butt joints to reinforce them.

• wood glue • 10d nails • wood putty • sandpaper

4 *Set the pine against the plywood,* attach it with clamps, and fasten it through the pilot holes with 10d finishing nails.

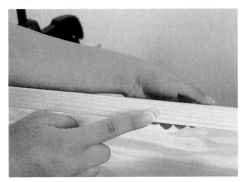

5 *Wipe off excess glue,* set the nails, and mix up a small amount of putty to fill holes on the exposed edge of the pine.

6 *Sand the trim seam* and the edges of the pine. The storage shelves can be 16 in. deep or more, with a durable, finished front.

shelving & storage

Bracket Options

There are two basic types of ready-to-hang shelving supports: stationary shelf brackets and shelving standards. Stationary brackets come in many sizes and styles, and range from utilitarian to decorative. Shelving standards are slotted metal strips that support various types of shelf brackets, including horizontal cantilevered brackets, adjustable arm brackets, adjustable end-clip brackets, and continuous Z-brackets.

Mounting Brackets

For maximum strength, anchor shelf supports to wall studs. If your shelf will carry a light load, you can anchor its supports between studs with mollies or toggle bolts. Attaching supports directly to the studs is always better, though, because sooner or later something heavy will wind up on the shelf. Use masonry anchors to attach shelf supports to brick or concrete. You can also attach shelf supports to a ledger attached to wall studs with

3-inch drywall screws.

Metal shelf standards can be mounted directly to walls or, for a more decorative look, you can insert the standards in grooves routed into the wood itself or into hardwood strips. (See below.) Cut the standards to fit with a hacksaw, and attach them to wall studs with 3-inch drywall screws. Use a carpenter's level to make sure that both standards are plumb and that the corresponding mounting slots are level. Mount standards 6 inches from the ends of shelving to prevent sagging. For long wall shelves, install standards every 48 inches.

Many kitchen and closet storage systems use wire grids that attach to walls with molded plastic brackets. If you anticipate light loads, you can mount these brackets to drywall using the screws and expansion anchors usually included with such systems. For heavier loads, use drywall screws to fasten the brackets directly to studs.

In the 1920s, Sears sold thousands of house kits complete with studs and joists, nails, paint– the works. Closets were part of the package, including No. 9266 triple-unit clothes closet, "the best closet arrangement known in architecture."

Brackets

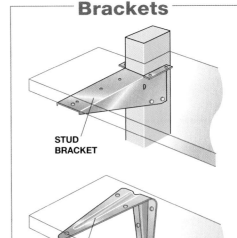

STUD BRACKET

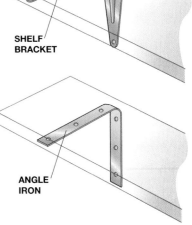

SHELF BRACKET

ANGLE IRON

Screw shelf brackets to wall studs with the longer arm attached to the wall and the shorter arm to the shelf.

Hanging Wood-Framed Standards

USE: ▶ table saw, circular saw, or router • power drill/driver • 4-ft. level • measuring tape • eye protection ▶ 1x4 lumber for frame • metal shelf standards

1 *Use a table saw* (or circular saw or router) to cut a groove down the center of the ¾-in. standard frame.

2 *Make the groove large enough* to hold the metal standard. Predrill in the grooves so that you can screw the frames to wall studs.

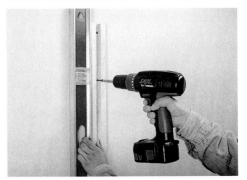

3 *Center the standard frames* on wall studs, level the bases, plumb them with a level, and screw them to the wall.

Z-Brackets

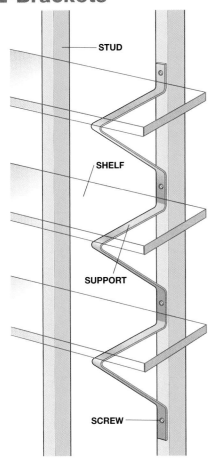

Continuous Z-brackets, often used for workshop or utility shelving systems, support multiple shelves.

Standards

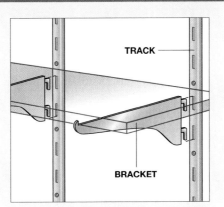

Slotted metal standards are leveled and screwed to wall studs. Shelf support brackets clip into the slots.

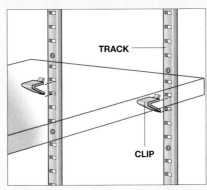

Adjustable end-clip standards can be surface-mounted on side panels or screwed into side-panel grooves.

Fastening

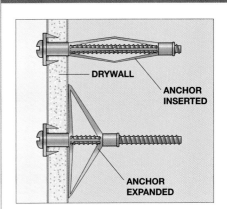

Screw shelf supports to wall studs whenever possible; otherwise, use hollow-wall anchors.

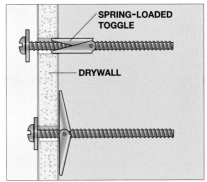

Some anchors expand when you tighten the mounting screw. Toggles have spring-loaded extensions.

• shelf brackets • boards for shelving • screws

4 Seat each standard in its groove, and tack it with a screw. Temporarily mount two standards, and double-check for level.

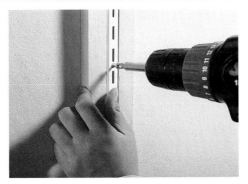

5 Once the slots are dead level, drive the rest of the screws. The standard should sit flush with the surrounding wood.

6 Fit shelf brackets into corresponding slots in the standards, adjust spacing to suit, and mount the shelves.

shelving & storage

Customized Storage

Built-in storage units are an excellent way to make the most of existing storage space in your home. Ready-made or custom-made built-in shelving units, entertainment centers, kitchen cabinets, medicine cabinets, window seats, and under-bed drawers are not only inexpensive and easy to assemble, they allow you to add a unique, personalized touch to your living spaces. (If you rent your home, however, make sure to check your lease and consult your landlord before embarking on one of these projects. Alterations may not be allowed.)

Built-in Shelving

A built-in shelving unit can create valuable storage capacity from an overlooked wall space, such as the area between windows or between a door and its adjacent corner. To construct the shelving, you'll need 1x10 or 1x12 lumber for side panels, top and base panels, and shelves; four 2x2 strips for spreaders; trim molding to conceal gaps along the top and bottom of the unit; 12d common nails and 6d finishing nails. If the unit will be bearing heavy loads, use hardwood boards, and make sure that the shelves span no more than 36 inches. To make installation easier, cut the side pieces an inch shorter than the ceiling height. (This way, you'll be able to tilt the unit into position without scraping the ceiling.) Paint or stain the wood pieces before assembling the unit. Hang the shelves from pegs or end clips inserted into holes drilled in the side pieces.

Plugging

USE: ▶ power drill/driver with plug-cutter bit • table saw or other saw ▶ lumber for plugs

1 *You can cut wood plugs* from dowels, or make your own from any wood with a plug-cutter bit.

2 *If you don't have a drill press,* try to keep your portable drill vertical, and drill to about the same depth on each plug.

3 *Remove plugs* by running the board through a table saw (or use a circular saw or handsaw) set to the plug depth.

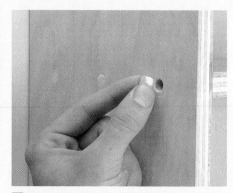

4 *Add glue to the plug,* and tap it into the hole. Trim excess wood with a saw or plane, and sand when the glue dries.

Filling Holes

USE: ▶ putty knife or flat-bladed screwdriver • container for mixing (if needed) ▶ wood putty • sandpaper • stain (if needed)

1 *Wood putty* comes premixed and as a powder. You can mix powder types to suit: thicker for holes; thinner for surface damage.

2 *Apply wood putty* by pressing it in the hole with a putty knife, flat-bladed screwdriver, or your fingertip. Leave a little excess.

3 *Small patches dry quickly* and sand easily. Because putty shrinks, you may need to fill deep holes with two applications.

Constructing a Built-in Shelving Unit

USE: ▶ pry bar • saw • measuring tape • hammer • drill/driver • square • miter box and backsaw ▶ shelving lumber • 2x4s • trim • common and finishing nails

1 *Use a pry bar* to carefully remove the base trim where you will install the built-in unit. Save it for reinstallation later.

2 *Build a box* out of 2x4s for the base of the unit. Use it to elevate the bottom shelf, and anchor the built-in unit to the wall.

3 *Cut 1x10s or 1x12s* for the sides. For adjustable shelves, mark your bit (or use a depth guide), and drill rows of peg holes.

4 *Make a support frame* from 1x4s for the ceiling, and tack the side panels. A finished shelf conceals the top frame.

5 *Add glue and nails* to secure the side panels to their support frames. You should add several support cleats along the sides.

6 *Nail the bottom shelf* in place. Make the shelf flush with the support box so that you can nail on baseboard trim.

7 *Cut trim pieces* to fit around the top of the unit (matching any existing wall trim), and fasten with 6d finishing nails.

8 *Replace the cut baseboards* around the unit. Miter-cut new matching trim pieces to fit around the base of the unit.

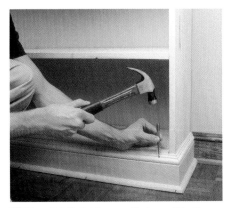

9 *Use 6d finishing nails* to nail in the base trim, set the nails, putty the holes, and finish the unit with paint or stain.

shelving & storage

Adding Closet Space

What homeowner or apartment dweller hasn't complained about having too little closet space? Fortunately, there are almost always ways to find a bit more closet space. You may have to put in some time and effort, but in the long run, it's always easier than buying a new house with bigger closets.

The easiest and most obvious solution is one of the many commercial closet organizing systems now on the market. But constructing your own version of a commercial closet organizer is far more economical. With a combination of shelves and plywood partitions, you can divide a closet into storage zones, with a single clothes pole on one side for full-length garments; double clothes poles on the other side for half-length garments like jackets, skirts, or slacks; a column of narrow shelves between the two for folded items, handbags, or shoes; and one or more closet-wide shelves on top.

Building a New Closet

Sometimes, taking away from your living space and adding a new closet is the only way to increase closet space. This will involve framing new walls (pp. 118–21), finishing them with drywall (pp. 180–85), adding matching trim (pp. 200–201), and hanging an interior door (p. 489) The closet's interior should be at least 24 inches deep and, for a bedroom closet, 48 inches wide. Try to locate the closet at a corner so that you only have to build two walls.

(pp. 118–21) ... (pp. 180–85) ... (pp. 200–201) ... (p. 489)

Closet Layout

It's always nice to have a lot of closet space. But given the high square-foot cost of a house, it is expensive to turn over a lot of floor space to storage space. The best plan is to minimize the closet footprint and maximize the closet efficiency by organizing the interior. For example, a typical closet has one shelf and one hanging pole. It also may be a full 24 inches deep, even though most clothes and many other kinds of storage will fit in a narrower area. Pick up 2 or 3 inches in depth at each closet in the house, and your kitchen is a foot wider or your family room a foot longer. One simple way to increase capacity is to install two storage shelves above the hanging pole. Allow a foot or so of clearance under the door opening for the first, full-depth shelf, and install a second, half-depth shelf above it. You also can divide up closet space with partitions so that one section has full-height hanging storage and another has two, half-height hanging poles for shorter items. The best plan is to build (or buy) a closet system with adjustable components to suit changing needs.

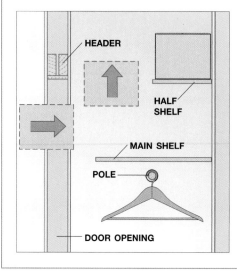

HEADER
HALF SHELF
MAIN SHELF
POLE
DOOR OPENING

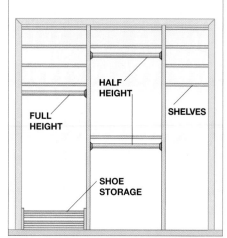

HALF HEIGHT
FULL HEIGHT
SHELVES
SHOE STORAGE

Framing a Closet

USE: ▶ circular saw or crosscut saw • hammer • measuring tape • framing square • chalk-line box • 4-ft. level • drywall tools • stepladder ▶ 2x4s for studs, wall

1 *Mark the closet outline* on the floor. Nail down the 2x4 soleplate every 2 ft. Mark the door, allowing space for jambs.

2 *Transfer the closet outline* to the ceiling using a chalk-line box and level. Nail on the outside studs and top plates.

3 *Set studs* 16 in. on center, and toenail them to the top plate and soleplate on all four sides. Nail crossbraces between studs.

Closet Systems

There are many types of closet systems. One of the most versatile is wire racks. Mix-and-match components include several stock lengths of shelving with integral hanging bars, plus support brackets and clips that allow you to install these systems in almost any configuration. They also are easy to alter. You can create the same kind of compartmentalized storage with custom and stock wood systems, or hire one of many specialized closet companies to build your system.

If you have a spare room to convert, you can design a wood storage closet system to create custom storage.

Use wire-rack components to build compartmentalized, multi-tiered storage into a standard closet space.

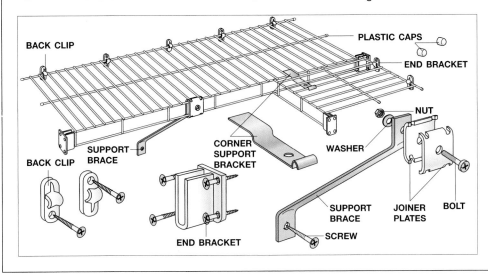

BACK CLIP • PLASTIC CAPS • END BRACKET • NUT • CORNER SUPPORT BRACKET • WASHER • SUPPORT BRACE • BACK CLIP • SUPPORT BRACE • END BRACKET • SUPPORT BRACE • SCREW • JOINER PLATES • BOLT

Use interlocking wire bins and box storage racks on tracks to increase the capacity of a closet and free floor space.

plates & braces • 2x lumber for header • common nails • jamb stock • drywall • drywall screws • joint compound • sandpaper • shelves & clothes poles as needed

4 *Nail jack studs* on each side of the doorway to carry the header. Install a double header across the opening.

5 *Remove the section of soleplate* in the doorway so that you can run finished flooring into the closet space.

6 *Install drywall inside and out,* and finish and sand the joints. Install the door, closet pole, and fittings.

shelving & storage

Ideas for Workshops

Workshops and other utility areas such as garages, attics, and basements can benefit from storage upgrades as much as any other room in the home—perhaps even more so, as utility areas are prone to clutter. Convenience, flexibility, and safety are the things to keep in mind when reorganizing your work space. Try to provide storage space for tools and hardware as near as possible to where they'll be used. In addition to a sturdy workbench, utility shelving is a mainstay in any workshop. You can buy ready-to-assemble units or make your own using ¾-inch particleboard or plywood shelves and ¾x1½-inch (1x2) hardwood stock for cleats (nailed to the wall), ribs (nailed to the front underside of the shelves), and vertical shelf supports (nailed to the ribs).

Don't forget about pegboard. To make a pegboard tool rack, attach washers to the back of the pegboard with hot glue, spacing the washers to coincide with wall studs. Position the pegboard so that the rear washers are located over studs. Drive drywall screws through finish washers and the pegboard into studs. (Use masonry anchors for concrete walls.)

Finally, try to take advantage of any otherwise wasted space. The area in your garage above your parked car is the ideal spot for a U-shaped lumber storage rack, made of 1x4 stock and connecting plates. The space in front of the car could be used for a storage cabinet or even a workbench.

Shop Storage

You can buy a ready-made workbench for your shop or build one yourself that is almost as sturdy. For a basic bench, use 4x4s (or doubled 2x4s bolted together) for the frame, and a double layer of ¾-inch plywood glued and screwed together for the work surface. There are hundreds of different storage products—from huge, roll-away tool carts to tiny bin dividers—but you can also build your own to use your work space efficiently. To protect children, provide locked storage for hazardous materials.

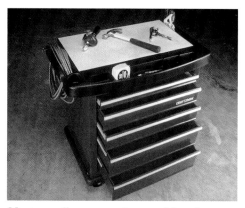

Move a roll-away cart *around the shop where you're working, and store it under a bench. Most are rated by weight capacity.*

An old-time storage technique *is still a good idea: screw lids to supports, and use jars to keep small items in plain sight.*

Lumber storage *can be portable, too, on a homemade rolling cart like this one—one side is for sheet goods and one is for boards.*

Attaching Casters

USE: ▶ power drill/driver • measuring tape or ruler • socket wrench • open-end wrench • pencil ▶ casters • bolts • nuts

1 ***Inset a caster*** *at each corner of your storage container, and mark the bolt-hole locations for drilling.*

2 ***Drill pilot holes*** *through the base of the container—in this case, two layers of plywood glued and screwed together.*

3 ***Bolt the casters*** *to the wood base. Use one wrench to hold the nut while you turn the bolt head with a socket wrench.*

Rack & Prefab Systems

When you need a few storage shelves but don't want to make a permanent installation on the wall, use metal rack or prefabricated wood units. Metal rack systems are held together with nuts and bolts. You can install shelves at any level using holes in the corner posts. The systems, often sold in kits, are not stable without the X-pattern bracing on the back. Prefab wood storage units assemble easily and hold a variety of tools and supplies.

Metal rack shelf units reinforced with X-braces are sturdy enough to hold heavy supplies, adjustable, and easily altered.

Prefab wood storage units, typically sold as knockdown kits, can be purchased with many shelf and drawer combinations.

Assembling a Wall System

USE: ▶ screwdriver • hammer or rubber mallet ▶ wall-system kit

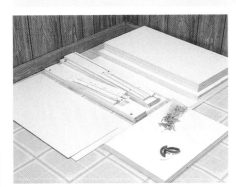

1 Before starting a kit project, read through the instructions, and make sure you have all the panels and hardware.

2 Panel sections may fit together with wooden dowel pegs. You tap them into one panel, and press them into mating panels.

3 Some panels join with threaded fasteners. The stud end mounts in one panel, and fits into a predrilled hole.

4 With threaded fasteners, once the stud end is in position, you use a screwdriver to engage and tighten the joint.

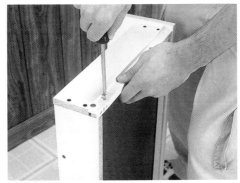

5 Assemble drawer sections with dowels and fasteners. Kits typically include full-extension drawer guides.

6 A modest-sized unit such as this can be assembled in under an hour. The plastic laminate panels require no finishing.

shelving & storage

Adding Storage Space

Few of us have the luxury of too much storage space. Yet if you look closely, odds are you will find places where the space you do have is being wasted or underutilized. Here are a few spots where dead space can be converted into handy places to put things.

Narrow hallways that end at a closet or door offer a surprising amount of storage space, especially if your ceilings are high. Install shelving around the doorway—or better yet, build a deep platform over the door supported by ledgers nailed to each side wall.

In the space under the eaves below a sloped attic roof or under a staircase, you can build a made-to fit bookcase or built-in cabinets. This is especially good in a child's bedroom, where it won't seem so low to the ground.

Garments hung on hangers usually do not take up a closet's full depth. The space you gain by moving the clothes pole toward the back of the closet may accommodate wire-rack shelves attached to the back of the closet door.

To utilize the overhead space in your garage, build deep storage platforms supported by ledgers screwed to wall studs and threaded rods hooked to ceiling joists or rafters. You can also hang tools from the walls by mounting pegboard. (See p. 258 for how to mount pegboard.) You can buy sets with a variety of hooks and brackets for tools. For small items, such as jars of nails, make shallow shelves by nailing 1x4 boards between the exposed studs.

Basic Toy Box

To make this toy box, first cut all the parts to the dimensions in the materials list. Rabbet the front and rear panels, and attach them to the side panels with glue and finishing nails. Square up the box with clamps; let the glue dry. Attach the trim and corner guards with glue and brads. Glue and nail cleats to the inside bottom of the front, back and side panels, and glue the bottom panel to the cleats. Paint or stain the wood. Attach the piano hinge to the box, and then to the lid. Attach the lid supports and handles.

MATERIALS

- ◆ **2 front/rear panels** ¾ x 17¼ x 38½
- ◆ **2 side panels** ¾ x 17¼ x 18
- ◆ **2 top trim strips** ¾ x 1½ x 20
- ◆ **2 top trim strips** ¾ x 1½ x 40
- ◆ **2 base trim strips** ¾ x 2½ x 20
- ◆ **2 base trim strips** ¾ x 2½ x 40
- ◆ **4 corner guards** ¼ x 1 x 1 x 13¼
- ◆ **2 cleats** ¾ x ¾ x 37
- ◆ **2 cleats** ¾ x ¾ x 15½
- ◆ **1 bottom panel** ¾ x 16⅞ x 37
- ◆ **1 lid** ¾ x 21 x 42
- ◆ **Hardware:** 36" piano hinge, 2 toy-box lid supports, 2 handles

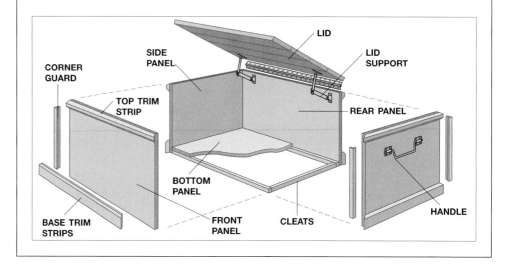

Cedar Closets

Both solid cedar boards and composite cedar panels have only moderate resistance to insects, and are used more for their pleasant aroma and appearance. The sheets of pressed red and tan particles are no less aromatic than solid wood, but the panels are 40 to 50% less expensive, and are easier to install. Solid boards require more carpentry work, and are likely to produce a fair amount of waste unless you piece the courses and create more joints. To gain the maximum effect, every inside surface should be covered, including the ceiling and the back of the door. The simplest option is to use ¼-inch-thick panels, which are easy to cut into big sections that cover walls in one or two pieces. Try to keep cedar seams in boards or panels from falling over drywall seams. No stain, sealer, or clear finish is needed; just leave the wood raw. The cedar aroma will fade over the years as natural oils crystallize on the surface. But you can easily regenerate the scent from the panels by scuffing the surface with fine sandpaper.

More Storage Ideas

You can squeeze extra storage space out of the tightest situations. On this page are eight ways to build more storage capacity into attics, basements, and other utility spaces: 1) on racks suspended from floor joists; 2) on furring strips screwed to joists; 3) in roll-out cabinets under stairs; 4) on shelves between studs in wall cavities; 5) on shelves built under steeply sloped roofs; 6) on shelves cut to fit into the spaces between rafters; 7) on high shelves suspended from rafters near the roof ridge; 8) on plywood panels fitted between truss webs.

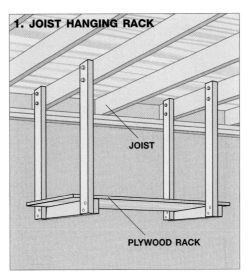

1. JOIST HANGING RACK

JOIST

PLYWOOD RACK

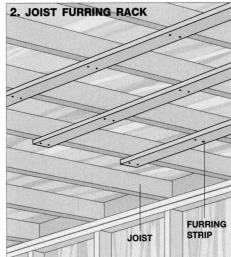

2. JOIST FURRING RACK

JOIST

FURRING STRIP

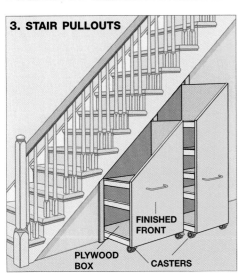

3. STAIR PULLOUTS

FINISHED FRONT

PLYWOOD BOX

CASTERS

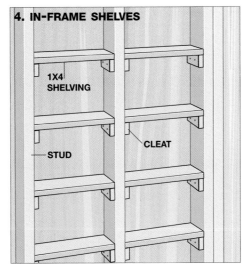

4. IN-FRAME SHELVES

1X4 SHELVING

STUD

CLEAT

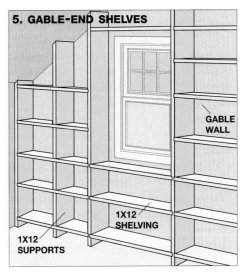

5. GABLE-END SHELVES

GABLE WALL

1X12 SHELVING

1X12 SUPPORTS

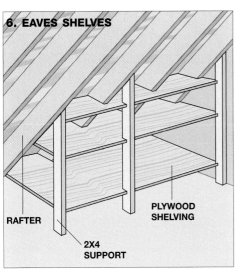

6. EAVES SHELVES

RAFTER

2X4 SUPPORT

PLYWOOD SHELVING

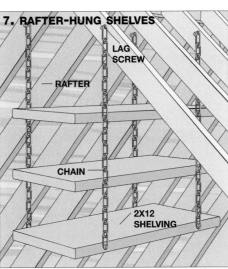

7. RAFTER-HUNG SHELVES

LAG SCREW

RAFTER

CHAIN

2X12 SHELVING

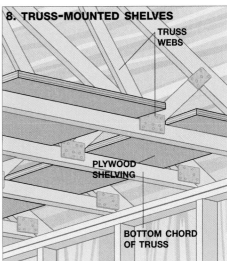

8. TRUSS-MOUNTED SHELVES

TRUSS WEBS

PLYWOOD SHELVING

BOTTOM CHORD OF TRUSS

furniture 14

Furniture Basics

Chairs, tables, beds, chests, and the like transform empty rooms into places where people can live comfortably. Even the plainest furniture has a functional value—imagine sitting or sleeping without furniture—but fine wood furnishings add a special beauty and elegance to a room. Plain or fancy, furniture is such a part of our daily lives that most people form sentimental ties to at least a few pieces.

Designing and building fine furniture from scratch is an art that requires excellent woodworking skills, experience, lots of time, and a shop with expensive tools. But there are easier ways of getting wood furniture into your home (and keeping what you've got). Many people with little more than average do-it-yourself skills have refinished old wood furniture in their spare time, turning garage-sale bargains into eye-catching showpieces. With a little know-how from this chapter, you'll be able to take on restorations that need repair work as well as refinishing, and maybe even fix that wobbly old rocking chair that has been in the family for as long as you can remember.

When it comes to restoring wood furniture, the three basic concerns are the type of wood it is made from, how the individual parts are joined, and the finish. (Value is another, of course; restoration of expensive antiques should be left to professionals.) The variety of wood has a lot to do with the range of color and grain pattern the refinished piece will have, while the type of joints used will determine its overall strength and level of quality.

Joinery

Mortise-and-tenon joints are among the strongest used in furniture-making. You form the tenon by cutting a square tongue (the tenon) on the end of one piece of wood and cutting a hole of equal size (the mortise) through the face of the second piece. Then, insert the tenon into the mortise, and glue it in place. Sometimes a pin or peg is also inserted perpendicular to and through the tenon to lock the joint together.

Many modern pieces, especially chairs, are built using joints held together by glue and wooden pegs called dowels. Dowel joints are shown in the illustrations for "Pinned Joints" to the right.

Simple Joints

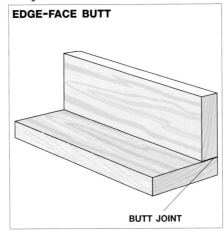

EDGE-FACE BUTT

BUTT JOINT

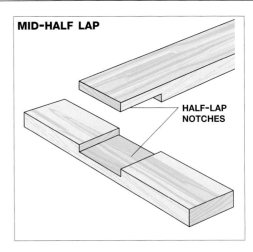

MID-HALF LAP

HALF-LAP NOTCHES

Mortised & Dadoed Joints

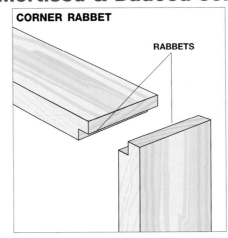

CORNER RABBET

RABBETS

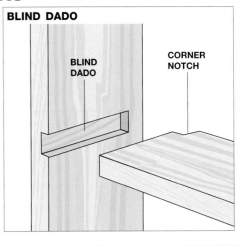

BLIND DADO

BLIND DADO

CORNER NOTCH

Pinned Joints

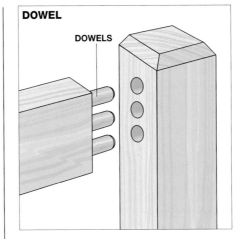

DOWEL

DOWELS

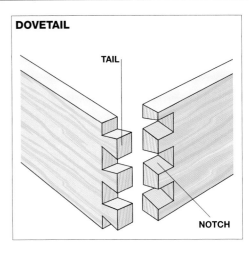

DOVETAIL

TAIL

NOTCH

CORNER FULL LAP

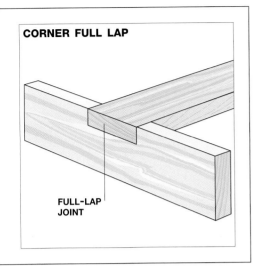

FULL-LAP
JOINT

CORNER MORTISE & TENON

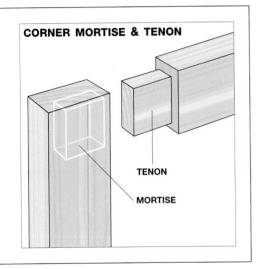

TENON

MORTISE

EDGE BISCUIT

BISCUIT
SLOT

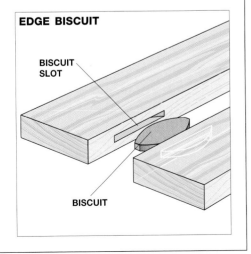

BISCUIT

Solids vs. Veneers

Solid wood is the traditional choice, but it's considerably more expensive than plywood and other panel materials covered with thin veneers. You can rout and shape the edges of solid wood because there is more of the same hue and grain underneath. With some veneers, you have to be careful when using a power sander so you won't sand through to the plain panel below. Solids are also easy to shape into tight-fitting patches for deep damage. Veneers are limited to skin-deep repairs on the wood surface.

Common Furniture Woods

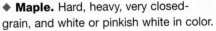 WHITE OAK

Furniture often is identified by the natural properties of woods—even plywood sheets covered with a thin veneer. But unless you use a clear sealer, most woods can be altered considerably with oils, stains, and other treatments.

 RED OAK

 MAPLE

 POPLAR

◆ **White Oak.** Has a pronounced open grain and a slightly gray-brown color.

◆ **Red Oak.** Has a pronounced open grain and a reddish-brown tinge.

◆ **Maple.** Hard, heavy, very closed-grain, and white or pinkish white in color.

◆ **Poplar.** A white or yellow hardwood with a straight, even, closed grain.

◆ **Cherry.** Closed-grained, with a light reddish-brown to brown color.

◆ **Mahogany.** Fine-textured, with an open grain; pink to brown in color.

◆ **Walnut.** Gray to chocolate brown in color; can have beautiful grain patterns.

◆ **Pine.** Soft, cream-to-yellow softwood now primarily used in furniture interiors.

 CHERRY

 MAHOGANY

 WALNUT

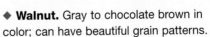 PINE

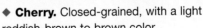

A Shaker Solution

Kit furniture was one of the Shakers' best ideas. Talented craftsmen designed and built prototypes; then, they were taken apart, and replicas of every component were cut and shipped out in neat bundles. Anyone with minimal woodworking skills could put the pieces together.

Furniture pieces in kit form usually cost only 50–60% of the assembled version. Materials are pine, maple, oak, cherry, and mahogany, not veneers glued over flakeboard, the material of most knockdown (KD) furniture sold at build-it-yourself stores. The joints in Shaker-style kits are traditional mortise-and-tenon, not nuts and bolts or snap-together KD hardware. And kit buyers enjoy the satisfaction of assembling and finishing quality furniture without struggling over a carpentry project.

$6.25

THE MOST WONDER-
FUL VALUE EVER
OFFERED IN A

**RECLINING
SWING CHAIR.**

THE EQUAL
OF
CHAIRS
SOLD
ELSEWHERE
AT
$12.00 TO
$15.00

Think that the reclining armchair with footrest was invented sometime after TV and canned beer? This affordable model dates from a 1908 Sears Catalog.

Building Your Kit

Typical reproduction kits require some woodworking skills—not complex measuring and cutting but an understanding of furniture assembly, a restrained and tidy use of glue, and the patience to sand imperfections before finishing. For example, the rungs in a chair kit may not fit smoothly into the leg-piece holes; even minor changes in humidity can make wood swell enough to disrupt a perfect match. Light sanding generally corrects the problem. With glue, you need to keep excess from oozing onto the grain of exposed surfaces, where it will keep stain from penetrating and create blotches.

Most kit furniture companies offer a wide selection of pieces, from large cabinets with over 100 components to simple candleholders made from 4 or 5 parts. It's wise to start small. Call the kit company if you have questions about the item you select from their catalog. Make sure no special tools or skills are needed for assembly—generally, a hammer and screwdriver will do the job. Read all instructions before gluing any parts.

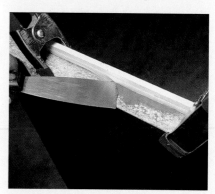

Some knockdown kits break along the edges where panels beneath the veneer are drilled for fittings.

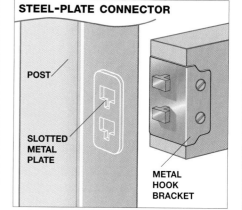

One solution is to form the broken area with a piece of wood and clamps, fill with epoxy, and then redrill.

Knockdown Hardware

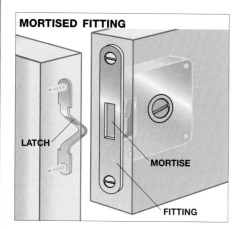

MORTISED FITTING

LATCH

MORTISE

FITTING

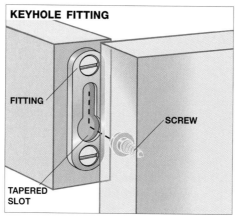

KEYHOLE FITTING

FITTING

SCREW

TAPERED
SLOT

STEEL-PLATE CONNECTOR

POST

SLOTTED
METAL
PLATE

METAL
HOOK
BRACKET

Assembling Kit Furniture

USE: ▶ hammer • carpenter's square • paintbrushes or paint pads • rubber gloves ▶ furniture kit • sandpaper • glue and nails (if needed) • stain • sealer

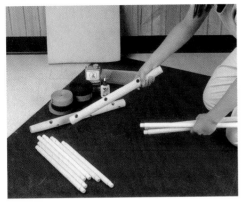

1 *It's wise to start a kit project* by laying out all the pieces and hardware in an exploded pattern of the finished kit.

2 *Many precut kits* require light finishing before assembly. Pieces may have swelled slightly from the time when they were cut.

3 *Kits often include* glue and nails. With this Shaker stool kit, rungs are glued into holes predrilled in the legs.

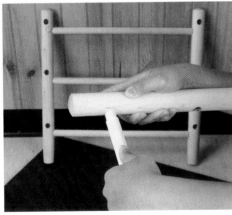

4 *Basic kits like this* can be assembled in modular sections; first one pair of legs with their rungs, and then the other.

5 *Square up modular sections* as you assemble them, and then put the assembled sections together.

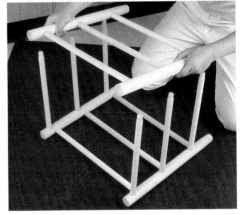

6 *Glue connecting rungs* into one leg assembly on the floor, add glue to the holes, and fit the other section on top.

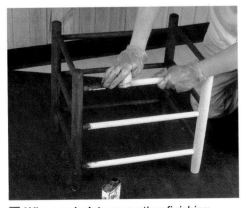

7 *When upholstery* or other finishing materials are used, stain and seal the wood before they are applied.

8 *The seat of this stool* is formed by a cross-weave of fabric strips, called chair tapes, with foam padding between layers.

9 *Weave alternate color tapes* (provided in the kit) to finish the project. The end of the last tape is tacked under the seat.

Refinishing Cautions

If you are lucky, restoring a piece of furniture will only involve cleaning up the original finish. More often, though, you have to remove the original finish, and prepare the bare wood for a new one. Old-timers used a caustic solution of lye and water to strip paint, but this mixture was so strong it loosened glue joints, discolored wood, and occasionally burned the user's skin and eyes.

Easier-to-use strippers, developed in the last 30 to 40 years, contain solvents such as toluene, methanol, acetone, and methylene chloride. These strippers, in liquid and paste form, are relatively safe to use as long as you follow the directions carefully. Strippers containing dibasic esters and N-methyl pyrrolidone are considered safer because of their slower evaporation rate. With any solvent-based stripper, always work in a well-ventilated area, and wear protective clothing, an apron, and safety glasses.

Heat-stripping a finish means using either a propane torch or a heat gun. The idea is to heat the surface enough to loosen or lift the finish but not enough to burn or scratch the wood underneath. Although this method of stripping may work fine for some situations, such as stripping household exterior woodwork that will be repainted, it's very risky for furniture. If you choose to strip any wood using a heat gun or torch, always keep a fire extinguisher close by, and wear an organic vapor mask, goggles, and heat-resistant gloves. Never use a heat gun along with chemical strippers.

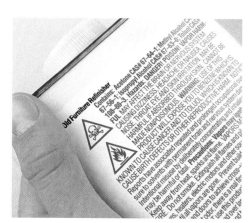

Always read and follow the manufacturer's cautions and safety standards, particularly for stains and other finishing materials.

Heat Stripping

USE: ▶ scraper • heat gun

1 *Use a sharp putty knife* or small scraper to remove any flaking or loose finish material.

2 *Carefully heat the surface* of the finish, watching for bubbles. Keep the gun moving steadily.

3 *As the surface layers* heat up and loosen, use a scraper to work with the gun and remove the finish.

Chemical Stripping

USE: ▶ brush • scraper ▶ stripper • sawdust

1 *Brush on a chemical stripper* in one small area at a time. Be sure to wear gloves and safety glasses.

2 *Spread sawdust* or wood shavings over the bubbled finish to consolidate the material for removal.

3 *Scrape off the stripper* and finish. You may need small knives to clean out molding and intricate patterns.

Scraping

This long-handled draw scraper has a crooked blade. The tool is good for removing finishes on flat surfaces.

Some scrapers have several different profiles built into the blade to remove finish from flat and curved surfaces.

This triangular scraper can reach into corners, grooves, and seams. Some have interchangeable heads.

Sanding

Most detail power sanders have a pointed tip to reach into tight spots. Some models are only half this size.

A belt sander is like a floor sander for furniture. The continuous belt can quickly strip and smooth a flat surface.

A random-orbit sander is ideal for finishing furniture because it can smooth opposing wood grains.

Detail Work

Professional refinishers may dunk an entire chair in stripper solution to remove every bit of old finish. Do-it-yourselfers have to tackle these projects one small section at a time, which can drag out a stripping project. To speed things up, use dunking where it's practical (to refurbish hardware), and use applied stripper paste, scrapers, and some specialized sanding products on the wood. A detail power sander with a pointed pad can reach into corners. Sanding tapes can handle small crevices.

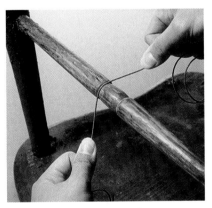

Sanding tape is like sandpaper on a string. A variety of grits are available to clean turned chair rungs and legs.

Mix a solution for stripping hardware by setting up a dunking bath. Wear goggles and rubber gloves.

furniture

Repairing a Joint

Chairs take plenty of abuse, so it should be no surprise if your first joint repair project happens to be loose chair legs or rungs. The best fix for loose furniture joints is to take them completely apart, clean them, and then reglue and clamp them in place. When that isn't possible, because the loose parts just won't separate or because other joints around it are still solidly glued, the next best repair is to inject glue into the joint. (See "Regluing," at right.)

If the joint hasn't already fallen apart, you'll have to separate the pieces. First, make sure the joint hasn't been locked with a small peg or pinned with tiny brads. Pegs can be hammered out—or if they resist, drilled out with a bit slightly smaller than the peg's diameter. Pull out pins, which may be hidden under wood putty, with diagonal pliers, or drive them through with a nailset. After removing the fasteners, apply a 50:50 solution of water and vinegar, and tap the joint apart.

Joint Reinforcements

Pegs and pins are not the only joint strengtheners you are likely to encounter. Depending on the joint being repaired, you may have to remove corner blocks, glue blocks, metal braces, and wood screws (along with wood buttons that hide them). Corner blocks may be glued and screwed to inside corners of chair frames; glue blocks often attach tabletops to the base. Pop glue blocks loose with a mallet and chisel after removing any screws or nails.

Where wood screws have been used to strengthen exposed joints, you will probably find they have been covered with a wood button or plug. You can remove buttons by inserting the tip of a scratch awl under the button edge and popping it out—or use two chisels, one on either side, to lift the button out. Avoid damaging the sides of the hole when removing the countersink screw because it makes replacing the button more difficult.

Once you have separated and cleaned the joint, test-fit the pieces. If they are very loose, further repairs are needed. Sometimes going to the next larger screw size does the trick, or tighten up the joint by cutting a slot in the end of a rung and inserting a wedge. Fill excess space in a joint using epoxy glue with a bonding filler.

Two Ways of Regluing

USE: ▶ drill • ¼- & ⅛-in. drill bits • hammer ▶ ¼-in. dowel • polyvinyl glue

1 *To strengthen a weak rung,* check your alignment, and drill a hole through the chair leg into the center of the rung.

2 *After injecting glue* into the hole, gently hammer in a dowel until it seats. Cut off the dowel with a backsaw.

1 *To strengthen a weak mortise,* drill a small hole at an angle into the joint through both mortise and tenon.

2 *Insert the syringe tip* into the hole, and inject a thinned-down polyvinyl glue. Wipe off the excess, and sand smooth.

Repairing a Rung

USE: ▶ utility knife • backsaw • band clamp ▶ precut wedge • wood glue

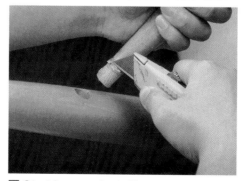

1 *Start by scraping off* any old glue from the rung using a utility knife. This helps fresh glue adhere to the old surface.

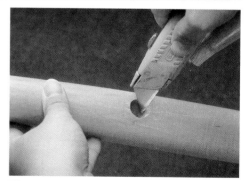

2 *Also scrape away old glue* from the mortise. A power Dremel-type tool with a burr attachment is handy for this job.

Wedging

One of the slickest ways to strengthen a rung is with the old-fashioned technique of inserting a foxtail wedge. First, cut a narrow groove down the center of the tenon on the rung. Then, partially insert a small hardwood wedge. It also helps to remove old glue and add a fresh application before seating the rung. As you clamp the connection tight, the wedge forces the rung slightly open, locking it into the mortise.

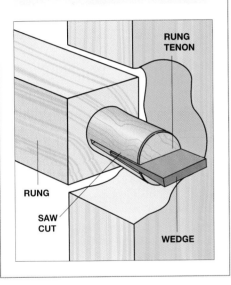

RUNG TENON

RUNG

SAW CUT

WEDGE

Before... and After

Angle Drilling

Because many joints between furniture components are at odd angles, you need to align the drill with mating parts.

To make sure that your angle is correct, set a bevel square to an existing component, and use it to guide your drill.

3 *Cut a kerf* in the end of the rung using a backsaw. Before assembling the pieces, coat all mating surfaces with glue.

4 *Cut a small, hardwood wedge* about as long as the saw kerf. Start the wedge in the kerf before seating the rung.

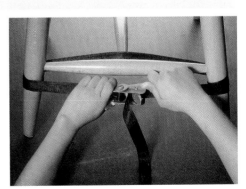

5 *Reassemble the chair* after applying glue. A band clamp that ratchets tight is ideal for tightening several joints at once.

Wear & Tear

Well-made wood furniture is long-lasting but far from indestructible. Older pieces especially will show signs of normal wear, not to mention abuse and neglect. Drawers, for example, are pulled out and pushed back in thousands of times over the years. Eventually the wooden runners wear down, and the drawer stops break loose. (See "Fixing a Drawer," below right, and "Cabinets & Counters," pp. 234–235.) Over the years, stresses from opening and closing a cabinet door or lid may also loosen hinge screws, and could even split the wood. Usually larger screws solve this problem.

Constant changes in temperature and humidity can affect the wood, too, causing drawers and cabinet doors to swell and stick, veneer to pop loose, or panel tops to split and warp. Years of use and the stresses that go along with it can loosen joints and even split wood parts, such as the rocker runner on a rocking chair.

Fixing Splits & Fractures

Breaks that occur in the direction of the grain will usually make strong joints that do not need reinforcing, as long as they're free from old glue and can be pulled up tight with clamps. You can generally fix a split by working glue well into the opening, using pressure from the clamp to close up the split, and allowing the glue to dry. If the split has been glued previously, clean the joint before regluing.

When wood breaks across the grain, the repair may need extra reinforcement. Likely places for cross-grain breaks are weaker points in the furniture, including delicate pieces such as finials; curved pieces; and legs, stretchers, and other turned pieces. (Turned pieces, also called turnings, have been shaped on a lathe.)

When repairing turnings broken across the grain, you need to reinforce the joint with wood or metal dowel screws. The trick is to glue the broken parts back together first. Then, if the break was near the end of the turned piece, drill the dowel hole down from that end and through the break. Otherwise, cut the reglued turning at the nearest shoulder above or below the break. Drill dowel holes into the ends of both pieces, going deep enough into one to drill through the break. Insert the dowel, and glue the cut parts back together.

Fixing a Frame

USE: ▶ backsaw • woodworking vise • wood chisels • utility knife • glue brush or palette knife

1 *Clamp the frame securely, and use a backsaw to cut a centered slot across both sides of the picture frame's miter joint.*

2 *Cut a wood spline from scrap wood the same thickness as the slot. It should be wider than the frame and trimmed later.*

Fasteners

Most wood furniture is held together by a combination of joinery, glue, and fasteners. When repairs are necessary, you're likely to use a combination of brads and nails, tacks to hold upholstery, and either wood screws or dowels to strengthen weak joints. While glue can hold many joints temporarily, you're likely to need the extra strength of screws. You can conceal their heads with wood plugs.

Fixing a Drawer

USE: ▶ framing square or other large square • block plane • palette knife • scratch awl • wood chisel

1 *To repair a damaged drawer runner, first scribe a straight line above the damaged area using a framing square.*

2 *Using a fine-toothed handsaw, cut away the damaged area—up to the drawer bottom if necessary.*

▶ wood for splines • wood glue

3 Spread glue onto the spline and into the slot. Push the spline into place, and clean the excess glue with a damp rag.

4 After the glue dries, cut the spline flush with the frame on both sides of the mitered corner using a backsaw.

5 To finish the repair, trim the spline with a sharp chisel or block plane. Sand smooth, and stain the spline to match the frame.

Glues

There is a type of glue to suit any furniture project. Basic yellow carpenter's glue is one of the most popular, general-purpose glues used today. Among many others are hide glue, a slow-setting mix that is reversible—even after drying, joints can be disassembled by applying heat and water. Epoxy works well on nonporous materials and is water- and chemical-proof. Contact adhesive is best for laminates.

Clamping pressure is critical for maximizing glue effectiveness. For instance, when using epoxy, too much pressure on a tightly fitted joint will create a weak, glue-starved connection. Using polyvinyl glue and less pressure on the same joint can produce better results. In most applications, contact glues work best with no clamping pressure. The label on the glue bottle should indicate what pressure is best.

• clamps • handsaw ▶ wood for new runner • sandpaper • wood glue • touch-up stain, finish, and wax • clean rag

3 Plane the bottom of the remaining runner to smooth it. Use a chisel to smooth hard-to-get-at areas.

4 Cut a new strip of wood for the runner. Glue and clamp the new runner in position on the side of the drawer.

5 Plane the runner edge until the drawer fits and works smoothly in the cabinet; then sand, finish, and touch up the patch piece.

furniture

Wood Preparation

Once you've stripped and rough-sanded a piece of furniture, you'll need to prepare for the new finish. Surface preparation is just as important here, if not more so, than with paint. Stripping, for example, probably will expose nicks and cracks that should be fixed with wood putty. Finish sanding is also important for smoothing out the wood surface.

For some open-grained woods, no amount of sanding will get you a smooth finish. Pros use a paste wood filler, a creamy substance that can be packed into the pores of open-grained woods to provide a smooth, even surface on which to apply the finish. Wood fillers are available in water- and oil-based mixes and in neutral or tinted colors to match the wood.

Small dings, holes, and cracks can be filled with the wood putty. Two of the basic types are nitrocellulose-based wood putties, which clean up with lacquer thinner, and acrylic-based putties, which clean up with water. You may also come across gypsum-based putties, which come in powder form. Because the putty may shrink, it's best to build the patch above the wood surface slightly. Once the putty has dried, sanding it down is easy enough.

Larger cracks and holes usually must be repaired by gluing in a piece of wood especially to fit or with a variation of two-part autobody filler, which was developed specifically for use on wood. However, you shouldn't use filler on antiques or other quality pieces.

Filling & Finishing

Apply wood putty *by pressing it into a hole with a putty knife or screwdriver tip. Leave excess to sand flush after drying.*

Small patches *are less noticeable if you match the wood and putty colors. Some dry-mix patches can be stained.*

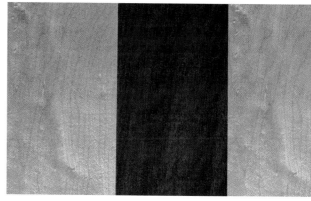

There is a stain *to simulate almost any wood hue, but appearance also depends greatly on the wood itself. In this picture, the same stain was applied to maple (far left), mahogany (second from left), poplar (second from right), and oak (far right).*

Sanding

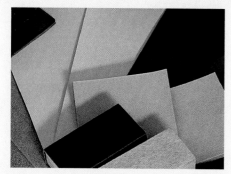

Even with the best tools *to cut and join wood, every project needs sandpaper for final smoothing and finishing.*

Description/grit	Purpose and comments
Extra coarse/12–36	Rough sanding, shaping; not recommended for furniture
Coarse/40–50	Rough sanding, shaping, paint removal, rarely used
Medium/60–80	Rough sanding to remove scratches; follow with finer grit
Fine/100–150	Preliminary sanding of wood before applying finish
Very fine/180–240	Pre-finish prep of hardwoods; between-coat sanding
Extra fine/280–320	Sanding and smoothing finishes between coats
Superfine/360–400	Sanding and smoothing finishes between coats
Ultrafine/500–600 and up	Sanding final finish coats, usually with water or oil

Repairing Veneer

USE: ▶ clothes iron • palette knife • veneer roller • utility knife • clamps ▶ wood glue • cotton cloth • wax paper • masking tape • stain and finish to match

Blisters

1 *To reactivate old veneer glue* and compress a blister, apply a hot iron to a damp cloth laid over the blister.

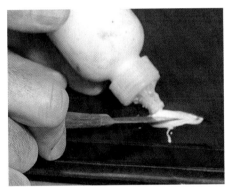

2 *You can slit the veneer* with the grain (if it isn't already split), and work wood glue under a blister.

3 *Once you force glue into a blister,* use a veneer roller to roll the area flat, and force out any excess glue.

Edges

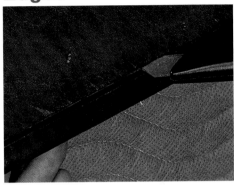

1 *Before regluing loose veneer,* clean out as much old glue as possible from under the edge using a knife or utility blade.

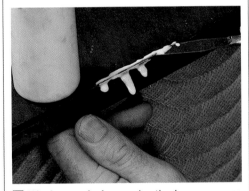

2 *Work wood glue* under the loose veneer using a palette knife or other thin-bladed tool, and clean the excess before clamping.

3 *Clamp the veneer tightly* using a piece of flat scrap wood over wax paper. Use several clamps to distribute pressure.

Patches

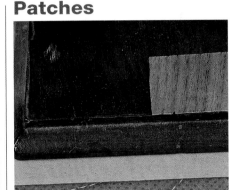

1 *To patch a chipped edge,* cut a similar piece of veneer, and tape it over the damaged area, lining up the grain.

2 *Make a V-shaped cut* over the damaged area. Make several passes to scribe the surface below.

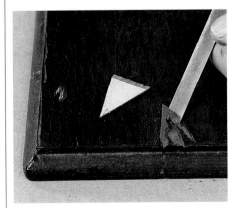

3 *Cut out the damage,* glue the patch in place, and clamp it. When dry, sand it flush, trim it, and apply a finish to match.

furniture

Replacing Cane

USE: ▶ screwdriver • mallet • utility knife

1 Remove damaged cane by lifting the spline that holds the sheet of cane into a groove around the seat.

2 Rough cut a new sheet, and install it glossy side up. Tap on a wood block to set the new spline in the groove.

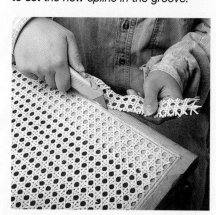

3 When the last section of spline is in place and the cane is tight, use a utility knife to trim off the excess.

Replacing Tapes

USE: ▶ hammer ▶ chair tape • tacks

1 Chair tapes are fabric strips used on chair seats and backs. Start a tape by tacking one end to the chair frame.

2 The tapes often are used in contrasting colors. You wrap one color side to side, and tack the end.

3 Start a second strip (or introduce a shorter repair strip) by weaving it at right angles through the first layer.

Fixing Wicker

USE: ▶ needlenose pliers ▶ glue

1 Nailing often splits older strips of wicker. It's better to add glue and tuck them into a wrapped section.

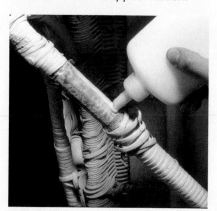

2 To repair loose wrapping of flat wicker, add glue to the supporting chair frame, and rewrap the section.

3 Don't rely on glue to hold the end of the wicker. Tuck the end under the last loop, and trim the excess.

Fixing Upholstery

USE: ▶ pliers • staple gun • hammer

1 To fix loose or damaged springs in upholstered chairs, turn the chair over, and strip off the cover fabric.

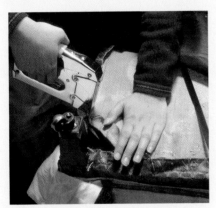

2 You may have to retie some springs, and hold them in tension by restapling strips or sheets of burlap.

3 If necessary, also straighten or replace the spring-holding straps. Nail the ends to the chair frame.

Replacing Webbing

USE: ▶ screwdriver ▶ webbing • hardware

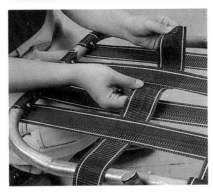

1 Plastic webbing used on lawn chairs may be pinned to the frame with either grommets or screws.

2 To reduce the strain at the end of the webbing, double-fold the end on top of itself to form a point.

3 Wrap the ends of a new seat or a single strip over the frame, and fasten with a washer and screw.

Replacing Canvas

USE: ▶ canvas • dowel

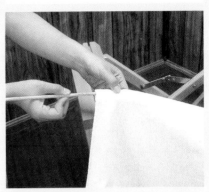

1 Secure canvas to a folding chair by fitting a new dowel through the sleeve on each side of the canvas seat.

2 Slide the reinforced sleeves into grooves on each side of the chair frame. Clean debris from old grooves.

3 To replace a back panel, slide the sleeve at each stitched end over the back frame of the chair.

furniture

Removing Blemishes

Polyurethane, wax, and other finishes are designed to take surface-level wear and tear and prevent damage to the wood below. But no matter how many coats you apply on furniture or floors, some dents and stains get through. Here are fixes—short of a complete refinishing job—for the most common wood blemishes.

Scuff & Burn Marks

Routine buffing should remove light scuff marks on well-sealed wood. Where damage tends to be heavy, rub the marks with a rag or fine steel wool and a wood cleaner.

For burn marks, the amount of refinishing needed depends on the depth of the burn. Light surface damage will respond to a household cleanser, but this will raise the grain slightly, which means you must give the spot a light sanding before you reseal the surface.

For deeper burns, use sandpaper, working with the grain; then clean and finish. Sanding a particularly deep burn may create a surface depression, so you might use bleach to remove all color from affected fibers. Successive treatments, if necessary, will leave a gray, weathered tone. You'll need to stain to match the undamaged wood before resealing the surface.

Dents

The easy fix for a dent is to fill small depressions with wood putty; stain the patch, if need be, and wax the area to match the surrounding gloss and make the repair blend in. On softwoods, you may be able to raise up the dented area. Try applying steam from an iron, or soak the dent with water and apply heat with a heat gun or hair dryer. The idea is to make the compressed fibers swell.

If you must use a filler (which you will on deep dents and scrapes that break the wood fibers), try a porous, sandable wood filler—such as a powder type—that can be easily sanded flush and will accept stain uniformly.

A burn-in resin stick will also remedy the problem. Melted with an electric heat knife, the resin packs the gouge with a pliable filler, which becomes sandable and stainable within minutes. The stick comes with instructions, but experiment with scrap wood before moving on to a piece of furniture.

Repairing Wood Damage

USE: ▶ wood chisel • brush ▶ wood filler • dry stain • touch-up stain and finish • sandpaper

1 *Use a wood chisel* to cut off loose wood from the damaged area. Don't smooth it out—filler bonds best to a rough surface.

2 *Mix the wood filler,* and apply it to the damaged area. Add enough material to allow trimming and shaping later on.

3 *When the filler is dry,* use a small, sharp wood chisel to shape the filled area close to the desired shape.

4 *Use sandpaper* to trim and blend in the repaired section. Small, Dremel-type tools make this sculpturing job much easier.

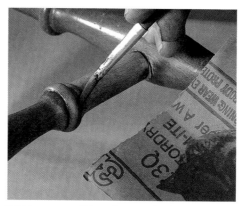

5 *Use a small brush* to stain the repaired area. Match the color of the surrounding wood as closely as possible.

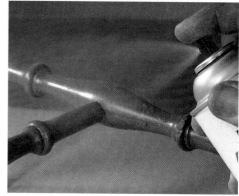

6 *After the stain dries,* apply as many coats of finish as necessary to blend with the surrounding finish.

Fixing Moisture Stains

USE: ▶ #0000 steel wool • 600-grit wet-or-dry sandpaper • sanding block • furniture paste wax • soft cotton rag

1 *Use fine steel wool* to rub over the stained area. Apply firm pressure in the direction of the grain.

2 *Use fine wet-dry sandpaper* to sand the area. It helps to use a small amount of mineral spirits as a lubricant.

3 *Rub the area again* with fine steel wool and paste wax. To help the repair blend in, finish by buffing with a soft cotton cloth.

Fixing Wax Drips & Stains

USE: ▶ plastic scraper (or plastic card) ▶ ice cube • #0000 steel wool • soft cotton rag

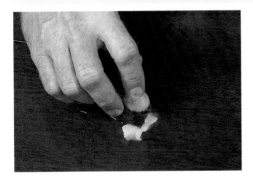

1 *Apply an ice cube* to the wax to make it harder and more brittle. This makes the residue easier to remove.

2 *Use the edge of a plastic card* or a nonmarring plastic scraper to scrape the wax off the wood surface.

3 *Apply cream polish* to the area with fine steel wool, rubbing in the direction of the grain. Finish by rubbing with a clean cloth.

Fixing Burns

USE: ▶ razor blade • burn-in knife • brush ▶ lacquer stick • wet-or-dry sandpaper • touch-up stain and finish

1 *One way to fix small burns* is to cut away loose and damaged fibers, and fill the spot using a heat tool called a burn-in knife.

2 *When the burn-in knife* gets hot enough to melt a color-matched lacquer stick, transfer some to the knife tip.

3 *Apply the lacquer* until it fuses and is slightly higher than the surface; use fine sandpaper and mineral spirits to sand flush.

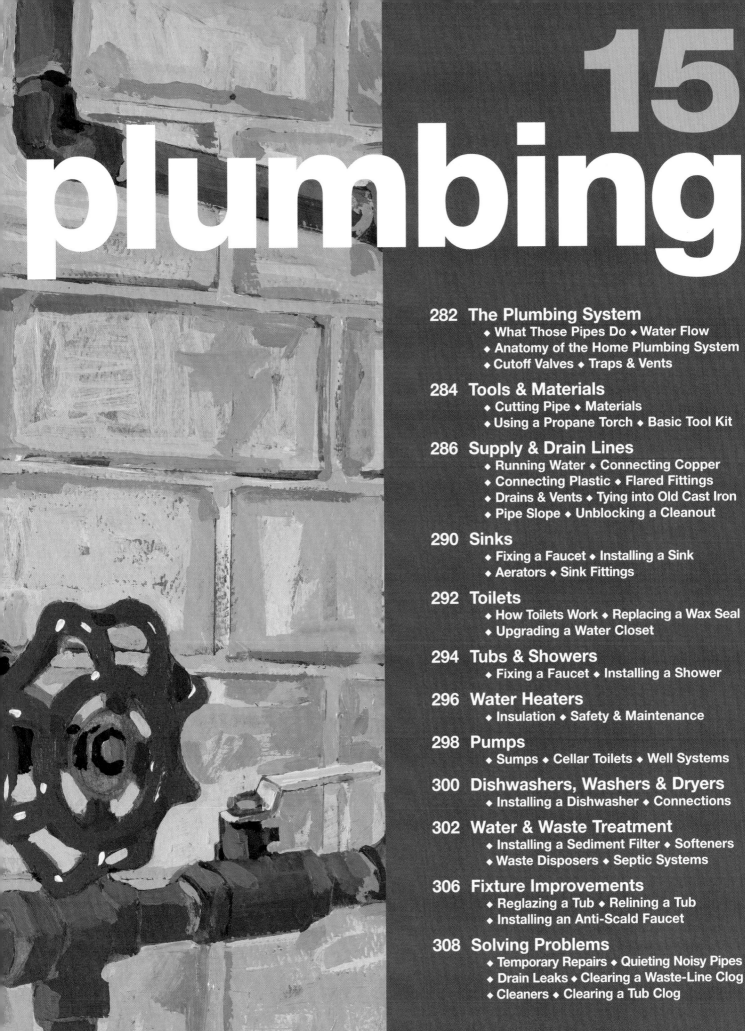

15 plumbing

plumbing

What Those Pipes Do

If dealing with plumbing problems seems like a pain, remember that before indoor plumbing, any water used for cooking and washing had to be carried into the house by hand, and whatever wastewater remained went out the same way. And then there was the outhouse, where answering the call of nature could mean trekking outside in the rain or dark of night.

Parts of the Plumbing System

A modern household plumbing system has three basic parts: water supply pipes that distribute water (hot and cold) throughout the house; appliances, faucets, toilets, and various other plumbing fixtures that draw water; and the system that carries wastewater out of the house (the DWV, or drain-waste-vent system). Country houses draw water from underground wells, but most houses today are supplied (for a price) by city water pipes. A water meter keeps track of how much is used.

Inside the house, the main supply line splits, with one branch feeding all the cold-water pipes in the house and the other supplying water to the water heater. The hot-water line coming out of the water heater branches, paralleling cold-water lines throughout the house. The two lines supply hot and cold water to sinks, tubs, showers, dishwashers, and all other plumbing fixtures as needed. (Toilets and outside faucets don't need hot-water pipes.)

When water goes down the drain, it enters the DWV system. Part of the system actually channels the water down to the main house drain; the other part consists of pipes (called vents) that rise up out of the drainpipes to the roof. Vents allow in outside air to replace the air displaced by flowing water; otherwise, the negative pressure would suck the water out of your traps. (See "Traps & Vents," at right.)

Besides supply lines and drainpipes, gas pipes and hot-water heating pipes may also run through your house. Gas pipes are usually iron or copper, and run between the gas meter and a stove or other appliance that uses gas. (Copper tubing may also be used for gas.) Other than shutting a gas cutoff valve in an emergency, you should always call professionals to work on gas pipes. The same goes for heating pipes: Steam and scalding water can be very dangerous.

Water Flow

If you use water from a municipal system, the main shutoff valve and the water meter are located where the water-company supply line enters your house, generally along a foundation wall. The water meter keeps track of how many gallons flow into your plumbing system. Most companies meter water by CCFs. One CCF is 100 cubic feet of water, which equals 748 gallons. Most bills also list use in gallons used per day for the billing period.

Water meters *are the property of the water utility. They should be called if it is leaking or not working properly.*

Anatomy of the Home Plumbing System

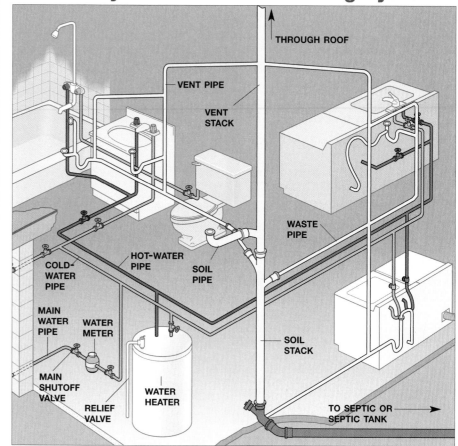

Residential plumbing has three basic components: supply pipes that deliver water (typically copper or plastic), drainpipes that carry away waste (generally plastic), and vent pipes (also plastic) that allow the system to drain freely.

Cutoff Valves

The main cutoff valve for your water supply system will be near the spot where the municipal water pipe enters your home or, if you have well water, near the storage tank. Other cutoff valves farther along enable you to turn off just part of the water supply system, allowing you to close a valve to fix a leak in the bathroom, for example, and still have water in the rest of the house. Though sometimes hard to find, there should be valves on supply lines near toilets and water heaters; other fixtures depend on local regulations.

Every water-using appliance or fixture, like this toilet, should be isolated with its own easily accessible cutoff valve.

If you can't find or turn a fixture cutoff and need to stop an emergency leak, use the main valve located near the meter.

Traps & Vents

Most people know about the drain-pipe running from each sink, bathtub, and other plumbing fixture in a house. It carries wastewater down to the main pipes of the drainage system. But the drainpipe for each one of those plumbing fixtures also has a trap—the curved section of pipe that you can usually see right below a sink.

The trap's main purpose is to prevent noxious (and potentially lethal) sewer gases from rising up through the drains. Because of their shape, traps always have water in them, which provides an airtight seal. The traps are always near a drain opening, although some may be hidden below the floor (such as those on tubs) or out of sight in the basement.

Each drain must be vented, as well. Vent pipes are usually located near the drain opening after the trap; sometimes multiple drains are served by one vent (called wet venting). Vents connect to a drainpipe and run either directly to the roof or horizontally to another vent. Without them, wastewater flowing down the drain would empty the trap due to siphoning action. Instead, vents allow outside air to flow into the pipe, breaking the siphon action.

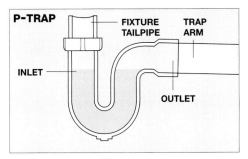

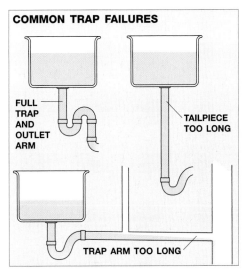

Traps are designed to keep a small amount of water in the drain line. The water effectively seals out sewer gas.

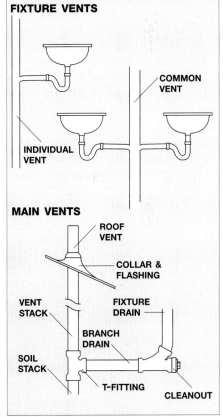

Vent pipes are designed to let water drain freely and to release sewer gas outside the house.

plumbing

Cutting Pipe

If you want to take care of plumbing repairs yourself, sooner or later you will have to cut pieces of pipe. For copper pipe, get a pipe cutter, which scores the pipe around its perimeter with a cutting wheel. It is possible to make clean-edged, accurate cuts using a hacksaw, but that can be difficult on existing pipes tucked between wall studs where there isn't much room. Wheel-type cutters work where hacksaws can't go because they are more compact.

Try out the cutter a few times on a scrap piece of pipe to get the idea. First, fit it around the pipe, and tighten the handle until you feel resistance. After you rotate the cutter around the pipe once or twice, you'll feel less resistance as the wheel deepens its cutting groove. Tighten the handle again to make the wheel bite in a little deeper; keep rotating and tightening until the wheel cuts all the way through the pipe. With some practice, you'll get the knack of tightening the handle gradually while you're rotating the cutter. If you find it difficult to rotate, the wheel is biting in too deeply, and you should back off on the handle a bit.

Sometimes even a relatively clean cut needs smoothing around the inner edges, which improves water flow and prevents buildup of mineral deposits on the pipe's inner wall. There are reaming tools for cleaning up burrs; many wheel cutters have fold-out reamers. You can also use carbide sandpaper or a round metal file.

Cutting Plastic & Iron

Cut rigid PVC plastic pipe with a coarse-toothed hacksaw or a fine-toothed carpenter's saw. To ensure a square cut, wedge the pipe firmly against a piece of wood screwed down to your workbench. Pipe already in place can be stabilized for cutting by taping it tightly to a nearby joist, stud, or pipe. The inside edge of cut plastic pipe must be cleaned and smoothed before installation. A razor knife works best.

Small iron pipe (½ to 2 inches) is best cut with a wheel cutter; a course-toothed hacksaw also works well. Larger iron pipe is cut with a tool called a chain cutter, which is available at rental stores. Alternatively, you can score a cut in the pipe with a hammer and a cold chisel.

Materials

COPPER

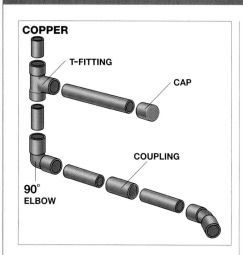

- T-FITTING
- CAP
- COUPLING
- 90° ELBOW

Soldered copper is the material of choice (and of many local codes) for carrying water to fixtures and appliances.

PLASTIC

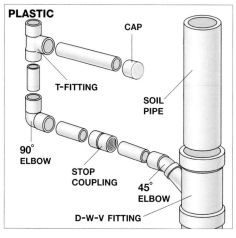

- CAP
- T-FITTING
- SOIL PIPE
- 90° ELBOW
- STOP COUPLING
- 45° ELBOW
- D-W-V FITTING

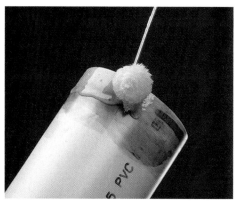

Glued plastic is lighter, less expensive, and easier to install than copper. It is widely used for water supply, drains, and vents.

GALVANIZED METAL

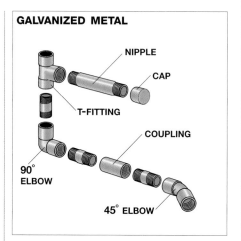

- NIPPLE
- CAP
- T-FITTING
- COUPLING
- 90° ELBOW
- 45° ELBOW

Threaded galvanized iron pipe is the standard for carrying natural gas but not for water or wastes.

Using a Propane Torch

Before you try to heat up a pipe with a torch—to thaw a frozen section or to resolder a joint—first drain the line. You can't get copper hot enough to make solder flow when it is filled with water. Also, open a faucet just beyond the repair so that any steam that develops can escape. Be careful using propane torches in tight spots where the flame may lick past the pipe and heat up building materials nearby. Use extra care working in framing cavities, particularly in older homes where the wood is very dry.

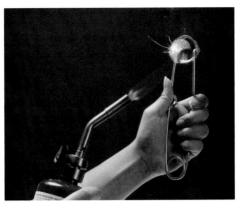

1 *Use a sparking tool* to safely ignite gas from the torch. Turn on a gentle supply of gas, and squeeze the sparker handle.

2 *Once the gas is ignited,* increase the gas flow to enlarge the flame. It's wise to wear gloves when you handle heated pipes.

Basic Tool Kit

There are some basic plumbing tools that every household should have on hand: a toilet plunger for freeing clogs in toilets and sinks; a closet auger for clearing out more serious blocks in drains, waste pipes, and soil pipes; and a variety of wrenches for making simple repairs to fittings. More complex repair work and installation requires different, specialized tools—not just specific wrenches but valve seat reamers, pipe cutters, and tube benders.

A round file and sandpaper also should be included in the basic tool kit. In place of a relatively expensive pipe reamer, use the file to remove burrs from the inner edge of freshly cut copper pipe. Medium-grit sandpaper or emery cloth is used to clean the exterior surface of the end of copper pipes, which is important when soldering pipes together. Then, too, you'll need the propane torch, flux, and solder for that job. A Phillips head and a standard screwdriver for #8 and #6 screws are also important basic tools because machine screws in faucets, sillcocks, and cutoff valves often need tightening or loosening during repairs.

A basic plumbing kit includes a hand auger (A), plumber's putty (B), adjustable wrenches (C & D), Stilson pipe wrench (E), slip-jaw pliers (F), solder (G), Allen wrenches (H), propane torch (I), tubing cutter (J), screwdriver (K), pipe-joint compound (L), basin wrench (M), soldering paste or flux (N), heat-proof grease (O), handle puller (P), packing string (Q), Teflon tape (R), gaskets and washers (S), toilet plunger (T), and saw (U).

plumbing

Running Water

Water supply lines, which distribute hot and cold water to all the plumbing fixtures in your house, are much smaller than drainpipes—usually they range from ½ to 1 inch in diameter. The pipe walls have to be reasonably thick, though, because the water these pipes carry is under pressure. (The pressure makes the water flow when you turn on the tap.) Houses built before the 1960s may have galvanized iron water pipes. Newer homes have copper or plastic pipes. Local codes regulate what kinds of supply lines can be used in your area.

Pipes & Fittings

Copper water supply lines inside the house come in two grades: Type M or the thicker-walled Type L. Plumbing-supply stores sell this kind of hard copper pipe in ½-, ¾-, and 1-inch diameters and 10- and 20-foot lengths. Type K copper pipe has the thickest walls and is used for underground water lines.

Plastic supply lines are CPVC (chlorinated polyvinyl chloride), which is rigid and off-white, or PEX (cross-linked polyethylene), which is white and flexible. PE (polyethylene), which is black, is most often used for underground watering systems. Black Schedule 40 ABS (acrylonitrile butadiene styrene) and white Schedule 40 PVC are both used for drain and vent lines.

Fittings, such as elbows and reducers, come in the same materials as the piping. You can also buy fittings for transitions between iron and copper pipe or CPVC and copper.

Connecting Plastic

USE: ▶ fine-toothed saw or tubing cutter • utility knife • felt pen (for marking) ▶ rigid plastic pipe

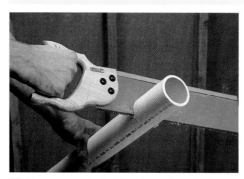

1 You can cut plastic pipes (supply lines, drains, and vents) with almost any saw, but a fine-toothed blade makes a cleaner cut.

2 When you cut through plastic, even a fine-toothed saw can leave burrs and small shavings. Trim them off with a utility knife.

Measuring

Until you get used to the system, you have to remember to measure the length of pipe between fittings, and add the amount of pipe that rests inside elbows, tees, and nipples. The safest approach is to hold a rough-cut length in place (with copper and plastic), and mark the overall distance from the barrel of one fitting to another. To be sure everything fits, test-fit several sections and fittings. Then, disassemble the pieces, make any adjustments, and solder or glue them together.

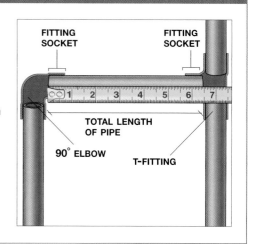

Connecting Copper

USE: ▶ hacksaw or tubing cutter • propane torch • spark lighter • wire brush or sandpaper • flux brush • work gloves • eye protection • rags ▶ copper pipe and

1 You can cut copper pipe to length with a hacksaw, but a tubing cutter that rotates around the pipe makes a much cleaner cut.

2 Plumbers use a small tool with metal wires inside to brighten copper for the best solder bond. Use sandpaper in a pinch.

3 To brighten the interior surfaces of a connection, use a wire-brush tool, and rotate it several times in the fitting.

& fittings • solvent glue • pipe primer

3 *You can use one coat of adhesive* in many cases, or start with a prep solvent that cleans the surface for better adhesion.

4 *Apply liquid adhesive for plastic pipe* to mating surfaces. Be sure to read and follow all label cautions.

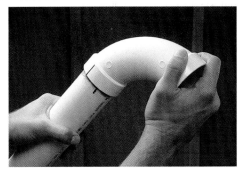

5 *Plastic pipe adhesive* softens mating surfaces. They become one when the surfaces harden. You need to work quickly.

Making Flared Fittings

USE: ▶ two-piece flaring tool ▶ copper pipe • brass flare fittings

1 *Use flared fittings* where soldering would be unsafe. The base part of a flaring tool clamps around the pipe.

2 *The top of the flaring set* forces the lip of the pipe against the clamp to create a bell-shaped flare.

3 *A flaring nut* on one side of the joint threads onto a flaring union on the other. Most codes don't allow flares in walls.

fittings • solder • flux

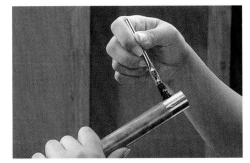

4 *To draw solder* completely into the joint (even uphill against gravity), coat mating surfaces with soldering paste, called flux.

5 *Assemble the connection*, and apply heat evenly to the entire joint. Wear gloves or use clamps to handle heated pipes.

6 *When the copper* is hot enough to melt solder, remove the flame and apply solder around the joint. The hot metal can scorch.

plumbing

Drains & Vents

Pipes in the drain-waste-vent (DWV) system rely on gravity to carry liquid and solid wastes downward to the main house drain and out to the underground sewer or a septic tank. Smaller drainpipes called waste pipes, usually at least 1½ inches in diameter, carry wastewater from sinks, showers, and appliances. Soil pipes, which handle solid wastes from toilets and serve as the main house drain, are larger: 3 or 4 inches around. Most drain lines lead to the house's main drain, called the soil stack. (The portion above the highest fixture that leads to the roof is called the vent stack.) The soil stack (and some fixture drains) lead to the house drain.

Both waste pipes and soil pipes have vent pipes that run upward to the roof or horizontal branch lines that tie into a vertical vent. The vents equalize air pressure inside pipes to keep the water from being siphoned out of the traps. Vent pipes tend to be slightly smaller than the drains they connect to—waste drains have, say, 1½-inch vents; soil pipes, 2-inch vents.

Soil pipes and their vents are made from cast iron or plastic. Waste drain lines and vents are usually iron, galvanized steel, or plastic.

Getting Good Drain Flow

If drainpipes always flowed straight downward they probably wouldn't back up as easily as they sometimes do. Instead, they must follow twisting paths inside walls and floors, and there will always be sections that run horizontally, not straight down. In these sections, the pipe still slopes downward, but the proper angle is critical—a ¼-inch downward slope for every foot of horizontal pipe is just right. Make the slope less than that, and water and solid waste flow too sluggishly and may back up. Make it steeper, and the extra slope causes the water to flow faster than the solids, which get left behind and build up in that section.

You can also improve drainage by avoiding 90-degree turns when laying out waste pipes; use two 45-degree elbows instead. If the space is tight, go with a long-sweep 90-degree elbow. Do not use tight-turning 90-degree vent pipe elbows in the waste portion of the drain system. And include Y cleanout fittings where pipes of the same size tie in and then make long horizontal runs to a larger waste pipe.

Low-Volume Toilets

In 1992, the Department of Energy mandated low-volume, 1.6-gallon toilets as a water-conservation measure. But a nationwide survey of builders and homeowners conducted by the National Association of Home Builders found that roughly four out of five experienced problems with low-flush units. Most builders surveyed said that they receive more callbacks on low-flush toilets than on anything else.

There are three common complaints: multiple flushes are needed to clear the bowl; residue remains even after multiple flushes; and they clog easily. New low-flush units work better than the first models, but many builders and owners still have to call in plumbers. And some service calls cost up to $500 due to damage from overflows. To deal with the problems, most people revert to double flushing, which defeats much of the water-conservation potential of the system.

If you have a choice, there are two basic types of low-flush units to choose from. Gravity-tank toilets, the most common and inexpensive, depend on the siphoning action of water in the tank to flush wastes. Pressure-tank toilets (pictured) have a secondary container inside. It uses the pressure of water coming into the main tank to compress air and give each flush a pressure assist to push out wastes. This hybrid design is roughly twice the cost of gravity units.

Low-volume toilets have the potential to save up to 12,000 gallons of water a year in a typical household. But even the best low-flush units can cause problems in bathroom remodeling projects

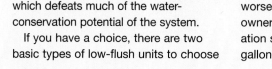

because drainage plumbing in some older houses is designed to work with a higher water-flow rate. If you have had intermittent drainage problems in the past, installing a low-flush unit will probably make them worse. This dilemma drives some homeowners to recycling yards and restoration suppliers in search of older 3.5-gallon toilets, no matter what their style.

Tying into Old Cast Iron

USE: ▶ riser clamps (strap hangers for horizontal pipe) • chain cutter • adjustable wrenches • chalk

1 *Support heavy cast iron* on both sides of the cut with riser clamps. Mount the upper clamp on blocks before cutting.

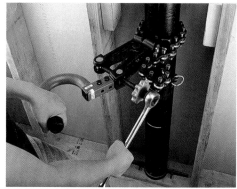

2 *To cut cast iron,* rent a chain cutter. Wrap the chain and its cutting wheels around the pipe, tighten, and twist.

Pipe Slope

Proper pipe slope is critical to maintaining efficient drainage and clean, non-clogging waste pipes. As a general rule, use ¼ inch of vertical drop for every horizontal foot of the pipe. Use a taut mason's string to determine where pipe hangers should be positioned before beginning to assemble lengths of pipe. Hang pipes to minimize cutting into joists. Observe local codes covering both incoming water and outgoing wastes.

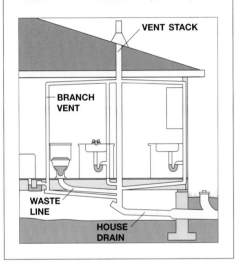

VENT STACK

BRANCH VENT

WASTE LINE

HOUSE DRAIN

Unblocking a Cleanout

USE: ▶ Stilson wrench • hand or power auger ▶ Teflon tape or pipe dope

1 Use a Stilson wrench to unscrew the cap on a Y-shaped cleanout fitting and gain access for clearing blockages.

2 Feed a plumbing auger into the cleanout extension. Provide ventilation to carry away noxious sewer gas.

3 To clear blockages, most pros use a power auger that extends and turns the snake line. (You can rent one.)

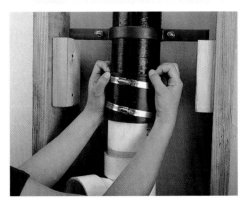

4 To provide a positive seal against sewer gas, add tape or pipe dope to the cap before tightening it in place.

• socket wrench • measuring tape • screwdriver • work gloves ▶ plastic pipe and fittings • rubber gaskets • banded clamps

3 New plastic fittings tie into cast iron with heavy rubber gaskets and banded clamps. Slip the gaskets over each cut end.

4 Fix short pipe stubs in the plastic fitting, set it in place, and slide the gaskets over the connecting joints.

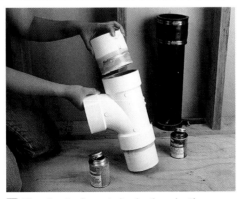

5 Leave the clamps loose, so you can maneuver the gaskets into position, and then tighten down the four clamp rings.

plumbing

Sink Basics

A sink is a sink, unless it's in the bathroom, in which case it's called a lavatory (from the Latin word meaning "to wash"). Sink or lavatory, the job it does is the same—to provide a basin to receive potable water, retain it as long as you want, and then drain it away when you're done.

If you ever have to buy a sink, you'll find out just how many different kinds there are. Sinks are made from enameled cast iron and steel, cultured marble, stainless steel, vitreous china, and even plastic. Bathroom lavs— round, oval, or square—can be mounted in the countertop of a vanity, hung from the wall, or supported on a pedestal attached to the bathroom floor. Kitchen sinks, often made of stainless steel or enameled iron, are usually mounted in kitchen countertops and may have one, two, or even three bowls.

Countertop-mounted sinks can be attached in three ways. Self-rimmed sinks have a molded lip that overhangs the edge of the hole in the counter and so holds the basin in place. Face-rimmed sinks are secured to the counter-top by a metal strip around the basin edge. Unrimmed sinks are mounted to the underside of the counter with metal clips.

Bathroom sinks also have a few features in common. Most have pop-up stoppers controlled by lift rods to keep water in the sink when needed and an opening called an overflow that allows water to flow out of a stopped sink after the water reaches a certain height.

Fixing a Faucet

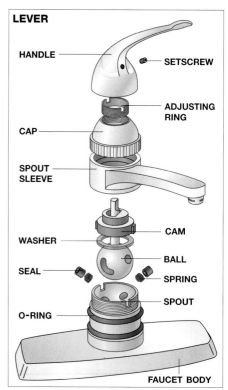

STEM

- TRIM CAP
- SCREW
- HANDLE
- PACKING NUT
- STEM
- PACKING
- THREADS
- SCREW
- SEAT WASHER
- VALVE SEAT
- FAUCET BODY

Many houses have stem faucets that screw up and down to open and close the water flow. The most common weak link is the washer at the base of the stem. You need to take the stem out and remove the holding screw to replace it.

LEVER

- HANDLE
- SETSCREW
- ADJUSTING RING
- CAP
- SPOUT SLEEVE
- CAM
- WASHER
- BALL
- SEAL
- SPRING
- SPOUT
- O-RING
- FAUCET BODY

Lever faucets come in several types, such as disk- and ball-types that do not use threads. The common weak link is wear between disks. You have to remove a small setscrew at the base of the lever to remove it.

Installing a Sink

USE: ▶ adjustable wrenches • pipe wrench • basin wrench • slip-jaw pliers ▶ sink • flexible tubing • coupling nuts • trap bend • trap arm • compression washer

1 *A counterset faucet* has an 8-in. spread between valves. Join the control valves to the spout with flexible tubing.

2 *Press putty* around the drain flange, and thread the flange onto the drain tube inserted through the sink drain opening.

3 *Tighten the nut on the drain tube* from below, and attach the pop-up lever to the lift rod inserted through the faucet.

Aerators

An aerator screws onto a faucet nozzle to decrease the force and amount of the water flow. If the flow seems sluggish, the aerator may be clogged. If you can't unscrew the aerator by hand, wrap electrical tape around the jaws of pliers, lock them on the aerator, and turn counterclockwise to loosen it; finish unscrewing it by hand. Flush out deposits from the screen and soak it in vinegar, or use a toothbrush to loosen residue. If that doesn't help, replace it.

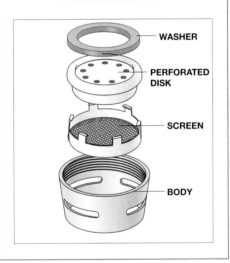

WASHER

PERFORATED DISK

SCREEN

BODY

Sink Fittings

To work in tight spaces under sinks, you need to use special tools. A spud wrench makes work on sink drains easier, while a basin wrench is indispensable for faucet work—its swiveling head can be wormed into spaces too confining for other wrenches. Plastic sink fittings are easier to work with than iron, copper, or brass, but be careful because plastic breaks more easily than metal. When working with threaded pieces, remember that they usually require only tightening by hand. If you have hard water, avoid mixing copper fittings with iron pipe.

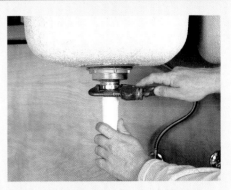

The nut joining the plastic tailpiece to the drain spud is metallic, so tighten it in place with a wrench.

Use a basin wrench to reach between the sink and wall to tighten the supply risers to the faucet.

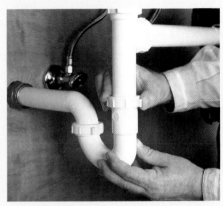

To connect a sink to the drain line, buy a plastic sink-waste kit. Tighten the fittings only hand tight.

• plumber's putty

4 *The trap for a pedestal lavatory* is hard to reach later, so attach it to the basin drain before setting the basin.

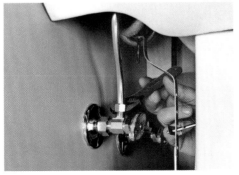

5 *Set the basin* on the pedestal, and join the faucet to the valves with chrome supply tubes. Tighten the compression nuts.

6 *To connect the trap,* slide a compression washer and nut onto the trap arm. Insert the arm into the drain and tighten.

plumbing

How Toilets Work

Though it may seem baffling when something goes wrong, there really isn't much to your toilet's inner workings. The two most basic parts are the toilet tank, which holds the water needed to flush, and the toilet bowl, which connects directly to the soil pipe by way of a built-in trap. (That's why there is always some water in the bowl.)

Pushing the toilet handle lifts a valve (often a rubber flapper type) and, thanks to gravity, water in the tank floods down into the bowl by way of the flush passages. As water rises in the bowl, it pushes the level up over the top of the internal trap. Water then flows down the drain, drawing with it any wastes in the bowl.

Meanwhile, back at the toilet tank, the flapper valve closes as the tank empties, and a float valve (or pressure sensor) turns on the water supply valve to refill the tank. The float rises with the water level and shuts off the supply valve when it reaches the preset level (or the water is deep enough to create the predetermined level of water pressure).

The tank also has an overflow tube that keeps water from running out over the top of the tank in the event the water supply valve fails to shut off. The small pipe running into the overflow tube is the bowl refill tube, which adds some water to the bowl after flushing ceases. That reseals the trap and prevents foul-smelling sewer gases from coming up through the toilet.

Replacing a Wax Seal

USE: ▶ adjustable wrench • hacksaw • putty knife or scraper • rags ▶ new wax ring • closet bolts

1 *Before working on a toilet,* turn off the fixture cutoff valve. Then disconnect the supply tube, and empty the holding tank.

2 *Empty the bowl,* pry the caps from the closet bolts, and undo the nuts. If the nuts are corroded, cut them off with a hacksaw.

Adjusting a Ball Float

You can adjust the ball float to change the height of the water in the reservoir. Adjust it too high, and the toilet runs constantly; too low, and flushing isn't efficient. Adjust the float by bending the brass float arm up or down, as needed. If the float is on a pull rod, adjust the spring clip on the lower end of the rod.

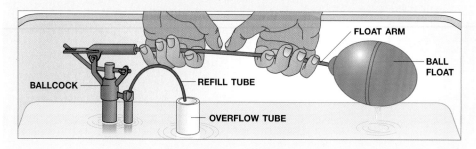

FLOAT ARM

BALL FLOAT

BALLCOCK

REFILL TUBE

OVERFLOW TUBE

Upgrading a Water Closet

USE: ▶ adjustable wrench • spud wrench • needlenose pliers • screwdriver • wire brush • masonry bit • work gloves ▶ fill valve kit • pipe dope

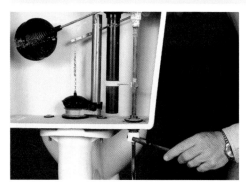

1 *To replace a fill valve,* drain the tank, loosen the supply riser fastening nut, and then loosen the jamb nut above it.

2 *Clean the tank around the opening,* coat the new fill valve's washer with pipe dope, and install the valve in the opening.

3 *Attach the fill valve's small tube* to the tank overflow; use the connecting clip packaged with the fill-valve kit.

• penetrating oil (optional)

3 To remove a toilet, *grip it by the bowl next to the seat hinges. Set it on newspaper, and stuff a rag into the soil pipe.*

4 Scrape away any old wax *from the worn gasket with a putty knife or scraper. Remove the old closet bolts as well.*

5 Install new closet bolts *in the flange and a new wax ring. Then, remove the rag, reset the toilet, and refasten the connections.*

Eliminating Tank Condensation

The cold water supply can make the bowl cool enough to cause moisture in warm interior air to condense. And flowing condensation can damage floors. To defeat this problem you can buy a toilet with factory-installed insulation, or use a retrofit insulation kit. Another option is a special mixing valve that adds hot water to temper the cold supply.

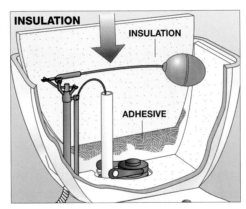

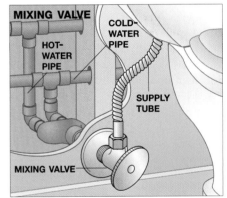

• household cleanser • new flapper valve • retrofit flush-valve seat kit • emery cloth

4 To upgrade a flapper *(sealing the outlet), remove the old flapper, and hook the eyelets of a new flapper over the flush-valve hooks.*

5 To install a retrofit flush-valve seat, *use the kit's epoxy putty to stick the new seat over the old.*

6 With the new seat fastened in place, *feed the plastic lift chain through the hole in the flush lever.*

plumbing

Shower Options

Over anything but the most heavy-duty walls, using tile for showers is a case of good looks overwhelming good sense. You're building a watertight enclosure to resist leaks and to withstand the weight of people moving around inside but including weak links—namely, the leak-prone grout joints between tiles. The result is an attractive maintenance nightmare.

A popular alternative is to replace the tile with a seamless, one-piece fiberglass or solid-surface-material shower. Choices range from very narrow units that trigger claustrophobia to spacious combination tub-showers—some with luxurious whirlpool jets, extra spray nozzles, and steam generators.

The smallest sizes of one-piece units generally can be maneuvered through existing halls and stairwells, but before you buy, be sure to check that you can get the unit through the front door and into the bathroom. If you want to use more spacious models, there are two options. One is to take out a few extra studs during your bath remodeling job and to make sure that the shower is ordered in time for delivery while the walls are open. Another option is to order a special remodeling unit that comes in two or three pieces.

Cracking

Even well-made, rib-reinforced fiberglass can flex under body weight. That can lead to hairline cracks in the shower floor finish, which eventually lead to larger cracks that leak. To prevent flexing, mound a light masonry mix under the shower floor before the unit is installed and plumbed.

Consider this a mandatory part of the installation—even if it isn't included in the instructions and even if your contractor says that the fiberglass is strong enough without it. Making this supporting mud pie takes all of 5 minutes and could save the entire installation.

Sound Insulation

Packing the walls around the shower with insulation is not really necessary, but it's a nice touch that reduces the kind of tin-roof echoing of water against the thin shower walls. Some are even available with soundproofing insulation molded right into the unit.

Drains

Pop-up and plunger tub drains are notorious for getting plugged up, usually with some combination of hair and congealed soap. This is a particularly difficult blockage to move using only a plunger. So when you install a new tub enclosure, it pays to take three precautionary steps. First, install a wide-mouth plunger drain with both a removable, fine-mesh screen that is flush with the shower stall floor, and another wide-mesh, or crosshair, screen directly underneath. These should catch most of the debris before it has a chance to move into the trap. Second, make sure that the drain linkages operate smoothly. Third, provide access to the trap, so you can take it apart and clear blockages.

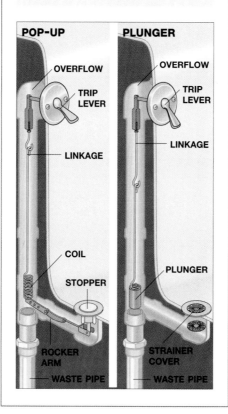

POP-UP — OVERFLOW, TRIP LEVER, LINKAGE, COIL, STOPPER, ROCKER ARM, WASTE PIPE

PLUNGER — OVERFLOW, TRIP LEVER, LINKAGE, PLUNGER, STRAINER COVER, WASTE PIPE

Fixing a Faucet

USE: ▶ slip-jaw pliers • socket wrench with deep

1 *To repair a deep-set tub faucet,* cut off the water supply, undo the handle, and back the retainer nut from the escutcheon.

Installing a Shower

USE: ▶ drill/driver • tubing cutter or hacksaw

1 *Use the preformed shower base,* pushed tightly against both walls, to mark the drain location on the floor. Cut the hole.

5 *Prepare the shower wall panels* by applying two-sided foam tape to the edges and panel adhesive to the fields.

socket for faucets • screwdriver ▶ replacement parts (as needed)

2 Use a deep socket kit *designed to reach deep-set faucet fittings to back the faucet stem from the faucet.*

3 Some older faucets *have stems that seat inside replaceable sleeves. Stem parts and worn sleeves can be replaced.*

4 Back the screw *from the base of the faucet stem, and replace the washer. Make sure the replacement is the same size.*

• propane torch (optional) • caulking gun • safety gear ▶ shower stall kit • cement board • pipes and fittings • insulation • solder and flux or adhesive • silicone caulk

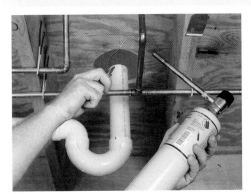

2 With the shower drain trap in place, *cut into existing hot- and cold-water lines, and solder in connecting fittings.*

3 Measure carefully *to establish the exact center of the faucet opening, and then drill the shower panel with a hole saw.*

4 Solder in the shower valve *about 48 in. off the floor, and secure it to a backing board in the wall with copper straps.*

6 Start each panel *against the shower pan base, and gradually arch it against the wall, pressing it in place.*

7 Set the vertical enclosure panels *in their tracks, and apply caulk along the side and base tracks.*

8 Set the end panel *into the base track, and snap it into its vertical track. Finish with the top track and door assembly.*

plumbing

Hot Water

Showers just would not be the same without plenty of hot water, and it's the water heater's job to keep it coming. The heater's capacity does matter—a 40-gallon tank should be enough for a family of four—but if two showers are running and the dishwasher is going, it may not be able to keep up. Suddenly that soothing hot shower turns tepid, and then icy cold.

Elements of a Water Heater

The two most common water heaters are gas and electric. Both have a water tank (capacities range from 30 to 80 gallons), a cold-water inlet, and a hot-water outlet pipe. Turning on a hot-water faucet causes hot water to flow out of the heater's tank and draws cold water in through the dip tube, which carries it to the bottom of the tank. With cold water flowing in, the tank's water temperature will cool below the preset temperature (usually about 120°F). That activates the heater's thermostat, which turns on the gas burner (or the electrode in electric heaters) to raise the temperature.

The recovery rate measures how fast the cold water in the tank heats up. Gas heaters heat the water more quickly, having a better recovery rate, and because of this, electric models must have a larger tank capacity.

Water heaters have a temperature and pressure (T&P) relief valve that prevents the tank from exploding. Most also have a magnesium anode rod, which sheds electrons as it corrodes, helping to keep the tank from rusting. The size and number of anodes determine the life of the heater.

Capacity & Recovery Rates

Before installing a water heater, first estimate how much hot water you will need during the peak hour of use—for example, in the morning when three or four people need to shower, breakfast dishes need to be washed, and Dad needs to shave. (See the table below.) But a large-capacity tank is not the only way to avoid having that fourth shower be ice-cold. The heater's recovery rate is the number of gallons per hour that the heater can produce. A 30-gallon heater might be able to recover 55 gallons of hot water an hour, more than a 50-gallon model.

Typical Hot-Water Use

Activity	Gallons Used
Showering	3 gals./minute
Bathing	15–25 gals./bath
Shaving	1–3 gals.
Washing hands	½–2 gals.
Washing dishes	4–6 gals.
Running dishwasher	5–20 gals./load
Running clothes washer	25–40 gals./load
Cleaning house	5–12 gals.
Food preparation	1–6 gals.

Gas Piping

The main supply line and valve may be black iron, although many building codes call for flexible copper tubing for gas lines, with flared compression fittings at the joints. To avoid kinks, bend tubing with a special spring-like coil. Where abrupt turns are necessary, use 90-degree flared compression fittings. Once the gas is turned on, brush soapy water on fittings to test for leaks indicated by bubbles. Most leaks can be fixed by tightening the fitting.

To test the seal at a gas fitting, brush the joints with soapy water. If bubbles appear, turn off the supply to the pipe.

Water Heater Insulation

Insulating your water heater, as well as the hot-water pipes, is the easiest way to improve hot-water efficiency. Where plumbing is exposed in a crawl space or cellar, cover hot-water lines with foam insulating tubes. Technically, heat radiating through pipe walls isn't lost because it helps to warm floors inside the house. But insulation that keeps water in the pipes warmer helps to deliver hotter water where you want it, and you waste less water running tepid water through the tap.

Cut partially across the top piece, and fit it carefully before taping it down. On a gas heater, be sure not to block the draft diverter.

Wrap the sides of the heater with the larger blanket, and tape the seams. Cut carefully around controls and the drain.

Tankless Heaters

These compact wall-hung units combine a coil of hot-water supply pipe and a heating element fired by natural gas, propane, or electricity. The idea is to heat water on demand instead of storing it. For example, when you open the tap, the heating element on a gas unit envelops the coil in flame and heats the water passing through. A small unit may work in a remote bath far from the main heater but may not be able to handle the demand of baths that are used often.

HOT-WATER OUTLET

COLD-WATER INLET

POWER SWITCH ASSEMBLY

HEATING COILS

ELECTRICAL TERMINALS

Safety & Maintenance

USE: ▶ socket wrench ▶ replacement valve • replacement anode rod • Teflon tape

All water heaters should be fitted with a pressure-relief valve. It's unlikely that the valve will be needed. But if problems in the heater developed to the point where the tank could explode, the relief valve would open and vent steam and overheated water. That's why the valve is connected to pipes that run to the edge of the heater and down toward the floor. You should test the valve periodically, and if it fails to operate, have a new one installed as soon as possible. Also periodically flush out sediments that collect in the bottom of the tank. Do this job once a year or more often if your water supply is hard and laden with minerals. Remember to turn off heating sources before draining the heater. Then attach a garden hose to the drain valve located near the bottom of the tank, open the valve, and let water flow out until accumulated sediment is cleared. To maximize the heater's life span, adjust the thermostat to maintain the water supply at approximately 120°F.

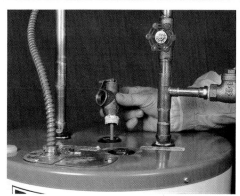

1 *All water heaters require* a valve to release pressure in an emergency. The fitting is threaded onto the top of the tank.

1 *To remove* your water heater's anode rod, use a 1¹/₁₆-in. socket wrench. If it's difficult to move, heat the tank fitting.

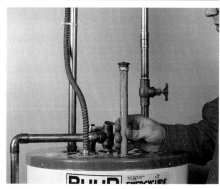

2 *Connect the replacement valve* with plumber's putty. A emergency discharge pipe from the valve leads to the floor.

2 *After removing* the old rod, feed a new rod into the tank and tighten. This can double the life of your heater.

plumbing

Defying Gravity

Pumps help us defy gravity by making water and other liquids flow uphill instead of down. Anyone who has a well, for example, relies on a pump to draw water from a hundred or more feet underground. Even municipal water systems use pumps—those water storage towers you see in towns and cities are kept full by huge pumps. But there are also pumps for the special situations covered here—sump pumps, wastewater pumps, and recirculating pumps.

Two basic types of pumps are reciprocating pumps and centrifugal pumps. A reciprocating pump uses a piston to draw water into a chamber. Then, after the inlet valve closes and an outlet valve opens, the piston pushes the water out of the chamber under pressure. Centrifugal pumps use a rotating impeller—a wheel with many blades—that draws water in at the center and forces it outward (by centrifugal force) along the spinning blades. This increases both the water's pressure and velocity of flow.

Well Pumps & Pressure Tanks

Because wells are located far belowground and the average person uses about 95 gallons of water a day, you need a powerful pump to supply a whole house. Submersible centrifugal pumps are commonly used—they have multiple impellers to increase lifting capacity and are powered by electric motors sealed in waterproof housings. The pump is attached to a drop pipe, and the whole unit is lowered into the well casing below the maximum draw-down level so that the pump's intake will always be submerged.

The pump's ability to send enough water up the pipe is one important concern, but it isn't the only one. For example, you also have to consider the well itself, which will only supply water at a given rate. Another concern is peak demand, which can outstrip the yield of even the best wells. A pressure tank helps solve that problem. With storage capacities of 20–80 gallons or more, it provides a reserve for those times when the washer is going, someone is filling a tub, and you are watering the lawn all at once. An air bladder inside the tank expands as the water is drawn out, keeping the pressure at about 40 psi. Meanwhile, the pump begins refilling the tank as water is being used and continues pumping until the tank is full again.

Sump Pumps

Sump pumps are the last resort against flooded basements. Typically, the pump is mounted in a small pit so water leaking into the basement will run into it. Because you may not be around to turn on the pump when the pit fills with water, there is an automatic switch triggered by a float mounted on a vertical rod set in the pit. When water fills the pit, the float rises, triggers the motor, and the pump runs until the water level recedes. It's wise to test your pump by dumping a pail of water into the pit.

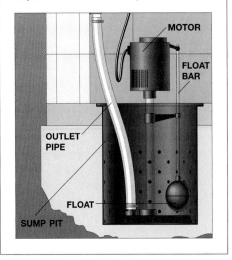

Cellar Toilets

Cellar toilets installed below the main waste pipe leaving the house require special plumbing. These units, called up-flush toilets, need an electrical connection and a pump to raise wastes up to the level where they flow by gravity to a municipal sewer line or private septic system. The expensive toilets require water supply and vent piping like standard installations, and a special valve, called a check valve, that prevents sewage from flowing back into the system if a blockage occurs anywhere in the house waste lines.

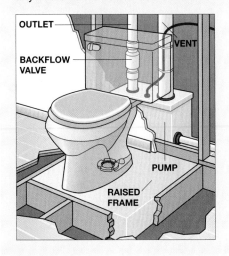

Installing a Recirculating System

This improvement can save 35–40 gallons a week of tepid water that pours down the drain while you wait for hot water to reach the tap. The system includes an extra pipe run from the heater and a small pump that keeps hot water slowly flowing through the loop. Hot water is always there when you want it because the pump recirculates water that normally would lose heat standing in the pipe. Installing the pump, electrical line, and extra pipe loop costs more up front, but the systems pays for itself long-term.

USE: ▶ adjustable wrench • propane torch

1 *Cut a tee* into the cold-water supply line, and install a check valve. This allows water to flow only one way, toward the heater.

Pump Piping

Preserve temperature with pipe insulation. Some foam tubes have zip-lock seams for easy installation.

Most pipe insulation comes partially split for retrofits. Trim to fit with a sharp knife, and tape over seams.

Most wells move water from a submersible pump at the bottom of a well casing into a pressurized tank in the house. When you open a tap, the pressure forces water through the pipes. This system conserves the well pump, which is costly to replace, by running the pump only periodically to refill the tank, not every time you call for water. If the power fails, the pump won't deliver more water to the tank, but you'll be able to use most of the water already stored under pressure.

The pressure in many holding tanks can be increased or decreased by pumping in or bleeding off air.

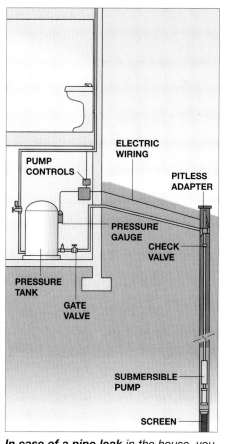

ELECTRIC WIRING

PUMP CONTROLS

PITLESS ADAPTER

PRESSURE GAUGE

CHECK VALVE

PRESSURE TANK

GATE VALVE

SUBMERSIBLE PUMP

SCREEN

In case of a pipe leak in the house, you need to shut off the pump motor, and close the cutoff valve at the tank supply.

• tubing cutter or hacksaw • work gloves ▶ check valve • in-line pump • pipe and fittings • solder • flux • pipe insulation

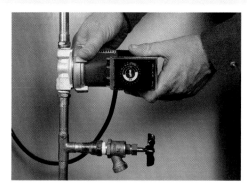

2 **Install the inline pump** on the return loop near the heater and a power outlet. Pumps with timers are most efficient.

3 **To make the return loop,** cut a new pipe into the existing hot water line near the fixture farthest from the heater.

4 **The loop should be insulated.** (See above left.) The line should also have a shut-off and a drain valve to allow service.

plumbing

Washers & Dryers

The most obvious yet essential advice about installing washers and dryers is to follow the manufacturer's instructions. Although all plug into standard electrical outlets and take stock plumbing fittings, there is enough design variation so that no one set of instructions will do. But some pitfalls are common to most installations.

Hooking Them Up

Where you're hooking up to existing wiring and plumbing lines, installation is definitely a do-it-yourself job. The hardest part is likely to be maneuvering the cumbersome machines into position without battering door frames and scratching floors. But with enough extra muscle or a dolly, it's certainly possible.

New all-electric models are already wired, so you can simply plug them in to existing washer-dryer outlets. With gas dryers you have to be more careful, making sure that the gas cutoff valve is closed before disconnecting an existing gas line. (The top bar of the valve should be perpendicular to the supply

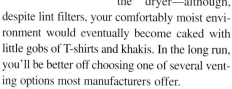

Back in 1908, washing machines weren't very automatic—you had to supply the hot water and hand-crank the tub. But this "Superba" model cost only $6.38.

pipe.) Also, take care after making a gas connection that you don't crimp the line as you nudge the dryer into its final position. If new wiring and plumbing lines are needed, you should call a licensed plumber and an electrician. After they provide the necessary electrical outlets, drainpipe, and water supply lines, you can continue on your own.

The new machines' height should not pose a problem unless you install cabinets over the new machines, a common setup. In that case, leave enough room to comfortably lift the doors of top-loaders (about 16 inches for most models) without banging into the bottom of the cabinet.

In a bone-dry climate, you may be tempted to skip installing an exhaust line for the dryer—although, despite lint filters, your comfortably moist environment would eventually become caked with little gobs of T-shirts and khakis. In the long run, you'll be better off choosing one of several venting options most manufacturers offer.

Connections

The drain hose from a clothes washer is connected to a pump at the base of the machine. To prevent siphoning and backflows, the hose typically rises above the level of the washer drum and fits into an open drainpipe. To fix or replace a leaking hose, you're likely to find factory-installed spring clips on the connections. Remove them by squeezing the ends with a pliers. Install banded clamps on the new hose, or to apply more pressure on the connections.

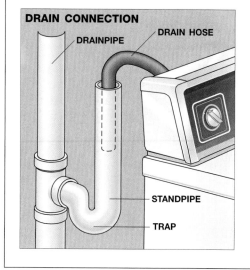

DRAIN CONNECTION — DRAINPIPE — DRAIN HOSE — STANDPIPE — TRAP

Installing a Dishwasher

USE: ▶ adjustable wrench • power drill/driver with hole saw • tubing cutter or hacksaw • wire strippers • screwdriver ▶ dishwasher • water-supply pipe • T-valve

1 *To supply water to the washer,* remove the hot line to the sink and the single cutoff valve. Install a T-valve with two outlets.

2 *Use pipe dope or Teflon tape* to install the new cutoff. Reconnect the sink line and tighten; then, feed the line to the dishwasher.

3 *Install an extension* with a dishwasher leg to the sink drain. Slip a clamp over the machine's drain hose, and fasten it to the leg.

HOSE-BIBB SHUTOFF

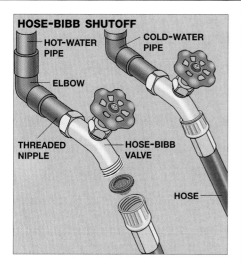

- HOT-WATER PIPE
- COLD-WATER PIPE
- ELBOW
- THREADED NIPPLE
- HOSE-BIBB VALVE
- HOSE

SINGLE-LEVER SHUTOFF VALVES

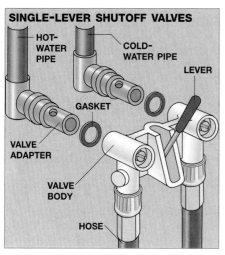

- HOT-WATER PIPE
- COLD-WATER PIPE
- LEVER
- GASKET
- VALVE ADAPTER
- VALVE BODY
- HOSE

Water Inlet Valves

To protect automatic solenoid valves in the machine that control fill cycles, inlet valves have filter screens.

To clean an inlet screen, pry it out of the hose, rinse, carefully remove debris as necessary, and reinstall.

Leveling

Even on the sloping floors of older houses, you can adjust the legs of washers and dryers to make them level front to back and side to side. Adding a few drops of liquid detergent to the legs beforehand can make this job a lot easier. It also helps to unload the weight of the machine—for example, by raising it slightly with a crowbar. Once level, adjust the leg locknuts to hold the leg adjustments in position. If the washer or dryer wobbles or rocks during operation, you need to readjust the legs.

Use a level to check positioning, and adjust each leg up or down. Tighten locknuts to secure the position.

• drainpipe • drain-line fitting • pipe dope or Teflon tape • banded clamp • wires and wire connectors

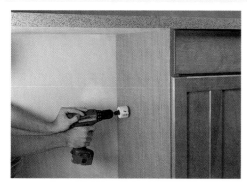

4 Use a hole saw (or a drill and a saber saw) to make an access hole from the sink cabinet to the dishwasher bay.

5 Make electrical connections according to manufacturer's directions and local codes. Secure the wires with wire connectors.

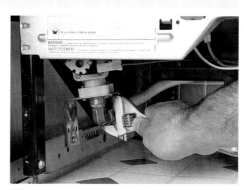

6 Route the water supply hose under the machine to the water inlet valve, and tighten the hose fitting with a wrench.

plumbing

Getting Better Water

No matter what kind of contaminants get into your water supply, and no matter how sensitive you are to slight alterations of taste and odor, there is some form of conditioning equipment to fix the trouble. The first step, of course, is to have your water tested by a reputable agency.

The test for bacterial content costs only a few dollars. Having a full test done, which includes an examination for organic compounds, pesticides, dissolved gases, and solid particles, can cost several hundred dollars. Before deciding which tests you want, consider where your home is located. Are there gas stations in the vicinity? Have there ever been manufacturing facilities or a dump nearby? Is your house on (or downhill from) land that used to be a farm? Local officials can also be of help in deciding which tests should be done.

Selecting a Water-Treatment System

A single water-treatment system cannot remove all possible contaminating agents, but you have eight different systems to choose from. The most commonly used are activated-carbon filters, reverse-osmosis (RO) filters, and distillation units. Each of these eliminates more than one type of impurity. The remaining systems—ultraviolet radiation, chemical treatment, ion-exchange, sediment filtration, and aeration—have more narrowly defined roles.

UV radiation and chemical treatment are effective against bacteria. An ion-exchange system (or water softener) is effective if your water has a heavy concentration of calcium, magnesium, and/or iron. This kind of water, usually described as "hard," is not considered to be contaminated. A sediment filter screens out particles that make water look cloudy. It is also effective if asbestos fibers are present in the water. Often this type of filter is used in combination with an activated-carbon filter.

An aeration unit and activated-carbon filter are effective against radon gas and the odor caused by dissolved gases (such as sulphur) in the water. Activated-carbon filters also eliminate organic chemicals and pesticides. These filters are available in a wide variety of sizes and prices. Smaller units are attached to the spout of a faucet, while larger ones are tanks that are connected to the water supply line at its entry point into the house. To maintain its effectiveness, an activated-carbon filter must be replaced periodically.

Both reverse-osmosis and distillation units remove a variety of heavy metals, such as lead, arsenic, and mercury. An RO unit will often be combined with an activated-carbon filter to weed out organic chemicals, pesticides, odors, and radon as well. Both units can cost from hundreds to thousands of dollars.

A distillation system doesn't filter the water but boils it and captures the steam in a condensing coil. This impurity-free water collects in a tank, where it is drawn off by the faucet. Distilled water, however, is flat and tasteless.

Water Treatments

Problem	Solution
Bacteria	Chlorine feeder with activated-carbon filter; distiller; RO unit; UV unit
Low suds	Water softener; RO filter
Rusty stains	Water softener; oxidizing or activated-carbon filter
Green stains	Limestone neutralizer; neutralizing filter
Cloudy water	Sediment or sand filter
"Rotten egg" smell	Oxidizing filter; chlorine feeder with sand filter; activated-carbon filter
Yellow/ brown tinge	Water softener; activated-carbon filter; distiller; RO unit
Chlorine odor	Activated-carbon filter; RO unit
Pesticides, VOCs, benzene	Activated-carbon filter; distiller; RO unit
Lead, mercury	Distiller; RO unit
Nitrates, sulfates	Anion-exchange unit; distiller; RO unit

Installing a Sediment Filter

Clearing up cloudy water is a job for a sediment filter, which removes the inorganic particles causing the problem. It's not unusual to install a carbon filter as well. Both types can be installed as in-line fixtures, making the installation easy to set up. You'll have to do some soldering once you cut the water pipe, and you'll need a couple of cutoff valves to isolate the filters. Be sure to locate the filters in an accessible area so that you can get at them easily and clean them out on a regular basis.

USE: ▶ tubing cutter • propane torch • adjustable wrench • hose (for backflush) • sandpaper or wire brush

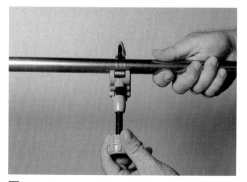

1 *Remove a section of the supply line* using a tubing cutter, to accommodate the filter and threaded fittings.

2 *To help new solder fittings* bond on existing copper pipes, use a wire brush or sandpaper to brighten the old metal.

Faucet Filters

Modern filters *can be built into faucets. This unit provides an aerated stream, spray, and filtered stream.*

To keep the supply clean, *regularly change the filter. On this unit, the cartridge tucks into the handle.*

Reverse-Osmosis Units

These units typically combine a reverse-osmosis membrane to filter out heavy metals, a carbon filter, a sediment filter, and a large tank to store the filtered water. Filtering membranes must be changed at least once a year or impurities will build up again. Although removing impurities is important, the taste of the water sometimes remains unaffected. Waterborne minerals such as manganese, iron, and sodium may need further treatment.

The combination of equipment *required for reverse osmosis generally fills the cabinet space under a sink.*

Softeners

Softening water is a process of reducing the amount of minerals that are picked up as water filters through the ground. Very soft water tastes bad but produces fewer deposits on fixtures, causes less corrosion in pipes, and creates more suds and cleaning action with soap. Effective systems split the supply between water for drinking, lawn watering, and such, and the softened supply for washing and cleaning. Installations such as these can cost between $1,000 and $3,000.

Water softeners *need to be located in a convenient spot for maintenance and drainage.*

▶ sediment filter • male adapter fittings • solder • flux • shutoff valves

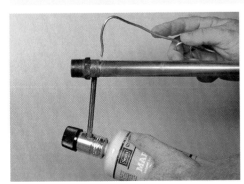

3 ***Solder a ¾-in. copper male adapter*** *fitting onto each open pipe end. Be sure to use lead-free solder.*

4 ***Install the filter body*** *with shutoff valves on each side. The shutoffs should be full-flow gate or ball valves.*

5 ***To backflush a sediment filter,*** *attach a hose, and drain it through the bottom. The element can also be replaced.*

plumbing

Treating Waste

Every ounce of water that leaves your house must be separated from solid wastes and treated before it can be returned to the environment. Homes that don't have septic tanks, as well as commercial properties and apartment houses, feed into enormous waste-treatment plants, some of which handle millions of gallons of sewage a day. These plants use the same chemical and biological processes that septic tanks do—and, like septic systems, they can be compromised by chemicals that are flushed into them. Pesticides, for example, not only interfere with the microorganisms that break sewage down but can find their way back into the area's fresh water supply.

Maintaining Septic Systems

A septic system has three main sections: the septic tank, the distribution box(es), and the leachfield (also called the drainfield). As sewage enters the tank, it is poured into a hot mix of waste and anaerobic bacteria, churning in endless loops inside the tank. Most of the solids are quickly digested, and the liquid effluent leaves the tank and enters the distribution box, from which it flows into the leachfield's perforated pipes and leaches into the ground. What remains behind in the tank are nondigestible solids called sludge (such as cigarette filters, apple seeds, and plastics), which sink to the bottom; and grease, which rises to the top. Accumulated sludge at the bottom of

the tank won't fill the tank to overflowing and stop up your drains, but it will reduce the tank's capacity. If not cleaned out, eventually new solids in the tank won't have enough room to settle properly and can infiltrate the leachfield, clogging its pipes. The grease layer, if also left to accumulate, can flow past the tank's outlet baffle and out into the leachfield, where it coats the pipes and limits absorption, evaporation, and microbial activity in the soil. If the sludge or grease gets this far, the entire drainfield must be dug up and replaced, at a cost of thousands of dollars.

To keep this from happening, you should have a septic tank professionally pumped out periodically. How often depends on the tank

Installing a Waste Disposer

Waste-disposal units can be convenient appliances, although they have some limitations. There are two basic types: batch-feed units that you load before running and the more common continuous-feed units that can run as you feed in wastes. To avoid problems with disposers—mainly jamming—always run cold water as you feed in wastes, and to clear the drain afterward. Don't grind wastes with metal or glass, and never use chemical drain cleaners: they can damage inner seals.

USE: ▶ socket wrench ▶ waste-disposal unit (with drain fittings/waste kit) • supply tubes • shutoff valves

1 *To install the sink drain,* press plumber's putty around the drain flange and insert the drain into the sink opening.

2 *Disposer drain fittings* come with several types of fasteners. In this case, the lower component is drawn up with a bolt.

4 *Lift the disposer* up to the drain fitting, and rotate the metal collar to engage the connection at the top of the disposer.

5 *Use a plastic disposer waste kit* to drain both sides of a double sink into the fixture trap. Connect the trap to the drain.

6 *If your disposer* has a cord with a household plug, provide a grounded, 15-amp switched outlet in the cabinet.

capacity and how many people live in your house. Two people using a 1000-gallon tank only need to pump it out every six years or so, but six people using a 2000-gallon tank should have it pumped out every three years. To help keep your tank working efficiently between cleanings, you should avoid flushing down a drain any chemicals that may kill the bacteria, such as paint thinner or photographic chemicals; instead, dispose of these at a local dump.

Major problems in a septic system will probably first come to your attention as a telltale sewage odor or permanently wet soil over the leachfield. Poor flow in every drain (not just one toilet) may also indicate a serious backup in the system.

Septic & Graywater Systems

If your home isn't connected to a municipal sewer system, you need a septic system on the property. A typical system has a tank for solids, which must be pumped out periodically, and a leachfield, where a series of perforated pipes gradually filters liquid wastes into the ground. Local codes for private septic systems are increasingly strict in most communities, and in some cases can cost up to $10,000 or more to install. The main concern is that the wastes do not contaminate underground supplies of water used for drinking, cooking, and washing. Expect to conduct a test of the soil, called a percolation (perc) test, and to excavate a substantial portion of the backyard. In some areas, you can install a complementary system to handle wastes from baths, showers, and washing machines called graywater. It may contain some soap and dirt but not sewage. With minimal treatment in a sand filter and a holding tank to eliminate contaminants, hundreds of gallons can be recycled for uses such as watering landscaping. Local codes are also strict about graywater; you can't simply dump soapy water on the grass.

• outlet box and wiring • plumber's putty

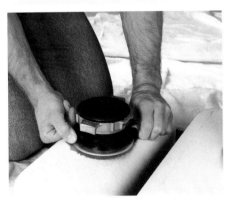

3 *This disposer's drain fitting* has a threaded collar with wings to help thread it over the drain extension, called a spud.

7 *When connecting* ¼-in. fixture supply tubes to ½-in. supply lines, use shutoff valves with compression fittings.

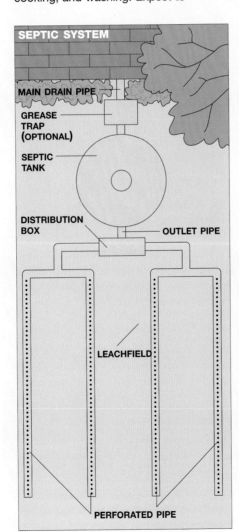

SEPTIC SYSTEM

MAIN DRAIN PIPE

GREASE TRAP (OPTIONAL)

SEPTIC TANK

DISTRIBUTION BOX

OUTLET PIPE

LEACHFIELD

PERFORATED PIPE

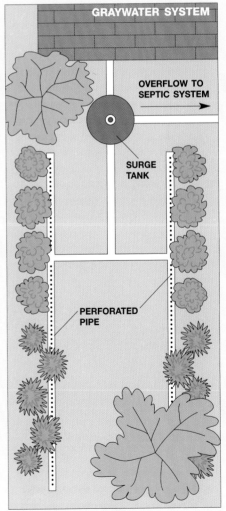

GRAYWATER SYSTEM

OVERFLOW TO SEPTIC SYSTEM

SURGE TANK

PERFORATED PIPE

plumbing

Cleanups

The improvements shown here are some of the upgrades you can make—for example, to install a new shower head and resurface an old tub or shower. Another way to spruce up plumbing fixtures is to get rid of mold, stains, and soap deposits with some heavy-duty cleaning.

To remove a buildup of soap residue on molded tubs and showers, spray the surfaces with an all-purpose nonabrasive cleaner, and let it soak in for a few minutes before rinsing. If some deposits remain, try a specialized product such as Tilex Soap Scum Remover or a liquid laundry detergent that also helps with mineral deposits left by hard water.

Try lightening porcelain stains by scouring with a proprietary cleaner such as Zud or a mixture of lemon juice and salt. For deep stains, add baking soda to the mixture to make a wet paste that you can leave on the stain overnight.

To remove mineral deposits on metal fixtures, use a softening solution of one cup of white vinegar in a quart of water or one of the specialized products such as Lime-a-Way. You may need to wash the area several times and scrub with a nylon sponge to dislodge multi-layer deposits.

Remove mold stains from tile grout with a household scouring powder, or add enough household bleach to an abrasive cleanser to make a paste, scrub it on, and then rinse. Don't add bleach to a cleaner containing ammonia; the combination produces dangerous fumes.

Reglazing a Tub

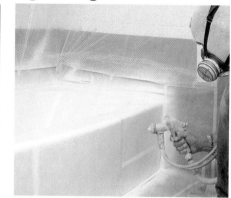

1 *A worn bathtub* can be refinished. A contractor first chemically etches the surface and then sprays on a new finish.

Replacing a Shower Head

USE: ▶ pipe wrenches ▶ new shower head • pipe dope or Teflon tape • scrap cloth

1 *To remove the old head* without marring the stem, wrap a cloth or thin towel around the fittings.

2 *Use two wrenches* to remove the old head: one to hold the stem in place and one to twist off the old head.

3 *To seal the connection* between the stem and head, wrap the threads with Teflon tape or add pipe dope.

4 *Screw the new shower head* onto the threaded stem. New heads will come with flow restrictors to save water.

Tub Surrounds

USE: ▶ saber saw • caulking gun • measuring tape

1 *Measure from the tub and sidewall* to fix the faucet and spout locations. Cut the openings with a saber saw.

3 *Mark the center of the tub* and the center of the final panel. Stick the bottom of the panel first, and then press upward.

2 *When the finish cures,* the final step is to buff it to a high shine. High-quality refinishing will last 10 years or more.

Relining a Tub

1 *Some contractors* offer custom relining of old tubs. This alternative to reglazing takes only a few hours to install.

2 *This before-and-after photo* shows half of the old tub and enclosure, and half relined with high-impact acrylic.

▶ tub surround • adhesive • caulk

2 *If the panels* are adhesive-backed, peel back the paper; otherwise, apply panel adhesive to the edges and center of the panel.

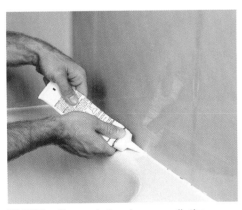

4 *With all panels in place,* caulk the vertical seams and the joint between the tub and surround.

Installing an Anti-Scald Faucet

USE: ▶ adjustable wrench • keyhole saw • torch • wheel cutter ▶ faucet • fittings • solder/flux

1 *Start by removing* the spout and faucet trim; the spout may thread or pull off. Look for an underside Allen screw.

2 *Cut the drywall* from the back of the plumbing wall, and cut out the old faucet with a close-quarters wheel cutter.

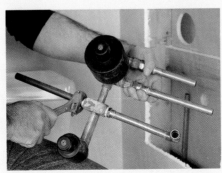

3 *Solder male adapters* to copper pipe stubs, and preassemble as much of the faucet piping as possible.

4 *With the faucet assembly* installed and secured, solder the remaining fittings with lead-free solder.

plumbing

Plumber's Helper?

Sometimes learning from experience can be expensive. You're looking over the plumber's shoulder, acutely aware that the meter is running, thinking that you could have done what he's doing. Everyone needs professional help on some repairs, but there are a few good candidates for do-it-yourselfers. If in doubt about your ability to tackle them, pay for the education and watch a contractor do it. Soak up the details; then you'll know whether you can handle the job yourself next time.

DIY Pipe Repairs

Here are some general rules to observe whether you're trying to fix copper or plastic pipe. Start by turning off a valve to stop feeding the leak. If, in an emergency, you can't locate this cutoff valve, shut off the main meter valve until you find it.

If you try to heat up a pipe with a torch—to resolder a joint—first drain the line. You can't get copper hot enough to make solder flow when it's filled with water. Also, open a faucet just beyond the repair spot so that any steam that develops can escape.

Most plastic pipe is a snap to repair compared with copper. It can be easily cut and cemented to new fittings. Plastic fittings do require a lighter touch when threading them onto nonplastic fittings—it's easy to over-tighten a threaded plastic fitting and break it. Cross-threading a plastic fitting is also a problem at least until you get the feel for it.

Temporary Repairs

USE: ▶ metal file • screwdriver ▶ rubber pipe insulation • banded clamps

If you don't have the time or tools to make a permanent repair when a pipe springs a leak, temporarily plug a tiny pinhole by jamming in a sharpened pencil. To plug a split pipe, wrap the area with a piece of thick rubber, and tighten it down with a banded clamp. If you can't find a local cutoff, turn off the main valve while you search. Remember that in houses with wells and pressure tanks, leaks continue to flow even if you turn off the well pump.

1 *To make a temporary repair that won't leak, first use a file to flatten out any ragged edges around the split.*

2 *Slit a thick piece of rubber or a short section of garden hose, and slip it over the damaged pipe.*

3 *Attach banded clamps over the rubber sleeve at each end of the split, and tighten the clamp screws.*

Installing an Anti-Freeze Faucet

To protect an outside faucet against freezing, replace it with a special anti-freeze valve. You can still turn the water on and off outside. But the long stem of the faucet extends through the wall and controls a valve inside the house. Water doesn't stand in the portion of the pipe or faucet outside the wall where it could freeze. These faucets don't need a cutoff valve. You should take the standard installation steps of caulking and insulating the hole through the siding.

SEAT WASHER
VACUUM BREAKER
STEM

USE: ▶ tubing cutter • reciprocating saw (optional)

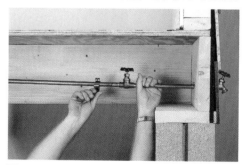

1 *Shut off the water supply,* and drain the system. Then, cut out the old faucet piping, including the shutoff valve.

Heat Cables

Heat cables look like extension cords, but they are designed to convert electricity into heat so that you can wrap them around pipes that might freeze. Sealing air leaks and insulating pipes should be your first step. But if you install heat cables, use only UL-approved products, and follow manufacturer's installation instructions. Models with a built-in thermostat can be left plugged in. But take care not to wrap the cable on top of itself. It produces enough heat to melt the wire insulation and could start a fire. Do not use old, cracked, or damaged cables.

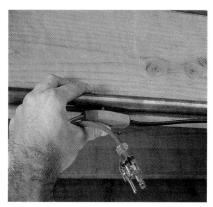

Modern heat cables have a built-in thermostat. Some do not have to be spiral wrapped around the pipe.

Quieting Noisy Pipes

To reduce the noise from supply and drainpipes, wrap them with foam tubes, and pack the wall cavities with insulation. (Cast iron drains are quieter than plastic ones.) Severe pipe banging, called water hammer, is caused by excessive water pressure or the abrupt shutoff produced by the solenoid valves on dishwashers and clothes washers. To fix water hammer, anchor the pipes to the framing with hangers or install a shock absorber. You can make a simple one by cutting in a T-fitting and a capped stem of pipe. Gas-and oil-filled shock absorber fittings also provide damping action.

To support water pipes and prevent rattling and banging against framing, use clip-on pipe hangers.

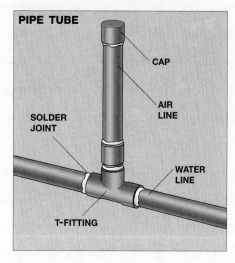

PIPE TUBE

CAP

AIR LINE

SOLDER JOINT

WATER LINE

T-FITTING

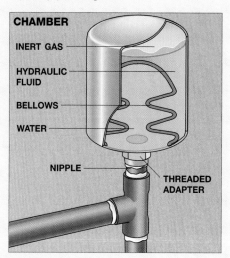

CHAMBER

INERT GAS

HYDRAULIC FLUID

BELLOWS

WATER

NIPPLE

THREADED ADAPTER

• propane torch • caulking gun • work gloves/eye protection ▶ anti-freeze faucet • screws • solder/flux • braces • caulk • insulation

2 Enlarge the wall opening if needed, and insert the freeze-proof faucet through the siding and band joist. Secure it with screws.

3 Solder the copper supply line to the faucet with lead-free solder. Brace the line to ensure adequate drainage.

4 Although the valve is inside, it pays to protect water pipes at outside walls with foam tubing or batts of insulation.

plumbing

Drain Troubles

What could cause gurgling in a rarely used wet-bar sink when water drains in the kitchen at one end of the house or in a bath at the other end? Chances are that the wet bar isn't vented or that its vent stack is blocked. You could check by looking for a plumbing vent pipe protruding through the roof above the area. It will look like the ones above the kitchen and bath.

Sluggish drainage is one symptom of this problem. Sewer smell is another. When water drains in the kitchen or bath, it siphons water out of the wet bar's drain trap, which produces a gurgling noise. Without the seal provided by water in the drain trap, sewer gas can rise up through the sink and into the house.

If you don't use the wet-bar sink because of these problems, call a plumber to install an auto-vent. With this in place, the other drains won't siphon water out of the trap. If you don't use it and don't really want it, have the plumber remove it and close the drain connection. In the meantime, you can reduce the sewer gas smell by periodically pouring some water in the wet bar drain to keep the trap full.

Big Backups

Even with proper venting, trap placement, and pipe sizing, drains still may be slow. This indicates a big blockage farther down the line. The best indicator that a blockage is in the waste line is sewage gurgling up through floor drains and basement fixtures. Solving this problem depends on your septic system type.

If you have a septic system with a leachfield, your septic tank may need to be pumped out. This is a job for a professional, but it's important to be around when the pumping concludes. Ask the pump operator if the tank was filled with enough greasy scum to cause the drain problems. If not, the pipes in the leachfield itself may be the problem. Digging them up may be the only solution.

If you're tied into a municipal sewage system, check to see whether any work has been done on your branch line lately. If so, it could have caused problems with your drainage. If not, tree roots may have gotten into the pipes. Hire a professional to auger the line and pull out the tree roots; thereafter, flush copper sulfate root treatment through the line twice a year.

Drain Leaks

To find out whether the sink drainpipe or the drain flange in the sink is leaking, pour water directly into the drain. If water leaks below, the problem is in the piping. If not, the problem is likely in the flange seal. You may need to unscrew the flange, clean off old caulk or plumber's putty, install a fresh bead of caulk, and retighten the flange. Leaks in the drainpipes generally occur in the trap. Some traps have a cleanout nut that makes it easier to clean blockages.

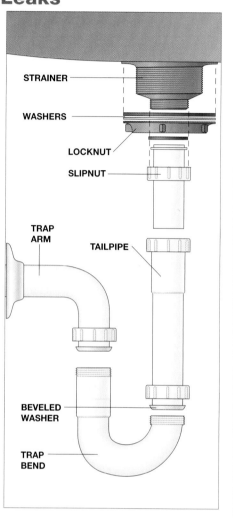

STRAINER
WASHERS
LOCKNUT
SLIPNUT
TRAP ARM
TAILPIPE
BEVELED WASHER
TRAP BEND

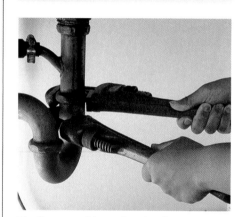

To disassemble a standard trap, use two pipe wrenches: one to hold the sink stem in place and one to turn the fitting.

Clearing a Waste-Line Clog

To clear a stopped drain, you should start by using a plunger. For best results, block the overflow and second-drain outlets, spread petroleum jelly on the rim of the plumber's helper, and (with 2 or 3 inches of water in the basin or tub) use steady, forceful downward strokes to clear the clog. If this doesn't work, you can try working a piece of wire through the cleanout plug and removing the blockage. However, snaking with a hand auger or power auger is much more effective. Disassemble the traps, insert the auger, and clear out any blockages.

To get the most force, plug the overflow fitting with a wet towel when plunging a bathtub. Standing water also helps.

Cleaners

A plumber's auger is the safest way to clear stubborn jams in household pipes. It won't damage metal pipes, which is a risk with some caustic chemical drain cleaners, such as those that contain acid or lye. An auger is simply a flexible wound-wire cable that you turn into the pipe either by hand or with a special drill. Another option is to use water and air pressure to dislodge a jam. These pneumatic devices typically fit over the stopped drain and release a charge of air into the standing water.

Position a pneumatic cleaner over the stopped drain, seal the connection, and release the air charge.

Clearing a Tub Clog

Tubs fitted with an internal drain stopper, called a tripwaste, require extra attention when they become clogged. Removing the linkage helps you diagnose the problem. Check the drainage flow by running water down the drain. If the drain fails to empty properly, the clog is farther down the line. If the drain flows freely, the tripwaste is stretched and the stopper is too low in the drain tee, blocking flow even when open. Shorten the linkage by ¼ inch, tighten the locknut, and replace the linkage—the drain should work fine.

2 *Sluggish tub drainage* may be caused by a stretched tripwaste linkage. Remove the linkage, and shorten it about ¼ in.

1 *To access a tripwaste linkage* for cleaning, remove both screws, grip the overflow plate, and lift out the linkage.

3 *Pop-up drain plugs* often clog with hair. Lift out the plug and linkage, remove the hair, and replace the assembly.

When snaking a kitchen sink line, remove the trap, and bore directly into the line with a hand-held drain auger.

To snake out a bath drain, remove the overflow plate, pull out the tripwaste linkage, and bore through the overflow.

When plunging won't clear a clogged floor drain, it's best to remove the plug and auger the line through the cleanout.

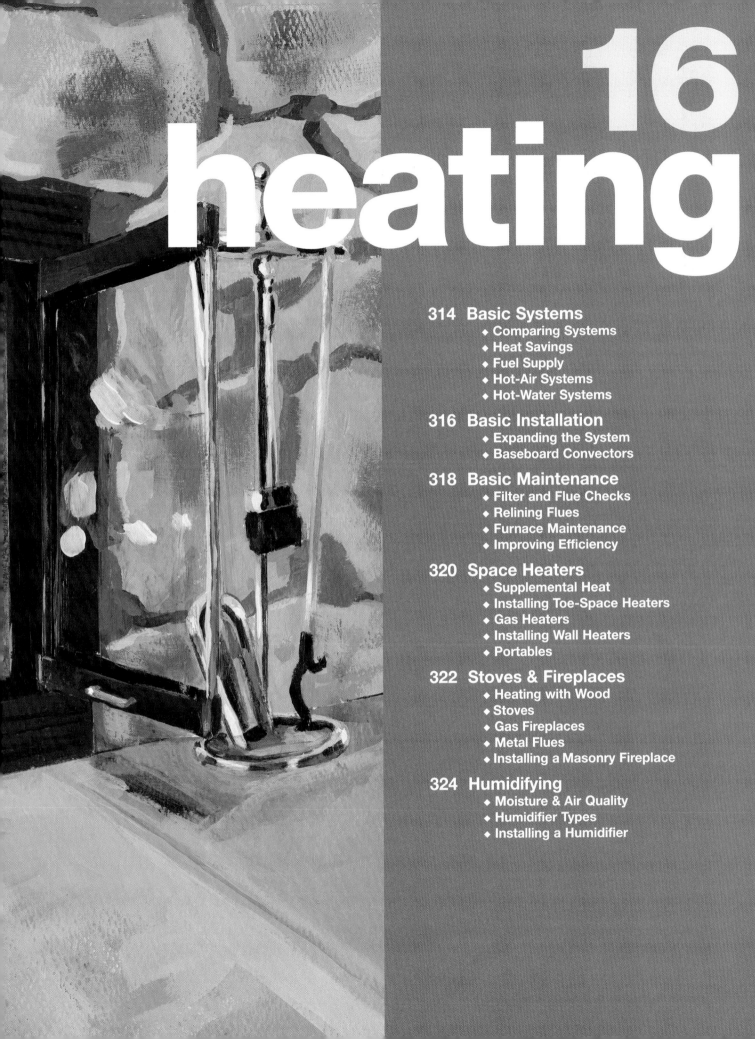

heating

16

heating

Comparing Systems

You can number-crunch comparisons among gas, oil, or electric furnaces, or even wood stoves, but when thinking about your home's heating system, don't forget to factor in basic, practical considerations. Switching to gas could mean that you'll have to pay to run a supply line into the house. Sticking with oil could mean replacing a rusting storage tank. Electric heat would cost more every month but save thousands on installation costs of alternative systems.

Ask heating contractors for installation estimates and fuel suppliers for approximate operating costs. Because all heat output is measured in British thermal units (Btu), you'll have a common denominator to make comparisons.

If you're thinking about replacing or upgrading an existing system, it's important to find out how efficient the new system will be compared to the old one. For a well-maintained existing system, you could subtract half the unit's age from the original efficiency rating—for example, rate a 20-year-old oil-burning furnace that was 65% efficient at 55%. Of course, if you pay a contractor to make combustion efficiency tests, you'll get a more accurate rating. Once you know the increase in efficiency with a new system, you can estimate how much less fuel you'll use every year, how much money this will save each year, and how many years of savings it will take to recover your investment in new equipment.

Fuel Supply

Gas-Fired

Gas-fired furnaces burn natural gas or liquefied petroleum (LP) gas to heat either air that is blown through a system of ducts or water that is circulated to radiators or baseboard convectors through pipes. Older gas-fired appliances have pilot lights that are burning all the time. Improved modern systems have electronic igniters to light the flame as the gas starts to flow. Gas furnaces burn cleanly and convert up to 95% of the fuel into usable heat.

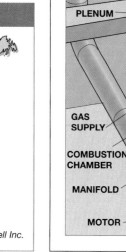

Heat Savings

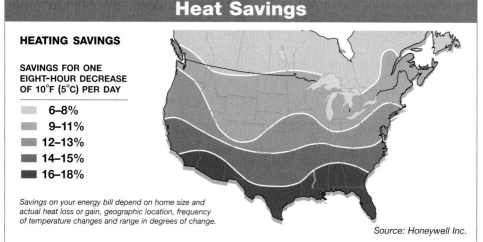

HEATING SAVINGS

SAVINGS FOR ONE
EIGHT-HOUR DECREASE
OF 10°F (5°C) PER DAY

- 6–8%
- 9–11%
- 12–13%
- 14–15%
- 16–18%

Savings on your energy bill depend on home size and actual heat loss or gain, geographic location, frequency of temperature changes and range in degrees of change.

Source: Honeywell Inc.

Hot-Air Systems

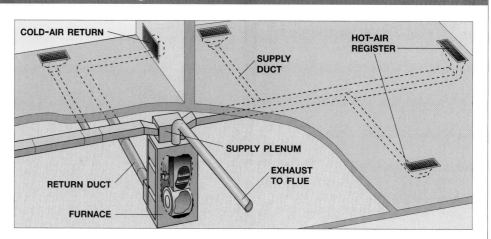

Hot-air systems use a blower to force heated air through a large supply plenum and into a system of ducts. The ducts lead to registers in the floor and walls of your living spaces. Cold-air registers and return ducts take cooled air back to the furnace for reheating. These systems require dust filters. Because they provide dry, hot air, a furnace-mounted humidifier often is needed to maintain indoor comfort.

Oil-Fired

A high-pressure oil burner, mounted either outside or inside the furnace, pumps a fine mist of oil and air into a combustion chamber, where it is ignited by an electric spark. This in turn heats a heat exchanger that passes the temperature onto air or water that circulates throughout the house. Unlike natural gas, which is fed from a gas main to provide a constant supply of fuel for gas systems, oil must be delivered. Oil burns less efficiently than gas, with furnace efficiencies under 90%.

Electric

Electric furnaces can heat air or water by passing current through heavy-duty heating coils. Electric heat elements also are included in heat pumps that provide both heating and cooling. Electricity can power central systems and is used to heat individual baseboard convectors. Electric systems require almost no maintenance because they generate heat without combustion. They are 100% efficient in your house but not at the utility plant where power is generated.

Heat Pumps

In summer, heat pumps run like air conditioners. In winter, the system reverses, extracting heat energy from the air (or from the ground, in the case of ground-source heat pumps) to warm air in the house. But when the outdoor temperature drops to about 35°F, a back-up system of electric coils takes over, and the system loses fuel efficiency. The units are most cost-effective in regions with roughly equal heating and cooling demand.

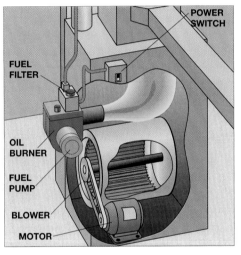

FUEL FILTER — OIL BURNER — FUEL PUMP — BLOWER — MOTOR — POWER SWITCH

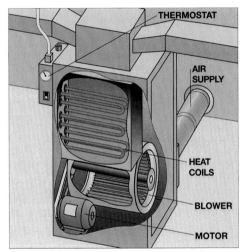

THERMOSTAT — AIR SUPPLY — HEAT COILS — BLOWER — MOTOR

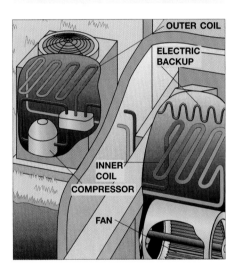

OUTER COIL — ELECTRIC BACKUP — INNER COIL — COMPRESSOR — FAN

Hot-Water Systems

Hot-water (or hydronic) systems use a pump, called a circulator, to force heated water from a boiler through a network of pipes. Heat transfers from the pipes to the air at radiators or baseboard convectors and continues back to the boiler for reheating. Older homes have one large pipe loop. Newer homes have two or more loops, each with its own thermostat, to heat different zones of the house more efficiently.

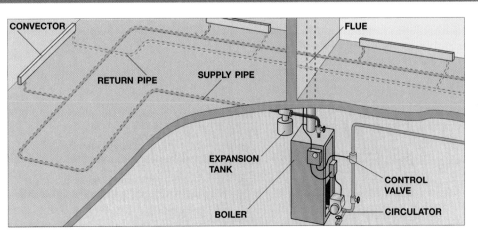

CONVECTOR — RETURN PIPE — SUPPLY PIPE — FLUE — EXPANSION TANK — BOILER — CONTROL VALVE — CIRCULATOR

heating

Expanding the System

Installing a furnace or an entire network of HVAC ducts or heating pipes are not DIY projects—they must be put in by professional contractors. However, when you've added new living space to your home—whether by finishing an attic or garage, enclosing a porch, or building an addition—you will need to provide heat for the space. You have the option of extending your home's existing system into those spaces or installing individual electronic heaters or portable space heaters. (For more on space heaters, see pp. 320–21.)

Hot-Air Systems

New runs of ducts can be extended from the furnace's plenum or from a main duct in an extended-plenum system. Cut a hole in the plenum or main duct using sheet-metal snips; the hole should exactly fit a metal collar, either straight (to run sideways from the plenum) or take-off (to run upward from a main duct).

Round metal ducts are then snapped or hammered together (depending on the type of duct) and attached to the system. There are T- and Y-fittings to make branches; for turns, use 45- and 90-degree-angle pieces or sections of flexible duct. Each new run must also have a damper, to shut off heat to that duct run and balance the system if needed. The final joint in a run of ducts should be attached with a drawband—a steel collar that is tightened with bolts (like a band clamp).

Use flexible metal straps, called hangers, to attach new ducts to basement ceiling joists. You can easily heat the first floor by placing heat registers (grilles with movable vents) in holes cut into the floor and running the ducts to the registers with transition fittings called boots. To bring heat to the second floor, you'll need to run the ducts up the wall or through closets, and box them in with studs and drywall.

In 1777–1778, Washington's Continental Army wintered in Valley Forge, PA, in these primitive log huts with chimneys made from log sections chinked with mud.

Hot-Water Systems

Hot-water heating pipes run in a circuit around the house. Usually, you won't need to add new pipes to the system to install a new convector but instead can tap into existing lines. Most systems have the excess capacity to handle one or two additional convectors.

There are three common layouts for hot-water systems. A series loop has the convectors as part of the circuit; hot water enters each unit through a supply riser and exits through a return riser, then moves on to the next convector in the loop. One-pipe systems have supply and return branch lines that feed each convector from a main supply loop. Two-pipe systems have entirely separate circuits for supply and return. You need to know what kind of system you have before you start cutting pipe. The main line may run around the perimeter of the basement or along a center beam. The steps for adding a hot-water convector are shown at right. (For information on cutting and soldering copper and cast-iron pipe, see "Plumbing," pp. 284–87.)

Electric Systems

It may not be practical to extend your home's heating system into a finished garage or attic. Your other heating options include installing a wood stove, space heater, or electric convector. Although electric heaters aren't as efficient as gas or oil systems, a single room unit is still far cheaper and easier to install than extending ducts or pipes. Wall-mounted baseboard convectors run along the bottom of the wall like hot-water convectors; recessed models are installed through the exterior wall. Smaller 120-volt heaters will plug right into wall outlets; 240-volt models will be more efficient, but you will need to have an electrician install a new circuit at the service panel to operate them.

Baseboard Convectors

USE: ▶ screwdriver • power drill/driver • clamps

1 *Locate the new baseboard unit* over a supply pipe in the floor below. Start by installing the reflector panel on the wall.

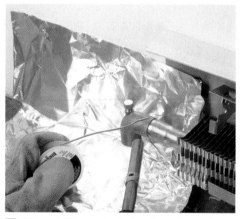

5 *After drilling a hole* for the return pipe at the other end of the convector, solder on a bleeder valve. Protect the wall from flame.

9 *To draw solder fully into the joint* and prevent pinhole leaks, paint the connecting pipe parts with flux.

• propane torch • pipe cutter or hacksaw • work gloves ▶ baseboard convector • pipe & fittings • bleeder valve • solder • flux • scrap Type X drywall & foil

2 ***Position the convector element*** *on brackets attached to the reflector panel. Be careful not to bend the heat-dispersing fins.*

3 ***Temporarily fit the cutoff valve*** *onto the end of the convector pipe, and mark the floor below where the supply pipe will rise.*

4 ***Remove the valve,*** *and drill a hole through the floor. The hole and valve will be hidden by the convector end cap.*

6 ***Test-fit pipes and fittings*** *to reach from the convector valves to the hot-water supply pipe below the floor.*

7 ***Cut off the water supply,*** *and use a pipe cutter to cut away a section of the supply pipe to install a T-fitting.*

8 ***Use a wire-brush tool*** *or sandpaper to brighten the mating edges (inside and out) of the old pipe and the new fitting.*

10 ***Take care to protect*** *surrounding wood from flames. A clamp holds this piece of nonburning drywall covered with foil.*

11 ***Once the pipe joints*** *are soldered, slide on the adjustable heat-control flap and the front cover of the convector.*

12 ***To finish the job,*** *clip an end cap onto each end of the unit. A front flap lifts to provide access to the cutoff valve.*

heating

Filter & Flue Checks

You'll probably remember to replace the big air filter in a forced hot-air system. If you don't, you'll eventually notice the reduced air flow—blocked by a thick mat of collected dust. But there may be several other potential clogs to remove. Before you work on them or on any electrical appliance, make sure that the system is turned off and its power supply is interrupted. Remember, a furnace that appears to be off can be suddenly triggered into operation by the thermostat.

On oil-fired systems, there is another filter to replace. Just like a car engine, the furnace has a filter in the oil line designed to trap sludge and other impurities that can clog the spray nozzle. They are very helpful if the furnace kicks in soon after an oil delivery, which stirs up sludge from the bottom of the tank.

A typical oil filter looks like a small canister attached to the oil feed line. The body of the canister unscrews to provide access to the removable filter cartridge inside. Because oil spills are smelly and difficult to clean up, put a pan beneath the filter (and wear rubber gloves) to make the change.

Some hot-air systems may have a filter on the return air grille—the oversized, centrally located, usually wall-mounted grille that returns cool air to the furnace for reheating. If an electronic air cleaner is added to the system, it's likely to have two filters—a wire-mesh grille for trapping larger particles of airborne debris, and electrostatic dust-collecting canisters. On most systems, the canisters are removable; you can pull them out of the cleaner and fit them in a dishwasher.

In addition to the seasonal maintenance on your furnace, normally performed by a contractor, it pays to check the exhaust flue. Aside from electric furnaces, which do not produce heat by combustion and don't need a flue, other systems require a clean, completely sealed escape route for exhaust. Even a small leak from a flue pipe inside the house can release carbon monoxide, which can be lethal.

In many houses, a metal exhaust pipe from the furnace leads into a masonry flue. It should have a lining, and be separated from other flues, such as a chimney flue, even when the two flues share one chimney. In older houses where brick chimneys deteriorate from exposure to the weather outside and exhaust gases inside, you may be able to reline the chimney instead of building a new one. There are two basic relining systems offered by specialty contractors. One is to insert a vibrating tube in the chimney, pour a fireproof cement mix around it, and gradually draw up the form, which vibrates to compact the mix. The other system relies on an inflatable form, which is centered in the old chimney while the fireproof mix is poured around it. The mix seeps into cracks and crevices, sealing and strengthening the chimney walls. When the form is removed, it leaves a newly formed flue.

Relining Flues

CEMENT LINER

- BRICK
- FORM
- CEMENT MIXTURE
- FLUE

STEEL LINER

- FLUE
- BRICK
- AIR SPACE
- STAINLESS STEEL PIPE LINER

Contractors can reline damaged flues by pouring cement around a removable form or with flexible pipe.

Furnace Maintenance

If you are restarting a furnace, and it hasn't been serviced recently, begin the cold season by paying a pro to clean and tune the system. It's wise to check older systems every year, particularly to be sure that combustion furnaces (both gas- and oil-fired) are properly vented to safely exhaust potentially lethal gases. Look for nests, twigs and leaves, ash and soot—anything that could block escaping gas. If you can't get on the roof to look down the flue and don't want to disassemble the exhaust pipe, hire someone to do it.

USE: ▶ screwdriver • vacuum • bucket or watering can ▶ replacement dust filter • lubricating oil

1 *Furnaces have air-intake grilles* that are easily removed. Turn off the power supply first, and follow manufacturer's directions.

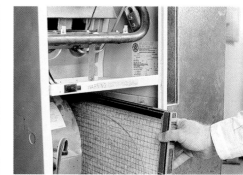

2 *The most basic job,* and one of the easiest, is to replace the dust filter. You may need to do this several times a year.

Improving Efficiency

Most hot-water heating systems have a sight glass you can check to be sure there is sufficient water in the boiler.

Improve the efficiency of both warm- and cool-air delivery by insulating ducts. Use spiked duct fasteners on large plenums.

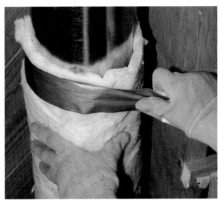

Where individual ducts run close to subflooring and framing, you can spiral-wrap them with batts and tape the joints.

Maximize heat from radiators and convectors by bleeding off trapped air. Open bleeder valves until water flows.

In single-pipe systems, prevent cool water (or condensed steam) from blocking the inlet by raising the far end of the radiator.

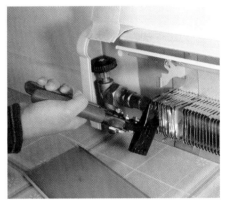

Increase the output of convectors by separating and aligning bent fin plates with pliers or a fin comb.

• disinfectant

3 Use the small brush on a vacuum to clean the furnace blower. Removing the blower can make complete servicing easier.

4 For smooth and quiet operation, oil the blower motor (typically only 3 drops) according to manufacturer's directions.

5 On modern high-efficiency furnaces that produce condensation, clean the drain tube with a disinfecting solution.

heating

Supplemental Heat

In many homes, there are times and locations when the main heating system could use a boost. There are circumstances where it is nice, if not necessary, to maintain an extra amount of heat—say, in a room farthest away from the furnace where long duct runs provide enough heat most of the time but not in really cold weather. Also, if you spend a lot of time in one room, it may be more efficient to add supplemental heat there instead of beefing up the central system.

An oil- or water-filled portable baseboard-type unit is preferable to a kerosene heater, which burns fuel without venting the combustion exhaust outside the house. Because of the double risks to your health (from the exhaust) and to you and your house (from an accidental fire), many localities have outlawed kerosene heaters.

Both oil- and water-filled units produce even heat—similar to the radiating heat from standard convectors in a house with hot-water baseboard heating. If you want to warm up a room quickly, however, a fan-assisted electric-resistance heater would be the best choice because it works more like a forced hot-air heating system and can raise room temperature much faster than a water system. That's why these heaters are often found in bathroom ceiling fixtures, where you want a quick blast of heat to keep you from shivering when you step out of the shower.

Installing Toe-Space Heaters

USE: ▶ power drill/driver • keyhole saw • utility knife • fish tape • screwdriver ▶ toe-space heater

1 *A booster heater* fits into the toe-space under kitchen cabinets. You have to drill corner holes, and make the cutout by hand.

2 *Cut out a section of drywall* for the heater switch, and run power lines through the wall according to your local codes.

Gas Heaters

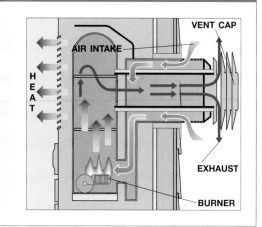

Gas space heaters are more expensive initially than electric models but will save you money in the long run because they produce heat more cheaply, from natural or LP gas. Unvented gas heaters are dangerous and often illegal. Direct-vent gas heaters require no exhaust flue and use separate channels built into a single pipe to bring fresh air in and take exhaust gases out.

VENT CAP
AIR INTAKE
HEAT
EXHAUST
BURNER

Installing Wall Heaters

USE: ▶ stud finder • drywall saw or saber saw • fish tape • cable ripper • combination tool • screwdriver ▶ wall heater & mounting box • cable (per code)

1 *Select a central location* where you can easily snake a supply wire through the wall, and cut out a section of drywall.

2 *Fish your supply cable* between studs, allowing slack to wire the heater. Check local codes and the manufacturer's instructions.

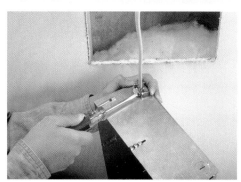

3 *Strip the wiring leads,* pull them through the heater mounting box, and tighten them in a strain-relief fitting.

• switch • electric cable (per code) • strain-relief fitting

3 Snake the supply cable out from under the cabinet. Allow about 2 ft. of slack so that you can remove and clean the heater.

4 Make electrical connections to the heater wires, including a strain-relief fitting on the cable, according to code.

5 When the wiring is complete at the heater and switch, slide the heater into place and secure it with screws.

Portables

Portable electric baseboard heaters work much like a baseboard convector. Most have a fan-assist and thermostat.

Ceramic heaters are good for heating small areas. They will shut off automatically if they are tipped over or start to overheat.

Portable electric radiators, which can be rolled on casters, use electricity to heat a fluid filling for even heat.

• strain-relief fittings • wire connectors • sheet-metal screws

4 Fold the cable into the wall cavity, and fasten the heater mounting box to an adjacent stud with screws.

5 Make the final wire connections with wire connectors, fasten the ground, and attach the heater to the mounting box.

6 Once the wiring is complete and the grounding wires are connected, the last step with this unit is to clip on the cover plate.

heating

Heating with Wood

Millions of households use wood as the primary source of heat, mostly in airtight woodstoves. Heating a house will use four to five cords of wood per year. (A cord of wood is a stack measuring 4x4x8 feet.) At prices in the neighborhood of $150 per cord delivered and stacked, even a modern EPA-approved stove with secondary chambers and catalytic combustors may not offer energy savings compared with oil or gas or even electricity, commonly the more expensive fuel source. (Of course, if you cut, split, and carry the wood yourself, you're gaining heat from all that exercise.) Seasoned (dry) wood provides more heat than green wood; hardwoods will provide more than softwoods. (See the table at right.)

Many more people burn wood in fireplaces, which are pleasing to look at but even less efficient than a woodstove: not only does most of their heat go up the chimney, but they actually draw warm air out of your house and suck in cold air from outside. A fireplace insert can greatly increase its efficiency.

Stoves are also available that burn pellets, which are made from wood by-products such as sawdust. In places where anthracite coal is cheap, a few people still operate coal stoves, which are slightly more efficient and burn longer and cleaner than woodstoves.

Stoves

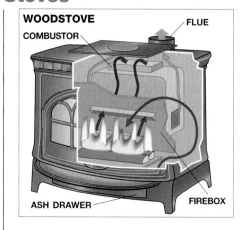

WOODSTOVE
COMBUSTOR
FLUE
ASH DRAWER
FIREBOX

Gas Fireplaces

There are gas fireplaces that fit in conventional chimneys, in freestanding islands, and against walls where there is no chimney. Some look like woodstoves with gas logs inside. Unlike open-hearth fireplaces, gas-fired units produce a predictable amount of warmth, from about 20,000 to 40,000 Btu/hour. With a blower to increase circulation, a large unit can provide supplemental heat for a 2,000-square-foot house.

Modern gas fireplaces look like the real thing (from a distance, at least), and stop and start at the touch of a remote control.

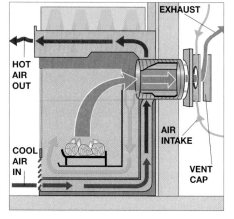

EXHAUST
HOT AIR OUT
COOL AIR IN
AIR INTAKE
VENT CAP

Metal Flues

Inside a standard masonry flue is a tile liner. This double-wall system provides good protection and separates both exhaust gases and sparks from combustible building materials that surround the chimney before it rises over the roof. To save both the time and expense of building with masonry, you can sometimes use interconnected triple-wall metal pipe. These flue systems are standard with prefab fireplaces and can be boxed in with wood framing. You need several components in addition to the pipe sections, including a connector ring at the firebox outlet and fire-stop spacers wherever the pipe travel through framing—for example, at the attic floor and roof rafters. Roof-level spacers have a flange that mounts to the roof deck, and an adjustable collar that allows you to fit the system to any slope. Most pipe systems are topped off with a cap that arrests sparks and keeps out animals.

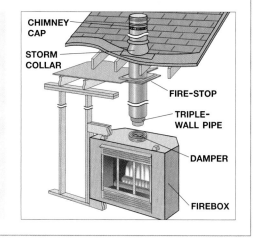

CHIMNEY CAP
STORM COLLAR
FIRE-STOP
TRIPLE-WALL PIPE
DAMPER
FIREBOX

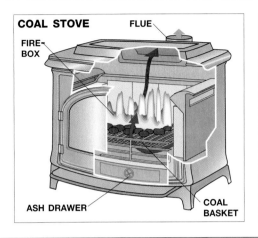

COAL STOVE — FLUE — FIRE-BOX — ASH DRAWER — COAL BASKET

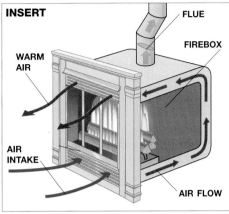

INSERT — FLUE — FIREBOX — WARM AIR — AIR INTAKE — AIR FLOW

Firewood

Species	Btu/cord
Hickory	26 million
White oak	23 million
Sugar maple	21 million
Red oak	21 million
Spruce/hemlock	15 million
White pine	14 million
Aspen	13 million

Installing a Masonry Fireplace

USE: ▶ trowels • 4-ft. level • work gloves ▶ fireplace parts (throat, smoke chamber, damper, air intake) • concrete block • firebrick • mortar • flue liner • flue cap

1 **This shallow but efficient** masonry fireplace, called a Rumford, combines traditional hand work and preformed parts.

2 **Once the opening is prepared,** a team of contractors raises the firebrick firebox inside the concrete-block chimney.

3 **A one-piece throat** rests on top of the firebox. At the back of the firebox is an optional air-intake grille.

4 **A two-piece smoke chamber** sits over the damper, which must be protected from excess mortar that could foul its operation.

5 **In about 4 hrs.,** this crew has completed the firebox. They continue to raise the block and interior flue.

6 **On the way to finishing in one day** (less the stucco and trim), the crew builds the chimney up around a clay flue liner.

heating

Moisture & Air Quality

To add moisture to dry winter air and create an indoor environment that's comfortable for you and good for your house as well, you can use a variety of portable or central humidifier systems. Here is a look at some of the options.

Portable & Central Systems

Portable, or console, humidifiers are concealed in small cabinets. They are helpful if one room is particularly dry or if you have a heating system without an air-distribution system, such as electric baseboards, that isn't suited to a central humidifier system. The drawback is that you have to add water to console storage tanks periodically. Also, they require maintenance much more often than central systems.

Central humidifiers are attached to the home heating system, normally at the plenum, where heated air is distributed to the ducts. The advantage is that the appliance is part of the house; you don't have to plug it in or add water. But an automatically replenished water supply can become a breeding ground for pollutants that are spread through the ducts and into living areas. Treating the water and doing seasonal maintenance can reduce this problem.

Types of Appliances

If you are shopping for a humidifier, bear in mind that two of the four basic types, just by their design, are more likely to disperse microorganisms. Ultrasonic humidifiers, which use high-frequency sound waves to generate a cool mist, and impeller humidifiers, which make a mist with a high-speed rotating disk, produce the greatest dispersions of microorganisms and minerals. Breathing misted air containing microscopic dust mites, mold, bacteria, and other pollutants can cause respiratory problems and allergic reactions.

The other two types of humidifiers generally disperse fewer pollutants. Evaporative units pick up water from a holding tank with a belt, sponge pad, or wick that is exposed to the airflow from the furnace. Warm-mist or similar steam-vaporizer humidifiers can completely eliminate pollution problems. A heating element boils the standing water before it is dispersed as mist into the air flow, which distills the minerals and kills bacteria and mold.

Humidifier Types

Heat from your furnace warms the air in your house, and dries it out, too. Forced-hot-air systems in particular can lower indoor humidity to the point at which people feel uncomfortable. You can add moisture to the air with portable humidifiers, although the most economical systems connect to the furnace. These have a moisture control, called a humidistat, and feed moisture directly into the warm air flow.

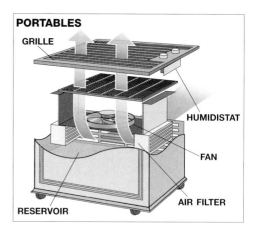

PORTABLES
GRILLE
HUMIDISTAT
FAN
AIR FILTER
RESERVOIR

Installing a Humidifier

USE: ▶ level • tape • marker • metal shears • screwdriver • adjustable wrench • needle-nose pliers

1 *In a typical installation,* you mount a paper template for the humidifier on the main return plenum above the furnace.

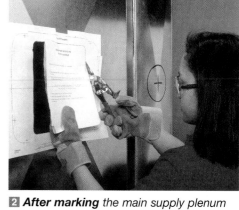

2 *After marking* the main supply plenum for the humidifier duct, cut the template through the sheet metal with a metal shears.

6 *A typical humidifier* has a solenoid valve to control water flow. This small pipe runs from the valve to the distribution tray.

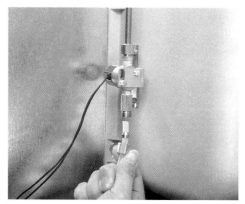

7 *To bring water* from your supply piping to the unit, most humidifiers supply either flexible copper pipe or hard plastic tubing.

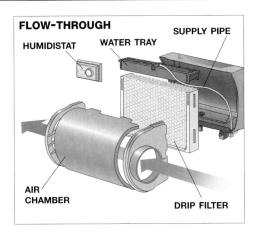

FLOW-THROUGH

HUMIDISTAT WATER TRAY SUPPLY PIPE

AIR CHAMBER DRIP FILTER

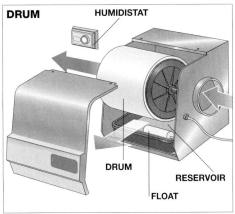

DRUM

HUMIDISTAT

DRUM RESERVOIR

FLOAT

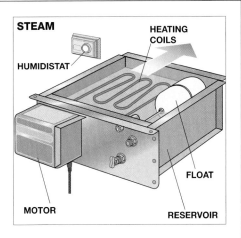

STEAM

HEATING COILS

HUMIDISTAT

FLOAT

MOTOR RESERVOIR

• pipe clamp • work gloves ▶ humidifier • humidistat • duct (flexible or metal) • mounting collar • saddle valve

3 *It's important to level* the humidifier for even water distribution. This unit has a small bubble level built into the water tray.

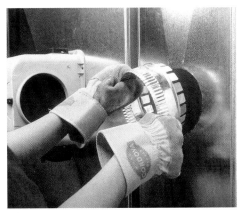

4 *Cut through the main supply plenum* to make a hole for the humidifier supply duct. This kit comes with a mounting collar.

5 *Use flexible duct* or a length of standard metal duct and an elbow fitting to connect the humidifier to the supply plenum.

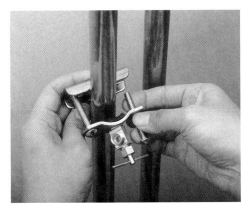

8 *Install a saddle valve* (if permitted by code) on the supply pipe. Clamp it to the line, and turn the handle to pierce the pipe.

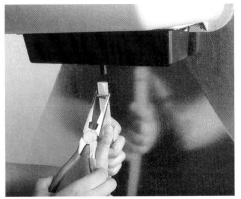

9 *Central-system humidifiers* typically have a catch basin that recirculates water, or an overflow drainpipe like this one.

10 *Install the humidistat,* which allows you to regulate indoor humidity, on the plenum or near the existing thermostat.

cooling 17

cooling

Choosing a System

The time to collect your thoughts about keeping cool this summer is before the weather gets too hot and humid. By planning early, you'll avoid making a rash decision or being stuck with what's left at the home center. Before buying an air conditioner, ask some basic questions: Will it fit in the window? Will it keep the room cool? Is it so noisy that you won't sleep?

Capacity

The cooling power of an air conditioner is measured is units of heat energy called British thermal unit (Btu). An air conditioner's Btu per hour (Btuh) rating indicates how much heat energy it can remove from the air in an hour. Some larger units are rated in tons, which measure the energy it takes to melt one ton of ice in a day. A ton is equal to 12,000 Btuh. As a general rule, 5,000 Btuh are needed to cool a 150-square-foot room. Add 1,000 Btu for every additional 50 square feet.

Central Air vs. Room Units

Central air conditioning is an attractive feature in the resale market, but it's costly and difficult to install in many homes. A contractor may be able to set up machinery and ducts in an unused attic or use forced-air heating ducts, but in a two-story house, you may have to give up some cabinet or closet space to install ducts on the first floor. In most homes, one or two window or in-wall units can keep crucial rooms comfortable and spill out enough cool, dry air to reduce heat and humidity in adjacent areas.

Types of Units

Central AC

Central ACs consist of an outside unit with a compressor, condenser coil and fan, and an interior evaporator coil installed in the supply duct of a warm-air furnace. Indoor heat is picked up and carried through pipes by a refrigerant to the condenser coil outside. Central air is expensive to install if your home lacks heating ducts but may still be cheaper (and quieter) than an array of room units. Modern, high-pressure lines can work with small-diameter hoses that are easy to install in existing spaces.

In-Wall Units

Individual room units can be installed through the wall to avoid blocking the view through a window or having to remove the unit when it's cold. Like window units, in-wall units have two coils made of copper tubing and aluminum fins, one facing inside and one facing outside. These machines work like central systems, but all the components are built into one box. Most room units can be plugged into a standard 120-volt outlet but some require 240 volts. You should be sure that the unit does not overload the circuit.

System Schematic

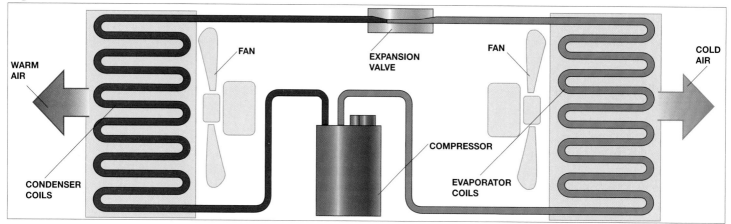

WARM AIR

FAN

EXPANSION VALVE

FAN

COLD AIR

CONDENSER COILS

COMPRESSOR

EVAPORATOR COILS

Window Units

If you need to keep one room or area cool in the summertime, the easiest solution is to install a window unit. You don't have to make a hole in your house or install extensive ductwork, and most units can be plugged in and working an hour after you open the box. The best location is a double-hung window with a wall outlet nearby. The weight of the unit is carried on the sill and held in position with brackets at a slight downward slope for proper drainage of condensation. Extensions on each side of the unit slide out to seal the opening.

Heat Pumps

Heat pumps can heat and cool your home. They have an outdoor coil and compressor and an indoor coil and fan. (There are also self-contained through-the-wall units.) In hot weather, the heat pump acts like a conventional air conditioner. In cold weather, the cooling cycle of refrigerant is reversed to create a heat gain inside the house. But as the temperature outside drops, heat pumps lose efficiency, and an electric back-up heater kicks in. The units are most economical in areas with roughly equal heating and cooling demand.

Chillers

Evaporative chillers (sometimes called evaporative coolers) are typically used to cool the air in commercial buildings or large homes in the Southwest. Chiller units can deliver from 10 to 500 tons of cooling. Modern chillers with heat exchangers and high-efficiency motors can use as little energy as 0.5 kilowatt per ton of cooling. Chillers usually flow water through evaporator and condenser tubes surrounded by refrigerant. Hot refrigerant is then condensed back into liquid in a cooling tower.

Efficiency

You can compare air conditioners by checking their Energy Guide labels. These stickers explain annual electrical costs, compare efficiency among several units, and list an Energy Efficiency Rating (EER) number—a Seasonal Energy Efficiency Rating (SEER) on central air systems. This rating is the ratio of Btu used per hour of cooling to the watts used to produce those cooling Btu—fewer watts per Btu means greater efficiency.

SEER Rating	Recommendation
less than 9.7	old unit; replace with newer model
9.7/10	nat'l min. standard for single package/split-systems
12	recommended min. (Dept. of Energy)
18	most efficient unit available

EER Rating	Recommendation
less than 8	old unit; replace
8	nat'l min. standard
9.2	recommended min. for all units (but see below)
10	recommended min. for louvered unit 6000–19,999 Btuh
10–11.7	most efficient available

cooling

Picking a Window Unit

If you don't have central air conditioning, you may find yourself lingering in front of the refrigerator this summer—unless you install at least one room air conditioning unit. And if you're only air conditioning one room, make it the bedroom. This way, you'll create an island of cool air where you can retreat on sweltering days and get a good night's sleep even if most of the house is hot.

There are many installation options for an individual room unit, but the basic choice is between a removable unit installed in a window or a permanent one built into a wall.

Site Requirements

Basic site requirements are similar for window and in-wall units. Look for a spot where the outside heat-dispersing coils won't broil under direct sunlight, which can decrease the unit's efficiency. You need a location near an outlet with sufficient capacity for the appliance. It's wise to pick a location away from a main entry or deck area where you spend time—so you won't be bothered by the humming and condensation dripping. An in-window machine may work if you have a convenient window. There are more design options with a through-the-wall machine because you can install it almost anywhere on the building.

Window units can be heavy—some big machines weigh over 100 pounds—but they are easy to install. Manufacturers include adjustable panels and foam weatherstripping that surrounds the machine and fills the gaps between the metal case and the window frame.

In-window machines look clunky and block some of your view, but they are portable. You could take the machine with you to another room (if it's not too heavy) or to another house. In-wall units are considered part of the build-

Invented in 1902, air conditioners were not common until the 1920s when they were installed in movie theaters. Stylish household units were not widely used until the 1940s.

ing, like a furnace, even though they plug into a wall outlet like other appliances.

How Much Do You Need?

There are three capacity formulas you can use to help you decide what size unit to buy. The most general rule of thumb would be to buy one ton of cooling (12,000 Btu) per 500 square feet of floor space.

The more complex WHILE formula takes into account several characteristics of a building. In this formula, each letter in the word WHILE stands for a building characteristic for which you substitute a numerical value as follows. W stands for width of the room in feet. H stands for room height in feet. I stands for the amount of insulation. (Substitute 10 if the room is covered by an insulated, ventilated attic or another cool room, 18 for a top-floor room under an uninsulated attic.) L stands for length of the room in feet. And E stands for exposure factor. (Substitute 16 if the longest wall faces north, 17 if it faces east, 18 if it faces south, and 20 if it faces west.) Multiply the numbers and divide by 60 to estimate required Btu capacity. Here's how the formula works for a 15x20-foot room with 8-foot ceilings that is insulated and vented above with a southern long wall.

$$W \times H \times I \times L \times E / 60 = \text{Btu needed.}$$
$$15 \times 8 \times 10 \times 20 \times 18 = 432{,}000 / 60 = 7{,}200.$$

The third capacity formula is found in the Cooling Load Estimate Form available from the Association of Home Appliance Manufacturers (also on its Web site, at aham.org/indexconsumer.htm). While considerably longer and more complicated than the other two formulas, it is the most precise.

Window Fittings

If you install a window unit improperly, it may fall from the window when you raise the sash, damaging the unit and whatever happens to be underneath it. Install all brackets with the hardware provided; if the wood of your sills seems soft and partly rotten, use another window or replace the sill. If your windows have metal sashes instead of wood, use sheet-metal screws to install them.

Installing a Window Unit

USE: ▶ pencil • measuring tape • level

1 *Older units (and some very large machines) rest on external brackets, but modern ACs rest on a sill-mounted support.*

5 *Extensions on both sides of the unit slide out to make a snug fit in the opening. Screw each extension to the sash.*

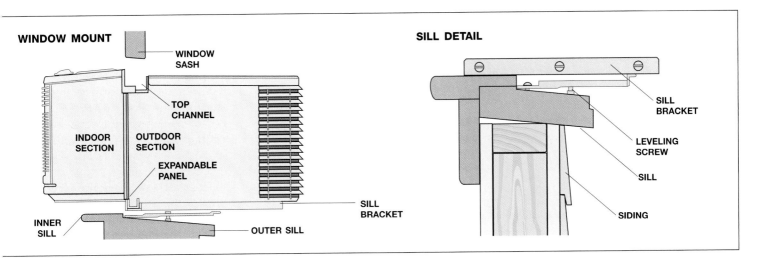

WINDOW MOUNT

WINDOW SASH

TOP CHANNEL

INDOOR SECTION

OUTDOOR SECTION

EXPANDABLE PANEL

SILL BRACKET

INNER SILL

OUTER SILL

SILL DETAIL

SILL BRACKET

LEVELING SCREW

SILL

SIDING

• screwdriver or power drill/driver • caulking gun ▶ window AC unit • waterproof caulk

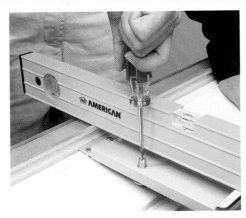

2 *One end of this bracket* is screwed to the sill. You adjust a center screw to level the unit and provide condensation drainage.

3 *This self-contained AC unit* has integral handles that make it easier to set in position on the sill over the mounting

4 *As you slide the machine* into the window opening, a pocket underneath the machine locks in place over the bracket.

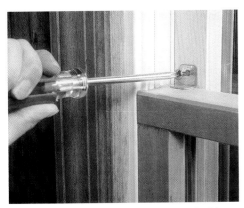

6 *Use the angle bracket* provided with most machines to secure the two window sashes to each other over the AC unit.

7 *To seal the installation inside,* use a foam strip (provided with most machines) to seal the air gap where the sash overlaps.

8 *Caulk the unit outside,* check the manufacturer's instructions for operation and maintenance, and plug in the unit.

cooling

In-Wall Unit Basics

To install an in-wall air-conditioning unit, you will need to make a hole through the exterior wall of your house—a daunting prospect for some DIYers. But if you select a section that is free of pipes and wires, basic carpentry skills and tools will get you through the job.

If you're placing the unit in a solid wall, you will have to build a header—a horizontal beam that picks up loads from studs that are cut short and carries them to the sides of the opening. In most cases, you can avoid this step by installing an in-wall unit beneath a window. The space already has a header and should have double studs running down each side all the way to the floor. You may have to make the air-conditioner space smaller than the window, which is easy, but you won't have to worry about supporting loads from above. An in-wall unit also looks better if it's installed under a window. A metal box poking through a clean wall of siding will grab your eye. It's less noticeable under a windowsill, particularly if you trim the exterior of the conditioner the same way the window is trimmed.

Making the Opening

When cutting and building an opening for an in-wall unit, always follow the manufacturer's directions. Unless you have some experience cutting through concrete, brick, or stone, leave installations through solid masonry walls to professional contractors.

Select a location above the height of wall outlets in order to avoid any buried cables. The best choice often is directly under the framing that supports the windowsill. Wiring may run in the wall under a window, but it's generally at the same height or lower than the wall outlets. If you install the air conditioner in a wall of full-length studs rather than under a window, check with your local building inspector for the size of the header you'll need to install.

Always start work on the inside of the opening before the outside. That way, if you

Installing an In-Wall Unit

USE: ▶ reciprocating saw, crosscut saw, circular saw, & saber saw (optional) • drywall saw & crosscut saw (optional) • pry bar • hammer • pencil • level • screwdriver

Before beginning your project, plan a convenient installation, such as a section of wall beneath a window where you won't have to reroute plumbing pipes or electrical wiring. The air conditioner's instructions should explain what additional framing, if any, will be required to support your unit. Additional trimmer studs and cripple studs may be required to safely hold the unit in place. It's also important to follow the manufacturer's instructions for setting the unit slightly out of level to drain condensation.

1 *Cut away a section of drywall* to expose wall framing underneath. Remove the insulation, and lay out the opening.

2 *Remove short studs* in the opening by cutting them in half and prying out each section. Pull or cut exposed nails.

6 *For a typical installation,* you remove the machine from its chassis, and mount the chassis in the opening.

7 *Use a level* to match the manufacturer's specifications for sloping the chassis slightly downward for proper drainage.

8 *Once the chassis* is screwed to the frame, slide the machine into position. For heavy units, you may need a helper.

uncover an unexpected obstruction—a gas pipe, for example—you'll only have to replace a section of drywall, and repaint the damaged wall. A pain, perhaps, but a much easier job than adding nailers to support the pieces of siding you've cut.

Don't cut blindly into a wall cavity with power tools such as a reciprocating saw or saber saw. Measure and mark the opening carefully, and then trim through surface gypsum by hand with a drywall knife or utility knife. This will produce clean edges that are easily trimmed and will help prevent surprise encounters with mechanical lines or hidden braces buried inside the wall.

Framing the Unit

To frame the unit, you can cut through studs under a window, and add cross timbers top and bottom and new side pieces. But for many people, it is easier to build a box—for example, from ¾-inch-thick plywood—to the manufacturer's specifications, and then use it to mark and cut away sections of studs. Allow an extra ½ inch of length and width so that you can plumb and level the box in the opening. Make sure the unit does not slope even the slightest amount to the inside. Pitch the casing slightly toward the exterior so that condensation will drain to the back of the unit and outside the house, not inside or into the wall cavity.

Transfer the perimeter of the opening to the outside wall by drilling small holes precisely at each corner or by driving nails through the corners. Then go outside, connect the dots, and cut through the siding and sheathing along the outline with a circular saw. For greater accuracy, nail a straightedge to the siding to serve as a saw guide.

Before installing the air conditioning unit in the box frame, reuse pieces of the old insulation to fill in any gaps between framing members. Then, before trimming the opening inside and out, seal small surface gaps with silicone caulk that is flexible enough to maintain a seal next to a vibrating machine.

---

or power drill/driver • drywall knives • caulking gun ▶ in-wall AC unit • 2x4s as needed • drywall • joint compound • sandpaper • caulk • framing & drywall nails

3 *Add framing* as specified by the manufacturer to build the rough opening and create support for the unit.

4 *When the frame is complete,* drive a long nail at each corner to mark the AC opening on the exterior wall.

5 *Mark the opening on your siding,* remove the nails, and cut through siding and sheathing with a saber saw or circular saw.

9 *With the unit secured* in the chassis, which should be flush with the finished wall, piece in drywall around the opening.

10 *After finishing, sanding, and painting* to conceal seams, trim the interior to suit, and reinstall your baseboard.

11 *Use a flexible caulk* around the exterior of the unit to seal the seams between the chassis and the siding.

cooling

Basic Maintenance

Air conditioners don't need a full seasonal tune-up the way most furnaces do. Some basic maintenance, however, will maximize cooling output. The well-maintained unit runs more efficiently, lasts longer, and makes rooms feel cooler at a lower, money-saving setting on the thermostat.

Before attempting anything more than superficial cleaning, unplug room units (or trip the breaker on central systems), and follow the manufacturer's directions for discharging the capacitor, an electrical storage device that can deliver a shock even when a unit is unplugged.

Room-Unit Maintenance

To clean the inside of a room unit, remove the access panel and the filter and, following the manufacturer's directions, either wash the filter or replace it. Clean the inside coil fins with a vacuum cleaner or a soft brush, taking care not to bend the fins. On the outside, remove the grille, and repeat the cleaning process on the exterior coils.

Even in a clean unit, the meeting of warm, wet air and cool, dry air produces humidity. In most room units, it collects in a pan at the base of the machine, which can stagnate. To keep the surrounding airflow clean, rinse the tray with a 50:50 solution of chlorine bleach and water. Be sure the tray drains when you rinse it with water so you won't get overflows.

To keep the fan from pulling warm air through to the inside, seal any leaks between the wall and the metal housing of the air conditioner. If you see moisture around the frame, warm air is probably seeping in, and you should caulk the seams inside and out.

Central-System Maintenance

The procedure for cleaning a central air system, illustrated below, is similar to that for a room unit, except that the machines are bigger, and the parts may be harder to reach—even though on most systems they are split into two sections. To clean the condenser fan and oil the fan motor (both in the outside unit), you will probably have to remove a cover grille, loosen a setscrew holding the fan on the motor shaft, and then remove the fan to gain access to oil ports on the motor. Typically, fan motors get two or three drops of non-detergent motor oil in each port, but follow the manufacturer's oiling guidelines.

Use a garden hose to clean the outside condenser coils, but only after removing the coil guard so you can spray from inside the unit. Otherwise, water-soaked debris will lodge in the fins. If the fins are bent against each other, which is more likely on exterior coils set away from the protection of the building, it's best to use a specialized tool called a fin comb to clean and straighten them. One of several sets of small teeth arranged around the tool head will fit between undamaged fins above the bent area. As you pull the tool downward, its teeth will separate the compressed fins.

Recharging

The refrigerant in older refrigerators, freezers, and air conditioners is typically an ozone-damaging hydrochlorofluorocarbon (HCFC) called Freon. Eventually, the closed refrigerant loop can develop a slow leak and cause the compressor to fail prematurely. As it's illegal to release HCFCs into the atmosphere, when an older machine needs repair, the service contractor is required to capture and recycle the refrigerant. Recycled HCFCs are used to recharge older machines. Most new models use less-damaging refrigerants.

Homeowners can take care of basic maintenance, but you need a contractor to recharge the refrigerant.

Basic Cleaning

USE: ▶ screwdriver • soft brush • fin comb ▶ lubricating oil • new air filter

Service on an AC compressor normally is left to professionals. But there are several steps you can take to improve the efficiency of your central AC system. Be sure to follow the manufacturer's instructions for basic cleaning, and always shut off power to the unit before working on it. Also take care not to compress the delicate rows of metal fins, which must be separated to transfer temperature efficiently.

1 The first step is to shut off power to the unit. Most systems have a cutoff box mounted outside near the fan unit.

2 Remove the access panel, and use a garden hose and brush to clear any debris or grass clippings from cabinet grilles.

Saving Energy

There are many ways to save on your air-conditioning bill—with high-efficiency windows, extra insulation, shades, and other devices. But the easiest way to save is simply to raise the thermostat a few degrees. Your savings will vary depending on where you live and how your house is constructed. But you can estimate a savings of 2% to 3% on your cooling bill for every degree of cooling you do without over 24 hours. You can also increase savings by installing a setback thermostat that can raise the setting automatically when you leave for the day, and lower it before you get home. (See "Thermostats," p. 339.)

You can also save money by improving the efficiency of the duct delivery system. Many systems lose 20% to 40% of the heating or cooling energy they carry, according to studies by the U.S. Department of Energy. The most obvious losses are at loose joints where you can stop leaks by reconnecting the ducts, securing them to each other with sheet metal screws, and wrapping the joints with duct tape. Insulating ducts helps as well. You can use plastic-wrapped sleeves or spiral-wrapped batts of wall insulation secured with tape.

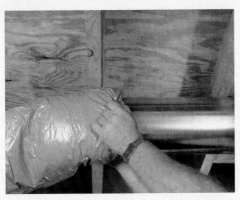

Slide on insulating sleeves, or spiral-wrap ducts with conventional batts to reduce temperature loss in the ductwork.

Secure insulating sleeves with twist ties, or use duct tape to close the seams in spiral-wrapped batts.

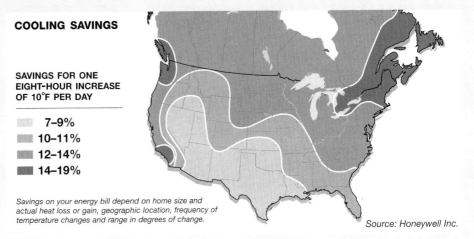

COOLING SAVINGS

SAVINGS FOR ONE
EIGHT-HOUR INCREASE
OF 10°F PER DAY

- 7–9%
- 10–11%
- 12–14%
- 14–19%

Savings on your energy bill depend on home size and actual heat loss or gain, geographic location, frequency of temperature changes and range in degrees of change.

Source: Honeywell Inc.

3 **Clean the fan blades** and fan motor housing, and lubricate the motor with oil as required by the manufacturer.

4 **Use a soft brush** to clear dust from coil fins. If some are bent, use a straightening tool or a fin comb to align them.

5 **One of the easiest steps,** but one of the most important, is to change air filters that keep dust out of the duct system.

cooling

Cleaner Air

Modern houses and apartments are built to be airtight for greater heating and cooling efficiency. They're so airtight, however, that new air circulates back into the house very slowly—it may take hours for the air in a new house to recycle itself. This creates not only stale air but a buildup of indoor pollutants. These pollutants include irritants such as dust, smoke, mold spores, pollen, and animal dander—which not only bother your lungs but clog up heating and cooling systems, computers, and other electronic equipment—but also more serious environmental hazards such as the outgassing of formaldehyde from construction materials.

Several devices are available to clean the air of a tightly-sealed house. Forced-air cooling and heating systems can have electronic filters installed right inside the HVAC ducts. If you don't have these systems, buy a portable air cleaner with a HEPA filter. Developed by the U.S. Atomic Energy Commission to remove almost all airborne particles, HEPA (high-efficiency particulate-arresting) filters are widely used in hospitals and labs where clean rooms are needed. A true HEPA filter removes 99.97% of particles as small as 0.3 micron. (A micron is one-millionth of a meter; the period at the end of this sentence is several hundred microns across.) An ultra HEPA, or ULPA, filter removes particles as small as 0.1 micron. HEPA filters need to be replaced periodically, typically every one to three years.

Portable Cleaners

A portable air cleaner may have several types of filters. The most basic filters are similar to the ones used in hot-air furnaces to trap dirt. Some have to be replaced, while others can be washed and reused. Some machines also include an ion generator to force particles against surfaces. The most effective filter is a HEPA filter, which removes nearly 100% of airborne particles. Manufacturer's literature, mainly the material data sheet, should list filter capacity and effectiveness against different pollutants.

This portable room air cleaner (about 18 in. wide and 12 in. high) will provide 6 air changes per hour in a 15x17-ft. room.

Air Exchangers

An air exchanger is often added to the ductwork of tightly built houses that have only minimal ventilation. Most are designed around the basic plan of two fan-assisted pipes: one to exhaust stale air and one to bring in fresh air. Where the pipes pass each other, a common wall or other media transfers up to 75% of the outgoing temperature to the incoming air supply. This way, you can exchange stale air year round without heating or cooling the fresh supply from scratch.

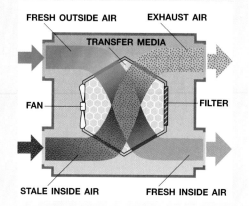

Cleaning Ducts

USE: ▶ screwdriver • glove • vacuum

1 *If your ducts have never been cleaned* (even if you use furnace filters), remove a register and check the duct walls inside.

2 *A household vacuum* may reach several feet down most ducts. A professional cleaning covers the entire duct system.

3 *Dust that gets past your filters* may eventually be trapped at the return-air grille, which also should be vacuumed.

Media Cleaners

A media air filter performs the same tasks as a standard fiberglass mesh furnace filter. However, it does the job more thoroughly because instead of using a loosely woven, flat mesh to trap particles, these filters are made of a tightly interlocking network of microscopic fibers folded like an accordion. The configuration creates a large surface area in a small space. The increased density helps to capture more particles in the airflow than a standard filter. The increased area makes some media filters ten times more effective than a typical disposable filter. Like an electronic unit, most media filters are mounted in the ductwork near your furnace. They are contained in a metal box frame that has an access door so you can remove the media filter for cleaning or replacement. These filters are passive compared to electronic systems. You need to make the same kind of alterations to existing ductwork to install them, but do not need to install wiring.

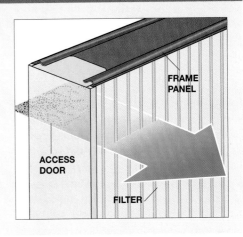

Electronic Cleaners

Electronic air filters are built into the ducts near your furnace. (A unit can be added to existing systems by modifying the ducts.) A typical electronic cleaner has a prefilter that is similar to a standard furnace filter. It traps large dust particles and can be removed for cleaning. Next in line is one or two metal boxes (also removable for cleaning) containing thin metal plates. Particles in the airflow, typically in the return duct, are positively charged on their way to the plates. The plates themselves are negatively charged to attract the particles, which are driven against the plate walls as they pass through the system. These appliances can remove over 90% of most airborne pollutants, including pollen and smoke particles. The drawback is that larger particles hitting the plates can make an annoying sound—like an outdoor bug-zapper.

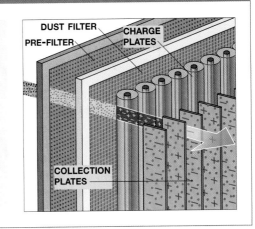

Electronic Air-Cleaning Installation

An electronic air cleaner can be mounted anywhere in the ductwork of a forced-air system. Generally, the most practical location is near the furnace at the end of the return plenum. Before dusty air from the house is sent back into the furnace for reheating, it passes through a prefilter (similar to a standard dust filter) and a row of removable cartridges that contain electronically charged plates. Aside from basic sheet-metal connections, you'll need to provide power for the plates and controls, including a sail switch, located in the return plenum. It activates the cleaner when the furnace blower runs and air flows through the ducts.

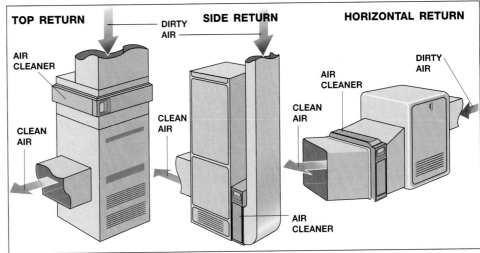

cooling

Dry Air

Moisture won't get a toehold in spaces covered by central air-conditioning or in the immediate vicinity of a room unit you run regularly. But many homes have a laundry, home shop, or storage room that doesn't really need cooler air, just drier air—that's where a dehumidifier comes in. These portable, plug-in appliances use a compressor to pump moisture out of the air, typically into a collection pan underneath the unit that has to be emptied periodically. To some extent, the same thing happens with a refrigerator, which collects condensation in a pan down by the compressor. You don't have to continually empty that pan because a fan blows air over the water to evaporate it. But if a dehumidifier worked this way, the appliance would be working at cross-purposes. Once a dehumidifier removes moisture from the air, you have to remove the moisture from the room.

Paying for reliable convenience features can wind up saving money and maintenance in the long run—even if you buy a machine with more capacity than you really need. Unlike air conditioners, where the costs of running high- and low-efficiency units varies widely, electric operating costs vary only marginally between the least and most efficient dehumidifiers. A Department of Energy analysis of the operating costs of dehumidifiers with a capacity of 20 pints per day running 1300 hours per year (from morning to night during the summer) found only a $9 per year difference between the least and most efficient models.

Dehumidifier Capacity

The industry standard for dehumidifier capacity is specified in pints per day. Unlike air conditioners and many other appliances, they are not rated by energy efficiency (an EER rating). Among the 300-plus models from 30 manufacturers that were rated by the Association of Home Appliance Manufacturers (AHAM), an industry trade group, the pints-per-day ratings range from about 10 to 50. Smaller units in the 15-pint-per-day range should handle most rooms and even full cellars (up to about 500 square feet) that are only moderately damp.

Increase capacity by about 25% if the area is very damp and moisture regularly condenses on walls during the summer. Units rated in the 20- to 25-pint-per-day range should be able to handle larger areas—for example, a 60x25-foot cellar. Units with capacities near the top of the range should only be necessary in very large, very wet areas. Large machines collect as much as 50 pints of water per day and generally include some warning system that automatically signals when the water collection pan is full and has to be emptied.

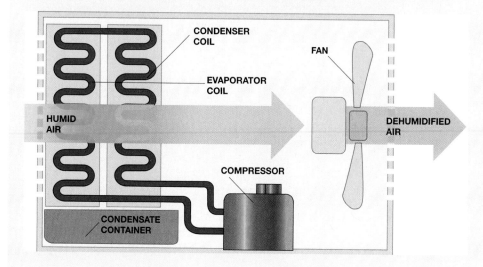

Servicing a Dehumidifier

USE: ▶ screwdriver • vacuum ▶ soap or disinfectant • lubricating oil

1 Remove the access panel, and you're likely to find a dirty air filter that can be replaced (or washed) at least once a year.

2 Behind the panel is a removable water tank where condensation collects. Follow manufacturer's directions for cleaning.

3 Even if you regularly empty the tank, you should periodically wash it with soap and water or a disinfectant.

Thermostats

Among many variations on the standard thermostat, one of the most valuable is the automatic setback. It can save about 3% of fuel costs for every degree of heating or cooling you do without over 24 hours, which makes these programmable units among the most cost-effective energy-saving improvements available. You can program these units to save while you're asleep overnight and at work during the day, and return to 68°F shortly before you rise and before you get home. A 10° setback twice a day can cut fuel bills by about 20%.

Setback thermostats are available in many configurations, including the traditional round shape. Some have enough built-in memory to allow complex programming that includes different weekday and weekend schedules. Several companies also make special thermostat controls with large numerals for visually-impaired people, and with a surrounding ring that makes a distinct click as you move up or down the temperature scale.

The standard round design is still made; it is available as a setback unit that changes temperature levels in preset time cycles.

This thermostat has a large-number sleeve, and a knurled outer ring that makes it easier to turn the dial.

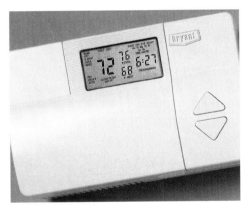

Modern setback thermostats have enough memory to update dozens of displays, aside from time and temperature.

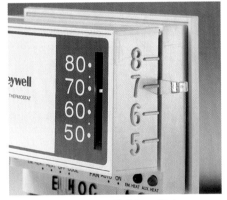

Some units are available with large type and either tactile or audible feedback as you change the setting.

4 *Behind the exhaust grille,* you will find condenser coils. Clean dust on and between the coils with a vacuum.

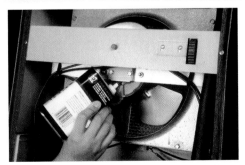

5 *To foster smooth and quiet operation,* oil the fan motor (typically with only three drops) following manufacturer's directions.

6 *Clean the intake and exhaust grilles,* install a new air filter or washable filter if called for, and reattach the access grilles.

electrical

18

electrical

Electrical Basics

Electricity enters your home through overhead or underground wires, where it passes through a meter before entering the main service panel (also called a fuse box or circuit-breaker panel). The meter measures how much electricity you use. At the main service panel, the electricity is divided into branch circuits, each of which is protected by a fuse or circuit breaker. Power travels in a closed loop through the circuit's hot wires to outlets or fixtures and returns to the service panel via neutral wires, unless it is interrupted by an open switch or short circuit. The fuses or breakers protect these circuits from overloading (drawing more power than the wires can handle).

Electrical Terms

Current flow is measured in amperes, or amps. The amp rating is marked on many appliances. Electrical suppliers have charts showing the amp rating for various American wire gauge (AWG) sizes. The rating for your house's circuits will be marked on the circuit breaker or fuse—generally 15 or 20 amps for most room circuits and 30 or 50 amps for heavy-duty circuits, such as those serving a kitchen range, a clothes dryer, or a water heater.

Voltage measures the force of electrical pressure that keeps the current flowing through the wires. Products are marked with a voltage capacity, usually 120 or 240 volts. You can't hook up a product designed to operate at 120 volts to a 240-volt electrical outlet—it will burn out. The shape of the receptacle will prevent you from inserting the wrong type of plug.

Wattage equals volts multiplied by amps. The wattage rating of a circuit is the amount of power the circuit can deliver safely, determined by the current-carrying capacity of the wires. Wattage also indicates the amount of power that a fixture or appliance needs to work properly. Appliances with large motors, such as air conditioners, should not exceed 50% of a circuit's capacity because of start-up overcurrent—motors need more current to start than they do to run. Large appliances often need their own circuits.

Grounding

Electricity always seeks to return to a point of zero voltage (the ground) along the easiest path open to it. If you touch an electric fence, elec-tricity will flow from the fence through your body to the ground—the electrical path is then "grounded" through you. A short circuit in wiring is a similar situation. Electrical current is able to leave the closed loop of the circuit—because, for example, a hot wire is off its terminal and touches the metal box of a light fixture, which is now charged—and return to the source by some other means. If the system is properly grounded, this short would be a fault to ground, and pose no hazard. If it's improperly grounded, and you touch the wiring path—and it could be something as innocuous as the metal pull cord on that light fixture—the electricity will seek to ground itself through your body.

To guard against this, your house's electrical system has grounding wires, which give the electricity a permanent alternative path for its return to the source. Each receptacle and fixture has its own grounding wires that return electricity to the main panel—the third, grounding plug of most appliances extends this protection to them. The entire system is also grounded to your cold-water pipes or (if you have plastic plumbing) to a grounding rod buried underground next to your foundation—or to both.

System Diagram

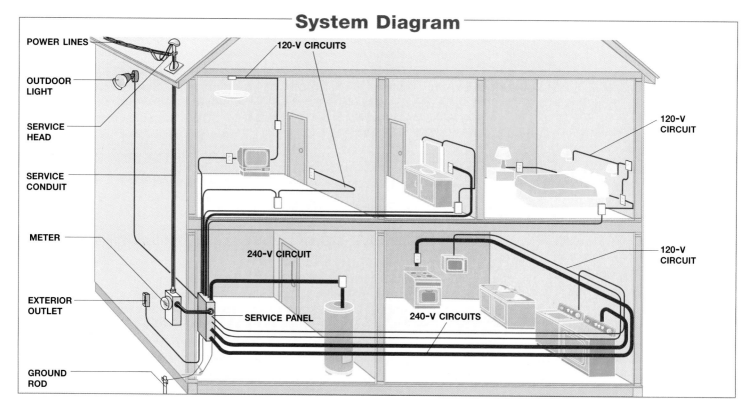

POWER LINES

120-V CIRCUITS

OUTDOOR LIGHT

SERVICE HEAD

SERVICE CONDUIT

120-V CIRCUIT

METER

240-V CIRCUIT

120-V CIRCUIT

EXTERIOR OUTLET

SERVICE PANEL

240-V CIRCUITS

GROUND ROD

Wire Types

Single wires can be insulated to carry electricity or bare for grounding. Most household wiring is contained in cable, inside flexible metal (such as BX, pictured at top), or plastic insulation (such as NM, 2nd from top). Cords (such as lamp cords, 3rd from top) are stranded wires in plastic insulation, not to be used as fixed wiring; low-voltage wire (bottom) is used to wire doorbells and thermostats.

Wire Sizes

Wires have size numbers based on the American wire gauge (AWG) system, which expresses wire diameter as a whole number. For example, No. 14 wire is 0.0064 inches in diameter; No. 12 is 0.081 inches. Smaller numbers indicate larger diameters that can carry more power. The National Electrical Code requires a minimum of No. 14 wire for most house wiring.

Cable Colors

Wires have color-coded plastic insulation to indicate their function in your house's wiring system. Hot wires carrying current at full voltage are usually black, red, or white with black marks (marker or bands of electrical tape), but can be other colors. Neutral wires carrying zero voltage are white or gray. Ground wires can be bare copper or copper clad in green plastic insulation.

Basic Tool Kit

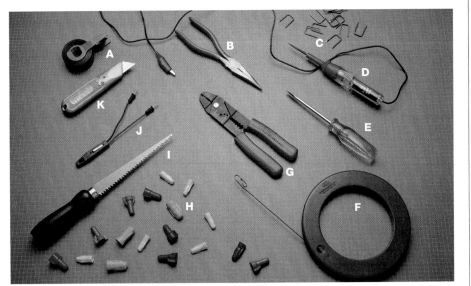

The basic electrical tool kit includes electrical tape (A), needlenose pliers (B), staples (C), continuity tester (D), insulated screwdrivers (E), fish tape (F), combination tool (G), wire connectors (H), utility saw (I), neon circuit tester (J), and utility knife (K).

Aluminum Wire

Many homes built in the 1960s and early 1970s have aluminum wiring, identified by the silvery color and an AL stamp. Because aluminum wire expands and contracts at a different rate than that of copper, it can work loose from copper or brass terminals. This mismatch of materials has been traced to many home electrical fires. If your home has aluminum wire, there are two ways to prevent trouble. One is to connect a short piece of copper wire (called a pigtail) to the terminal, and tie it to the aluminum wires with a wire nut. The other is to use aluminum-compatible connectors marked CO/ALR or CU/AL.

electrical

Electrical Cautions

Electricity can be dangerous, but if you use common sense, you can work with it quite safely. The most important thing to remember is to always, without fail, turn off the power at the main service panel before working on a circuit. Only use one hand to disconnect or reactivate a fuse or circuit breaker, and keep the other hand in your pocket or behind your back. Before starting work, check the circuit with a voltage tester to make sure that it is powerless. If you follow this rule, you will never suffer an electrical shock.

Confine your projects to outside the main service entrance. Do not go in the fuse/breaker box to add new circuits or into a transfer panel for a backup generator unless you have the professional know-how. You can wire in new circuits, repair old ones, and make countless other improvements, but call a licensed electrician when it is time to hook up the project to the entrance panel. The cost is not prohibitive, and the pro will check your work.

Codes

All electrical procedures and materials are governed by local building or electrical codes. They may prohibit the use of a certain type of cable or require a particular size wiring or minimum number of circuits, for example. The codes are for your protection. You may need a permit before beginning some projects; always consult with a municipal building inspector.

Testing

Testing tools let you know that wiring is safe. Use a neon circuit tester to see whether power is present, an important safety step even when you have tripped a breaker or removed a fuse. Touching the probes to a hot circuit causes an indicator to light. Use a continuity tester when a circuit is turned off to check whether an electrical path is uninterrupted. A multitester, which has a voltmeter on its face, performs both functions and is essential for measuring low voltages.

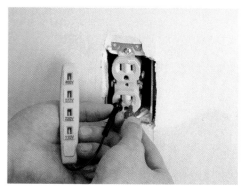

Cut off power at the service panel, and insert the metal probes of the tester into each slot of the receptacle.

Testers

Use a continuity tester on wiring and appliances to pinpoint trouble by determining if a complete circuit exists.

Some analyzers can test for power, reversed wire connections, and other conditions of your electrical system.

Cutting Off Power

Touch only the insulating rim when removing a fuse. An overload melts the fuse's ribbon; a short discolors the window.

A tripped circuit breaker can be in the off position or between on and off. Reset it by switching it to off, then pressing it back on.

Ground-fault circuit-interrupter receptacles cut power automatically. They are required in many locations.

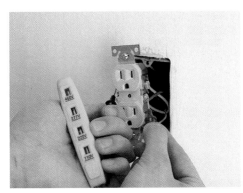

Touch brass and silver terminals with the probes; if the bulb glows, you have to shut off the circuit at the service panel.

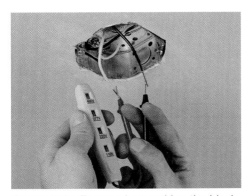

Check light fixtures by touching the black wire and the box or grounding wire, or by touching the black wire and white wire.

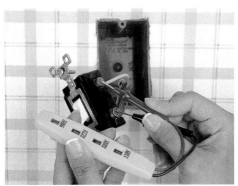

Touch the outlet box or grounding wire of a switch while touching each brass terminal. Again, no glow means no power.

Fixing a Cord

USE: ▶ cutting pliers • screwdriver ▶ new plug

1 Cut a frayed cord below the damage, expose the individual wires inside, and strip ¾ in. of insulation from each one.

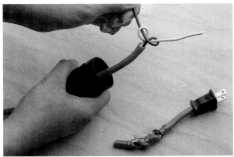

2 Choose a new plug rated for your wire. Some need an Underwriter's knot to prevent wire stress; some have a built-in clamp.

3 Hook exposed leads clockwise on the terminal screws (the way they are tightened), and clamp the cord.

Socket Safety

Three-slot outlets are built to accept a standard two-wire plug with a third grounding leg to reduce shock hazards.

Place protective plastic caps onto receptacles near the floor to keep young children safe from electrical shock.

A receptacle cover closes over plug and outlet to shield connections and prevent accidental pull-outs.

electrical

Basic Materials

House circuits are usually wired with non-metallic sheathed cable, with metal-armored cable, or with insulated wires running through metal or plastic pipe called conduit. For most projects, you will be working with flexible nonmetallic sheathed cable known as NM (or by the trade name Romex). Armored cable is often called BX, also a trade name. Conduit, according to code, can be galvanized-steel pipe or plastic pipe. Metal conduit comes in an array of sizes and three types: rigid (often preferred for outdoor use), intermediate, and electrical metal tubing (EMT). Special tools are used to bend metal conduit, or shaped fittings are available to join sections.

Cutting Armored Cable & Conduit

To cut armor-clad cable, use a hacksaw to cut the flexible steel wrapper about 8 inches from the end. Make the cut diagonally across two metal ribs, and stop sawing as soon as the blade cuts through the metal or you will damage the wires. With your fingers, bend the cable back and forth until the metal snaps apart; then slide the armor off the cable.

Conduit, both metal and plastic, can be cut with either a pipe cutter or a hacksaw. A pipe cutter is the best tool—the shoulders of the cutter keep the pipe square in the device and ensure an even cut. When cutting with a hacksaw, wrap the cutline with masking tape first to reduce burring. (For more information, see "Cutting Pipe," p. 284.)

Wire Terminals

Wires attach to screw terminals *around threaded screws. Wire insulation should stop just short of the screw.*

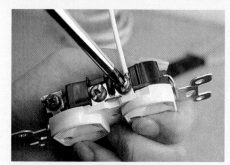

Push-in terminals *feature molded-in gauges to ensure proper wire length. Strip the wires, and push them into the holes.*

Fastening Cable

Fasten cable *along framing with code-approved staples or plastic fasteners. Keep cable 1¼ in. back from the edge.*

Hammer galvanized metal nail guards *onto studs and joists to protect hole-threaded cable from nails or screws.*

Stripping Cable Sheathing

USE: ▶ cable ripper • combination tool ▶ cable

1 Slide the cable ripper *onto the cable, and squeeze it 8 to 10 in. from the end to force the point through the plastic sheath.*

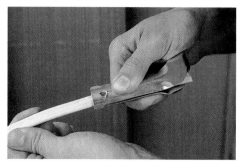

2 Grip the cable tool *in one hand and the cable in the other, and pull the ripper toward the end of the cable.*

3 Expose wires *by peeling back the plastic sheathing and paper wrapping. A cable ripper won't damage individual wires.*

Attaching Wires

USE: ▶ combination tool • needlenose pliers • insulated screwdriver ▶ wire • switch or outlet

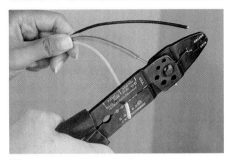

1 Clamp the wire in the proper gauge slot of a combination tool, and strip ¾ in. of insulation from each wire end.

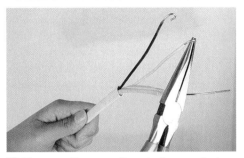

2 Use needlenose pliers to form a clockwise half-loop at the end of each wire. Avoid making nicks that could weaken the wire.

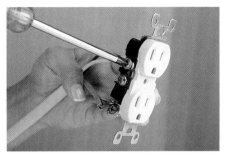

3 Hook the looped wire end onto the screw terminal. The clockwise wire loop will close as you tighten the screw.

Capping Wires

USE: ▶ needlenose pliers • combination tool ▶ wire • wire connector

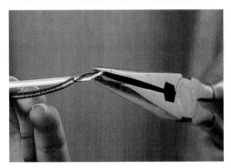

1 To join wires, strip ½ in. of insulation, hold the wires parallel, and twist them together clockwise with pliers.

2 The twisted part should be long enough to engage the wire connector without exposing any bare wire when it is applied.

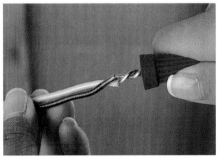

3 Screw down on a wire connector so that the exposed wires are covered. Use hand pressure only, not the force of pliers.

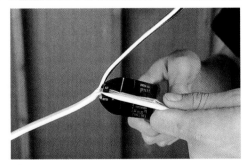

4 Use a combination tool's cutting jaws to trim away excess plastic sheathing and paper wrapping inside the sheath.

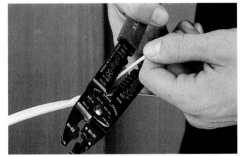

5 Use the cutting jaws of the combination tool to cut individual wires in the cable to length, if needed.

6 A combination tool has slots for different gauges of wire. The correct one will remove the sheath without crimping the wire.

electrical

Plugging In

Outlets, or receptacles, are the devices into which you plug appliances. They're housed in metal or plastic boxes that are attached to the framing. Behind a metal or plastic faceplate, the outlets are held by two screws to a metal mounting strap and the box. When these screws are removed, the outlet may be pulled from the box.

Some outlets are designed exclusively for use outside; some are made to handle heavy-duty appliances such as air conditioners, dryers, and ranges, and have distinctive "faces" that won't accept ordinary two- or three-prong plugs. The most common home receptacle is the duplex receptacle that is rated at 15 amps and 120–125 volts. A duplex receptacle has two outlets and accommodates two plugs. Ground-fault circuit interrupter (GFCI) outlets may be code-required for kitchens, bathrooms, garages, crawl spaces, and other damp locations. GFCI outlets have a safety device that compares the amount of current flowing in the black and white wires of the circuit, and breaks the circuit if it detects a difference as little as 0.005 amp.

If you buy a replacement outlet, make sure it matches the circuit—the markings and ratings on the old and new outlets should be the same. Amperage and voltage ratings indicate the maximums that each outlet can handle. The type of current indicated (such as "AC ONLY") is the only one that outlet can use. The wire in your house must also match the outlet: either copper (CO or CU), copper-clad aluminum (CO/ALR), or solid aluminum (ALR).

Typical Outlet Wiring

Side-wired receptacles generally have two screws per side: one brass or black pair and one silver pair. The brass terminal connects to a hot (red or black) wire and the silver to a neutral (white) wire. (Some outlets have back-wire slots.) Newer outlets also have a green screw at the bottom for a grounding wire. Most outlets are always hot, but you can wire one or both receptacles to be controlled from a switch—say, to control a plugged-in lamp.

In the middle of a circuit, two cables with black, white, and bare copper wires enter a box. Power continues to other outlets in line.

Grounding Boxes

All outlets must be properly grounded to prevent short circuits. Metal outlet boxes require that a grounding wire is pigtailed to the grounding screws of the outlet and the box. With plastic boxes, the cable grounding wire attaches directly to the outlet's grounding screw. Wiring configurations differ from outlet to outlet, however. Houses more than 50 years old may have metal-armored cable, called BX or Greenfield, connecting all outlets and fixtures. In this case, the metal wrapping serves as the ground.

Most electricians now use plastic boxes. With older metal boxes (above), the box must be part of the ground system.

Outlet Boxes

SIDE CLAMP & EARS

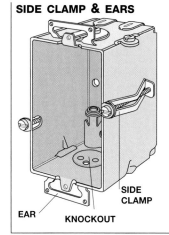

EAR KNOCKOUT SIDE CLAMP

FLANGED

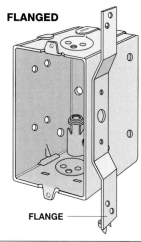

FLANGE

PLASTIC

NAIL

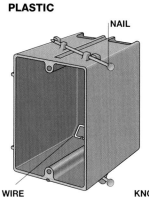

WIRE INLET

GANGED

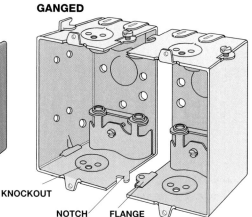

KNOCKOUT NOTCH FLANGE

outlets

At the end of a circuit run, power feeds the last outlet. In all cases, the grounding wires must be connected at the green terminal.

With a switch-controlled outlet, you can turn a lamp on and off from a switch, useful in a room without a ceiling fixture.

Ground-fault interrupters are wired like conventional outlets but provide extra safety with a built-in circuit breaker.

Installing an Outlet

USE: ▶ measuring tape • pencil • hammer • cable stripper • combination tool • insulated screwdriver ▶ cable • outlet box with screws • common nail

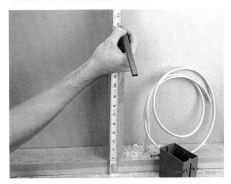

1 *Bring your cable* into the framing bay through the soleplate, and mark the box location 12–18 in. from the floor.

2 *Most boxes have a slot* through which you drive a mounting nail. Set the box ½–⅝ in. proud of the stud to be flush with drywall.

3 *Pull the cable* through the box; many have self-clamping inlets. Allow enough wire (at least 6 in.) to make connections.

4 *Use a cable stripper* to slit open the cable sheath and expose the individual leads inside without crimping the wires.

5 *Use a combination tool* to strip the insulation from individual wires. Match the tool stripping slot to the wire gauge.

6 *Connect wire leads* to the screw terminals, fold the wire bundle behind the outlet, and screw the outlet to the box.

electrical/outlets **349**

electrical

On & Off

A switch controls the flow of power in a circuit. Most residential switches are toggle types, also called snap switches. Older houses might have push-button or dial switches. There are other options, however, that can add convenience and save electricity. Timer switches, for example, are used to control fans in kitchens and baths so that you can turn them on and leave without turning them off.

Illuminated switches are handy if a switch controlling an overhead light isn't at the entry to a room. Instead of groping for a lamp, change the nearest standard switch to an illuminated one. Some have a small pilot light under the toggle; others have a toggle that emits a glow so that you can't miss it. You can also exchange standard toggles that click on and off for more modern units such as paddle switches or silent switches that don't click.

Switch Stamps

Switches are stamped with code letters and numbers detailing operating specifications and safety information. Learn how to read these so that you buy the right switch. The switch in the illustration below is rated for 20 amps and both 120- and 240-volt circuits on alternating current (AC) only. CU WIRE ONLY shows that it can't be used with aluminum wire; CU/AL or ALR switches can be used in that case. UL or UND. LAB. means that the switch has been tested by Underwriters Laboratories. (CSA is the equivalent Canadian organization.)

Typical Switch Wiring

A switch with two terminals (plus ground) is called a single-pole switch; it alone controls a circuit. The incoming hot wire is hooked to one terminal screw and the outgoing hot wire to the other. A switch with three terminal screws (plus ground) is called a three-way switch; these control one fixture from two places and will not have ON/OFF on the toggle. There are also four-way switches, which control lights from three locations; and double switches, which serve more than one circuit in the same switch box.

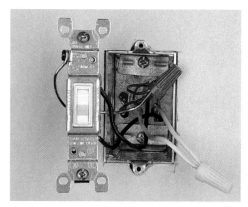

A single-pole switch in the middle of a circuit has two cables entering its box, each with hot, neutral, and grounding wires.

Dimmers

Dimmer switches allow you to control the amount of light—for example, by dialing the power up or down.

Dimmer switches are available in many configurations, including toggles that look like standard on-off switches.

Special Switches

Pilot-light switches have toggles that show when a light has been left on in an attic, basement, or other infrequently used spot.

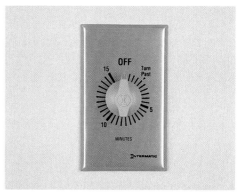

A timer switch has a spring-wound dial that shuts off a light or appliance, such as a bathroom fan, after a set period of time.

Switch Stamps

USE CU WIRE ONLY

UND. LAB. INC. LIST SPECIFICATION GRADE

AC ONLY 20A—120/277V

1HP-120V 2HP-240V

A single-pole switch at the end of a circuit has cable coming into the box but not going out. Cable clamps at the back of the box.

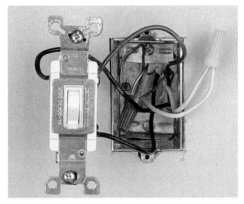

Three-way switches in the middle of a circuit have a red traveler wire. These switches control one light from two locations.

Three-way switches at the end of a circuit run still have a red traveler wire to connect switches—for example, at each end of stairs.

Slide-switch dimmers translate the allocation of power to a vertical scale. Some push to turn off power completely.

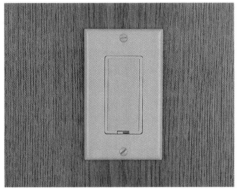

Universal-design dimmers with large paddle switches make it easier for people with disabilities to adjust lighting.

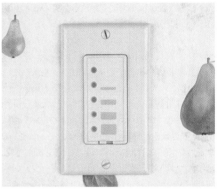

Built-in circuitry in some dimmers will remember lighting levels and recall them with a push of a button.

A clock switch turns appliances and lights on and off at preset times. They can be fitted with adjustable on/off trippers.

Programmable switches with digital controls can provide security with up to four on/off cycles per day.

A motion-sensor switch continuously monitors an area of the room and turns lights on and off as people come and go.

electrical

Lighting Basics

Lightbulbs are rated by lumens, which measure the amount of nondirectional light the bulb produces, and watts, which measure the rate at which the electrical energy is used. The ratio of lumens per watt is an indicator of a bulb's efficacy. Watts don't measure brightness: though a 100-watt incandescent bulb is brighter than a 40-watt one, a 13-watt compact fluorescent bulb may be brighter than the 40-watt as well.

Compared with an energy-guzzling 100-watt incandescent, compact fluorescents use 75% less electricity and last longer—but you can't dim them without installing special ballasts and wiring. The harsh, bluish light of a fluorescent is also not what most people want in the dining room or next to the sofa. For some uses, fluorescents are fine—for example, over the washer and dryer or tucked under upper kitchen cabinets for task lighting. If you are stuck with fluorescent fixtures, a lighting expert can help by choosing warmer bulbs or cooler tubes to suit the situation.

Halogen bulbs have a kind of clear-white quality, are about 25% brighter than standard incandescent bulbs of the same wattage, and can be dimmed without special wiring—but they do require special fixtures. They are also extremely hot and should be treated with caution. High-intensity-discharge (HID) bulbs, such as halide and high-pressure sodium, are also bright and efficacious, but require special fixtures. They are often used outdoors because of their brightness and long lifetime.

Common Bulbs

Common bulbs *(from left): incandescent A-bulb, fluorescent tube, metal halide bulb, and compact fluorescent.*

Bulb Type	Lumens/ watt	Life (hrs.)
Standard A-bulb	14–18	750–2500
Standard 3-way	10–15	1000–1600
Halogen	15–22	2500–3500
Fluorescent Tube	up to 105	6000–24,000
Compact Fluorescent	up to 105	9000–10,000
Halide	71–100	7500–20,000
High-press. Sodium	64–95	16,000–24,000

Lamp Repair

Bulb lamps usually fail from heat or wear that breaks continuity between the hot terminal (brass or black screw) and the base of the socket, or between the neutral terminal (silver screw) and the socket. After unplugging the lamp, your first step in a repair is to test for continuity between the screw terminals and these points.

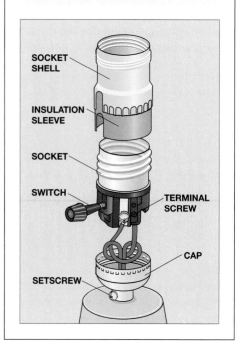

Boxes

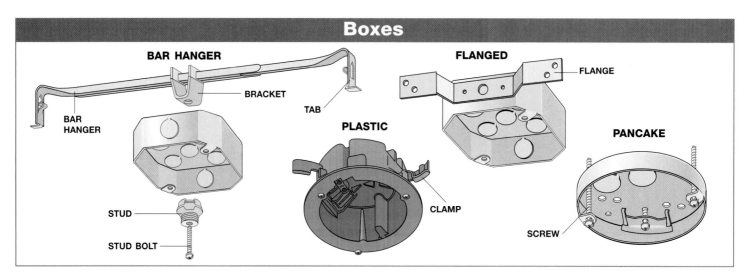

Installing a Ceiling Box

USE: ▶ pencil • keyhole saw or saber saw • screwdriver ▶ ceiling fixture box • screws • wire connectors

1 *A cut-in box* *lets you add a fixture without the support of joists or studs. First, mark and cut the drywall opening.*

2 *Bring cables into the box,* *and press the box into the opening. Engage the holding tabs with a screwdriver.*

3 *Connect* *the circuit/switch-loop wires to the new fixture with wire nuts. Then, screw the fixture to its base.*

Installing a Fluorescent Fixture

USE: ▶ neon tester • keyhole saw or saber saw • screwdriver • combination tool • fish tape (optional) ▶ fluorescent fixture & box • wire connectors • screws

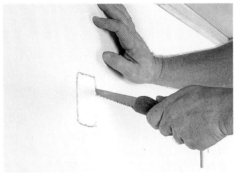

1 *Take power* *from a nearby fixture box—in this case, in the floor below an installation of kitchen cabinet lights.*

2 *After securing connections* *with wire connectors and closing the box, mark and cut an opening in the wall for your switch.*

3 *Fish the power leg* *up through the wall and the switch leg down from an opening in the back of the cabinets.*

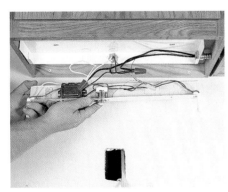

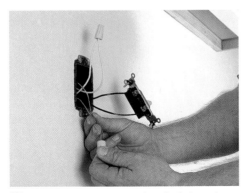

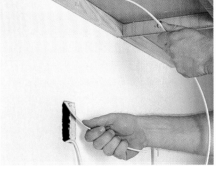

4 *Screw the lamp fixtures* *to the cabinets, and wire them to each other through flexible conduit.*

5 *Clamp the power and switch legs* *in the wall box, strip the leads, and connect the black wires to the switch.*

6 *Finish by clipping diffusers* *on the lamp cases. They help fluorescents cast a more even light on the counters.*

electrical

Low-Power Circuits

Doorbells and thermostats need less than 120 volts of power to operate. To install either one, you will also have to install a transformer to step down the house voltage to 12 or 24 volts.

A doorbell circuit must have three connections: a transformer to 120-volt house current and two low-voltage wires, one from the transformer to the bell and one from the bell to the button. The transformer may be wired directly into a junction box in a basement, attic, or above a dropped ceiling. Use transformer wire, 20-gauge or larger, or equivalent bell wire rated at 30 volts.

Remote Switching

In new wiring, you can save a great deal of time and money by installing a low-voltage remote control. Standard 12- or 14-gauge wire is used only between the main panel and the outlet or fixture boxes. Switches are wired with low-cost 18- or 16- gauge wire that does not have to run in conduit, and the switches do not have to be mounted in boxes (unless this is required by local codes). The lightweight wires are easy to run, strip, and connect.

You need three kinds of devices for a low-voltage remote-control system: a transformer, a switch, and a relay. A transformer takes the 120-volt primary power from the service panel and supplies 24 volts to the switching system. Wires between the transformer and the remote switches connect through a relay, an electromagnetic switch that acts as a go-between.

Phone Wiring

You can run phone wires in or on the wall. Partially conceal exposed wires on molding, secured with non-pinch staples.

If a phone works plugged into the company's exterior jack but not inside, the fault is in your interior wiring.

Installing a Transformer

USE: ▶ screwdriver • needlenose pliers • combination tool ▶ low-voltage transformer • transformer wire

1 Select a junction box near the bell or other transformer-fed appliance. Cut power to the box, and remove its cover.

2 Bend and remove a metal knockout in the side of the junction box where the transformer will be mounted.

Fixing a Doorbell

USE: ▶ screwdriver • soft-bristled brush • utility knife • continuity tester ▶ grommet

1 When the bell won't ring, check wiring connections behind the exterior button, which may corrode or come loose.

2 If the wiring is okay, try cleaning dust from the bell contacts. An unlikely tool (a soft-bristled toothbrush) works well.

3 If the bell tone sounds like a dull thud, cut out the grommet that helps to suspend the tone bar. It may be brittle or broken.

Replacing a Thermostat

USE: ▶ screwdriver • combination tool • pen ▶ thermostat • masking tape

1 Loosen the old thermostat from its wall mount, and mark the terminal location and color of each wire you disconnect.

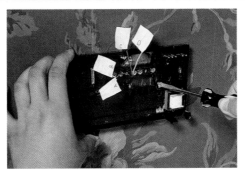

2 Mount the base of the new thermostat in the same location (away from heat sources), and pull through the tagged wires.

3 Remove the tags, and attach old wires to the new thermostat one at a time. Finish by installing the new faceplate.

• wire connectors

3 Mount the transformer to the box by inserting its threaded stub through the knockout and securing it with a nut.

4 After removing the old wire connectors, join the transformer leads to their corresponding power leads in the junction box.

5 Run transformer-gauge wires from the bell, thermostat, or other appliance, and connect them to the transformer terminals.

4 Add a new rubber grommet if needed, so that the tone bar can vibrate freely and create sustained bell tones.

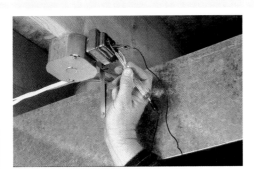

5 Use a continuity tester to check electrical circuits at the transformer that powers the low-voltage bell system.

6 If the transformer is not working, cut power to the junction box, remove the wire leads, and install a new transformer.

electrical

New Wiring Options

If you are building new or remodeling old construction where the framing is exposed, wiring in new circuits and fixtures is easy—there's nothing in your way. Stringing wire or cable through existing walls and ceilings, however, is akin to fishing in a muddy creek: you can't see where the line is going.

Wiring in Open Walls

To add new wiring, you can drill holes in the studs for the cable using a ⅝- or ¾-inch bit. Holes should be at least 1¼ inches from the facing edge of the stud. If you can't leave that much space, attach a steel nailing plate on the outside of the stud to keep any drywall or paneling fasteners from being driven into the wires. You can also cut notches into the front of the studs, about ¾ inch deep and 1 inch apart. Once the cable is in position, cover the notch with a steel plate. If the ceiling framing is also exposed, cable can be run through the joists and down the wall, stapled to the studs.

Edison produced the first practical lightbulb in 1879. He then had to build a power plant; by 1882, his New York City plant had 203 customers.

Wiring in Closed Walls

If you have access to walls from an unfinished basement or attic ceiling, you can add new wiring by fishing the cable down or up (through a hole drilled in the top plate or soleplate) instead of across. Otherwise, you'll need to "fish" the cable through the closed walls by cutting additional openings in the drywall surface, such as behind the base molding, and then drilling holes in the studs. Pull the cable through using fish tape—wires with hooked ends that pull the cable between studs or joists.

Surface Wiring

Surface wiring—wiring installed in a raceway (a protective plastic or metal casing)—eliminates behind-the-wall cable fishing. The raceway is permanently attached to the wall, usually at the base molding or the ceiling. Raceway wiring can include outlets, switches, and ceiling fixtures. Special connectors turn corners and provide intersections for branches.

Fishing Connections

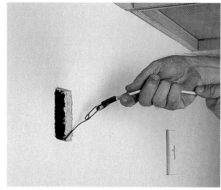

1 *Instead of trying to thread* bendable cable through wall cavities, thread a more controllable steel fish tape.

2 *Bend wire leads* around the fish tape end hook, tape the leads down, and roll up the tape to pull the cable through.

Fishing Routes

ATTIC WALL

FISH TAPE

2ND FLOOR CEILING

1" HOLE IN TOP PLATES

WIRE HOOK

CABLE

1" HOLE IN SOLEPLATE

1" HOLE IN TOP PLATES

1ST FLOOR WALL CAVITY

FLOOR JOIST

1" HOLE IN FLOORING & SOLEPLATE

CABLE

BASEMENT

Installing Surface Wiring

USE: ▶ metal snips • hacksaw • screwdriver • combination tool • neon tester ▶ raceway channels, trim & clips • wiring & connectors • screws • boxes & fixtures

1 *Plastic surface wire channels,* called raceways, are easy to cut—use metal snips on the base channel and a hacksaw on trim.

2 *Screw the base channel* to the wall with plastic anchors. At a tee, clip the edge to clear a path for wires.

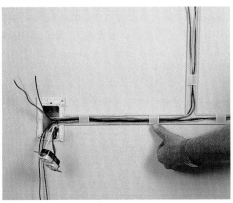

3 *Install a box plate* over an existing outlet, and extend wires from that circuit. Hold the wires with clips.

4 *Once all wiring* is in place, clip trim channel over the tracks. There are special connectors for T- and L-joints.

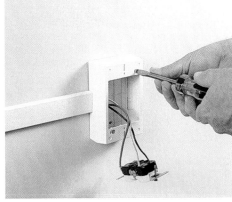

5 *Where raceway wiring* feeds power to a new outlet, you can mount a matching plastic outlet box on the wall.

6 *Strip the wire leads,* connect them to the terminals on the outlet, and screw the outlet to the plastic wall box.

7 *To feed power to a ceiling light,* run a raceway up the wall and across to the fixture. Cover the corner with an L-clip.

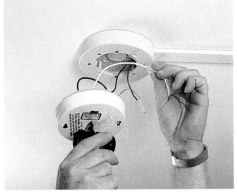

8 *Raceway systems* have surface mounts for outlets and switches—and ceiling fixtures. Connect the leads with wire connectors.

9 *Once the wiring is complete,* screw the fixture base to the raceway ceiling mount, and fasten the diffuser to the fixture.

electrical

Outside Power

Outdoor wiring is needed for the same reasons you put electrical lights and outlets inside: to light living space, to make steps and walks safer at night, and to run fixtures and appliances (such as hot tubs). There are also motion-sensor lights that are installed to startle intruders. Installing outdoor wiring is similar to doing it indoors, but it's done with special weatherproof switches, outlets, and light fixtures.

Generally, local codes require that outdoor wiring be protected by rigid metal or intermediate metallic conduit (IMC) whenever it is installed aboveground. Most codes allow buried cable to be Type UF (underground feeder); some require that Type TW (thermoplastic—wet) wire and conduit be used. Always check your local codes before planning an outdoor wiring project.

Installing Outdoor Cable

The most difficult part of installing outdoor wiring is digging trenches for the cable; the longer your cables, the more time-consuming the project will be. Cables need to be buried 18 inches underground (12 inches if the circuit is less than 20 amps and is protected by a GFCI). Weatherproof receptacles can be attached to the side of your house, screwed to a deck post, or left freestanding. (Freestanding outlets must be supported by a footing, like a buried bucket filled with concrete). Outlet boxes are attached to the conduit with watertight compression fittings.

Outdoor Circuits

There are two basic types of outdoor systems. One includes outlets and floodlights and is like your standard house circuits. But the outlets must be waterproof and in many regions must include a built-in circuit breaker (GFCI). Also, wiring run outside the building must be shielded from exposure, typically in metal conduit. The other basic system is low-voltage lighting, typically to light a walkway. These are easy to install, and are run from a transformer plugged into the house.

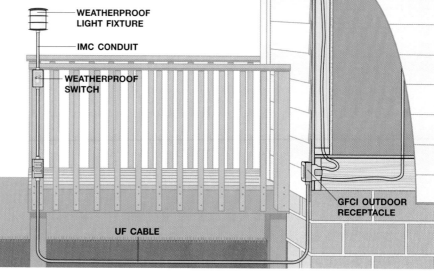

- SECURITY LIGHT
- NM CABLE
- SWITCH FOR SECURITY LIGHTS AND GFCI RECEPTACLE
- WEATHERPROOF LIGHT FIXTURE
- IMC CONDUIT
- WEATHERPROOF SWITCH
- GFCI OUTDOOR RECEPTACLE
- UF CABLE

Installing a Floodlight

USE: ▶ screwdriver • power drill/driver • caulking gun ▶ floodlight • weatherproof fixture box • wire connectors • cable • staples • screws • caulk

1 *To bring power* to your new floodlight, punch a knockout opening in an existing ceiling electrical box.

2 *Extend power* to the switch box, stapling the cable as you go, and then continue to the exterior light location.

3 *A typical box fitting* has a mounting stub for the light fixture. The box must be installed securely to support the lights.

Installing an Exterior Outlet

USE: ▶ measuring tape • power drill/driver • fish tape • combination tool • screwdriver • neon tester ▶ weatherproof box • galvanized screws • cable • staples

1 Mark the outlet location, *measuring to a point at least 4 in. above the foundation and 12 in. above ground level.*

2 Drill through the wall's rim joist, *and fish across the basement ceiling to bring cable outside.*

3 Pull the power cable *through a knockout in a weatherproof box, and mount the box to the wall with screws.*

4 Wire the receptacle *to a GFCI circuit. The black wire goes to the brass terminal, and white goes to silver.*

5 Fasten the outlet *in the box. Most exterior fittings include foam-rubber gaskets to help seal out the weather.*

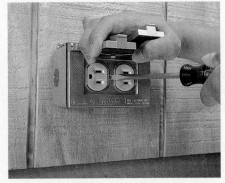

6 Finish by installing *a weatherproof receptacle cover. They are spring-loaded and close automatically.*

4 Most fixtures have two lamp holders *that swivel to cover a large area. Many also have motion sensors and timer switches.*

5 Connect wire leads *from the lamps to the power leads (and ground) in the box with wire connectors. Caulk the top of the box.*

6 Mount the box cover, *and adjust the lights to suit. Use bulbs rated for outdoor use, even under a roof overhang.*

insulation 19

insulation

Insulation Basics

Like clothing, insulation comes in all shapes and sizes, but each has an R-value, the measure of its resistance to heat flow. In general, light-weight, air-filled materials such as fiberglass insulation batts have high R-values per inch of thickness and are good insulators. Standard fiberglass is rated at about R-3.5 per inch. Heavy, dense materials such as brick (R-0.2) and gypsum plaster (R-0.2) have R-values so low it's difficult even to think of them as insulators. R-values are stamped on the insulation itself and displayed in all insulation advertising. It is the only reliable way to determine how effective the insulation will be, and the only way to compare one type with another.

Comparing R-Values

Thicker is not necessarily better when it comes to insulation. That sometimes confusing subject becomes clear when you compare materials. For example, these three alternatives are rated at R-11 and offer the same thermal protection: 1½-inch-thick polyurethane board, 3½-inch-thick fiberglass batts, or 4 inches of loose-fill vermiculite. That means you can't pick one insulation over another based only on thickness. A full 5 inches of a traditional, poured-in insulation such as perlite rated at about R-13 would provide only about 60% of the thermal protection offered by an inch less (4 inches) of polyurethane board rated at about R-23. So in order to reach an insulation rating of R-11 in walls, R-19 in floors, and R-30 in ceilings, you would need different thicknesses of commonly used insulation materials.

Comparing R-values without splitting hairs should show which one of several alternatives will provide the most resistance to heat loss. But some insulation materials are better suited to certain kinds of installations. That means you must consider other insulation characteristics in addition to the R-value. (See "Choosing Insulation," p. 364.)

Also bear in mind the law of diminishing returns as it applies to insulation. This means that the first inch in an uninsulated wall offers the greatest benefit, while the second inch offers a bit less, and so on, even though the last inch costs as much as the first.

Thermal Envelope

Heat moves toward colder surfaces and is conducted through walls and windows to the colder air outside. Insulation materials are poor conductors of heat—they slow the escape of warm air from your house.

ATTIC

RAFTER

CEILING JOIST

LIVING SPACE

HEAT LOSS

WINDOW

HEAT SUPPLY

FLOOR JOIST

STUD WALL

CRAWL SPACE

R-Value Zone Map

Recommended R-values

	A	B	C	D
■	30	0	11	11
□	30	0	11	19
▨	38	19	11	19
▨	38	19	11	19
▨	38	19	11	19
▨	38	19	11	19
▨	49	19	11	19
▨	49	19	11	19
▨	49	19	11	19
▨	55	19	11	19

A=Ceilings below ventilated attics
B=Floors over unheated basements
C=Exterior walls (wood frame)
D=Crawl space walls

Be sure to check general R-value recommendations against the requirements of local energy codes.

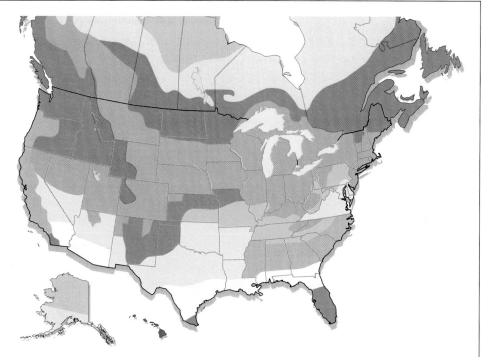

AVERAGE R-VALUE RECOMMENDATIONS FOR U.S./CANADIAN CLIMATE ZONES

Insulation Performance

The most common type of insulation is fiberglass, which has R-values ranging from R-11 to R-38, depending on thickness. Other types of materials include blown cellulose, several varieties of rigid boards, sprayed foams, and many less common materials, such as cotton fiber and aluminum foil bonded to plastic bubble pack.

The table at right compares approximate R-values for different types of common insulation. Each material is evaluated on how much resistance to heat change it offers. Values can be slightly different for very similar materials. To be certain of the value (and be sure that you meet local energy codes), check product labels. All are required to list the R-value per inch.

Generally, extruded plastic boards like polystyrene and polyisocyanurate offer the highest R-values.

R-Value Comparisons

Fiberglass Batts

3½"	R-11
6½"	R-19
7"	R-22
9"	R-30
13"	R-38

Rigid Board (per inch)

Expanded Polystyrene	R-4
Dense Polystyrene	R-4
Extruded Polystyrene	R-5
Polyurethane	R-6
Polyisocyanurate	R-6–7

Loose Fill (per inch)

Cellulose	R-3
Perlite	R-3
Vermiculite	R-2

Sprayed or Foamed Fill (per inch)

Cellulose	R-3–4.0
Polyurethane	R-5.5–6.5

insulation

Choosing Insulation

Two main factors affect your choice of insulation: the configuration (for instance, loose fill or rigid foam board) and the R-value. There are many types available, so you can pick the most efficient product for the job. Some do-it-yourselfers also may consider ease of application, how the material is packaged, and potential drawbacks such as possible skin irritation. But many lumberyards and home centers stock only fiberglass and a few types of foam boards.

Basic Configurations

Insulation is commonly available in five forms: batts to fit between 16- or 24-inch-wide framing, either paper or foil-faced; loose fill to blow or pour into structural cavities; and foam boards, used mainly on roofs and on the outside of walls and foundations. The two other types, sprayed-in-place cellulose foams and foamed-in-place urethanes, are more expensive and not used as widely.

Some materials come in only one configuration, others in several. You can get by using scraps of one material in spaces where another product would offer more protection. But to do a thorough job of creating a thermal envelope around your living space, particularly in the framing compartments of an existing building, you may want to use more than one type of insulator.

Materials

Cellulose fiber is a paper-based product and has roughly the same R-value as fiberglass, about R-3.5 per inch. Typically, it is made from shredded recycled paper combined with a fire retardant. Loose fill can be blown in using a pressurized air hose. Several newer insulating materials use a mix of about 75% recycled cotton fiber (even scraps of old blue jeans) with 25% polyester to bind the fibers together. The material comes in batts and as loose fill. Its R-value is generally about the same as cellulose.

Polyurethane foam can be sprayed by contractors into open framing cavities where it provides a thorough seal against air leaks and a thermal rating of about R-6.0 per inch. It also comes in pint-sized quantities—in a can with a nozzle so you can use foam to fill small openings in the building envelope.

Common Types of Insulation

FIBERGLASS

MINERAL WOOL

CELLULOSE LOOSE FILL

EXTRUDED POLYSTYRENE

POLYURETHANE

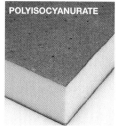
POLYISOCYANURATE

◆ **Fiberglass**
The most common of wall and ceiling insulation materials, fiberglass insulation is installed in 80 percent of new homes. R-values available in a variety of different thicknesses range from R-11 to R-38. Unfaced batts can be laid on top of themselves to create super-insulated attics. Most residential applications use either rolls or precut batts.

◆ **Mineral wool**
Like fiberglass, mineral wool is made from a hard mineral slag and spun into a soft material. Mineral wool gets clumpy when wet and will lose R-value. When dry, mineral wool has the same R-value as fiberglass.

◆ **Cellulose loose fill**
Cellulose is made from shredded newspapers that have been chemically treated with a fire retardant. It is sold in large bags and can be easily poured in between attic floor joists or professionally blown into wall cavities. When it is blown into walls some settling can occur, creating under-insulated slices along the ceiling line.

◆ **Extruded polystyrene**
This form of rigid board insulation has an R-value of about 5.0 per inch. The extruding production process creates a denser layer of polystyrene than expanded polystyrene. Boards are usually pink or blue in color. A similar material, called expanded polystyrene (EPS), has many tiny foam beads pressed together, like a styrene foam coffee cup or cooler. EPS is commonly called "beadboard" and has an R-value of about 3.5 per inch of thickness.

◆ **Polyurethane**
This versatile type of foam has a white or yellowish color, and an R-value of about 6.0 per inch. Rigid panels can be faced with foil for radiant heat deflection. Used on a large scale on exposed framing, the material also can be mixed on site and sprayed into place as a dense liquid that fills both large areas and small spaces in irregular framing bays. The material bubbles up after application, and is later trimmed flush with framing.

◆ **Polyisocyanurate**
This plastic has an R-value of approximately 6.0 per inch. It has a white or yellowish appearance and is usually backed with foil for radiant heat reflection.

Cementitious foam is made from magnesium oxide compounds extracted from sea-water—a natural alternative to synthetic foams. This material (rated at about R-2–3 per inch) will not burn and does not shrink, but like polyurethane, is relatively expensive.

Expanded polystyrene board (beadboard) is similar to the material used in disposable coffee cups and is the first in a line of foam boards. Each offers a step up in quality, R-value, and, of course, cost. All are highly resistant to moisture and water damage. Expanded board is crumbly but can add R-4.0 per inch under new roofing and siding or over foundation walls when covered with an exterior finish. Extruded polystyrene board is a more expensive, somewhat denser board that offers R-5 per inch for more insulating value. Polyisocyanurate board is a more rigid foam board that carries a very high rating of about R-6.3 per inch. In one inch of space you get almost double the thermal resistance provided by fiberglass.

Bubble pack is a flexible, foil-backed sheet of plastic with air-filled bubbles. (It looks like packing material.) Use it where there isn't room for batts or foam boards. You can wrap the ¼- or ⁵⁄₁₆-inch-thick sheeting around ducts and even use it under new drywall, say, between the house and garage.

Foil Insulators

Foil-covered bubble pack sheets are thinner and more flexible than rigid boards, which makes them more versatile in their insulating applications. Foils are also impermeable to vapor, which allows them to double as a vapor barrier. Cold, sweaty pipes and air-conditioning vents benefit most from vapor-resistant insulation. Foil's flexibility makes it very useful in wrapping pipes and ductwork, and no safety precautions against airborne fiberglass particles or skin irritation are needed.

Foil also can be draped underneath plywood roof sheathing to improve energy efficiency. Laboratory testing of foil has shown that 90% of radiant heat can be reflected from a foil's surface. Depending on how and where the material is applied, the R-values can range from R-6 to R-18 or more in highly controlled and stable environments.

Foil sheeting installed under the roof deck between rafters can cut A/C bills by reflecting radiant heat.

New wall spaces can also be insulated with foil-backed bubble pack, which has an R-value around R-18.

Tools & Special Handling Equipment

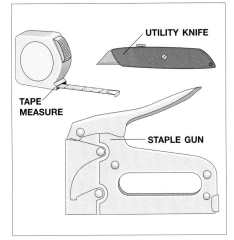

UTILITY KNIFE

TAPE MEASURE

STAPLE GUN

Most insulation is installed with simple tools that are probably already in your garage or workshop.

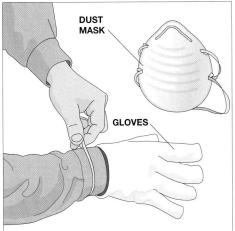

DUST MASK

GLOVES

Protective gear for installing insulation includes gloves, dust mask, and a shirt with long sleeves secured with rubber bands.

An advantage rigid board and foil bubble pack have over fiberglass is that they require no protection against airborne particles. You can easily cut rigid boards using a utility knife, and you don't need to wear gloves and a dust mask. With fiberglass insulation, however, care must be taken to protect your eyes and lungs from glass fibers that can become lodged in your skin or breathed into your lungs. *WARNING: If you encounter asbestos insulation on old pipes, do not attempt to remove it yourself— call in a professional.*

insulation

Foundations

Foundations can be insulated in two ways: from the inside and from the outside. Attaching insulation on the inside is much easier, but over the long term, insulating outside is more effective. Ideally, foundations should be insulated and waterproofed from the outside before they are backfilled during construction. But if your foundation is not insulated, and you are thinking about fixing basement leaks—which will require digging out around the foundation anyway—this may be the time to consider it.

From the Outside

An outside foundation insulation project requires digging out the backfill from the entire perimeter of your house—not an easy job. But if you go that route, remember to repair cracks with cement and check the over-all foundation for signs of deterioration. Once the foundation is exposed, trowel a liberal layer of liquid asphalt on the outer surface for waterproofing; then attach rigid insulating board, and backfill the foundation. The backfill should consist of mainly gravel for the below-grade level and at least 1½ feet of topsoil for plantings and shrubbery.

If your house is built on a perimeter foundation with a shallow crawl space instead of a full basement, digging from the outside to expose the wall surface may be easier than trying to apply insulation from the confined space inside the foundation.

From the Inside

First, clean and paint the walls with a masonry paint. If efflorescence (white, powdery spots) occurs anywhere, then water is coming from the outside into the basement and should be addressed as a separate problem. (See "Foundations," pp. 76–79.) If your basement is dry year-round and you want to add insulation, you can apply rigid foam board or batts and a modular system of furring strips or studs to hold a finishing layer of paneling or drywall.

You can stuff fiberglass insulation around openings in the foundation, for instance, where plumbing pipes exit the house, and then seal the opening with caulk or cement. Another option is to spray foam around the hole, and trim the expanded material flush with the wall.

Insulating Foundation Exteriors

USE: ▶ shovel • chalk-line box with plumb bob • hammer • trowel • hose • straightedge ▶ rigid insulation

1 Excavate the dirt around the foundation. Check for cracks and holes, clean with a garden hose, and let dry.

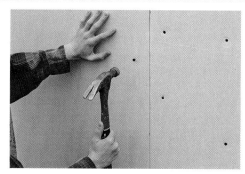

2 Nail rigid foam board insulation directly into the concrete or block foundation using masonry nails.

Insulating Foundation Interiors

USE: ▶ 4-ft. level • hammer • work gloves ▶ rigid insulation • drywall • masonry nails • wood shims

1 Install furring strips to support rigid foam panels. Use wood shims and a spirit level to plumb the strips.

2 Nail the strips in place with concrete nails once you have shimmed them the correct distance out from the wall.

Insulating Crawl Spaces

USE: ▶ staple gun • dust or respirator mask • work gloves ▶ batt or blanket insulation • heavy-duty staples

1 Batts of fiberglass insulation should be installed in the bays between the floor joists.

2 Staple wire mesh onto the joists, to keep out animals and prevent the insulation from sagging.

• stucco • masonry nails

3 *Apply cement plaster* to protect the above-ground insulation from the weather and present a finished surface.

• 6-mil polyethylene vapor barrier

3 *Attach the foam* between or on top of the furring, or both to increase the R-rating. Then cover with drywall to finish.

• wire mesh

3 *Staple fiberglass insulation* batts onto knee walls above foundations. You can let the batts drape down over the masonry.

Diagnosing Wall Insulation

To rate the energy efficiency of your house, conduct an energy audit. The most thorough version, handled by professional testing firms, checks air leaks, insulation values, the efficiency of glazing, and more. Many utility companies provide this service free. Some also recommend specific improvements and estimate the expected return on your investment in the form of lower utility bills.

One easy way to discover if your home needs an audit is to conduct an insulation test with two thermometers. Tape one on an exterior wall; set the other in the middle of the room—off the floor and away from direct sunlight or heat registers that could skew the results. If the wall surface is within 5° of the ambient room temperature, the wall is adequately insulated.

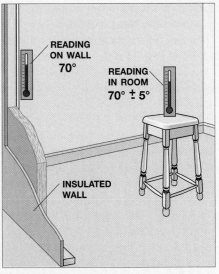

If a thermometer on an outside wall registers 5° less than one in a heated room, you could use more insulation.

To reduce drafts and cut energy loss around windows, fill narrow gaps around the frame with loose-fill insulation.

To stop air and water infiltration on the outside apply a bead of flexible caulking, such as silicone, to exterior seams.

A thermographic picture of your house can reveal where energy is escaping. This temperature-sensitive photograph highlights heat leaks in bright colors, typically at windows and doors. Also notice heat leaks under the double garage doors.

insulation

Adding Insulation

If adding some insulation is a good idea, more must be better—but only up to a point. With insulation there is a law of diminishing returns: the first inch offers the greatest benefit and makes the most noticeable difference in comfort. But layer upon layer provides less and less benefit—even though the last one costs as much as the first.

So when is enough insulation enough? One sensible guideline is to fill the space between framing members. For instance, you can add 3½ inches of insulation to wall cavities framed with 2x4s, but trying to cram in 7 inches of insulation is counterproductive.

Interior Coverage

If you do decide to add to existing insulation, be sure to install only insulation, not a vapor barrier. A layer of plastic or foil buried between layers of insulation can cause condensation problems, decay surrounding wood, and greatly reduce the insulation's effectiveness.

For example, if you have only a few inches of cellulose between floor joists in the attic, you could add unfaced batts, rolls, or loose fill. You could build up the insulation depth between joists, and if you don't need the storage space, spread rolls of insulation above the joists at right angles to the framing.

This over-layer insulates the attic floor framing as well as the spaces between joists, which are in direct contact with the ceiling of the living space below and act as heat conductors. Because heat rises, extra ceiling insulation is often a cost-effective improvement.

Exterior Coverage

You can gain the same frame-covering benefits outside the house, too, and eliminate thermal weak links (such as the seam between foundation and framing) by cladding walls with a layer of rigid foam board. It can run from underneath the siding, down the exposed foundation wall, and into the ground because foam board won't rot.

Even with a layer of foam, it's important to fill spaces that don't match the size of standard insulation, such as openings between unevenly spaced framing members and gaps around window and door frames.

Insulating Walls

USE: ▶ staple gun • dust or respirator mask • work gloves ▶ batt or blanket insulation • heavy-duty

1 *Wear gloves* and a long-sleeved shirt when you unroll fiberglass. Cut it to length using a sharp bread or paring knife.

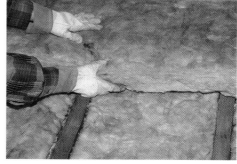

2 *Fit the batt* between framing members by hand. You should wear a dust or respirator mask and gloves for protection.

Insulating Ceilings

USE: ▶ utility knife ▶ batt, blanket, or loose-fill insulation • plywood baffles

1 *To avoid condensation* due to trapped moisture, slit the facing of new batts or use unfaced blankets over existing insulation.

2 *For maximum thermal effectiveness,* run new insulation over both the old insulation and the framing members.

Insulating Roofs

USE: ▶ staple gun • dust or respirator mask • work gloves ▶ batt or blanket insulation • air baffles

1 *Staple air-chamber baffles* to the underside of the roof sheathing before installing batts between rafters.

2 *Because air can circulate* through the baffles, you can fill the remaining space between rafters with batts.

staples • 6-mil polyethylene vapor barrier

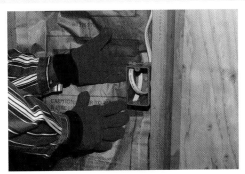

3 ***Run the insulation*** *behind pipes, outlet boxes, and other obstacles to reduce thermal loss and prevent pipe freezing.*

4 ***Flatten out the flanges*** *extending from each side of the batt, and then staple them to the wall studs.*

3 ***Loose fill*** *is poured into the spaces between joists. Keep it a few inches away from obstructions such as recessed lights.*

4 ***Install plywood baffles*** *above exterior walls to prevent loose fill from blocking vents in the roof overhang.*

• heavy-duty staples • 6-mil polyethylene vapor barrier

3 ***Position and flatten the insulation*** *the same way you would between wall studs. Batts should not compress the air baffles.*

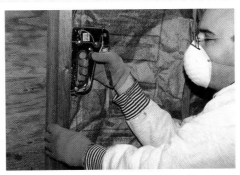

4 ***Trim and fit insulation*** *in irregular openings and around obstructions to create a complete thermal barrier.*

Insulated Headers

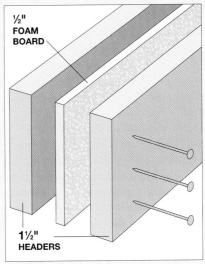

Headers that bridge openings over windows and doors normally have two timbers, a plywood core, and low insulation value. Where codes permit, raise the value by replacing the plywood with ½-inch foam board.

Air-Space Baffles

Air baffles stapled to the roof decking moderate roof temperature and protect against damage due to condensation problems. Air can travel beneath insulating batts from vents in the overhang to the ridge.

insulation

Blowing-In Insulation

Blowing-in insulation makes the most sense when the framing cavity is empty. New material won't be blocked by old batts and thermal improvement will be dramatic, even though the dead air trapped in an empty wall cavity does provide some insulation. A contractor can fill the empty space by cutting small holes through the drywall, inserting a hose, and pumping insulation into the bay between each pair of framing members. You do wind up with a row of little cutouts, but they can be patched, sanded, and painted.

Access from the Outside

It may be easier for the contractor to gain access from the outside, by removing a course of clapboards and cutting a channel in the sheathing over the studs. It depends on which way into the wall cavity causes the least damage while providing the best access. In most cases, it's simpler to remove and replace exterior siding than it is to patch and repaint dozens of small holes in an interior wall. But even working blind with a hose through a hole, experienced contractors should be able to gauge how much insulation the cavity should take and know when the flow of loose fill has been blocked—say, by a construction brace or plumbing. In those cases, they may have to make a second hole to be sure that the bay is completely filled.

You might want to make a thermographic or thermometer test when the job is done to confirm results—although to be completely fair, you would have to duplicate weather conditions of the first test. (See "Diagnosing Wall Insulation," p. 367.)

Insulating the Attic

Unlike wall cavities, you can't just fill all the empty spaces in the attic with blown-in insulation. You might find that there is room for a lot of new insulation—under the roof edges, for example—but you have to leave at least 1½ inches of air space under the roof for ventilation. Why? Because even when the ceiling insulation is protected with a vapor barrier, some moisture from the living space below gets through. Water vapor simply seeps through the insulation, rises against the cold roof, condenses, and drips back into the fiberglass or cellulose. This reduces the insulation's effectiveness and causes mildew, wood rot, and water "leaks" that, in the rooms below, will seem to be substantial enough to have come through the roof, not just from condensation beneath it.

Forming Dams

You need insulation directly over the exterior wall frame, but loose fill won't stay in neat piles along the wall until you close up the roof. And even if it did, over time the loose fill would spill down onto the soffit (the plywood running parallel to the ground on the underside of the overhang) and block the vents.

One way to solve this problem is by stapling foot-long batts of foil-backed fiberglass on their edges between the joists to form a dam running from the exterior wall back up and into the bays. Air coming up through the soffit vents can flow freely over the short batts and across the loose fill, which can't spill out onto the soffit.

Because of a lack of wood, early homesteaders in Nebraska built well-insulated houses out of sod—the 3-foot-thick walls (seen in the doorway) kept them warm in winter, cool in summer.

Obstructions

Blown-in insulation works best on walls where the wall cavities are empty. You won't gain much insulating value if existing insulation already fills most of the cavity. Another potential problem is that even if there is no insulation in the wall, some cavities will always be partly blocked by pipes, wires, and built-in obstructions such as horizontal fire-stops. Sometimes, the blown-in insulation will fill around the blockage. Usually, however, a new hole will have to be drilled higher on the wall to feed insulation into the blocked section.

Insulating Existing Walls

USE: ▶ blower equipment • blower hose with nozzle • drill/driver with hole saw attachment (optional)

1 Remove vinyl siding *using a zip tool. Once the seam is separated, slide the zip tool along to free the panels.*

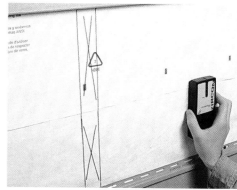

2 Use a stud finder *to locate the studs beneath the sheathing. A hole will be drilled into each stud bay.*

Obstructions

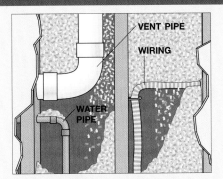

Pipes and wires can block the flow of loose insulation blown in through a hole in the top of the wall.

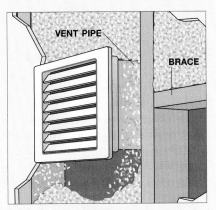

Vents and cross braces may create pockets without insulation. Another hole must be drilled to fill them.

Insulating Attics

You should keep loose fill away from recessed light fixtures in ceilings, which need air flow to prevent overheating. Also keep loose fill blown into attics away from eaves vents. It's pointless to continue insulating out onto the roof overhang. Install some form of dam above the exterior stud wall to hold back the loose fill, preserve its loft, and prevent it from retarding ventilation by spilling onto the soffit vents.

Spraying loose fill is a great way to add insulation in your attic and cut your heating bills.

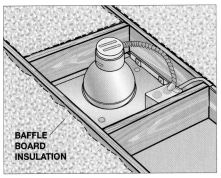

Keep loose insulation away from recessed ceiling light fixtures. Heat from the lamp could start a fire.

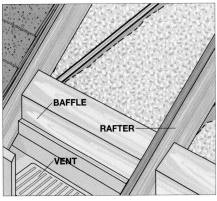

Wood dams between the joists help keep loose fill insulation from spilling onto soffit vents and blocking air flow.

• saber saw • pry bar (for wood siding) • stud finder • zip tool (for vinyl siding) ▶ cork or plastic plug • loose-fill insulation • yellow wood glue

3 *After you've shut off the power* to the circuits in that wall, drill a hole with a saber saw or hole saw chucked into a power drill.

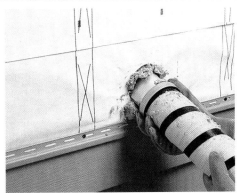

4 *Place the nozzle in the hole,* and load the hopper, operating the blowing machinery per the manufacturer's instructions.

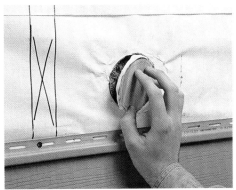

5 *After a bay is filled,* plug the hole with a cork or plastic plug, replace the siding, and move about 4 ft. up the wall; then repeat.

insulation

Preserving Heat

Insulation's main job is to keep heat from escaping from inside the house. So in many homes, heating ducts that run through the cellar or a crawl space are not insulated. They're not outside, after all. And any heat that radiates from the ducts is still inside the building. That's good and that's bad—good because the heat isn't lost; bad because it's not going where you need it, down the duct to a chilly bedroom far from the furnace.

In any case, the solution is simple enough: Wrap the ducts in insulation. The exact configuration (batts or rolls) or type (cellulose or fiberglass, for instance) hardly matters. And you don't have to hermetically seal each seam. Improvement in heat delivery from the ducts should be noticeable, particularly if the ducts travel through a chilly, vented crawl space.

The major sources of heat loss in a home, which obviously can't be fixed with insulation, are windows and doors. A popular method of sealing windows involves taping a thin sheet of shrink-wrap polyethylene over the window frame and blow-drying it for a shrink fit. On old double-hung windows with single glazing, this is a much cheaper plan than replacing the windows, although it is unsightly. Drafts are contained, and a layer of dead air is trapped between window and plastic, adding extra insulation.

Doors can be upgraded by attaching thermal stripping along the jambs and nailing a flexible threshold to the door's bottom edge. When installing weatherstripping, make sure you don't prevent the door from seating.

Preserving Hot Water

What's good for ducts is good for water pipes, too. Like a tea cozy on a teapot, insulation helps keep the hot-water pipes hot and will keep cold-water pipes from sweating in summer. You could wrap the pipe with insulation rolls or batts, or use widely available foam tubes made for the job. They are neater than a do-it-yourself spiral wrapping of batts but not any more effective.

If you are replacing or adding insulation in a wall and discover water pipes, be sure to place the insulation between the pipes and the outside wall. Don't bury pipes under insulation.

Eight Ways to Conserve Temperature

Seal sills
In new construction, the space between the top of the foundation and the sill can be sealed with a narrow strip of foam insulation. Foam will expand to fill cracks that open as a house settles.

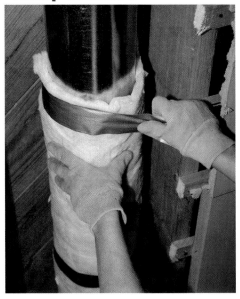

Wrap ducts
Ducts can be wrapped in paper-backed fiberglass insulation or foil-backed bubble wrap. Where ducts enter and exit through walls, ceilings, and roofs, seal the edges with foam insulation.

Seal holes
Foam expands like shaving cream out of its can, and can be messy to work with if it's not contained in a hole or crevice. But foam is a good choice for where pipes go into walls.

Close gaps
Windows are often a major source of thermal loss. If you can feel a draft, remove the casing and stuff pieces of fiberglass insulation in any cracks between the window jambs and the framing.

Vapor Barriers

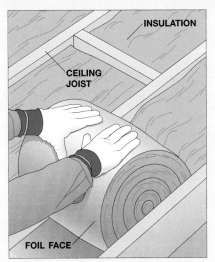

Vapor barriers block both air and water vapor. The only impervious barrier is foil. But you need to install foil-faced batts carefully, and tape the seams for maximum effect. Plastic sheeting is second best, and often used over paper-faced batts to improve moisture resistance. Clear polyethylene sheets 6 mils thick are standard. All vapor barriers are rated by permeance (the ability of air to penetrate). To be reasonably effective, the perm rating should be less than 1. Polyethylene sheets have a perm rating of 0.04 to 0.08.

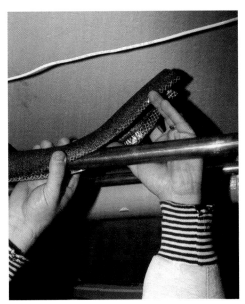

Wrap pipes
To insulate pipes, buy preformed pipe sleeves that fit over the pipe, or wrap the pipe in thin fiberglass strips and secure them with duct tape. Both will prevent pipe sweating in the summer.

Encase water heater
A water heater can be wrapped in a fiberglass thermal blanket to cut down heat loss. Water-heater blankets are sold in kits that include tape and a thermal blanket encased in a plastic sleeve.

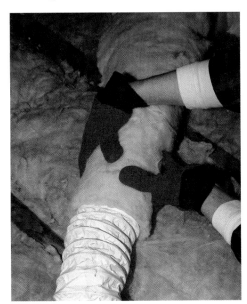

Insulate ventilation ducts
Wrap attic ventilation ducts with thin batts of fiberglass insulation. This insulation prevents condensation from forming—and then leaking down through the ceiling—where hot vented vapor meets cold attic air.

Seal utility boxes
An insulating pad inserted between a switch or receptacle and its cover will stop airflow. You can also inject silicone caulk around all wires inside the box and around the drywall or plaster.

ventilation 20

ventilation

Ventilation Basics

Water, in any form, can be one of the most destructive forces on a house. While most buildings are designed to cope with water from the outside—even if you need to replace a few new shingles or some caulking after a storm—many are not well-equipped to deal with moisture that is trapped inside in the form of vapor-laden air. It is good for houses to be able to "breathe". The East Coast is dotted with 200-year-old houses that have been breathing like crazy from the day they were built. Houses need to breathe out some cool, conditioned air in summer and some warm, heated air in winter. It costs you money on your heating and A/C bills, but it will take some of the 7 to 10 gallons of potentially harmful moisture produced daily inside a home with it.

This moisture comes from many sources: cooking, washing clothes, watering plants, taking showers, and humidifying the air during winter. Unless indoor air and the moisture it contains has some way out of the house, you're in for lingering odors, stale air in general, mold growing on wall paint, and even enough moisture condensing on cold windows to make puddles that peel paint and rot window sills.

You may picture insulation company ads of dollar bills flying out leaky windows. But those ads don't show all the dollar bills that must fly back in to pay for a vent fan in the stagnant kitchen, new tile to replace the buckled floor in the bath, new paint or wallboard to replace the mold-encrusted walls in the cellar—only some of the problems caused by trapping moisture inside.

Ventilation Systems

There are several ways to alleviate ventilation problems, which often are most troublesome in the more energy-efficient houses and apartments built since 1980 or so. Many of these homes are so airtight that they trap too much moisture and stale air. The solution is to vent excessive heat during the summer (especially in the attic) and excessively warm, moist air during the winter. One easy, low-tech way to do that in winter is to open a few windows a crack. It costs a bit more in heat, but the fresh air can correct moisture and stale odor problems.

Some parts of the house may need more attention. Moisture can condense during winter months in a poorly ventilated attic. In the summer, heat can build up in that same attic, resulting in higher A/C bills and a shorter life span for the roofing shingles. Think of your roof as a passive heating and cooling system that needs a constant flow of fresh air to function properly.

Roofing Vents

For roofing vent systems, the most important thing to know is how much air is exchanged. About 1.5 cubic feet of air exchanged per minute will adequately vent a typical attic in both winter and summer. In some situations, particularly in modern, tightly constructed houses, you can improve energy efficiency by exchanging temperature between a flow of stale indoor air being exhausted and fresh air pulled in with a fan.

It's difficult to figure out air-exchange rates without sophisticated equipment, but knowing the differences between venting systems can help you make informed choices. Roof vents, for example, come in five types: continuous ridge vents, soffit vents, gable vents, turbine vents, and motorized fans. Some vents are active (electrical), and some are passive. Both can work in other areas in the house, particularly where moisture is produced, such as kitchens, baths, and laundry rooms.

Ventilation Paths

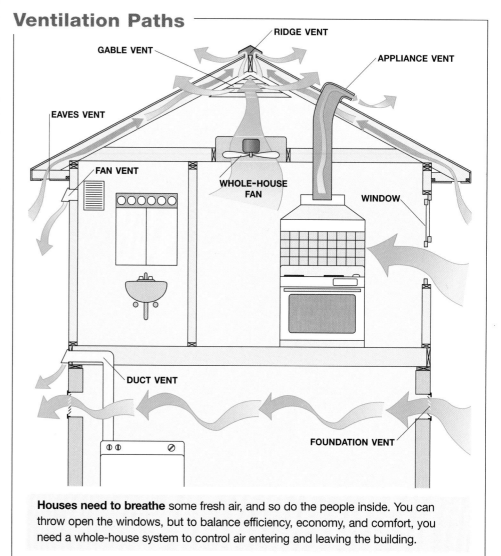

Houses need to breathe some fresh air, and so do the people inside. You can throw open the windows, but to balance efficiency, economy, and comfort, you need a whole-house system to control air entering and leaving the building.

Crawl-Space Venting

Dirt floors require more ventilation than concrete floors. If the floor of a crawl space is concrete and the walls are insulated, you can ventilate with a series of small foundation vents. The number of vents depends on the total square feet in a given space. A general rule is to have 1 square foot of vent area for every 150 square feet of floor space. Sliding metal vents are designed to replace the space of one 8x8x16-inch concrete block. A ventilated crawl space needs to be screened, with either pressure-treated-wood or PVC lattice and a welded wire netting.

Plastic lattice *provides venting in many shapes and colors—and when it gets dirty you just wash it down with a hose.*

PT (pressure-treated) lattice *has built-in resistance to water damage and rot, even near ground level.*

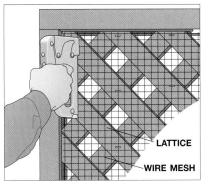

LATTICE

WIRE MESH

Use galvanized wire mesh or plastic screening to keep insects and animals from entering.

Ventilation Requirements

Basements & Crawl Spaces

There are many formulas contractors use to gauge ventilation requirements—and a few DIY rules of thumb, such as providing 1 square foot of vent per 150 square feet of floor space. But every case is different. You'll need more venting in a damp climate with a shaded site and a dirt floor, and less in a dry climate with more sun and wind and a concrete slab on the crawl space floor.

Roof & Attic Ventilation

Flat and Sloped Roofs:
$\frac{1}{300}$ of the area of the space being ventilated, uniformly distributed between eaves and ridge vents.

Unheated Attics:
Same as above for gable roofs, plus at least two louvers at opposite ends near the ridge. Same for hip roofs, plus $\frac{1}{600}$ at ridge, with all vents interconnected.

Installing Foundation Vents

USE: ▶ drill • hammer • trowel • cold chisel • masonry bit • work gloves ▶ vent grille • mortar

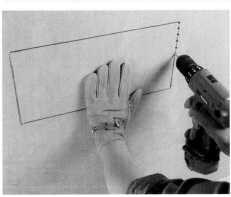

1 ***To break through the foundation,*** *drill closely spaced holes along the vent outline with a masonry bit.*

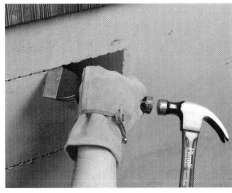

2 ***Use a cold chisel*** *along the outline to weaken and clear away the masonry. Always wear eye protection.*

3 ***Smooth out rough edges*** *around the opening as needed for fit, and set the vent in a bed of cement.*

4 ***Secure and seal the vent edges*** *with a surface coat of cement. Don't clog the fins on adjustable vents.*

ventilation

Venting Baths

No room will produce more water vapor than a bathroom. For this reason, bathrooms are usually finished with a moisture-resistant gypsum board or cement panel. All this extra protection from water vapor, will probably escape your eye—until the mold and mildew start to develop and the tile grouting turns black. If you have a bathroom with persistent mold and mildew problems, chances are that your real problem is inadequate ventilation.

Bathroom vents are typically electric fans recessed in walls that vent directly outside (on a first-floor bathroom) or through the roof soffit (on a second-floor bathroom). The fans are either connected to a timer to ensure full clearing of water vapor or connected to the light switch. If your bathroom vent doesn't have an independent switch, it's a good idea to have an electrician install one.

Some older houses were built without any bathroom ventilation. An open window served as the means of ventilation—not a very economical or pleasant way to vent a bathroom, especially on a cold winter day. Sometimes windows have even been placed inside of shower stalls. Such designs are a disaster in the making, and almost always result in water damage deep inside the walls. If you have one of those bathrooms on your hands, installing an electric vent (and getting rid of the shower window) will solve a lot of moisture problems.

Vent Placement

A bathroom vent should be able to exchange the entire volume of air from the room in 30 minutes. The best place to put the vent is near the ceiling or within the ceiling itself, to ensure that warm moist air is adequately vented. The ductwork from the vent can be routed either directly to an outside wall or through the attic to a soffit vent.

You'll have to remove insulation from the access area along the joist where you'll place the bathroom vent. You can pack the outside of the ductwork itself with insulation—a good idea for keeping down condensation inside the ductwork.

Direct, through-the-wall installations are usually the easiest, particularly when you save the electrician some work by picking a spot in

Design Options

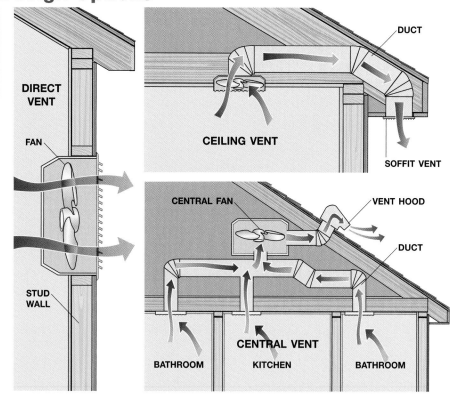

Direct vents are the easiest to install but often the least energy efficient. Ducts from ceiling vents should be insulated to prevent condensation problems. Central fan systems reduce noise while serving several rooms at once.

Installing Bath Vents

USE: ▶ reciprocating saw • drill • screwdriver • caulking gun • measuring tape • pencil ▶ cover grille

1 *Mark an unobstructed release point* outside the house, and screw the fan housing to the nearest stud inside.

2 *Connect the duct* to the inside housing and outside vent. Flexible ducts allow an offset between inlet and outlet locations.

the same framing bay as an electrical outlet. Mount the fan in an open area where it can easily collect moisture.

All this may change if you have a plaster interior wall or if you have to punch through a brick exterior wall. Although it can be done, it's wiser to make a ceiling installation and route the fan duct to an outlet either in the roof or in the roof soffit.

Vent to the Outside

If you take the ceiling route, don't simply dump warm, moist air into an attic where it will condense. Use the space between ceiling joists to route ducts to a soffit or roof vent.

The soffit outlet is preferable because it doesn't put a hole in the roof and because warm, moist air in the duct will condense where it is exposed in an unconditioned space such as an attic. When the duct walls are cool, moisture will form before the air is exhausted and then drip back down the duct into the fan and back into the room. Avoid those problems by taking the duct straight up from the ceiling grille into the bay between ceiling joists and then turning it toward the outside wall and running it with a slight slope downhill to the soffit outlet. The duct will also be out of the way if you decide to use the attic or crawl space floor for storage.

Installing Timer Switches

USE: ▶ circuit tester • screwdriver ▶ switch box • timer switch with coverplate • NM wiring • wire nuts

1 *Once you're sure power to the old* switch is cut, remove the holding screws and disconnect the wires.

2 *Connect the new switch* to the wires. Make sure the wire loops around the terminal and that the screw is tight.

When moisture lingers as you're ready to leave the bathroom—after a shower when you're dry but the mirror is still foggy—replace the fan's standard on-off switch with a timer switch. (You can find them in an electrical supply house or a store that sells saunas.) It has a knob that you can rotate to set an extended run time. Then, sometime after you leave the room, the fan shuts off automatically. You don't have to remember to turn it off, and you won't waste energy running it all day.

3 *Most timer switches* are spring-loaded. Just turn the switch to select the amount of run time, and leave the room.

• switch box • vent hood with backdraft damper • vent kit • fan switch with speed control • flexible duct • duct clamps • insulation • NM wiring • screws • wire nuts

3 *Make code-approved* electrical connections to the housing, and install the fan motor—often a plug-in component.

4 *To finish the inside,* tuck loose-fill insulation (or use spray-foam) to seal around the housing, and clip on the cover grille.

5 *Cover the exhaust end of the duct* with a vent hood. Some backdraft dampers prevent air leaks when the fan is off.

ventilation

Venting Kitchens

Kitchen ventilation requires extra consideration because cooking creates grease as well as water vapor. While oil may have a higher boiling temperature than water, it does not need to boil to produce vapor, which will condense into a greasy film over all kitchen surfaces if not properly vented.

Vent Hoods

Ovens are often sold with a vent hood as an attachment; hoods are either vented or ventless. A vented hood is the most effective method for removing cooking odors, moisture, and grease directly at their source. Ventless hoods function primarily to collect airborne grease. Filters on ventless hoods need to be changed every so often, and they do not contribute to the exchange of air in a closed kitchen.

If you have a ventless hood in your kitchen, or no vent at all, consider installing a ceiling fan. A ceiling fan can work in conjunction with an open window or doorway. The cross-

Settlers in Texas' hot and dry Hill Country solved their ventilation problems with a dog-trot—a breezeway through the middle of the house, seen here in Lyndon Johnson's grandfather's cabin, located at LBJ National Historical Park in Johnson City.

ventilation this creates helps reduce the buildup of cooking odors.

Wall & Ceiling Vents

Another approach besides installing a range hood is installing ceiling- and wall-mounted vents. Wall vents should have a swinging louver on the outside vent to prevent air and insects from getting inside. When selecting the vent fan (or even an unvented range-hood unit), be sure to match the fan's capacity with the size of your kitchen. Fans are rated by the cubic feet of air that they can vent per minute—abbreviated cfm. To size a fan correctly, one rule of thumb is to use 150 cfm per linear foot of range surface along walls, and 180 for ranges on islands. Using this rule, a 30-inch-wide range (2.5 linear feet) times 150 cfm would require a range hood fan rated at about 375 cfm if it were installed along a wall, and a 450 cfm fan if it were installed on an island.

Wall vents and ceiling vents can become cold spots during very cold weather, and there is no real way to avoid this weakness. The trade-off is between ventilation and insulation, and you should take that into consideration when planning kitchen ventilation. A perfectly insulated kitchen with no air flow is neither desirable nor healthy. Because kitchen vents should operate only when needed, they should have a backdraft louver.

Other options in kitchens and baths (or both) is to use a centralized system with one motor that is large enough to pull air from several locations. One advantage of this type is noise reduction because the fan motor is not in the wall or ceiling, but mounted in the attic. For the whole house, large fans located in central areas, such as stairwells, can pull enough air through the house to create a quick air change.

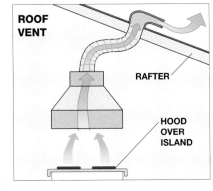

Range Venting

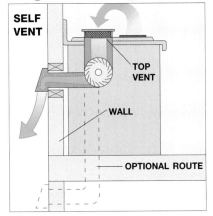

SELF VENT

TOP VENT

WALL

OPTIONAL ROUTE

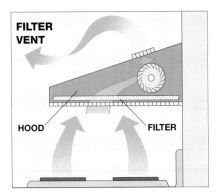

FILTER VENT

HOOD

FILTER

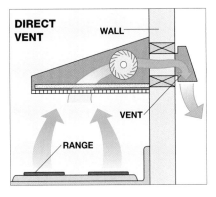

DIRECT VENT

WALL

VENT

RANGE

ROOF VENT

RAFTER

HOOD OVER ISLAND

Vents can be a focal point of the kitchen with multiple built-in fans and filters.

Laundry Venting

Clothes dryer vents always vent directly to the outside of the house because the air that comes out of the clothes dryer is a combination of heat, moisture, and fine lint. Several types of vent materials will do the job, including flexible plastic that is generally the easiest to install. But noncombustible metal duct is best for fire protection and required by most building codes.

You should take that into consideration when planning the installation because a clogged dryer vent can be a fire hazard when lint builds up and prevents the escape of air. For this reason, dryer vents should be as short as possible, and run directly from the back of the dryer to the outside wall.

Most dryers heat with electricity, but some produce heat with natural gas. If you have a natural-gas dryer, it is important to make sure that the vent system is up to code.

To cut down blockages inside a vent, position the outlet at the same level as the dryer's vent, and avoid sharp bends in the line and circuitous routes from inlet to outlet. In basements, route dryer hoses to vent above the foundation sill, so you drill through wood instead of masonry.

Installing Dryer Vents

USE: ▶ saber saw • screwdriver ▶ dryer vent • flexible duct • vent hood with damper • duct clamps • caulk

1 *Pick a spot between studs,* and trace and saw a hole the diameter of the vent line.

2 *Transfer your cuts* through the outside wall, and mount the vent cover.

3 *Inside,* one end of the flexible duct fits over the vent cover pipe.

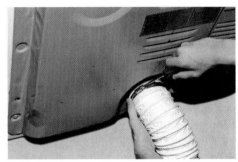

4 *The other end* fits over the dryer outlet. Attach both ends using clamps.

FIRE WARNING

The U.S. Consumer Product Safety Commission estimates that 14,000 fires related to clothes dryers occur every year. A main cause: lint buildup in the dryer filter or vent line.

Solutions

▶ Clean the lint filter before or after drying every load of clothes.

▶ Make sure the exterior vent outlet and cover flap are not clogged.

▶ If the dryer runs hot, disconnect the vent to check for hidden clogs.

▶ To trap less lint, use smooth-wall duct instead of ridged material.

▶ Check manufacturer's instructions. Many UL-rated machines require metal vent duct, not plastic.

▶ Install a smoke detector and fire extinguisher in the laundry room.

Dryer Vent Options

Dryer vents should be routed the shortest possible distance from the dryer to the outside of the house. However, you may want to extend the vent hose in a basement to reach framing that is easier to drill through than masonry. Where vents may be unsightly on the outside of the house, you can hide them behind shrubbery. But do not use long, twisting lengths of vent tubing only for cosmetic reasons. Also, do not vent the dryer directly into the laundry room, even on winter's coldest days. You might save a little heat, but the open vent will deposit gallons of water vapor and a cloud of lint into the air.

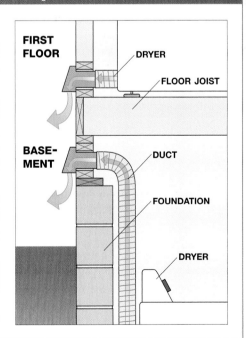

FIRST FLOOR — DRYER — FLOOR JOIST — BASEMENT — DUCT — FOUNDATION — DRYER

ventilation

Ventilating with Fans

You can easily vent your entire house with a big electric fan installed into the gable end of the attic. Depending on the size of the unit and the speed of the fan, air can be completely exchanged throughout a house in a matter of minutes. During hot weather, the fan will keep your house cool until the peak of the afternoon, when the air conditioner can take over. In the winter, it can vent moisture more quickly than passive vents and help prevent the formation of ice dams. If the fan system is connected to a series of vents that can be opened or closed to regulate the flow of air, then the bathrooms, kitchen, and attic can be vented individually or together.

Installing a whole-house fan requires more work, but the project is within the range of many do-it-yourselfers. The fan will probably need its own electrical line, and you may want an electrical contractor to install it, especially if it is a 220-volt line. (See "Electrical," pp. 348–49.) For fans mounted in gable ends, be sure the fan and electrical connections are designed for exposure to rain and snow. Water is usually not a problem with fans installed in attic floors over a stairwell, but be careful about locating one near a gable-end vent.

Ceiling Fans

Ceiling fans are a good choice for circulating air, especially in rooms with high ceilings. Ceiling fans can also work in conjunction with whole-house attic fans for a highly efficient air exchange system. Warm air rises naturally and remains at the top of a room until it cools and then descends. A ceiling fan operating at the same time as an attic fan will help to remove moist or stagnant air from a room much more efficiently than an attic fan acting alone.

Ceiling fans with multiple speeds are the best option for doing the twin tasks of circulating and ventilating. Some fans come with three speeds—the slowest speed will keep warm air circulating downward, the middle speed will create noticeable cooling drafts in the room, and the highest can actually clear a room's air. A kitchen with an open window or door and a ceiling fan set on high can eliminate the aftermath of a burnt roast or a fish fry in a matter of minutes.

Installing Whole-House Fans

USE: ▶ crosscut saw • utility saw • wire cutters • wrench • circuit tester • hammer • screwdrivers • dust mask

1 *Mark an opening* in the ceiling below the framing of the attic floor, and cut through the drywall with a utility saw.

2 *Span several ceiling timbers* to make a sturdy work platform, and cut through the joist that crosses the fan opening.

House Fan Design Options

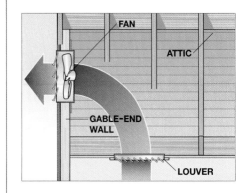
FAN
ATTIC
GABLE-END WALL
LOUVER

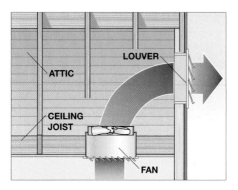
LOUVER
ATTIC
CEILING JOIST
FAN

Installing Ceiling Fans

USE: ▶ drill • hammer • long-nose pliers • saber saw • screwdriver • wire cutter • wrench • circuit tester

1 *Cut an opening* for the special ceiling-fan junction box, and screw the box to a nailer cut to fit between joists.

2 *Run required electrical cables* into the box, position the box over the hole, and then fasten the nailer between the joists.

▶ whole-house fan • fan switch with speed control • switch box • saber saw • 2x joists • joist hangers • nails • NM wiring • rubber washers • screws • wire nuts

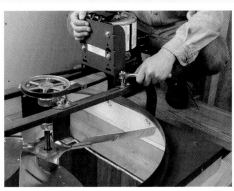

3 *Set double headers* across the cut joist one piece at a time to facilitate nailing, and double the full-length side joists if required.

4 *Mount the fan housing* on the opening. Make the electrical and motor connections according to manufacturer's instructions.

5 *On most models,* louvers in the cover grille mounted below the fan open automatically when the fan is turned on.

ELECTRICAL SAFETY

▶ **Don't overload the circuit.**
Attic fans and ceiling fans come with information on electrical requirements, including specific wattage ratings. Some may require power for a fan motor and a light, and some large fans may require 220 volts. To plan a safe electrical installation, be sure the total circuit demand does not exceed the rating of your fuse or circuit breaker.

Reducing Fan Vibration

WASHERS
RUBBER WASHERS
FAN BRACKET
FRAME

FAN BRACKET
RUBBER STRIP
FRAME

▶ ceiling fan • fan switch w/speed control • mounting bracket • switch box • NM wiring • octagonal electrical box • nails • screws • wire nuts • wood blocking

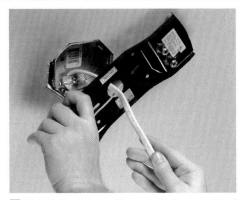

3 *Bring the wiring* through holes provided in the mounting bracket, and secure the bracket to the nailer and joists.

4 *Attach the fan motor* to the bracket following manufacturer's directions. Make secure connections that can't vibrate loose.

5 *Install the fan housing and blades* to finish the job. The fan should have its own wall switch if there is no pull chain.

ventilation

Venting the Roof

A well-vented roof keeps a house cool and cuts down on the air-conditioning bills in the summer, prevents the formation of ice dams and condensation in the winter, and helps prolong the life span of asphalt shingles. A good ventilating system is simple to install and inexpensive—it may even eliminate the need for mechanical air conditioning entirely.

Ridge Vents

A recent innovation in roof ventilation systems is the continuous ridge vent. This system allows the natural flow of air along the roof rafters and the wind outside to create negative air pressure that will also draw air from the attic. Continuous ridge vents are the most energy-efficient method of exchanging attic air.

The ridge vent covers a slit that runs along the roof. It "caps" the opening with screening and a small roof of plastic that keeps rain from entering the vents.

Install a ridge vent by removing the capping shingles along the roof ridge to expose the roofing felt; then, cut away the roofing felt 3 inches from the top to expose the roof sheathing. Snap a chalk line 2 inches from the top of the ridge on each side of the roof. Cut out the sections with a circular saw set to the exact depth of the roof sheathing (usually ½ to ⅝ inch). Attach the ridge vent with caulking and roofing nails.

Ridge vents work by allowing air to flow from the soffit vents out through the peak of the roof. Turbine vents also draw air up through the roof, but here the heat rising up into the vent turns the fixture's turbine blades and so helps pull more air out of the attic space. The hotter the air becomes, the faster it turns the turbine.

Other Roof Vents

Other common types of vents include fixed grilles (usually in soffits and high on gable ends), which allow air to pass through louvers and a variety of power fans. The venting ability of these systems depends on the size of the opening being vented. Building codes usually require the area of attic vent openings to equal at least $\frac{1}{300}$ of the total ($\frac{1}{150}$ if no vapor barrier in ceiling) square feet of attic space being ventilated.

Roof Vent Combinations

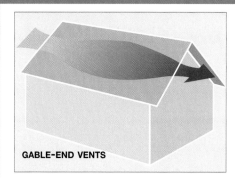

GABLE-END VENTS

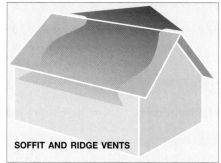

SOFFIT AND RIDGE VENTS

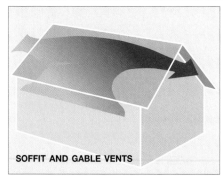

SOFFIT AND GABLE VENTS

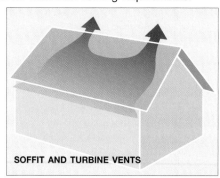

SOFFIT AND TURBINE VENTS

Attic vent combinations. Top left: gable vents provide end-to-end ventilation. Top right: soffit and ridge combination. Bottom left: soffit and gable. Bottom right: soffit and turbine combination. Check local codes for minimum venting requirements.

Maintaining Attic Air Flow

Air baffles keep loose fill added to attic floors from blocking air flow through soffit vents. To add baffles, first scrape away excess insulation, then set the forms between rafters and staple the flanges into the roof sheathing.

Soffit Vents

Soffit vents come in three basic configurations: round, rectangular, and perforated. The round variety, called plug vents, are easier to install than rectangular, or strip-grille, vents. You need only an electric drill and an auger bit, or a hole saw, to cut the hole for plug vents, whereas continuous vents require a circular saw to cut the opening. It is easier and safer to drill an overhanging section than it is to cut it with an upside-down circular saw—especially if you're working on a ladder. If you are installing rectangular vents, have someone hold the ladder steady.

Another option for installing soffit vents is to remove the plywood, cut the holes (circular or rectangular) while the plywood is secured to a worktable, insert the vents, and renail everything back in place. This is a viable option if the soffit has dry rot and is in need of replacing anyway. If you're planning to install rectangular vents, this approach tends to be best.

Continuous perforated soffits are manufactured in preformed sheets of vinyl or aluminum, and can be installed once the old soffits have been ripped out. Perforated soffits eliminate the need for cutting plywood, but they may not come in the size or color that you require. Home centers usually have manufacturers' catalogs listing the sizes and colors of their products.

Clearing an Air Path

After you've decided how to vent your soffits, inspect the areas between the ceiling joists to make sure insulation is not blocking air flow. Insulation in the soffit space will completely defeat the purpose of soffit vents, and a section-by-section inspection is the best way to ensure air flow through the vents.

Homes with blown insulation are more likely to have this problem because the insulation is loose and tends to drift. One way to keep blown cellulose away from soffit vents is to construct barriers to act as dams, separating the ceiling area (where insulation is needed) from the soffit area. Make the dams from rigid material, and cut them to fit between the joists.

With fiberglass insulation, simply fold back the batt or tuck it under itself to keep the end section away from the soffit.

Installing Strip-Grille Vents

USE: ▶ circular saw • wood chisel • drill • hammer • screwdriver ▶ strip-grille vents • screws

1 Use a circular saw (very carefully, in this position), to make parallel cutouts for the long edges of the continuous vent strip.

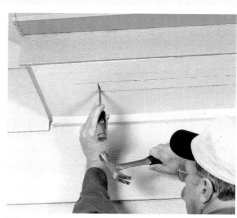

2 Slice through the short ends of the cutout with a sharp chisel, or drill a small starter hole and use a reciprocating saw.

3 Some vent strips have flanges that must tuck under the exposed edges of plywood along the cut; others screw down.

4 Attach surface-mounted strip vents to the soffit using ½-in. screws spaced about a foot apart.

Plug Vents & Perforated Soffits

Plug vents are the easiest vents to install. Drill a hole in the soffit between pairs of rafters, and press the vents in place.

Perforated soffit vents typically are made of vinyl panels that are perforated to supply ventilation through the entire soffit area.

ventilation

Through the Roof

Even in areas with moderate climates year-round, air temperatures in attics can soar on sunny days. That may not seem like a problem if the space is used only for storage. But the floor of an unfinished attic is the ceiling of a finished living space below. And even if the common floor/ceiling is insulated, oven-like temperatures of 125° F and higher can radiate through to the living space and increase the load on air conditioning.

But reducing attic temperatures to increase cooling efficiency is only one reason for ventilating an attic. You also need attic airflow to carry away moisture that rises from the living space. Even if the floor-ceiling is insulated and protected with a vapor retarder (commonly 6-mil polyethylene sheeting), some of the moisture produced in cooking, washing, and other household operations inevitably seeps into cracks and seams. Again, that may not seem like a problem if the space isn't lived in. But moisture collecting in the attic can condense on wood framing to foster rot, and drip puddles onto insulation and ceiling drywall.

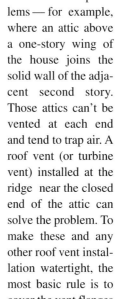

VENT PATH

GLASS

FRAME

VENT FLAP

Some roof windows have a vent flap in the frame so that you can circulate air even in bad weather with the unit closed.

To prevent these problems, the best approach is to treat unfinished attics as outdoor space. Wrap the living areas below with layers of insulation and vapor barriers, but flood the attic with fresh air. There are several ways to provide thorough ventilation. Most of the systems are easiest to install on new construction, where they can be conveniently woven into weatherproof layers of shingles and siding. But the three main options of soffit vents (shown on the previous page), as well as roof vents, gable vents, and ridge vents, also can be installed on existing homes.

To handle the installations, you will have to do some of the work from the attic and some from a ladder to reach the triangle of siding just under the roof ridge, or from the roof itself.

If you do the job yourself, make a safe working platform that bridges open framing in attic floors; use ladders safely; and work on roofs only if they have a low slope. Bear in mind the most important safety rule of all: if you feel uncomfortable or unsafe working high off the ground, don't. Hire a contractor, and devote your DIY energy to a ground-floor project.

Roof vents come in many forms, but generally include some type of weather-shedding hood and a flange around the base that forms a seal between the vent and the surrounding roofing material. These vents are a good choice if you want to solve "dead-zone" problems — for example, where an attic above a one-story wing of the house joins the solid wall of the adjacent second story. Those attics can't be vented at each end and tend to trap air. A roof vent (or turbine vent) installed at the ridge near the closed end of the attic can solve the problem. To make these and any other roof vent installation watertight, the most basic rule is to cover the vent flanges with roof material on the high side and along the edges of the vent, and cover the roofing material with the vent flange on the low side.

Gable vents require a similar installation, except on an existing building you'll have to cut through siding instead of roofing to reach the plywood sheathing.

Ridge vents, which ventilate the full length of the attic, require a little more work. In addition to stripping shingles along the ridge, you will have to trim back the wooden roof sheathing on each side of the ridge. The narrow gaps will create a continuous flow from soffit vents up and out of the roof.

Installing Roof Vents

USE: ▶ reciprocating saw • 4-ft. level • pry bar

1 Determine the vent location between rafters inside the attic, and drive a nail to mark the location outside.

Installing Gable Vents

USE: ▶ circular saw • hammer • level • staple gun

1 Frame out a rough opening, and install headers between studs in the end wall to form the required rough opening.

Installing Ridge Vents

USE: ▶ chalk-line box • circular saw • hammer

1 Strip ridge-cap shingles to expose about a 2-in. section of roof deck on both sides of the ridge.

• putty knife • hammer • measuring tape • pencil • utility knife ▶ roof vent • replacement shingles • galvanized roofing nails • roofing cement

2 ***Mark the opening*** *required by the vent manufacturer, centered around the nail. Then cut back the shingles.*

3 ***Once you've trimmed the shingles,*** *cut through the roof deck with a reciprocating saw to make the vent opening.*

4 ***To shed water,*** *slip flanges on the upper section of the vent underneath shingles. Seal nails with roofing cement.*

• caulking gun • measuring tape • pencil ▶ gable vent • 1x4 casing • screening • 2x framing lumber • caulk • galvanized nails or screws • heavy-duty staples

2 ***Use nails driven from inside*** *to locate and mark the opening at the top of the gable-end wall outside.*

3 ***Strip back tar paper,*** *or air barrier paper, as needed. Then cut through the plywood sheathing with a circular saw.*

4 ***Caulk under the edges*** *of the vent, and nail it per manufacturer's instructions. The back should be screened.*

• pry bar • putty knife • straightedge • utility knife ▶ galvanized roofing nails • replacement ridge-cap shingles • ridge vent • roofing cement

2 ***Peel back shingles and tar paper,*** *snap a chalk line as a guide, and cut through the plywood roof deck along the ridge.*

3 ***Nail down the ridge vent*** *on top of the ridge. The flexible vent material conforms to the roof, while baffles allow air to escape.*

4 ***Conceal the vent*** *without decreasing its effectiveness by installing a new line of overlapping ridge-cap shingles.*

safety & security

21

safety & security

A Sense of Security

No home can ever be made absolutely burglar-proof: if a burglar really wants to get in, even elaborate electronic security systems probably won't stop him. It's a question of degree: not enough protection can be foolhardy, while too much can be overbearing. What makes one person feel safe at home may leave another fearful.

You can achieve a comfortable level of security in many ways, ranging from taking such commonsense precautions as not advertising your absence, to installing expensive electronic alarms linked to a security station that monitors them. But some of the most beneficial security measures are relatively simple. Begin by strengthening the most basic defenses you already have, including door locks, window latches, and lights, before adding to your home security arsenal. That way you can make your home more secure without disrupting your day-to-day life—or denting your checkbook.

Locking Up

There's a reason castles were built with moats around them: limiting intruders to one point of entry makes a building easier to defend. The average home, however, provides a dozen or so points of entry: all your doors and windows.

You need a good lock on the front door, of course, but no burglar will waste time on double dead bolts if you've left a first-floor or basement window open a crack for ventilation. It makes more sense to build in a reasonable amount of protection at every point of entry. Windows need locks, and you have to remember to use them when you go out for the evening. If you want to leave a window open a crack for ventilation in hot weather—just install a second lock in the cracked-open position as detailed under "Locking an Open Window," p. 392.

Basement windows are especially easy targets for burglars; they are so low to the ground it's hard to see anyone breaking in. To make them more secure, you can install scissor-type gates and a lock on the inside of the window or custom-made iron grilles on the outside. A less prison-like solution would be to use glass blocks to replace the windows—you'd lose the ventilation, but not the light. (See "Glass & Mirrors," pp. 198–99, for installation information.)

Keys & Combinations

While a standard lockset is relatively easy to break through, the dead bolt above is not because it locks the door to the frame.

This type of keyless lock has a combination cylinder on the dead bolt, and a regular keylock in case you forget the combination.

Key Lock Cutaway

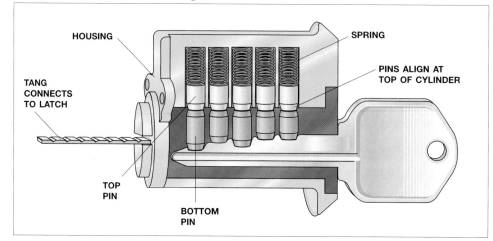

HOUSING

SPRING

TANG CONNECTS TO LATCH

PINS ALIGN AT TOP OF CYLINDER

TOP PIN

BOTTOM PIN

Fixing Common Lock Problems

When a lock sticks or is slow in responding, it may be clogged with dirt. Lubricate the cylinder with penetrating oil.

If you can't push in a key because of ice in the lock, thaw it out with a hair dryer, or heat the key with a match and work it in.

Many people enter through the garage, where computer chips in modern remotes can set new code combinations every day.

The cylinders of most locks have the same basic design. Two opposing rows of spring-loaded pins are cut at different lengths so that they align (and you can open the door) only when the pins are shifted into position by a particular key. The system provides reasonable security and convenience. Unfortunately, many burglaries today are kick-ins where the door and jamb are smashed. Long screws that join jamb and house frame will help; so will a dead bolt. Some codes may not allow dead bolts with an inside key (instead of a thumb latch) because you may have to search for the key in a fire emergency.

When a key breaks inside a lock, lift up the broken end with a narrow piece of metal, and remove the stub with pliers.

Security Programs

In some areas, there are so many false alarms from security systems that police reduce their level of response—or stop responding altogether. Electronic systems are a deterrent, but there is no substitute for high-quality locks on windows and doors, good exterior lighting so that burglars can't conceal themselves, and good neighbors who watch out for each other.

A crime watch program, like a security company sticker, may not stop a determined thief but may deter a casual one.

Vacation Security

If you have piles of cash in the house, burglars may fight through a pack of rottweilers to get it. But if your cache is like most people's— TVs, stereos, and such—most burglars are likely to break in only if they're sure you're not there. Below are several ways to make your home look like a bad risk by simulating normal activity with light timers and other devices—even if you're away on vacation.

A stuffed mailbox and a pile of newspapers is a clear signal no one's home— have deliveries held while you're away.

VACATION CHECKLIST

▶ **Don't close up**   Leave signs of normal activity, like a rake on the front lawn

▶ **Stop deliveries**   Don't let mail or newspapers accumulate while you're gone

▶ **Phone calls**   Leave your answering machine on (and clear the messages from your vacation spot) or have your calls forwarded

▶ **Outside lights**   Put outdoor lights on a timer, photoelectric switch, or motion-sensor switch

▶ **Inside lights**   Mimic your normal schedule by putting upstairs and downstairs lights on automatic timers

▶ **Trigger activity**   Put some indoor lights on special switches that turn on when they detect noise or motion—such as lamps near your front porch

safety & security

What Locks Do

Good locks help keep the honest people honest and provide you with a sense of security on a dark and rainy night. Of course, burglars know plenty of ways to defeat even the best locks. But jimmying a locked door or smashing a window can be noisy or take too long to do—either of which may convince an intruder to look elsewhere for a less risky target.

Door Locks

The easiest type of standard door lock for a burglar to open is a key-in-knob lock. These are the locks that can be opened with a credit card: just slip the card between the strikeplate and the spring latch to pop it open. Some of these locks have a separate tongue on the latch that makes this more difficult. But the lock can still be easily stripped out with a screwdriver, or simply removed from the door.

To give would-be intruders more trouble, attach a separate dead-bolt latch above the existing lockset, or remove the old knob and reinstall a stronger lockset, one with a full mortise dead bolt or spring-latch rim lock. The rim lock is easier to install than a dead bolt and somewhat stronger but has a clunky appearance. The dead bolt is hidden from view.

Locking an Open Window

On windows, permanent locking clips and screws are no help if you want an occasional breath of fresh air; window locks need to be secure yet allow at least some ventilation. You can solve this problem with proprietary hardware or some do-it-yourself installations.

On a double-hung window, the plan is to lock the two sashes together in a partly opened position—say, with the upper sash cracked 2 inches. To make your own lock, set the sash in a vented position, then drill a hole through the frame of the inner sash and three-fourths of the way into the outer sash where they overlap. The two frames then can be joined solidly but temporarily by a dowel or a common nail.

Several manufacturers also offer more attractive alternatives, such as elegant brass-capped sash bolts. A small, threaded receptacle fits into, but not through, the outer sash. It accepts a 2¼-inch-long threaded bolt that slips through a corresponding hole in the inner sash.

Basic Door Locks

Passage locksets that have no key are commonly used on interior doors where there is no need for security.

Standard keyed locksets used on exterior doors have a key cylinder on the outside and a thumb latch inside.

Installing a Peephole

USE: ▶ power drill/driver ▶ peephole

1 *Use a sharp bit* to drill a centered, eye-level hole the same diameter as the cylinder of the peephole.

2 *A typical peephole* has an eyepiece attached to a cylinder that goes through the door and screws to a cover plate.

Window Locks

This rotating lever lock slides under the adjacent housing on the outer sash to join the two sections together.

This rotating cam lock is harder to pick from the outside because it clips around the housing on the outer sash.

Combination locksets may have a separate latchset and dead bolt, or they can be connected on the same face hardware.

Dead-bolt locks make any key-lock door more secure by connecting the door to the frame with a long-throw bolt.

Exterior keyed locks come with many types of handles, including lever types that are easier to use for people with disabilities.

Sliding Door Locks

The typical in-line hook lock on sliding doors can't offer the degree of security that a lockset provides on a swinging door. The best bet is a bar lock. One end is hinged to the far jamb and can fold down out of the way when you're using the door. The other side folds down into a U-shaped bracket on the sliding panel and is pinned there with a small key. You can also install a sliding bolt lock that ties the movable panel to the fixed panel. Fixed panels should be permanently clipped to the door frame.

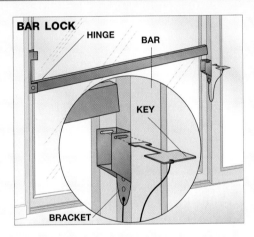

BAR LOCK — HINGE — BAR — KEY — BRACKET

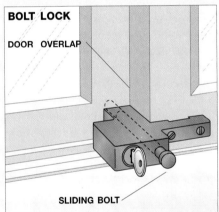

BOLT LOCK — DOOR OVERLAP — SLIDING BOLT

Keyed window locks are secure, but can be inconvenient if you need to find and use a key every time you want some ventilation.

This window lock increases security with a small stop that prevents the lock from turning unless you squeeze the handle.

This sash lock has a stub that travels in a slotted bracket. In this position, the stub is out of the way so the sash opens.

safety & security

Doors & Jambs

A good place to start making your home more secure is the point that a burglar is most likely to attack: the door. Invest in strong locks, but remember that locks only make a connection between exterior doors, which are pretty solid, and door jambs, which aren't. An intruder may not bother to pick or drill through an expensive dead bolt lock when one swift kick can break loose the door jamb that holds the dead bolt keeper. The entire assembly may stay securely locked while swinging into the room with the jamb. You can fix this weak link in your household security by making the door frame part of the building frame, as shown at right in "Strengthening Frames."

Sliding Glass Doors

This method of strengthening the jamb won't work on a sliding glass door, and their locks tend to be very small. Here's what you can do to beef up sliding-door security. First, replace the screws that came with the door with ones that reach several inches into the structural house framing. Then, install a special dead-bolt lock or commercial security bar (as described in "Sliding Door Locks" on p. 393). You could also cut a piece of broomstick or a 2x4 to place in the track between the door and the side jamb instead. Then your door is secure, short of someone smashing the glass—a step many intruders won't take because it makes such a racket.

Strengthening Frames

USE: ▶ pry bar • power drill/driver ▶ shims • wood screws

1 *Prevent kick-in entries* where burglars crash in the door and jamb with the lock intact. First, remove the trim.

2 *Insert blocks of wood* at several points into the gaps between the door casing and the house wall framing.

3 *Remove the stop* or weatherstripping so you can drive screws through the door casing and blocks into the house frame.

4 *Use screws long enough* to reach at least an inch into the nearest wall stud. Replace the stop to conceal screwheads.

Security Hardware

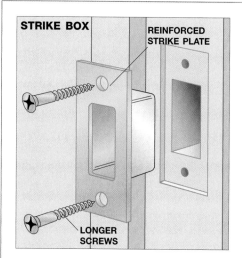

STRIKE BOX
REINFORCED STRIKE PLATE
LONGER SCREWS

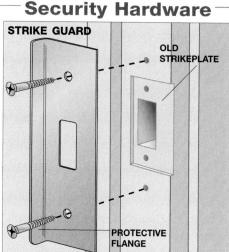

STRIKE GUARD
OLD STRIKEPLATE
PROTECTIVE FLANGE

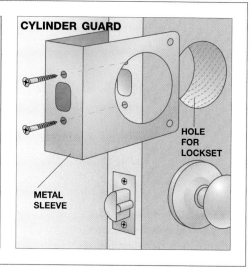

CYLINDER GUARD
HOLE FOR LOCKSET
METAL SLEEVE

Installing a Dead Bolt

USE: ▶ power drill/driver • hole saw • spade bit • wood chisel • utility knife • screwdriver • pencil or scratch awl ▶ dead bolt kit

1 Use the paper template *provided with the dead bolt to mark the center point of the holes you will need to drill.*

2 Bore a hole *in the door face using a hole saw. When the tip breaks through, drill from the other side to prevent tearout.*

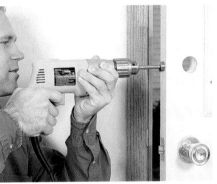

3 Bore a hole *in the door edge for the latch bolt. To keep the drill (and the hole) level, it helps to sight along the drill.*

4 Set the latch bolt *in its hole, and make a tracing of the latch plate on the door edge with a utility knife.*

5 Chisel out a mortise *to match the size and depth of the latch plate. Turn the chisel over to clean the bottom of the mortise.*

6 Insert the latch bolt *(this one being for a new dead bolt) on the door edge, and fasten it in place with the screws.*

7 Install the lock cylinder *by sliding its metal extension bar, called a tang, through the latch mechanism.*

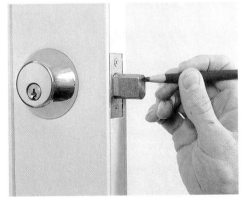

8 To line up the bolt keeper *on the jamb, color or chalk the end of the bolt, close the door, and turn the lock to make an imprint.*

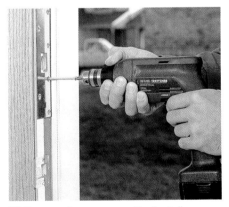

9 For maximum security, *install a heavy-gauge keeper using screws long enough to reach into the house framing.*

safety & security

Wired for Security

For most people, alarm systems should be considered only a last resort. A good system is very expensive, often requiring monthly monitoring fees, and you will still need other security measures, such as window locks.

Too often, elaborate alarms have also one of two undesirable by-products: they either produce a false sense of security because no single system can keep out a determined burglar, or they become a nuisance—because of all the arming, disarming, and false alarms. That only makes you overly security-conscious and more fearful than you reasonably need to be.

Types of Alarm Systems

Alarm systems are either wired directly into your house's electrical system or are radio-controlled. A radio system uses battery-powered transmitters to send alarm signals to the master control unit. For a wired system, you need to loop wiring to and from each component of the system. A radio-controlled system is much easier to install but more expensive, and the batteries must be checked periodically.

Sensors installed at entry points in your home feed signals to the master control panel. Typical sensors are magnetic switches set on door jambs or first-floor window sashes; trap switches that string across an air-conditioner or casement window; and metal-foil alarm tape that detects movement in a window.

Basic System Layout

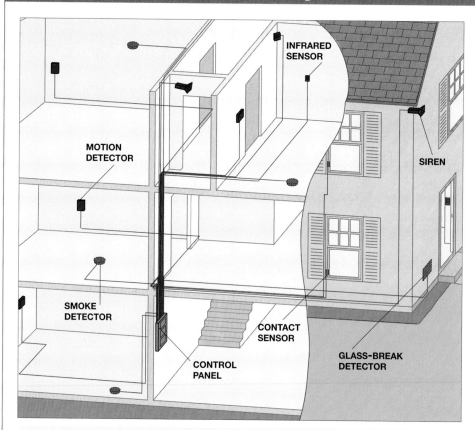

A complete home alarm system can combine many different security functions: monitoring entry at windows and doors, sensing motion inside rooms, and reacting to signals from a variety of sensors such as smoke alarms.

Common Components

A whole-house security system may include dozens of components, including inside and outside sensors and alarms.

Sensor packages at a window can be wired or remote. When a connection between units is broken, the alarm sounds.

Remote sensors also work on doors. A wired alternative, a plunger switch in the jamb, releases when the door is opened.

Auto-Dialers

Some security systems offer off-site monitoring or some other way to respond to an emergency, even if you're not home. When an alarm is triggered at your house, it shows up at the security company's monitoring station. One alternative to this is an auto-dialer. When a security system sensor is triggered, the auto-dialer automatically calls the telephone numbers that you programmed it to call. Any auto-dialer that uses regular phone lines (that is, nonwireless) won't work when lines are down.

Some security systems tie the entry sensors and other components in your house to a central monitoring location.

CAUTION

▶ Before investing in an expensive security system that automatically reports trouble to local authorities, check with local police about their policy on false alarms. In some areas, the police may not have the manpower or the budget to cover every alarm. There may be a penalty for repeated violations. In some cases, police may not respond at all after there have been a certain number of false alarms from the same address.

Remote Sensors

Remote sensors are like wireless phones. They do the same job as standard security-system components, but they broadcast trouble to the central control panel instead of relaying it by wires strung through your house. Remote sensors make installation easy in an existing home where it may be difficult to conceal wiring. Most types of sensors are available as remote units, including motion detectors and sensors that monitor glass breakage and basement flooding.

A remote sensor has circuitry to monitor entry at windows and doors, for example, and battery power to signal the entry.

Many remote sensors are barely noticeable (only twice the size of a quarter) and do not require hard-wire connections.

Many whole-house systems include a remote trouble switch—a panic button— that can trigger an alarm from any room.

One economical alternative to a detector at every window is a centrally located audio unit that detects glass breaks.

Motion detectors are installed inside to signal movement in rooms and outside to trigger lights. Their range is adjustable.

safety & security

Preventing & Detecting

Many house-fire tragedies that make the news could have been prevented. But because the possibility of one's own house burning down seems so remote, many homeowners don't take even the most basic preventive measures. Many are surprisingly simple and inexpensive, yet very effective at saving both lives and property.

Smoke Detectors

Smoke detectors may be the most cost-effective consumer product on the market. Just consider what it costs (about $15), how easy it is to use (just screw it to a ceiling), and what it can do (provide a warning in enough time to save lives). Detectors should be installed on every level of a home, high on the walls, or on ceilings in open areas like hallways. Because deaths are most likely from fires that start at night when everyone is asleep, it's important to install detectors in halls just outside bedrooms. Be sure your detectors are working by trying the testing mechanism, normally a button that triggers a brief warning blast to prove readiness.

Heating Equipment

Regular checkups are the best preventive measure for your heating system. Annual tune-ups are recommended for oil-fired furnaces; once every 3 years for gas-fired units. Electric units, which do not produce any combustion by-products, normally do not need regular tune-ups.

If you burn wood or coal regularly, have the flue cleaned annually by a chimney sweep. Wood and coal combustion in a stove is dirtier than other types of heating—you need the sweep because the worst hazards are out of sight: creosote, a gummy and flammable product of wood combustion that collects inside the chimney, and cracks in the chimney liner or bricks, which could let smoke and fire escape.

Escape Routes

Fire departments call it an alternative means of egress—a second way out of a room. On the first floor you could climb out a window. On second stories, you may need a portable safety ladder with metal arms that hang on the window sill and steps that unroll to the ground below. It's important to go over escape routes with children, and walk through the route to make it familiar.

Battery-Powered Detectors

Each year, more than 3,700 people die in over 400,000 residential fires. The best way to prevent property damage and injury is to install smoke detectors. About 90% of U.S. households have at least one, but up to 16 million detectors don't work, due mainly to dead or missing batteries. You should test battery-powered units monthly, and replace batteries that are low on power. (Most units warn you by beeping or chirping.) Some hard-wired units also have a battery backup.

Most safety organizations *recommend that you change the batteries in your smoke detector at least once a year.*

Typical Detector Locations

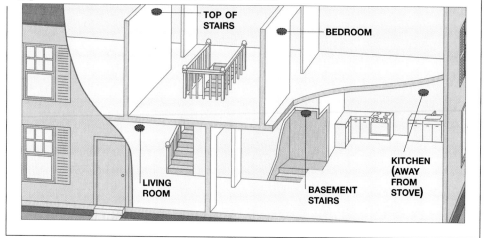

TOP OF STAIRS

BEDROOM

LIVING ROOM

BASEMENT STAIRS

KITCHEN (AWAY FROM STOVE)

Hard-Wiring a Detector

USE: ▶ circuit tester • combination tool • screwdriver • drywall saw • pliers ▶ hard-wired smoke detector

1 ***The most convenient power source*** *is a junction box mounted to a ceiling joist. Cut power to the box before opening it.*

2 ***Check your local codes*** *before running a new supply line from connectors in the junction box to the detector mounting box.*

Home Fire Extinguishers

Most homes need at least two extinguishers: a small unit in the kitchen, and a larger, wall-mounted unit (generally installed in a closet) to use elsewhere. To avoid confusion in a fire emergency, choose A-B-C-rated units that work on all types of fires. To use an extinguisher effectively, remember the acronym P A S S—Pull (the pin), Aim, Squeeze, and Sweep.

Use an all-purpose A-B-C extinguisher against paper, grease, and electrical fires. Aim at the base of the fire.

Typical Clearance Codes

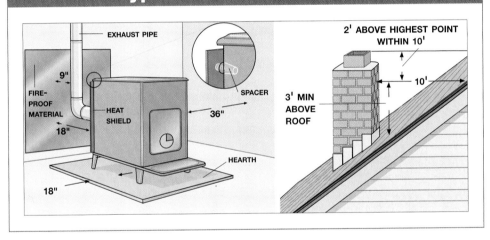

EXHAUST PIPE

9"

FIRE-PROOF MATERIAL

HEAT SHIELD

18"

36"

SPACER

18"

HEARTH

2' ABOVE HIGHEST POINT WITHIN 10'

10'

3' MIN ABOVE ROOF

SAFETY CHECKLIST

▶ **Don't overload:** Do not plug more than one heat-producing device into an outlet.

▶ **Maintain smoke detector:** Replace battery and vacuum the unit annually; test a detector monthly and replace it every 10 years.

▶ **Provide safe egress:** Have two ways out of every room—a door and a code-compliant egress window—including rooms in finished basements.

▶ **Fire-safe security:** Don't use security locks, bars, or devices that make it difficult to escape a fire.

▶ **Clean your chimney:** Have wood-burning chimneys inspected annually and cleaned as needed.

▶ **Store inflammables safely:** Store inflammable liquids in original containers with tight-fitting lids. Keep them away from heat sources or flames, preferably in a shed.

▶ **Be prepared:** Keep an extinguisher handy to stop a small fire from spreading. In other cases, call 911.

• cable • wire connectors

3 *Most hard-wired detectors* have a surface mounting plate that attaches to the electrical box above the drywall.

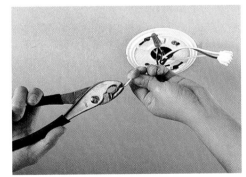

4 *Following the instructions* supplied by the manufacturer, join the detector leads to the power-supply cable.

5 *The leads* are attached to a harness that plugs into a receptacle on the detector. Twist the detector onto the mounting plate.

safety & security

Dangers at Knee Level

Don't put off babyproofing your house until the little one can walk—a fast-crawling baby can find plenty of trouble. Crawl around your house yourself, and you'll discover many dangerous things at infant eye level: outlets, rickety TV stands, appetizing potted plants. And when a toddler learns to stand, he or she will hold onto anything to get upright, including the tablecloth dangling from a table full of bone china.

Storing Hazardous Items Safely

Any potentially harmful item should be either locked away or kept in cabinets and drawers with childproof safety latches. This includes knives and the obvious poisons such as medi-cine and cleaning products, but also mouth-wash, shaving cream, perfume, and deodorant, which can be harmful to curious toddlers who like to put things in their mouths. Even high counters are not necessarily safe places; you need to put away that decorative knife rack because toddlers will figure a way to get up on a counter well before you think they can. It's a good idea to have one cupboard or drawer full of safe distractions, such as plastic containers or wooden bowls, that a toddler can get to.

Leave small appliances unplugged, and store them as far out of reach as possible. Plastic bags and plastic wrap also need to be kept in a high place. When discarding the plastic bags from dry cleaning, tie them into knots before throw-ing them into the garbage. Buy garbage cans with secure lids that kids can't open.

Keeping Rooms Safe

Get safety gates to close off stairs or any room where you don't want the baby to go and you don't have a door to lock. Guards or gates are also needed to keep them away from fireplaces, wood-burning stoves, or space heaters.

One door lock that kids figure out quickly is the push-button on bedroom and bathroom doors. For bathrooms, an adult-height bolt would be a better option for a house with young children. You won't have time to look for a bobby pin to unlock the door if your child slips in the bathtub.

Built-In Features

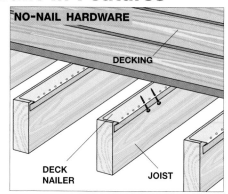

Remove one source of accidents on decks (raised nails) with hardware that allows you to fasten boards from below.

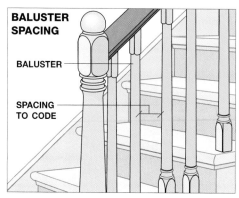

Codes control spacing (often only 4 in.) between parts of stairs and railings so that children can't get caught between them.

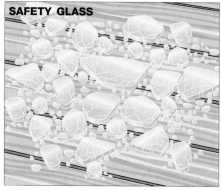

Unlike standard sheet glass that breaks into razor-sharp shards, tempered safety glass breaks into pebble-like pieces.

Openings

Safety grates can prevent falls. Building codes will not allow locks if the window is a potential fire-escape route.

Safety gates can prevent accidents on stairs and wall off rooms. This model has mesh panels that won't trap children.

Reduce the risk of accidents with landscaping tools and materials by walling them off with a hinged lattice gate.

Soft Surfaces

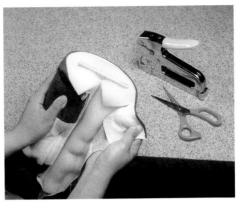

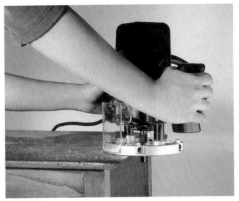

To reduce noise transmission *through the floor and take the edge out of falls, install wall-to-wall carpet over a thick pad.*

This cushioned chair rail *for a child's room has thick foam stapled around a strip of plywood and covered with fabric.*

On furniture *where you can't create cushioned surfaces, you can at least reduce hard edges with a roundover bit and router.*

Hazardous Materials

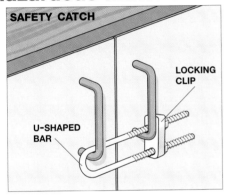

SAFETY CATCH

LOCKING CLIP

U-SHAPED BAR

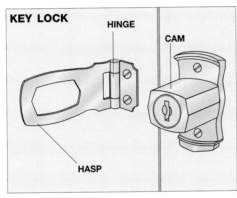

KEY LOCK

HINGE

CAM

HASP

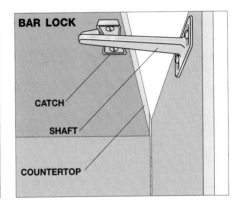

BAR LOCK

CATCH

SHAFT

COUNTERTOP

When you can't remove all hazardous materials from children's reach, lock up the cabinets that contain them.

There are locks to fit every type of door and cabinet combination, including hasp locks that can't be opened without a key.

Where only minimal security is needed, this under-counter spring lock will keep a door from opening fully.

Electricity

Short cords *are inconvenient on counter-top appliances, but they keep the wires from hanging within the reach of children.*

To eliminate shock hazards *when an electrical outlet is not in use, plug a plastic insulator cap into the receptacle.*

Required by code in many locations, *circuit-breaker outlets (ground-fault circuit interrupters) reduce shock hazards.*

safety & security

Bad Air & More

If you are a nonsmoker or allergic to dust, you can tell as soon as you walk into a room that these common pollutants are present. But some air pollutants can be harder to identify; fumes from volatile organic compounds (VOCs) and high levels of carbon monoxide are prime examples.

VOCs

VOCs are released as gases from many ordinary products, including wood finishes, paints, adhesives, rug and oven cleaners, dry-cleaning fluids, furnishings, and office equipment. Some (not all) VOCs have a distinct odor, and some (not all) products containing VOCs come with caution labels.

Health problems resulting from exposure to VOCs include skin rash, upper respiratory irritation, nose bleed (from formaldehyde glues), headache, nausea, vomiting, fatigue, and dizziness. Because VOC emissions are greatest in new materials and gradually dissipate, symptoms are likely to be triggered during or shortly after remodeling and cleaning work.

At home, there are several things you can do to reduce your exposure. Meet or exceed label cautions for ventilation when using products that emit VOCs. Don't store opened containers of paint and other materials containing VOCs in the house. To reduce emissions from composite boards used in some cabinets, seal the interior surfaces with two coats of polyurethane.

Carbon Monoxide

Carbon monoxide (CO) gas is made whenever fuels such as gas, oil, kerosene, wood, or charcoal are burned. A properly used (and maintained) stove or heating appliance won't leak a significant amount of the gas. But CO poisoning is tricky to detect, and the initial symptoms (dizziness, headache, nausea, shortness of breath) are easily mistaken for other illnesses. The best preventative measure is to have heating appliances inspected annually by a professional. CO detectors are widely available but should only be used as a backup for yearly maintenance. Performance of these detectors varies widely, and because CO is colorless and odorless, it's easy to think the real thing may be a false alarm.

Lead Paint

Many house paints made before 1978 contain lead, which is a threat to children and can cause cause permanent brain damage, behavioral problems, and other serious health problems. If you live in a pre-1978 home, you should contact the EPA National Lead Information Center (800-424-LEAD) for free information on testing and safety precautions and for guidelines on whether the paint should be left alone, covered, or removed.

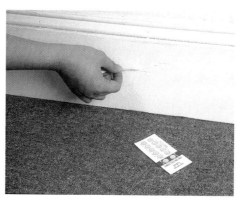

You can test existing paint for lead with a simple kit. Following instructions, scrape the surface, apply the activator, and wipe.

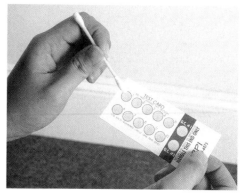

The activator makes a liquid sample on the swab that you then apply to the test card, to find out the lead-content reading.

Lead in Water

Sources of lead in drinking water include lead pipes (common until around 1930), brass faucets or fittings than contain some lead, or copper pipes soldered with material containing lead. If you suspect there is lead in your water, have it tested. To reduce the lead you may be consuming if you're at risk, use cold water for consumption (it doesn't sit in pipes for long), and run the tap 1 or 2 minutes before you drink. You may have to replace old pipes.

To take a sample of water for testing, first use the flame from a match to burn off impurities on the faucet head.

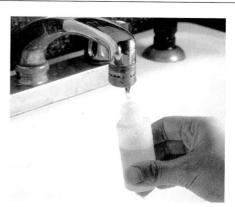

Fill a small, clean container with a sample, which can be tested by some town health departments or a private lab.

Radon

Radon (a colorless, odorless gas) is the second-leading cause of lung cancer after smoking. This naturally occurring gas comes from the ground, well water, and some building materials. Nearly one out of every 15 homes contains high levels. It's easy and inexpensive to test your home or well for radon with a canister kit. Indoor levels of 4 picocuries per liter or more need to be fixed. Contractors can install an air-pumping system that vents radon from the ground under your house to the outside.

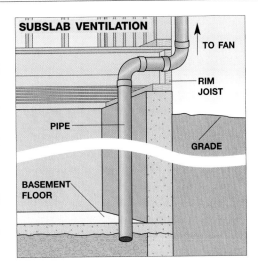

SUBSLAB VENTILATION

TO FAN

RIM JOIST

PIPE

GRADE

BASEMENT FLOOR

A radon test kit consists of a small canister that you leave in your living areas. You mail it to a lab for results.

Asbestos

Asbestos is often found as insulation and fire protection on pipes. You also may find asbestos in old cement roofing and siding shingles, insulation (in houses built between 1930 and 1950), walls and floors around wood-burning stoves, and hot water or steam pipes in older houses. The safest course of action is usually to leave it undisturbed—asbestos material in good shape won't release fibers. If it needs to be removed, hire a state-licensed abatement contractor.

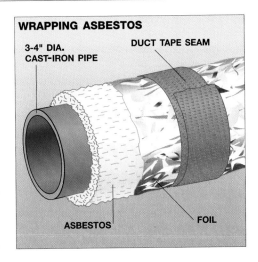

WRAPPING ASBESTOS

3-4" DIA. CAST-IRON PIPE

DUCT TAPE SEAM

ASBESTOS

FOIL

Asbestos was often used to insulate heating pipes in older homes. You should test a sample before deciding on removal.

Gas

A natural- or propane-gas leak is detectable due to mercaptan, an additive in gas that has a rotten-egg smell. If you suspect a gas leak, the safest course is to leave the house immediately and report it to 911 and the utility's emergency number. If you suspect problems in a gas-fired appliance but don't smell the overwhelming aroma of a major leak, you can turn off the gas valve near the appliance or the main valve at the gas meter.

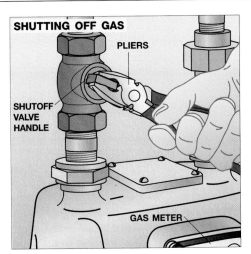

SHUTTING OFF GAS

PLIERS

SHUTOFF VALVE HANDLE

GAS METER

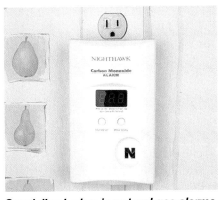

Specialized, plug-in natural gas alarms can detect small amounts of leaking methane and propane in your house.

safety & security

Universal Design

Making homes accessible for disabled people was once considered an extra that added to the cost of building it. But the trend in residential design today is to include features that make a building accessible for a disabled person and easier and more convenient for anyone else, too. It's called accessible or universal design. Here are some of the basic principles that can be incorporated into new construction and remodeling projects.

Entrances & Floor Level

Even in single-story homes, level changes are common at the entrance because the floor level is generally higher than ground level. There are a few good ways to eliminate this barrier without sticking a wood ramp on the front of the house. One is to create a gradually bermed, or earth-ramped, entrance with landscaping timbers.

In new construction, you can lower the foundation or floor level. Typically, the foundation is several inches aboveground; the first floor is a foot or so higher than that. But when building a home, you stop the foundation at grade and use a combination of pressure-treated plywood sheathing and a waterproofing barrier to prevent leaks at the critical transition between foundation and frame. Another way to reduce floor height is by creating a ledge in the top inside of the foundation equal to the depth of the floor framing. To reduce the chance of damage from wood rot if water seeps in, the joists can be set onto metal hangers attached to a pressure-treated ledger board bolted to the foundation.

Other Features

There are other universal design alternatives to standard architectural details. For example, a round, easily grasped stairway banister makes a safer, more convenient handrail than the typical 2x6 wood cap piece that is too wide to hold onto firmly. Another design defect is common to bypassing closet doors and cabinets that have inset pulls. They put even more stress on finger joints than round knobs. Instead of applying the strength of your whole arm, these pulls focus all the stress on the ends of your fingers. D-shaped pulls with at least 1½ inches of clearance to the door surface make the job easier.

Access

HALLWAYS

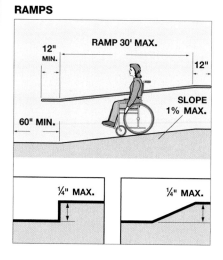

RAMPS

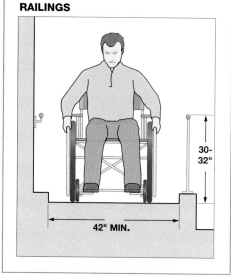

RAILINGS

Kitchens

STOVE CLEARANCES

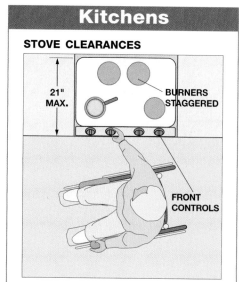

SINK CLEARANCES

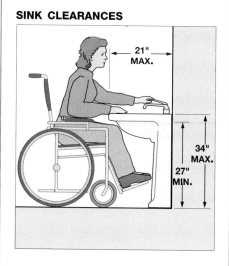

TABLE CLEARANCES

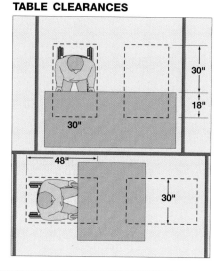

Baths

TUB LAYOUT

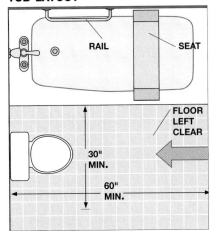

RAIL

SEAT

FLOOR LEFT CLEAR

30" MIN.

60" MIN.

SHOWER LAYOUT

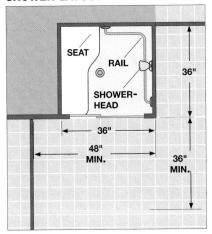

SEAT

RAIL

SHOWER-HEAD

36"

36"

48" MIN.

36" MIN.

TOILET LAYOUT

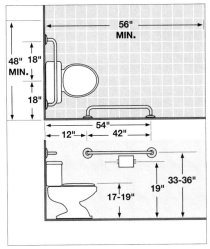

56" MIN.

48" MIN.

18"

18"

54"

12"

42"

33-36"

19"

17-19"

Universal design seeks to make houses easy to use and accessible for almost everyone. Overall, rooms don't look much different, although this space has a raised dishwasher, lowered dish cabinets, open-plan sink, pull-out steps and stools, and many similar features.

Special Fixtures

This sink *has flexible plumbing connections and an electric motor to raise and lower the sink platform.*

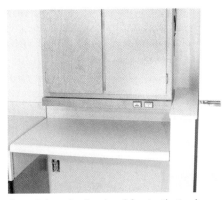

Special motorized cabinets *that raise and lower also are available to make storage more accessible in kitchens.*

Counters are more versatile *when they have several levels and pull-out extensions near appliances.*

To reach higher shelves, *the door on this bin-storage cabinet is equipped with a sturdy (four-legged) fold-down stool.*

roofing 22

roofing

Roofing Language

Standing out in the yard with a pair of binoculars at the ready, you might be mistaken for a bird watcher by your neighbors. How would they know you are only following the advice of the Asphalt Roofing Manufacturers Association on the best way to inspect your shingles. If your knees get a little wobbly when you climb a ladder, using binoculars is not a bad idea. Of course, you could ask two or three roofing contractors to take a look instead. But it is good policy to know something about the condition of your roof—and the language roofers use—before asking for estimates. The following chapter covers each type of roofing material in turn, from asphalt shingles to slate. But before getting into the particulars, it's worth taking time to nail down a few basic terms.

Roofing Speak

One square of shingles is the amount needed to cover 100 square feet of roof surface. This is the standard measure you'll find in contractor's estimates, and it is the way to order shingles and most other roofing materials. To cover that area you may need more of one type of shingle than another, depending on their size and configuration. But a square of standard asphalt shingles (the material most used on residences) is composed of three bundles of 27 shingles each.

Coverage refers to the number of layers of roofing protection provided. For example, standard modified bitumen for flat roofs, or asphalt shingles for sloped roofs, provide one layer. Dimensional asphalt shingles that show a more textured, shake-like roof, may provide two layers of coverage.

The slope of a roof is expressed as a ratio: inches of rise (vertically) per inches of run (horizontally). For example, a low-slope, 3-in-12 roof gains 3 inches of height every foot. On a 16-foot-long run from the eaves up to the ridge, the roof would rise 4 feet. Just measure a set distance along the side wall in from the eaves (run) and then a straight line up to the roof (rise) to find the slope on your roof. You could use slope to help calculate an order or to determine what type of roofing to use. For example, on standard asphalt shingle bundles you might read that the manufacturer doesn't recommend installation (or has special requirements) on roofs with a slope of less than 4-in-12.

As a safety guideline, you may use slope to decide if a roof is walkable. That means you can work on it without scaffolding. For most people, the cutoff point is a 6-in-12 slope, which means that a 16-foot-long run would rise 8 feet from the eaves to the ridge. But use some common sense too: For example, wear sneakers, and go up only when the roof is dry. And if you feel uneasy about being up there, even on a low-slope roof, stay on the ground.

Estimating the Order

There are several ways to estimate roof surface area. The most obvious and reliable is simply to go up on the roof with a tape measure.

From the ground, you can measure the floor

Anatomy of a Roof

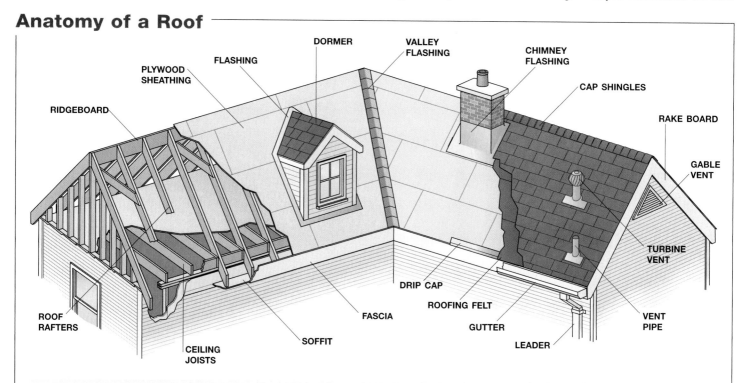

The elements of most roofs are similar to those of the gable roof, shown above. Rafters carry the weight down to the house frame. Plywood sheathing supports water-shedding shingles. Flat roofs, the exception, have joists like floors instead of rafters.

plan of the house, add on overhanging areas, and then multiply by one of many conversion factors based on the roof slope—for example, by 1.03 for a nearly flat roof with a slope from 1-in-12 to 3-in-12, by 1.12 for a 6-in-12 slope, and by 1.45 for a steeply pitched roof with a slope of 12-in-12. After that, you add on 10% to cover ridge tabs, hips, valleys, and starter courses, and round up to the next full square.

Multiplying by conversion factors is not necessary if you measure on the roof. But you should figure in extras—for example, four full shingles for every 5 linear feet of hip or ridge, or about 30 linear feet per square of shingles, which builds in some waste. To save money, buy nails in bulk; figure to use about 2 pounds of standard 1¼-inch galvanized roofing nails per square.

When ordering roofing felt, remember most manufacturers assume a 2-inch overlap, and one 432-square-foot roll will cover about 400 square feet. If you decide to overlap more, you'll need more rolls of felt.

Special Tools

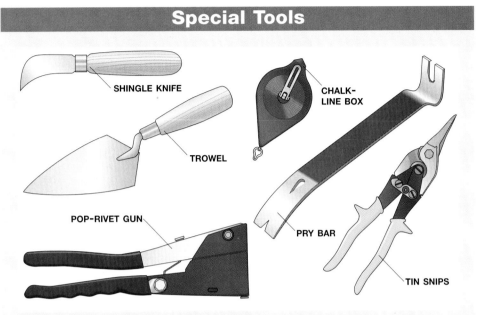

Roofing tools include the basics like a hammer, of course, and a few you might not have in the toolbox: a shingle knife, trowel, pop-rivet gun, chalk-line box, pry bar, and metal shears. Professional roofers generally use air-powered nailers to speed up the job.

Ladders & Scaffolds

Take a warning from the construction industry, where the most serious accidents are the result of falling. In plain language, you need to be particularly careful working on a roof, as you will be anywhere from 10 to 30 feet off the ground. You can make the job safer, though, by using the variety of ladders, scaffolds, and fall-arrest devices on the market today. Use extension ladders in good condition rather than stepladders to gain access to your roof. Scaffolding and working platforms make a roofing job even easier, and can be rented for the duration of a job. The simplest are metal cleats or roof brackets anchored to the roof itself. Ladder jacks, pump jacks, and scaffolding provide movable platforms for working. Those rated for construction will support you and piles of shingles at the roof edge.

roofing

Roof Design

Roof designs have changed over the years, reflecting a general trend toward cost savings, efficiency, and ease of installation. Victorian-era mansard slate roofs, with geometric patterns of multicolored tiles, are perhaps the most artistic and difficult roofs to build (and fix). If you're lucky enough to own a house with a roof like that, you may question your luck after getting a bill for fixing a leak.

With modern roofs, the major cost in repair and replacement is labor. Older homes with slate roofs have the dual expense of labor and material. Sometimes homeowners who need to replace a slate roof will opt for asphalt shingle replacement, because the price of new slate roofing can be as much as 10 times that of asphalt shingles.

Roofs can be pitched at almost any angle, from nearly flat to almost vertical. While a roof's pitch is mostly a matter of design, the roofing materials that can be used are beholden to the pitch, if they are to shed water, snow, and debris. Flat roofs cannot be covered with asphalt shingles; mansard roofs cannot be made with built-up roofing.

Climate

Climate and weather patterns are the primary concerns for the general design of the roof. A flat roof, for instance, is impractical in a part of the country with a great deal of snow or rain—that's why houses in New England generally have steeply pitched roofs.

The type of roofing material needed to meet weather conditions and the slope of the roof are secondary concerns. Clay tile roofs, for example, look beautiful on Spanish-style

Roof Types

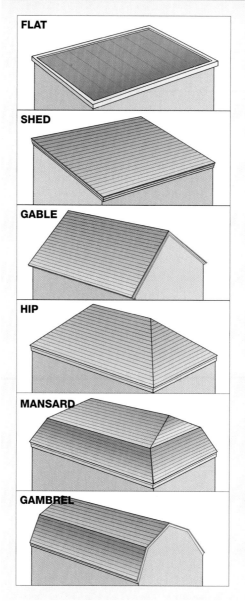

FLAT

SHED

GABLE

HIP

MANSARD

GAMBREL

- ◆ **Flat roofs** are easiest to install and fix for do-it-yourselfers. Made with built-up roofing material or roll roofing, they last 10–15 years.

- ◆ **Shed roofs** are similar to a flat roof, only they are pitched at an angle. They can be roofed in metal, roll roofing, shingle, or tile, depending on the pitch.

- ◆ **Gable roof** is a simple A-frame roof with a single ridge, no hips or valleys. It can be sheathed in any roofing material, except roll roofing.

- ◆ **Hip roofs** have all roof sections sloping toward the roof ridge. Hips are capped with shingles to keep out water.

- ◆ **Mansard roofs** slope steeply at first, then flatten out. Typical in Victorian designs. Done in slate or shingle, sometimes copper metal.

- ◆ **Gambrel,** the basic barn roof design, has a slope that flattens near the top. This allows for more storage space in an attic. Needed extra support is provided by interior cross beams. Roofed in most materials.

Ventilation

Ridge vents run along the top of the roof. They allow optimal attic ventilation by creating a strong flow from vents in the soffit overhang. In many cases, they are woven into the shingles so you don't even notice them.

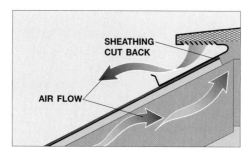

SHEATHING CUT BACK

AIR FLOW

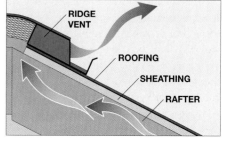

RIDGE VENT

ROOFING

SHEATHING

RAFTER

homes in the Southwest. However, clay tile does not perform very well in colder climates, where ice and snow can back up into the tiles and cause roof damage. A slate roof with a steep pitch, on the other hand, performs very well in cold climates, but may not shed heat very well in hot climates.

Seasonal weather should also be taken into account when choosing a color for your roofing material. Asphalt shingles, for example, come in a variety of colors, from white to pitch black, with shades of gray, green, and red also available. As you would guess, a black roof pitched at a low angle on a house in Florida is not the brightest idea for keeping a house cool. In hot climates, white shingles, Spanish tiles, and wood shakes or shingles will help deflect the sun's heat. In cold climates, slate and dark asphalt shingles will absorb the sun's heat.

Trusses

If you're nervous about cutting rafters from scratch and you don't mind not having open attic space and dormers, roof trusses are a good framing option. Roof trusses are difficult to install, but you can get them made to order, which eliminates cutting. Trusses are essentially framed triangles, with 2x4 or 2x6 chords (the outside lines of the triangle) and 2x4 webs (supporting members, most often in W- or M-shapes inside the triangle) held together by gussets, which are flat metal or plywood plates. The two top chords and the long bottom chord form the shape of a gable roof.

You erect trusses right on the top plates, with one truss per stud bay. If you've framed the walls at 16 inches on center, for example, then the trusses will occur every 16 inches on-center as well. This is why you lose the attic space—every 16 or 24 inches there's a bunch of intruding supports from roof to floor. Also, you can't cut into a truss to install dormers, because cutting any one of the framing members compromises the structural integrity of the entire truss. For this reason, trusses are common in storage buildings and garages.

You order trusses from a local truss manufacturer or building-supply store, by specifying the desired length of the bottom chord. There may not be a wide variety of ridge heights for you to choose from, however.

In a warm climate where you rely more on air conditioning than heating, use light colored shingles; they reflect more heat.

Aluminum paint (applied mainly over flat roofs) is another way to reduce heat buildup. It also reduces surface cracking.

Rise & Run

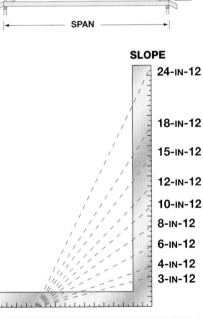

12 / 6 SLOPE

TOTAL RUN

TOTAL RISE

SPAN

SLOPE

24-IN-12
18-IN-12
15-IN-12
12-IN-12
10-IN-12
8-IN-12
6-IN-12
4-IN-12
3-IN-12

The rise and run of your roof should suit house style and regional climate. Generally, cold, wet locales require houses with steeply pitched roofs to shed snow and rain. In hot, arid locales, low-slope and flat roofs are more suitable.

Overhang Options

NARROW OVERHANG

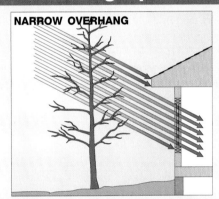

A narrow overhang can be the best design where you want the greatest heat gain and maximum light through the windows.

WIDE OVERHANG

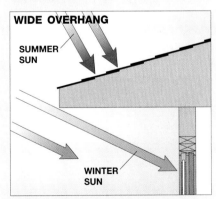

SUMMER SUN

WINTER SUN

A wide overhang is good in wet climates to shed water, of course, and to block more of the harsh rays of the summer midday sun.

roofing

Flat Roofs

Flat roofs look good on modern houses in architecture magazines, but they have problems. They would be great in a climate where it rarely rained. And some houses just don't work with a steep gable or Prairie-style hip roof, so they're stuck with a water-collecting top, which is bound to need repairs.

Old-style flat roofs were built up from as many as five layers of asphalt felt paper, each one sandwiched between beds of molten tar, applied with the kind of labor-intensive steps builders don't have the time for today. But if you have an old built-up roof, don't be too eager to tear it off. First, removal of so much heavy material is a major project. Second, if the roof was applied over a solid frame and covered with gravel (called ballast) to keep it flat and shielded from sunlight, the surface could last 40 years or more. Third, most of these flat roofs just don't spring a leak somewhere in the middle of the interlaced layers, where it is difficult to make a long-lasting repair. They normally open up along the edges, at seams protected by metal flashing, which are easier to fix.

Fixing Edge Leaks

Along the edge of a flat roof, water enters where metal flashing is raised. Hairline breaks can be sealed with a liberal coat of roof cement and reinforcing fabric. Larger and longer openings need to be reset. After cleaning out any debris, trowel as much tar as you can fit under the raised edge and re-nail the flashing to the roof. Add a coat of tar on top of the metal and over the new nails, extending it past the flashing onto the roof a few inches. Then embed in the tar a layer of fiberglass roofing tape, and add a final, top coat of tar.

Repairing Newer Flat Roofs

With modern coatings such as modified bitumen, bubbles, punctures, and other openings are easier to fix—with one caution. The rubbery sheets of these roofs are not joined to each other with tar. They are fused by heating the material until it begins to melt, making it easy to add a waterproof cover. The old section can be cleaned, scarified, and then heated to fuse with a patch piece. But because of fire danger, this is best done by a professional roofer.

Typical Flat-Roof Systems

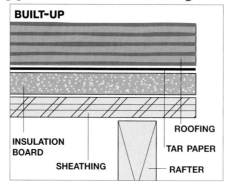

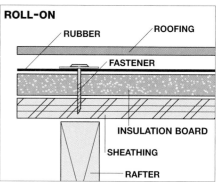

Built-up and roll-on roofs. Built-up roofs (left) have several layers of roofing felt and asphalt under a final layer of asphalt and gravel. Modern roll-on roofs (right) have a single layer of synthetic rubber, attached with nails and roof cement.

Flat-Roof Details

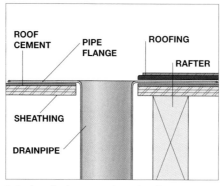

Interior drains are placed at low spots, and carry water through part of the structure en route to an exterior outlet.

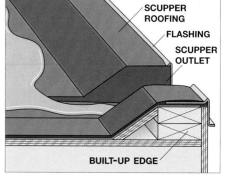

Scupper troughs are cut into the built-up roof edge so that collected water can drain to an exterior downspout.

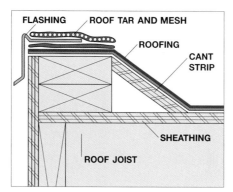

Edge flashing is essential to protect the roof from seepage. Typically, the flashing is coated with roof fabric and tar.

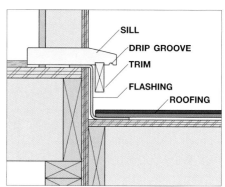

Where a flat roof meets a second-story wall, the entire seam needs flashing. Its upper edge must be protected.

Repairing a Flat Roof

USE: ▶ spade • utility knife • putty knife • trowel • broom ▶ roof cement • roof patch • gravel

1 With a flat spade, scrape away surface gravel from the damaged area.

2 Cut away a rectangular piece around the damaged section with a utility knife.

3 Fill up the removed patch with a generous amount of roof cement.

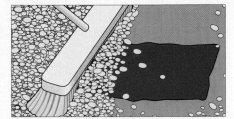

4 Tamp down the patch material, generally more roofing or fiberglass mesh.

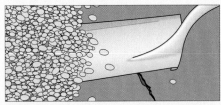

5 Using a mason's trowel, cover over the patch with roofing cement.

6 Cover the patched area with gravel, called ballast, that protects the surface.

Roof Decks

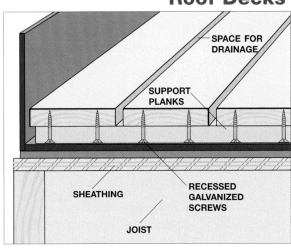

SPACE FOR DRAINAGE
SUPPORT PLANKS
SHEATHING
RECESSED GALVANIZED SCREWS
JOIST

Install a doorway to a flat roof (and railings according to local codes), and the roof can become a deck. To protect the roofing and still have access in case of leaks, cover the surface with duck boards, which are removable sections of spaced planks laid on sleepers.

3 Common Flat-Roof Problems

1. Too many roofers leap to the ultimate solution for a leaky flat roof: a whole new roof. Sometimes, of course, that's the best advice. But in general, don't opt for removal and replacement until you take a shot at fixing spot leaks, particularly when they occur anywhere near a protrusion through the roof surface. That includes the edges, interior drains (drainage holes in the roof overhang that connect to down spouts), the perimeter of skylights, chimneys, and plumbing vent pipes.

2. You're likely to need a new roof—if not immediately, then in a year or two—if there are bubbly areas that compress when you walk on them. They might be the size of your foot or larger. Bubbles indicate that some of the layers of roofing have delaminated. If you step down and hear the sucking sound of water, you'll need the roof much sooner than later—there's water trapped inside your roof, rotting it away.

3. Most flat roofs retain some water in puddles. Standing water can result because the roof was not built with enough slope or because the building—or even a few supporting joists—have gradually settled over the years. These depressions can cause problems where water that doesn't immediately drain stands against seams. In the summer, large puddles also can become stagnant. Depressions in modern flat roofs made of rubber-like sheets can be filled before they begin to leak by bonding on pieces of new roofing contoured to raise the low spot.

roofing

Choosing Shingles

Four out of five residential roofs are made of asphalt shingles or continuous sheets of asphalt called roll roofing, which is usually reserved for low-slope roofs not visible from the ground.

You may be asked to chose between regular asphalt shingles or fiberglass, with a bottom mat of fiberglass mesh that is lighter, stronger, and longer-lasting than asphalt. Fiberglass-mat shingles are a good choice for reroofing jobs, as they reduce the load carried by the rafters without giving up durability. About 80% of all shingles sold for new homes and reroofing are the fiberglass-mat variety, including almost all the heavyweight, overlay-type shingles.

Shingle Weight

Shingle weight is an important factor on both new roofs and on reroofing jobs because heavier shingles last longer, carry a longer warranty, and generally offer a better fire rating. Of course, they are more expensive than lighter shingles. The weight rating (240 pounds for a standard shingle) denotes the total weight of a square of shingles (enough to cover 100 square feet of roof).

The heavyweight shingles are those over the 240-pound rating—generally 300 pounds per square or more. Individual shingles in this category often are configured in layers—like a shingle on a shingle—that simulate the dense pattern of slate or wood shakes. The heavyweights are a good choice for new homes and additions, but a questionable choice for reroofing jobs, where the weight can overload the roof structure.

Color

You don't often see a bright green, blue, or red roof—even though asphalt shingles are available with granules in those colors—because they can become a bit oppressive after a few seasons. Off-white or light gray shingles make a house look larger, but will mar more easily than dark shingles and show wear sooner (even though they will not wear out any faster than dark shingles). Light colors on the roof can reflect more sunlight than dark, which will keep the house cooler in summer and reduce air-conditioning costs. If gaining heat is more important, a dark shingle would be the most energy-efficient choice.

Installing Asphalt Shingles

USE: ▶ ladder or scaffolding • hammer • chalk-line box • shears • utility knife • work gloves ▶ metal drip

1 ***Roofers have different techniques,*** *but all start with a sound plywood roof deck where nail heads are driven flush.*

2 ***Nail on a metal drip edge*** *at the edge of the eaves with roofing nails. This protects the fascia boards from rot.*

6 ***Start each new course*** *at a 6-in. offset, to stagger the seams in adjacent courses in a water-shedding layout.*

7 ***To trim shingles in valleys*** *and other areas, use shears or a utility knife. This is a closed valley with interwoven shingles.*

TOOLS AND MATERIALS

◆ **What you'll need.** You need only basic tools to install asphalt shingles. You can cut them with shears or a utility knife, and nail them in place with a standard hammer. For reroofing jobs, a pry bar and flat shovel are handy for removing old shingles.

◆ **Types of shingles.** Dimensional shingles (bottom) are thicker than regular flat-tab shingles (top) and are not uniform in color, which produces a three-dimensional look similar to slate. Heavier shingles also last longer and have better fire ratings.

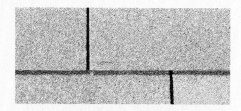

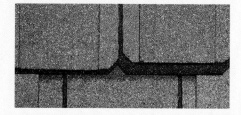

edge • roofing nails • roofing felt • shingles • roof cement

3 ***Roll roofing felt*** on top of the decking, nailing it every 10–12 in., 3 in. from the edge. Overlap rows by several inches.

4 ***For the starter course,*** snap a chalk line and lay the shingles with the tabs pointing up. Put one nail through each tab.

5 ***The first course covers*** the starter course with the tabs pointing down. Each shingle should have at least four nails.

8 ***To shingle around a vent stack,*** trim to overlap only the upper half of the vent collar, and seal underneath with roof cement.

9 ***To shingle the ridge,*** cut single, slightly tapered tabs from whole shingles and wrap them across the ridge, nailing on both sides.

10 ***To save time,*** let full shingles extend past the roof overhang, and trim all of them at once with shears.

Shingle Repair

USE: ▶ pry bar • hammer • caulking gun ▶ new shingles • roofing nails • roofing cement

1 **Remove** all damaged shingles, and pull any protruding nails with a pry bar.

2 **Nail all new shingles** in place but the topmost course (which must be cemented).

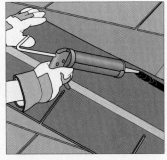

3 **Apply roofing cement** to the underside of the topmost course of shingles.

4 **Slide the new shingle** into place, and tamp down on the surface so it sets firmly.

roofing

Reroofing Asphalt

Most asphalt shingles should last without leaking for 15 to 20 years. Some last longer—even 25 or 30 years. After about 15 years, however, you might start checking for signs of wear. But don't jump the gun. There is no advantage in reroofing a building ahead of time—before the shingles have started to deteriorate and years before they are ready to spring a leak.

Reroofing consists of applying new shingles over the existing roofing material. This is less expensive and easier than a tear-off job, which requires that the old roofing be striped off and hauled away.

Tear-Off or Reroof?

The first step in determining whether or not to reroof is to check the rake of the roof to find out how many roofing layers there are. (The drip edge sometimes is applied before reroofing and may hide evidence of previous layers.) Once you determine the number of layers, check local roofing codes for the maximum number of roofing layers allowed—the figure will be different depending on the type of roofing and pitch of the roof. For asphalt shingles, codes usually allow the original plus two layers of reroofing.

All rotten boards under the old roofing must be replaced. Go to the attic and examine any suspicious spots, including voids and separating plywood. Check for rot by poking with a screwdriver or awl. If rot is limited to a few places, you need only remove the old roofing and replace the boards in those spots. Where necessary, build up the roof above the replacement sheathing with extra layers of shingles to make a flush surface for the new roof.

Checking Wear

Here are the four progressive stages of shingle wear to look for. First, you may notice the tiny chips embedded in the surface of asphalt shingles, called granules, accumulating in gutters and at downspout outlets. Second, you will see bare black patches of tar appearing as more granules are lost. This is hard to see on a dark roof, even with binoculars, but obvious on shingles with white or gray surface granules. Roofs at this stage probably will not leak—not yet. But in a few years they probably will.

In the third stage, exposed sections of the shingles, called tabs, have lost most of their surface granules and start to become brittle. You have to touch the tabs to detect this condition. Within a few seasons, however, the tabs will start to curl noticeably. Even then, the roof may not leak. But now is a good time to reroof—before the curling becomes excessive, and gets in the way of new shingles. In the fourth stage, brittle shingle tabs crack and break. Bare, black patches that appear as the tabs break off are unmistakable. You also may see nailheads holding down the shingles beneath the broken tabs. At this point, you are likely to have small leaks that may start to rot the wooden roof deck and rafters even if you do not see large water stains on the ceiling. After all, nails put holes in the shingles, and are placed so that they would be covered by those broken tabs.

Preparing for Reroofing

USE: ▶ pry bar • hammer • trowel • utility knife • paint scraper ▶ shingles • roofing nails • flashing

1 *Before roofing over old shingles,* strip a few sections down to the deck to check the decking for water damage.

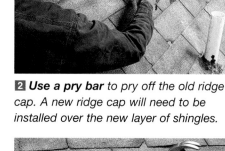

2 *Use a pry bar* to pry off the old ridge cap. A new ridge cap will need to be installed over the new layer of shingles.

3 *The new layer needs a level surface;* broken or bent tabs must be replaced. Cut them away with a sharp utility knife.

4 *Cut a tab from a new shingle,* and nail it in place with two or three roofing nails to fill the space in the existing roof.

5 *Scrape away old roof tar* around plumbing vent stacks to clear the way for a new piece of molded flashing.

6 *Install new flashing* made from molded plastic or metal over the new roofing. The top edge will be shingled.

Installing Double-Layer Roll Roofing

USE: ▶ chalk-line box • broom • hammer • trowel ▶ roofing felt • roofing nails • roofing cement

1 *Snap a chalk line* 35½ in. from the eaves, roll out the first layer on top of the roofing felt, and nail at 12-in. intervals.

2 *After the first layer is installed* (with courses overlapped about 6 in.), spread roofing cement on the first course.

3 *Roll out the first course* of the second layer, nailing it in place every 12 in. with roofing nails.

4 *At course overlaps,* trowel on roof cement. Some roll roofing is designed to overlap up to half the previous layer.

5 *Successive courses* cover the strip of roof cement. Some roll roofing is available with light-colored granules.

6 *Long roofs may need vertical seams.* These should be nailed and cemented like the horizontal laps.

Signs of Deterioration

The signs of shingle wear are easy to spot, and indicate both the degree of decay and the roof's expected life.

1. Loose granules will appear in the gutters while the shingles still look like new.

2. Spottiness of shingles, with bare areas where granules have worn away, indicates the next stage of decay.

3. Shingle tabs will eventually curl at the edges, and become brittle. Roofs at this stage are about to spring leaks.

4. The final stage of a shingle's life span are broken tabs. At this point you need to reroof or install a new roof from scratch.

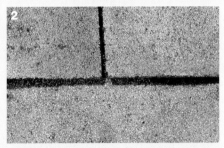

roofing

Roofing with Slate

Perhaps no other roofing material lasts as long as slate. Incredibly, some old churches and homes from America's colonial period still have their original slate roofs. Slate is still in demand for upscale custom homes, churches, and country-club clubhouses, but most new homes today are roofed with asphalt shingles instead, because they are so much cheaper.

Like asphalt shingles, slate comes in many colors, sizes, grades, and weights. Due to its weight—three times that of asphalt—roof rafters and roof sheathing need to be up to code to support slate's heavy load. Slate can be placed over a layer of composition shingles only if the slope of the roof is 4-in-12 or more, and only if a structural engineer has confirmed that the roof framing can bear the weight of 7 pounds per square foot.

Today, only a handful of roofing companies specializing exclusively in slate are in business. Most roofing contractors will do occasional slate roofs. And because it is difficult to cut and apply, slate roofing is not an easy job for the do-it-yourselfer. If you do decide to do

For a longer-lasting roof than slate, how about slabs of rock? Used as early as the eighth century, the type of roof found on this Scandinavian barn will last for centuries rather than decades.

the work, expect to make a considerable investment in time and materials.

Installing Slate

Slate should be installed tilted slightly upward at the eaves, extending ½ inch beyond the rake and 1 inch beyond the eaves. Use a piece of lath to shim the starter course, which is made up of slates set lengthwise.

Slate is often laid on top of one layer of 30-pound roofing felt. Some contractors prefer to use individual felt strips under each course to provide additional cushioning. Two copper or brass nails, installed in predrilled holes, hold each slate. The slates are set so their beveled edges show, with about a ¼-inch gap between slates. The gaps from one course to the next should be offset by at least 2 inches.

To cap each side of the ridge, use slates that are the same width. Alternate the overlap at the peak from one side of the roof to the other. Slates are fastened to the ridge with two nails.

Working Slate

USE: ▶ nail set • hammer • work gloves ▶ slate roofing • scrap wood

1 *To cut a slate roof tile,* first use a nail set to punch a series of holes along your cut line on the back of the tile.

2 *To complete the cut,* place the slate between two pieces of wood at the score line, and tap lightly with a hammer.

3 *Smooth out any rough spots* along the edge with gentle taps from a hammer, supporting the slate as you work.

MATERIALS

◆ **What you'll need.** To work on a slate roof you need three specialized tools: a nail ripper (which is used to cut an old nail flush to the decking surface), a slate hammer (which has a sharp edge for cutting shingles and a point for poking new nailholes), and a T-bar (to use as an edge for trimming shingles).

◆ **Selecting slate.** Slate comes in a variety of colors, from green to gray to red. The colors are generally muted. The material is sold in uniform lengths but varying widths. The thickness may also vary to some degree. A batch of slate sold in one color will also have natural variations. This is considered desirable, and will then create a slightly mottled appearance as opposed to one color.

Slate is applied in an overlapping pattern with staggered seams. You can use one color, or a mix.

Repairing Slate

USE: ▶ nail ripper • hacksaw blade • hammer • screwdriver ▶ new tile • S-hook • scrap wood

1 To remove a cracked slate, hook the nail ripper onto the nail shaft and hammer the ripper to cut the nail.

2 Using a hacksaw blade instead of a ripper, you can reach under a damaged slate to cut the nails.

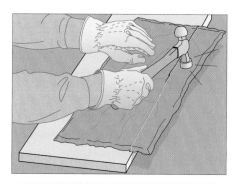

3 To cut the new tile, punch a series of holes in the back of the slate with a nail set, and tap with a hammer.

4 Hammer an S-hook between slates to hold the bottom edge of the replacement slate in position.

5 Insert the new slate where the old slate was removed, gently prying up on the course above to make room.

6 To avoid breaking existing slate as you slide in the new piece, you may need to use a temporary wedge.

Slate Tips

◆ Use solid-copper or brass nails driven through factory-punched holes in each slate.

◆ Practice cutting slates on the ground—it's safer than cutting on the roof. Always wear eye protection.

◆ Rent a wet saw for complicated edge cuts. This will save time and allow for accurate cuts.

◆ Give new slate roofs extra pitch at the eaves. Nail a ¼-inch-thick strip of wood along the eaves so the bottom course turns upwards slightly. This gives the roof a classic appearance and provides drip protection for the fascia.

◆ Slate cannot be nailed over asphalt or other types of roofs and cannot be fastened with pneumatic nail guns. Slate must be nailed firmly but gently, by hand, so nailheads seat without over-stressing and cracking the slate.

◆ Slates with hairline cracks should be discarded; cracks only worsen with exposure to the weather.

roofing

Clay Tile

A clay tile roof is what most people picture when they imagine a house in the American West. An adobe stucco house, designed in the Spanish mission style, would look incomplete with a roof made from anything but naturally colored, terra-cotta, red clay tiles. Like slate, clay tiles are heavy, weighing as much as half a ton per square. If you're considering installing clay tiles, check with a local roofing supply source and your municipal building department to make sure your roof's structure can handle the tiles you choose. Do not tile a roof with a slope flatter than 3-in-12.

Installing Clay Tile

Clay tiles will come with instructions, which will tell you whether or not they require underlayment. Some tiles are nailed directly to sheathing, while others require battens to be laid first. These battens are 1x2 strips of redwood or pressure-treated pine that are spaced at intervals to match the tile exposure. (14 inches is typical.) Further preparations may be called for, such as one 2x2 along all ridges and hips, 1x2 starter strips along eaves and rakes, or 1x3s nailed to rake rafters to allow the tiles to extend further sideways.

Use nails and flashing that will last as long as the tiles—copper is preferred. You should apply a metal drip edge along the eaves before the underlayment is installed. Take special care in the valleys: put down 90-pound mineral-surfaced roll roofing, then W-metal (ridged) flashing at least 2 feet wide. Cover hips and ridges with a double layer of felt.

MATERIALS

- **What you'll need.** Copper flashing and nails are best with clay tiles. To cut tiles, you'll need a circular saw equipped with a masonry blade, and a good pair of safety glasses for eye protection.

- **Special installations.** If your roof has a steep slope of 7-in-12 or more or if you live in an area subject to high winds, fasten every third or fourth course of tiles with metal clips, observing local codes.

Repairing Clay Tile

USE: ▶ pry bar • hammer • wet saw (optional) ▶ new tile • tile clips • scrap wood

1 Wedge up tiles above the damaged course with wood strips, and remove old tile nails with a pry bar.

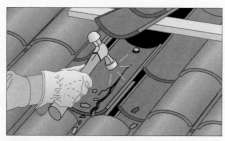

2 Break the old tile with hammer, and remove debris to clear the area for a new clip. Be careful not to hit good tiles.

3 Attach the tile clip to the roof support on one end and to the underside of replacement tile at the other end.

4 New tile should fit in without stressing adjacent tiles. If need be, shave edges with a wet saw.

Concrete Tile

If you want the look of slate or clay but don't have the money to invest in it, you can substitute a cheaper alternative: concrete tile. These roofing tiles—sometimes referred to as synthetic slate or fiber-cement roofing—imitate these looks at a much lower cost while keeping much of their durability. Made from cement on a fiberglass backing, the tiles are light, attractive, and warranted for 40 years. Besides the lower cost, another advantage of concrete tile is its uniformity—you are less likely to get defective tiles or mismatching colors when purchasing synthetic slate. Concrete tile also has an excellent fire rating.

Concrete tiles are manufactured in a number of geometric shapes, rather than all being flat like real slate. This allows for a much greater variety in your design and will give the roof a stylish look that can greatly enhance the value of your home.

Installing Concrete Tile

It is not advisable to put concrete tiles over old asphalt shingles, because the slates will outlast the underlying asphalt. Any potential problems with old roof sheathing, roof rafters, fascia boards, or soffits should be addressed before a house is roofed (or reroofed) with concrete tile.

As with natural slate and clay tile, concrete tiles are installed on clean decking, with freshly laid roof felt if an underlayment is required. (The manufacturer will specify.) Copper flashing is preferable to aluminum, so the flashing does not wear out before the roofing material. Use W-metal flashing in the valleys.

Some tiles are nailed directly to the sheathing, while other ones must be attached to 1x2 wood battens. The strips are then nailed in place at intervals matching the tile exposure, which is usually about 14 inches. Wood strips along the eaves, rakes, ridges, and hips may also be needed.

Repairing Concrete Tile

USE: ▶ hammer • pry bar • pliers ▶ new tile • copper nails • hanger strip

1 Break cracked tile with a hammer, taking care not to break adjacent tiles. Clear out debris to expose the support.

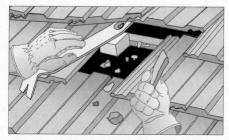

2 Raise the upper course, and set in wedges to provide access to the supporting batten. Clean batten for nailing.

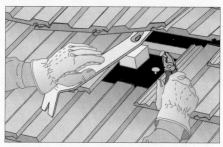

3 Pull any old nails that protrude—they can break new tiles. Repair any openings in the felt with roof cement.

4 Slide a new concrete tile into place under the top course, and clip it into a hanger strip. (See clip detail on p.420.)

MATERIALS

◆ **What you'll need.** Concrete tile is brittle and can be difficult to cut without a wet saw fitted with a masonry blade, a tool you can rent. Wear safety glasses when cutting through masonry material.

◆ **Tile styles.** Concrete tiles are made in the classic barrel shape of Spanish clay tile, in curved S-shapes, and interlocking flat tiles that resemble slate shakes (above).

roofing

Wood Shingles

Wood shingles and shakes usually are made from western red cedar, a long-lasting, straight-grained wood. The grain is what gives this wood surprising strength, whether it's cut thick or thin. Straight-grain wood generally does an excellent job of shedding water, even after years of weathering. Shakes and shingles also resist heat transmission twice as well as composition shingles.

However, wood shingles require more maintenance than other roofing options, especially if you live in a region with a harsh climate. In such areas it is advisable to treat the roof with a preservative every 5 years or so. Regular cleaning is also recommended to clear away the debris that traps moisture and, in turn, breeds fungus, mildew, rot, and insect borers.

Wood shingles are not fire-resistant; some local codes may require that wood roofing be pressure-treated or installed over fire-retardant plywood. Some localities have banned wood roofing altogether; check with your local codes before proceeding. (You might also want to check with your home insurance company to see if your premiums will be affected.)

Shingles or Shakes?

Shingles are thinner than shakes and are sawn smooth on both sides. Shakes are often split by hand and have an irregular surface. They are thicker and therefore more durable than shingles, which last no more than 20 to 25 years. Shakes are either taper split (which are split on both sides) or hand split and resawn (which have one split and one sawn face). There are also straight-split shakes, which do not taper and are not intended for residential use.

Both shakes and shingles are available in number 1, 2, and 3 grades. Grade 1 is cut from heartwood, and is both knot-free and more resistant to rot than the other two grades. Grade 2 has a limited amount of sapwood; grade 3 shakes, knotty and mostly sapwood, should be used only for outbuildings.

Shingle length is determined by the desired exposure (the length of the shingle exposed to the weather). Exposure is determined by pitch: shingle widths vary from 3 to 9 inches. One advantage of shingles is that you can add a new layer of shingles over an old one.

Installing Wood Roofing

USE: ▶ hammer • carpenter's pencil • spacing jig • staple gun ▶ roofing nails • heavy-duty staples • skip

1 *Wood roofing* can be applied over rafters and horizontal skip sheathing.

2 *Today, most wood roofing* is applied over decking and a layer of roofing felt.

5 *The starter course* should be two shingles thick and overlap eaves by 1 in.

6 *When the roof* butts against a second story, install step flashing at the joint.

MATERIALS

◆ **What you'll need.** To install or repair wood shingles, you can use the same basic tools used on asphalt roofs. The main difference is that asphalt is trimmed with a utility knife, while wood shingles are either sawn or split. Many pros use special hammers with a hatchet on the end instead of a standard nail-pulling claw. If you're not used to this tool, it's safer to use a standard hammer.

◆ **Shingle sizes.** Shingle widths vary from 3 to 9 inches. There are numerous grades and surface finishes, ranging from thin shingles with a smooth surface to thick shingles that are hand split.

sheathing or roofing felt (over decking) • plastic mesh • drip edge • step flashing • shingles or shakes

3 *Over sheathing and felt paper,* apply plastic mesh to provide air circulation.

4 *Nail on drip edge* along the rakes and eaves before installing the starter course.

7 *Keep about ¼-in. of space* between shakes by holding a pencil between them.

8 *Keep the exposure consistent* by using a homemade spacing jig (see p. 441).

Exposure & Pitch

In order to install shingles and shakes, the roof must have a steep enough slope. Unlike composition shingles or roll roofing, voids remain between courses of wood shingles and shakes. With enough pitch for quick runoff, this poses no problem, but when installed on a low-slope roof, the roofing is not protected from windblown rain and snow. Wood shingles are not recommended for roofs with less than a 3-in-12 slope. Shakes are not recommended for roofs with a slope of less than 4-in-12. Exposure must also be limited for slight pitches. With a 3-in-12 slope, 16-inch shingles must have a maximum 3¾-inch exposure (5 inches on a 4-in-12 slope). Eighteen-inch shingles may be exposed a maximum of 4¼ inches (5½ inches on a 4-in-12 slope). Shingles that are 24 inches long can have the greatest exposure: 5¾ inches on a 3-in-12 slope roof and 7½ inches on a 4-in-12 slope.

Repairing Shingles & Shakes

USE: ▶ wood chisel • hacksaw blade or nail ripper • hammer ▶ roofing cement • nails

1 **To replace damaged shingles and shakes,** remove the damaged piece by first splitting it with a wood chisel. **2** Then wedge up the upper course, and cut the nails with a hacksaw blade or nail ripper. **3** Finally, after trimming the edges of a new shingle or shake to size, nail it in place, and cover exposed nailheads with roof cement.

roofing

Metal Roofing

The look of corrugated metal covering a Quonset hut at an army barracks is still most people's idea of a metal roof, and few would consider that suitable for their home. Recent advances in sheet metal, however, have turned the metal roof into an attractive option for certain types of homes. It costs as much as three times more than composite shingles but can last up to 50 years with almost no maintenance—a longevity surpassed only by slate and tile. Unlike the old galvanized tin roofs, metal roofing today is made of steel with a coating of aluminum or a durable polymer.

Metal Roof Options

Many different profiles are available, but simple standing-seam metal roofing (where overlapping ridges run parallel to the eaves) is the most appropriate for older homes that might have had a tin roof at one time. Standing-seam panels, being a light material (just one pound per square foot), may even be used over three layers of composition shingles (local building codes permitting). For roofs that have irregularities, narrow, textured, and dull-finish panels work best. Metal roofing (even individual shingles) can also cover low-pitched roofs that have a slope of at least 3-in-12; some metal roof systems can handle slopes as slight as ¼-in-12 (usually a job for built-up roofing).

The installation process involves laying 12- to 16 ½-inch-wide panels and joining them at the seams, wall flashing, valleys, and ridges. The panels are precut to the exact length ordered, up to 40 feet long—for this reason, horizontal seams are unlikely on most homes. Metal roofing can be applied over plywood decking with an underlayment of 30-pound felt. Laying and joining the panels is not difficult, but handling eaves edges, rakes, and ridges can be. Most metal roofing manufacturers will provide an installation guide.

Care should also be taken not to walk on the metal roof, as dents, scratches, and depressions can easily occur. Be sure to replace all copper, lead, and other metal roof fittings, which might corrode the metal panels. Metal roofs should also be grounded with lightening rods in the event of an electrical storm.

Standing Seam

Standing-seam metal panels are one of the most expensive ways to cover a roof, but also one of the longest-lasting applications. Panels run vertically up the roof slope and interlock at the seams. They are made from aluminum or galvanized steel and are available in a variety of finishes, including a wide array of factory-applied paints. Panels can be flat or ribbed between seams, and ordered in lengths up to 40 feet.

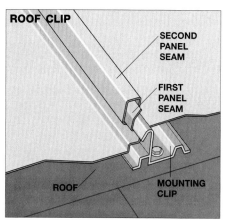

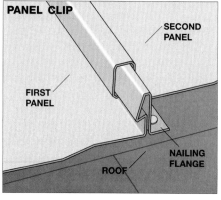

Painted metal roof panels can lace into flashing to shed water at roof openings.

MATERIALS

◆ Most metal roofing systems are installed by contractors. They fasten mounting clips to the roof over felt paper and attach the panels to the clips. Some panel seams are not preformed but joined on site where contractors use a special machine that travels on wheels down the roof one seam at a time, folding the sections together. The simplest systems for do-it-yourselfers to handle has panels without mounting clips. Instead, each panel has a nailing flange that is fastened directly to the roof. Successive panels simply snap down onto this seam on one side, and fasten with nails on the other as you work across the roof.

Two Ways to Repair Metal Roofs

USE: ▶ shears • wire brush • soldering gun • flat knife ▶ patch material • flux or roofing cement

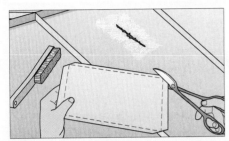

1 Cut a metal patch piece from the same metal as the roof, and nip off the raised edges. Wire brush the repair area.

2 Weight the patch in place; then apply flux and heat to make a solder bond around the edge of the patch.

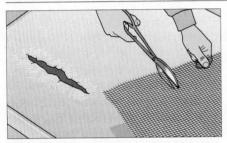

1 Aluminum roofs cannot be soldered. Instead, cut a patch of roofing mesh, and set it in a bed of roof cement.

2 Cover the mesh patch with a second coat of roof cement. Work it through the mesh to join with the undercoat.

Metal Edging

In regions with a lot of snow, consider this variation on standing-seam roofs. Instead of covering the entire surface, only the first few courses of shingles along the eaves are clad in metal. The idea is to encourage snow to slide off the roof instead of building up in ice dams at the roof overhangs.

The bargain-basement version of this installation is simply a long roll of sheet metal (aluminum flashing material) rolled onto the roof and tucked under a course of shingles. The drawback is that the sheet metal has to be face-nailed, which creates leak-prone holes.

Corrugated Panels

METAL PANELS

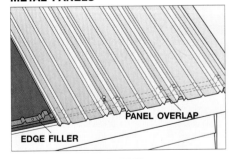

PANEL OVERLAP

EDGE FILLER

SEALING PANEL SEAMS

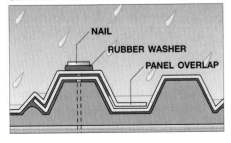

NAIL

RUBBER WASHER

PANEL OVERLAP

Corrugated aluminum and galvanized steel panels (the kind of roofing you might see on barns), are long-lasting solutions for utility buildings. Corrugated panels made of plastic or fiberglass can provide a watertight yet translucent covering for decks, carports, and greenhouses. Panels of both types are typically sold along with manufacturer-specific nails, filler strips, and caulk. The filler strips fit the contours of the panel, and are installed along the eaves. The nails are compatible with the metal (aluminum or steel). Because these panels do not interlock like standing-seam panels, they have to be face-nailed. To prevent leaks at the nailholes, every nail is set with a rubberized washer. The trick is to set nails just firmly enough to seat the washer without deforming it and causing a leak.

PLASTIC PANELS

Translucent corrugated panels can let light into breezeways and decks but keep out most of the rain. At least one curve of the corrugation along the edge of a panel is covered by the next panel in line to prevent leaks at seams.

roofing

Skylights

The extra natural light flooding through a skylight can dramatically change the look of a room, which is one reason why adding a skylight is such a popular home-improvement project. Another reason is that it is fairly easy to do, although the job does involve cutting a hole in your roof. Skylights can be easily added to rooms of a one-story house or on the top floor of a multi-story house. It's a simple matter of mounting the skylight on the roof and building a short light shaft to the room. Where an attic has been converted to a living space, the job is even easier—you don't need the light shaft. (A skylight or two might also eliminate the need for dormers.)

Types of Skylights

As long as you are going to cut that hole in your roof, you might as well pay the extra money for what's called an operator skylight (the industry's way of saying it opens). The added fresh air, as well as the light, is welcome in most kitchens.

Aside from inexpensive all-plastic bubbles, most quality skylights have a glazed section attached by the manufacturer to a frame that raises the glazing several inches above the roof. There are two basic types of operator skylights: bubbles, which are hinged on the high side and open a few inches at the bottom, and roof windows, which are flat frames that pivot about halfway up the frame. In both cases the entire assembly, frame included, is installed in the roof. In addition to being cheaper, clear-bubble skylights expand and contract with changes in temperature. That motion stresses the site-built seam between the roof and the bubble, even if the installer sets the bubble on some type of frame added to the roof. For skylights with an integral frame, the manufacturer takes into account movement at the critical seam between glazing and frame.

Installation

No matter which type you use, the installation consists of attaching the frame of the skylight to the roof. Both fixed and operator frame-mounted skylights should install in approximately the same amount of time and require the same amount of maintenance.

Installing a Skylight

USE: ▶ framing square • pencil • measuring tape • hammer • circular or saber saw • skylight • T-bevel

1 *Lay out openings* for the skylight and its light shaft between rafters and joists.

2 *Drive nails* from the inside to mark the corners of the opening in the roof.

5 *Cut the center rafter,* and install same-dimension headers to pick up its roof load.

6 *The opening in the ceiling* requires similar headers where joists are cut.

Design Options

Skylights in cathedral ceilings (above) offer direct exposure. The section view of a roof and ceiling (right) shows how a light shaft can be angled on both ends to allow for maximum light entry.

▶ 12d and 16d nails • 2x4s • 2x6s • drywall • drywall screws or nails • joint compound • drywall tape

3 *Reinforce the framing* with 2x4s across the rafters before cutting the opening.

4 *Strip roof shingles,* and peel back felt paper to cut the plywood sheathing.

7 *Frame the light shaft with 2x4s* running between the rafters and joists.

8 *With the skylight in place,* finish the light shaft surfaces with drywall.

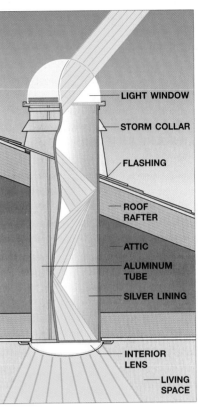

LIGHT WINDOW

STORM COLLAR

FLASHING

ROOF RAFTER

ATTIC

ALUMINUM TUBE

SILVER LINING

INTERIOR LENS

LIVING SPACE

A solar tube makes only a small opening in the roof and the ceiling, and reflects light down its shaft.

Skylight windows (above) can be opened manually or electronically. Some models have fold-out sections (right), so you can stand outside the roof surface.

Solar tubes concentrate natural light that radiates into the room below through a diffuser.

roofing

Flashing

One of the most vital parts of any roof is largely invisible—the flashing. Its function is to provide a watertight seal at points where the covering on the roof is interrupted by chimneys, plumbing vents, air vents, and skylights. Without flashing, a roof would leak around all these edges.

Flashing is made from sheet metal, usually copper or aluminum. It can also be made from flat roll-roofing material and plastic. Copper is the most expensive flashing material, but it also lasts the longest. Roll-roofing flashing lasts the shortest time—about 10 to 15 years. If you're investing in a long-term roof of slate, concrete tile, or clay tile, you should use copper flashing.

If your roof has a leak, check the flashing points first. Sometimes it's only a matter of corroded or punctured flashing that needs nothing more than a coat of roofing cement.

Types of Flashing

Chimney flashing is the most complicated of roof flashing jobs because it involves at least three types of flashing: base, step, and counterflashing. Counterflashing is tucked into the mortar joints between layers of brick. The function of counterflashing is to keep water away from the point where step flashing meets with the chimney. Sometimes the freezing and thawing of ice loosens this flashing, which must then be recemented in place.

Other flashing sections that need periodic checking and occasional minor maintenance are valley flashing and sidewall junctures. Check for punctures and corrosion, and repair them with roof tar.

Installing Step Flashing

USE: ▶ metal snips • rubber mallet • vise • hammer ▶ step flashing • shingles • roofing nails

1 Cut flashing from rolls of aluminum into squares with shears or metal snips.

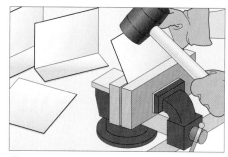

2 To bend flashing, place it between boards, and tap it with a rubber mallet.

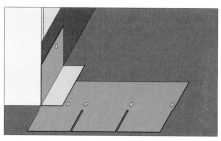

3 The first piece of flashing is laid on top of a course of shingles.

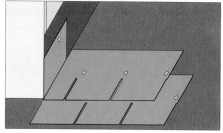

4 The next course of shingles is laid over the flashing, covering its lower half.

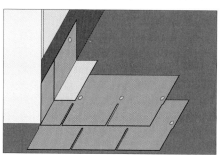

5 The second piece overlaps the first, with the same exposure as the shingles.

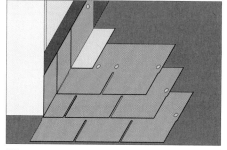

6 Shingle courses are staggered to keep their seams from aligning.

Valleys

Woven valleys don't have any exposed flashing. They use interlaced shingles from both sides of the valley to keep water from penetrating.

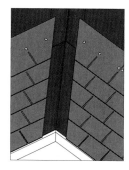

Open valleys have shingles that are trimmed back on both edges of a metal channel. Extra protection is provided by a wide strip of roll roofing beneath the metal.

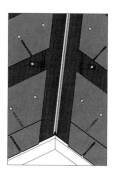

W-flashing, held to the deck with nailed clips, has a center ridge to keep water from flowing sideways and bent-up edges that prevent water from flowing under the shingles.

flashing

Flashing & Counterflashing

Base flashing seals the roof seams, and a cover piece seals the flashing.

The covering pieces, called counterflashing, are sealed into mortared joints.

Even on low-slope roofs, flashing has a bend to deflect water past the chimney.

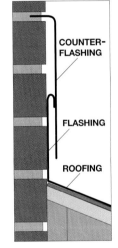

COUNTER-FLASHING

FLASHING

ROOFING

Counterflashing is installed over flashing to further protect chimney joints. The top lip of the counterflashing is inserted into a mortar joint and secured with mortar. It should overlap the base flashing by at least 4 in.

Pipes & Vents

Vents are best sealed with formed flashing. A rubber collar seals the pipe.

Hoods are flashed similar to vents, with upper and side edges under the shingles.

Flashing Repairs

USE: ▶ chisel • brush • jointing tool
▶ brick mortar • new flashing if needed

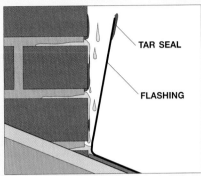

TAR SEAL

FLASHING

1 Chimney counterflashing sealed only with tar will eventually break away from the masonry. Then water seeps behind it, into the roof.

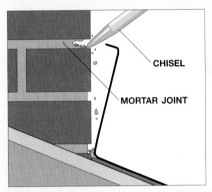

CHISEL

MORTAR JOINT

2 To repair leaks, chip out mortar from the joint between bricks, and fold the flashing into the seam.

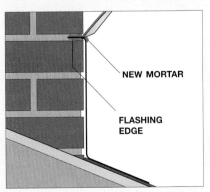

NEW MORTAR

FLASHING EDGE

3 Brush out the old mortar, tuck the flashing into the space in the joint, and secure it by filling the seam with fresh mortar.

roofing/flashing   429

roofing

Winter Problems

When snow, ice, and freezing rain land on the roof where you live, chances are the coat of frozen stuff will last a while, melting and refreezing several times before finally disappearing. This is not a problem unless your roof overhangs freeze solid, creating an ice dam, which can push water underneath the shingles and cause leaks.

If you can get at the roof edge safely, break off icicles before they become heavy enough to dislodge the gutter. Some homeowners attack ice-choked gutters with a hair dryer or pour hot water in gutters and downspouts to hasten melting. Start at the critical joint between gutter and downspout. Once this area is clear, melting ice will have a drainage channel as you work backward along the rest of the gutter.

Preventing Ice Dams

There are several possible solutions to ice-dam problems. Working from the outside, you can install a strip of sheet metal over the shingles covering the overhang. This method is fairly common in the rural Northeast—it is most effective on steeply sloped roofs, where gravity and the slick metal surface encourage ice and snow to slide off the roof.

Another approach is to install heat cables in a zigzag pattern along the shingles on the overhang. The resistance wiring, which looks like a long extension cord, is attached with small clips tucked under the shingles and even can be

Ice Dams

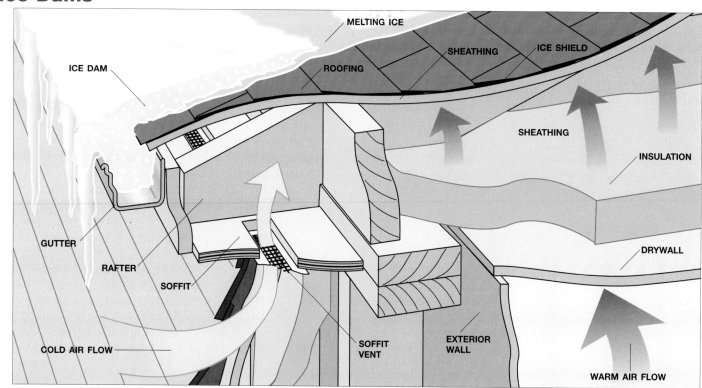

To install an ice shield, peel the paper backing on the rubberized sheet.

How Ice Dams Form

Ice dams form as snow on the roof melts and then refreezes along the eaves. Even in houses with insulation in the ceilings, enough heat can rise through the blankets or batts to gradually warm the bottom of the roof over the attic. In the right conditions, the heat causes the snow blanket to melt from the bottom up, and water trickles down toward the gutter. It may be cold outside, but the trickle is protected from freezing by the snow above. However, when the melted water reaches the roof overhang, there is no longer a heat source from below because the overhang is outside the exterior wall. That's where the water begins to freeze. It forms a dam, and the water above can back up under shingles.

extended into gutters to help them remain unfrozen. These cables are designed to produce enough heat to prevent freeze-ups.

Because warmth rising through the ceiling or attic is often the cause of ice dams, you can also alleviate the problem by working from the inside to reduce the heat flow with extra insulation. In a typically constructed wood frame attic floor, for instance, the spaces between floor joists should be filled with insulation. An additional layer, even the 3½-inch batting used in walls, can be set on top of and perpendicular to the joists for more protection. At the same time you can increase the vent size in the attic or crack a window at each end. This will make the bottom of the roof colder and closer to the temperature outdoors, which will prevent melting, while the extra insulation will retard heat flow from living spaces below.

On new construction jobs or reroofing projects, consider installing a rubberized ice shield membrane on the roof deck. It should cover the overhang and at least a few courses of shingles over living space. This provides a backup barrier just in case an ice dam does form and works under the shingles.

Usually, these membranes are made of waterproof, rubberized asphalt and polyethylene in self-adhering sheets that bond directly to the roof deck and to each other at overlaps. The material is installed beneath the shingles, and it seals itself around punctures from nails protruding through the shingles above.

Ice Control

There are many ways to keep ice from forming on roofs and in gutters where it can leak and damage shingles and flashing:

◆ Draw enough outside air through the attic so that heat rising through insulation in the ceiling of your living space will be diluted and carried away before it can warm the roof and melt snow. You can ventilate with plug vents, strip-grille vents, or perforated panels in the roof overhang. (See "Ventilation," pp. 384–385.)

◆ Where ceiling insulation extends toward the overhang, cut it back at the exterior wall, and make sure that it does not block vents.

◆ Keep gutters and leaders clear of debris and free-draining so any melting water won't be trapped.

◆ Install a rubberized barrier under shingles on the overhang. (See photo at left.) This self-sealing membrane closes around nail shanks driven through shingles and protects the overhang from water that may back up and seep through the overlapped courses.

Temperature Extremes

The best policy is to stay off the roof during any period of extreme temperature. But the weather won't always cooperate when you need to make repairs. When the weather is hot, bear in mind that asphalt shingles become soft. You are more likely to slip and to dislodge surface granules. Also remember that working in extreme heat taxes you as well as the roof. You should be exceptionally careful—work only in shoes with non-slip soles, and only from a safe position. Protect yourself further by wearing a hat, drinking a lot of water, and taking regular breaks. In extreme cold, even with only a few scattered patches of ice and snow, the roof surface may be so treacherous that you should call in a professional. If you must make emergency repairs, use a trowel or drywall knife to spread roof cement under and over shingles in the leaking area. If you want to clear ice-filled and icicle-laden gutters (which can be surprisingly heavy), start work at the corner of the house out from under the main gutter. Some homeowners try a hair dryer or a propane torch, which might clear a relatively small frozen bottleneck. Electric heat cables that can prevent freeze-ups in leaders and gutters should be used with extreme caution. Use only UL-approved units installed exactly to manufacturer's specifications.

When it's very hot outside, the best policy is to work on the roof either early or late in the day. Under midday sun, asphalt shingles soften and mar easily.

When it's very cold outside, let cap shingles warm up inside, and bend slowly into shape. Bending them outside can cause cracks that lead to leaks.

roofing

Maintaining Gutters

Many old roofs have no trouble shedding water—as long as the water continues to flow off it. The trouble starts when it backs up in the gutters and drains. Leaves, twigs, animal nests, and other debris can block drain outlets, clog gutters and downspouts, and stop up underground drains that take water away from the building where it won't cause any damage.

There are many products designed to prevent blockages, such as wire baskets and gutter screens. In theory, wet leaves are supposed to pile up on them, then dry out and blow away, leaving a clear path for drainage. In reality, the screens and guards often clog themselves, particularly on flat and low-slope roofs. So instead of cleaning out the gutters, you have to clean off the gutter guards: same dreary job; slightly different location.

You may have seen advertisements for a supposedly clog-proof gutter, basically a strip of louvers. It simply breaks the flow into a series of small streams that drop off the edge of the roof, including down your neck while you're fumbling for the door key. They don't clog like a gutter because the louvers don't collect water like a gutter. They aren't really gutters at all.

Blocked Downspouts

If water collects in a cleaned-out gutter instead of draining freely or you hear dripping in the downspout, some debris may have gotten hung up at one of the fittings. The most likely bottleneck is the S-shaped piece of pipe that carries water from gutters at the edge of the roof overhang and curves back toward the house wall to a downspout.

Most downspout systems have enough play that you can take them apart to get at a clog. Some are simply pressure-fitted together; some are joined with small sheet-metal screws you have to remove. But try flushing the debris out with a garden hose first. If you are lucky, you will be able to clear the blockage without taking the pipes apart.

Spikes and ferrules *are the standard hanging system. The ferrule (a tube around the spike) prevents crimping.*

Brackets *nail into the fascia board and clip into the gutter edge. Space brackets about 3 feet apart.*

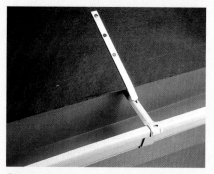

Straps *wrap around the gutter and are nailed to the roof deck under the first course of shingles.*

System Assembly

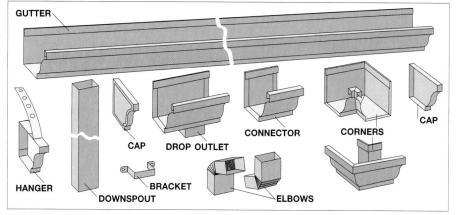

GUTTER

HANGER

CAP · DROP OUTLET

DOWNSPOUT · BRACKET

CONNECTOR · CORNERS · CAP

ELBOWS

Metal and vinyl gutter hardware includes a full line of fittings. In addition to U-shaped gutters (and end caps), there are inside and outside corner pieces, connectors to link sections of gutters, drop outlets, downspout pipes, and a variety of brackets and hangers that hold the system to the house.

Slope

Gutters should slope about 1 in. for every 10 lin. ft.—more for better drainage. Place downspouts every 35 ft.

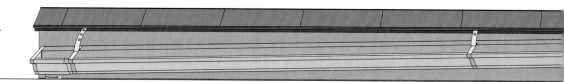

Gutter Cleaners

Keeping gutters clean will help to prevent backups and leaks in bad weather. Clean gutters in the fall after all the leaves have fallen, and in the spring. Start by pulling out all debris by hand; then flush the entire system with water from a garden hose.

A wire basket that rests in the gutter over the downspout opening will keep debris out of the pipe.

Screens that cover the entire gutter are designed to trap wet debris where it can dry and blow away.

Some systems replace standard gutters with louvers that disperse the flow onto the ground.

Repairing Gutters

USE: ▶ wire brush • power drill • pop-rivet gun ▶ patch • rivets • caulk

1 *Use a wire brush* around the hole to clean and scuff the metal. Cut a patch from the same metal as the gutter.

2 *Set the patch piece in position,* and drill pilot holes for pop rivets through the patch and the gutter.

3 *Caulk the area* covered by the patch and the back of the patch with silicone, and press the patch into place.

4 *Secure the patch* with pop rivets. Install as many as you need to make the caulk ooze out on all sides.

Downspout Extenders

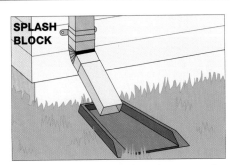

SPLASH BLOCK

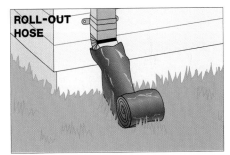

ROLL-OUT HOSE

Splash blocks are designed to prevent water leaving the downspout from draining directly down along the foundation wall. Some innovative fixtures, such as a roll-out hose, extend to carry off water during heavy rains, then coil up again, out of the way.

siding 23

siding

Siding Choices

Siding problems usually can be fixed by making spot repairs—such as replacing a rotted clapboard or cutting out a cracked piece of vinyl siding. But when it comes to completely re-siding the house, you'll have to decide whether to use vinyl, aluminum, wood, or masonry veneer. Every material has its proponents, but it's important to remember that the siding you finally pick will change the look of your home for years to come and may require alterations in trim details that can loom as large as the re-siding job itself.

Many people think vinyl siding looks synthetic, even when it is embossed with a simulated wood grain. But vinyl is usually the least expensive option because it is so easy to install. Aluminum siding tends to look more like painted wood clapboards, but the patter of rainfall takes on a metallic tone and a wayward baseball can leave a dent—a repair you should need to make on cars but not houses.

Wood siding looks like wood, and for many homeowners holds a special appeal. But it needs regular repainting or restaining—a big job that has convinced a lot of people to switch from wood to vinyl or aluminum.

Getting to the Top

Tackling siding jobs means spending time on ladders and scaffolds, so it's worth going over some basic safety tips. For starters, you need a Type I extension ladder, rated to carry up to 250 pounds per rung. Set the ladder's bottom feet far enough out from the wall so that it won't tip backward, but not too far out—about a quarter of the ladder height is a good rule of thumb. Put pieces of wood under the feet if the ground is soft or uneven. When you're on the ladder, wear shoes or boots with heels for the best grip, and don't overreach—leaning over to the side can tip a ladder.

For more ambitious siding jobs that cover more than one story, you'll want to use scaffolding. You can rent ladder jacks that hold a scaffold plank, pump jacks that rise vertically, or pipe scaffolding equipment. Pipe systems provide the most stable work surface, but it takes time to set up the pipe framework and wooden decks. Scaffolding higher than 12 feet should be anchored to the wall for stability.

House Wraps

Building wrap, or house wrap, is an improvement on the felt paper that was once commonly installed over wood sheathing. It is designed to be a one-way material, somewhat like the fabric used on rainwear and parkas, called Gore-Tex. It is woven tightly enough to prevent air infiltration, which improves energy efficiency and comfort by cutting drafts at leak-prone seams in corners and around windows and doors. But the fabric will allow interior moisture to escape, something that tar paper does not do. This is an important distinction, because if interior moisture is trapped in the wall, it can soak insulation, reducing its thermal value and causing rot in the plywood sheathing and framing.

Lightweight house wrap is easily installed with staples. Run wide rolls horizontally to cover one story at a time, with edges tucked into the openings.

Scaffolding

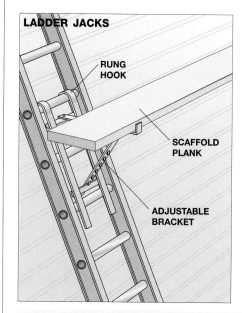

LADDER JACKS

RUNG HOOK

SCAFFOLD PLANK

ADJUSTABLE BRACKET

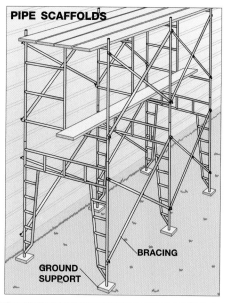

PIPE SCAFFOLDS

BRACING

GROUND SUPPORT

If you have two ladders, the most economical and versatile scaffolding is an adjustable ladder jack for each one and a scaffold plank. Scaffolding made of interconnected pipe sections can stack on each other as work proceeds.

Materials

Wood shingles and shakes

Siding in these small sections is easy to work with because the joints don't fit tightly like cabinetwork, and the layout does not have to be precise. The main drawback is that the installation is labor-intensive, which can drive up a contractor's price. But repair is easy—split damaged shingles into small pieces for removal, and weave replacement shakes into the wall so there is no noticeable line around the repair.

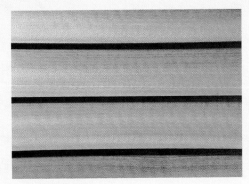

Wood boards

Solid wood siding can be installed vertically, horizontally, and even on an angle. Cost ranges from moderate to very expensive, depending, of course, on the wood species you use. Although wood siding will need periodic restaining or repainting, it's difficult to match its natural beauty. Stagger joints by at least one stud course to course and when you make repairs. Cut out a damaged section between studs, and conceal the new piece with paint or stain.

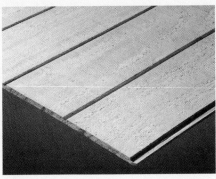

Panels

Panel siding can be made from hardboard or plywood. It's usually less expensive than other types of siding and easy to install (at least on the first floor) because each sheet covers so much area. Some panels are made to resemble materials ranging from shingles to stucco, while others are available in a variety of finishes, including smooth surfaced, rough-sawn, and with grooves every 4 or 8 in. to resemble planks.

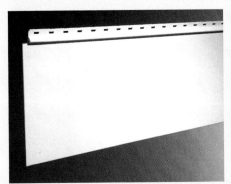

Aluminum

Aluminum siding is moderately expensive and somewhat difficult to install. It is a lot stiffer than vinyl, the number-one choice today, but any scratches that expose base metal through the finish are noticeable. Metal also dents, a problem that generally requires replacement instead of repair. But from a distance, aluminum looks more like painted wood clapboards than many vinyl products, and unlike wood does not need repainting every few years.

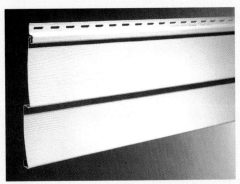

Vinyl

Vinyl siding is typically less expensive than aluminum or wood, is easy to install, and requires little to no maintenance. The trade-off can be a synthetic look and a plastic-like shine in the sun, even when the vinyl is embossed with a wood-grain finish. Vinyl siding is more likely than aluminum to fade in sunlight or crack in cold weather. But damaged vinyl can be patched; you have to unlock the interconnected pieces and make a visible lap joint where the replacement meets undamaged material.

Brick and stone

Brick and stone facing materials are both beautiful and durable, but they cost more than other siding materials, mainly because of the time and skills needed for installation. Standard sizes of bricks are easier to install than irregular stone. Arranging an attractive and functional collection of rocks borders on being an art and requires difficult cutting and shaping. But modern face stone—cast masonry that is colored and textured to look like rocks—makes the job easier.

siding

Panel Advantages

Because labor accounts for so much of the final bill in a re-siding job, plywood panels can be an attractive, cost-saving alternative. Typically, just two workers can panel an average-size house in about a weekend, and the skill needed is within the range of many DIYers. Also, panels are often available in 4x9- and 4x10-foot sheets that reach from foundation to roof edge.

Many lumberyards carry one of the most popular plywood panels, called Texture 1-11. These sheets have grooves cut into the face 4, 8, or 12 inches apart to simulate separate planks. But many other styles and surface treatments are available, although not all plywood can be used for siding—only sheets rated for exterior use, assembled with special glue that can withstand the exposure.

While the panel surface will be coated with stain or paint for appearance and protection against the weather, panel edges often are not coated. They are the weak links, because layers of thin plywood laminations are exposed along the edges. If they soak up water, the panel is likely to delaminate, which can pop nails and create an array of repair problems. You can protect against this deterioration by brushing a primer coat on the edges prior to installation or by concealing the edges with trim, such as vertical corner boards. It's also important to caulk or flash seams around windows and doors, and on two-story projects where one sheet rests on top of another.

Sample Materials

Surfaced panels come in a variety of styles. The final appearance is mainly a product of the wood species, of course, but also depends on how the wood is sawn. The surface texture can be smooth, rough-sawn, striated, or brushed. These panels are often stained or covered with clear sealer for a rustic look, and their mating edges are covered with trim.

Composite panels are made of engineered materials, often including sawdust, wood chips, and other parts of the tree that used to be considered waste. Without a natural grain that could twist one way or another, the panels are stable. Many manufacturers sell either solid-wood or engineered trim pieces matched to the panels to finish off the job.

Grooved panels offer a variety of looks, depending on the groove profile. A wide spacing between grooves generally looks best on a big wall, while narrower spacing fits the scale on smaller surfaces and smaller houses. These panels are built to join in a lap at the last groove with a thin edge of one panel crossing over the other panel so seams aren't noticeable.

Board and batten panels have a wide, flat groove cut at regular intervals along the length. This configuration is designed to resemble a twist on the typical board-and-batten design, called a reverse batten, where a narrow board is set behind the simulated planks. In traditional board-and-batten siding, plank seams are covered by narrow boards.

Installing Panels

USE: ▶ circular saw or saber saw • sawhorses • ladder • power drill/driver • combination square • 4-ft. level • hammer • C-clamps • plumb bob • work gloves

1 *Establish a level line* on the foundation, and nail a 2x4 ledger in place to support the panels.

2 *Starting at a corner,* make sure the sheet is plumb, and nail into studs using fasteners specified by the manufacturer.

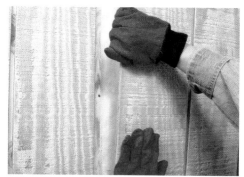

3 *On panels with built-in laps,* tack the edge of the last panel; then install the next sheet, and nail through the lapped section.

Trim

Panels can be joined edge to edge on an uninterrupted surface and mitered at corners. But the most-efficient installations use trim to frame the house and all openings in the walls, and siding panels to fill the spaces closed in by the trim. This plan will conceal plywood edge grain, giving the job a more finished look. Most panel manufacturers produce trim to match their siding materials. Some offer trim made of composites bonded together with plastic resins. Composite trim is typically less expensive than solid wood and less likely to warp and twist.

Choose trim pieces to suit the style of the house and siding. Plan the installation to minimize cutting and maximize the coverage of the panels—for example, by using trim between stories on high walls.

Install ornamental base trim before the siding panels. Outside corner trim is often made by butting together two 1x4s. You also can use one board or a piece of cove molding to trim an inside corner. Windows and doors can also be trimmed, but most often exterior casing is used. Drip-cap trim and flashing over windows and doors keep water from getting under the siding.

Panel Laps

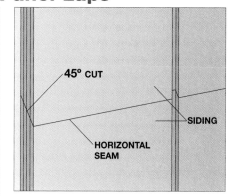

On horizontal joints between sheets of siding on two-story jobs, there are two good ways to protect the seams from the weather. One is to cut 45-degree angles along the mating edges and install them with a bead of caulk. Water would have to run uphill to get behind the siding. The other method calls for a piece of Z-flashing tucked up behind the top panel and extended onto the face of the bottom panel. No 45-degree cuts are needed, but you will see the flashing.

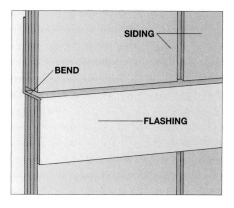

▶ building wrap • plywood siding panels • 2x4 ledger boards • Z-flashing • corner boards • galvanized nails • screws

4 **To install corner boards over panels,** *mount the first one flush and the second one lapping the first, covering its edge.*

5 **To accommodate protrusions,** *measure out from the corner and up from the level base line to mark your cutout.*

6 **You can create** *double corner boards at inside corners, too, or conceal the plywood seam with molding.*

siding

Plank Siding

Clapboard or plank siding is well suited to a wide range of architectural styles. Real wood offers flexibility and an attractive look—so much so that there are many imitations available in vinyl, aluminum, and other synthetics. The biggest disadvantage of wood siding is that it must be repainted about every 7 years or restained every 3 to 5 years, depending on conditions at your site.

Cedar and redwood are preferred woods for siding, but Douglas fir, larch, ponderosa pine, and local species are also used. You will pay more for cedar and redwood, but these two are naturally more resistant to decay than most other woods and are available in prime-quality grades that look good enough to protect with a clear sealer, instead of coats of paint or stain.

Like panel siding, plank siding can also be made of hardboard. It's cheaper than solid wood but less durable. You also must be careful during installation to prevent damaging moisture from getting in. Hardboard plank siding is generally available in two forms. One has splines that hook over the course below and allows blind nailing. The other is rabbeted along the bottom edge.

Level & Plumb

Though plank siding usually is installed horizontally, it can be applied vertically or diagonally as well. For a good-looking, professional-quality job, horizontal siding must be level, and vertical installations must be plumb.

The layout of the first board is critical, as this board is the base for all successive rows. Even a slight error in measurement during the early stages can lead to noticeable problems after several courses. To keep the installation on track, double-check horizontal installations after every fourth or fifth course—or more often if you haven't installed siding before. Don't measure from course to course, but go all the way back to the first one. After measuring the vertical spacing at the corners, snap a chalk line at the point where the top of the next piece will be installed.

If you find that boards are beginning to run out of level (or plumb on vertical installations), make several small adjustments in the next few courses instead of one big fix that stands out.

Material Options

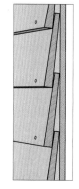

Plain bevel (clapboard) siding is used for horizontal applications. It comes in clear and knotty grades for a more rustic look. The boards are thick along the bottom and taper toward the top.

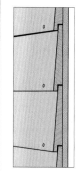

Rabbeted bevel siding (Dolly Varden) is used only in horizontal installations. It is thicker than beveled siding and has a rabbeted overlap. It comes with a smooth or saw-textured face.

Shiplap siding provides the weatherproof security of a lap, and a decorative bend that looks like quarter-round molding below each seam. Overlaps can absorb movement of the house frame without opening.

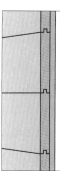

Tongue and groove siding is available in a variety of patterns and sizes from 1x4 to 1x10. Some versions have a chamfer or bead along the edge to create a more finished appearance.

Corner Design

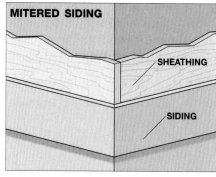

MITERED SIDING — SHEATHING — SIDING

OUTSIDE CORNER BOARDS — SHEATHING — SIDING

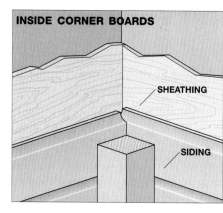

INSIDE CORNER BOARDS — SHEATHING — SIDING

Corner boards protect leak-prone siding joints at the corners of a house. Mitered joints look neat and elegant but aren't as durable as other options, and the technique requires laborious hand-fitting. Butted outside corner boards are easier to install—you nail them in place, then cut the siding to butt squarely against them. Also, at inside corners, you can butt clapboards or simply nail trim boards in place on flat siding.

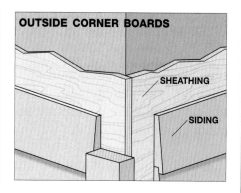

Spacing Jig

You can speed up the installation of clapboard or shakes and increase the overall accuracy of the project at the same time by relying on a simple siding jig that you can build yourself. (Jigs save time on clapboards, shakes, and any siding installed in horizontal courses.) The idea is to create a moveable measuring tool that duplicates the overlap on each course. Every few rows you still should measure back to the base course, and check the current course for level. But you won't have to stop work and check each piece if you use a jig. To construct the jig, screw a small cleat to a rectangular piece of wood in a square T-shape. (1x4s work well.) Use a square to check alignment; then, clamp the pieces and screw them together. Be sure to use screws that won't protrude through both pieces and scratch the siding underneath. To use the jig, slide the cleat section along the bottom edge of the last piece of siding you installed, and make a pencil mark, or simply set the next course in position on top of the jig. The long riser of the upside-down T will gauge the amount of exposure on the next piece and keep your clapboard installation uniform.

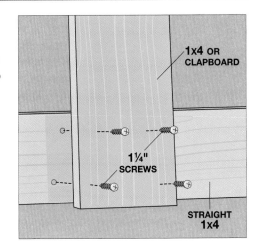

1X4 OR CLAPBOARD

1¼" SCREWS

STRAIGHT 1x4

Installing Clapboard

USE: ▶ circular saw • drill • spacing jig • ladder • 4-ft. level • hammer • measuring tape • work gloves ▶ clapboard • building wrap • corner boards • nails

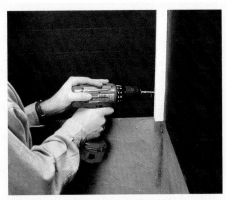

1 ***Install prefinished*** *inside and outside corner boards to provide square edges against which the siding can butt.*

2 ***Snap a level line*** *for the base course, and nail a starter strip of lath along the bottom edge of the sheathing.*

3 ***Overlap the starter strip*** *with the first board, and drive nails high enough to be covered by the next course.*

4 ***Periodically check the weather*** *exposure at the ends and middle of each row as you progress, even if using a jig.*

5 ***Joints should be staggered*** *at every course. Place joints at random intervals spaced a minimum of 16 in. apart.*

6 ***Cut around obstructions*** *as you go. Always overlap boards and fittings so that rainwater will run off, not in.*

siding

Buying Wood Shingles

Wood shingles and shakes are not just for roofs alone—they also make an attractive siding material for many house styles. Although you can buy traditional and fancy-cut wood shingles made especially for siding, it's okay to cover walls with roof shingles and shakes as well. But because weathering on siding is not as severe, you can save by using a lower grade of roof shingle.

Shakes are machine- or hand-split from blocks of wood called bolts. They're thicker than shingles and less uniform along the exposed edges, but they last longer. Wood shingles are sawed smooth. Both types come from woods like western red cedar and redwood, and are available with a fire-retardant treatment. It's wise to allow an extra 10 percent for waste.

Choosing an Exposure

The amount of the shingle surface exposed to the weather is called the exposure. Manufacturers should specify the allowable exposure, since it varies depending on the material. But as a general guideline, calculate the maximum exposure by subtracting ½ inch from half the overall length of the shingle. You can reduce the exposure for looks and greater weather protection, but remember that smaller exposures use more shingles. A typical exposure requires about four bundles of shingles per 100 square feet of wall area.

Design Options

RANDOM STRAIGHT

RANDOM DROP

SCALLOPED

ARROW/DIAMOND

Estimating Guide

Square Footage Coverage of Four Bundles of Shingles (Single Coursed)

Length	Exposure								
	4"	5"	6"	7"	8"	9"	10"	11"	12"
16-inch	80	100	120	140	—	—	—	—	—
18-inch	72	90	109	127	145	—	—	—	—
24-inch	—	—	80	93	106	120	133	146	—

Installing Shingles

USE: ▶ block plane • sliding T-bevel • story pole • 4-ft. level • hammer • ladder • measuring tape • pencil • plumb bob • utility knife • work gloves

1 *Build up the first course* with starter shingles. Snap a chalk line, or string a level line as a leveling guide.

2 *The first course* covers the starter course. Select shingles by width to cover all joints, overlapping gaps by at least 1½ inches.

3 *Mark the weather exposure* at the middle and ends of each finished course; then snap a chalk line to guide your row.

Shingle Corners

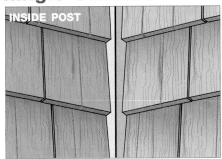
INSIDE POST

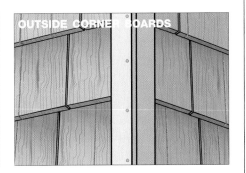
OUTSIDE CORNER BOARDS

INSIDE WOVEN

OUTSIDE WOVEN

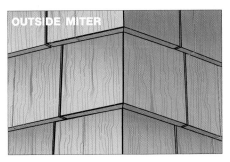
OUTSIDE MITER

At corners, you can butt shingles together, or weave them against trim. Mitering looks good, but it's time consuming and doesn't weather well. Woven corners offer better protection but require cutting and fitting. Butted corners offer the most protection.

Final color depends on the wood hue and the stain color, of course, but also on how long you leave the stain before wiping or brushing out.

The same stain can create different effects, from a wash that resembles a semitransparent coating to a rich tone that conceals most wood grain.

▶ wood shingles (or shakes) • building wrap • edge molding • corner boards • 1x4 ledger board • galvanized nails

4 *To keep the courses level* and make the installation easier, install a temporary guide board leveled across the wall.

5 *Drive galvanized nails* about ¾ in. from shingle edges and 1 in. above weather exposure. Space shingles ⅛ to ¼ in. apart.

6 *Use a hand block plane* to dress shingle edges for fit. Stagger seams so they don't line up course to course.

siding

Routine Repairs

Siding, and the roof, are your home's first line of defense against the elements. Wood naturally responds to changes in temperature and humidity, which over a winter can pop nails, open joints, and cause siding to crack or distort. Leaks can do even more damage—to the siding and structural members. It's tempting to smooth over trouble spots with caulk and paint, but if you bury the problem without fixing the cause, it will just work its way back through the refinished surface. Eventually it may require an even bigger repair.

Shingles, Shakes & Clapboards

Damaged shingles and shakes are easy to remove because they come out in small, easily split pieces. This also makes new shakes easy to weave into the wall so that there is no noticeable line around the repair. The most difficult part of shingle and shake repair is removing the nails in a way that won't damage adjacent shingles. New shingles on walls not painted or sealed will weather in after a few months and eventually match the surrounding color, so long as the new shingle is made of the same type of wood.

Clapboards are a little more difficult to replace than shingles or shakes, but adding new boards, though a slow process, is well worth the effort, especially if it saves you from having to re-side an entire wall. If damage is caused by rot, check the extent of the problem by poking the wood on each side of the damaged area with a knife or screwdriver. Mark the points where the wood changes from dry and crumbly (punky) to solid. The damage may extend only a few inches, but to make a repair that blends in, you may have to remove some good wood, too.

Repairing Panels

You can patch small punctures or rotten areas of plywood siding with an epoxy compound, but if the damage is major or there is veneer failure, you will have to replace it. Buy the new panels to match the thickness of the existing panels, and prime them with a primer that is compatible with the final finish before installation. Paint or stain the replacement panels as soon as possible to protect them from the weather.

Repairing Bows

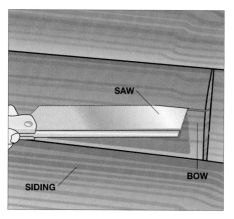

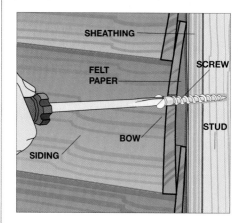

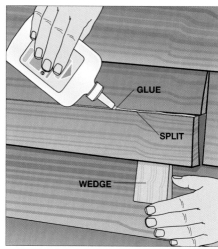

R eattach bowed pieces of siding by fastening them into the studs with long screws. Drill pilot holes for the screws to avoid splits; recess the screwheads, and conceal the heads with putty or caulk. If the siding is heavily bowed, saw a relief cut into each end of the board before screwing it down. To stabilize a large split for caulking, wedge out the split portion, drill pilot holes, apply waterproof glue or construction adhesive, and screw both sides of the split to the wall.

Replacing Shingles

USE: ▶ mini-hacksaw blade • pry bar • hammer • wood chisel • safety goggles • work gloves

1 *Drive wood wedges* under the course directly above the damaged shingle. Take care not to split the shingles above.

2 *Use a hammer and chisel* to split the damaged shingle into several narrow pieces that can be removed without pulling nails.

Repairing Panels

USE: ▶ crowbar • drill • hammer • paint brush or pad • caulking gun ▶ caulk • galvanized screws • wood stain

1 Where panel seams have popped, *pull the nails with a crowbar or hammer, and check for water damage underneath.*

2 Instead of driving down old nails, *use new galvanized screws driven into wall studs through the old nailholes.*

3 To conceal the screwheads, *set them slightly below the surface, add caulk or filler, and touch up with matching wood stain.*

Repairing Clapboards

USE: ▶ hammer • paint brush or pad • pry bar • wood chisel ▶ 1x2 ledger board • exterior paint • exterior wood glue • galvanized finishing nails

1 If the board is split *but still intact, hold the split open with a chisel or pry bar while you inject exterior wood glue.*

2 Place a 1x2 support *beneath the split to hold it closed while the glue sets. Fill the nail holes later with putty.*

3 After the glue dries, *remove the 1x2 and fill the nailholes; then anchor the repair with finishing nails above and below the split.*

▶ replacement shingles • wooden wedges • galvanized nails

3 Cut away hidden nails *using a flexible hacksaw blade. Wrap the blade with tape, or wear gloves to protect your hands.*

4 Fit the new shingle *to fill the damaged area, and gently tap it home. Remove the wedges under the shingles above.*

5 Nail the new shingle *just beneath the butt of the course above. Set the nails, and fill holes with caulk.*

siding

Brick & Stone Siding

Few materials are more durable than brick and stone. They don't catch fire or fall prey to rot or insects. And they are so tough that most problems occur at the weak links in the walls—the mortar joints and flashing seams. But they do require considerable skill to work with. Actually building brick or stone walls for a house—and even replacing old siding with brick or stone veneers—are all projects beyond the range of most do-it-yourselfers.

But there are many maintenance and repair jobs on brick and stone walls that DIYers routinely take care of themselves, including cleaning and repointing masonry joints. See "Spot Repairs" in this chapter (p. 450), as well as "Brick Basics" (p. 52), "Brick Maintenance" (p. 54), "Working with Stone" (p. 56), and "Cleaning Masonry" (p. 58) in the Masonry chapter.

Veneers

Masonry veneers add a look of substance to a house and provide a low-maintenance exterior surface. These advantages come at a price, however—brick and stone veneers are the most expensive siding, and they must be professionally installed. Stone veneers are anywhere from 1¼ to 4 inches thick and bricks from ½ to 4 inches. Both individual pieces and preformed panels can be held securely to wall surfaces with metal ties.

To Paint or Not to Paint?

You can paint brick the way you can paint almost anything else. But unless you want to sign up for the periodic repainting job that homeowners with wood siding have to endure, consider other repairs and coatings that let the brick wall be brick.

You can repoint eroded mortar joints to preserve the structure and its appearance. Once the wall is sound, you can seal it with a clear, silicon-based sealer. There are several types of clear coatings that help the wall shed water and dirt and make the surface easier to clean. Also, most clear coatings tend to wear away gradually without becoming the kind of eyesore you can get with flaking and peeling paint. If you must paint, the National Decorating Products Association suggests an alkali-resistant primer coat, followed by a top coat of latex house paint.

Setting Veneer Stone

USE: ▶ jointing trowel • mason's trowel • pointing trowel • brick hammer • grout bag • pitching chisel

1 *Start by making a dry layout,* placing the stones in approximate position on the ground to see how the joints will fall.

2 *Install wire mesh on the wall* to help support the mortar. Trowel on a base coat that bonds into the metal weave of mesh.

Stonework Types

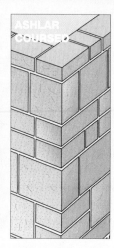

RUBBLE | RUBBLE MORTARED | ASHLAR COURSED | ASHLAR UNCOURSED

Setting Face Brick

USE: ▶ joint spacers • jointing trowel • notched trowel • string level • hacksaw • hammer • plumb bob

1 *For the adhesive mortar* to bond on the wall, start the job by using galvanized nails to attach sheets of wire mesh.

2 *Install an embedding coat of adhesive* mortar by troweling the mix onto and into the mesh. Work on one area at a time.

• mason's twine • 4-ft. level • measuring tape • plumb bob • wheelbarrow • work gloves ▶ stone • mortar mix • welded or woven wire mesh (or metal ties)

3 *Butter the backs of stones* with mortar. You can work in long rows or build up short sections of several courses at once.

4 *Fill seams* with mortar. To avoid discoloring the surfaces, some manufacturers recommend that you use a grout bag.

5 *Smooth the grouted seams* with a tooling blade. Fill all gaps around the edges of the stones to keep out water.

Brick Bond Patterns

RUNNING

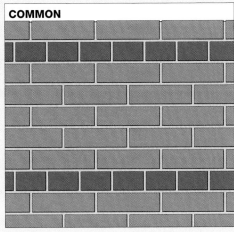

COMMON

GARDEN

▶ face brick or brick tile • adhesive mortar • welded or woven wire mesh

3 *Follow manufacturer's specs* for spacing; measure the space of two or three courses, and string a level guideline.

4 *Use a hacksaw* to trim bricks and to cut half pieces for alternate courses so that joints will be staggered.

5 *Mortar the joints* to a uniform depth and shape. Tooling blades commonly are concave but also flat and V-shaped.

siding

Stucco Pros & Cons

Stucco is again popular because of its durability and its uniquely textured appearance. Still, problems can arise in this weather-resistant shell. If the house foundation sinks unevenly or new framing members shift and shrink as they dry out, the movement can create enough stress to crack the rigid stucco walls.

Problems can also arise in the stucco itself. Fresh stucco (and the masonry wall underneath) may contain salt-based compounds that can be carried to the surface of the material. As the moisture evaporates, the salt deposits leave a residue (efflorescence) on the surface. Although the alkalinity of the stucco material normally neutralizes during the curing process, this residue can create discoloration. The presence of alkali may cause expansion and subsequent cracks.

A type of synthetic stucco system (called EIFS) is also widely used for all types of residential applications. The material can be problematic unless applied correctly. (See the facing page for more information.)

Installation

Stucco is made from portland cement, sand, lime, and water. You can mix your own or buy it premixed. (Unless you're experienced, it's advisable to buy premixed stucco.) Because stucco can be tricky to apply—and preparing frame houses for stucco installation can be time-consuming and labor-intensive—consider hiring contractors or at least one professional to work with you during application.

When you're about to begin the job, take care to choose an overcast day to stucco walls with a southern exposure. Excessive heat can dry the stucco prematurely, which causes shrinking and cracking. Conversely, cool temperatures make the stucco too stiff for proper troweling. The ideal temperature for installing stucco is between 50 and 80° F.

Changing Appearances

The finish coat of stucco, if made using white portland cement, can be colored with pigments in a variety of earth colors. The texture results from the technique used to apply the finish. You can create a variety of looks by using different finishing tools.

Stucco Systems

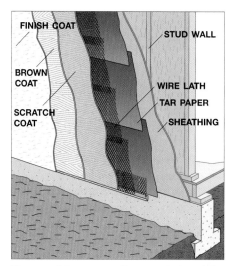

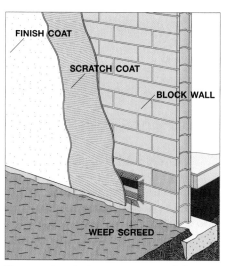

On wood frames, nail expanded metal lath, wire mesh, or woven wire to the sheathing over building paper, and apply the stucco in three separate coats.

Two coats of stucco are enough if you're stuccoing over a solid, stable substrate like concrete block or other masonry walls (or over old stucco).

Stucco Textures

For a smooth texture, trowel on stucco and finish with a wood float.

Create a swirled texture the same way as a smooth one, only leave the swirls.

Hit a paintbrush dipped in thinned stucco against a stick to spatter-coat.

To create a ridged finish, use a steel trowel with a waffling motion.

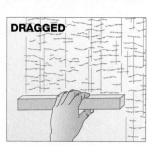

To produce a dragged finish, scrape a piece of 2x4 down the surface.

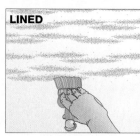

For a lined finish, pounce whisk broom bristles into the final coat.

Installing Stucco

USE: ▶ notched trowel • scratch tool • chalk-line box • hammer ▶ stucco • base strip • nails • wire mesh

▶ **EIFS** is a type of synthetic stucco. It stands for Exterior Insulation and Finish System. The components of the system typically are an adhesive, insulation board, a base coat of cement, fiberglass mesh, and a finish coat. When all the components are installed correctly by contractors (this is not a DIY job), EIFS can be a cost-effective and low-maintenance finish. However, many applications have caused problems to house structures—mainly rot stemming from leaks and moisture trapped in the wall. The most modern EIFS systems attempt to remove these problems by incorporating a system for evacuating moisture—for example, by using insulating panels with narrow grooves on the back.

1 Most stucco installations are anchored with a base strip. To set it, make level marks at corners, and snap a line in between.

2 Set the base strip along the level line, and fasten it to the wall through the mesh portion of the strip with galvanized nails.

3 Above the base strip, fasten sheets of mesh. Extend the bottom edge of the first sheet onto the base strip.

4 Mix the base coat to manufacturer's specs, and trowel it on, using enough pressure to set the mix into the weave.

5 To maintain a bond between coats, scratch the surface before it hardens. A homemade tool with spaced nails will do.

6 In most applications, the top coat is only ⅛ to ¼ in. thick. You can try to make a smooth finish or create a texture.

siding

Spot Repairs

Make it a point to fix cracks in brick, stucco, and stone as quickly as you detect them. Even small cracks in either the material or the mortar joints in between will let water seep into the underlying structure, where it will eventually cause damage. Over time, water and the winter freeze/thaw cycles will turn minor cracks into major problems, which are both more difficult and costlier to fix.

Brick

Brick repairs usually consist of either replacing crumbling areas of mortar or removing and replacing a cracked or damaged brick. If you shop around, you can usually find replacements for damaged bricks or facing stones that closely match the existing material; mortar, however, is far more difficult to match. Typically, it's necessary to try out a few test batches before you get one that will blend in with the rest of the house. Add powdered colorant, if necessary, to duplicate the existing mortar. Always wait for the mortar mix to dry before making any decisions, so you can make valid comparisons.

The first step in replacing a broken brick is to chisel it—and the surrounding mortar—out of the wall. After cleaning out the hole and spritzing it with water, you should first spread some mortar on the bottom. Then spread mortar on the top and sides of the brick, and slide it into place.

Stucco

Patch large cracks and gaps in a stucco surface with the same stucco mix that was used on the walls. Fill small cracks with all-acrylic or siliconized-acrylic sealants. If you spot large cracks but don't have time to make a thorough repair, at least seal the openings with a bead of silicone caulk to keep out water. The caulk can be peeled away when you get around to making permanent repairs.

Stucco can be difficult to color-match. If the surface requires many patches, it may be easier to cover it with a cement-based paint or an acrylic exterior paint. (Let the stucco patches cure at least 30 days beforehand.) Dampen the wall with water before painting. Cement-based paint will need a primer coat to prevent blotches, but acrylic paint won't.

Stone

When the joints between stones are the problem, follow the color-matching advice discussed for brick repairs. Chip out the old mortar to between ½ and ¾ inch deep, forming a groove with square sides, one side of which goes down to bare stone. After cleaning and misting the joint with water, add mortar to the groove. Tool the joint when the mortar has cured enough to retain a thumbprint.

For a loose stone, remove it and clean the joints. Butter the back with mortar, and then replace the stone and repoint the mortar joints around it.

Replacing Brick

USE: ▶ cold chisel • hawk • jointing trowel

1 Use a cold chisel and heavy hammer to chip away the damaged brick. Work from the joints in, wearing safety glasses.

Chalking Paint

Many contemporary exterior paints are specially formulated to shed dirt: the topmost surface of the paint breaks down into a chalklike powder and sloughs away slightly with each rainfall or cleaning. This chalking keeps the surface looking clean, but it will not allow a new coat of paint to properly adhere to it. Before painting over a chalking type of paint, scrub the old surface with detergent, and rinse well.

Repairing Stucco

USE: ▶ cold chisel • hawk • mason's trowel • short-handled sledgehammer • safety glasses • work gloves ▶ stucco • straight-edged board • welded wire mesh

1 Use a cold chisel and heavy hammer (while wearing gloves and safety glasses) to chop out loose material.

2 If the underlying wire mesh is damaged (or missing), cut a new piece and attach it to the wall with galvanized nails.

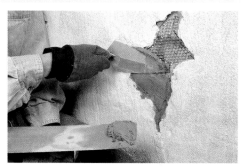

3 Mix more than enough patch material to fill the hole, and trowel it on the mesh so the patch is thicker than adjacent stucco.

• mason's trowel • mixing trough • safety goggles • short-handled sledgehammer • wire brush • work gloves ▶ mortar mix • replacement brick • water

2 Break away remaining chunks of mortar, and then wire-brush and sweep out the surrounding surfaces to remove debris.

3 Mix enough mortar to thoroughly coat the mating surfaces of the replacement brick, a process called buttering.

4 Force more mortar into the joints as needed (some will likely fall off); then tool the seams to blend in the repair.

• galvanized nails

4 Use the surrounding wall as a level guide, and smooth the patch surface by sliding a straightedge back and forth.

Wall Cleaning

Power washing uses a pressure washer to remove tough dirt. Some grime may need a non-abrasive detergent. Test the treatment on a patch of wall using a low-pressure setting (under 700 pounds per square inch). In older buildings, mortar may break away under high pressure. Protect nearby shrubs and flowers with drop cloths or plastic sheeting. When using a pressure washer, keep the spray moving. Most power washers come with nozzles offering both a wide spray at a lower pressure and a narrow jet at a higher pressure—you risk less damage by using the nozzle with the wider arc.

Excessive cleaning pressure can erode mortar joints and pit the brick surface.

Cleaning can reveal a sound brick wall that requires only minor repointing.

Spray at an angle to keep the water jet from digging into the mortar joints.

siding

Vinyl & Metal Styles

Siding textures in vinyl and aluminum are typically made to resemble wood clapboards or shingles. They come in a variety of colors and styles with matching trim and architectural details. Both vinyl and aluminum siding can be installed horizontally or vertically. When you get a siding estimate, it will likely come with an insulation option. Because both aluminum and vinyl are preformed sheet materials (not solid like wood), the space behind them can be filled with molded panels of insulation, called backer boards. Some vinyl siding comes with an insulated backing attached.

Aluminum siding is paintable, and many vinyl siding manufacturers now claim their products can be painted, too. But painting usually isn't necessary for many years, which makes aluminum and vinyl truly low-maintenance materials. But you will have to wash accumulated dirt and grime off the siding from time to time.

Installation

Both vinyl and aluminum sidings are installed in much the same way, using lock-together components designed to expand and contract with temperature swings. Trim pieces cover expansion joints, give the job a finished look, and help hide minor mistakes. Mounting systems differ slightly depending on the brand, so it's important to use the tools and techniques specified by the manufacturer.

Materials

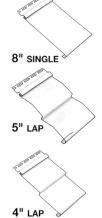

8" SINGLE

5" LAP

4" LAP

Aluminum siding covered millions of homes through the 1950s and 1960s. It was sold as the last siding you would ever need, and it would never need painting. Most homes now are covered in vinyl—it's less expensive and easier to work with, which saves labor costs on contracted jobs and allows handy do-it-yourselfers to tackle siding projects without contractors. But some vinyl can crack in cold weather, distort if not installed properly, and fade over time. While aluminum is structurally more durable, it dents and scratches easily—and even minor damage is difficult to conceal. Both vinyl and aluminum are sold in complete interlocking systems that cover everything from the roof line to the foundation, including matching systems for covering soffits and fascias.

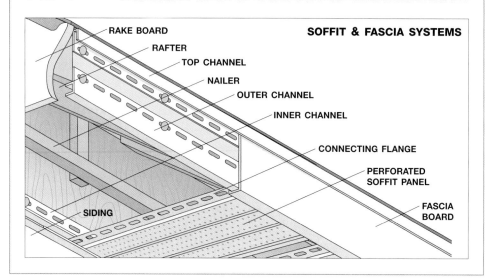

SOFFIT & FASCIA SYSTEMS

RAKE BOARD
RAFTER
TOP CHANNEL
NAILER
OUTER CHANNEL
INNER CHANNEL
CONNECTING FLANGE
PERFORATED SOFFIT PANEL
FASCIA BOARD
SIDING

Installing Vinyl

USE: ▶ nail-slot punch • snap-lock punch • zip tool • metal snips • 4-ft. level • hammer • ladder • straightedge • utility knife ▶ vinyl siding • vinyl trim (corner trim,

1 *Install preformed corner trim* first. *Siding ends fit into vertical channels on this piece to seal out the weather.*

2 *At window and door openings,* vinyl J-channels butt against the trim. Their outer edges conceal the edges of siding.

3 *Level and nail a starter strip* for your first course. The first full row of siding locks into the lip on this preformed strip.

Details & Finishes

The pros of vinyl siding are its low cost, easy installation that even some do-it-yourselfers can handle, and exceptionally easy cleanup (with no painting or staining), which every DIYer can appreciate. The downside—at least for some people—is the synthetic appearance, which is no match for real wood. Using vinyl with embossed wood grain may help. Installing clean-lined architectural details in vinyl, such as complete door surrounds, helps even more. Modern trim systems are available to suit many house styles and can dress up the siding behind them.

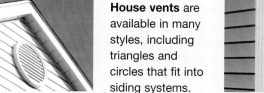

Use a plain siding on the bulk of the house, and cover small, independent sections with a decorative scallop.

House vents are available in many styles, including triangles and circles that fit into siding systems.

Detailed cornices with dental block and surround trim for windows and doors can tie into wall siding above.

Detailed trim pieces, like fluted corner posts, add a custom touch to a house clad in vinyl or aluminum.

Before...

...and after

fascia panels, F-channels, J-channels, starter strips, under sill trim, etc.) • rigid insulation (for retrofits) • soffit panels • building wrap • galvanized nails

4 *Push up on the siding butt* to lock it in; then nail into place through the top flange. Overlap panel end joints by 1 in. minimum.

5 *Nail through the center of flange slots* at a 90° angle, leaving nails loose enough to allow siding to expand and contract.

6 *Cut around windows,* using aviation snips for vertical cuts and a utility knife to score and snap horizontal cutouts.

siding

Fixing Damaged Vinyl

Vinyl is tough, but not indestructible—it often cracks under impact. This is especially true at low temperatures. Patch small cracks by removing the damaged piece, cleaning the crack with PVC primer, and gluing a patch of scrap siding from behind with PVC cement.

If large areas are damaged, the entire piece may have to be replaced. This isn't a major undertaking, since replacement pieces are fairly easy to install. But vinyl siding does fade with time, so your patch or replacement piece may not be a perfect color match—at first.

It's easy to remove a damaged section because each course of vinyl locks into the course below or beside it. The siding is nailed through a flange molded into the top of the course. All you need is a simple tool, called a zip tool, to unlock the courses. You wedge the device under the lower edge of siding and pull it horizontally to unlock the pieces. When working with vertical siding, you pull the zip tool down the seam.

Restoring Aluminum Siding

Although aluminum siding provides good weather protection and is easy to maintain, a stray baseball or large hailstones can dent it. Slight damage can be patched—the procedure for repairing dents in aluminum siding is a lot like repairing a dented car fender. It consists of pulling out the dent, sanding the area, and applying two-part auto-body putty (or auto-body filler for very slight imperfections). Once the surface is dry, you can sand, prime, and paint it. For minor surface imperfections, you can use steel wool. It also helps to know the manufacturer and color of the siding, because you may be able to purchase a touch-up kit in the original color.

You may need to replace areas with more serious damage, although you should try other repairs first for two reasons. First, aluminum isn't as flexible as vinyl; it's more difficult to weave one piece into an existing wall. Second, you may not find replacement pieces that match your old siding. If the repair is in a conspicuous place, you may want to consider removing and using a piece from a less obvious part of the house and then replacing that piece with the new material.

Repairing Vinyl

USE: ▶ zip tool • metal snips • hammer • nail set • pry bar • utility knife ▶ replacement vinyl • wedges

1 *Use an installer's zip tool* to unlock siding above the damaged piece. Pry down and slide tool along the edge to free it.

2 *Fit temporary wedges* under the loose siding course to hold it out of the way while you work on the damaged piece below it.

3 *Carefully pry out nails* directly above the damaged section. If necessary, protect the piece with tape or scrap beneath the flat bar.

4 *Cut out the damaged area* with snips or a razor knife. Avoid cutting the siding or locking edge of courses above and below.

5 *Cut a replacement section* 2 in. larger than the damaged piece you removed to allow a 1 in. overlap on both ends.

6 *Fasten the replacement* through the top flange, using a nail set to reach under the course above. A zip tool will relock all edges.

vinyl & metal repairs

Repairing Aluminum

USE: ▶ drill • pliers • sanding block • screwdriver • drywall knife ▶ auto-body putty • emery cloth • exterior spray paint • metal primer • sheet-metal screws

1 *Drill one or more holes* at the center of the dent; run a screw into the siding only. Pull the screw to pop out the dent.

2 *Remove the screws,* roughen surface with sandpaper, mix two-part auto-body filler, and smooth it onto the dented area.

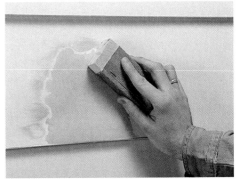

3 *After the patch dries,* sand filler and paint it with primer. When dry, spray on two coats of finish paint to match siding.

Painting Aluminum

USE: ▶ caulking gun • bucket • 4-in. paint brush • steel wool pad ▶ exterior paint • metal primer • caulk • mild detergent • water

1 *For the best adhesion,* use steel wool to smooth rough spots, and wash with a mild detergent and water.

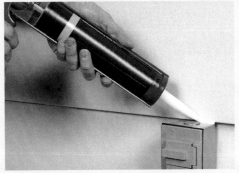

2 *Caulk around all openings* in the siding. Use a flexible caulk that can maintain the seal when siding shifts.

3 *Fill small punctures* with caulk. Also cover the heads of nails or screws used to make repairs prior to painting.

4 *Seal leak-prone seams* around windows and doors where aluminum J-channel trim laps onto wood casing.

5 *Once aluminum siding is prepared,* treat it like any other wall, and use a latex acrylic or oil-base exterior paint.

6 *To help disguise the repaint job,* carefully cut in around openings, and paint the aluminum trim as well as the siding.

siding

Re-Siding Options

When it comes to siding renovation, you have three options. Removing old siding costs time and money, but it lets you open up your exterior house walls. This gives you the opportunity to replace outdated plumbing pipes or damaged framing, string new electrical wiring, or add insulation. The second option, re-siding over existing material, saves you the cost of demolition and carting but adds the cost of coping with new trim work to accommodate an extra layer of siding.

When making your decision, don't overlook the obvious third option, cleaning, which can save you a bundle of time and money. Too often homeowners confuse excessive dirt and dinginess with more permanent deterioration. A thorough washing with soap and water can actually reveal bright paint beneath and make re-siding unnecessary.

If you do decide to re-side directly over the old material, invest some time and effort in surface preparation. Before covering old clapboard siding, for example, wash it with a mild solution of household bleach and water to kill off mold. If major sections of the old siding are deteriorated, don't bury the problem. Where wooden clapboards are rotting, twisted, and split, and many nailheads have popped, leaks or condensation are the likely culprits. Unless you find and fix the source, the problem will only work its way through your expensive new siding.

Vapor Barriers

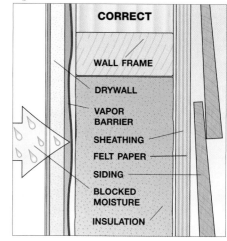

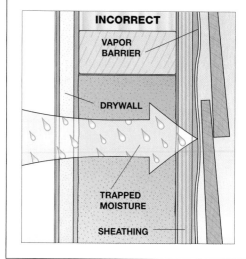

A vapor barrier is a layer of thin material, typically thin plastic sheeting and sometimes foil, that prevents moisture generated inside the house from seeping into exterior walls and condensing. It lies over the wall frame, under the drywall. Without this barrier, which is standard in modern homes but lacking in many built before 1960, moisture working through the wall can meet a surface that is below the dewpoint temperature. That's when moisture becomes water that can soak insulation, cause rot in the wall frame, and peel paint. If you are installing new siding, don't add a vapor barrier over the outside wall. It will stop moisture from escaping. And much of the damage can be hidden until the problems mushroom into major repair projects. House wrap is the right material to use outside the house under new siding because it allows the house to shed any moisture that might get by the vapor barrier inside. Moisture passes out through this fabric, but drafts can't get in.

Re-Siding

USE: ▶ nail-slot punch • snap-lock punch • zip tool • metal snips • 4-ft. level • hammer • ladder • staple gun • straightedge • utility knife ▶ vinyl siding • vinyl trim

1 If you're re-siding over existing siding, secure split, loose, and warped boards to ensure a solid nailing base.

2 Re-siding gives you the option of adding insulation through wall openings or applying insulating foam to the wall surface.

3 Building wrap protects interiors from drafts and heat loss. It can be stapled directly over existing siding.

Asbestos Shingles

When asbestos siding was popular decades ago, no one knew that it was carcinogenic: Now we know. Asbestos does a good job of protecting houses, but the striated, often powdery, and brittle shingles contain cancer-causing fibers. The material is not a hazard until it is disturbed—for example, by sawing shingles to install a new window. In theory, you could cover old asbestos siding with new vinyl siding. But in practice, nailing on the vinyl would fracture the older shingles. The piles of pieces would get in the way and create a health hazard. On small repairs you can install a fiber-cement board made to look like asbestos (above). On large projects, the safest plan is to have shingles removed by contractors licensed to handle asbestos and who have permits to dispose of it.

Flashing Windows

Above a window you need strip flashing to shed water. Tack the top to the old siding and bend the leading edge over the window frame. Use this flashing as a back up even with aluminum or vinyl siding that has its own trim. There are two ways to flash the sides of a window. When the wall is built out with extra insulation, you may need to install J-channel on the frame (below left). It looks better to butt J-channel against the side of the frame (below right).

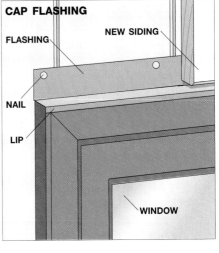

CAP FLASHING

FLASHING NEW SIDING

NAIL

LIP

WINDOW

Extend frame *with trim to add a layer of insulation with new J-molding for siding.*

Insert siding *into the J-molding slot to cover cut ends as you add each course.*

(F- and J-channels, starter strips, etc.) • building wrap • rigid insulation board (optional) • soffit panels • furring strips • galvanized nails • heavy-duty staples

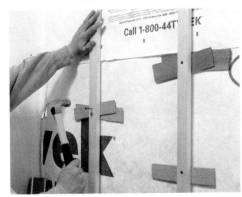

4 ***Furring strips*** *create a smooth, even nailing base where walls are uneven or out of plumb. Use shims under strips as needed.*

5 ***Install inside and outside corner posts*** *first, hanging them from top nails so that they are vertically plumb before fastening.*

6 ***Add each course of siding,*** *tapping it upward to lock it onto the course. Nail through the flange into furring strips.*

siding

Paint vs. Stain

Most people stain floors, cabinets, furniture, decks, and just about every other piece of wood, except the siding. Siding gets painted—despite the fact that while you're in the middle of the long, tedious, and expensive job, you know that in a few years you'll be doing it all over again. That's because paint lies on the surface of siding like a blanket. Stain, on the other hand, seeps more deeply into the wood grain and becomes a part of the siding. So what makes more sense: paint or stain?

Color & Coverage

Most homeowners use slightly muted shades, but paint is available in every color in the spectrum. Your house can be bright white, of course, or fire-engine red if you can stand the intensity. But penetrating stains offer almost as wide a variety. There are dark wood hues, brilliant blues, and potent reds, but also very light whites. And if you prefer that one shade you can't find on a paint chip, you can mix stain to a custom shade the same way you mix paint.

Typical stains let some of the wood grain show through, while most paint applications are designed to provide a solid, opaque surface. Both materials can be applied in thick coats or thin coats. You can thin paint to create special effects (generally inside the house), and you can buy heavy-bodied stain that creates the same appearance as full-strength paint on siding. If you choose paint, you'll be covering the wood completely, which may not be the best approach if you have elegant redwood or cedar underneath. In that case, the best choice may be a clear sealer that protects the wood but lets the natural beauty come through. If you choose stain, you can use a full-bodied material to conceal an average grade of pine, or a semitransparent mixture that gives the wood an overall color hue and lets some of the natural beauty come through.

Maintenance

On a modern home with vapor barriers in the wall, paint may last as long as stain. On older homes without vapor barriers (sheets, usually thin plastic, that stop interior moisture from entering the wall), stain will last longer. Here's why:

Moisture from cooking, washing, and other household operations can eventually reach the solid paint film and push it off the wall. But moisture is more likely to seep through a semitransparent stain. Also, when paint finally deteriorates, the results are obvious and sometimes an eyesore. However, as stain deteriorates, it tends to fade. More wood grain will show but the siding will look basically the way it did a few years ago—just a bit more washed out and weathered.

MATERIALS

◆ **Clear coatings** are solvent-based and they contain no pigments. Both the wood color and the grain remain visible.

◆ **Semitransparent coatings (stains)** have a solvent base of oil, oil/alkyds, resin, and/or emulsions. They are lightly pigmented to reveal the grain of the wood.

◆ **Opaque coatings (paints or stains)** can be water- or solvent-based. They conceal the natural color and grain of wood yet allow the texture to show through. **Latex stains** retain color well and are available in a range of finishes. They clean up easily with soap and water. **Oil stains** are more durable than latex stains because they penetrate into the wood. The finish and solvent used for the clean-up, however, create toxic fumes.

◆ **Stainkillers**, such as pigmented white shellac, are used to conceal blemishes and discolorations, such as bleeding knots.

Finishing New Siding

USE: ▶ 4-in. exterior wall brush • 1½-in. sash brush • caulking gun • drip rags • dropcloths • ladders • putty knife • sanding block • scaffolding (optional)

1 *Wrap sandpaper* around a block of wood to smooth out minor splits and other small imperfections.

2 *Fill holes* with putty. Deep holes will need two coats. Then prime the dry patch so that it doesn't show under paint or stain.

3 *Apply a weather-resistant caulk* around window and door openings and where siding butts against corner trim.

Applying Paint

A good paint job on bare wood begins with the primer coat. The primer coat seals the surface, hides imperfections and stains, and improves paint adhesion. Use a primer that is compatible with the final top coat you will be using. An oil-based primer works with both water- and oil-based top coats. A water-based primer is generally covered only with a water-based top coat. Be sure the surface being primed is clean and dust-free to ensure good adhesion.

Two coats of paint over a primer or over existing paint provide the longest-lasting, most durable results, particularly on the south and west sides of a house, where the sun is most intense. One coat of paint will last about 5 years; two coats lasts up to 10 years. Apply the first coat no later than two weeks after priming and the second coat when the first coat is dry.

Following a few rules will help make your paint job look professional. First, never paint when rain is in the forecast. The surface must be clean and dry before you begin, and a new coat of paint can be washed off or seriously affected by rain before it dries. Second, use a mildewcide before painting. Don't simply paint over mildew, as it will grow under the paint and cause blistering and discoloration. Lastly, paint at temperatures no lower than 50° F for latex paint and 40° F for oil-based paint.

Paint can be applied with brushes, rollers, paint pads, or a power sprayer. With any of these, make sure to coat the underside of the siding laps, and always be sure to check the undersides of the courses from the ground. It's easiest to detect drips and skipped areas from below.

In the last century, there was no precut siding but plenty of cheap lumber. This New York farmer saved some measuring by trimming the clapboards right on the house.

▶ primer • exterior paint (or stain) • caulk • sandpaper • wood putty

4 *There is no set application rule* for paint or stain. But it works well to cover seams before brushing out the surface.

5 *On the finish coat of paint or stain,* work on small sections between trimmed borders. Start by cutting in the edges.

6 *Work high to low* so you can pick up any drips before they dry, or scrape them away with a taping knife.

siding

Evaluating Problems

Preparing the surface of siding before repainting is probably one of the most important aspects of the job. Paint won't adhere to an improperly prepared surface, and you can be sure that any underlying problems that caused damage to the original paint job will soon reappear to ruin the new coating.

Of these problems, moisture is perhaps the biggest culprit. Water vapor from cooking, washing, and other normal household operations can migrate through walls until it reaches the building skin. On many homes the outermost skin is paint. It is applied to beautify and protect the house on the outside, but it can be cracked, bubbled, and peeled by moisture breaking through from the inside.

Another problem results from painting over thick layers of paint. After 20 or 30 years, many houses have been repainted several times. Not every homeowner scrapes and sands the siding each time it needs new paint. Even when carefully done, the paint coat may be only scraped away in small patches, leaving most of the old paint on the walls. The multi-layer skins are the most likely to crack, often in a pattern resembling an alligator's skin. This condition can quickly resurface in a fresh layer of paint. In this case, rather than scraping off the paint—a task which is laborious, and costly—many people choose to re-side the house with new material.

Water Spots

These gray, milky areas appear on exterior wood near the ground. They're usually caused by sprinkler systems used to water shrubs or flowers near the foundation. Any minerals in the water then get deposited on the siding and cake in place as the water evaporates.

Although hard-water deposits can be softened with white vinegar and other solvents, it's often easier to scrape the surface with a draw-type, razor-blade paint scraper, followed by sanding and refinishing. Since it isn't economical to use softened water on garden plants, the only way to prevent this problem from recurring is to shield the siding during watering or to redirect sprinklers away from the siding. If after scraping and sanding some deep stains linger, cover them with two coats of pigmented white shellac.

Diagnosing Surface Problems

◆ BLISTERING

Blistering appears as a series of bubbles in the paint. These blisters form when paint is applied to a wet surface. It can also occur when paint is applied in direct sunlight. Moisture migrating outward from inside the wall or in the house itself can also cause paint to blister, even though the surface was dry when it was applied.

Causes
Cut open a blister to diagnose the cause. If raw wood is under the blister, the problem is moisture. If paint is under the blister, the top coat was probably applied in the hot sunlight.

Solutions
Scrape off the blistered paint, and sand the area smooth. If the blistering is caused by moisture migration from the interior, there is no point in repainting until the source of the moisture problem has been fixed.

◆ PEELING

Peeling paint is characterized by paint flakes or strips that don't stick to the surface. Several factors can cause peeling, including the application of a very thick layer—the two-coats-in-one approach. But the problem is most commonly due to interior moisture working through the exterior wall.

Causes
Paint peels when it does not bond sufficiently to the surface. A dirty surface, a surface coated with many paint layers, or moisture migration from the inside can all cause peeling.

Solutions
Scrape the paint to the surface of the siding, and then recoat with high-quality paint. Where the peeling has been caused by migrating moisture, fix the problem before repainting.

◆ ALLIGATORING

Alligatored paint has small connected cracks that resemble the skin of a reptile. It often occurs on siding where multiple layers of paint have been applied, making it difficult for the outermost coat to adhere properly. The newer paint may have been incompatible or applied to a moist surface.

Causes
This results when one layer of paint doesn't adhere to another. It also happens when incompatible paints are used, the surface is poorly prepared, or the previous coat has not dried.

Solutions
Scrape the paint down to the raw wood; then prime and recoat the surface with high-quality paint. Where many layers of old paint are the cause, you may want to consider replacing the siding altogether.

◆ MOLD

Mold and mildew are fungal growths that appear on siding, causing it to look dirty. Growth of the spores is encouraged by soiled, moist, or warm surfaces and lack of adequate sunshine and fresh air. Once the green and gray-green growths take hold, they can discolor most of the wall, prematurely age the paint, and make repainting more difficult.

Causes

Mold and mildew thrive on damp surfaces that are shielded from the sun and prevailing winds. Problems often are worst under wide roof overhangs and wherever siding is concealed by shrubs.

Solutions

Wash mold and mildew with a scrub brush and a solution of up to half household bleach and half water. Try the solution on an inconspicuous area first because the bleach could discolor the siding.

◆ RUST

Rust is the reddish-brown coating formed on iron or steel by oxidation when the material is exposed to water and air. Metals that are unprimed or poorly primed are most likely to develop problems with peeling paint, which exposes the metal and promotes rust that can leave a telltale streak.

Causes

Rust stains can be spread onto the siding by rainwater when metal components such as flashing, gutters, ungalvanized nailheads and shutter hardware begin to oxidize.

Solutions

Try a 50–50 bleach/water solution. If that doesn't work, use oxalic acid, a chemical that must be handled with care. You can also try commercial cleaning products for cleaning rust stains off surfaces.

◆ BLEEDING

Some materials can show through two coats of paint or stain, even when most of the surface is smooth and even in color. This bleeding can come from many sources, including rusting nailheads, resin seeping from wood, and knots that are too hard to accept much stain or paint. The most common fix is to coat trouble spots with pigmented white shellac.

Causes

Bleeding comes from uncoated steel nailheads or nails that are coated with a low-quality zinc plating. It also can stem from knots and tight sections of wood grain that produce resin.

Solutions

Prevent bleeding by using noncorrosive stainless-steel or aluminum box nails on siding. To remove existing stains, scrub with a 50-50 bleach/water solution. Coat discolorations with a stain killer.

Stopping Moisture

Problems with moisture build-up can damage a paint job. Inadequate venting is often the cause, and permanent cures are possible only when venting is improved. Moisture around windows and doors can also cause problems—gaps should be caulked as part of routine maintenance.

When insulating, *install foil or asphalt-impregnated kraft-paper vapor barriers toward the heated areas.*

Staple through *the insulation batt edge flaps every 6 in. or so to create the best possible seal along the studs.*

Installing a layer of plastic sheeting *is the easiest way to build a complete vapor barrier over paper-faced batts of insulation.*

Use clear tape *(or duct tape) to seal all tears or gaps in the vapor barrier, and around all pipes and vents.*

siding

Repainting Basics

Don't decide to repaint your house until after you have washed the siding and exterior trim. Scrubbing with a soft brush and a solution of warm water and nonabrasive household detergent (about ⅓ cup detergent to a gallon of water) can sometimes be as effective as repainting. As dirt accumulates on siding over several years, you may not notice the gradual increase in dinginess—until you wash one of the dull spots and find surprisingly bright paint underneath.

If repainting is called for, there are a few guidelines that can help make the finish more durable. Scuff the painted surface by sanding lightly. Washing the siding is also a must, because the new paint won't adhere over dirt, mold, or other surface deposits such as grease from a kitchen exhaust fan.

Prepare thoroughly before repainting. On a two-story project or any place you need ladders and scaffolds, it may be tempting to prepare the surface and paint in one step. But chips of old paint, dabs of caulk, and sanding dust may settle onto areas you're about to paint or have just painted.

Hairline cracks can be filled with paint, but caulk larger openings, such as where ends of siding butt against the trim. Use a flexible butyl or paintable silicone caulk there and where dissimilar materials like wood and masonry meet. Don't use old paint, which can be damaged by improper storage and will not match with new paint. And don't try to get by with one thick coat of paint—that causes sagging, wrinkling, and peeling. Wherever you sand, scrape, set nails, or make other repairs that expose raw wood, prime the area before painting. If you don't, these raw patches will pull too much water out of the surface paint, creating dull spots and weakening adhesion.

In addition, limit yourself to working on one manageable area at a time. Trying to cover too much surface from one spot is unsafe and undercuts job quality.

Lastly, always work from high to low. The paint you are using will probably cause drips and splatters, which you can fix on your way down. If they have solidified by the time you get there, scrape them off instead of trying to blend them in.

Wall Cleaning

With extension wands on hose-end cleaners, you can cover large walls.

Hose-end washers: While power washers use a high-pressure water stream that can sometimes strip paint and cause leaks, hose-end cleaners use standard household water pressure. Many extension wands and cleaning heads are available to suit almost any job, although tough dirt may require vigorous scrubbing by hand. Some systems use cleaning tablets sold by the manufacturer; many allow you to add whatever cleaner you need to the water stream.

Stripping

There are several ways to strip layers of old paint. You can use chemicals that soften the paint so you can scrape it away, a heat gun that does about the same thing without chemicals, sandpaper, sharp scrapers, and more. The trick is to pick the most practical method for the job at hand. On large surfaces like the side of a house, for example, applying gallons of caustic chemicals would make a mess and be difficult to handle. Those surfaces should be scraped. Chemical strippers and heat are better on small jobs such as taking layers of paint off molding. Where grooves and other details in the wood are almost filled with old paint, you may need several applications. On flat surfaces, you can use a putty knife to clear the softened paint. In tight spots, use a shaped scraper blade. There are hand-held models and tools with interchangeable heads designed to dig into all kinds of beading and channels. Before stripping, be sure that the paint is not lead-based. Have a sample checked if you're not sure. Also bear in mind that your town may have restrictions on disposing of the waste. If you use a chemical stripper, wear rubber gloves and safety glasses.

Use chemical strippers in small areas. Allow the reaction to take place (you'll see the paint wrinkle) then scrape.

Heat guns don't add any potentially toxic chemicals to the job but can make paint hot enough to burn you.

Stain Over Paint

Besides giving siding a natural look, stain has a major advantage over paint. Instead of cracking, peeling, or blistering, it tends to age gracefully and just fades away to a paler but recognizable version of what it once was. That means you're likely to get more years without major maintenance if you use stain instead of paint. So how about switching in midstream and covering paint with stain? It's worth a try on an old house, particularly one without vapor barriers where interior moisture works through the wall and disrupts the paint film every few years. It's wise to try it on an out-of-the-way section of wall. Ideally, you should scrape the siding down to bare wood. But you can get by simply by removing any loose material and leaving a thin paint film that is so well-adhered, you can't easily scrape it away. Pressure-washing is another option. Sand the entire surface with medium to rough paper, and wash the wall clean (if you haven't pressure-washed). Then apply at least one coat of stain. A semitransparent exterior stain that is a close color match for the underlying paint color often works best.

Repainting

USE: ▶ 4-in. wall brush • 1½-in. sash brush • caulking gun • hammer • nail set • scrapers • sanding block ▶ primer • exterior paint • caulk • putty • sandpaper

1 *Use a nail set* to recess popped nail heads below siding surface. If additional repairs are needed, do them now.

2 *Fill nailholes with putty,* allow to dry, and then sand the patch smooth. Also fill any gaps, nicks, and other damaged areas.

3 *Scrape paint* that is blistered or peeling to provide a smooth surface and good adhesion base for the new coat.

4 *Recaulk* around windows, doors, and openings for pipes and vents. Use a quality, nonshrink, elastic acrylic caulk.

5 *Spot-prime* sanded and scraped areas, places that have been caulked and puttied, and inside and outside corners and edges.

6 *Paint from top down* to catch drips and missed spots. Pros apply one primer coat, followed by two finish top coats.

24 windows & doors

windows & doors

Windows, Inside & Out

Most homeowners just accept their windows as they are, even if they are too small or poorly positioned in a room. Remodeling windows definitely involves more work than some other DIY projects—you can't just rip holes in the side of your house without doing some basic structural work—but the effect of new windows can be dramatic. The extra sunlight can brighten drab rooms and make them seem larger. Repositioning a window may open up an eye-catching view of a backyard garden, warm up part of the house by letting in more sunlight during winter, or improve ventilation by catching prevailing summer breezes.

You do have to consider other things before redoing windows, however. Privacy is one—most people don't want a picture window in their bedroom or bathroom, and it is best to avoid placing windows so people can easily see into the house. Fire codes generally require that at least one window in each bedroom be suitable for emergency escape. You also have to think about how the window will affect the appearance of the outside of the house. The size, style, and position of the new window should be compatible with the rest of the house.

The ideal height of the window off the floor varies according to the use of the room, however—for example, the window's bottom end should be about 3 feet 6 inches above the floor in a kitchen, to allow for counters and cabinets; 2 feet 5½ inches in the dining room; and as little as 1 foot above the floor for a picture window in the living room. You should always consult your local building codes before determining the size and location of a new window.

Before You Begin Work

After deciding on the style and positioning of the new window, the next step is to determine what is lurking behind the drywall. It could be a jungle of wiring, plumbing and heating pipes, or ductwork that would have to be rerouted. Moving the new opening may be easier.

When you order the new window, note the dimensions of the required rough wall opening. You'll need to include them on a scale drawing of the wall, with the location and size of existing and new wall framing. Take the drawing when you apply for a building permit.

Styles

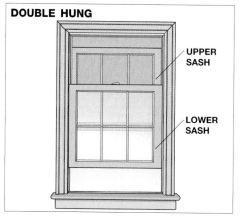

Double-hung windows have a traditional look that is suitable for most home styles. New models have tip-out sash for cleaning.

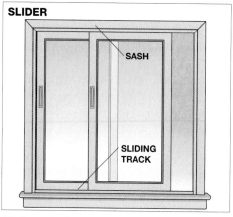

Sliding windows are like small sliding glass doors. For ventilation, one sash slides in a track slightly in and past the other.

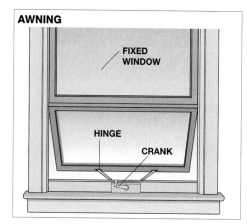

Awning windows are like casements turned sideways. The design can shed rain and still provide ventilation.

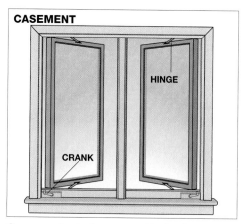

Casement windows are attached to their frame with side-mounted hinges. A crank or slide allows the window to swing out.

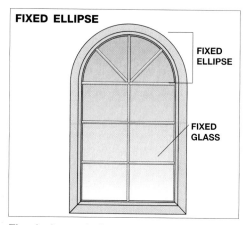

Fixed-glass windows, which are available in many styles, can be used by themselves or paired with operating windows.

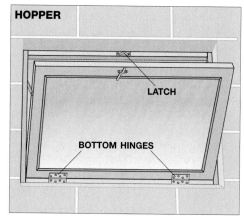

Hopper windows, often used in basements, are hinged at the bottom and open from the top—venting that works well in fair weather.

Window Anatomy

TRIM

UPPER SASH

JAMB

MUNTIN

RAIL

LOWER SASH

STOOL

APRON

SILL DETAIL

STOOL

APRON

DRYWALL

SIDING

LOWER SASH

SILL

MATERIALS

◆ **Wood** offers good insulating value. It accepts paint or stain but requires periodic maintenance.

◆ **Vinyl** windows generally require less maintenance than wood and are less expensive. It is the most-used material for replacement windows.

◆ **Vinyl-clad wood** windows have the advantage of low-maintenance exterior cladding and the look of real wood windows on the interior.

◆ **Aluminum** windows with a baked-on or anodized finish are less energy efficient but are low-maintenance.

◆ **Aluminum-clad wood** offers the same advantages as vinyl-clad units and is more paintable.

◆ **Steel** makes the strongest window frame, but it can rust and is usually more costly and less energy efficient.

◆ **Fiberglass** has strength, durability, stability, and energy efficiency. It's maintenance-free and easily painted.

Dividers

Years ago, when window glass was weaker and more difficult to manufacture, panes had to be small. Muntins—narrow strips of wood—held panes together in a larger sash. Now muntins are no longer needed. In fact, they reduce the energy efficiency of double glazing. (True divided lights in double-glazed windows are costly.) There are several other options, such as a variety of snap-on muntin grilles that simulate divided-light patterns without compromising efficiency.

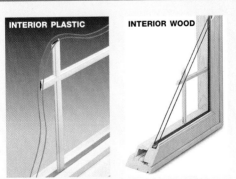

INTERIOR PLASTIC

INTERIOR WOOD

TWO-SIDED

TRUE DIVIDED

Many codes today have energy standards that require double glazing. To maintain a dead-air space between panes, use interior grilles made of plastic or wood, a combination of materials inside and out, or true divided lights with individual double panes.

windows & doors

Better Windows

Older homes had single-glazed windows—only one layer of glass separated the inside from the outside. Unless you wanted chilly rooms and high heat bills, every fall you got out the ladder and put up the storm windows. They provided a second layer of glass over the window and slowed the heat loss. Then, every spring, you took down the storm windows and put up screens for ventilation.

New energy-efficient windows eliminate all that hassle with double glazing—two panes of glass separated by an air space are built right into the window frame. The added glass and the air space provides enough insulation to slice anywhere from 10% to 25% off your heating bill.

Double glazing is a good compromise between cost and energy efficiency in most parts of the country. But if you live where winters are very cold, you may want triple-glazed windows, which have three layers of glass. They cost more and are heavier, but you may save enough on heating to make up the difference.

It was such a novel idea that C. G. Johnson, who invented the uplifting garage door in 1921, promoted his space-saving design on the back of a Model T— complete with tracks, pulleys, and springs.

Some other high-tech options will conserve even more of your energy dollars. You'll pay about 15% more, but windows with low-emissivity (low-E) glass have a microscopically thin metallic coating that blocks heat loss. You may also want to try double-glazed windows with argon gas between the panes. With an insulating value equivalent to 2 inches of fiberglass, some high-tech windows can reduce heating bills in cold climates by 30% or more.

Window Frames

When choosing a new window, consider the framing material as well. Wood is a better insulator than many other window frame materials. But wood must be protected from the weather with paint or a coat of vinyl or aluminum.

Framing made from solid vinyl and aluminum generally needs less maintenance, but these materials are not good insulators. To limit the rapid heat loss through these frames, quality windows must have a thermal break between the inner and outer halves of the frame.

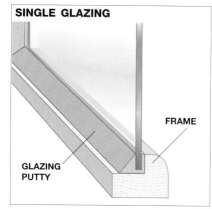

SINGLE GLAZING

FRAME

GLAZING PUTTY

Single glazing is the easiest to install, but it has an insulating value of only R-1, and it fosters condensation.

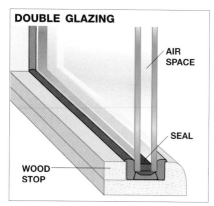

DOUBLE GLAZING

AIR SPACE

SEAL

WOOD STOP

Double-glazed windows provide about an R-2 by trapping a small area of dead air between the panes.

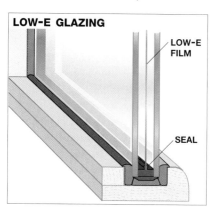

LOW-E GLAZING

LOW-E FILM

SEAL

Low-E glazing can more than double the efficiency of double glazing with a reflective film between panes.

Fogging

One by-product of high-tech windows is less condensation, particularly on windows with what's called warm-edge technology—low-conductance spacers that lower heat transfer near the edge of insulated glazing. When it's 20°F. outside, single glazing can sweat when the indoor air has only 20% relative humidity; a double-glazed low-E window won't sweat until the interior air has 70% relative humidity.

Thermal Breaks

Years ago, metal windows were constructed with one-piece frames, which conducted temperature so fast that the interior surface would freeze when the outside temperature hit 32°F. These frames sweated and corroded. Today, manufacturers provide new and replacement windows with a thermal break using two-piece frames separated by and connected to a piece of rubber or reinforced foam that retards temperature transfer. Windows with energy-efficient frames cut drafts at openings.

Many modern windows with energy-efficient, thermal-break frames have a nailing flange to make installation easy.

You need to caulk drop-in replacement sash to provide a thermal seal between the new window and the old casing.

Special Glass

Standard glass breaks into dangerous, razor-edged shards. There are several types of glass that are safer; these may be required by local building codes in different locations in a house. For example, tempered glass is designed to break into pebble-like pieces. Safety glass, generally required on nonplastic overhead glazing, can be reinforced with wires so that that pieces hang together even when broken. Tempered glass has increased resistance to shattering but must be cut by a professional glazier.

Most residential glass (in both operating and fixed windows) has a small stamp in the corner that specifies the glass type.

Wire-reinforced glass will break under pressure, but the bulk of the glass shards will be held in place.

High-Efficiency Windows

When the need for energy efficiency is paramount and you have taken the many less-costly steps to make your home energy efficient, it may pay to upgrade to one of the super glazing systems. Spectrally selective coatings are the latest low-E technology. Glass with these coatings can block from 40% to 70% of the heat normally conducted through glass without reducing transmitted light.

Low-E , or low-emissivity, uses one or more invisible metallic coatings suspended between two or more sheets of glass. The glass can be fitted into standard or curved frames. Heavy, triple-glazed units (right) may require special installation.

windows & doors

Cutting Openings

Installing a new window in an existing exterior wall is not easy work, even if you don't have a brick wall to contend with. Cutting a hole in the exterior wall of your house can cause irreversible damage. Be sure to locate the new window in a wall section free of wires, pipes, or ducts, and never start the work until after you've actually received the new window.

Begin by marking the exact position of the rough opening—two vertical lines from floor to ceiling (using a long level or plumb bob) and one horizontal line across the top of the rough opening. Cover the floor with a tarp, and use a handsaw to cut through the drywall. (Power saws could cut into buried wires or pipes.) Remove the drywall and insulation underneath.

Before cutting existing studs in the rough opening, build a temporary support for the affected ceiling joists. Make it with 4x4s or doubled 2x4s, and set it up no more than 2 feet from the existing wall. This support should extend at least 2 feet beyond each side of the rough opening. Cut existing studs to be removed into sections to make them easier to pry out. Don't cut through the siding at this point.

Framing the Opening

With the existing studs out, toenail full-length king studs into the soleplate and top plate on either side of the rough opening—or drive in angled screws. Cut and nail up the shorter jack studs to the inside face of the king studs. Trimmer studs support the header, which forms the rough opening's top.

You'll have to make the header by sandwiching a piece of ⅜-inch plywood between two sections of 2x10 and nailing them with staggered 16d nails about 16 inches on center. The required width of the two-by varies with the length of the span between trimmer studs, however. Check local building codes.

Nail up the header and the short cripple studs above it. Cut and nail in the sill and the jack studs supporting it. Add insulation in stud cavities before nailing up drywall around the opening. If you have wood siding, drive nails through the corners of the rough opening to transfer the outline to the exterior siding. Cut the opening from the outside. Tack a board to the siding as a guide for the power saw.

Drip Cap

A piece of flashing called a drip cap, made from either aluminum or plastic, must be installed to form a barrier between the window and the sheathing to prevent water from seeping inside the wall. One flange of the drip cap is installed under-neath the siding above the window; the other folds down over the window frame. Install the drip cap with a downward slope to deflect rainwater.

Although windows *generally come supplied with flashing, you can cut and bend your own out of aluminum.*

Caulking

Seal the gap between the window casing and the sheathing with an exterior-grade polyurethane caulk. This bead of caulk, along with flashing, will prevent air and water from seeping between the window and the wall, where it can cause rot. After you've installed the window trim, you can also run a second bead of caulk between the trim and the siding. It pays to check the caulk around the windows periodically. By filling cracks (or replacing old caulk), you can cut down on drafts and save on heating costs.

On a new window *with an integral nailing flange, add a liberal bead of caulk to help seal the window perimeter.*

Edging

To seal side seams between windows and wood siding, you need to rely on caulk. With vinyl siding, use molded J-channel. It has a lip that wraps around the ends of the vinyl and a nailing strip where you can attach it to the wall. No matter what type of siding you install, first staple up a layer of felt paper or air-stopping house wrap. Trim the corners, and tack the overage back into the frame opening.

Vinyl J-channel *fits against the side edges of the window and is nailed through its perforated flange.*

Installing a Window in New Construction

USE: ▶ measuring tape • circular saw • staple gun • caulking gun • level • hammer ▶ new window • exterior-grade caulk • nails • shims • insulation • trim

1 **You can cut sheathing** *around window openings, but it is often easier to sheathe the entire wall and cut the openings later.*

2 **After marking the rough opening,** *set a circular saw to the depth of your sheathing (typically ½ in.) to make the cuts.*

3 **When you install** *felt paper or house wrap, leave enough to tuck back and staple onto the sides of the framed opening.*

4 **To make a weathertight seal,** *add a bead of exterior-grade caulk to the back of the nailing flange before installing the unit.*

5 **Set the window unit** *in place, resting it on the sill so you can tip it in place. Add a few temporary nails for security.*

6 **Use pairs of tapered shingle shims** *to adjust the window on all sides in the opening, checking for plumb and level.*

7 **Cut drafts** *and improve energy efficiency by stuffing insulation into gaps between the studs and the window frame.*

8 **Once the window** *is plumbed and leveled, fasten it by nailing on all sides through the perforated flange.*

9 **With the window fastened,** *you can add caulk and trim: J-channel for vinyl siding or a variety of wood trim for clapboards or shakes.*

windows & doors _____

Finishing Touches

Once a new window has been leveled, shimmed, and nailed in place, it's time to begin working on the trim. Factory-built windows won't have anything beyond the bare essentials, and what's there might not match the style used on your house.

Exterior trimwork begins with the factory-supplied exterior casing. It is usually one of two types of bare-minimum molding: brick-mold, a narrow molding with a little detail; or a flat ⁵⁄₄ casing, which is just a narrow, flat strip alongside the window's outer edge. By themselves, they don't look like much. Probably the best way to fix factory casing is to just add more molding over or around it. For example, you can widen the flat casing by adding ⁵⁄₄ stock; then cover both pieces with stock molding to add detail to the profile.

You could leave the side casing alone and replace the top piece, called the head casing, instead. This works well with brickmold casing, which is harder to add to because the face is not flat. Replace the factory head casing with a ⁵⁄₄x6 board nailed over the window frame, and apply trim to it—quarter-rounds, coves, drip caps, and other shapes to make the trim as elaborate as you like. When planning your new trim design, it's probably best to tack samples to a wall so that you can step back and take a look. But mixing and matching from stock molding shapes available at lumberyards will surely produce a combination that does the job.

Interior Trim Options

PLAIN

SIDE CASING

REVEAL

MITERED CORNER

DECORATIVE

ROSETTE CORNER BLOCK

STOP

STOOL

APRON

FLUTED CASING

Some windows come with exterior trim already mounted. That system works because windows are installed from the outside. Inside, you have to add trim. Flat or clamshell shapes generally are best suited to casements and fixed glass, while double-hungs can be trimmed with beaded casings and corner blocks.

Installing Window Trim

USE: ▶ power miter saw or miter box and backsaw • power drill/driver • hammer • saber saw • eye protection ▶ side trim • stool • apron • return pieces

1 Cut top and side pieces at 45°, add glue to the joints, predrill to avoid splitting, and secure with finishing nails.

2 Use a saber saw to cut the deep, interior sill, called a stool, where it extends beyond the window frame and side trim pieces.

3 Add glue, predrill the stool, and drive finishing nails at an angle into the window frame. You can fill and sand the holes later.

Exterior Details

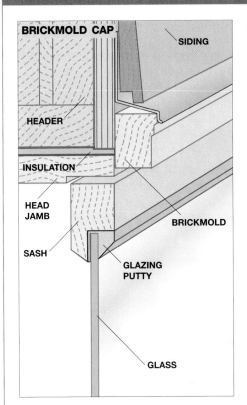

BRICKMOLD CAP

SIDING

HEADER

INSULATION

HEAD JAMB

SASH

BRICKMOLD

GLAZING PUTTY

GLASS

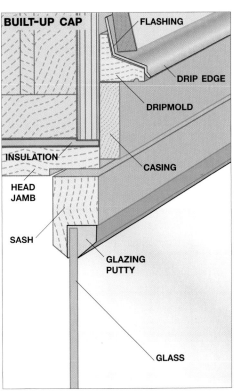

BUILT-UP CAP

FLASHING

DRIP EDGE

DRIPMOLD

INSULATION

HEAD JAMB

CASING

SASH

GLAZING PUTTY

GLASS

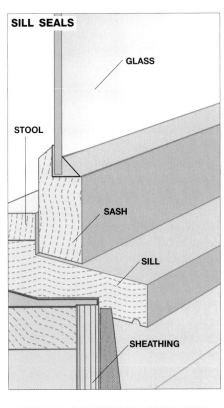

SILL SEALS

GLASS

STOOL

SASH

SILL

SHEATHING

To protect the top edge of windows with standard brickmold trim, tuck flashing under the siding and across the top of the frame.

Provide extra protection for windows under a shallow roof overhang by adding an extension of angled cap trim above the window trim.

For the best seal at windowsills, siding should tuck into a slot in the sill. The small outer groove is a capillary break to shed water.

• finishing nails • wood glue • wood putty • sandpaper

4 *Use a power miter saw* or *backsaw and miter box to cut a miter at each end of the trim that supports the stool, called the apron.*

5 *After predrilling,* drive finishing nails at a slight upward angle through the apron and into the wall and window frames.

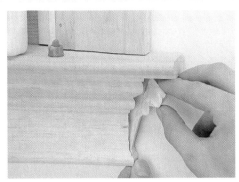

6 *Make and glue on small return pieces to complete the apron miters. Without this step, you would see the apron end grain.*

windows & doors

Old Windows

After years of use and layer upon layer of paint, your windows may not be broken, but they won't work as they did when they were new. On older homes, single-pane glass and worn jambs aren't doing much to keep the heat in during winter, and that old paint can make windows nearly impossible to open and close.

You could spend hours scraping the windows down to bare wood and wind up with the same old energy-inefficient model. Replacing them makes better use of your time and money. These days you can get inexpensive, custom-made replacement windows with double glazing that drastically improves the unit's insulating value. You could also opt for low-emissivity glass or even triple glazing if you live in an area with very cold winters. (See pp. 468–69 for more on window glazing.)

Replacement Options

You have three basic choices—sash kits, replacement windows that fit into existing frames, or entirely new windows that have their own frames and casing. With sash kits, you get new standard-sized sashes—the window glass and the frame around it—plus new jamb liners, which are the tracks that hold the sash in place. Sash frames can be wood or vinyl with double glazing. Your existing window frame, casing, and trim all stay in place, and all installation work is done from the inside. On the downside, a sash kit typically is not as energy-efficient as a new window.

Replacement windows are entirely new, energy-efficient units custom-made to fit into an existing window frame (usually at no extra cost). These windows have less glass area than the old ones, but if cost is a major consideration, vinyl replacement windows are the way to go.

New windows give you a wider range of options—you can go to larger sizes and different shapes—but the installation involves a lot more work because you have to rip out the old window entirely. If the new one is only a little larger, you may be able to take advantage of extra space in the rough frame that was formerly occupied by the sash weights. For larger windows, it means cutting a bigger wall opening and installing new framing. See pp. 470–71 for more on installing a new window.

Cutting Back Siding

To cut back vinyl siding, use a zip tool, which unlocks the joint between courses, and trim with metal shears.

Wedge wood siding to make room for your saw blade, and finish the cuts at the top with a sharp wood chisel.

Curved Windows

To set and flash windows with curved frames, you need special flashing. Generally, it is supplied by the window manufacturer, often as a premolded flexible vinyl strip that conforms to the curve. Curved shapes are difficult for DIYers to make because the edge must be snipped and tucked every few inches to create the curve—and every cut is a potential leak. It's better to have flashing made up by a metal shop.

Joining New and Old Siding

You can butt seams where you stagger joints around a new window, but cuts at 45° offer more protection.

Should new siding shrink and open the joint, you'll see more wood instead of a gap. Predrill at the ends of boards.

Installing a Replacement Window

USE: ▶ pry bar • hammer • chisel • reciprocating saw • level • plumb bob ▶ replacement window • 2x4s • ½-in. plywood • nails • shims

1 To remove an old, single-glazed window, use a pry bar, hammer, and chisel to pry loose the surrounding trim.

2 Use the same techniques inside to remove interior trim. If you want to reuse it, pry gradually as the trim may be brittle.

3 To release the window, cut through the nails that extend from the frame into the house-wall studs.

4 Once the nails are cut, you can pry out the window. First, you may need to release shims at the sides of the frame.

5 Pack out the old opening as required, using 2x4s or other lumber to make a rough opening matched to the new window.

6 The new 2x4 will not be as thick as the adjacent wall. You need to add drywall inside and plywood sheathing outside.

7 Add an overlapped strip of felt paper or house wrap, and plumb and level the replacement window.

8 Tack the window in place, add pairs of tapered shingle shims from the inside, and finish nailing the exterior flange.

9 You can cut back alternate courses of siding so that joints won't align as you fill in around the new window.

windows & doors

Unsticking Windows

Once spring arrives and the weather warms up, you'll want to open all your windows all the way and let the fresh air in. But moving parts that have been locked in place over the winter may refuse to budge. So start small: just try to get the windows cracked. If the frame is swollen from moisture or the window sash and the surrounding frame are sealed by paint, you could be in for a wrestling match.

If a double-hung window won't move, first try a sharp push with the heel of your hand on the sash at the center of the window—by the window lock. A good crack may break a thin paint bond. Do not use a hammer and wood block—they may break the window.

Before going too far, make sure the window is unlocked and that no one has set a finishing nail through the sash or installed some other security device. It's embarrassing to curse at a window that won't move when it's locked.

Usually, the trick is to slice apart the painted seams between the window sash and the trim piece, called a stop, that makes a track for the sash. You can use a utility knife, a tool called a paint zipper, or even a sharp pizza cutter. Don't forget to do the outside seams, too.

If all else fails, try forcing the window with a flat pry bar set between the windowsill and the bottom of the sash. The tool will likely gouge the wood, but the only alternative is prying off the stop, which holds a double-hung window in place.

USE: ▶ scoring tool or wheel cutter • straightedge • eye protection • work gloves ▶ glazing panel

1 Use a scoring tool (left) on plastic glazing panels and a wheel-type tool (right) on single-thickness glass.

2 Work on a flat surface with a square or straightedge to guide the cutter. Sheets of newspaper provide a cushion.

3 Press down firmly as you draw the cutter across the glass. A small wheel scores the glass surface.

4 Set a narrow wood dowel under the score line, and apply pressure on both sides to snap the glass or plastic cleanly.

Replacing Glass

USE: ▶ putty knife • paintbrush • glass cutter (if needed) • eye protection • work gloves ▶ new glass • primer • glazing compound • glazier's points

1 On an older window, the exterior putty may pop off the glass and frame easily when you scrape it with a putty knife.

2 On some frames, you may need to dig out the putty. Once the glass is free, also scrape the wood underneath.

3 Prime raw wood where new compound will rest. This keeps moisture from seeping into the wood and weakening the bond.

Freeing a Stuck Sash

To free a sash stuck in place by many coats of paint, use a utility knife to make several scoring cuts between sash and stop.

On older windows, particularly those that are not regularly opened, layers of paint can seal the sash in its track. Instead of forcing the sash or prying at the base and damaging the wood, release the painted-on seal. You can slice along the seam with a utility knife, making repeated passes to cut through the paint. A circular cutting wheel also works well and is easier to keep in the seam. Sometimes the only permanent solution is to pry off the stop, and remove the window for a thorough scraping and sanding.

A wheel cutter rides along the seam between the sash and the stop. You may also need to cut the paint film outside.

Glazing Compounds

Traditional compound is an oily putty. You need to work it smooth until it's soft like dough, form a ball, and roll the ball into strips.

At seams between dissimilar materials, such as glass and wood, which expand and contract at different rates, you need glazing compound. To form the compound, work it in your hands or roll it out on a board. If you need to make a glass repair in cold weather, first prepare the compound inside so that it's pliable when you work it along the window. The wood against which the compound rests should be primed. Otherwise, the compound can dry prematurely and crack.

Preformed compound is available in plastic-backed strips. Peel the backing, and push the strip of compound in place.

4 Roll out a rope of fresh compound to back up the glass, set it against the sash, and press it in place with your fingers.

5 To secure the glass, set small holders, called glazier's points. Use a putty knife to force the points into the sash.

6 The exterior layer of compound covers the points. Spread this layer with a putty knife, and use the edge to trim any excess.

windows & doors

Making Windows Glide

A window doesn't have to stick to be a pain. Some windows still move but demand a workout to get opened or closed. On a wood window, built-up paint layers can simply make the sash too big for the sliding track. The solution is to scrape or sand off enough paint so that the sash will be a hair thinner. Make sure all exposed wood has been covered with paint (or sealer) to minimize swelling on humid days.

An easier way to make the sash move more freely is to increase the clearance between the sash and stop. Do this by scoring the seam between the sash and the stop with a utility knife, then a metal-cutting jigsaw blade, then a slightly thicker wood-cutting blade.

Adjusting the Friction

On many windows, tension that holds the sash in place is supplied by some type of spring clip, usually in a tight V-shape, that is built into the window frame. It presses against the sash. To decrease the tension, place a 1x2 over the spring clip, and give it a few shots with a hammer. You may find that you have to use some really firm blows before noticing any difference. You can increase the tension by slipping a screwdriver into the V-clip and prying it open a bit—use only a little pressure.

Improve old double-hung windows that use the weight-and-pulley system by installing new friction channels. (See below.) Your sash will operate more smoothly and leak less air.

Removing an Old Sash

USE: ▶ utility knife • wood chisel • pry bar • work gloves

1 To remove an old sash for scraping, painting, or other repairs, start by scoring the painted seam along the stop.

2 Use a chisel to break the bond between the stop molding and the window casing.

3 Use a pry bar to gradually pry off all the stop. An old stop, which you can reuse, is likely to be brittle and snap easily.

4 With the stop removed, you can lift the sash out of its tracks. On some units, you need to disconnect slide systems.

Improving Windows by Using Friction Channels

USE: ▶ pry bar • hammer and wood chisel or small saw • block plane or scraper • paintbrush • plumb bob • power drill/driver • work gloves ▶ friction channels

1 To improve an old window with a loose sash, you can install friction channels. Start by removing the inside and outside stop.

2 Set the new channel in place to mark its location on the existing top trim. You'll have to notch the trim to install the channel.

3 Use a small saw or a hammer and chisel to trim away the end of the trim so that the molded side channels will fit.

New Flashing

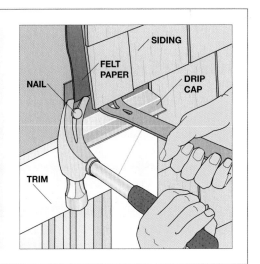

When a window leaks, often the problem stems from the most exposed seam along the top. It should be protected by flashing, which sheds water running down the siding. When flashing deteriorates, particularly synthetics that can become brittle due to constant exposure and the sun's UV rays, you can replace it. The trick is to gently pry up and wedge shakes or clapboards above the window, and pull or cut the old flashing nails. Then you can caulk, and slip in a new piece.

New Sills

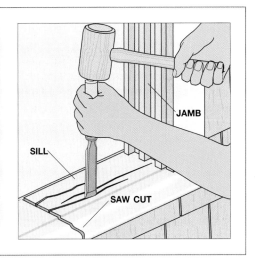

Windowsills can rot on the outside from exposure and on the inside from condensation that runs down the glass. When the wood is beyond repair, you can buy a replacement sill to install without replacing the entire window. To remove the old sill, cut all the way through to make two big pieces. Then use a chisel to split each piece into small sections that you can slide out from under the jamb. You may also need a hacksaw to cut nails.

• primer • screws

4 *You probably will need to scrape* or plane down the sides of the sash so that they move smoothly in the new channels.

5 *After priming any raw wood,* fit the sash into the appropriate sides of the channels, and reinstall them as one unit.

6 *Plumb the channels,* slide the sash out of the way, and permanently fasten the channels to the window frame with screws.

windows & doors

The Case for Storms

With so many high-tech alternatives, you may wonder why there is still a market for storm windows. They're old-fashioned, a nuisance, and easily replaced with energy-saving double-glazed windows (two sheets of glass sandwiching an insulating "dead air" space).

In homes with single-pane glass, new double glazing certainly makes a noticeable difference in your comfort and utility bills. However, you can also make a difference for far less money and effort by putting up storm windows. There are many types available. And in almost all cases, adding a removable storm, even triple-track storms with screens, is less costly and less work than ripping out old window sashes and frames and installing completely new units—with trim, touch-ups, and all the other work that goes along with opening a large hole in the side of your house.

And for less than $10 a window, you can add a layer of clear plastic film on the inside during the winter. It is almost unnoticeable, just as energy-efficient as storms and double glazing, and an easy do-it-yourself project. Replacement windows cost more—a lot more.

If you prefer ⅛-inch thick rigid plastic, you can make custom frames for interior-mounted storms using U-shaped plastic or aluminum channels. Many casement windows have interior sash slots that allow you to clip framed storm panels in place.

Installing Heat-Shrink Plastic

USE: ▶ hair dryer • utility knife ▶ heat-shrink plastic • double-faced tape

1 Interior clear plastic traps a layer of dead insulating air next to the glass. It mounts with double-faced tape.

2 Unfold the plastic, spread it evenly over the window, and press onto the tape. There are kits for windows and doors.

3 Use a hair dryer to apply heat. This causes the film to shrink, which removes the wrinkles and leaves a clear film.

4 Trim excess plastic using a utility knife. If the material is well installed, it can last through a heating season.

Replacing Screens

USE: ▶ small pry bar • pliers • screwdriver • C-clamps • staple gun • utility knife • straightedge • hammer ▶ blocking • new screening • staples • finishing nails

1 To replace damaged screens on a wood frame, start by prying off the trim pieces that hold the screen edges.

2 Use pliers and a screwdriver to pull the old staples and remove the old screen. You may want to sand and paint the frame, too.

3 Use clamps to create a downward bow in the center of the frame. When the raised ends are released, the screen will tighten.

Glazing Connections

There are many types of storm windows, including the old-fashioned sash frame that is glazed like a regular window. To replace or repair those glazing joints, scrape off old putty, prime raw wood, and spread a new layer. Most aluminum storm units have a rubber gasket to hold the glazing in place. You need to disassemble the frame and strip out the gasket to make repairs.

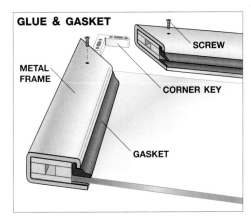

GLUE & GASKET
SCREW
METAL FRAME
CORNER KEY
GASKET

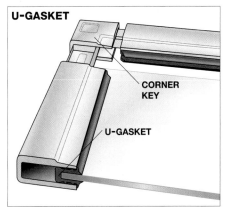

U-GASKET
CORNER KEY
U-GASKET

Screening Frames

Use shears or a utility knife to cut new screening with a 2-inch overage on all sides. Lay it over the frame, and roll the screening into the channel with the wheel of a screen roller. Then roll the spline into the channel to tighten and hold the screen in place. Keep the screen tight as you work. With fiberglass or metal screens, it works best to install opposite sides in order.

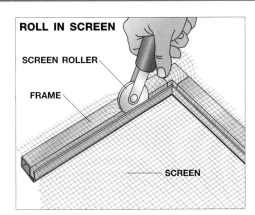

ROLL IN SCREEN
SCREEN ROLLER
FRAME
SCREEN

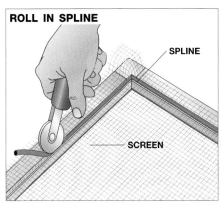

ROLL IN SPLINE
SPLINE
SCREEN

4 *Spread a new piece of screen* over the bowed frame, and staple it in place, starting at the center and working out.

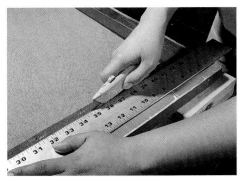

5 *Use a utility knife and a straightedge* to trim away excess screen. You have to staple in a straight line to get a neat edge.

6 *Finally, nail down the trim pieces* that help to hold the screen tight and cover the rows of staples.

windows & doors

Door Basics

Doors, like windows, serve various purposes. On the functional side, they provide a way into and out of the house, give us privacy when we want it, and keep out unwanted noise, cold drafts, bugs, and people who bug us. But doors (and doorways) also figure in home design. The front door is an important architectural focal point, and interior doors help express the style of the house or complement a room's decor.

A new front door with sidelights can make your entry hall seem brighter and more inviting, while switching from a painted to a wood-finish door adds a touch of elegance. You can improve traffic flow between parts of the house by installing a new door or two, but it comes at a cost. Because the traffic lanes take up space, the more doors a room has, the smaller it seems. Every new door also needs enough space to swing open and closed.

Don't count on just adding or moving a door in just one afternoon, because there is a lot to the job. You have to locate and cut a hole through an existing wall, remove the old wall framing, frame the rough opening, and install the door itself. You'll need good carpentry skills and a building permit in many locales, but the job is within the range of many DIYers.

Buying Doors

The wood doors you'll find at building-supply centers are either panel doors, which have anywhere from one to ten panels set in a solid wood frame, or flush doors, formed by covering a solid wood core or a lightweight hollow core with thin sheets of wood veneer. While panel doors come in a wide range of wood types, flush doors usually are faced with lauan mahogany or birch, and they are less expensive.

Doors are sold prehung (where the door is mounted in a frame, sometimes with holes for the lockset predrilled) or as individual components. Unless you have hung a door before, spend the extra money for a prehung unit. It's not that the skills required to assemble a frame and hinge a door are all that difficult, it's the time you'll save. On an exterior door, you will also be assured of a tight weather seal. If you want to replace or upgrade an old door, just buy the door alone and use the original as a template for mounting hinges and the lockset.

Types

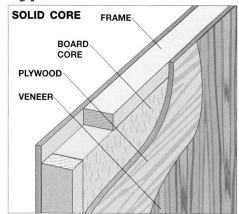

Solid-core doors are used on exterior openings for security and durability. They often need three hinges due to their weight.

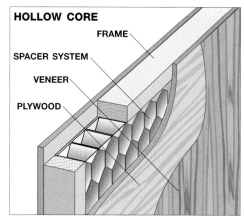

Hollow-core doors are used on interior openings. They are much lighter because the core is an air-filled spacer system.

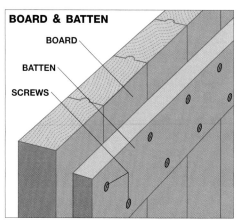

Board-and-batten doors generally are used on sheds and other outbuildings. The batten ties together several boards.

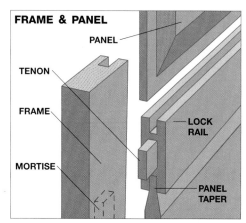

Frame-and-panel doors typically are used on cabinets. Interlocked rails are permanently fixed, and the panel floats inside.

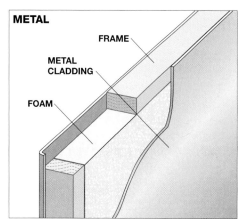

Metal-clad doors are increasingly popular because the metal needs little maintenance, and the foam core is energy efficient.

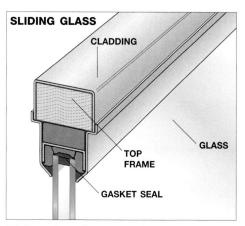

Sliding glass doors may be wood- or metal-framed. One panel is fixed with hardware; the other slides in a track.

Anatomy

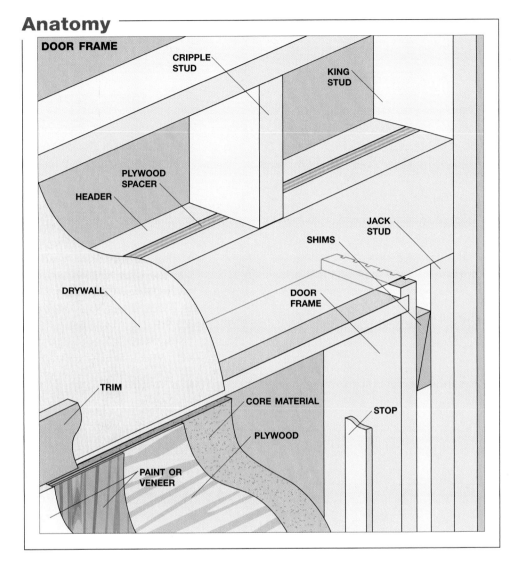

Door Actions

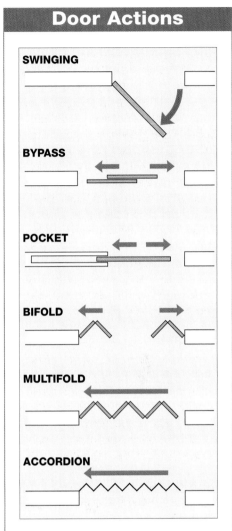

Hinge Swings

When you order a prehung door, you need to specify how it will swing. The convention is to order a door by its hand, which means that the door has either a left-hand or right-hand swing. This is determined by the side of the door that is hinged when you stand on the outside of the room or street side of an exterior door. When you open the door away from you, right-hand doors will swing to the right, left-hand doors will swing to the left. Reverse models are available for doors that swing toward you.

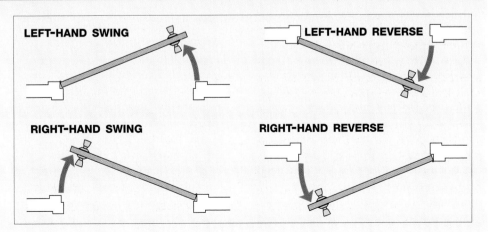

windows & doors

More Than a Door

Doors don't just hang by themselves; other structural pieces surround the door and provide support. Buried beneath drywall and trim is the door frame, which forms the door's rough opening. It is composed of vertical 2x4s and a horizontal piece called a header. The header is needed for extra support over doorways in load-bearing walls, because some wall studs have been removed to make room for the door.

The doorjambs—two side jambs and the head jamb across the top—form the finished opening for the door itself, as well as the mounting point for the hinges and the lockset. The door sill, or threshold, lies below the door, and the door stops—narrow strips of wood nailed to the jambs—keep the door from swinging beyond the closed position. Trim, also called casing, covers gaps between the rough opening and the jambs. The gaps provide room to level and plumb the door and jambs.

Installing a Prehung Door

To start, don't remove shipping braces from the door—they keep the frame square. If the floor is not level, cut one leg of the frame. Prehung doors are built to allow for thick carpeting, so you may need to cut both legs if the bottom of the door is too high off an uncarpeted floor.

Center the unit in the opening, and check that the top is level. Insert shims in the gaps between the doorjambs and rough framing to square and plumb the door opening. Use prepackaged shims sold for this purpose, tapered wood shingles, or homemade shims.

Remove the stops, and set a pair of shims with tapers opposing between the frame and stud at each hinge location—and if there are only two hinges, in the middle. Increase or decrease the overlap of the shims to adjust the frame until it is plumb. Drive a finishing nail through the jamb, each shim set, and partially into the stud. Then install three sets of shims on the other side jamb and one set above the head jamb. When all shims are in place, the frame is plumb and square, and there is a uniform gap between the door and the jamb, then add a second nail at each shim and drive all nails home.

On an exterior door, stuff insulation behind and above the jamb before installing the casing.

Exterior Details

Exterior door frames are constructed differently from interior doors. Because exterior doors provide protection from rain and seal out drafts, the perimeter must be weatherstripped, even at the sill. The sill must slope down away from the house so that water runs off. It should also have a drip edge to prevent water from seeping underneath. A drip cap above the door and caulk around the casing completes the weather protection.

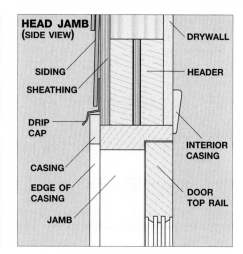

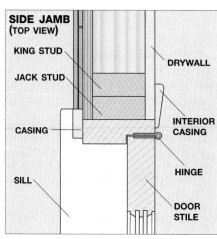

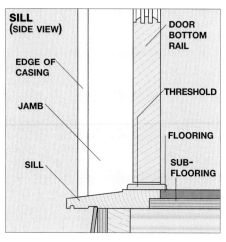

Glass vs. Security

Glass will let in light, but a large panel makes an exterior door vulnerable to break-ins. To minimize your risk, you can use tempered or safety glazing that is harder to break. (Double glazing is also more resistant than single glazing.) The problem is that by breaking the glass, a burglar can simply reach inside to undo the locks. To prevent that easy entry, use glass panels on top of the door or small panes that don't allow access to the locks.

Installing a Prehung Door

USE: ▶ utility knife • staple gun • level • drill • hammer • putty knife ▶ prehung door & lockset • caulk or flashing • 2x4 brace • shims • nails • wood putty

1 Cut the felt paper or house wrap *across the door opening, and staple back the excess against the sides of the framing.*

2 You can install flashing *under the sill, although many manufacturers suggest using a waterproof caulk instead.*

3 You set a prehung exterior door *from the outside of the house. The door already has exterior molding attached to the frame.*

4 Working from the inside, *use a level to plumb the door. Put a brace across the outside to keep the door in the opening.*

5 As you check for level, *insert shingle shims in the gaps between the door frame and the 2x4 wall studs.*

6 When the door is correctly positioned, *predrill and nail through the frame (and hidden shims) into the wall framing.*

7 Also drive finishing nails *through the face of exterior molding into the wall framing. Set the heads, and fill with putty.*

8 You can order most prehung doors *with locks already installed or with the holes predrilled so you can install your own.*

9 A lockset plus dead bolt *provides extra security. Use long screws in the keepers that reach through to the house framing.*

windows & doors

Keep Cold Out

Weatherstripping an entry door used to be a job for pros because interlocking metal channels had to be routed into the door and jamb and mated precisely for the door to close. Sealing up doors today is child's play by comparison, and the weatherstripping itself does a much better job of keeping the heat in and the cold out.

As long as the door itself is solid and there are no cracks in the wood panels, your main concern will be sealing up the narrow space around the door's outer edge. Jamb weatherstripping takes care of the space along the sides and top of the door. Sill weatherstripping seals the bottom to keep out cold drafts and water.

Weatherstripping a Door

Home-supply centers sell nail-on and self-adhesive weatherstripping for the sides and tops of doors. Both must be cut to length and mounted on the jamb so that when the door closes, it presses against the rubber or foam sealer on one edge of the strip. Neoprene rubber sealers last longer than foam, and nail-on weatherstripping stays put better than the self-adhesive type. You need a perfectly clean, smooth surface for self-sticking weatherstripping, and it may not last more than a season.

Vinyl, wood, and aluminum door-stop trim, edged with a sealer, comes precut with coped joints on the side pieces. You only have to square-cut to length the top piece and the bottoms of the two side pieces. Then, with the door closed, nail the trim to the jamb with 4d finishing nails so that the weatherstripping compresses very slightly against the door. If you pack in so much that it compresses a great deal, it does no good.

Manufacturers offer a greater selection of weatherstripping for the door sill than for the jambs. Simple door sweeps attach to the inside face of the door and hang down to make a seal with the sill. Usually you don't have to cut down the door itself. Sweeps and any other type of weather seal attached to the door may not work if you have a thick mat inside.

Other types of sill weatherstripping include a U-shaped brass frame and an aluminum threshold with a vinyl sealer. Mount the U-shaped sealer with screws, adjusting to seal the space under the door. On the aluminum threshold, install it and set the height of the vinyl sealer.

Installing a Door Shoe

USE: ▶ chalk-line box • circular saw • paintbrush • hacksaw • screwdriver • drill ▶ door shoe • sealer

1 *Exposure to the weather* sometimes can cause extensive rot along the bottom edge of an exterior wood door.

2 *Snap a chalk line*, and cut off the damaged base of the door. An inch or more can be concealed with most door shoes.

Sill Weatherstripping

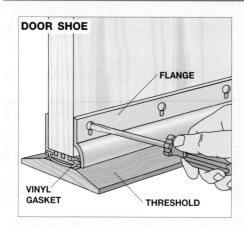

DOOR SHOE
FLANGE
VINYL GASKET
THRESHOLD

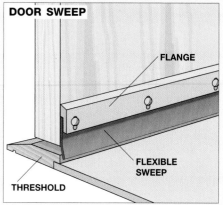

DOOR SWEEP
FLANGE
FLEXIBLE SWEEP
THRESHOLD

Replacing a Threshold

USE: ▶ saw • wood chisel • pry bar • caulking gun • putty knife ▶ threshold • waterproof caulk or flashing

1 *When the weather causes cracking* and rotting in an exposed door threshold, you can buy and install a replacement.

2 *To remove an existing threshold* without removing the door casing and trim, cut through the middle of the board.

- screws

3 *Apply at least one coat of sealer* to the raw wood along the bottom edge of the door before installing the shoe.

4 *Cut the extruded aluminum shoe* to length with a hacksaw, set it onto the trimmed base of the door, and drill pilot holes.

5 *Fasten the shoe* with screws. This shoe covers the trimmed base and provides a flexible weatherstripping seal.

Jamb Weatherstripping

Most modern exterior doors are sold ready-to-install on their hinges in a frame with integral weatherstripping. To bring an older door up to modern standards, you can add jamb weatherstripping to the existing frame. J-strip is a flexible aluminum strip that fills the gap between the door and the frame. Gasket weatherstripping has a flexible vinyl tube to provide a seal when the door closes.

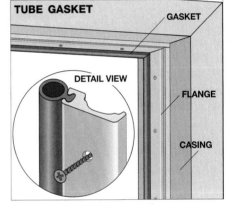

J-STRIP
J-STRIP
DETAIL VIEW
JAMB

TUBE GASKET
GASKET
DETAIL VIEW
FLANGE
CASING

- wood plugs or wood putty

3 *With the threshold in two pieces,* it's easier to split the shorter sections using a chisel and pry them out with a pry bar.

4 *To keep water from seeping in,* you can install threshold flashing or use a double bead of waterproof caulk.

5 *Notch out* for the threshold extensions, slide the new piece in place, and fasten it using screws that are plugged or puttied.

windows & doors

Saving Space

Where there is room to swing open and closed, standard doors work as well as any other for interior rooms, closets, and storage areas. But in a hall without much room, you can gain space by reducing the swing.

You could use several single doors in small openings, but each door requires framing, trim, and hardware, which takes time and money. At the other extreme are pocket doors, which slide sideways into the wall. They save the most hall space but provide limited access because, for every foot of open wall, you need a foot of closed wall into which the door can slide. (And you have to find wall space free of pipes, wires, and ducts.) Another drawback is that the pocket section of the wall has skimpy surface framing instead of full-depth studs. So, unlike other partition walls, if you push on the pocket section, the framing may give a bit.

Another option is to make one large opening and hang two or more sliding doors. But they provide limited access because one door width always stays in the opening. So the best bet for a hall may be a compromise—either double doors or bifold doors. Double doors that meet in the middle of the opening reduce the swing by half. Bifold doors swing over on themselves like an accordion and use even less floor space.

For more money but less work, use prehung doors already hinged in the frames. Don't remove the bracing until the unit is plumbed, shimmed, and nailed.

Interior doors also are often bought prehung. If the unit comes from the supplier with at least one cross brace to keep the door and frame aligned, leave it on until the door is set. On partition walls that do not bear structural loads, you can use 2x4s on the flat across the top of the opening. Load-bearing walls require a structural header. On each side of the opening there is one full-height stud and a shorter stud that helps support the header.

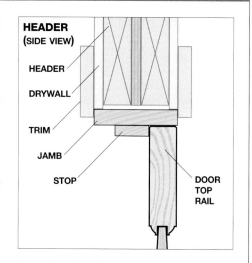

HEADER (SIDE VIEW)
HEADER
DRYWALL
TRIM
JAMB
STOP
DOOR TOP RAIL

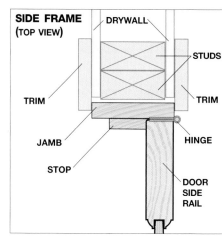

SIDE FRAME (TOP VIEW)
DRYWALL
STUDS
TRIM
TRIM
JAMB
HINGE
STOP
DOOR SIDE RAIL

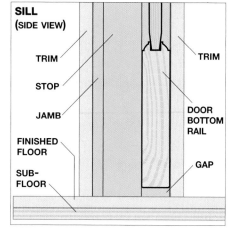

SILL (SIDE VIEW)
TRIM
STOP
JAMB
FINISHED FLOOR
SUB-FLOOR
TRIM
DOOR BOTTOM RAIL
GAP

Pocket Doors

Although pocket doors require special framing and more installation time than a standard door, they save floor space by sliding directly into the wall instead of swinging through an arc and taking up wall space when open. New units come with a double-sided frame around the sliding pocket space. Because this framing is not as thick as normal 2x4 wall studs, you have to install it carefully, often with screws instead of nails. The frame must be plumb for the door to slide smoothly on its track.

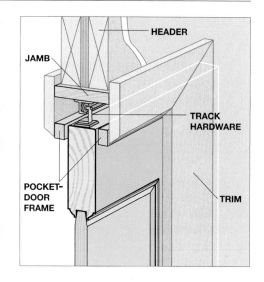

HEADER
JAMB
TRACK HARDWARE
POCKET-DOOR FRAME
TRIM

Installing an Interior Door

USE: ▶ power drill/driver • hammer • framing square • level ▶ prehung interior door • 2x lumber for header • 2x4s • cross brace • shims • nails • trim

1 *To fit an interior door* into a non-load-bearing partition, lay out the rough opening, allowing for two jack studs.

2 *A jack stud* nailed onto a full-height stud helps to support the header. Pack out vertically set headers with ½-in. plywood.

3 *With the door framing in place,* install drywall panels (typically ½ in. thick) using wide-threaded drywall screws.

4 *Although this prehung door* is hinged in its frame, it pays to check for square and lock the position with a cross brace.

5 *Tip the door into place* and hold it temporarily with shingle shims. The cross-brace keeps the frame flush with the drywall.

6 *Working from the inside of the wall,* use more shingle shims and a level to plumb the door in the framed opening.

7 *When the door is plumb,* drive 10d finishing nails through the jamb and shingle shims into the 2x4 wall framing.

8 *Select trim for the outside face* that matches other trim in the room. Cut mitered corners, add glue, and nail.

9 *It's wise* to order doors predrilled. You can buy the hardware you like and easily fasten it in the factory-drilled holes.

windows & doors

Sticking Doors

Hot, humid summer days don't have to mean a wrestling match with sticking doors. You can minimize this seasonal headache by making sure all edges and door faces are sealed with varnish or paint. If the door rubs only slightly in summer, leave it alone. But if it sticks or needs a real shove to open or close it, it's better to adjust the fit. Eventually all that sticking and shoving may cause the hinges to loosen, which will only aggravate the problem. Bear in mind that a small adjustment will probably do the trick and that if you cut off too much in summer, the door may be too loose in winter. Often you will need less than a ¹⁄₁₆-inch clearance.

Resetting Hinges

Make sure that a loose hinge is not causing the door to bind. Tightening the screws on a loose hinge pulls the door edge closer to the frame on the hinge side. That widens the gap on the handle side, and your binding problem disappears.

If the screws you try to tighten spin in their holes instead of digging in, you have to fix the hole. Dip slivers of wood or toothpicks in glue, and drive them into the hole in a tight pack. When the glue dries, the screw threads will have something to bite into. You can also substitute longer screws that will extend into the framing behind the jamb. This is a good idea for the top hinge of a heavy door and will often solve your problem, even if the hinge is already tight. The longer screw actually draws the jamb closer to the studs, producing extra clearance on the handle side of the door.

Shaving It Down

Unless the binding problem is clearly caused by built-up paint, save sanding or planing the door edge for a last resort. Take off only a little at a time, but remove enough to make room for a new coat of paint. Medium-grit sandpaper is best for small adjustments. If you can't tell where the door is rubbing, sprinkle colored chalk on the edge of the open door. Closing the chalked door will leave smudges on tight spots.

If all else fails and you have to remove a significant amount of wood from the door edge, it's usually best to take the hinges off the door and plane the hinge side. Be sure to deepen the hinge mortises by the same amount.

Tightening a Loose Hinge

When hinge screws on a door work loose, you can solve the problem by installing longer screws with thicker shanks. The idea is to use screws that bite into fresh wood and provide more holding power, with an inch or so more of thread. You can also increase a screw's holding capacity by filling in the existing holes. There are several DIY fixes, including wood filler, a short length of dowel, or even a bunch of toothpicks packed into the old screw-hole to provide material for the screws to bite into.

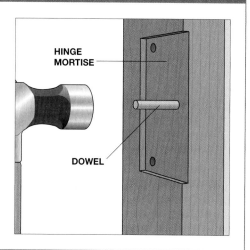

HINGE MORTISE

DOWEL

Repairing a Slider

If a sliding door no longer glides, remove it by lifting the panel straight up and edging the bottom out of the lower track. Then examine the wheels, and replace them if they are badly worn or broken. Also check the ribbed channel on the door sill, and straighten out any dents or bends. If the door still rubs after you reinstall it, see whether the ends of the panel are low. Sliders have an adjustment screw recessed in the end of the door that raises and lowers the wheels.

USE: ▶ whisk broom • pry bar • screwdriver

1 *To help the door glide smoothly,* sweep debris from the ribbed channels of the track, and add a few drops of oil.

Adjusting a Closet Door

Most closet doors have top-mounted wheel assemblies that travel on a ribbed aluminum track. Bypassing doors also have a plastic guide on the floor to keep the doors in alignment. When doors don't operate smoothly, first check the track to make sure that it is tight against the header. Then adjust the wheels to raise or lower the doors as needed. To adjust bifolding doors, loosen the bifold pivots at the bottom and top of the door, adjust as needed, and retighten.

USE: ▶ screwdriver

1 *Bypassing or bifolding doors* will not operate smoothly unless the aluminum track is securely screwed to the header.

Adjusting Bound Hinges

When door hinges close but the door doesn't, even though the door is not rubbing against the frame, the hinges are binding. This problem can occur when hinges sit too deeply or not deeply enough in their mortises. The face of the hinge leaves should be flush with the surface of the door and jamb. Check to see if the hinge is properly aligned and that the screws are tight and don't protrude above the face of the hinge. If that does not work, remove the hinge. Deepen the mortise or add a cardboard shim as needed.

HINGE MORTISE

SHIM

▶ lubricating oil • wood block

2 *To gain more clearance* for the door, first unload its weight by lifting the door slightly with a pry bar on a wood block.

3 *Hold or brace the door* in its unloaded position; then use a screwdriver to turn the adjustment screw and raise the wheels.

2 *To raise or lower bypassing doors,* use a screwdriver to turn the adjustment mechanism attached to the track wheels.

3 *To keep bypassing doors* from banging into each other, you may need to adjust or tighten the plastic floor guide.

Refinishing Metal

USE: ▶ sanding block • putty knife
▶ sandpaper • auto-body filler • paint

1 *To repair surface damage* on metal-clad doors, lightly sand the area and fill with auto-body filler.

2 *When the compound cures,* smooth the finish with fine sandpaper. Use a block to keep the repair flush.

3 *You can prime and paint* the area with a brush, but a sprayed finish will closely match the factory paint.

windows & doors

Locksets

The term lockset describes the whole mechanism of a door handle, whether it locks the door or latches it. A lockset includes the door knobs, a latch bolt or locking mechanism, and decorative plates (escutcheons or roses) that cover the lock mechanism. Latch bolts are spring-loaded and may have a locking mechanism. A dead bolt is not spring-loaded and locks and unlocks only with a key or thumb turn.

Locksets fall into two basic categories, although you'll find many variations. Cylindrical locksets are usually installed in 2⅛-inch-diameter holes drilled into door faces. Their latch bolts fit in ⅞-inch-diameter holes drilled into the edges of doors. The other type includes the rectangular, full-mortise lockset, which is mounted in a deep mortise (hole) dug into the edge of a door. Small holes are cut into the door faces to accommodate the spindle, on which doorknobs are mounted. Cylindrical locksets are the more common and stronger of the two and are easier to install because you don't have to dig out the deep mortise cavity.

Entry-door locks can be locked and unlocked from both sides of the door. One type will lock automatically when the door closes and unlock with a key from the outside or by turning a knob from the inside. For added security, exterior doors are often fitted with a separate dead-bolt lock, located above a door's key-in-knob lockset. Interior doors may have only a latch or a button that when pushed locks the door.

Common Locks

Standard keyed locks have a key knob outside and a thumb-lever knob inside that engage the strike assembly.

This combination lockset includes a keyed latchset with a traditional handle and a keyed dead bolt with thumb lever.

Passage sets have a thumb-lever knob inside. In an emergency, open them by pushing a long nail into the outside hole.

Installing a Privacy Lock

USE: ▶ power drill/driver • hole saw • spade or Forstner drill bit • utility knife • wood chisel • screwdriver ▶ doorknob with privacy lock • paper template

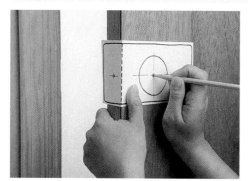

1 **Locate the hole centers** on the door face and edge using the paper template supplied by the lock manufacturer.

2 **To cut clean-edged openings,** use a hole saw. Bore through until the pilot bit emerges; then drill from the opposite side.

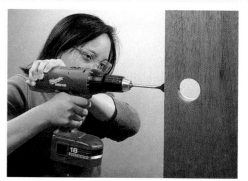

3 **Make the connecting hole** for the latch with a spade or Forstner bit. Keep the drill level as you drill through the door edge.

Special Hinges

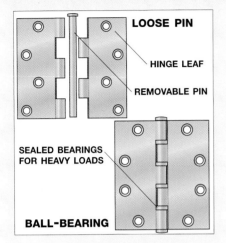

LOOSE PIN

HINGE LEAF

REMOVABLE PIN

SEALED BEARINGS FOR HEAVY LOADS

BALL-BEARING

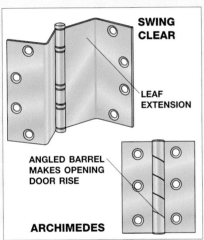

SWING CLEAR

LEAF EXTENSION

ANGLED BARREL MAKES OPENING DOOR RISE

ARCHIMEDES

Closers

The same kind of pneumatic piston *closer used on exterior screen and storm doors also works inside.*

Typical interior closers *have a door-mounted piston and a roller arm that travels on a trim-mounted track.*

Bumpers

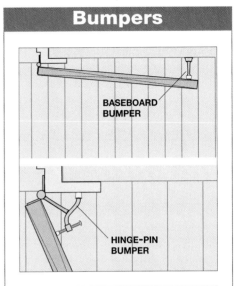

BASEBOARD BUMPER

HINGE-PIN BUMPER

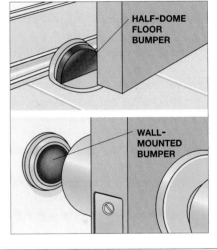

HALF-DOME FLOOR BUMPER

WALL-MOUNTED BUMPER

4 ***Mark the latch mortise,*** *trim around the edges with a sharp utility knife, and clean out the mortise with a chisel.*

5 ***Repeat the mortising sequence*** *for the strike. You can color the end of the sliding bolt to accurately locate the strike.*

6 ***When the bolt and strike*** *are aligned, tighten the screws that hold the latch mechanism and both knobs to the door.*

windows & doors

Overhead Doors

Unless you have lived in a house with the old-fashioned swinging doors on the garage, you probably take the convenience of your overhead garage doors for granted. Springs and rollers make sliding the horizontally hinged sections up into the overhead track relatively easy, and if you have an electric motor attached, it only takes the push of a button to open or close even the biggest of garage doors.

The most common type of residential overhead door has an extension spring mounted above the horizontal section of each track. A torsion-spring design has a single, horizontally mounted spring parallel to and above the door.

Installing an overhead door, or installing a new door that opens automatically, is certainly trickier than most other kinds of doors, but it's not beyond most do-it-yourselfers. The key is to identify and organize the dozens of parts and follow the step-by-step instructions that come with the door. You'll need a drill and a socket wrench set in addition to a level, measuring tape, and some other basic carpentry tools.

Overhead doors are typically trouble-free, provided you keep the hardware tight, clean, and lubricated. It's also important to maintain the exterior finish, particularly on raised-panel-style wood doors, which are subject to rot. Water inevitably seeps between the panel and the frame and has no way to drain. Check these areas annually for cracks in the paint, and caulk seals along joints.

Door Maintenance

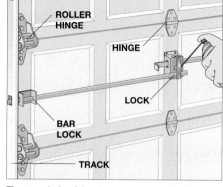

To make the lifting operation smoother (and quieter), add a few drops of machine oil to the spring-mounted pulley.

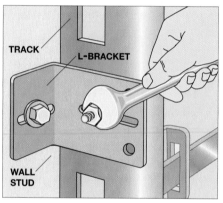

To reach inside the crossbar locking mechanism, use a spray lubricant with an extension straw.

Reduce the friction and clatter of door rollers in their tracks by cleaning the tracks and wiping them with silicone.

Check and tighten bolts on the frame-mounted L-brackets that hold the door to the frame and overhead track.

Automatic Opener Safety Features

Since 1982, when the Consumer Product Safety Commission began keeping accident records, automatic garage-door openers have caused many injuries and over 100 deaths. Several improvements have been made over the years. They are designed to meet an Underwriters Laboratories standard, which includes these four key provisions. First, garage-door operators must reverse a downward moving door within 2 seconds after the door contacts a 2-inch-high test block in the door's path. Second, door operators must reopen the door within 30 seconds of the start of downward movement if the door does not fully close to the garage floor. Third, once the door is moving down, it must stop, and may reverse, if the control button is pushed again. If the door is moving up, pushing the control button must stop the door and prevent it from moving downward. Fourth, door operators must have a manually operated way of detaching the operator from the door.

Following manufacturer's directions, install a UL-approved device that reverses the door when an obstruction is in its way.

Installing a Garage-Door Opener

USE: ▶ measuring tape • wrench set • power drill/driver • hammer • level ▶ garage-door opener • carriage bolt • 2x4 cleats • angle irons • nails • screws

1 *The heart of the system* is an electric motor that is mounted on the drive track along the centerline of the door.

2 *The chain or rubber drive belt* fits around the drive sprocket on the motor. It moves the trolley (and door) back and forth.

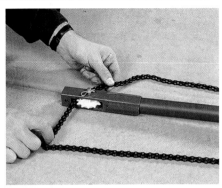

3 *The drive belt* loops around the plastic idler sprocket that is built into the other end of the main drive track.

4 *Bolt a 2x4 cleat* to the ceiling frame, and secure the motor with angle irons. A diagonal piece prevents lateral motion.

5 *Mount a cleat* over the door, and mark a centerline for the header bracket that holds the other end of the drive track.

6 *The track* (with the drive belt threaded around the idler sprocket) is held in the bracket with a clevis pin.

7 *A two-part arm* (predrilled so you can adjust the length) reaches from the drive track trolley to a bracket on the door.

8 *A terminal block* with a keypad, installed on the door frame, can control opening and closing, locking, and lighting.

9 *Follow the manufacturer's directions* for adjusting the up and down limits and the force applied to the door.

25
decks
& porches

decks & porches

Planning a Deck

Building a deck is usually a satisfying and hassle-free do-it-yourself project. With an outdoors project like this, you don't have any of the difficulties associated with projects inside the house—installing wiring, plumbing, and cabinetry in bath and kitchen renovations. Unlike interior alterations, decks are built in unencumbered free space, allowing you to swing around 12-foot joists without worrying about damaging anything.

With a deck, you expand your living space and increase your home's value for a tiny fraction of what it would cost to build an addition. Homeowners who don't have the time, skill, or inclination to build it themselves might hire a contractor. Although contracting out the job is more expensive than doing it yourself, decks are highly rated features in surveys of home buyers, so the cost is usually justified.

Design Decisions

There are several design decisions common to every deck project. Although most decks are simply platforms raised above the yard, they are an extension of the house—more like living space than yard space. Replacing a solid wall with sliding glass doors leading to an expansive deck is a quick and relatively inexpensive way to make a room seem larger. Considering the connected inside and outside space as one unit, deck additions are likely to be most useful when added onto living or family rooms and kitchen/dining areas.

Because wooden decks are exposed to the elements year-round, the wood must have weather-resisting characteristics built in or brushed on. Common framing material such as construction-grade fir is more than strong enough and can be treated with penetrating wood stain, clear wood preservative, or both to resist deterioration. In most regions, particularly the Northeast, this protective coating should be reapplied every 2 or 3 years. For example, even in wet New England a 20-year-old fir deck that has been drenched in clear preservative five times over the years will show few signs of rot.

Another option, pressure-treated lumber, has chemical preservatives injected throughout. It may take several seasons for the characteristic greenish tint to weather to a more natural tone. This type of decking has a long life and requires only periodic sealing or staining.

For more money (sometimes a third or even half again the cost of fir), you can use redwood or cedar, both of which are more naturally resistant to the elements. Although these woods have an extraordinary appearance when first installed—some select redwood has a unique cinnamon hue—they will weather. Most woods used for decking eventually turn a driftwood gray color. Redwood may turn much darker unless protected with a clear sealer. Even then it gradually changes to an elegant silvery tan. (See "Rot-Resistant Wood," p. 90.)

Deck Levels

Most decks have four structural levels. From the top down they are: the surface (often 2x4s, and generally 2x6s on large decks); the joists (at least 2x6s and as large as 2x12s), usually set 16 inches on center at right angles to the surface boards; one or more beams such as a 4x10 at right angles to and supporting the joists; and posts or piers that support the beams and transfer loads to the ground.

The deck surface is usually the controlling feature of a deck plan. Because it ties into the house, it should be built even with or a few inches below the house floor. The joist and girder dimensions are controlled by the structural requirements specified by an architect or contractor and verified by a building inspector. The posts are the only easily adjustable element, taking up as much or as little space as required between the beam and the ground.

Drafting Your Design

Decks are also among the easiest home improvements to commit to paper—even if you

Deck Anatomy

Labels: POST, BALUSTER, RAIL, JOIST HANGER, DECKING, LEDGER, BRIDGING, JOIST, GIRDER, POST HARDWARE, POST, PIER, STRINGER

don't have drafting experience. A few preliminary drawings on graph paper will help you decide what deck design will be most attractive and useful, and what will fit in best with the layout of your house and yard; it will also aid contractors in estimating the job. Many lumberyards will take even a rough plan and do a take-off, or estimate of materials and costs.

However, bear in mind that areas defined on uncluttered scale drawings tend to look larger than they actually will be. To avoid disappointment, transfer the scale drawings to the actual building site. Use stakes driven into the ground connected with string to outline the deck. Deck labor is two to three times as costly as the materials, so extending the deck using 12-foot instead of 10-foot joists has little effect on labor costs and increases material costs only marginally, but may increase the usefulness and sense of space dramatically.

Nails vs. Screws

Most decks are fastened with galvanized common nails. It's still an adequate way to build, but the convenience and fastening power of cordless drill/drivers and exterior-grade screws have upped the ante. Screws are more work and slower to use, but they are better in many ways—nails are more likely to pull loose under any load; screws won't back out of deck boards after a few years of service. Professional deck framers still use pneumatic nailguns, though, because nothing is faster for nailing off large areas of decking.

Air-powered nailguns *take time to get used to but speed the work of decking. You can rent the gun and a compressor; you also need special nails for the gun.*

Raised

Structure: Raised decks stay cooler on summer days and are easier to keep clean. To meet building codes, you need a solid foundation, sound attachments to the house itself, and a sturdy railing.
Advantages: A deck with a view adds an entirely new dimension to a home. Upper-story decks retain valuable space below.
Disadvantages: The higher you go, the higher the costs. Raised decks can be a danger in homes with small children.

Roof

Structure: Like raised decks, roof decks provide owners with a unique perspective. Access may be from inside the house or by an outside stairway.
Advantages: Roof decks offer maximum privacy, make excellent outdoor living areas, and utilize wasted space.
Disadvantages: Perhaps the most difficult to build. Areas below must be reinforced to carry the added load of deck materials and occupants. Extra waterproofing is needed.

Ground Level

Structure: The simplest deck to build is situated on or slightly above grade. Often, foundations and posts are unnecessary.
Advantages: Ease of construction tops the list, but on-grade decks also improve access and can make a smaller home appear larger.
Disadvantages: Without an enclosed yard, ground-level decks offer little privacy. Also, wood touching the ground is more susceptible to insect and rot damage.

Multi-Level

Structure: The most complex, and usually more costly, type of deck. Generally not a project for the novice builder.
Advantages: The different levels may be used for privacy, to add interest to larger decks, negotiate a steep building site, or connect the home with a pool.
Disadvantages: Too many levels can look busy and can be hazardous after dark if not adequately illuminated. Maintenance is more difficult and time-consuming.

decks & porches

Choosing Wood

There was a time when the word redwood was synonymous with "deck." But when decks became more popular, the supply of redwood couldn't keep pace with demand, and not everyone could afford what was available. Other woods were used in its place—cedar was a good substitute, also naturally decay- and insect-resistant, but fir and other softwoods didn't last as long or weather as nicely. So chemical treatments were developed to give ordinary woods the resistance they needed to withstand insect infestation, decay, and sometimes even ultraviolet degradation.

This hierarchy of wood remains unchanged, with redwood regarded as the premier deck material, followed by cedar. Pressure-treated woods make up the bulk of the lumber sold for decks today, though. Before you choose any one for your deck, it pays to know the differences not only between these woods but also the grades of each that are available. There is also a growing category of artificial wood—plastic or composite plastic and wood—now being sold for deck surfaces.

Redwood & Cedar

The range of grades and prices within these related species is so broad that you'll want to be sure to choose the correct grade for your application, and that you get what you pay for. Ask to see a grading chart before you make any purchase. The most expensive, highest-quality woods, for example, are architectural grade Clear All Heart, which are typically used indoors where their decorative beauty shows to its best advantage. This grade may be used for decking because it is also the most decay resistant, but the cost is usually too steep to be practical. Farther down on the chart, but still superior for most outdoor purposes, are construction or garden grades, selects, and common lumber. You won't pay as much for these woods, which contain more

knots and less-resistant sapwood, but you'll still get most of the natural benefits of redwood and cedar.

Those benefits include not only long-lasting appearance but wood that is structurally strong and can be used in contact with the ground. Redwood is generally stronger than cedar, and both were once the preferred woods for deck posts and other underpinnings most susceptible to decay. Today, because of their higher cost, redwood and cedar are often reserved for decking and decorative features such as benches, while less expensive pres-

sure-treated wood carries the load and remains hidden from view.

Pressure-Treated Wood

Most homeowners are familiar with the green-hued outdoor lumber commonly known as CCA, or pressure-treated, wood. Its color (and three-letter designation) comes from chromated copper arsenate—a chemical infused deeply into the wood cells under high pressure. Although this treatment has been certified to be inert, the wood should not be burned, and wearing gloves and a dust mask is advised

Special Tools

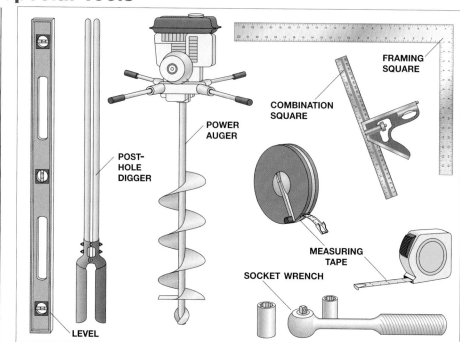

Key tools of the trade: Leveling tools include a carpenter's level, line level, torpedo level, water level, and post level. You will also need a combination square, angle square, framing square, hammer, saws, drill clamps, and ratchets for lag screws. Measuring is done with tape rules and reels. A posthole digger, chalk-line box, wheelbarrow, and plumb bob are used for layout and excavation.

Water Levels

A water level is made from a long hose, like a garden hose, with two transparent tubes at each end. It can pinpoint two level spots spanning long distances.

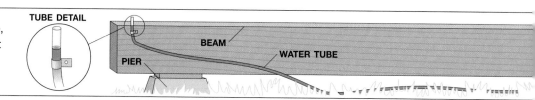

when cutting it. There is also some question of whether it is safe to use near gardens or for pet enclosures. (See "Pressure-Treated Wood," p. 91.) Earlier chemical treatments, such as creosote and penta (pentachlorophenol), are suspected carcinogens. Products containing them are no longer available.

Pressure-treated deck lumber can be any one of several softwood species, most often southern yellow pine, fir, or hemlock. Although newly treated wood is soft at first, the chemical treatment leaves it difficult to nail and cut. This wood is also prone to warping and twist-ing, and you should use it as soon as possible after delivery to minimize these problems. All chemically treated wood must be labeled by grade and chemical content. Wood for above-ground use is commonly treated to 0.25 or 0.40 (pounds of chemical per cubic foot). If you need to set posts or landscape ties below grade, you can special-order wood to 0.60, which is recommended for this use.

Buying Lumber

For all but the smallest decks, you will probably want to have the lumber trucked directly to your home. Most lumberyards are happy to deliver large orders for free or for a small fee, and the obvious advantage is that you don't have to load and unload a big pile of wood before you even start on the deck.

But you pay a price for the free delivery. You are pretty much stuck with whatever boards they put on the truck—at least some warped, split, knot-infested, or otherwise undesirable pieces are sure to come your way. Wood is not perfect after all, and often you can find uses for all but the worst pieces. But to protect yourself, ask what the yard's policy is on returns.

Common Lumber Options

Douglas fir is one of the more common types of construction lumber but is not suitable for areas where wood meets the ground. Also, fir needs application of protective coatings to prevent wood rot.

Pressure-treated wood is infused with copper arsenate compounds and will resist rot and insects. PT will turn from green to gray after several seasons and can be stained with an oil-based decking stain to retain color.

Redwood is considered the premier decking wood. It resists rot and insects and has a desirable salmon tint that will turn to gray after several seasons. Select, or knot-free, redwood is rare and expensive.

Cedar is also insect- and rot-resistant and will turn gray after two or more years of exposure. Cedar can be stained in a semitransparent or solid color stain. It's more expensive than PT wood but less costly than redwood.

Fastener Options

Nails or screws? Beams, joists, and posts should be secured with nails. Galvanized wood screws are used to secure decking, stair treads, and railings. Nongalvanized fasteners will bleed rust through the wood.

Lag screws and carriage bolts secure ledger boards to the house and beams to the support posts. Lags are first tapped in an inch and screwed in with a ratchet. These fasteners come in a variety of sizes and diameters.

T-braces, strap ties, and post caps function to keep large pieces of lumber securely tied to each other. Use special nails available for these hangers or galvanized wood screws to attach hardware to wood.

Joist hangers support joists between beams and ledgers. They give better load support than nailing joists straight into beams. Don't skimp on buying these inexpensive hangers, as most building codes require their use.

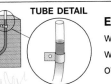

TUBE DETAIL

Electronic units sound a tone when the water levels out, which helps when working alone. You can also make your own water level from clear plastic tubing.

decks & porches

Supporting the Deck

Whatever style of deck or porch you plan to build, the first step is to get the structure off the ground. Because these outdoor platforms don't enclose living space, they don't need a conventional, continuous foundation. A few piers will do, and handling concrete on a small-batch scale is a job most do-it-yourselfers can handle.

Posts on Piers

On many first-floor decks where the lumber stack is approximately the same depth as the floor frame inside, it's likely that the concrete piers will have to extend only a few inches aboveground. In situations where piers would have to extend a few feet above grade, it's often easier and better looking to make up the height with posts (4x4 or larger).

On decks that are elevated well above ground and where the ground beneath the structure varies several feet in height, posts are the way to go for several reasons. First, it's difficult to build tall, free-standing masonry piers without making them massive and heavy. Second, you would need a substantial footing to prevent sinking. Third, when you use posts, the piers don't have to be level with each other, which makes them much easier to build—a major advantage for the do-it-yourselfer.

Pier Depth

To avoid frost heave, which can crack concrete and disrupt the structure above, piers must extend down into the ground and reach below the level where groundwater usually freezes in the winter. That dimension, called the average frost depth, is available from your local building department. (See "Average Frost Depth," p. 63.)

To dig this kind of deep but small-diameter hole, you can use a posthole digger or rent a gas-powered auger if you have many holes to dig. Minimize settling by digging down to the required depth and pounding the dirt at the bottom of the hole with the end of a 2x4. That way the pier will rest on a solid base.

Pouring Piers

On most projects, you won't use enough concrete to order it delivered to the site. The best bet is to mix your own from ready-mix bags.

If the sides of the holes aren't crumbling, you could use them as rough forms. Build a box staked at ground level to contain the concrete above grade. But to avoid mixing in any dirt and weakening the concrete, use lightweight form tubes, available at lumberyards and masonry-supply yards. You cut them to the height you need, and then insert them into the ground.

(See "Average Frost Depth," p. 63.)

Mixing Concrete

Deck footings generally don't require much concrete, unless you're putting in a lot of them. It's easy to mix one batch at a time in a wheelbarrow or tub, working as you go.

Formula for cubic feet in a box: To determine the cubic footage of a box, multiply the height times the width times the depth (all in inches), and divide the result by 12.

$$(h \times w \times d) \div 12 = \text{cu. ft.}$$

Formula for cubic feet in a cylinder: To determine the cubic feet in a cylinder, multiply the radius (half the diameter) by itself (square it), and then multiply by its height and 3.14. Divide the result by 12.

$$(r \times r \times h \times 3.14) \div 12 = \text{cu. ft.}$$

Setting Piers

USE: ▶ posthole digger • mason's hoe • mason's trowel • mixing trough • 4-ft. level • hammer • wrench • wheelbarrow • work gloves ▶ fiber-tube formwork

1 *Dig a hole* with a posthole digger (or power auger) to below frost depth. Large rocks may require extra digging. Fill the bottom with 2 in. of gravel for drainage.

2 *Insert a form tube* into the hole. It should protrude from soil level about 6 in. Cut off excess with a handsaw. Plumb the inside of the form to ensure straightness.

3 *Backfill the form* after it has been made plumb using a level. Avoid backfilling with large rocks. Small rocks from the fill can be added to the gravel at the base.

Surface Forms

Concrete footing forms can be any shape. The most common are cylindrical tubes made from heavy-duty fiber. Square forms, custom made, are the preferred option in areas where heavy loads meet soft ground. If you have questions regarding soil in your area, consult with an engineer or building inspector. Forms can be made from one-bys or plywood and should be backfilled. The bottom of the form should be filled with 2 inches of gravel.

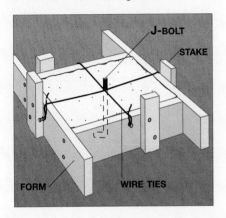

Laying Out Piers

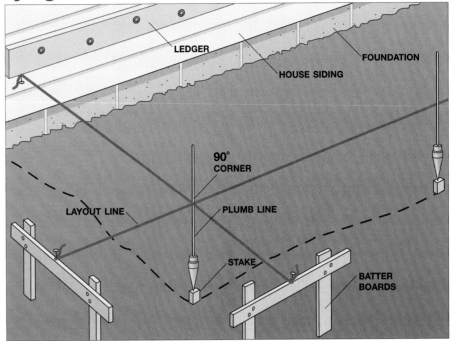

Determine the exact location of the concrete footings by using mason's line, measuring tape, batter boards, and a plumb bob. Using the scale of your site plan, map out exact measurements above the ground with mason's line. Attach the line to the batter boards, square the corners, drop a plumb bob, and mark the footing spot.

• cement mix • J-bolt with washer and nut • post base anchors • pressure-treated posts • galvanized nails • wire ties

4 *Pour concrete from a wheelbarrow* directly into the form. Before it hardens, insert a J-bolt into the center, leaving ¾ in. of threads above the concrete surface.

5 *After the concrete sets,* attach the post base hardware using a washer and nut. The post sits on a metal standoff that allows for drainage and keeps the post's bottom dry.

6 *With the standoff in place,* set the post in the metal base. Nail through the base holes into the wood. Bend the remaining base side up, and nail it off.

decks & porches

Deck Framing

House framing can be cratered with misguided hammer blows and studded with bent nails because you won't see the mistakes under siding and drywall. But you will on a deck. Because it is out in the open, you want framing to have both strength and a finish-quality appearance. So consider some of the following tips on both form and function.

Posts on Piers

Keep the support system neat by limiting concrete piers to a couple of inches aboveground—even if the ground is uneven—and make a uniform transition to wood by topping the piers with galvanized post anchors. Often, one end has a pin that embeds in the concrete while it's still wet, and the other has a U-shaped bracket that secures the post.

There are many post-anchor varieties—some that hold 4x6s or 8x8s if your deck needs the support, even some with a threaded rod and nut so you can adjust deck height where a section settles slightly out of level. Although this hardware keeps posts out of the dirt, soak the end grain with wood preservative prior to installation, particularly when it is a fresh cut.

This combination of piers and posts is durable and the easiest way to take up uneven slack between ground and deck. You don't have to establish precise levels and cut posts to exact size ahead of time. You can let them run long and trim to final length when the girder is placed. Posts are more practical than high, aboveground concrete piers and are better-looking, too. While a deck seems perched on top of high concrete piers, posts reaching to grade level seem to anchor it to the site.

Extended Posts

If you are taking the time to set posts that rise from the ground to a girder, you may want to get more for your efforts with longer posts that extend past the girder to anchor the railing, too.

In a typical deck plan, posts reach up to a pair of spiked-together 2x10s or 2x12s that carry the joists and decking above. With minor span adjustments (checking your plan with the local building department), you can make way for the post extensions by assembling the girder in two parts—one on each side of the posts, bolted in position. Figure the approximate post height you need to reach the deck floor, plus another 3 feet or so for railing.

This elegant detail provides many options and makes finishing railings easy because there are solid vertical supports in place every few feet along the deck edge before you start

J-bolts and post anchors are attached to the concrete footing, and the anchor bracing is nailed or screwed to the post. Soak post ends in preservative before attaching.

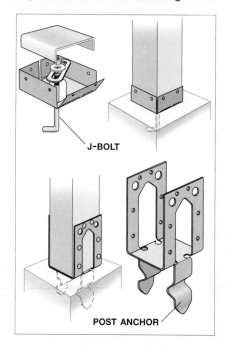

J-BOLT

POST ANCHOR

Installing Girders

USE: ▶ circular saw • C-clamps • 4-ft. level • hammer • work gloves ▶ ½-in. pressure-treated plywood • pressure-treated 2x4s and 2x10s • 3-in. galvanized nails

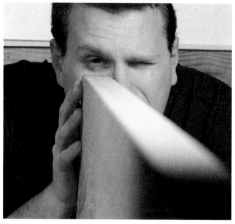

1 *Sight a 2x10 beam for crowning* or any arching along the length of the wood. Install the beam with the crown side up, not down, to compensate for stress loads.

2 *Double up support beams* and increase their width to 3½ in. by adding ½-in. pressure-treated plywood between beams. Beams will sit flush on top of posts.

3 *Nail beams together* using 3-in. galvanized nails. Set nails 16 in. apart in two separate rows. Make sure both beams are crowned upward and nailed flush.

adding railings and balusters. And no nailed-on, screwed-on, or even bolted-on railing system applied to the finished deck platform can provide the security of a row of full-height, solid 4x4s.

Dressing Posts

On low decks where supports are recessed, the scruffiest lumber will do as long as it's solid. But on some decks, post supports loom large from the yard. You don't gain anything structurally with a solid 4x4 versus two 2x4s spiked together, but you won't see a seam between boards or nailheads or discolored dings where you swung the hammer and missed.

Also, solid posts can be dressed up with nice touches of carpentry that once were used on exposed beams in early colonial houses. To make tree-size timbers appear more finished and graceful, reduce the hard edges with a chamfer—a 45-degree slice across the corner. Run it across most of the timber length, and taper it away near the top and bottom to make the beam square-edged near the joints.

Another option is to clad the wood posts with one-by facing. You can use quality wood to match your siding or choose a rustic, rough-sawn grade for a contrasting look. Clad 4x4 posts with 1x6 boards and 6x6 posts with 1x8s.

Post Assembly Options

ONE 4x4

TWO 2x4s

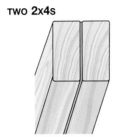

COMBINATION

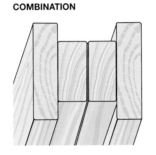

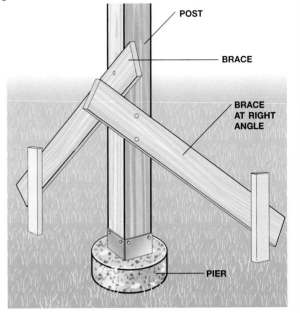

One 4x4 post is easier to erect than doubled 2x4s, which require assembly and may not cost less in the long run. Using larger posts may save you money, but they should be through-bolted to secure them. Two angle braces will hold each post plumb in both directions.

• wood shims

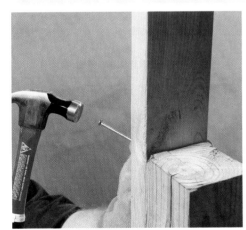

4 To temporarily position the girder, face-nail a 2x4 to the back of the post, extending up several inches. When you set the girder in place, it will rest against the extended 2x4.

5 To keep the girder from falling while you work on the installation, clamp the face to the 2x4 brace. Another option is to install two braces and set the girder between them.

6 Place a level on top of the beam, and use wood shims on posts to make the beam level. Also, shim any gaps in post-beam joints as needed.

decks & porches

Choosing Joists

Most deck designs call for 2x8 or 2x10 joists set 16 inches on center. The length of a joist's span from ledger board to beam also depends on the species of wood and the width of the joist. Naturally, thicker boards can span longer distances and support greater loads than thinner boards. To find out what the allowable measurement should be between joists and how far they can span, consult a span table—your local building department should have them available for your reference.

Wood & Fastener Options

Your deck's joists, beams, and ledger should be made from pressure-treated wood to stand up to the elements, particularly any timbers near the ground. But you can also use standard construction grades if you first coat them with wood preservative. To build a deck economically without sacrificing either strength or durability, you might want to consider using pressure-treated wood for the joists, ledger, and beams, as these parts of the deck generally are out of sight.

For maximum strength (and to satisfy most local building codes), joists are attached to supporting timbers with metal brackets called stirrups or joist hangers. These hangers will support more weight than nails can and reduce the chance of wood splitting at joints. Joists are often doubled up for extra support or to accommodate designs where surface boards require increased nailing support. But there are double-wide hangers to cover those situations—and hardware designed to reinforce just about every structural connection you can make on a deck. Even where hardware isn't required by code, you may find that bridging joints with metal brackets makes construction easier.

Hanging Joists

One good way to hang joists is to first build the deck's outer perimeter, with outside joists nailed to a belt (also called a header) at the outside of the deck and to a ledger board at the house. Pros who can easily envision the complete layout ahead of time can stack up the components and mark them prior to installation. But for many do-it-yourselfers, it's easier to take one step at a time: build the basic post-

Frame Design Options

Joists are connected to beams with joist hangers. Hangers give more support than toenailing into the beam.

Joists on top of beams is one framing option. Use metal framing ties along beam; joist hangers for ledger board.

Decking options include one-by and ⅝-by boards; thinner boards require closer joists to prevent sagging and breaking.

Typical deck setup calls for two-by decking with joists spaced 16 in. on center. Wider spacing makes decks less stable.

Cantilevers

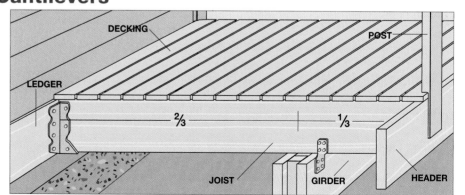

As a rule, no more than one-third of a deck's framing should extend past its support.

and-girder support system, box in the deck space, and then fill in that frame with joists.

As mentioned, most deck designs call for joists on 16-inch centers. But this rule depends on the thickness of your decking material and deck design. If your deck has a herringbone design, for example, which calls for a diagonal pattern of decking boards, the joists may have to be on 12-inch centers. Your plans will only be approved by a building inspector if they specify the placement and thickness of joists.

After you've marked the modular layout of the deck joists on the beam and ledger, check to make sure your frame is square overall by measuring the diagonals from inside corner to inside corner. If the deck is square, the measurements will be equal. You can clamp or temporarily tack the outermost joists in position to complete the deck perimeter. But don't fix them permanently in place until the perimeter is square.

To install the joist hangers, slip one of the brackets around a short section of joist, and set the sample assembly in position. The trick is to position the bracket so that the top of the joist it holds will be flush with the adjacent ledger. If it's not flush, the deck boards—even beefy 2x4s and 2x6s—will ride up and down over their supports. Once you are sure of where the bracket should be, you can use the position of the sample to fix all the brackets in place.

Your joists should fit snugly between the ledger and header. Again, the best bet is to cut a sample joist and test it in place. Then you can use it as a template to cut the other joists.

Setting Joist Hangers

USE: ▶ joist template • combination square • hammer • marker ▶ joist hangers • galvanized nails

1 *Make a template* to fit just below the flashing, and then mark reference lines for plumb and horizontal placement.

2 *Size hangers* correctly for joists and ledger, and set them plumb to avoid twisted or uneven joists.

3 *Use nailing clips* stamped into the hanger to position it and galvanized common nails to install it in place.

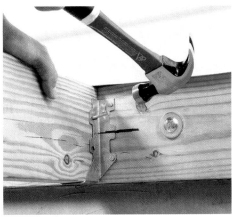

4 *With the hanger fastened* to the ledger, set the joist, and nail it in place. Use short nails that won't protrude.

House-Mounted Ledgers

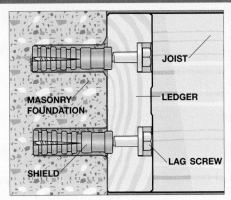

When attaching ledger boards to masonry, predrill the ledger, and use holes as guides for masonry holes. Place board onto the masonry wall, level it, and use a marker to indicate drill points. Then drill and insert shields or anchors. Don't confuse masonry with stucco; ledgers on stucco must be bolted into the house's frame. On other exteriors, strip siding to expose the sheathing; bolt the ledger into the frame. To preserve this crucial timber, use pressure-treated wood and cover the top edge with flashing.

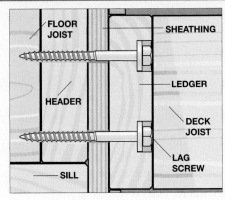

decks & porches

Decking Basics

Using elegant, high-quality decking materials such as cedar and redwood is one sure way to make a deck look good. It also is an easy way to empty your checking account. But even plain, construction-grade fir 2x4s, complete with knots and rough edges, can be joined with some high class carpentry and design detailing to make an elegant structure.

Nailing Decks

Without careful attention to the spacing and nailing of decking, even a simple symmetrical design can present a haphazard appearance. Usually, 2x4s, 2x6s, or 5/4-by boards are attached to larger supporting joists with two 10d galvanized common nails driven through each board at every point where it crosses a joist—a time-consuming job. Although one nail at each crossing point would hold the board in place, it would allow the board to cup, or turn up at the edges. Two nails about ¾ inch from each edge keep the board flat.

There are many such crossing points, even on a small deck. Without a system for this kind of repetitive work, you have a tendency to lose concentration after a while. That may not seem important, but such lapses can create irregular gaps between boards and erratic nailing patterns—sloppy-looking work.

Experienced carpenters can repeatedly and accurately gauge such distances by eye, but many use a low-tech distance-estimating system anyway. For example, to create an even gap between boards, drop a nail into the space between boards or tack a nail onto the joist. Because the nail shanks are the same size, they create a uniform spacing between boards—about ⅛ inch for good drainage.

To nail at the same margin from the edge of the 2x4s, it's convenient to use some form of human measuring template. For instance, you might grip the nail between thumb and forefinger just below the head, rest your thumb at the edge of the board, and then press down on the head to leave a slight depression where the nail should be driven. Using this type of human engineering can be surprisingly accurate. Mechanical aids such as rulers or pre-marked nailing templates are too cumbersome in this type of operation.

Other Systems

A more time-consuming but totally concealed nailing system called Dec-Klip uses T-shaped clips nailed onto the joists. One flange of the clip is toenailed through the decking board, while a spur on another flange secures the adjoining board.

You can also eliminate the splinters and chips of wood entirely by using vinyl decking. Hollow, ribbed vinyl boards (tooled to provide traction in wet weather) are held on by clips screwed into the joists—either wood or proprietary vinyl deck systems. Although they're more expensive than most types of wood decking, they are both longer-lasting and stronger: Some systems allow you to span joists set 32 inches on center.

The deck is vinyl, but it looks like wood— and you can clean it the way you clean siding.

Deck Lumber Options

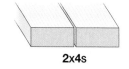

2x4s

2x4s will give a deck a busy look, due to their relatively thin widths. If not pressure-treated, 2x4s must be coated with a preservative; they will also need periodic maintenance. Soak 2x4 ends in preservative before nailing. When you can, check wood for crowns, cups, and warps before purchasing.

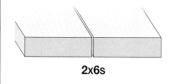

2x6s

2x6s are a better decking option than 2x4s, as they require less time to install. These boards can also be used as joists if the span is short, but check first with building codes. Use two nails over each joist to minimize cupping. 2x6s are heavier than 2x4s; an extra set of hands will help for long boards.

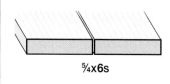

5/4x6s

1x4s, 5/4x4s, and 5/4x6s are some of the more popular choices for decking. Joists may have to be on 12-inch centers, depending on wood species and grade. This decking size is sold in many different grades and different species. Pressure-treated, cedar, and redwood are the most popular.

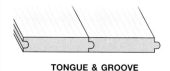

TONGUE & GROOVE

Tongue-and-groove boards fit into each other for a tight seam. Used mostly on porches with a roof, tongue-and-groove decks should be pitched to shed water and waterproofed against the elements to prevent swelling. They are not recommended for use on open decks where the wood will be exposed to the elements.

Deck Fasteners

◆ **Nails** should be galvanized when used for exterior building projects such as decks. Some hammering skill is needed to avoid "crests" and "moons," unsightly indentations in the wood from an errant hammer. It is also hard to remove nails without gouging the wood.

◆ **Screws** have better holding power than nails and are easier to drive in tight spots. Some drills come with a depth-gauge attachment that will set the screw just below or exactly flush with the wood surface. Screws should be galvanized or stainless steel.

Deck Edging Details

Miter-cut framing sections take a bit more time and attention than butted joints. On outdoor wood, subject to expansion and contraction, a mitered edge may lose its tight look after a few seasons. Treat the open grain of a freshly cut mitered edge with wood preservative before installing.

MITERED FRAME

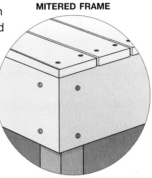

FLUSH DECK

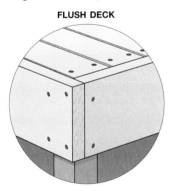

A flush edge is more resistant to general wear and damage, particularly where deck elevations change. Also, with this type, board ends are less prone to splitting and breaking. Deck boards are nailed to a sistered joist set 1½ inches lower than the outer face joist.

OVERHANG DECK

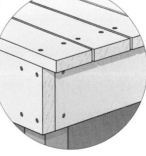

Overhang is perhaps the most forgiving design option for decking. Snap a line 1 or 2 inches from the outside joists, and cut with a circular saw. You don't have to worry about blade depth unless there are underlying obstructions. Treat cut edges with wood preservative. Wear a dust mask and eye protection to cut pressure-treated lumber.

Hidden Fasteners

An alternative to surface nails or screws, deck fasteners are specially made to secure decking to joists from the underside. This not only improves the deck's appearance, it also eliminates nail pops and rot spots that can develop over time in nail and screw holes. Fasteners cost more and take longer to install but result in a longer-lasting and cleaner-looking deck. Hidden fasteners are the best if you're building a deck with expensive, high-grade redwood.

USE: ▶ chisel • hammer • measuring tape • 10d or 16d nail ▶ deck boards • galv'd. nails

1 *Space the boards* a full ⅛ in. apart with a 10d or 16d nail.

2 *Use a chisel* or special lever tool to pull boards tight as you nail.

3 *Spacing measurements* should be equal at both ends and center.

4 *Use two common nails* per board at each joist to minimize cupping.

decks & porches

Laying Out Stairs

Stairs can be a simple matter of a few steps, or they can be as complicated as a convoluted, two-story spiral. But all stairs and ramps are based on a couple of simple rules that can help you calculate how many steps you need and just how far out the staircase must extend to connect the upper and lower levels.

Because most decks are fairly close to ground level to start with, you can probably get by with a simple, straight staircase that has just a few steps. You may need to remeasure and refigure to get exactly the right angles on stair stringers, but the assembly is a project most do-it-yourselfers can handle.

Stair Anatomy

There are three basic parts to a stair: the stringer, the riser, and the tread. The dimensions and relationships of all three come together to form a typical staircase. But on many decks, stairs are basically platforms that are built without stringers along the sides.

The tread is the flat board that your foot steps on. It is usually at least 11 inches deep from the outer edge to where it meets the riser, but it can be wider to create platform steps.

Not all stairs have risers, the back board which rises up from tread to tread. All stairs do have a rise, however, which refers to the height from step to step. The rise must be the same for every step, because people will trip if they encounter even a slight variation in height. Generally, the height of the rise, combined with the thickness of the tread, is about 6 or 7 inches, but you should check this dimension (and details of stairway hand rails) with your local building department.

To find out how many treads and risers your staircase needs, you must first determine what the total rise and total run are for your stair area. After you've measured rise and run, you can calculate the unit rise and unit run, and divide the space into steps.

Measure your total rise in inches, and divide this figure by the 6- or 7-inch riser height you want. Then round off the result to the nearest whole number. This is the number of steps. Next, take the vertical rise in inches, and divide by the number of steps. This will give you the exact riser height.

Stair Layout

Exterior stairs are generally not as steep as interior stairs because of the more-hazardous conditions that exist outdoors. Wider treads and lower risers make safer exterior steps. Tread and riser tables are available to help you determine the correct number of stairs and angle of the staircase.

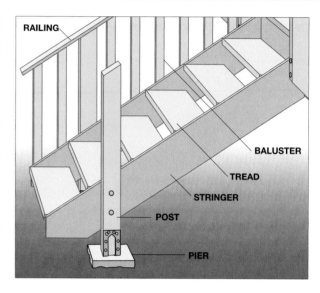

RAILING

BALUSTER

TREAD

STRINGER

POST

PIER

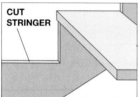

CUT STRINGER

Precut stringers can be purchased at most home centers.

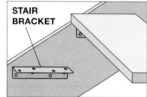

STAIR BRACKET

Metal brackets can replace cutout portions of the stringer.

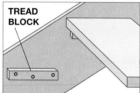

TREAD BLOCK

Wood blocks can also support stairs if metal brackets are unavailable.

Installing Stairs

USE: ▶ circular saw • combination square • framing square • spirit level • drill/driver • hammer • pencil

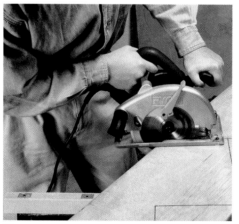

1 *Measure twice and cut once* is a carpentry rule, especially on stair stringers that can be difficult to calculate.

2 *Mark the location of the stringers* on the header or rim joist. Measure rise and run from the deck to where stringers will end.

Platform Design

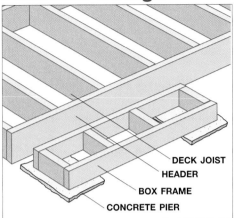

DECK JOIST
HEADER
BOX FRAME
CONCRETE PIER

Platforms break up the monotony of a large, flat surface and provide areas for planters, seats, and furniture. They can replace a few stairs and give a deck a classier look. Building a platform area is done by first framing out the intended area. Use the same lumber species and sizes for joists, decking, and stringers as on your original deck, but use pressure-treated framing on the piers. The stairs should rise no higher than 7 inches and no less than 5 inches from the deck. Before you build, check your local building codes for loads on decking.

Accessible Ramp Layout

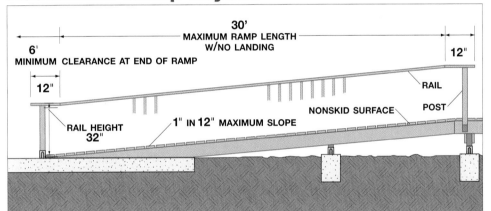

30'
MAXIMUM RAMP LENGTH
W/NO LANDING

6'
MINIMUM CLEARANCE AT END OF RAMP

12"

12"

RAIL HEIGHT
32"

1" IN 12" MAXIMUM SLOPE

NONSKID SURFACE

RAIL

POST

Standards established in the federal Americans with Disabilities Act (ADA) are designed to facilitate access while preventing injury to persons with limited mobility. All public buildings must conform to these design standards, but many homes also are being retrofitted with barrier-free devices, such as lever door handles and access ramps instead of steps and stairs. Because ramps can pose a hazard if improperly designed, it's a good idea to follow the ADA model if you plan to build one.

• measuring tape ▶ pressure-treated 2x lumber • angle brackets or sloped hangers • stair brackets • galvanized nails or ¾-in. lag screws • J-bolts with nuts

3 *Nail or screw on an angle bracket* or *sloped hanger to strengthen the connection between each stringer and the rim joist.*

4 *Install stair brackets* if the stringers *are not cut out. Angles should be slightly shorter than the overall tread depth.*

5 *Fasten treads to brackets* with nails or *screws. Avoid splits on ends of treads by predrilling nailholes.*

---

decks & porches

Finishing Touches

Because decks are relatively easy to design and build, even for amateurs, exercise your creativity when planning it out. Decks can conform to slopes, wind their way around building angles, incorporate seats and planter boxes, or have interesting patterns underfoot. They can be whimsical or practical, exotic or prosaic, but there is really no excuse for a deck to be boring.

Curved Railings

A long piece of wood beefy enough to serve as a deck railing (even against the house wall) is difficult to bend. So the best option is to use several thin pieces of wood that, taken individually, can be bent easily and then laminated into one beefy railing. If you use multiple pieces of thin stock—only ¼ or ⅜ inch thick—each piece can be bent to shape in place. For example, you could install the railing hardware, bend one piece into place, clamp it, and then do another, and so on.

Deck Seats

It's not difficult to add seating to your deck for convenience and comfort. To support a seat on the perimeter railing of a deck without adding legs that will block the edge, use the posts to support the seat the same way they support the deck joists—as the core of a structural sandwich that takes the overall shape of a triangle. One leg is the existing post, the other is the horizontal seat support, and the third (the hypotenuse) is an angled brace.

The brace can slope back from the seat to the post at the edge of the deck—out of the way. At its top, the brace is buried between two horizontal 2x4s that support the seat platform. Each pair of 2x4s can be bolted around the 2x6 railing post at one end and around the main brace at the other. To assemble each triangle, sandwich the pieces between clamps, make minor adjustments as needed, and then drill through for bolts. If the deck is square and level, you should be able to make one triangle, and use the pieces as templates to cut others. To make the triangle frames blend in, use finishing details such as recessed, round-headed carriage bolts instead of machine bolts, and comfortable, rounded-over square edges on seating that might otherwise catch you under the knees.

There is no limit *to what you can create when you build a wood deck. A simple box can be enlarged to become a planter or railings extended into built-in seating. Level changes are also easy to make and create decks that look interesting and inviting.*

Deck Details

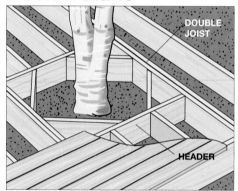

Tree boxes are framed with headers between double joists. Tree holes should be planned and built before decking is laid.

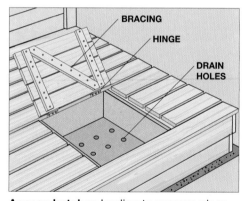

Access hatches leading to sewage pipes or storage areas can be cut out after the decking is constructed.

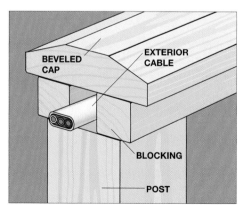

Wiring for outlets and lights can be hidden within the railing. Be sure the wiring conforms to local codes.

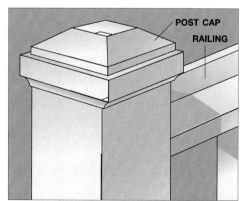

Details such as fancy post caps and railings can be purchased at millwork shops or created with a router and plane.

Installing Railings

USE: ▶ combination square • drill & 1-in. spade bit • level • hammer • handsaw • socket wrench • measuring tape • router (optional) ▶ lumber • lag screws/washers

1 Railing posts are installed after the deck and stairs. Posts are usually 4x4s; balusters can be 2x2s and 2x4s.

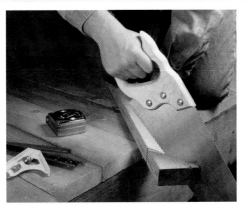

2 For improved drainage and appearance, trim each 2x4 baluster with a 45-degree angle at the top and bottom.

3 Countersink screws on balusters for neatness. Make countersink holes for washers and lag screws using a 1-in. spade bit.

4 Set balusters in place with a single lag screw at bottom; then, use a level to plumb before drilling the second hole.

5 Place a washer on each lag screw before tightening it down. A socket wrench makes quick work of this job.

6 Measure and mark for each baluster, being sure your lines are plumb and square on the header and equally spaced.

7 Level and clamp the top rail, in this case a 2x6, to one of the installed balusters at each end of the railing run.

8 Use a lag screw to anchor the end balusters; then, drill pilot holes and install the other balusters with screws or lags.

9 For an attractive finish and to make the rail easier to grasp, use a router to give the railing a chamfer or roundover edge.

decks & porches

Porch Construction

Unlike decks, most porches are not big, elaborate affairs. They are incorporated into a house's architecture, more so than a deck. Porch floors are usually constructed with tongue-and-groove decking, waterproofed or painted, and pitched at a slight angle for water runoff. Also, porches have roofs supported by columns. These obvious differences aside, the principles and methods of porch construction vary little from deck construction.

Porch Design

If you're thinking of adding a porch onto your house instead of a deck, your plans will probably be limited by exterior design details. Victorian houses, for example, lend themselves well to porch construction, whereas modern homes (such as ranches and split-levels) are better candidates for decks than porches. It all comes down to what will look good on your house.

If you're considering building a porch, you should first have a set of architectural drawings made up, and have those plans approved by your local building inspector.

The roof of the porch will tie directly into a ledger board bolted to your house's exterior, just like the beginnings of a deck. The floor will be supported by a ledger and posts and beams, rising up from concrete footings. From there, the construction techniques of the porch are identical to building a deck, except the fact

Porch Layout Options

3/4 VIEWS

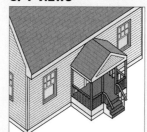

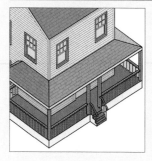

Add-on porches project out from the house. To blend in, a porch roof would have the same slope as the main roof. Here, the porch stands out by having its own gable roof with slopes perpendicular to the main roof.

Recessed porches forming balconies or private nooks are usually seen on Victorian homes, as well as some modern homes. They can have a sloped roof, or a flat one that can be used as a second-story balcony.

Wraparound designs require carpentry expertise for creating angled fascias, railings, and deck floors. Making miter cuts for rafters of hip-style roofs also requires knowledge of complicated roof framing.

SIDE VIEWS

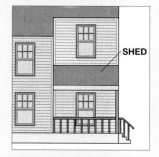
GABLE

SHED

HIP

Shed-Roof Details

Shed roofs are the easiest to build—they're like a floor with one end tipped up. The design eliminates complex miter cuts and makes an uncomplicated seam between the roof and the house wall. Along the top of the roof, where you need to pull away siding to anchor the main ledger and rafters, pry up one more course. When it comes time for re-siding, slide a piece of flashing underneath so that water runs down the house, across the flashing, and onto the porch roof.

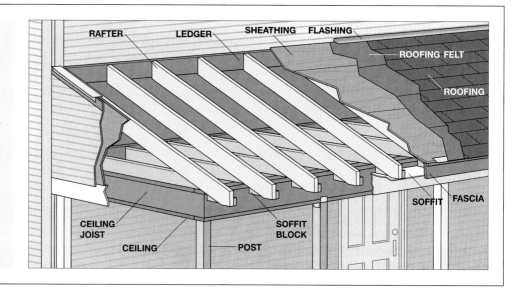

RAFTER   LEDGER   SHEATHING   FLASHING
ROOFING FELT
ROOFING
SOFFIT   FASCIA
CEILING JOIST
CEILING
POST
SOFFIT BLOCK

that the porch is covered by a roof. Most porch roofs are built at the same angle as the house's roof; a different roof angle may make the porch look like it's not part of the house.

Porch Construction

Building a roof entails many steps using special tools and materials. (See "Roofing," pp. 408–33.) Flashing, roof felt, shingles, roofing nails, and gutters are all a part of a roof's structure. Even a small roof can take a lot of careful planning and labor before it's completed.

Before the roof is built, the support columns are erected and secured in place. These posts are usually 4x4s; they can be covered over with boards for a square column or prefabricated sections for a round column. The style of column you choose should reflect the overall design of your house.

After the beams are set in place on top of the posts, a ledger board is secured to the house. From the ledger board, the roof rafters are screwed into joist hangers and extended to the beams spanning the posts. The roof rafters should be cut at the same angle as your house's roof. Be aware that this job requires knowledge of how to use a framing square, some heavy lifting, ladder work, and an extra person for help. Building a full porch with a roof will take several weeks to complete, and the roof especially may be a job better left to an experienced, knowledgeable carpenter.

Porch Roof Ceilings

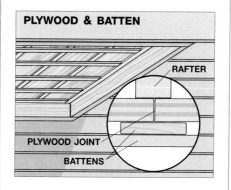

PLYWOOD & BATTEN

RAFTER

PLYWOOD JOINT

BATTENS

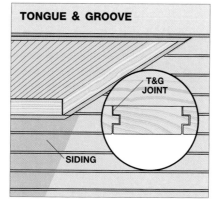

TONGUE & GROOVE

T&G JOINT

SIDING

Porch roofs are usually built with a decorative underside. Use batten construction, for installing traditional beadboard slats or paneling, or solid tongue-and-groove boards.

Hip-Roof Details

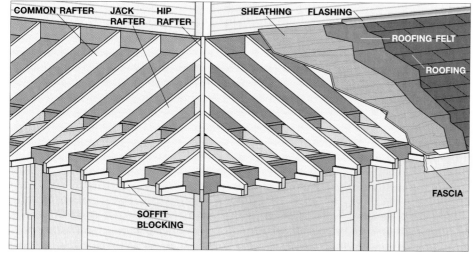

COMMON RAFTER
JACK RAFTER
HIP RAFTER
SHEATHING
FLASHING
ROOFING FELT
ROOFING
FASCIA
SOFFIT BLOCKING

Wraparound porch roofs are a traditional and handsome complement to many homes, but they are complicated to design, cut, and install. Consider hiring an architect and professional carpenter to do the work. Roofs of this type are generally hip constructions, which require intersecting rafters of sequential length cut on compound angles or miters. It takes an experienced hand to follow a layout and cut these rafters correctly, but these roofs are often unequaled in detail.

decks & porches

Finishing the Porch

The key details of porch design are support columns, handrails, and balusters. Most home centers don't carry a wide selection of this type of millwork; to get a good idea of what's available, consult millwork catalogs at your local lumberyard. You should be able to find made-to-order columns and many varieties of railings and balusters, but you'll have to special-order these items, and some assembly may be required. When ordering, make sure you have the exact measurements of your porch. If you're installing railings on a stairway, measure the exact nailing points on the posts, and add a few inches on the handrail you're ordering to give yourself some extra cutting length.

Decorative detailing, sometimes referred to as gingerbread, can give a porch a cozy, homey appearance. It's installed like regular trim, with finishing nails. Gingerbread woodwork looks best on Victorian-style homes. It can be a fun woodworking project, but only if you have the proper tools (at least a saber saw, drill, and wood files).

There are many approaches to making a porch look inviting, cozy, and livable. Plants play a big part in effective porch design, with roses on trellises among the more popular choices. Trellises add privacy and beauty and can easily be installed against porch columns. They're sold at garden and home centers and are modestly priced.

Trim Details

Exposed joists can be decorated with lattice work, or skirting, to hide the raw appearance of unadorned lumber.

Turned or carved post finials are available ready to install. You can finish them to match or contrast with the railing.

Some construction details are decorative enough to be left exposed, like these cut and stained support beams.

Fret work and fancy detailing can often be seen on original or reproduction Victorian-style homes.

Installing Porch Railings

USE: ▶ drill/driver • hammer • socket wrench • C-clamps ▶ top and bottom filler strips • top and bottom rails • balusters • newel posts • post finials

1 An easy way to lay out balusters is to install intermediate top and bottom filler strips, hidden by the finished rails.

2 Attach the baluster assembly to the railing with galvanized wood screws so that no nails or screws show.

3 Fasten railings to posts using wood screws. To prevent splitting the end grain, predrill pilot holes into the railings.

Interior Drains

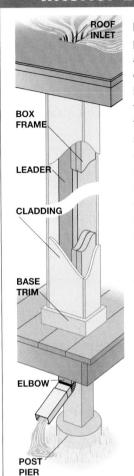

ROOF INLET

BOX FRAME

LEADER

CLADDING

BASE TRIM

ELBOW

POST PIER

Drainage, as part of a porch and roof design, can be hidden from view by running the downspouts behind or within columns. If you opt not to have gutters on your porch roof, soil around the base of the porch may wash away during heavy rains. The dirt should be sloped away from the house, and a bed of gravel should also lay beneath the soil to facilitate drainage and avoid puddling.

• galvanized nails or wood screws

4 *After counterboring screw holes* for the top and bottom rails, use a deep-socket ratchet wrench to secure the rails.

Columns

BOX

Box columns are made by covering posts with 1x6 or 1x8 boards. Use 1½-inch galvanized finishing nails; then belt-sand the seams flat. Fill any cracks with wood putty, and then finish-sand.

ROUND

Manufactured from layers of wood turned on a lathe, solid round columns can hold substantial loads. A good alternative to 4x4s, as no carpentry work is required to alter their appearance.

PREFAB

The look of a round column with the core of a 4x4. This option may be less expensive than a solid round column, but requires some carpentry expertise to assemble over 4x4 posts.

CAPITALS

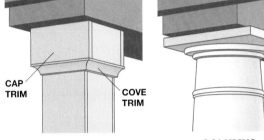

CAP TRIM

COVE TRIM

COLUMNS

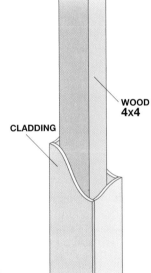
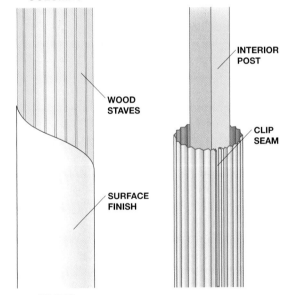

CLADDING

WOOD 4x4

WOOD STAVES

SURFACE FINISH

INTERIOR POST

CLIP SEAM

BASES

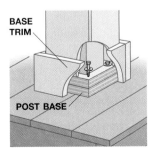
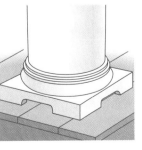
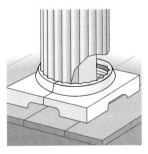

BASE TRIM

POST BASE

Sealing the Surface

Some of the most common problems with decks are not related to the type of wood you use—for instance, mold, mildew, and stains. However, the more unusual and more serious long-term problem is wood rot, and pressure-treated lumber offers the most resistance to it.

Non-pressure-treated wood also offers resistance to rot, so long as you seal it and periodically renew the coating. Wood on a deck surface that is not pressure-treated and not sealed also can survive without rot for years—maybe a decade or more if the deck gets plenty of ventilation and sunlight. Under the surface, however, where girders and joists may be close to the ground and shielded by the deck from air and sunlight (the natural mold, mildew, and rot inhibitors), raw wood needs protection.

Because pressure-treated wood is more expensive than untreated wood, a reasonable compromise might be to build in extra protection on the deck girders and floor joists—the timbers that would be the most difficult to replace if they did rot—and select a less expensive and more attractive wood for the surface.

Color is another question. The green tinge of pressure-treating is no match for the elegant hues of redwood, cedar, or even construction-grade fir. But using pressure-treated surface decking does not eliminate the perennial project of resealing the deck every two years. It does build in extra protection for uneven wear on a deck surface, where surface sealers can wear out along natural traffic paths long before the rest of the deck needs recoating.

Even the best surface sealers are only skin deep, while pressure-treated lumber has wood-preserving chemicals driven deeply into the wood grain. And if the green color is unappealing, you can apply a grayish semitransparent stain to simulate the more weathered appearance treated wood takes on after a few seasons out in the weather.

Solid-Body Stains

If you want to completely hide the natural color of your deck's wood or you prefer a bold rather than subtle tone, you can use a penetrating stain finish that performs more like a paint. In fact, the only real difference between solid stains and paints is the relative amount of resin, or solid, suspended in their liquid base. These solids harden to create an opaque surface film. Solid-color stains are more appropriate for siding than for decks, however, because they will wear away quickly under foot traffic. There are also paints sold as porch and deck finishes, but these should be used mainly for covered porches with good drainage. On a deck exposed to the weather, these film-forming finishes can create problems when water gets under the paint film and is trapped there. It may lead to rotting, warping, and cracking.

Penetrating Stains

Semitransparent stains contain smaller amounts of pigment than solid-color stains, and they don't completely mask the natural wood grain. Although they penetrate the wood surface to seal out moisture, on the surface they can appear either glossy or flat, depending on the sealer's formulation. Clear finishes also penetrate and seal, but they impart little color to the wood.

Deck sealers contain oils, resins, or wax additives that enable them to repel water. You can tell that these products are still working when rainwater beads up on the deck like on a freshly waxed car, instead of soaking into the wood. This beading effect doesn't last, though, especially if your deck gets a lot of use or your area gets a lot of rain. However, it's much easier to renew a sealer than it is to renew a coat of paint; old paint must first be scraped or

Finishing Options

◆ **Semitransparent**
These stains will allow the grain to show through, and will hide the gray. Semitransparent stains come in many colors and will last up to 3 years. They are sold in water-based and oil-based solutions.

◆ **Solid Body**
Solid stains completely cover the wood grain. They are a good option on wood that has gone gray, started to splinter, and shows signs of age. Quality exterior stains can add a few years to a deck's life.

◆ **Paint**
The pigment in paint is heavier than in stains, and the penetrating power of a heavy paint may not be as effective as a stain. On decks, use an epoxy-based or oil-based deck paint.

◆ **Solvents**
Coating solvents are water-based (vinyl acrylic, latex, epoxy), oil-based, or alcohol-based. Use solvent thinners that are specified on the label of your container. Avoid using old paints and stains.

◆ **Clear Latex**
A base solvent for a variety of coatings, including primers, paints, and stains. They feature easy clean-up and nontoxic fumes but have limited durability on unfinished wood. Apply over an oil-based primer.

sanded before repainting can begin. A sealed surface will only need to be power-washed before you apply another coat of sealer.

Both clear and semitransparent finishes also may contain ultraviolet (UV) inhibitors, which block or slow the deteriorating effect of strong sunlight on wood. Like waterproofing sealers, these products can withstand only so much sunlight and must be reapplied frequently—as often as every year in extreme situations.

Refinishing & Restaining

No finish is weatherproof—not even several coats of sealer on pressure-treated wood. Eventually, exposure to the ultraviolet rays of the sun can cause fading, and exposure to water along foot-worn paths can cause rot and

other problems. Before the skin-deep deterioration fosters more damage (and to improve appearance), give the deck a fresh layer of protection. Start by cleaning the surface the same way you clean interior walls before repainting. This step improves the adhesion and durability of a new coating. And you may find that a good scrubbing with a solution of household bleach and water (as much as fifty-fifty) does such a good job of removing mold and other discolorations that the old deck looks nearly new.

You can add more color to the old wood with a solid-body stain, or use a semitransparent stain that adds some tone without completely concealing the grain pattern. If you use a clear sealer, pick one with an ultraviolet inhibitor to retard fading.

For older homes, porches provide not only an inviting entrance but a naturally cooled living space in the summertime, as seen here on Ulysses S. Grant's home in Wilton, New York.

Renewing a Deck

USE: ▶ planer/belt sander • pressure washer • hammer • sandpaper block • steel rake • stiff-bristled brush ▶ bleach • galvanized screws • stain • wood sealer

1 Drag the back of a rake across boards to find protruding nailheads. Hammer the popped nails back down.

2 Replace popped nails with screws for greater holding power. Use galvanized screws about ½ in. longer than the nails.

3 Reduce raised edges with a hand planer or belt sander. Shave or sand lightly to avoid gouges and splinters.

4 Bleach gray or dirty wood with a solution of 1 cup bleach per gallon of water. Use a stiff-bristled scrub brush.

5 Power-wash the deck with a pressure washer, but use caution to avoid damaging soft wood.

6 After the deck is clean, apply stain or wood preservative. Make sure the deck is dry before applying sealer.

decks & porches

Fixing Old Decks

Decks never look as good as they do on the day they are nailed down. After that, it's all downhill. Redwood and cedar lose their rosy hues, flat boards start to twist, and smoothly sanded surfaces start to roughen or rot in the weather. Even if you have periodically resealed the deck, it may finally be time for a face-lift.

Cleaning Old Decks

The easiest improvement is to scrub the deck with a solution of household bleach in water. Experiment on a discolored section with weaker and stronger (up to half bleach, half water) solutions, letting the area dry for inspection before tackling the entire surface. The more muscle power you supply to a stiff scrub brush, the better the result, even on decks with stubborn mold and mildew stains.

If you plan to refinish the deck, one option is to use a commercial deck brightener. Most of these products contain a caustic chemical solution that removes both dirt and a microscopically thin layer of the wood itself, revealing a new, lighter surface. Take care to protect nearby walls, furniture, and shrubs with plastic sheeting, and wear protective clothing.

You may want to rent a power washer to apply cleaning solutions, but be sure to use a low setting to avoid damaging the wood. And just to be safe, try it out on an inconspicuous area first.

Improving Drainage

CLEAN DEBRIS

Good spacing between deck boards is the best method for draining water. For decks that have become clogged with debris, clean between the boards with a 1-inch paint scraper, or use a circular saw to make wider cuts between them. For decks that have cupped boards that are now collecting water, just flip them over and renail them. If your deck has sagged over the years, add shims under the posts.

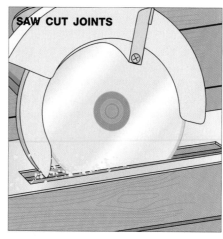
SAW CUT JOINTS

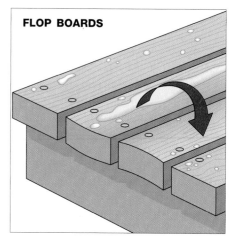
FLOP BOARDS

Refacing Edges of Old Decks

USE: ▶ block plane or belt sander • circular saw • hammer • chalk-line box • measuring tape ▶ 2x2 or 2x4 pressure-treated wood edging • 2-in. paintbrush

1 ***To reface edges of old decking*** *and provide edge support, measure the amount of overhang beyond the joists.*

2 ***Snap a line*** *to guide your cut. Include a large part of the damaged area, but be sure the line is not inside the supporting joist.*

3 ***Don't use a rip fence*** *that would ride unevenly along the rough edge of the deck. Follow the chalk line, cutting freehand.*

Repairing Boards

Once the deck surface is cleaned, there may be a few boards that are beyond recovery, due to rotting, splitting, deep scars, and stains you can't remove by bleaching or sanding. Pull the nails, and replace these boards with good lumber. To minimize the difference in appearance, choose a few weathered boards from the pile at the lumberyard, and wash them with the bleach solution two or three times to help them blend into the color scheme.

If you didn't discover raised nailheads while washing the deck, check for them now. One easy method is to slide a rake or snow shovel across the surface until you hear a "ding" or feel resistance on raised heads. If the nail is barely above the wood surface, just hit it with a hammer. But if the nail has worked loose, pull it and drive in a longer nail, or better yet, a decking screw, which will bite more deeply into the wood to hold the board in place.

Some surface boards may have swelled or worked against their nails to close off the joint. This stops surface drainage and catches little bits of debris and foliage. You can clear these seams by digging your way along with a knife, or take the time to pull nails and remove boards. But one short cut is to run a saw blade down the seam using a circular saw. Be sure to adjust the depth of cut to equal the thickness of your decking. Then cut slowly and carefully to avoid binding the blade in tight cracks.

Jacking

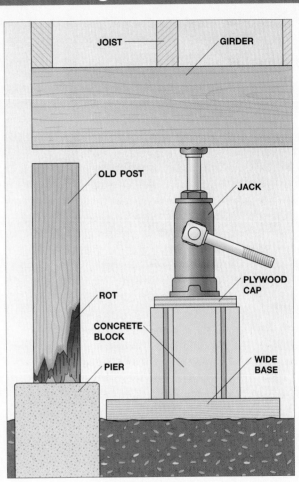

Structural repairs on support posts can be done if you jack up the main support beams. Set the jack on top of a concrete block with plywood cap positioned directly below the beam. Slowly pump the jack until the beam starts to lift. Remove the old post by cutting through with a circular saw, then banging out the bottom section with a hammer. Remove the top section of the post with a pry bar or wrench; then replace the post with a new 4x4. Before replacing, soak the ends of a 4x4 in wood preservative. (PT chemicals don't always penetrate into the core of thick wood.) After the posts have been replaced and secured, lower the jack from the beam. Posts should sit straight on top of piers.

• sealer • stain • wood preservative

4 **Seal the cut ends** with wood preservative. Rough end grain can soak up a lot of moisture, often deteriorating the ends first.

5 **Set a 2x2** along cut ends or a 2x4 to create more of a border. Drive at least one nail into each board, or use galvanized screws.

6 **Use a block plane or belt sander** to dress the seams between the new edging and the decking; then seal or stain to suit.

26

walks, patios & drives

walks, patios & drives

Design Basics

Well-designed walks, patios, and drives can unify outdoor and indoor areas as well as create valuable new outdoor living spaces. Your site is unique, presenting its own set of challenges and opportunities, but a few rules of thumb can guide your design.

The first task is to identify your site's desirable views and natural features, such as trees, rocks, and streams. Next, plan your new walk, patio, or drive to enhance these features. Part of planning is to decide whether you want a formal or informal look; this will influence your choice of materials and plants. Generally, a symmetrical layout tends to appear more formal, while an asymmetrical plan is more casual. Feel free to mix formal and informal layouts in your overall design. For example, you might try a formal patio layout integrated into a system of informal, curvilinear walks and planting areas.

When designing the site plan, you can unify your landscape by selecting and using elements that share a common trait or characteristic. By choosing items that are similar in size, shape, color, material, texture, or detail, you can create cohesiveness among the various elements of the site. Avoid a bland, uniform look by incorporating at least some variation. This will help you add interest and introduce a focal point into the total composition. Just remember that too much variety can be worse than too much unity, resulting in a confusing, chaotic jumble.

Slopes

There's no reason why drives and walks made of certain materials can't travel along a slope, but a patio must be installed on a level surface. If your site slopes, you'll need to terrace it by cutting away sections of the slope and using the dirt to fill adjacent areas. (See "Terracing," pp. 564–65.) Terracing offers a number of advantages: it creates a flat buffer zone for good drainage around the base of the house; it provides areas for landscaping that are easy to maintain; and it affords opportunities to use walkway materials that wouldn't suit sloping terrain. Retaining walls built of stone or railroad ties are commonly used to edge terraces.

Soils

Coarse soils rich with gravel and sand will support more weight and drain much better than fine soils such as clays and silts. Fine soils and topsoil (usually the first 6–12 inches) are relatively unstable; excavate these to a suitable depth, and replace them with coarser soil.

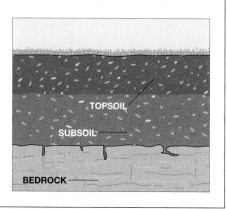

Slopes

Area	Recommended Slope		
	Maximum	Minimum	
Patio	2%	1%	
Walk	5%	0.5%	
Yard	4%	0.5%	
Bank	25%*	—	

For a bank planted with grass; a slope of up to 50% is acceptable for banks with unmowed groundcover.

To find the slope of an area of your yard, divide the vertical distance (rise) by the horizontal distance (run). A slope that drops 2 ft. in 25 ft. has an 8% incline. In the absence of surveying equipment, you can measure rise and run with a yardstick, twine, and level. The twine measures the run (if kept level), and the point at which it meets the yardstick downhill indicates rise. A slight slope provides drainage for patios and walks, but too great an incline can create erosion problems.

Front Yards

The front entry of a house usually serves as the focal point of its design. Front walks typically approach the house in a straight or gently curving—but not circuitous—fashion. Elevated porches and patios adjoining the house provide a sense of security as you approach. The best offer a sense of enclosure, even outside.

A curving front walk adds character and privacy to a home.

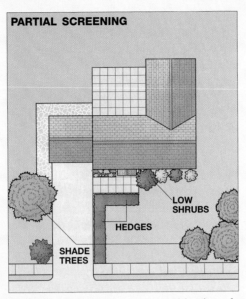

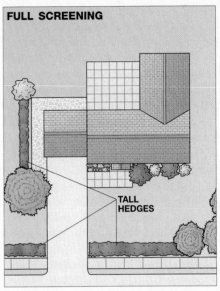

Partial screening—here, a combination of setback trees and low hedges along the entry route to the house—reduces street noise and increases privacy.

By relocating the same landscaping, you can more fully shield the house from the street and create a more enclosed and private front yard.

Side Yards & Backyards

Backyard patios, decks, and walkways also can be shielded and defined with landscaping to create distinct outdoor spaces. While old-fashioned plans often called for shrubs to be set directly against the house, modern layouts use banks of landscaping to extend the living space outside.

Good landscaping can screen the house and still let in light and air.

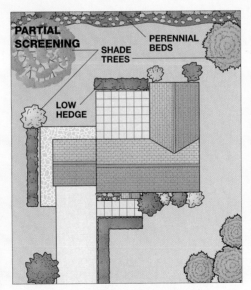

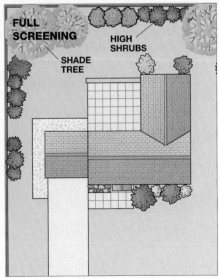

To create partial screening, plant low hedges and build low boundary walls. Shrubbery set directly against the building can foster mold and mildew.

To fully screen a yard and create maximum privacy, use high walls (the limit of which is generally controlled by codes) and rows of fast-growing trees.

walks, patios & drives ___

Designing a Walk

Walks should be designed to complement fences, gates, patios, and other yard features. They should measure at least 2 feet wide, enabling one person to walk comfortably. Garden walks should be 3 feet wide to accommodate wheelbarrows and other equipment; a 4-foot walk allows two people to walk side by side or pass in opposite directions. A walk leading up to a house should measure 5 feet wide to permit wheelchair access.

Walks are considered hard or soft, depending on their material. Hard walks are made of brick, stone, or concrete, while soft walks consist of loose aggregate or wood chips. The simplest walk to make would be gravel or wood chips scattered between plastic edging or landscape ties. Hard walks are a little more complex, requiring a foundation and heavy labor. A walk made of rot-resistant redwood or cedar adds beauty but also a good deal of expense; pressure-treated pine rated for ground contact has less visual appeal but also costs considerably less. (For more on PT wood, see pp 90–91.)

Safety

The safe travel of people along the walkway is essential. Features that add to the safety of walks include textured surfaces, such as a broom finish for concrete, and lighting at critical points, such as steps and landings. A slight slope will allow water to drain off the walkway instead of puddling, which can ice up in winter.

Forming Curves

USE: ▶ spade • garden hose • handsaw • hammer • 4-ft. level • power drill/driver ▶ scrap 2x4 lumber

1 *Lay out the curve* with a garden hose or stakes and string. Excavate the sod to make way for the curved form.

2 *Make stakes* from foot-long pieces of 2x4 with the ends trimmed to a point. Set the first one at the start of the curve.

Reinforcing Concrete Walks

To resist cracking and shifting, reinforce poured concrete walkways with wire mesh (also called welded wire). Flatten the unrolled mesh by walking on it, and cut it to fit with heavy wire cutters or bolt cutters. If you need more than one piece, overlap the seam by at least 6 inches, and secure the sections with wire. Elevate the mesh on small metal risers called chairs, so it will embed itself in the middle of the concrete slab.

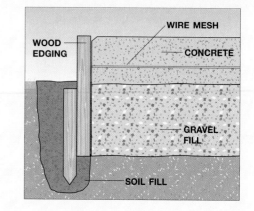

Forming Walks

USE: ▶ 4-ft. level • mason's twine • wheelbarrow • mason's hoe • screed board • mason's trowel or magnesium float • spade • work gloves

1 *After laying out forms* and before pouring, check for level. Consider a slight slope away from the house for drainage.

2 *Pour concrete* from the front of your wheelbarrow to maintain stability, in batches small enough to control and work.

3 *Strike off the surface* as you go, working a screed board back and forth with a sawing motion on the tops of the form.

• ⅛-in. hardboard • deck screws • nails

3 *Use a level* long enough to span the walkway to set consistent stake heights through the curving corner.

4 *Attach ⅛-in.-thick hardboard* to the inside corners of the form frame to create a curve. Drive 3-in. deck screws at all corners.

5 *Reinforce the curve* against the force of poured concrete by driving support stakes every few feet outside the form.

Finishing Concrete

To add a non-slip surface to your walkway, finish the surface with a broom, working with more or less pressure to create a light, medium, or heavy texture. Use the broom after the concrete is troweled smooth but before it sets up. To make a pebbled surface, embed aggregate (colored pebbles or gravel) into the poured concrete before it sets. You can also add pigment to the concrete, or throw rock salt onto the surface, which leaves behind an interesting texture of small holes.

▶ 2x4 lumber for edging • concrete • gravel • rebar or wire mesh (optional)

4 *If you can't use forms* to screed the surface, embed pipes in the pour and use them as a level guide.

5 *When you lift out the screed pipes,* fill the void with extra concrete. Also tap the forms with a hammer to settle the mix.

6 *Smooth screed lines* and the entire surface with a trowel or float, making large arcs with the front edge slightly raised.

walks, patios & drives

Grading & Drainage

Your site's terrain, soil conditions, and drainage requirements, as well as the walkway materials to be used, determine how you must prepare the ground for your walk. Virtually every walk project will require some excavation to create a level surface and provide a stable base for the paving materials. This is especially true of concrete. If poured concrete or concrete pavers are not laid on a firm, well-compacted, and well-drained base, they will likely buckle, crack, or sink. A base consisting of 4 inches of compacted gravel or crushed stone topped by 2 inches of builder's sand should suffice. Soils that drain poorly—or those subject to frost heave, settling, or erosion—may require a thicker base of 6 to 8 inches of gravel or crushed stone.

Drainage Systems

There are two basic ways to drain soggy soil: construct a surface drain system or install a subsurface system consisting of area drains, catch basins, trench drains, dry wells, or drain tiles. In wet soils, you may need to bury perforated drainage pipe in a gravel subbase. However, due to the expense and work involved, consider a subsurface system only as a last resort.

Surface drain systems consist of shallow drainage ditches, called swales, and built-up mounds that direct runoff, called berms. After you've identified the area where runoff enters your site, the next step is to decide where to channel the water. Generally, you'll want to direct it to an existing storm sewer located in the street, channeling the water with swales, berms, and retaining walls. If it's impossible to channel storm water to the street system, look for an alternative outlet. But take care to respect your neighbors' property, and don't divert your water into their yards.

Don't install walks that cross swales or run across slopes. Such walks can act as dams; they'll impede natural drainage patterns in the yard and even cause problems with flooding.

In the good old days when wood was cheap, this hotel in Bermuda thought nothing of building a walkway to the beach that was wide enough for an early-1930s sedan to drive across it.

Edges & Joints

USE: ▶ edging and jointing trowels • metal float

1 *Form the perimeter of the slab* with an edging trowel. Run it slowly back and forth to smooth the mix and release the form.

Control-Joint Spacing

Slab thickness	JOINT SPACING	
	Aggregate < ¾ in.	Aggregate > ¾ in.
4 in.	8 ft.	10 ft.
5 in.	10 ft.	13 ft.
6 in.	12 ft.	15 ft.

Control joints reduce surface cracking in concrete. The thicker the slab the fewer you need.

Cracks & Breaks

USE: ▶ whisk broom • cold chisel • hammer • paintbrush • mason's trowel • safety glasses ▶ concrete repair caulk • masking tape • bonding adhesive

1 *To make minor repairs* of small cracks, start by cleaning out dirt and debris with a whisk broom.

2 *Concrete repair caulk* provides a quick fix for minor cracks. It prevents further damage but is only a temporary repair.

3 *To patch larger areas and edges,* clear out loose debris with a cold chisel. Add a form board to contain the patch material.

• trowel ▶ poured concrete walk (see "Forming Walks," pp. 526–27)

2 *Form control joints* with a jointing trowel run against a squared-up 2x4 for a straight-edged guide.

3 *The jointing trowel* leaves a smooth groove in the surface, but you may need to clear out the interior seam with a trowel.

4 *Use a float to smooth the surface* and any marks left by edging or jointing. Try not to overwork the surface and puddle water.

Stamped Concrete

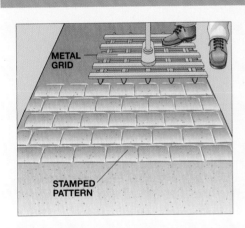

METAL GRID

STAMPED PATTERN

If you like the look of a patterned masonry surface but prefer to use one big pour of reinforced concrete instead of pavers, talk to a contractor about stamping. On a driveway, for instance, workers come back over the surface with a metal grid tool to make an imprint of squares or other shapes in the mix—a little like turning soupy pancake batter into waffles. As the surface wears and weathers, these recesses tend to darken and give the impression of individual tiles.

• vinyl-reinforced patching compound

4 *Use masking tape* to protect any adjacent surfaces where you don't want any fresh masonry to bond.

5 *Apply a thin layer* of bonding adhesive, which will help create a strong bond with the patch material.

6 *Fill the damaged area* with vinyl-reinforced patching compound in thin layers. Wait 30 min. between coats.

walks, patios & drives

Brick & Paver Basics

Bricks and concrete pavers make ideal materials for do-it-yourselfers. Because they're packed into a sand base without mortar, installation is forgiving—you can make minor adjustments along the way as needed. Edging keeps the paving material and sand in place.

Bricks and pavers produce beautiful, durable walkways and patios. When selecting brick, choose a type rated for exterior use, with a slightly rough surface that will provide traction in wet weather. (See "Brick Basics," p. 52.) Check with your building department to find out the type of brick that works best in your area.

Concrete pavers come in a variety of shapes and sizes. Most are modular, meaning they fit together in a variety of geometric patterns. Unlike bricks, concrete pavers usually have rounded edges; spacers on the sides keep you from setting them so closely together that there's no room for sand.

Estimating

It will take an average of four-and-a-half 4x8-inch bricks or pavers to cover a square foot of surface area. For example, a 12x20-foot patio (240 square feet) would require approximately 1,080 pavers. Order 5–10% extra to allow for miscuts, breakage, and future repairs. Some brick patterns, such as herringbone and basket weave, require a paver type whose length measures exactly twice its width.

Calculate the sand you'll need at a rate of 9 pounds per square foot of surface. Filter fabric goes under the sand to keep down weeds and prevent sand erosion, so you'll need to buy some of this material as well.

Installation Tips

The most difficult step in laying bricks or pavers is creating the gravel and sand bed to set them in. The gravel must be firmly compacted: add one layer, compact it, add a second layer, and compact that, too. Add the edging, which must be deep enough to contain both the paving material and the sand layer. Otherwise, the sand can wash under the edging, causing the pavers above to sag. Shovel in the sand, and tamp it down. Then wet it, fill in any low spots, and wet it again. Smooth and level the sand by pulling a notched 2x6 board along the edging.

Paver Patterns

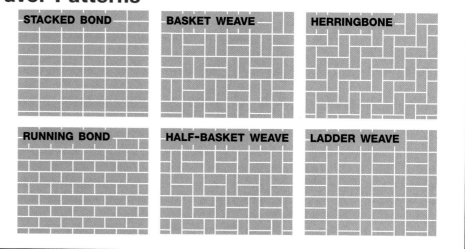

STACKED BOND   BASKET WEAVE   HERRINGBONE

RUNNING BOND   HALF-BASKET WEAVE   LADDER WEAVE

Edging Options

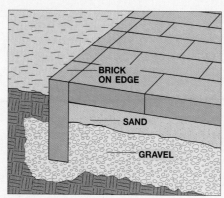

A perimeter row of pavers, called a soldier course because it is set vertically, contains the supporting base.

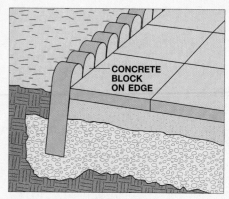

Molded blocks in several shapes also can form a soldier course to prevent undermining from drainage.

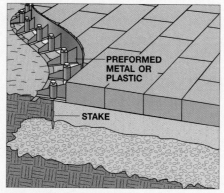

To contain curved edges made of smaller, less stable blocks, use flexible plastic forms staked into the ground.

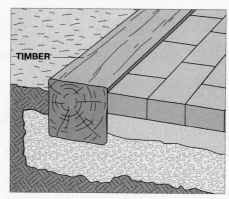

PT landscaping timbers also can provide edge support. They should be nestled in gravel and staked or spiked.

Installing a Paver Patio

USE: ▶ power tamper • circular saw & masonry blade • sledgehammer • rubber mallet • broom ▶ pavers • sand • gravel • filter fabric • pipe • edging • 2x4

1 *Once you dig out the sod,* rake away stones and twigs. Use a 2x4 to create a roughly level subbase for the patio.

2 *To minimize shifting and settling,* rent a power tamper to vibrate and compress a 4–6-in. bed of gravel over the dirt.

3 *Prevent erosion from drainage* through pavers by covering the compacted base with filter fabric.

4 *There are many ways* to contain the edge blocks. On of the most efficient is plastic trim secured with oversized stakes.

5 *Shovel a bed of sand* over the prepared base. Use pipe set in the sand as screed boards to level the sand bed.

6 *Pull the screed pipes,* fill in the narrow troughs with sand, and start laying pavers. Use a level to check the surface.

7 *You can try to break* pavers with a cold chisel and hammer, or make precise edge cuts with a saw and masonry blade.

8 *Use a level or straightedge* to check the surface level, and tap raised blocks down into the sand with a rubber mallet.

9 *To help the interlocked blocks* stay in position, dump some sand on the surface, and sweep it thoroughly into the joints.

walks, patios & drives

Stone Paving Systems

Like bricks, both stone and interlocking pavers can be dry-laid—that is, installed on a simple sand bed. This creates an attractive, intricate-looking walkway that requires little preparation. Large flagstones and fieldstones can also be installed directly on compacted soil in warmer areas where frost heave is not a problem. Sand or dry mortar swept between the embedded paving materials keeps them from shifting, as does the edging on each side of the walkway. Sand is best used between interlocking pavers because the units fit closely together. Sand can also be used to fill joints between regular-shaped stones, but wide joints between irregular shapes require joint stabilizer.

Interlocking pavers are installed in the same manner as bricks and concrete pavers. Because it's important to compact the sand and gravel subbase thoroughly, plan on renting a power tamper. These machines work better and faster, and require less effort than tamping by hand.

Depending on the shape of the pavers, you may end up with voids or chinks along the edges of the walk. You can buy special edging pieces to create a straight edge, if your local dealer sells them. Otherwise, you'll have to cut the pavers to fit the spaces.

Modular Concrete

In this process, concrete is poured into molds to make big foundation blocks. The concrete can also be worked into a variety of smaller, stone-like shapes and sizes using a special form. Manufacturers offer a range of earth-tone colors that you can mix and match to create subtle gradations, giving your walkway an appearance more like that of real stone at far less cost.

Concrete slabs or smaller areas of fake "stones" should be supported on a 2-inch bed of sand, or 2 inches of sand on 4 inches of compacted gravel. When making areas of stone, it's a good idea to experiment with color and practice using the form before starting on the real thing. You place the form, fill it with the colored concrete, lift the form, and then move on to an adjacent section. After pouring each section, clean up the edges of each stone with a pointing trowel. As a final step, sweep sand into the joints between the fake stones.

Interlocking Paver Patterns

Interlocking pavers come in a variety of sizes and shapes, but most of them measure 2⅜ to 2½ inches thick, about the same size as a standard brick. Grass pavers have an open-grid shape for planting grass or other ground cover. They help to make a durable and natural-looking walk, and the turf itself (or structural edging) holds the pavers in place. Depending on the walkway design—for example, if you lay the stone in a grid or randomly—they can look casual or formal. Keep in mind that curved patterns will require a lot of difficult cuts on the edge blocks.

ZAG

HEXAGONAL

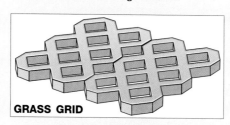
GRASS GRID

DIAMOND

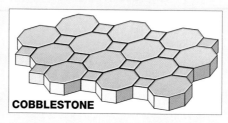
COBBLESTONE

MULTI-WEAVE

Laying Stone Pavers

USE: ▶ power tamper • shovel • mason's twine • rubber mallet • short-handled sledgehammer • cold chisel

1 *You can use forms* to level a sand base, or temporarily set pipes in the bed and level the sand by dragging a 2x4 over the pipes.

2 *Use accurate sod cuts* on the border or string guides to position the first few stones. Set them with a rubber mallet.

Cutting Stone

Mark your cut line across the stone, and score it with a cold chisel and hammer, working back and forth.

With the score line etched in the surface, set a board under the stone for leverage, and break the stone.

Stone in Sand

A 2-inch sand bed is adequate for stones of similar thickness; use a thicker sand bed for stones of varying thickness. To create a level walk surface, remove as much sand as needed. Finish by sweeping sand between the joints with a stiff broom, working a 5- or 6-foot section at a time. A light spray of water will pack down the sand and wash it off the surface. Allow the surface to dry; then repeat the process until all the joints are filled and compacted. Replenish the sand as necessary, usually once a year.

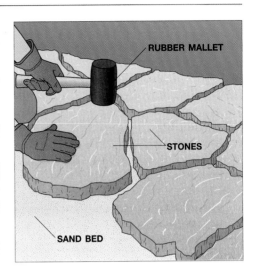

Stone in Mortar

To make a mortar-bed walkway, pour a 3½- to 4-inch concrete slab over a compacted gravel subbase. Then, embed the stones in the concrete slab. The concrete provides support for the stones and keeps them from separating as the ground shifts. As with sand-bed walks, the base must be set on a firm, well-drained bed— usually a 4-inch layer of gravel. The joints between stones are typically filled with mortar but may also be filled with sand or even topsoil.

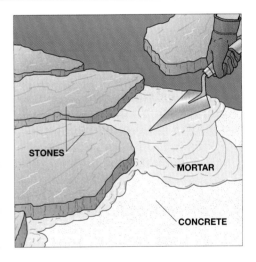

• 4-ft. level • push broom • garden hose ▶ stone pavers • mason's sand • gravel (optional) • pipe (optional) • 2x4 scrap • 2x lumber for forms (optional)

3 *Check the surface* with a level, and run a straightedge across the seams to identify any high spots.

4 *Brush sand across the surface,* working your broom back and forth to fill the joints between stones.

5 *Spray the surface with water* and brush on another layer of sand. Repeat the process until the joints are full and firm.

walks, patios & drives

Backyard Boardwalks

Boardwalks transplant the advantages of wood decks to the turf, a place normally reserved for more cumbersome concrete and stone. By setting pressure-treated (PT) timber supports and covering them with redwood, cedar, or PT 2x4 decking, you can make an elegant, ground-hugging walkway.

Wooden walks can be built with concrete foundations that extend below the frost line, but most soils can support a simple, less expensive structure. These economical ground-level installations can rise and fall with the frost heaves. In nearly all cases, that's acceptable; wooden walks are flexible enough to bend without breaking.

Basic Walkway Construction

The easiest approach is to embed in the ground parallel pressure-treated boards (called sleepers), setting them on edge 3–5 feet apart, depending on how you plan to use the walk. (See "Designing a Walk," p. 526.) The top edges of these boards, like joists on a deck, carry short lengths of 2x4 or 2x6 decking—the surface you walk on.

To help secure the embedded sleepers, you should add stakes. One way is to drive pointed, pressure-treated 1x4s a foot or two into the ground every 2 feet inside the 2x10 sleepers. Trim them flush with the top edges, and nail them to the sleepers. They'll add strength and help keep the sleepers from tipping. To add even more strength, nail on cross braces, embedding them at right angles to the sleepers (and at the same depth) every 4 to 6 feet. To finish, nail on the decking perpendicular to the sleepers—just the way you would on a deck. (See "Decks," pp. 508–9 for more on this.)

Other Design Options

Some situations may call for more elaborate construction methods. For more stability in sandy soil, replace some of the stakes with 4x4 posts sunk in holes that reach the frost line. If the land rolls up and down, go with 2x12 joists. Use these to help level the terrain, allowing them to sit completely aboveground for a stretch (which may require a railing or even steps) and run belowground where necessary. Keep in mind that walkways needn't be level.

Forming a Gravel Walk

USE: ▶ garden hose • shovel • wheelbarrow • garden rake • hand tamper ▶ gravel • mason's twine

1 Use a length of garden hose to lay out curves in the walk. Cut several sticks the same length to keep the width consistent.

2 Spray-paint the grass outside of the hose, and remove the hose and wood to start digging out the sod.

4 Dig a trench along the edges with a shovel, deep enough so that the edging will rise a few inches above grade.

5 Set edging blocks into the trenches. This perimeter course will contain the surface material and prevent erosion.

Building a Boardwalk

USE: ▶ shovel • wheelbarrow • garden rake • tamper • measuring tape • 4-ft. level • framing square

1 After laying out your walk with string, dig a trench at least 4 in. deep and wider than the walk by 4-6 in. on each side.

2 Lay down landscape fabric to prevent weed growth, and backfill the trench with 4 in. of gravel raked level and tamped.

• 2x4 scraps • spray paint • bricks or other edging

3 *Dig up the grass* between the painted lines along with 2–3 in. of soil, and rake the ground free of stones and twigs.

6 *Spread the gravel onto the walk* in layers, and tamp each layer until it's about ¾ in. below the edging.

Installing In-Ground Steps

USE: ▶ power drill/driver • sledgehammer • saw ▶ PT lumber • rebar • screws

If your steps will be on a slope, you often can build them directly into the ground. Carve the steps into the hillside and build them with landscape timbers and brick or other walk materials. These steps work well on a hillside where the run equals 24 to 32 inches per foot of rise. (See p. 168 for how to calculate rise and run.) To determine the number of steps, divide the rise by the height of a landscape timber. Treads on these types of steps usually measure about 15 inches deep, but they can be as deep as 17 inches.

2 *To minimize shifting,* drive a piece of rebar down through the timbers and into the soil.

1 *Use pressure-treated lumber* to build an edge for the steps, and drill landscape timbers retaining the steps.

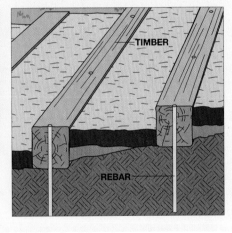

• power drill/driver or hammer • router (optional) ▶ gravel • stakes • mason's string • PT lumber for sleepers • decking • decking screws or galvanized nails

3 *Lay pressure-treated sleepers* (anything from 2x4s to 2x12s) on the gravel, and screw them to 2x4 stakes in the ground.

4 *Cut decking boards to length* and attach them to the sleepers with 3-in. deck screws or 10d galvanized nails.

5 *For a more finished look,* use a router with a round-over bit to give the rough edges of the 2x4s a smooth, uniform shape.

walks, patios & drives

Driveway Basics

Sand and gravel make up the basic ingredients of driveways. Sometimes these materials are combined with cement to make concrete. More often, they are bound together with liquid asphalt to make blacktop. Bricks, pavers, stone, or crushed gravel can also be used to construct driveways.

Driveway Design

The driveway serves as the main access to your home. It should accommodate not only the family's everyday vehicle use—including work if you run a home business—but also special purposes such as deliveries and entertaining. As you plan your driveway, keep in mind accessibility and visibility. Offer as clear a view of the road as possible, and get rid of any overgrown plantings that could make it difficult to see oncoming traffic.

Size the main part of the driveway between 10 and 12 feet wide for a one-car garage, and 16 to 24 feet wide for a two-car garage. (If the drive will form part of a walkway, add another 2 feet.) While a narrower drive (6 to 8 feet wide) may suffice, it's better to go wider so that people can step out onto the pavement and not onto grass or flower beds. An apron that tapers outward to meet the street makes it easier to back your car in or out. Extra parking that doesn't obstruct normal activities is extremely useful; allow 12 feet per vehicle for cars, more for trucks and RVs. You can screen these parking areas with plantings or fences, but make sure that the design is proportional to the rest of your yard. For safety's sake, don't crowd the walkway from the parking area to the entry door with plantings or other obstructions. Keep this area fully visible to maximize security and deter trespassers.

A concrete driveway need be only 4 inches thick for normal car traffic. However, if you expect heavy trucks, you should increase the thickness to at least 6 inches. Because a variety of vehicles might use the end of the driveway to turn around, you should make that part at least 8 inches thick. Keep in mind that proper drainage is critical. Any water that collects on the driveway will produce dangerous ice in the winter and will puddle near your house during heavy rains.

Design Options

Safety is the most important thing to consider when designing your driveway. If your house is on a busy street, take extra yard space for a turnaround so you don't have to back out. The figures given in these diagrams should be considered minimums; always consult with your building inspector before beginning work; local codes may be different.

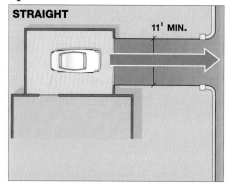

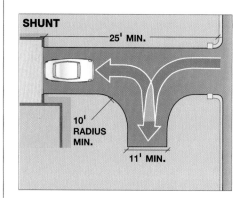

Slope & Drainage

If there is no natural slope to your driveway, it must be shaped to allow for drainage. Three possibilities illustrated at right include the crown (top), concave (middle), and cross-slope (bottom). The ramp can have a slope of anywhere from 4–8%; the steeper the ramp, the gentler the slope of the apron. Ramps with 6–8% slopes should have aprons with 2% slopes or less.

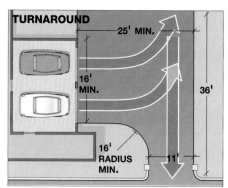

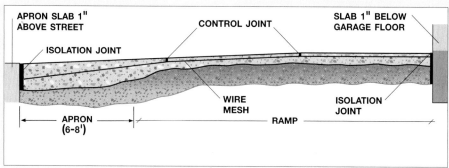

Material Options

◆ **Concrete slabs** make strong, long-lasting driveways as long as the ground underneath is relatively stable and has been prepared thoroughly. The material can be slightly commercial-looking and without much visual interest—unless it is stamped with a pattern when poured. Light-colored concrete will show oil stains. Concrete generally costs more to install than asphalt.

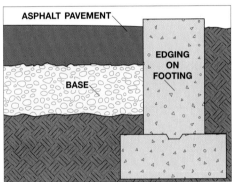

◆ **Asphalt** doesn't offer the strength of concrete, but it is more malleable, so you can form a shallow swale to carry water away from a garage door or mound up a speed bump. Asphalt also repairs easily. While concrete cracks tend to drift apart no matter how you patch them, asphalt can be made whole, even regraded, and sealed to look new.

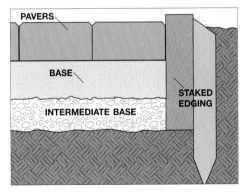

◆ **Concrete pavers** have the same durability as concrete; some blocks can withstand up to 2,000 psi of pressure. They come in a wide range of colors and styles, so it's easy to complement the look of your home. While fairly simple to install yourself, pavers cost more than plain concrete or asphalt. They are cheaper than stamped concrete, however.

◆ **Stone and brick** make durable drives, but they're not a good choice for steep driveways; they tend to get slippery when wet and ice easily in cold climates. In terms of installation, if you're looking to save money, brick set on a sand bed costs less than brick set on a concrete slab. Stones can be set in a mortar or sand bed, or placed directly in the ground.

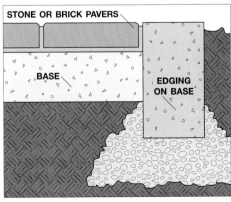

walks, patios & drives

Asphalt Problems

Although asphalt driveways are fairly durable, they do require some maintenance, especially in cold areas where freeze/thaw cycles are the norm. Small cracks let in water that will freeze and expand, causing existing minor damage to become major. Periodic sealing will help keep these cracks from starting, but they won't prevent damage caused by settling of the ground under the driveway or improper installation.

Minor Repairs

Before you apply any filler or sealer, brush out loose material or vacuum it up with a wet-dry vac. Use blacktop crack filler, which comes in cartridges like caulk, applying it in a continuous bead with a caulking gun. Check the instructions for set time (about 10 minutes). When the material settles, compact and smooth out the surface with a putty knife. Fill deep cracks with sand, compacting it to within ½ inch of the surface before applying the filler.

For small holes, clear away loose chunks and break off any unsupported edges of old blacktop. A wire brush will dislodge debris. Then, use paste-like asphalt patching compound. This material contains fine aggregate and is malleable enough to be feathered to the edges of depressions. It works well where asphalt is broken out along curbing. In the middle of the driveway, a repair will last longer if you dig out around the edges of the hole and make the patch uniform in thickness. Lay in the patch material with a trowel to create a mound about ½ inch higher than the driveway, and then tamp it with the end of a 2x4.

Filling Potholes

Use cold patch for street-sized repairs. It has larger aggregate than paste patches and comes in 60- to 70-pound bags. This material resembles the asphalt your driveway is made of, but it's treated with chemicals that keep it workable. If the temperature stays above 50° F, you don't have to heat it the way highway crews heat fresh asphalt—but you do have to roll it.

After clearing loose debris, remove jagged edges around the hole with a hammer and cold chisel. Then, pile on enough cold patch to leave a slight mound after tamping. Fill deep holes in two stages, tamping in between, to avoid leaving a water-collecting depression. Next, apply the weight of your car, driving it slowly over a piece of ¾-inch plywood or a layer of sand spread over the cold patch.

Surface Sealing

To determine whether blacktop needs resurfacing, pour a bucket of water on it on a hot day while the sun is out. If the surface water dries leaving a dark circle that takes much longer to dry, the water has soaked in, which indicates that resurfacing is needed.

A stable asphalt surface that was properly installed needs only occasional sealing. New drives won't need it for at least a year. Older drives should be washed using a household cleaner and water—about a quart per 1,000 square feet of asphalt—and then rinsed.

Sealing will make grayish, drying asphalt look better and keep out water that causes erosion and cracking. However, don't expect sealing to take the place of resurfacing, which involves topping an old asphalt drive with at least 2 inches of new material. And no coating can rescue one of those jobs that consists of a 1- or 2-inch layer of asphalt applied over loose gravel.

Sealer comes in 5-gallon cans, enough to cover about 250 square feet. Older, porous drives will soak up more, newer drives less. For extra protection, apply two thin coats, and allow 36 hours between applications.

Replacing Expansion Joints

USE: ▶ wet-dry vacuum • putty knife • caulking gun ▶ foam backer rod • urethane sealant

1 *Fiberboard and lumber* used to form expansion joints in concrete eventually wear away in the weather.

2 *To replace the joint,* dig out old pieces of lumber and debris, and clean out the crack with a wet-dry vac.

3 *To allow for some shifting* and to minimize cracking, pack a strip of foam backer rod into the joint.

4 *Cover the backer rod* and seal the joint against the weather with a liberal layer of self-leveling urethane sealant.

Cleaning Concrete

USE: ▶ brick • bucket • stiff-bristled brush • 4-in. paintbrush ▶ commercial absorbent or other material • concrete cleaner • clear concrete sealer

1 *Use a commercial absorbent,* sawdust, or kitty litter to lift deep oil stains. Work the absorbent around with a brick.

2 *Use a stiff brush* and concrete cleaner to scrub out stains. It also helps to wash the entire surface before sealing.

3 *A clear concrete sealer* improves the appearance of a concrete driveway and helps it shed water.

Repairing Asphalt

USE: ▶ mason's trowel • caulking gun • utility knife • rubber gloves ▶ cold patch • asphalt-based caulk • asphalt rolls

1 *Use cold patch,* a workable blend of asphalt and aggregate, to fill small holes. Clean out debris before mounding the mix.

2 *Patch asphalt cracks* so they don't let in water by sweeping them clean and filling with asphalt-based caulk.

3 *Asphalt rolls* are a convenient way to patch small cracks. Peel off the backing and press the self-adhering mat in place.

Sealing Asphalt

USE: ▶ garden hose with hose-end sprayer • pressure washer (optional) • push broom or squeegee • work gloves ▶ cleaner • asphalt sealer

1 *Wash the surface* to improve sealer adhesion. Use a hose, hose-end sprayer with detergent, or a pressure washer.

2 *Use full-strength cleaner* on tough stains. Most solutions can be diluted (1 cup to a gal. of water) for general cleaning.

3 *Most sealers* can both fill and coat cracks up to ⅛-in. deep. Spread them with a squeegee or an old push broom.

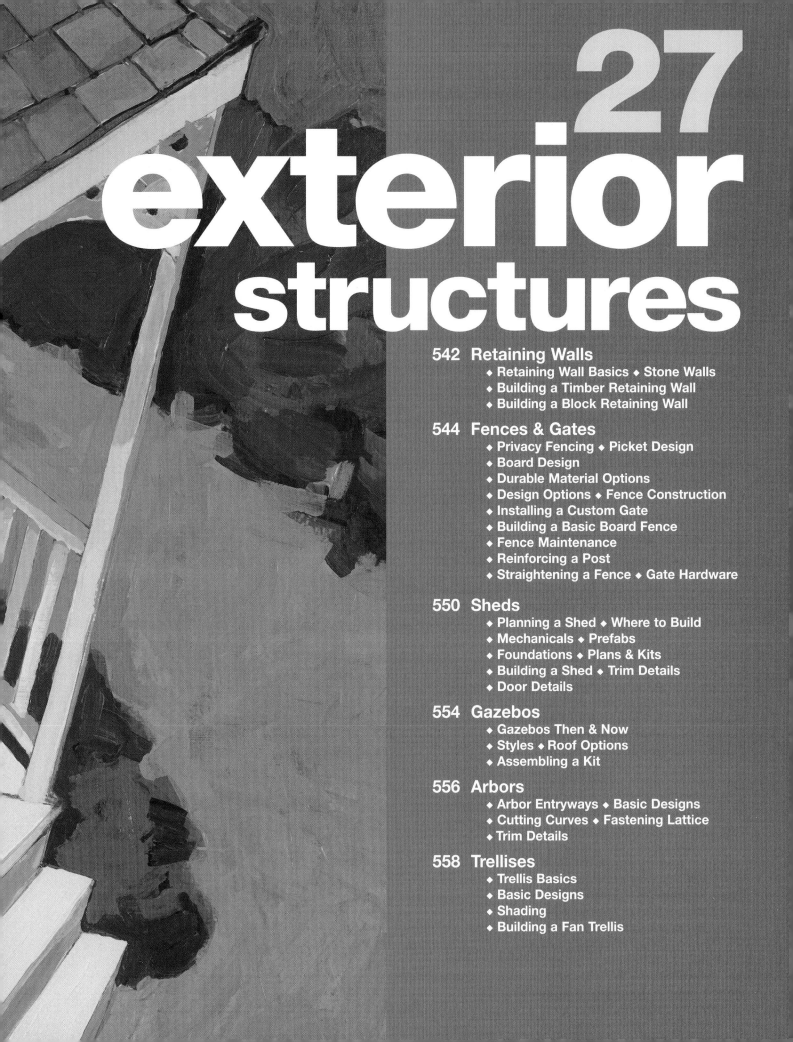

27
exterior
structures

Retaining Wall Basics

Retaining walls keep soil from eroding down a slope. They can also transform a hilly backyard into a series of terraces for lawns, planting beds, or patio areas. On flat sites, low retaining walls can create raised planting beds or borders, adding a sense of visual depth to an otherwise uninteresting landscape.

You can make retaining walls from a variety of materials: stone, pressure-treated lumber, brick, and concrete blocks. The easiest material for DIYers to work with is mortarless interlocking concrete blocks specially designed for retaining walls. But no matter what material you choose, the wall must be strong enough to hold the weight of the soil and the pressure of groundwater against it.

Drainage

A retaining wall must have provisions for drainage. Typically, you lay perforated pipe at the base of the wall before you backfill it with gravel. The gravel drains the water from the surface, and the pipe carries it away from the footing. Adding weep holes will allow some of the subsurface water to drain through the wall, relieving part of the pressure. In brick and block walls, just omit the mortar from some of the vertical joints, or insert 1- or 2-inch plastic pipe every 4–6 feet along the base of the wall as you build it. In timber walls, insert pipes in holes drilled into the wood. Always cover the back of the holes with landscape fabric before you backfill the wall, to prevent the drainpipes from clogging with dirt.

Footings

Most retaining walls require footings for support. Specific requirements depend on soil conditions, the size and type of wall you're building, and local codes. Generally, the width of the footing should be at least two-thirds the total height. The top of the footing should be at least 12 inches below grade on the downhill side of the wall. The footing should be as thick as the wall width (a minimum of 8 inches).

Mortared masonry retaining walls generally have poured-concrete footings with rebar running the length of the footing. Timber and interlocking-block walls need a gravel footing, poured in a trench dug below the frost line.

Building a Timber Retaining Wall

USE: ▶ circular saw • drill/driver • spade • sledgehammer • level ▶ 8x8 timbers • rebar • gravel • spikes

1 Cut 8x8 pressure-treated landscape timbers to the length you need, and start the first course on a gravel foundation.

2 Drill holes in the timbers for rebar every 4 ft. using a power drill and spade bit the same size as the rebar.

3 Set the first course on the gravel foundation, and drive lengths of rebar about 2 ft. long into the holes.

4 To resist tipover, set a few timbers, called deadmen, perpendicular to the wall, and spike them in place.

5 Check each course for level, particularly where long timbers are cut short to fit around deadmen.

6 When the wall is finished, backfill behind the wall with dirt and gravel, burying the perpendicular timbers.

Stone Walls

A stone retaining wall can be mortared or dry-stacked. Dry-stacked walls can be set without a footing but generally should be no higher than 3 feet. Most mortared walls need a concrete footing below the local frost line and should be thicker at the base to increase stability. To reduce tipover forces, provide drainage for water on the high side of the wall. It also helps to angle the wall slightly back into the raised bank.

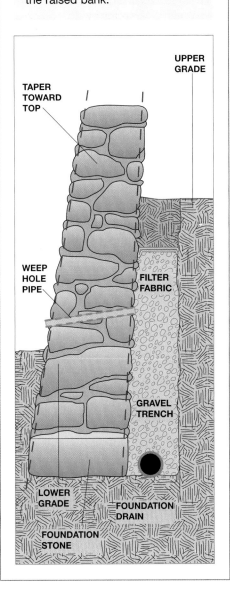

UPPER GRADE

TAPER TOWARD TOP

WEEP HOLE PIPE

FILTER FABRIC

GRAVEL TRENCH

LOWER GRADE

FOUNDATION DRAIN

FOUNDATION STONE

Building a Block Retaining Wall

USE: ▶ 4-ft. level • chisel & hammer ▶ interlocking blocks • plastic connectors • gravel • adhesive

1 *After digging a trench* and filling it with gravel, lay the first course of blocks, checking them for level as you work.

2 *Provide extra drainage* on steep slopes by burying a perforated drainpipe in gravel behind the block wall.

3 *To stagger the joints,* cut the first block of the second course in half using a hammer and cold chisel.

4 *Proprietary block systems* have different types of interlocking systems. This one uses hard plastic connectors.

5 *Set plastic connecting pins* into holes to align blocks vertically and into formed slots to align them horizontally.

6 *Finish the wall* with cap blocks cemented in place with adhesive recommended by the manufacturer.

exterior structures

Privacy Fencing

To make your yard really secure, you could surround it with a solid brick wall. To keep a dog from roaming, chain-link might be the ticket; or, for peace and quiet, densely interlocked evergreens. But if you just want a little more seclusion, the answer is a privacy fence—an inexpensive wood screen that makes backyard sunbathing a private event.

Of course, you can build privacy walls with masonry, such as concrete blocks that have perforated sides or bricks with spaces between them. But these walls are very heavy and need a footing. Even chain-link can be turned into a privacy fence by weaving plastic strips through the links, although this never quite overcomes the utilitarian appearance. Wood is the best bet for do-it-yourself projects because it is easy to work with and comparatively inexpensive. And if you use pressure-treated lumber or naturally durable cedar and redwood (which cost more than pressure-treated pine), you can expect the fence to last many years.

Design Components

A basic privacy fence has three components: posts spaced from 4 to 8 feet apart, top and bottom horizontal rails running between posts, and a filler nailed to this structural grid. The framework may be square or rectangular, ground hugging or raised a bit.

Once the structural grid is erected and braced, you add the filler. There are so many options that it's best to experiment a little. For example, you could tack vertical slats between the top and bottom rails or horizontal slats between posts. The screening boards could be plumb or diagonal, set very close together for optimum privacy or farther apart to allow for a breeze and preserve a bit of a view.

Although screen walls are not adjustable, you can make them directional by using vertical slats set at an angle. With such designs, the screen wall virtually disappears when you see only the edges of the boards from one side of the yard. But from a position at the other side of the yard, the slats appear full face and form an almost solid screen.

Picket Design

Some lumberyards carry precut pickets (or even premade 6-foot fence sections), but the design choices are often limited. To make your own simple pickets, clamp two or three boards together, and cut the tops with a hand saw or circular saw. For fancier cuts, cut with a saber saw. Add a finishing touch, and cover exposed end grain on posts by installing decorative caps and finials, which screw into the post top.

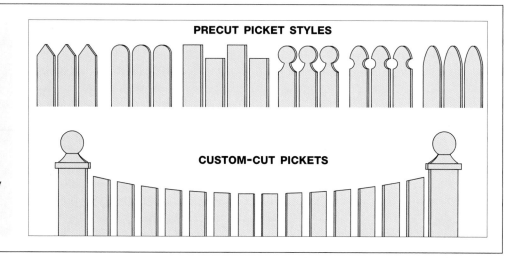

Board Design

Add interest to a vertical-board fence by varying the board tops or the widths of the boards. Board fence rails should be attached to posts before the boards are installed. Cut all the board tops before you attach them to the rails, except for an arched design. For that configuration, stretch a level string between the posts at the highest point, and make sure that all the boards extend at least up to this string. Then trace the arch pattern onto the boards, and make the cuts with a saber saw.

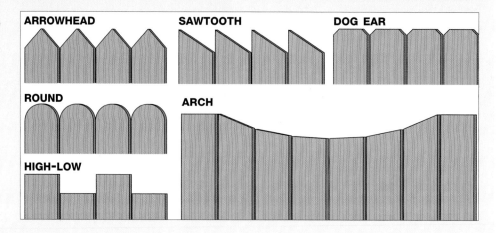

Durable Material Options

PRESSURE-TREATED WOOD

REDWOOD

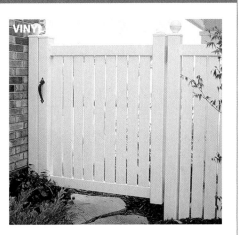
VINYL

Design Options

PICKET

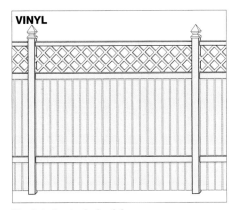

Picket fences have a traditional appearance. You can vary the amount of privacy by adjusting the picket spacing.

BOARD

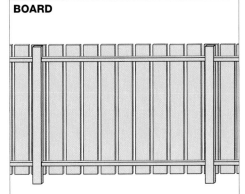

Board fences, usually used for backyards and side yards, provide more privacy and security than picket fences.

METAL

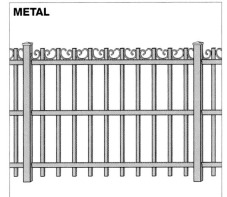

Prefabricated metal fences, in styles ranging from Victorian to modern, can be ordered through a fence supplier.

VINYL

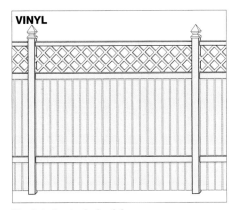

Prefabricated vinyl fences are manufactured to look like wood or metal but require less maintenance.

CHAIN-LINK

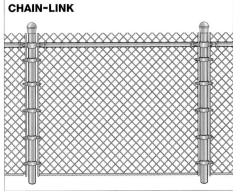

Chain-link fences are durable and provide excellent security; inserts can be woven into the chain to provide privacy.

WIRE

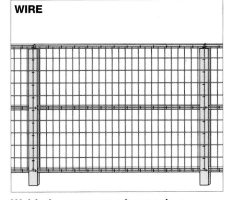

Welded- or woven-wire mesh on a wood frame makes a lightweight and economical fence.

exterior structures

Fence Construction

Fence building requires basic carpentry skills and hand tools. You may also want a circular saw, a power miter saw, and a power drill/driver. If you are planning to do the work yourself, choose a design suited to your skill, and make sure you have a helper to share some of the post-hole digging. You'll also want help plumbing and bracing posts and installing rails or fence sections.

Installing Posts

A hand-operated post-hole digger (a rental item) is usually all you need for digging post-holes. (Getting the dirt out of a deep hole with a shovel forces you to dig too wide a hole.) If you have a lot of holes to dig, consider renting a power auger. This heavy, corkscrew-like digging machine will drill a perfectly round hole in about a minute. However, if the auger hits a large rock or tree root, the kickback can cause serious leg bruises or worse, so avoid using one in rocky soil or around large trees.

Set posts below the frost line and on top of a 6-inch-thick tamped bed of crushed rock or gravel so the bottom end grain of the posts does not sit in water. Then fill the area around the posts with a well-tamped mix of earth and gravel or with concrete for extra strength at corners and gate openings. Space posts evenly about 6 feet apart. Dig holes for and install the corner posts first; then, stretch a taut mason's line between them to help locate the intermediate holes and posts.

In most cases, the fence top will either be level or stepped in sections to follow a significant ground slope. It's usually best to cut the tops in place—at an angle to shed water or straight across if a post cap is planned.

Holding Things Together

A couple of quick bar clamps are great for holding things in place until you've leveled and squared up posts and rails. So, too, are screws and a battery-powered drill/driver. Use fasteners rated for exterior use. Rust causes ugly stains, loose fasteners, and eventually complete failure. Hot-dipped galvanized nails are best; avoid the less durable electroplated ones. Because of their holding power, screws are often better than nails for attaching rails to posts.

Installing a Custom Gate

USE: ▶ drill • hammer • socket wrench • saw ▶ 1x4s • fence boards • gate hardware • nails or screws

You can buy a prefabricated gate, but to add a custom finishing touch, you may prefer to make one using the same materials that went into the fence. To remain square and solid despite heavy use, the gate must be diagonally braced. Exterior screws and a drill/driver simplify the work and make strong connections that won't loosen over time. Due to the extra load on the main gate support post, you may want to sink it deeper than other posts, and provide a concrete collar for more stability.

1 *To build a fence gate,* lay it out on a smooth surface, and screw the frame and cross members to the pickets.

2 *Firmly brace the gate* while you attach the hardware. It's wise to set the swing side slightly high to counteract initial sagging.

3 *Use a cedar or redwood 1x2 strip* as a gate stop. Nail it in place with 8d galvanized nails on the post opposite the hinges.

4 *Attach a gate spring,* if desired, to automatically close the gate—a good feature if you have small children or pets.

5 *Finish* with a matching gate handle. On this gate, the spring closure eliminates the need for a latch.

Building a Basic Board Fence

USE: ▶ paintbrush • measuring tape • circular saw • power drill/driver • shovel • level ▶ 4x4 posts • 2x4 rails • 1x4 or 1x6 boards • galvanized deck screws

1 Before setting the posts, coat the ends with a waterproof deck sealer. Then lay out the post holes with mason's twine.

2 Set the post in the hole, and gradually add soil, tamping every 4 in. Lift with a shovel handle as you check for plumb.

3 Establish a level for the lower rail at least a few inches above the ground, and mark above and below the rail.

4 Between the marks, make several kerf cuts 1½ in. deep with a circular saw. Chisel out the post to accept the rail.

5 At the corners, inset both rails, and screw them in place (after predrilling to avoid splits) with galvanized deck screws.

6 Fasten the end post next to the house. You may need to add spacers or shims against irregular or slanted siding.

7 Where support rails meet, center them in the post notch, and predrill before screwing them in place.

8 Cut a ½-in. spacer to simplify the installation of the pickets. Periodically check for plumb as you work along the rails.

9 To preserve the boards and keep your fence looking new, apply a deck sealer with UV protection.

exterior structures

Fence Maintenance

If you want a fence to last for the long haul, you will have to maintain it. Just how much work is required depends on local weather and your fence design, including the materials used to make it. In any event, it's a good idea to inspect fences and gates annually.

Inspect & Repair

Look for obvious signs of rot on square-cut post tops, any horizontal surfaces where water can collect, and all joints where water can get trapped. Probe with an ice pick to locate soft spots, especially where paint is peeling. Shake the fence at each post to see if it is solid. If not, excavate as needed to determine why—perhaps wood rot or erosion due to poor drainage. Look along the length of the fence—or use a level if you don't trust your eye—to see if any posts have been pushed out of plumb by frost heave.

If a post is not solid or plumb, dig out around it as needed, and replace the soil with a well-tamped mixture of gravel and soil or with

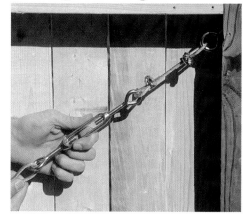

Simplex Portable Outhouse.
4 ft. Square.

55C14

$39⁰⁰

This turn-of-the-century outhouse kit weighed 720 pounds, but still shipped for only $39. It came with prefab wall sections, roofing, vents, and finished seats. And no chemicals in this portable john—you had to dig your own hole.

concrete. If the post is rotten below grade, it's easier to cut off the rotten portion and reinforce it as shown below than it is to replace the post.

Also make sure gates are square and fasteners are tight. To fix an out-of-square gate, install a turnbuckle diagonal brace or remove the gate, square it up, and add a wood brace.

Painting a Fence

Paint or stain a new fence as soon as possible after it has been installed—you should wait only if the lumber is green. Stain will be easier to maintain than paint, which must be scraped before a new application.

Previously painted fences must be scraped to remove all loose paint and scrubbed clean with a brush and a detergent/water solution or with a power washer. Use a 50/50 bleach/water solution to remove any algae or mildew. Feather-sand scraped areas to smooth between unpainted and painted surfaces. Spot-prime these areas before applying paint to the entire fence.

Straightening a Fence

Straighten a leaning post *with a turnbuckle and cables. Mount the assembly to eye screws, and tighten the turnbuckle.*

Gate Hardware

Gate hinges can be concealed (a butt hinge between the edge of the gate and the face of the post), mounted on the private (inside) face, or shown off on the outside face. The most durable finish is hot-dipped galvanized steel. Gates can be made self-closing with a gate spring and either a thumb latch or self-latching hardware mounted on the inside. The L-screw type supports the most weight.

Reinforcing a Post

USE: ▶ spade • garden trowel • screwdriver or awl • power drill/driver • hammer • cold chisel • sledgehammer • handsaw • socket wrench ▶ 2x4 brace

1 ***To check for post rot,*** *dig down to the gravel or concrete collar, and probe the post with a screwdriver or awl.*

2 ***Set a brace*** *on the upper portion of the post to keep it in position while you remove the rotten section below.*

3 ***Use a cold chisel and hammer*** *to break up the concrete, if necessary, or dig out the gravel at the bottom of the post.*

To reinforce a sagging fence or gate frame, attach a metal bracket to the corners where the rails and posts meet.

A galvanized metal brace placed underneath a joint will also keep a fence or gate connection secure and square.

Plywood gussets screwed to the corners reinforce the connections. Use exterior-grade plywood cut in a decorative shape.

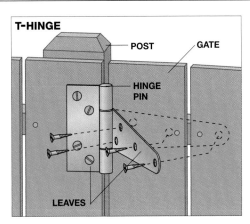

T-HINGE
POST   GATE
HINGE PIN
LEAVES

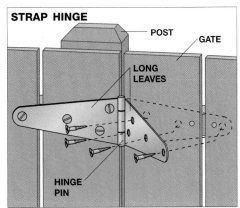

STRAP HINGE
POST   GATE
LONG LEAVES
HINGE PIN

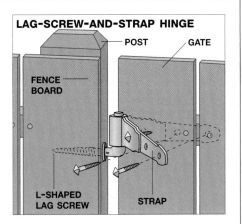

LAG-SCREW-AND-STRAP HINGE
POST   GATE
FENCE BOARD
L-SHAPED LAG SCREW   STRAP

• PT post piece to match • carriage bolt and nut • concrete • wheelbarrow

4 **After disconnecting the rails** and siding, cut off the rotten portion, and clamp a new section of solid post next to it.

5 **Drill through the support** and main post, and tie the two together with galvanized bolts. Bevel the top to deflect rain.

6 **Refill the hole** with concrete or with gravel tamped down in layers. Leave the brace on until the new post base has set.

Planning a Shed

The design and location of your new shed will depend on how it will be used—a shed for storing tools will be much simpler than one you intend to use as a small shop. For example, a large shed for housing wheeled equipment will need a ramp leading up to a double barn-style door or an overhead garage door and perhaps a concrete floor. A shed that doubles as a workshop may have plywood floors, insulated walls, windows for light and ventilation, overhead lights, and a few GFCI electrical outlets.

Although no rule says a shed must match the style of the house, using elements of roof design, siding treatment, or paint color can help unify the property and make the shed an attractive feature of your yard rather than an obvious add-on.

Building Codes & Permits

The building codes you must follow for a shed differ depending on whether it will just be for storage or will have plumbing, heating, wiring, and interior walls. Another set of rules could apply if you want to house livestock. Contact your local building department before you begin. In some localities, you may not need to get a building permit if the shed is under a certain size and is not built on a permanent foundation. There may also be rules about location (setbacks from property lines or existing structures on your property), size, and roof design that will affect your plan. After determining what codes apply, choose a plan that fulfills your overall requirements and can be built within your budget.

Siting & Orientation

Put your shed in a convenient location: a potting shed goes best near the vegetable garden; a bike shed, near the driveway. But also take into account such things as terrain and soil drainage, easy access to utilities, sun exposure, and view. If the shed will be visible from the house, particularly an often-used kitchen sink window, that will be an important factor in siting and orientation. And as much as possible, don't forget to be considerate of your neighbors as well. Discuss your plans with them, and look at the site from their point of view (especially from their kitchen window).

Where to Build

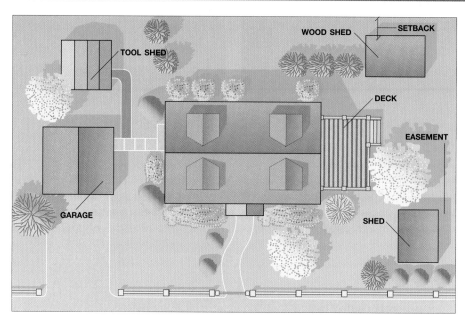

A utility shed should be in a convenient location for easy access to tools and materials inside. Local zoning laws may control how close a shed can be to your property line, and (on a small lot) even how big it can be.

Mechanicals

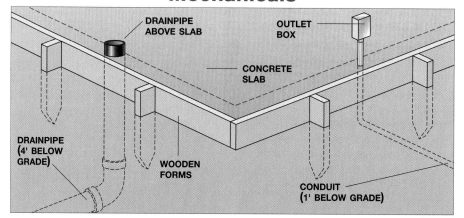

Plumbing, heating, and electricity can make a work shed more practical, but they also raise safety concerns. Avoid temporary measures, such as running an extension cord from the house. Instead, invest the time and money to install permanent utility service (in a permanent shed), even though it may require a subpanel. Although permits and inspections will likely be required, you may need only a 110-V underground cable running from your existing circuit panel to a GFCI-protected outlet in the shed. If your outbuilding rests on a full slab, position lengths of rigid plastic pipe in the masonry as it's poured to create access for wiring and outlets for drains.

Prefabs

If you want a nearly instant outbuilding, you can buy a prefab. Some of these units are delivered and set up by trained installers or subcontractors. Others come in kit form for you to erect on site. Before you buy, compare construction details, options, services, prices, warranties, and the company's reputation. You probably will be responsible for some or all of the site preparation. You may be able to support a small shed on pressure-treated landscape timbers or a bed of gravel. Larger sheds will need piers or a foundation matched to the structure.

This hip roof prefab has an overhang on all four sides. One of the standard end panels is exchanged for double doors.

This garden shed prefab is upgraded with shutters and windowboxes, and a fully glazed front door panel for more light.

Foundations

The foundation provides a stable base for the shed. The type you need depends on the size and weight of the structure, and to some extent the type of ground it rests on. A small shed of less than 100 square feet generally can sit on pressure-treated 4x4 skids or concrete blocks that have been cut into the sod and set level. If there is minimal or no frost heave in your area, you can also pour concrete into parallel trenches 8–10 inches wide and 12 inches deep. Skids may be considered nonpermanent foundations and eliminate the need for a permit. Be sure to check before building.

A larger shed will generally require a traditional foundation—pier-and-girder, concrete or block wall, or concrete slab—with footings that extend below the local frost line.

One of the most economical and easiest ways to support a heavy shed is with a combination of concrete piers and posts. Even on a sloping site you can pour piers into preformed tubes that extend a few inches above ground, and insert a post anchor in each one before the mix hardens. Then you can mount posts and cut them all off at the same level to support the shed floor frame.

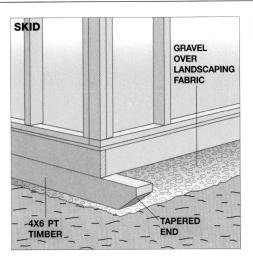

SKID

GRAVEL OVER LANDSCAPING FABRIC

4X6 PT TIMBER

TAPERED END

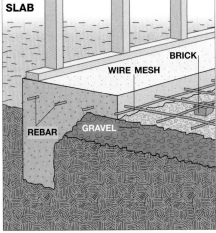

SLAB

BRICK

WIRE MESH

REBAR

GRAVEL

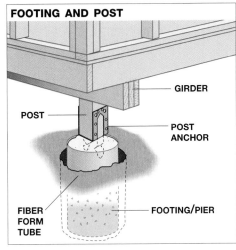

FOOTING AND POST

GIRDER

POST

POST ANCHOR

FIBER FORM TUBE

FOOTING/PIER

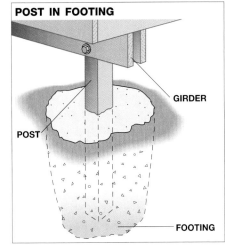

POST IN FOOTING

GIRDER

POST

FOOTING

exterior structures

Plans & Kits

Building a shed from a plan with stock materials is well within the range of most do-it-yourselfers. A good set of plans will provide detailed materials and cutting lists, clear diagrams, and step-by-step instructions that people with basic carpentry skills should be able to handle. Typically, when starting with a level site, building a small shed from scratch will take at least two or three weekends.

The Kit Advantage

Easy-to-build kits for the do-it-yourselfer are available in wood, vinyl, or metal. Prices often are comparable to the retail cost of the materials alone. Most retailers also offer professional installation or can refer you to a local contractor. As with prebuilts, the assembled kit can range from a barely acceptable and not the least bit attractive utility shed to a fine-looking, durable building that rivals house construction.

The pieces are all precut; some elements, such as roof trusses or wall sections, may be preassembled. Depending on the shed size, design, and the degree to which the kit comes preassembled, you and a helper may be able to erect the shed in as little as a few hours with only a hammer, drill/driver or screwdriver, measuring tape, and level. A weekend of work is probably more typical. Kits may or may not come with materials for a floor, but you must always provide the foundation.

Trim Details

Corner trim *may seem like an elaborate extra, but corner boards make it possible to install full-wall siding with no joints.*

Building a Shed

If you're a first-time builder with only basic tools and skills, work from a reliable plan with detailed instructions. Take the lead from professional kit builders, and precut your lumber, or at least all the pieces as needed for each stage (such as for floor, wall, and roof systems). If you want more details about this project, check these sections: "Framing," pp. 106–19 and 124–25; "Roofing," pp. 408-25; "Siding," pp. 436–45; and "Windows & Doors," pp. 470–73. For storage options in the finished shed, see "Shelving & Storage," pp. 250–53 and 261.

USE: ▶ drill/driver • hammer • measuring tape • framing square • 4-ft. level ▶ 2x4s and 2x6s for frame

1 ***Use 2x6s*** *to build a frame of floor joists set 16 in. on center, and attach ¾- or ⅝- in. plywood or OSB subflooring.*

2 ***Frame up the walls*** *with 2x4 studs set 16 in. on center. Check each wall for square, and nail on plywood sheathing.*

6 ***Set and brace the end roof trusses*** *first. Then you can string guidelines, and tip up and nail the trusses between them.*

7 ***One option*** *is to finish the gable ends of the roof structure with an extra layer of framing covered by a rake board.*

8 ***These trusses*** *have an overhang that protects the siding. You can add a fascia and soffit, and rake board to the eaves.*

To keep out the weather, *run a liberal bead of flexible exterior caulk, such as silicone, between the trim and siding.*

Door Details

Use stock double doors, *or build one large door on site out of plywood or boards joined on a braced back frame.*

Because an oversize *door is heavy and may get rough use, hang it with at least three hinges bolted to the shed frame.*

• plywood or other sheathing • siding • roofing material • window (optional) • 1x8 boards for door • nails/screws • door hardware & other hardware

3 Raise the first wall *into position, adjusting it until it is plumb. Use a 2x4 brace to keep the first wall in position.*

4 Cut out the sheathing *over a framed opening, and install a small window for natural light. Siding will run up to the trim.*

5 You can make your own roof trusses *by joining timbers with plywood gussets or truss plates, or use solid rafters.*

9 Leave the sheathing unfinished *on the inside but protected by siding that matches the house siding on the outside.*

10 Apply tar paper *to the roof and either roll roofing or strip shingles. With two coats of paint on the trim, the shed is ready for use.*

exterior structures

Gazebos Then & Now

By definition, a gazebo is meant to be a "gazing room," an isolated structure intended to offer a panoramic view of the surrounding landscape or garden area. Once a focal point of any proper Victorian or Edwardian English garden, the gazebo's popularity waned as lifestyles changed. Decks became the principal place for outdoor living. Today, gazebos are being added to homes with decks, thanks to advantages they offer that most decks don't—shade, isolation, charming appearance, and more.

Location is primarily a matter of aesthetics and function—are you looking for poolside shade, garden solitude, or a place for outdoor dining? Depending on that, you may also want to add a water-shedding roof, insect screens, and the like.

Building a Gazebo

Gazebos are among the most complex outdoor structures to build. Watch one being built from a plan and you'll see a lot of head scratching—even by experienced house carpenters—and multiple trips back to the saw to recut compound angles. Most gazebo designs are many-sided and highly decorative, with fancy railings, exposed framing, and ornamental friezes and corner brackets. This complexity, coupled with the fact that a gazebo is usually a focal point, makes it an ideal candidate for a kit approach. The kit's precut parts eliminate much of the guesswork.

Styles

A gazebo can be a simple structure with a deck, four posts, and a slatted, lattice-like roof. But most models are more complicated—and more difficult to build—whether you work from plans and cut each piece from scratch, or buy a precut kit. As a rule, the more sides on a gazebo, the more difficult it will be to build. If you cut your own pieces, use a jig or template to create uniform parts. If you buy a kit, lay out the pieces like an exploded-view drawing to make sense out of the assembly.

You can build up curved rafters *in lapped sections, or cut them from sheets of exterior-grade plywood.*

This custom-built redwood gazebo *joins to the deck with steps and railings, and hugs the site with lattice skirting.*

This prefab kit *is fully glazed to keep out the weather. Some firms also can provide removable screen panels.*

Roof Options

Roofing on multisided gazebos is often the most complicated part of the structure. For novice do-it-yourselfers, it may be the first encounter with a difficult rafter joint called a compound miter—a single cut that accounts for both the downward slope and sideways slant of a rafter. Curved rafters that create mushroom-shaped roofs should be cut from a template that is carefully tested for fit. Some gazebo kits include fully finished roofs shipped in overlapping, bolt-together sections. Some kits include precut rafters, but leave the sheathing and roofing for you to buy and install on site. (It makes sense not to ship materials available locally.)

Each roof panel on this kit *covers one plane of the complex roof shape. The panels have skip-sheathing and shingles attached.*

Frames around the roof panels *bolt together. Roofing (including flashing) extends from one panel onto another.*

Assembling a Kit

1 *On most gazebo kits,* you have to lay out the site, dig holes, and pour concrete footings before assembling the floor structure.

2 *On many kits,* anchors and bolts take the place of nails. Some timbers come predrilled for electrical lines.

3 *These posts are anchored* to metal brackets with bolts. Wall panels are fixed to the posts with rods and cap nuts.

4 *Prerouted panel caps* are installed between posts to create openings in the wall frame and tie the structure together.

5 *Some gazebo kits* use preassembled sections of small boards and decorative moldings, called fretwork, between posts.

6 *This gazebo kit* has a two-tiered roof, with fretwork and precut post tops separating the two roof decks.

7 *Assembling a prefab kit* is like putting together a jigsaw puzzle. Here, a shingled section of the upper roof is installed.

8 *One upper roof panel* is left off to make it easier to set the cupola. The preassembled section is attached to hardware on the roof.

9 *Most kits* have many optional features, such as wraparound benches, steps and railings, and varieties of finish trim.

Arbor Entryways

Ancient Egyptian wall paintings depict vine-covered structures that resemble the arbors of today. But it was the Romans who developed the arbor to its fullest. The structures, then as now, provide shade but are more familiar in today's homes when used as the entryway to a garden. They differ from their lighter cousin, the trellis, in that they are designed to support the heaviest of vines.

Building an Arbor

Start by using a wood that is naturally rot-resistant, such as cedar or redwood, pressure-treated lumber, or a combination of the two. (See "Wood," pp. 90–91.) Of the three, redwood is probably the best choice for a painted arbor. Pressure-treated lumber does not accept paint well, but it can be stained, and should be—not only for appearance but to protect the wood from warping, cracking, and other problems caused by exposure to weather.

Posts set directly into the ground provide vertical support; cross beams and joists form the open framework of the roof. Grid facing or sturdy lattice can be fastened to the posts to give climbing vines additional support or to create a more enclosed space.

Planting for Arbors

Grapes, climbing roses, clematis, honeysuckle, wisteria, and Carolina jasmine, all available from nurseries, make good plantings for covering arbors. Sweet peas, morning glory, and hyacinth bean are popular varieties planted from seed. Once they're started, climbing vines will scramble up posts, but they will climb better if they have more to hang on to—lattice, vertical slats, even nylon cord stretched between a few eyebolts. Some plants, such as climbing roses, need to be tied to posts. After the first year, most vines should be pruned annually in the spring to remove any dead, damaged, or straggly growth. Annual vines give you an opportunity to repaint or restain, but perennials must be cut back before painting. If the vines grow too long, you can cut them back, and they will branch out below the cut.

Basic Designs

Arbors can range in width from a narrow arched passageway to a huge pavilion that covers a whole patio. They can be freestanding or provide an entranceway to a fenced area. The top of an arbor can be curved, gambrel, peaked, or flat; flattop designs generally work best for large-scale arbors, such as those with bench seats. But not all arbors are designed to be walked through. An arbor with a closed back, such as one backed up against a fence, can be used as a decorative niche in a garden or backyard.

Many of the most popular arbor designs are available in prefabricated kits. However, unlike trellises, which are often supported by other structures, an arbor must be tied directly into the ground. The easy way to accomplish this is by setting pressure-treated posts below the frost line and bracing them in plumb position as you backfill and tamp the dirt. Always leave the braces in place as you gradually add lattice and other framing members that tie the structure together. The other option is to pour concrete piers for the main posts, and tie the post lumber to the piers with galvanized post-support hardware.

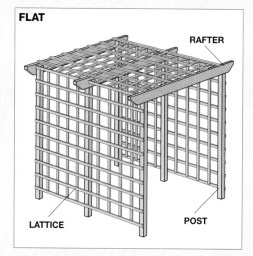

FLAT

RAFTER

LATTICE

POST

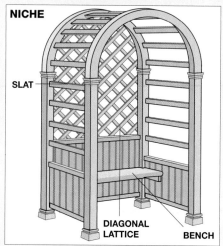

NICHE

SLAT

DIAGONAL LATTICE

BENCH

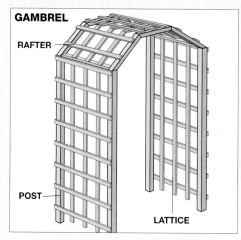

GAMBREL

RAFTER

POST

LATTICE

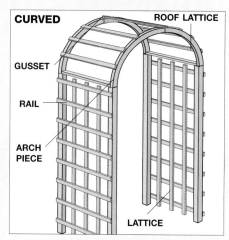

CURVED

ROOF LATTICE

GUSSET

RAIL

ARCH PIECE

LATTICE

Cutting Curves

USE: ▶ string compass • saber saw bit ▶ plywood

1 Lay out arched frames on a piece of plywood. Use a strip of wood tacked to the centerpoint to trace the curve of your arch.

2 Cut out along your layout line with a saber saw. For strength and stability, make arches out of double-thick exterior plywood.

3 To assemble the arch, spread a liberal bead of construction adhesive on one panel, and screw the second panel in place.

Fastening Lattice

USE: ▶ paintbrush • circular saw • measuring tape • hammer • eye protection ▶ lattice • primer and exterior-grade paint

1 Before you install lattice, take the time to prime and finish-coat support posts that the sheets will be fastened against.

2 Use a circular saw to cut stock-size sheets of lattice to fit between posts. Set the blade just slightly deeper than the lattice.

3 Where cut sheets join over support posts, you can conceal the cut ends, and secure the sheets with cover trim.

Trim Details

USE: ▶ power miter saw or miter box & backsaw • hammer • putty knife • paintbrush ▶ trim & finials • glue • finishing nails • wood putty • primer & paint • sandpaper

1 Trim posts with a combination of stock parts, such as this finial and molding. This also protects the post's end grain.

2 Cut miters at a 45° angle at the ends of the molding, and secure them to the post with glue and finishing nails.

3 Before priming and painting, wipe off excess glue, fill the nail holes with putty, and sand the molding smooth.

Trellis Basics

Trellises are simple structures that resemble arbors but are typically made with lighter materials; and if they support climbing plants at all, the vines themselves are usually lighter, too. Some trellises are vertical, like a free-standing framed lattice set between posts or a custom trellis attached to a chimney or house wall. Horizontal trellises may sit atop posts and have one or more sidewalls; or they may have one edge attached to a house wall and the other supported by posts or angled corner brackets.

If you place your trellis next to a deck or other structure, keep the trellis simple. If, on the other hand, you want to create a focal point, consider a more complex design such as a fan trellis mounted to a wall. If possible, construct lattice sections that mimic other details in your yard or house, such as a fencing pattern.

Building a Trellis

A well-designed horizontal trellis will filter most of the midday sun without blocking all light and will allow plenty of air circulation. To create a shading grid, rafters are normally spaced either 16- or 24- inches on center and are topped by one or more layers of progressively smaller cross members, such as 2x2s or 2x4s set on edge at right angles to the rafters.

When you settle on a pattern, consider interlocking heavier members by cutting a shallow notch in the bottom of each piece wherever it crosses a rafter or other support member. Don't notch the tops of the support pieces; this may cause rot problems. Exposed framing also looks better when made in this manner. The interlocked joints are stronger and help prevent the boards from twisting, too.

Clamp a number of boards together at a time to cut the notches in an assembly line fashion. If your design includes decorative cuts on the ends of rafters or cross members, make a template from ¼-inch hardboard or plywood. Clamp it over each board, and scribe the outline to guide your saber saw cuts.

If you are building a trellis attached to a wall, use hinges or other fasteners so it can be easily removed when the wall needs painting.

Basic Designs

You can create almost any type of screening structure using the basic combination of 4x4 posts, a variety of rafters, and an even greater variety of slatted roof screens. You can assemble the structure from pressure-treated lumber (including pressure-treated lattice in 2x8 and 4x8 panels), or use redwood, cedar, or fir with several coats of exterior-grade sealer, stain, or paint.

Because trellises do not have to shed water, you don't have to build sloping rafters. It's often easier to use horizontal layers, for example, on the trellis (bottom right) that is designed to extend from a wall of your house. Like a deck, it has posts and a girder to support the main rafters. (They attach to a ledger board on the house.) In this design, the ends of the rafters are shaped into a step-down. On the extension, you can use 2x2s for screening. On the main section, you can use 2x4s on edge. Notch the rafters so the screening timbers set in them instead of on them. You can also add a layer of top screening.

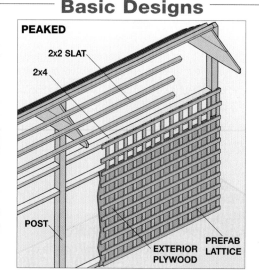

PEAKED

2x2 SLAT
2x4
POST
EXTERIOR PLYWOOD
PREFAB LATTICE

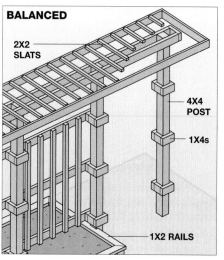

BALANCED

2X2 SLATS
4X4 POST
1X4s
1X2 RAILS

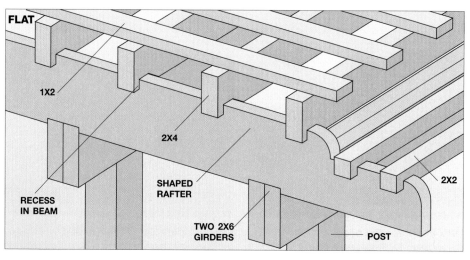

FLAT

1X2
2X4
RECESS IN BEAM
SHAPED RAFTER
TWO 2X6 GIRDERS
POST
2X2

Shading

The ultimate trellis would be a Venetian blind; you could adjust the slats to block more midday sun and open them on dark days to let in more light. Because a wood trellis is fixed, you have to decide on the degree of shading ahead of time. The best way to plan the project is to build the basic frame, temporarily tack several boards in position, and observe the results. Generally, use wider boards, steeper angles, and smaller spacing to block more light.

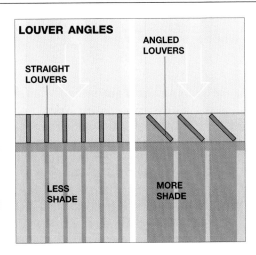

LOUVER ANGLES
STRAIGHT LOUVERS
ANGLED LOUVERS
LESS SHADE
MORE SHADE

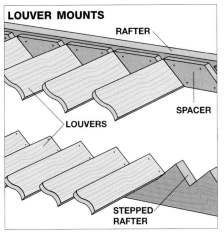

LOUVER MOUNTS
RAFTER
SPACER
LOUVERS
STEPPED RAFTER

Building a Fan Trellis

USE: ▶ clamps • power sander • power drill/driver • hammer ▶ PT 1x1s or 1x2s • carriage bolts, nuts & washers • nails • glue • stain or paint

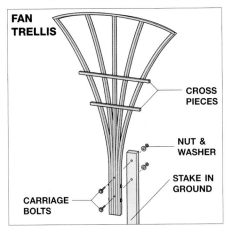

FAN TRELLIS
CROSS PIECES
NUT & WASHER
STAKE IN GROUND
CARRIAGE BOLTS

1 *Clamp or tack together* all the lattice strips for sanding. Use stock pressure-treated strips, or cut your own from boards.

2 *Clamp the sanded strips* at the base, and predrill two holes where you can bolt the pieces together.

3 *Use carriage bolts* with washers and nuts to tighten the base of the fan trellis. Then you can spread the strips.

4 *Lay out the fan pattern* on a work surface, clamp or tack each strip in position, and add the cross braces.

5 *Use a long strip* across the top of the fan, gluing and tacking each strip. Finish the fan with exterior stain or paint.

28 yards

yards

Maintaining Tools

Tools will last longer and do their job better if you maintain them properly after use and when you put them away for the season. At the end of the day, tools should always be put away clean and dry. Wipe off dirt and moisture with a rag; dip small tools in and out of a bucket of sharp builder's sand to get the dirt off them. Don't scrape metal tools with other metal tools, because it will scratch their finish and encourage rust. You can buy or make a tool called a wood man (a wooden spatula made for this purpose) to scrape off dried mud. Saws and bladed tools should be stored so that their sharpened edges won't rub against other metal tools or abrasive surfaces. Sharpen them often. Most saw blades can be touched up with a mill or bastard file. Most cutting tools, such as chisels, can be touched up on a small grinding stone.

End-of-Season Maintenance

Before you put your tools away in the fall or winter, remove any rust using a wire brush. Wooden handles that are cracked can be glued or taped for a temporary fix, but they will need to be replaced in a season or two. Clean and coat wooden handles with boiled linseed oil; give very old handles several coats of varnish, sanding them between coats, to rejuvenate them. Clean all metal parts thoroughly, polish them with steel wool, and apply a protective coating such as mineral oil to prevent rusting. Any moving parts should be coated thoroughly with lubricating oil. Drain gasoline from fuel tanks of powered tools.

Special Tools

BOW SAW

BULB PLANTER

LOPPER

PRUNING SAWS

TROWEL

CULTIVATOR

GRASS SHEARS

TILLER

STRING TRIMMER

It takes more than a lawn mower, a rake, and a shovel to care for your yard. Among the other tools you might need are a hedge trimmer, a spreader, spray equipment, and others shown above.

Mower Maintenance

USE: ▶ adjustable wrench • blade sharpener • screwdrivers • socket wrenches • wire brush • funnel • siphon • cleaning rags • gas can • safety goggles

1 *Replace the mower's air filter* per manufacturer's recommendations—it is held in place with a spring clamp or screws.

2 *At least once a year,* remove the blade for sharpening, and replace the engine oil to get the most out of the engine's life.

3 *The blade housing* should be scraped clean after each use. Also scrape off dried grass on the clipping bags and chutes.

Mower Blades

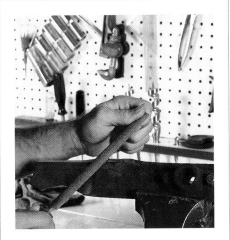

To sharpen rotary mower blades with a file, first disconnect the engine's spark plug before removing the blade. While sharpening, preserve the original angle of the sharpened edge as you stroke the file across it. File in one direction only—away from you. After you've sharpened each blade end, check the blade balance by slipping the center hole over a nail protruding from the wall. If the blade dips to one side or another, file away some more metal from that end.

Chain Saws

A sharp chain saw blade cuts through logs effortlessly, like a knife through soft butter, while a dull one can keep you bent over a log for what seems like an eternity just to make one cut. Dirt and grit can dull a chain in a matter of seconds—sometimes the stuff sticks to the bark of a fallen tree, but more often than not accidental contact with the ground is what takes the edge off. When a tree limb is down flat on the ground, it can be hard to avoid, though. That's one reason why most cutters keep a spare sharpened chain handy. A log lifter is a safe and easy way to pick up a tree trunk a few inches off the ground—just enough to keep the chain saw blade from hitting dirt.

For trimming high branches, a power pruner is much easier than a pole saw.

Hearing protection, such as this unit with helmet and visor, should always be used when chain sawing.

Chain saws with bars over 36 in. long are expensive, and heavy—most people can get by with a 16- to 20-in. bar.

• aluminum can ▶ air filter • engine oil (check whether 2-cycle is required) • lubricating oil • spark plugs

4 *Change the spark plugs* regularly—you'll need a socket wrench and a deep-well socket to loosen the plug.

5 *Controls* should be cleaned out and coated with a lubricating oil at the beginning of each season.

6 *Check the oil* after each use, and top it off whenever necessary. It will keep the engine running smoothly and extend its life.

yards

Landscape Planning

Landscaping is a natural extension of every home, whether you have acres of sculptured gardens or only room for a few potted plants by the front door. The arrangement of trees, shrubs, grasses, and flowers that you choose can provide a wide range of benefits aside from natural beauty alone. Good landscaping will define and protect private areas of the yard, establish an entryway, and enhance the architectural lines of your house. The right plantings can cut noise transmission from a nearby street, provide shade on hot summer days, and let the sun through when you need it in the winter. And landscaping is one of the best ways for do-it-yourselfers to improve property value. The key is to develop a plan for the entire property, even if you can complete only one small piece of it at a time.

Mapping Your Site

Begin with a site plan of your property. Your original survey or deed map is a good place to start. Enlarge it if necessary, and reproduce it on a large sheet of paper, preferably one with graph lines on it. The map should show overall dimensions, its orientation to north, the location of the house and other existing structures, the setback distances from the street and property lines, and the entrances and parking areas.

To the base map, add the features that aren't shown on the deed map or survey. Include the size and locations of trees and shrubs as well as lawn areas, gardens, flower beds, and borders. Show other factors that affect the yard as well. These include the direction of prevailing winds and existing sun and shade patterns for morning, noon, and afternoon. Note the drainage patterns and any other factors that affect the yard, such as noise or privacy problems, and any views that you want to retain or obscure. If the base map gets too cluttered, you may want to show these features on a separate overlay of tracing paper that can be attached to the map with tape.

Terracing

A good solution for lawns with steep slopes is "cut and fill"—to cut away sections of the slope and use the dirt to fill adjacent areas, creating a terrace. There are many ways to retain dirt at the edge of a terrace. On a small step you might use a pressure-treated 2x12 secured with 2x4 stakes. On a larger step you could build a retaining wall using stones from the excavation, or interlocking masonry blocks, or a more rustic wall of railroad ties. On steep slopes, it's difficult to calculate the forces pushing against the wall. But almost any slope can be tamed with the combination of a strong wall, such as reinforced concrete, and a system for releasing hydrostatic pressure, such as weep holes.

A comprehensive landscape plan can include several outdoor spaces, from fenced yards to open gazebos (with or without walls), and use natural features of the site to create distinct areas and levels that make an ordinary yard more usable and attractive.

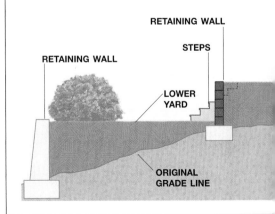

RETAINING WALL

STEPS

RETAINING WALL

LOWER YARD

ORIGINAL GRADE LINE

Your Design

Start your design by considering what you want from your yard, and establish a set of priorities. If you entertain often, allow for extra parking as well as an area for outdoor cooking. If you have children, consider a play yard or pool. If you are an avid gardener, the location of the sun will become important in selecting an area for a garden. Attach an overlay of tracing paper to the map, and then draw in the exact location of new fences, terraces, gardens, tool sheds, play yards, trees and shrubs, and any other proposed landscape features. Note the heights and construction materials on the overlay. If the lot will require extensive regrad-

ing or excavating, your local building department may want to see spot elevations of the lot on the final plans. This is best left to a surveyor or landscape architect.

Once you have the final plan, place the overlay sheets beneath the base map, and trace in the new features. This will be your final drawing, used to coordinate your efforts or to submit to the building department if a permit is necessary. You don't need anyone's permission to undertake most landscaping projects, but there are some exceptions. For example, there are codes called setback restrictions that control how close you can build to your property lines—even though you own the property.

Prepare the Yard

Now take your drawing out to the yard. See how your plan fits into the landscape and what will need to be changed. Depending on how drastically different your current landscape is compared with what you want it to be, there will be prep work to do. Rocks may have to be removed, above and below the soil, before you can dig holes for plantings. Tree limbs may have to be cut to allow more sunlight in for the garden. Weeds, of course, will have to be pulled. It's a good idea to start this preparation work four to six weeks before ideal planting time. Allow extra time for bad weather—and some time to rest.

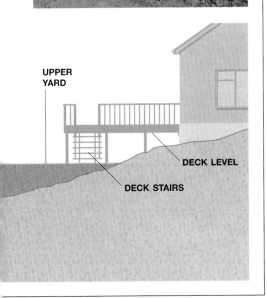

UPPER YARD

DECK LEVEL

DECK STAIRS

Sketching Your Design

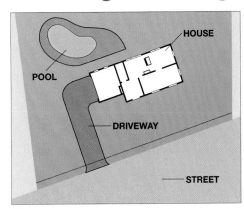

HOUSE

POOL

DRIVEWAY

STREET

1 **Before planning your landscape,** make a map showing your house and other permanent structures around it.

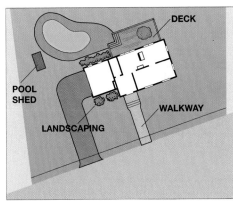

DECK

POOL SHED

LANDSCAPING

WALKWAY

2 **Add other features** such as decks, outbuildings, and your existing landscaping plants and walkways.

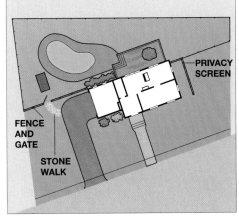

PRIVACY SCREEN

FENCE AND GATE

STONE WALK

3 **Also important to your design** are the wind directions, the sun's orientation, and other environmental factors such as a slope.

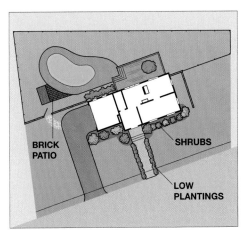

BRICK PATIO

SHRUBS

LOW PLANTINGS

4 **With this information** on your plan, you can begin to experiment with different landscaping ideas.

yards

Trees & Shrubs

Before planning your landscape, learn about the plants that grow best in your area by visiting a large nursery or consulting a landscape architect. Walk through an arboretum or public garden to get design ideas. Keep in mind the mature size of each plant and the scale of different plants to one another for a balanced design. Ideally, the finished landscape should be neither too crowded nor too sparse, should provide a diversity of colors and textures, and should require a minimum of maintenance.

Plant Hardiness

Plants thrive in an environment that approximates that of their natural range. Check the map on page 576 to determine your USDA Hardiness Zone, and pick plants that have a range that covers your zone. The numbers are not absolute: if you live in Zone 7, you can try a plant with a hardiness rating of Zone 3–6 if you shade it from summer sun, or a plant with a rating of 8–10 if you give it extra protection from winter cold and wind. Also, pay attention to microclimates: Cold air tends to collect at the bottom of hills, while southern slopes will be considerably warmer than northern ones.

Disease Resistance

The right trees, shrubs, and perennials are those that grow vigorously in your environment and require almost no help in fighting pests and diseases. Many such plants are new hybrids of old favorites that breeders have developed: Look for improved dogwoods, pest-resistant crab apples, mildew-free crape myrtles, even disease-resistant elms. Other good plants are the rugged native trees and shrubs that are becoming more widely available. It's a good idea to consult local nurseries for advice and to see examples of species that do well in your growing area.

Color & Habit

Not every plant is green, and many green ones aren't green all year. Take into consideration the color of a plant's foliage (in spring and autumn), whether it is evergreen or deciduous, and if and when it will flower. Try picturing your design in all four seasons, and add color or other interest to the design when it will be needed. Another important asset of a plant is its form or structure, referred to as its habit. Some common habits of trees and shrubs are pictured at the right on page 567.

Digging

Not all soils are easy to dig. If you're unable to make headway with a shovel, try breaking the ground with a pick before you dig. A pick also helps with rocky soil. A 6-foot wrecking bar is a handy tool for prying huge rocks out of the ground. Unless you can borrow a tractor with an auger bit, or rent a power auger, dig deep, narrow holes for piers and fence posts with a posthole digger.

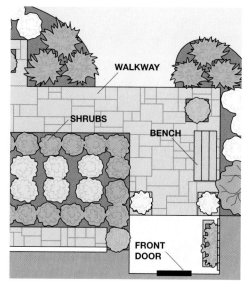

Plantings will enhance the entryway to your home. Here, shrubs and other plants border the walkway to the front door.

Planting Bushes

USE: ► garden fork • round-pointed shovel • garden hose • watering can • wheelbarrow • wooden stakes (optional) • soft-cloth or rubber-strip ties (optional)

1 *Cut away the sod* where you will be planting the bush. Clear an area about 1½ times wider than the root ball.

2 *Dig a hole* as deep as the root system of the bush, and loosen the dirt around and inside the hole with a garden fork.

3 *Water the roots* of the plant before transplanting, to minimize shock. Also water the empty hole and the ground around it.

Shapes & Profiles of Trees & Shrubs

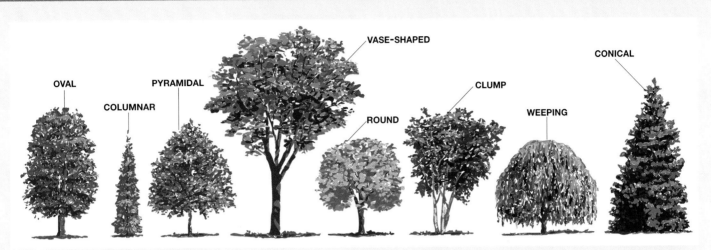

Trees come in a variety of shapes and sizes, which is called their "habit." Remember that a deciduous tree changes shape over the seasons. A tree that has leafed out in summer to shade the house and save on air-conditioning bills will drop its leaves and allow sunlight to illuminate and warm the house in winter—without your having to turn up the heat too much.

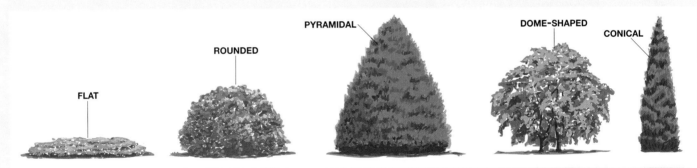

Shrubs have just as wide a variety in their habit as trees. Different shapes can define borders, screen out unpleasant views, or frame desirable vistas. Thorny hedges such as barberry, rugosa rose, or cotoneaster discourage unwanted animals—maybe a burglar, too. Also, consider the color of the foliage as well as the flowers and the time of year they bloom.

work gloves ▶ bush to be planted • fertilizer or compost (optional) • mulch

4 *Place the bush* in the hole, and shovel in fill, firming the dirt to avoid air pockets. Stake the bush if it needs support.

5 *Soak the dirt thoroughly* immediately after planting; come back and resoak periodically after the water has perked down.

6 *Mulch the bare earth* with bark, leaf mulch, or wood chips, in order to keep the soil as moist as possible.

yards

Drainage Paths

Spring thaws pose no problems if your home is built on an elevated site where water runs away from the foundation. But in many yards, groundwater flows toward the house instead of away from it—straight for that big hole in the ground you call a basement. If you have drainage problems, the best bet is to start with easy, inexpensive improvements, and opt for more elaborate solutions only if the problem persists. Often, the easiest approach is to stop water before it reaches the house—say, with an area drain that captures water and releases it well away from the house. But it also pays to make foundations more water resistant.

Increasing Drainage Capacity

Many basement leaks stem from ground water pushing against the foundation walls. At first, water is absorbed as if the ground were a dry sponge. But as spaces between specks of dirt fill with water during heavy rains, the drainage capacity of your yard can be overwhelmed. Water can puddle and overflow into basement light wells, and increasing hydrostatic pressure can force water through small cracks in the foundation.

One way to reduce puddling and relieve some of the hydrostatic pressure is to increase the water-holding capacity of the yard with a dry well. It's not a hole you dig to draw water from, but a porous, rock-filled hole you dump water into—for example, with a pipe connected to a downspout. If the yard puddles easily because water has to settle through layers of compacted dirt, a porous dry well can collect the puddles. The bigger the hole, the more water it can hold, of course. But size often is limited by the kind of soil you're digging into and what you're digging with. A backhoe can make quick work of a 6-foot-deep hole with a 4-foot diameter. You might want to settle for less capacity if you're digging by hand, one shovelful at a time.

If the well has no surrounding structure, it will work but not for long. As water streams in, it will wash in dirt, too. The sides of the hole will begin to collapse, and dirt will settle between the rocks and gradually clog the system. It happens to most dry wells, eventually. To make a dry well last longer, you can construct it with walls using concrete blocks (without mortared joints), or substitute a 55-gallon drum that's perforated to encourage drainage. Rocks that fill the well can be topped with fine gravel for appearance. Or you can conceal the well with a layer of gravel covered by a double layer of filter fabric under topsoil and grass, then sod.

Foundation Waterproofing

The traditional treatment is hot-mopped asphalt applied during construction. But if it cracks and leaks, it can't be repaired unless the foundation is reexcavated. Beware of quick-fix systems that pump a clay-type mixture into the soil to save the excavating; they don't work.

Modern systems may take many forms and use several layers to create a hydrostatic barrier. Some have a rubberized sheet on the outside of the foundation, and then a layer of open mesh an inch or so thick covered by water-filtering fabric. The fabric stops dirt so the mesh won't clog, but lets water seep through to drop down the porous mesh to foundation drains. It may never test the rubberized barrier.

If water is seeping inside through cracks in a wall, close them with hydraulic cement, which swells as it hardens to make a tight seal, even when a crack is wet from an active leak.

> ### DIGGING DETOURS
>
> ▶ Excavation contractors should plot the exact location of underground utilities such as natural-gas pipes and sewer lines, but it pays to check on them yourself with the local utility company before anyone starts digging.

Building Area Drains

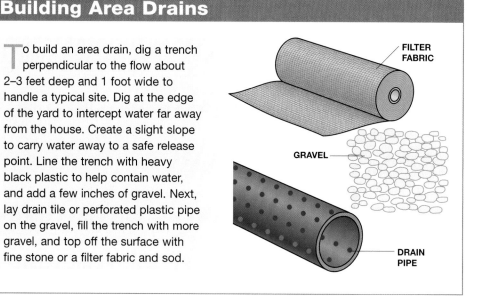

To build an area drain, dig a trench perpendicular to the flow about 2–3 feet deep and 1 foot wide to handle a typical site. Dig at the edge of the yard to intercept water far away from the house. Create a slight slope to carry water away to a safe release point. Line the trench with heavy black plastic to help contain water, and add a few inches of gravel. Next, lay drain tile or perforated plastic pipe on the gravel, fill the trench with more gravel, and top off the surface with fine stone or a filter fabric and sod.

FILTER PAPER

GRAVEL

PIPE

GROUND

FILTER FABRIC

GRAVEL

DRAIN PIPE

6 Ways to Keep Basements Dry

1. **Surface regrading.** To improve drainage around the house, fill in gullies that send water toward the house and any depressions along the foundation. Add compacted dirt to create a slope away from the building. Even a few inches of slope in the first 2 feet will help.

2. **Water diverters.** Keep roof water from the foundation by extending downspouts. An elbow fitting starts the flow away from the building. A splash block takes water a few feet farther and prevents water-trapping erosion along the foundation.

3. **Dry wells.** Add more water-holding capacity with a dry well. (See below.) The porous well can reduce surface puddling in heavy rains and provide a drainage outlet for downspouts. If you don't want to see rocks, cover them with a double layer of filter fabric and sod. The fabric lets in water but screens out dirt that can clog the system.

4. **Area drains.** To intercept water before it gets to the house, dig an area drain. (See at left, bottom.) The best place for an area drain is the edge of the yard or the high side of the house, where it can collect water before it reaches the foundation. Ground water drops down through the porous gravel, collects in the pipe, and flows to the new release point. You can lay filter fabric and sod over the gravel.

5. **Last-minute trenches.** When heavy rain saturates the ground, puddles in the yard, and heads for the house, divert at least some of the surface flood by digging a shallow trench. As a last resort, cut out sections of sod and deposit them like a seawall on the house side of the temporary drainage ditch.

6. **Last-minute coverups.** Temporarily cover window wells and doors so that water won't flow into the basement. Roll plastic sheeting or a tarp around a strip of wood, tack it onto the house above the opening, and weight the other ends to create the slope of a water-shedding roof.

Dripping roofs and leaking gutters can create a gully at the foundation that traps water and fosters leaks.

Turning a gully into a hill that slopes away from the building helps to take the strain off leak-prone foundations.

Building Dry Wells

DRUM DRY WELL

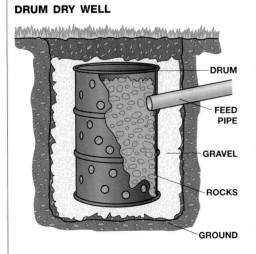

DRUM
FEED PIPE
GRAVEL
ROCKS
GROUND

Many older houses have excellent drainage features such as downspouts that empty into clay pipes near the foundation and drains in basement light wells—except they don't work because the pipes empty into clogged dry wells. You may be able to restart dead drains by building a new well and running new feed pipes to the old drain outlets. Check your trench slope between house and well with a level on top of a long, straight 2x4. The feed pipe should enter near the top of the well.

BLOCK DRY WELL

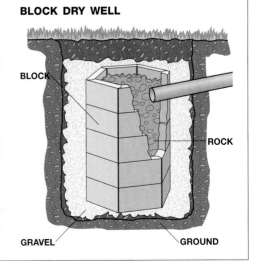

BLOCK
ROCK
GRAVEL
GROUND

yards

Pond Essentials

At one time, building a garden pond required yards of concrete, an expert mason, and a lot of money. Today, synthetic liners and fiberglass shells have made ponds easier to build and much more affordable. Whether it's a quiet reflecting pool tucked in a far corner of the yard or an elaborate water-scape complete with fountain, fish, and water lilies, a well-designed pond will provide hours of pleasure and increase your property value.

You may already have a perfect location in mind, but ponds built into level ground are easiest to set up and maintain. If possible, do not place them under trees. The shade keeps sun-loving water plants from thriving, and their leaves clog drains and filters.

You can build a pond that will fit with the style of your house—for example, a formal pond that conforms to the geometric shapes of nearby planting beds and hedges. You can make the pond more informal by blending it in with the natural surroundings; for instance, by making a border of randomly

Bred in China as early as the tenth century, goldfish were first imported to the U. S. in the late 1800s. Many varieties of goldfish are suitable for ponds, and thrive where water is deep enough to prevent large temperature swings and full-depth freezing.

placed rock. Color also can help. If you use a flexible pond liner, available in both blue or black, choose black to make the pond look real. A blue liner will make the pond look more like a swimming pool.

Lighting will allow you to enjoy the pond day or night. In addition to floodlights, consider submerged lighting, as long as you have clear water and the lights are positioned to avoid glare.

Installation

Basic installation steps are similar for ponds formed around a shell or a flexible liner, but check the manufacturer's instructions for your unit. Start by outlining the shape of the pond on the ground. For irregular shapes, use a long garden hose or rope as a guide.

To determine the right size liner, measure the width and length of the pond. Then add twice the pond depth to each dimension, plus 2 feet. If your pond is 24 inches deep and fits inside a 10x12-foot rectangular outline, to figure the liner width, add 10 feet (the width) plus 4 feet (the depth doubled) plus 2 feet (for overlap) for a total of 16 feet. The

Building a Pond

USE: ▶ backhoe (optional) • shovel • garden hose • hand tamper • steel rake • wheelbarrow • mason's twine • measuring tape • work gloves ▶ pond liner or shell

1 *If you're using a liner,* outline the shape you want your pond to be on the ground with garden hose or rope.

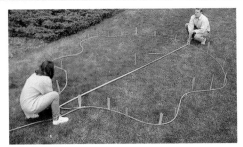

2 *Measure the area you have outlined,* and calculate the size liner you will need using the information above.

3 *Dig out the hole for your pond—small* ones can be dug by hand, but larger projects will require a backhoe.

liner length would be 12 feet plus 4 feet plus 2 feet—a total of 18 feet. You would need a 16x18-foot liner for a 10x12-foot pond.

To install the pond, dig along the perimeter of the hole to the depth of the shovel blade; then, remove all dirt within the pond area. Repeat the process until you reach the proper depth. For a shell-formed pond, dig the hole slightly larger, and backfill with damp sand or finely sifted soil. Make sure the pond bottom is level. Remove any sharp stones or projecting roots, and pack an even layer of sand into the hole to cushion the liner or protect the bottom of the shell. Set the shell in place, or drape the liner over the hole, and weight down the edges with rocks. Begin filling the pond with water. As the liner fills, stretch it to remove any wrinkles, and fold excess material into neat pleats. Ease off the stones as the water pulls the liner into the hole. When the liner is full, secure the edges with a few rocks. Cut off the excess (saving scraps for future repairs), and set coping stones around the liner or the shell to hide the edges and hold them in place.

Basic Maintenance

Test the water quality at least once a month, and remember to refresh the supply on a regular basis during hot weather, when water evaporates rapidly. Throughout the growing season, clip dead leaves and fading blossoms from aquatic plants to keep the pond clean. Water-garden suppliers sell pool sweeps, which help to remove leaves and silt from larger ponds. If you stock the pond with fish, don't use herbicides or insecticides on the landscape near the water—many can kill fish.

Pond Plant Varieties

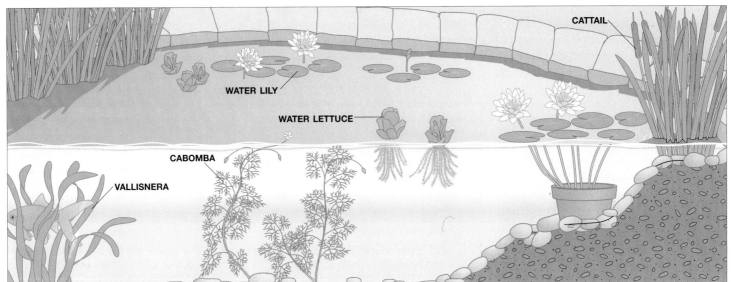

Beneficial pond plants range from submersibles that oxygenate the water, to surface floaters that require only occasional thinning, to marginal bog plants that do well around the edges of a pond in rich soil topped with 2 to 3 in. of water. Because many of these plants thrive in full sunlight, it is best not to locate the pond near trees that will shade them.

• water pump • water filter • aquatic plants • sand or finely-sifted soil • stones

4 *Rake out the base* of the pond to remove rocks, expose tree roots that might be cut, and help level the pond bottom.

5 *After pouring in the sand* to protect the liner, pack it down with a tamper. Make sure the bottom is still level.

6 *Set in the liner,* hold its rim down with stones, and add water. For shells, backfill the edges before filling with water.

yards

Watering the Lawn

The two biggest lawn-care questions you face during the hot summer months are "When is the best time to water?" and "How much water is enough?" Give your lawn too little and it will slowly turn depressingly brown. Pour on too much, especially at the wrong times, and you'll not only waste money, sooner or later you'll see a disease spreading through the once healthy turf.

Answering "When?" is easier than "How much?" During hot, dry spells, give your lawn a thorough watering about every week to ten days, although this varies somewhat depending on the type of grass, how well your soil retains water, and whether the grass is newly planted. Twice weekly waterings may be necessary.

Time of day also counts. Mornings are the best time to water, in part because more of the moisture soaks into the ground. During the afternoon and on windy days, large amounts of water evaporate into the air instead. Avoid watering in the evenings because the dampness and lack of sunlight promote lawn diseases—many diseases, particularly fungi, thrive in cool, damp conditions.

How much water is enough may require a little digging, literally. The object is to moisten the soil down to your lawn's root zone, but no farther. The actual amount needed varies according to your soil type (more or less porous), the length of the grass roots (tall fescue has long roots), and how hot and dry the weather is.

You can find out the amount you need to water with a simple test. After four or five rainless days, set out a number of cans on your lawn, and run the sprinklers until the water in them reaches 1 inch. Record how much time the sprinklers ran.

A full day later (half a day if the soil is porous), use a shovel to dig up a slab of sod and the soil beneath it. The darker colored band at the top is moist soil. If it doesn't extend down to the root depth, try running your sprinklers longer next time. If it goes well beyond the roots, reduce the sprinkling time.

Sprinklers

Aboveground sprinklers come in a variety of types—oscillating, pulsating, and revolving—

Installing Underground Sprinklers

USE: ▶ wrenches • screwdrivers • pressure gauge • shovel ▶ sprinkler pipes (feeder & water lines) • sprinkler heads • control box & wiring • control valve • drain valve

5 *Check your water pressure* to help decide the minimum number of watering zones your system can handle.

2 *Install a drain valve* so that you can drain water out of the system over the winter months.

3 *The main control valve,* located on the outside of the house, charges the system with water when it's time to start sprinkling.

5 *Glue the watering zone valves* to the feeder lines. Zones can be turned on or off manually or via a control box.

6 *Dig trenches* for the water lines. They don't need to be deep, as you will drain the system in the fall.

7 *Install pop-up sprinkler heads* spaced evenly across the lawn. The top of the head should be just about flush with the ground.

each with its own advantages and disadvantages. However, they are all easy to set up, can be moved if needed, and are inexpensive to buy. When used individually, they cover a small area, but connected in tandem by hoses they can water a whole lawn.

In-ground sprinklers require substantially more work and expense to install. You must plan the location of sprinklers very carefully, because they can't be moved after installation. Once you've laid out the system on paper, you may want to get a contractor to do the work, which involves digging trenches for water pipes throughout the yard, laying pipe, and backfilling the trenches. But once it's in, you won't have to fiddle with moving hoses or sprinklers again.

- zone valve adapter (transition fitting)

4 *An adapter* *or transition fitting connects water supply pipe to the system's plastic pipe, which will be buried in the ground.*

8 *Wire up a control box* *for an automatic system. Timers will turn on sprinklers in different zones at different times.*

Fountainheads

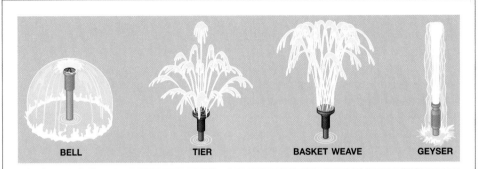

BELL   TIER   BASKET WEAVE   GEYSER

A small-scale fountain with a concentrated stream can release water into a small shell or pond liner with a pump at the bottom. In ponds, you can attach jet nozzles to pipes directly off submersible pumps and create wider sprays.

Hose Repair

So you didn't see the garden hose when you ran it over with the mower. But unless it has been hopelessly shredded, you can still get some life out of it with a repair kit available from most hardware stores. The fix is easy, and it costs less than a new hose. With a sharp knife, cut away the damaged part, leaving two squarely cut ends. The kit should contain two hose clamps and a plastic bushing about the diameter of the inside of your hose. Loosen the clamps, and slip one over each cut hose end; then push the bushing into the hose ends. The bushing should fit snugly. Now tighten the clamps just back from the cut ends. Leaks around male and female connectors can also be fixed with clamp-on replacement fittings.

Soaker hoses *leak on purpose—and get more water to plant roots.*

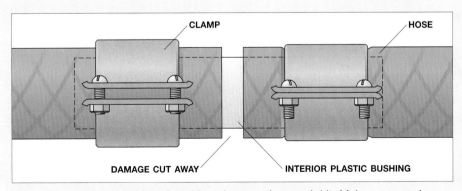

CLAMP   HOSE

DAMAGE CUT AWAY   INTERIOR PLASTIC BUSHING

Fix in-line garden hose breaks with an inexpensive repair kit. Make sure you know what the inside diameter of your hose is before buying the kit—garden hose comes in various diameters, including ½-inch, ⅝-inch, and ¾-inch.

Assessing Soil

Even the most attractively designed lawn can deteriorate if the soil is in poor condition, in need of fertilizing, or infested with weeds, bare spots, and insects. The size of the sand, silt, and clay particles that make up your soil affects how well it can sustain grass and, in turn, how nice your yard looks. Granular soil, with a balance of air, water-retention ability, and drainage, helps grass grow the deep, strong roots it needs to maintain a healthy appearance.

The main enemy of good soil structure in lawns is compaction due to the heavy traffic of people and equipment. When the ground feels almost like concrete underfoot, the soil is so compacted that it probably lacks oxygen, has poor water retention, and doesn't contain enough of the essential microorganisms for plant growth.

You can get a rough idea about soil compaction by pushing a long screwdriver into the ground after three or four rainless days. If you have trouble pushing the screwdriver in, your soil is probably compacted. You can loosen these areas with a manual or machine-powered aerator, or run a tiller back and forth, setting the tines more deeply with each pass.

Lawns also can suffer when dirt contains either too much sand or too much clay; when it lacks organic matter, nutrients, and minerals; and when it has a poor balance of alkaline and acidic components as measured in a pH rating.

Nutrition & pH

Nutrition and pH can be determined by testing the soil. The nutrients usually tested for are nitrogen, phosphorus, and potassium (usually referred to by their abbreviations, N-P-K). Nitrogen gives grass a deep green color, promotes dense growth, and helps grass bounce back from injury. Phosphorus fosters vigorous growth and root systems. Potassium increases disease resistance and improves hardiness. A soil that is low in nutrients can be fed with compost or a slow-release lawn fertilizer with a N-P-K rating of 3-1-2.

Most grasses grow best in a soil with a neutral pH (near 7.0). A low pH, indicating acidic soil, can be brought up ("sweetened") with ground limestone. A high-pH, alkaline soil can be brought closer to neutral with elemental sulfur.

Types of Mulch

Inorganic mulches include: **1** granite, **2** beach pebbles, **3** crushed brick, **4** crushed marble, **5** brown lava, **6** red lava and **7** beach stones. **Organic mulches** include: **8** aged hardwood chips, **9** fresh hardwood chips, **10** red-dyed cedar, **11** shredded cedar, **12** pine-bark nuggets, **13** shredded pine bark, **14** shredded hemlock, **15** pine needles and, **16** shredded cypress.

Determining Soil Type

1 *To start the test,* form the soil into a ball in your hands by pressing it firmly between your palms.

2 *Bounce the soil ball* up and down several times gently to see how well compacted it is.

3 *Soil that's mostly sand* crumbles easily. If it stays intact, it's silt or clay. If it crumbles as shown, it has a good balance of all three.

4 *Rub the soil* between your fingers. Sandy soil feels gritty; clay soil feels slippery; silt soil feels silky.

Testing Soil

Simple soil tests are widely available at garden stores and nurseries. These home tests will tell you your soil's pH and sometimes an analysis of N-P-K. Private labs or your local Cooperative Extension Service will be able to provide a more detailed test, including dozens of micro-nutrients and recommendations for soil amendments (the gardening term for additives).

Common Fertilizers and Soil Amendments

Material	Description	Approx. lbs./100 sq. ft.
Bagged steer manure	A weak, all-purpose fertilizer	6–8 lbs.
Dried poultry manure	A high-nitrogen fertilizer	2 lbs.
5-5-5 all-purpose fertilizer	An inexpensive and popular synthetic fertilizer	2 lbs.
Superphosphate or rock phosphate	Supplies phosphorus; work into the soil as deeply as possible	2–4 lbs.
Greensand	Supplies potassium, trace elements	2–4 lbs.
Limestone	Used to sweeten acidic soil	5 lbs.
Gypsum	Used to loosen clay soil and reduce salt buildup in roadside soil	2 lbs.
Wood ashes	Supplies potassium, phosphorus, lime	2–4 lbs.

Restoring a Lawn

USE: ▶ drop spreader • hopper spreader • rotary aerator • spading fork • thatching rake • wheelbarrow ▶ seed • fertilizer/compost • lime • sulfur • topdressing

1 ***Begin by dethatching the lawn*** *with a thatching rake, which pulls out dead grass and exposes soil for planting seed.*

2 ***Adjust the soil pH*** *by adding lime or elemental sulfur with a drop spreader. Lime raises the pH; sulfur lowers it.*

3 ***Fertilize the lawn*** *to promote good growth. Test results on your soil will determine which nutrients are needed.*

4 ***Add a topdressing*** *to restore organic matter in the soil. You can buy a 40-60 topsoil/compost mix for this purpose.*

5 ***A rotary aerator*** *helps restore lawns with compacted soil. Do not aerate in hot summer months.*

6 ***Fix bare patches and overseed*** *the whole lawn. Overseeding is best done in late summer, early fall, or early spring.*

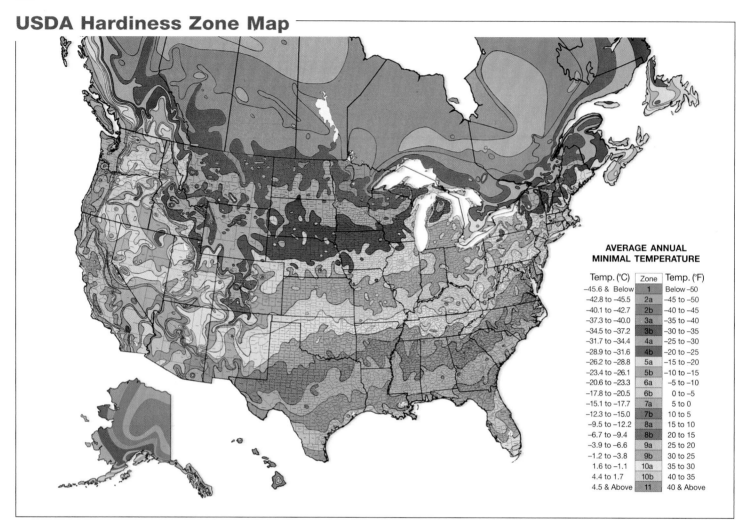

AVERAGE ANNUAL MINIMAL TEMPERATURE

Temp. (°C)	Zone	Temp. (°F)
−45.6 & Below	1	Below −50
−42.8 to −45.5	2a	−45 to −50
−40.1 to −42.7	2b	−40 to −45
−37.3 to −40.0	3a	−35 to −40
−34.5 to −37.2	3b	−30 to −35
−31.7 to −34.4	4a	−25 to −30
−28.9 to −31.6	4b	−20 to −25
−26.2 to −28.8	5a	−15 to −20
−23.4 to −26.1	5b	−10 to −15
−20.6 to −23.3	6a	−5 to −10
−17.8 to −20.5	6b	0 to −5
−15.1 to −17.7	7a	5 to 0
−12.3 to −15.0	7b	10 to 5
−9.5 to −12.2	8a	15 to 10
−6.7 to −9.4	8b	20 to 15
−3.9 to −6.6	9a	25 to 20
−1.2 to −3.8	9b	30 to 25
1.6 to −1.1	10a	35 to 30
4.4 to 1.7	10b	40 to 35
4.5 & Above	11	40 & Above

Plant Growing Zones

Plant hardiness zones have been identified and mapped by the U.S. Department of Agriculture (USDA). The lower the number, the colder the average winter. Low winter temperatures can kill plants that are rated for warmer zones.

Mail-order sources of plants and seeds rate their offerings as to hardiness, allowing you to judge whether a plant will survive in your area. Although the USDA hardiness ratings are useful, certain factors can affect their accuracy. Urban gardeners should consider that city temperatures tend to be 5–10° F warmer than the surrounding countryside, raising the rating of the city garden by a zone. Be sure that plants you select for their flowers are well within their cold-hardiness range—late frosts can devastate flower buds, or the plants may thrive but never flower. In general, plants growing at the coldest

and warmest borders of their hardiness zones are at greatest risk. A range of hardiness ratings that reads "USDA Zones 4 or 5 to 7 or 8" suggests that the plant may survive winter cold with protection in the warmer parts of Zone 4 but is safer in Zone 5; likewise, plants in Zone 8 may need shading from summer heat but are more likely to thrive in Zone 7.

While cold can be a threat to plants, excessive heat can be just as deadly. Temperatures above 86° F actually damage cellular proteins, and plants not suited to hot climates are likely to die during hot spells. To help identify areas that might be too hot for certain plants, the American Horticultural Society has compiled a Heat Zone Map. It divides the country into 12 zones, according to the average number of days the mercury tops 86°, and is especially helpful to those living in the South and in tran-

sitional zones. As is the case with the Hardiness Zone Map, urban areas in any given zone are likely to be an average 5–10° warmer.

Extending Your Range

Every location has microclimates that you can use to advantage, even when only a small area differs from its surroundings. It may be warmer or cooler, sunnier or shadier, drier or more humid. Delicate plants can be coaxed through a winter near a heat-absorbing wall or large rock or near a light-reflecting surface. In summer, heat-sensitive plants may thrive in the shade or on a northern slope.

You can also extend a plant's hardiness zone with a protective cover. A 3-inch mulch over plant roots will buffer extremes of soil temperature. And snowy regions have snow cover as a natural hardiness zone extender.

Basic Pruning

There are many reasons to prune—to make a tree or shrub healthier by removing dead or dying limbs; to provide more sunlight for a garden by eliminating branches from a tree; to shape shrubs and control future growth of a tree; or just to remove a hanging branch that's in the way. Pruning is best done in late winter or early spring—except for maples, birches, and other trees that produce large amounts of sap. They shouldn't be pruned until fall.

To removing an entire branch, *always cut just outside the slightly thick area, called the branch collar, where the branch grows out of the trunk.*

Selective pruning *involves removing weak, spindly, bent, or broken shoots. Where two branches rub together, remove the weaker or the one pointing inward.*

For rejuvenation pruning, *cut all stems close to the base in late winter or early spring. Use this technique on old, over-grown, or badly pruned shrubs or trees.*

To remove damaged branches or thin a tree, *cut the limb in a convenient location near the trunk, and make a final trim cut flush with the branch collar.*

It's still an undecided question: *whether to leave wounds or fresh cuts bare, or seal them with tar against insects and diseases—a toss up.*

BALLED PLANTS

Balled-and-burlapped
If you're certain that the material wrapped around the root ball is burlap, a natural fiber, leave it in place but loosen it. Remove any synthetic material because it won't decompose and will eventually strangle the roots of the new shrub or tree. Plant the root ball so the top is level with the surrounding soil. Fold down the burlap, and refill the hole with unamended soil.

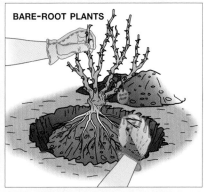

BARE-ROOT PLANTS

Bare-root
Dig a planting hole wide enough so you can fully spread out the roots. Then lay a stick across the hole as a depth guide, and set the plant at a depth where the section between the root and the trunk, called the crown, aligns with the stick.

resource guide

1 EMERGENCY REPAIRS

American Red Cross
Public Inquiry Office, 11th Floor,
1621 N. Kent St., Arlington, VA 22209
Phone: (703) 248-4222
E-mail: info@usa.redcross.org
Web site: www.redcross.org
The American Red Cross provides support for people involved in natural disasters and wars worldwide. Their Web site provides information on subjects such as repairing a flooded home, the risks of mudslides, how to prepare for a hurricane, as well as up-to-date information on Red Cross activities throughout the world.

Federal Emergency Management Agency (FEMA)
500 C Street, SW, Washington, DC 20472
Web site: www.fema.gov
FEMA is the federal agency that helps people before, during, and after natural disasters. FEMA runs several consumer education campaigns focusing on safety planning, makes financial assistance available to states, administers both national flood and crime insurance programs, and provides advice on building codes and safe building sites.

National Oceanic and Atmospheric Administration (NOAA)
U.S. Dept. of Commerce, 14th Street & Constitution Ave., NW, Room 6013,
Washington, DC 20230
Phone: (202) 482-6090 / Fax: (202) 482-3154
Web site: www.noaa.gov
NOAA, part of the Department of Commerce, includes the National Weather Service; National Environmental Satellite, Data, and Information Service; and the Office of Oceanic and Atmospheric Research. Their Web site provides up-to-date weather information, 3-D weather images and satellite photos, information on natural disasters, and other statistics.

2 TOOLS

Hitachi Power Tools
3950 Steve Reynolds Blvd., Norcross, GA 30093
Phone: (800) 59-TOOLS
Web site: www.hitachi.com
Hitachi makes a wide range of hand-held power tools and bench tools such as table saws for working with wood, metal, and concrete. They also manufacture a line of pneumatic tools, such as nailers and staplers, and the air compressors to power them. Call for more information or to locate a dealer or service center near you.

Makita USA
1301 W. Copans Rd., Pompano Beach, FL 33064
Phone: (954) 970-0806
Web site: www.makitausa.com
Makita manufacturers portable power tools, including saws, planers, drills, hammers, grinders, sanders, as well as pneumatic tools and outdoor power equipment. The U.S. operation includes over 1000 authorized service centers and a dealer network handling Makita's 65 tool models, which are manufactured in Buford, Georgia.

Pg. 22

Porter-Cable Corporation
4825 Hwy. 45 North, P.O. Box 2468,
Jackson, TN 38302-2468
Phone: (800) 4US-TOOL
Web site: www.porter-cable.com
Porter-Cable, a subsidiary of Pentair, Inc., is a leading manufacturer of portable electric and cordless power tools, nailers, staplers, compressors, and related accessories for the professional woodworking, commercial and residential construction, plumbing, and electrical markets.

Pg. 22

Ryobi North America
1424 Pearman Dairy Rd., Anderson, SC 29625
Phone: (800) 525-2579
Web site: www.ryobi.com
Ryobi produces portable and benchtop power tools for contractors and do-it-yourselfers. It also manufactures a line of lawn and garden tools. Call their toll-free customer service line for free literature, or go on-line for customer service, a power tool forum, warranty registration, and sales of selected products and accessories.

Pg. 22

The Stanley Works
1000 Stanley Drive, New Britain, CT 06053
Phone: (800) STANLEY
Web site: www.stanleyworks.com
The Stanley Works, founded in 1843, provides a line of hand and power tools for contractors and homeowners. Their speciality products include a series of ergonomically designed products and a line of extra-durable contractor tools for the job site. For information, call their toll-free information line or visit their Web site.

Pg. 18

3 FASTENERS & ADHESIVES

Elmer's
180 East Broad St., Columbus, OH 43215
Web site: www.elmers.com
Elmer's markets over 200 products, from school glues to home repair and woodworking products. Its range of products covers nearly every adhesive and home solution need of students, do-it-yourselfers, and even the professional contractor.

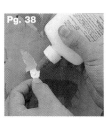

Pg. 38

Simpson Strong-Tie Company

4637 Chabot Dr., Suite 200, Pleasanton, CA 94588
Phone: (800) 999-5099
Web site: www.strongtie.com
One of the most widely used brands of framing hardware, with hundreds of different fasteners. Call for free catalog and free plans for deck construction and other home projects.

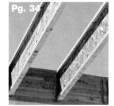

3M

3M Center, Bldg. 304-1-01,
St. Paul, MN 55144-1000
Phone: (800) 3M-HELPS / Fax: (800) 713-6329
E-mail: innovation@mmm.com
Web site: www.3M.com
3M, founded in 1902, started as a mining and abrasives company, but they now make thousands of products in manufacturing facilities located in more than 60 countries. Among 3M's developments are masking tape, cellophane tape, waterproof sandpaper, and magnetic sound recording and videotape.

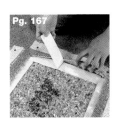

Vermont American

1980 Indian Creek Rd., P.O. Box 340,
Lincolnton, NC 28092
Phone: (800) 742-3869 / Fax: (704) 736-8092
Web site: www.vermontamerican.com
Vermont American Tool Company is a leading manufacturer of hand tools and power-tool accessories, including bits, gauges, cutters, blades, guides, and hard-to-find tools such as nut splitters. For more information on products and services, call their toll-free number.

4 MASONRY

Brick Industry Association

11490 Commerce Park Dr.,
Reston, VA 20191-1525
Phone: (703) 620-0010
E-mail: brickinfo@big.org
Web site: www.brickinfo.org
The Brick Industry Association is a national trade association representing brick manufacturers and distributors in the U.S. Write or call for a free catalog listing various do-it-yourself brochures and videos on brick.

Eldorado Stone Corporation

P.O. Box 489, Carnation, WA 98014
Phone: (800) 925-1491
Web site: www.eldoradostone.com
Eldorado Stone manufactures realistic simulations of different types of stone. The lightweight, precast architectural veneers can be applied inside or outside the house directly to walls—you don't need a special foundation.

Prosoco

3741 Greenway Circle, Lawrence, KS 66046
Phone: (800) 255-4255 / Fax: (785) 830-9797
Web site: www.prosoco.com
Prosoco is a custom formulator of specialty cleaners and protective treatments for masonry and concrete, designed to improve their appearance and performance. Products and services developed by Prosoco have been used on the U.S. Capitol, the World Trade Plaza, and the Smithsonian, among many others.

5 FOUNDATIONS

Concrete Foundations Association

107 First Street West, P.O. Box 204,
Mount Vernon, IA 52314
Phone: (319) 895-6940
Web site: www.cfana.org
The CFA was established in 1974 to improve the quality and acceptance of cast-in-place concrete foundations. The Association provides educational seminars and a newsletter to foundation contractors and suppliers in 26 states and Canada. The Web site has several construction publications available to non-members (for a fee), and links to other Web sites.

HouseGuard

8600 Berk Blvd., Hamilton, OH 45015
Phone: (800) 560-5701 / Fax: (513) 874-6870
Web site: www.houseguard.com
HouseGuard is a professionally installed system for new construction and existing homes that waterproofs, insulates, and drains water away from the basement. Call for a dealer near you or for your own consultation.

National Concrete Masonry Association

2302 Horse Pen Rd.,
Herndon VA 20171-3499
Phone: (703) 713-1900 / Fax: (703) 713-1910
Web site: www.ncma.org
The NCMA, established in 1918, is the national trade association representing the concrete masonry industry. It offers a variety of technical services and design aids through publications, computer programs, slide presentations, and technical training.

Portland Cement Association

5420 Old Orchard Rd., Skokie IL 60077
Phone: (847) 966-6200 / Fax: (847) 966-9781
Web site: www.portcement.org
Since 1916, PCA has conducted market development, research, education, and public affairs on behalf on the cement companies of the U.S. and Canada. You can order research reports and

resource guide

handbooks from their large collection. Their Web site contains numerous resources, including an on-line tour of the cement-making process.

6 WOOD

APA—The Engineered Wood Association

P.O. Box 11700, Tacoma, WA 98411
Web site: www.apawood.org
APA is a nonprofit trade association whose U.S. and Canadian members produce a variety of engineered wood products. Primary functions include quality inspection and product promotion. Write for free brochures.

California Redwood Association

405 Enfrente Dr., Suite 200, Novato, CA 94949
Web site: www.calredwood.org
This nonprofit trade association offers extensive technical information about redwood, including grade distinctions, structural applications, and finishing characteristics. The Association also has design and how-to help for consumers. Write for a free brochure.

Southern Pine Council

P.O. Box 641700, Kenner, LA 70064
Web site: www.southernpine.com
A nonprofit trade promotion group supported by manufacturers of Southern Pine lumber. Construction details and building tips, complete project plans, and other helpful information is described in a free catalog.

Western Wood Products Association

522 SW 5th Ave., Suite 500,
Portland, OR 97204-2122
Phone: (503) 224-3930 / Fax: (503) 224-3934
Web site: www.wwpa.org
WWPA establishes standards and levels of quality for Western lumber and related products in Western softwood species. Technical information is available via fax or on their Web site.

7 FRAMING

Lindal Cedar Homes

4300 South 104th Place, Seattle, WA 98178
Phone: (800) 426-0536 or (206) 725-0900
Fax: (206) 725-1656
Web site: www.lindal.com
Lindal builds solid cedar homes that can be shipped precut and assembled on your site. Walls, roofs, and other components are made of milled timbers with interlocking joints. The company offers their models in a book of plans, a video, and a CD-ROM. They have a large dealer network in North America.

Manufactured Housing Institute

2101 Wilson Blvd., # 610, Arlington, VA 22201
Phone: (703) 558-0400
Web site: www.mfghome.org
The MHI represents companies that build houses off-site and ship large sections or even complete homes. About 25% of all new single-family homes are built this way. MHI provides several consumer services and is a good starting point if you're interested in these low-cost homes.

North American Steel Framing Alliance

1726 M Street, NW, Suite 601,
Washington, DC 20036
Phone: (800) 79-STEEL / Fax: (202) 785-3856
Web site: www.steelframingalliance.com
NASFA was formed in 1998 to foster the use of steel framing in residential construction. Publications, including a directory of builders in the U.S. and Canada, are available through their toll-free hotline or their Web site.

Rocky Mountain Log Homes

1883 U.S. Hwy. 93 South, Hamilton, MT 59840
Web site: www.rmlh.com
Creating log homes for over three decades, this company offers a wide range of home designs, layouts, options, and materials, including homes made of large-diameter, hand-crafted logs. Write for free information or check their Web site.

8 REMODELING GUIDE

American Arbitration Association

335 Madison Ave., 10th Fl.,
New York, NY 10017-4605
Phone: (800) 778-7879 / Fax: (212) 716-5905
Web site: www.adr.org
This organization is available to resolve a wide range of disputes through mediation, arbitration, elections, and other out-of-court settlement procedures. They provide a forum for the hearing of disputes in 37 offices nationwide, using a roster of 17,000 impartial experts.

Council of Better Business Bureaus

4200 Wilson Blvd., Suite 800,
Arlington, VA 22203-1804
Phone: (703) 276-0100 / Fax: (703) 525-8277
Web site: www.bbb.org
The mission of all local Better Business Bureaus is to promote and foster the highest ethical relationship between businesses and the public through voluntary self-regulation, consumer and business education, and service excellence. The CBBB is the umbrella organization for the 132 local bureaus, supported by more than 250,000 local business members nationwide.

ImproveNet

Web site: www.improvenet.com

ImproveNet is a nationwide team of home improvement experts whose mission is to make the home remodeling process more successful for both homeowners and service providers. ImproveNet helps homeowners through every step of their home improvement projects, by providing how-to advice and matching homeowners with qualified remodeling industry professionals who are available to help them.

National Association of the Remodeling Industry (NARI)

4900 Seminary Rd., Suite 320,
Arlington, VA 22311
Phone: (703) 575-1100 / Fax: (703) 575-1121
Web site: www.remodeltoday.com

Members of NARI are full-service contractors, design-build firms, manufacturers, suppliers, distributors, subcontractors, lenders, and other related professionals in the remodeling field. NARI certification provides the industry with a formalized standard of expertise. Their Web site allows you to search for pros in your area.

9 FLOORS & STAIRS

Carpet and Rug Institute

P.O. Box 2048, 310 Holiday Ave.,
Dalton, GA 30720
Phone: (800) 882-8846 / Fax: (706) 278-8835
Web site: www.carpet-rug.com

CRI provides material—some items free of charge and some at a small charge—for consumers, including guidelines for carpet/rug selection, installation, daily maintenance and long-term care, and information on carpet's role in indoor air quality and the environment.

Pg. 164

Crain Cutter Company

1155 Wrigley Way,
Milpitas, CA 95035-5426
Phone: (408) 946-6100 / Fax: (408) 946-4268

Crain Cutter produces tools for the floorcovering trade, such as stretchers and kickers used to install carpeting. Product catalogs are available by calling the number listed above.

Pg. 166

National Oak Flooring Manufacturers Assoc.

P.O. Box 3009, Memphis, TN 38173-0009
Phone: (901) 526-5016 / Fax: (901) 526-7022
Web site: www.nofma.org

NOFMA is the main trade association for hardwood flooring manufacturing and grading. Their Web site includes information on estimating, installing, refinishing, and repairing hardwood floors. You can order how-to flooring pamphlets.

Pg. 149

10 WALLS & CEILINGS

Brewster Wallcovering Company

67 Pacella Park Dr., Randolph, MA 02368
Phone: (800) 366-1701 / Fax: (781) 963-8805
Web site: www.ewallpaper.com

Brewster manufactures wallpaper, borders, fabrics, and accessories including valances, shower curtains, and chair pads. Free consumer brochures, how-to-decorate videos, and referral to local retail stores is available by phone or by visiting their Web site.

Pg. 193

Celotex Corporation

4010 Boy Scout Blvd., Tampa, FL 33607
Fax: (813) 873-4058
Web site: www.celotex.com

Celotex produces consistently high-quality gypsum board, as well as tile backer board, interior ceiling board, and related gypsum products for use in residential and commercial construction, plus specially formulated products for fire-resistance-rated designs.

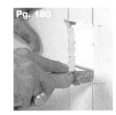
Pg. 180

Chicago Metallic

4849 S. Austin Ave., Chicago, IL 60638
Phone: (800) 323-7164 / Fax: (800) 222-3744
Web site: www.chicago-metallic.com

Chicago Metallic produces suspended ceiling grids and panels in several materials, including fiberglass, vinyl-covered gypsum, and stamped metal. Their roofing products include Shingle Shield roof and deck cleaner and Shingle Shield zinc strips. Call the samples and literature hotline listed above to request brochures.

Pg. 20

Pittsburgh Corning Corporation

800 Presque Isle Dr., Pittsburgh, PA 15239
Phone: (800) 624-2120 / Fax: (724) 327-5890
Web site: www.pittsburghcorning.com

Pittsburgh Corning provides a full line of glass block products and accessories, including fully-assembled LightWise windows and Pittsburgh Corning glass-block shower systems. Call the toll-free number to reach the Glass Block Resource Center with distributor locator, product information, and answers to frequently asked questions regarding products and installation.

Pg. 199

The Tile Council of America

100 Clemson Research Blvd.,
Anderson, SC 29625
Phone: (864) 646-8453 / Fax: (864) 646-2821
Web site: www.tileusa.com

The Tile Council of America provides technical assistance and literature to the tile industry. To receive technical assistance in reference to tile installation and maintenance, visit their Web site.

Pg. 194

resource guide

U.S. Gypsum Corporation
125 South Franklin St., Chicago IL 60680-4124
Phone: 1-800-USG4YOU
Web site: www.usg.com
USG is a major manufacturer of gypsum panels (drywall) and related products. Sheetrock—their brand name of wallboard—is among the most widely recognized names in the building industry.

White River Hardwoods—Woodworks Inc.
1197 Happy Hollow Rd., Fayetteville, AR 72701
Phone: (800) 558-0119
Web site: www.mouldings.com
White River has manufactured architectural molding since 1981. They specialize in decorative hardwood moldings and authentic hand-carved wood carvings: over 450 profiles with five different price ranges. Available nationwide through lumberyards and fine millwork houses. Contact them for samples, design assistance, free brochures, and various catalogs.

11 UNFINISHED SPACES

CraftMaster Door Designs by Masonite
One South Wacker Dr., Suite 3600,
Chicago, IL 60606
Phone: (800) 405-2233 / Fax: (312) 634-2856
Web site: www.masonite.com
CraftMaster is a leading brand of interior molded door facings in the U.S. and around the world— a superior alternative to both solid wood and flush doors. Their full-color, 21-page Idea Book shows the dramatic difference a door makes. Call their toll-free number for a free copy.

Murphy Bed Company
42 Central Ave., Farmingdale, NY 11735
Phone: (800) 845-2337 / Fax: (631) 420-4337
Web site: www.murphybedcompany.com
Murphy beds were originally designed to save space in small apartments. They still save room by tipping up into a self-contained wall unit. Dimensions, specifications, and photos of Murphy beds are available in a free brochure— just call their toll-free number.

Pet Doors USA
4523 30th St. W., #E502,
Brandenton, FL 34207-1072
Phone: (800) 749-9609 / Fax: (800) 283-8045
Web site: www.petdoor.com
Pet Doors USA makes 150 models of pet doors in sizes to accommodate everything from a cat to a Great Dane. The framed units can fit into walls, house doors, windows, and patio doors. They also offer electronic pet doors. Contact them for a free catalog and free technical support.

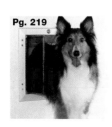

Robern
7 Wood Ave., Bristol, PA 19007
Phone/Fax: (215) 826-9800
Web site: www.robern.com
Robern, Inc. offers a wide variety of storage products, furniture, and accessories. Call or write for information about innovative mirrored cabinets, lighting, or bath accessories.

12 CABINETS & COUNTERS

Corian
Phone: (800) 4-CORIAN
Web site: www.corian.com
DuPont Corian is a solid-surfacing material used for kitchen countertops and bathroom sinks that is easy to clean, resists stains, and is available in over 70 colors. Visit their Web site or call their toll-free number for details.

Dura-Oak Cabinet Refacing Products
863 Texas Ave., Shreveport, LA 71101
Phone: (800) 228-7702 / Fax: (318) 424-8252
Web site: www.dura-oak.com
Dura-Oak's products include doors, drawers, veneer, valances, molding, and hinges. Cabinets come in many different door styles and species. They offer 33 wood colors and nine Giazo colors. Call the toll-free number for a free full-color brochure and a list of local dealers.

Ilco Unican Corporation
2941 Indiana Ave., Winston-Salem, NC 27105
Phone: (800) 849-8324
Web site: www.ilcounican.com
Developers of the first push-button lock, Ilco Unican provides electronic control, key blanks, key machines, and push-button locks to residential, commercial, and ADA-compliant areas.

KraftMaid Cabinetry
P.O. Box 1055, Middlefield, OH 44062
Phone: (800) 571-1990
Web site: www.kraftmaid.com
KraftMaid makes semi-custom cabinets in a wide selection of styles. The modular units can be combined to fit existing spaces with only minor adjustments. Call for free product literature, planning guide, and locations of nearest dealers.

Merillat Industries
P.O. Box 1946, Adrian, MI 49221
Phone: (800) 575-8763
Web site: www.merillat.com
Merillat manufactures cabinets in a full complement of styles and prices. Visit their Web site for product information, design tips, and a dealer locator, or call or write for free product guides.

National Kitchen & Bath Association (NKBA)

687 Willow Grove St., Hackettstown NJ 07840
Phone: (908) 852-0033 / Fax: (908) 852-1695
Web site: www.nkba.org

NKBA is a national trade association that provides information for professionals and homeowners involved with remodeling a kitchen or bath. The Association can provide help with planning and design guidelines for your project, including actual projects that you can review. NKBA also will help you locate a design professional in your area.

13 SHELVING & STORAGE

ClosetMaid

P.O. Box 4400, Ocala, FL 34478
Phone: (800) 874-0008
Web site: www.closetmaid.com

ClosetMaid makes a wide variety of storage products, including wire rack and wood storage systems for every room in the house. For a free brochure, a listing of stores near you, and installation assistance, call their toll-free number or visit the Web site.

Craftsman Tools (Sears, Roebuck & Co.)

3333 Beverly Rd., Hoffman Estates, IL 60179
Phone: (800) 349-4358
Web site: www.craftsman.com

Craftsman has been manufacturing hand and power tools for the professional carpenter, mechanic, as well as do-it-yourselfers for over 100 years. To store them, they also make an extensive line of tool storage boxes from work-site portables to huge roll-away drawer sets. All of their extensive line of mechanic's hand tools come with a lifetime guarantee, and all can be purchased at Sears stores nationwide and at the Craftsman Web site.

14 FURNITURE

Adjustable Clamp Company

417 N. Ashland Ave., Chicago, IL 60622
Phone: (312) 666-0640 / Fax: (312) 666-2723
E-mail: adjclp@ix.netcom.com

Adjustable Clamp, founded in 1903, offers 43 styles of clamps in 130 sizes and models, including a variety of adjustable pipe clamps. Other products include vises, miter boxes, motor saws, and related fine tools. Write or E-mail to purchase their catalog or for free brochures.

E. C. Mitchell Company

88-T Boston St., Middleton, MA 01949
Phone: (978) 774-1191 / Fax: (978) 774-2494
This company, established in 1919, makes a

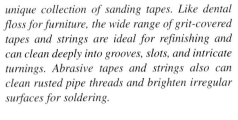

unique collection of sanding tapes. Like dental floss for furniture, the wide range of grit-covered tapes and strings are ideal for refinishing and can clean deeply into grooves, slots, and intricate turnings. Abrasive tapes and strings also can clean rusted pipe threads and brighten irregular surfaces for soldering.

Shaker Workshops

P.O. Box 8001, Ashburnham, MA 01430-8001
Phone: (800) 840-9121 / Fax: (978) 827-6554
Web site: www.shakerworkshops.com

Shaker Workshops makes chairs, tables, clocks, and other reproductions of Shaker furniture (plus baskets, boxes, and other accessories). The company offers the furniture either fully assembled and finished or in kit form. In the kit business since 1972, the company provides all pieces precut, stain, nails, chair tape fabric for seats, and a good set of instructions.

15 PLUMBING

American Standard

One Centennial Ave., Piscataway, NJ 08855
Phone: (732) 980-3000
Web site: www.americanstandard.com

American Standard manufactures technologically advanced air conditioners, bathroom and kitchen fixtures and fittings, among other systems. Its internationally recognized brand names include Trane, American Standard, and Armitage Shanks and Dolomite for plumbing products.

Moen

25300 Al Moen Dr., North Olmsted, OH 44070
Phone: (800) BUY-MOEN
Web site: www.moen.com

Moen, Inc., manufactures a wide variety of faucets for the kitchen and bath as well as bathroom accessories, kitchen sinks, showering products, and plumbing parts/accessories. They also feature a line of pure-touch filtering faucet systems, improving taste, reducing odor, and removing harmful bacterial from your water.

Plumbing Manufacturers Institute

1340 Remington Rd., Suite A,
Schaumburg, IL 60173
Phone: (847) 884-9764 / Fax: (847) 884-9775
Web site: www.pmihome.org

The Plumbing Manufacturers Institute is the voluntary, not-for-profit national trade association of manufacturers of plumbing products, serving as the voice of the industry. Member companies produce a substantial quantity of the nation's plumbing products. Call or write for free water-closet installation troubleshooting guide.

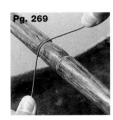

resource guide

Re-Bath Incorporated
1055 South Country Club Rd.,
Mesa, AZ 85210-4613
Phone: (800) 426-4573 / Fax: (480) 833-7199
Web site: www.re-bath.com

Re-Bath manufactures and distributes a variety of bathroom retrofit products including bathtub liners, wall surrounds, shower base liners, shampoo shelves, and soap dishes. Re-Bath products are manufactured from a lustrous impact-resistant acrylic. Product brochures and information on dealer locations are available. Call their toll-free number or visit their Web site.

Pg. 307

Sloan (Flushmate Division)
10500 Seymour Ave., Franklin Park, IL 60131
Phone: (800) 982-5839 / Fax: (847) 671-4611
Web site: www.flushmate.com

Flushmate is a pressure-assisted flushing system for low-consumption toilets. It uses water and line pressure to more effectively clean the bowl with one flush. Available through leading toilet manufacturers worldwide. The company also offers a free brochure, "How To Choose the Right Toilet," which includes pictures of low-volume units and a listing of toilet manufacturers.

Pg. 288

16 HEATING

American Gas Association
400 N. Capitol St., NW, Washington, DC 20001
Phone: (202) 824-7000 / Fax: (202) 824-7115
Web site: www.aga.org

AGA represents 189 local natural gas utilities that deliver gas to 54 million homes and businesses in all 50 states. AGA acts as a clearinghouse for gas energy information, including data on appliances and energy efficiency.

Pg. 315

Heat-N-Glo
20802 Kensington Blvd., Lakeville, MN 55044
Phone: (888) 427-3973 / Fax: (800) 259-1549
Web site: www.heatnglo.com

Heat-N-Glo offers a complete line of energy-efficient and clean-burning gas fireplaces, fireplace inserts, and log sets for almost any design application. They offer a wide variety of single- and multi-sided woodburning fireplaces as well. Call toll-free to receive a free brochure or to locate a dealer near you.

Pg. 322

Holmes Products Corporation
233 Fortune Blvd., Milford, MA 01757
Phone: (800) 5-HOLMES
Web site: www.holmesproducts.com

Holmes offers a comprehensive line of heaters, fans, humidifiers, air purifiers, and lighting products distributed through all major retail outlets.

Pg. 321

Holmes also offers the FamilyCare line of products, designed to help parents create a healthier home environment for their children.

17 COOLING

AHAM
1111 19th Street, NW, Suite 402,
Washington, DC 20036
Phone: (202) 872-5955 / Fax: (202) 872-9354
Web site: www.aham.org

AHAM—the Association of Home Appliance Manufacturers—provides programs and services regarding home appliances, including data compilation, technical standards development, and public information. Their Web site contains information on room air conditioners and dehumidifiers, as well as most other major appliances.

Pg. 328

ASHRAE
1791 Tullie Circle NE, Atlanta, GA 30329
Phone: (800) 527-4723 / Fax: (404) 321-5478
Web site: www.ashrae.org

ASHRAE, the American Society of Heating, Refrigerating, and Air-Cooling Engineers, is an international organization of 50,000 persons organized for the sole purpose of advancing the arts and sciences of heating, ventilation, air conditioning, and refrigeration for the public's benefit through research, standards, continuing education, and publications.

Pg. 328

Carrier Corporation
Phone: (800) CARRIER
Web site: www.carrier.com

Carrier Corporation is a major manufacturer of heating and air-conditioning equipment that includes a wide range of portable and central systems. The company (a subsidiary of United Technologies Corporation) now supplies cooling units with Puron, a replacement for freon, that is designed to meet the latest EPA standards.

Pg. 330

Honeywell
101 Columbia Rd., Morristown, NJ 07962
Phone: (800) 421-2133 or (973) 455-2000
Fax: (973) 455-4807
Web site: www.honeywell.com

Honeywell produces a wide range of residential and commercial heating and cooling controls and security systems. Honeywell's diversified subsidiaries also produce a variety of other products for your home, office, and automobile.

Pg. 336

Lennox Industries
2100 Lake Park Blvd., Richardson TX 75080
Phone: (800) 9-LENNOX
Web site: www.lennox.com

Lennox, founded in 1985, is a premium manufacturer of residential and commercial heating and air-conditioning equipment and related products. It is recognized as the leader in high-efficiency comfort conditioning. Lennox markets its products via one-step distribution, directly to its network of 6,000 independent dealers.

18 ELECTRICAL

Electrician's Web
Web site: www.electriciansweb.com
This Web site is one of the growing number of sites that matches consumers and contractors. You can search electronically for an electrical contractor in your area. The location also contains numerous links to industry sites, on-line periodicals, and how-to forums.

Underwriters' Laboratories
333 Pfingsten Rd., Northbrook, IL 60062
Phone: (847) 272-8800
Web site: www.ul.com
UL is an independent, not-for-profit product safety testing and certification organization. Each year, more than 14 billion familiar UL marks are applied to products worldwide. Since their founding in 1894, UL has held the undisputed reputation as the leader in product safety and certification for electrical products in particular.

19 INSULATION

North American Insulation Manufacturers Association (NAIMA)
44 Canal Center Plaza #310,
Alexandria, VA 22312
Phone: (703) 684-0084 / Fax: (703) 684-0427
E-mail: insulation@naima.org
Web site: www.naima.org
NAIMA is a trade association of North American manufacturers of fiberglass, rock wool, and slag wool insulation products. NAIMA's role is to promote energy efficiency and environmental preservation through the use of these products, and to encourage their safe production and use. Visit their Web site for publications on application and benefits of these products.

Owens Corning
1 Owens Corning Parkway, Toledo, OH 43659
Phone: (800) Get-Pink
E-mail: answers@owenscorning.com
Web site: www.owenscorning.com
Owens Corning offers a full array of products and systems for the home, including roofing, exterior, insulating, and acoustical. Call the toll-free number for free information.

20 VENTILATION

Benjamin Obdyke
65 Steamboat Dr., Warminster, PA 18974
Phone: (800) 523-5261
Web site: www.obdyke.com
Benjamin Obdyke has been a leading manufacturer of roofing products for over 130 years. They manufacture Cedar Breather, a unique underlayment for wood shakes and shingles designed to maximize performance and life of wood roofs and siding. For more information about Cedar Breather and other ventilation products, call (800) 346-7655.

CertainTeed
3000 West Commerce St., Dallas, TX 75212
Phone: (800) 247-8368 / Fax: (800) 635-7006
Web site: www.certainteed.com
CertainTeed is a leading manufacturer of attic ventilation products, including ridge vents, power fans, static vents, whole-house fans, and wind turbines. They make several types of low-maintenance, self-venting soffit systems. Call the company for a free video.

Cor-A-Vent
P.O. Box 428, Mishawaka, IN 46546-0428
Phone: (800) 837-8368 / Fax: (800) 645-6162
Web site: www.cor-a-vent.com
Cor-A-Vent manufactures ridge/soffit vent systems for residential and light commercial buildings. Shingle, shake, tile, metal roofing—any type of roof material can be used with Cor-A-Vent. Cor-A-Vent works on all styles and types of roof. Call the number listed above for free brochures, catalogs, and information.

Vantage Products
1665 Dogwood Dr., Conyers, GA 30012
Phone: (800) 241-7421
Web site: www.vantageproducts.com
Vantage Products makes Elite open louver and raised panel shutters, custom shutters, gable vents, siding accessories, and more—all backed by a lifetime warranty. Call for information, free catalogs, and brochures, as well as a list of distributors in your immediate area.

21 SAFETY & SECURITY

AD • AS
2728 S. Cole Rd., Boise, ID 83709
Phone: (208) 362-8001
Web site: www.ad-as.com
AD • AS (Accessible Design–Adjustable Systems Inc.) makes height-adjustable sink systems, height-adjustable cooktop systems, height-

adjustable wall cabinets, ergonomic office furniture, accessible computer furniture, library furniture, and rehab furniture. Call for a free catalog.

ASTM
100 Barr Harbor Dr.,
West Conshohocken, PA 19428-2959
Web site: www.astm.org
ASTM (the American Society for Testing and Materials) develops standards for a wide variety of materials, for example, so that light bulbs from different manufacturers all fit in one kind of socket. Their Web site contains numerous safety standards for a wide variety of products.

Children's Safety Network
55 Chapel St., Newton, MA 02458-1060
Phone: (617) 969-7101 x2207
Web site: www.edc.org/HHD/csn
The Children's Safety Network provides resources and technical assistance to child health agencies and other organizations seeking to reduce injuries to children and adolescents. Their Web site contains publications and resources produced by CSN, links to other resources, and a catalog of their publications.

Environmental Protection Agency
401 M Street SW, Washington, DC 20460-0003
Phone: (202) 260-2090
Web site: www.epa.gov
The EPA's extensive Web site contains special areas on children's health, air quality, and water quality. You can search for information based not only on keywords but your own zip code.

National Fire Protection Association
1 Batterymarch Park, PO Box 9101,
Quincy, MA 02269-9101
Phone: (800) 344-3555 / Fax: (617) 770-0700
Web site: www.nfpa.org
The mission of the NFPA (organized in 1896) is to reduce life and property losses from fires. The Association provides scientifically based consensus standards, research and training. Their Web site has information on the National Electrical Code, the Fire Prevention Code, the National Fuel Gas Code, and the National Fire Alarm Code, as well as answering FAQs on fire safety.

National Manufacturing Company
P.O. Box 577, Sterling, IL 61081
Phone: (800) 346-9445
Web site: www.natman.com
National Manufacturing is a leading supplier of home, farm, and builder's hardware products to the retail home-improvement industry. Call the toll-free number above for customer service.

U.S. Fire Administration
16825 S. Seton Ave., Emmitsburg, MD 21727
Phone: (301) 447-1000
Web site: www.usfa.fema.gov
The United States Fire Administration, a division of FEMA, has a mission of reducing life and economic losses due to fire and related emergencies. Their Web site contains numerous fire safety tips, a kid's page, links to publications, and information on product recalls.

22 ROOFING

Alum-A-Pole Corporation
1011 Capouse Ave., Scranton, PA 18509
Phone: (800) 421-2586
Web site: www.alumapole.com
Manufactures and sells the Alum-A-Pole Scaffolding System—a brake upgrade system for bending and working efficiently with vinyl or aluminum coil—and various other products. Call or visit their Web site for information.

Amerimax Home Products
P.O. Box 4515, Lancaster, PA 17604
Phone: (717) 299-3711 / Fax: (717) 299-3014
Web site: www.amerimax.com
Amerimax products include metal and vinyl rain gutters, soffit and fascia, drip edges, screen door guards, and others. Write for a free catalog.

ATAS International
6612 Snowdrift Rd., Allentown, PA 18106
Phone: (610) 395-8445
Web site: www.atas.com
ATAS is a manufacturer of metal roofing and wall panels, roofing trim, and rainware. They also provide technical assistance with design and shop drawings. Call or E-mail for a free brochure.

Englert
1200 Amboy Ave., Perth Amboy, NJ 08862
Phone: (732) 826-8614
Web site: www.englertinc.com
Englert manufactures a full line of formed residential metal roofing and aluminum gutters (including raw materials and accessories) mainly for independent installation contractors.

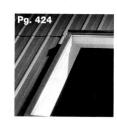

Metal Roofing Alliance
Phone: (888) METALROOF
Web site: www.metalroof.org
A coalition of metal-roofing manufactures and related companies in the metal-roofing industry, whose primary focus is to educate homeowners on the many benefits of metal roofing for residential applications. Call or visit their Web site for a free video on metal roofing.

Rainhandler

2710 North Ave., Bridgeport, CT 06604
Phone: (800) 942-3004
Web site: www.rainhandler.com
Rainhandler is a long grate used instead of a gutter. The idea is to break the water running off the roof into a spray. In the process, there are no gutters to clog and no leaves to remove.

23 SIDING

Alcoa

201 Isabella St., Pittsburgh, PA 15212-5858
Phone: (412) 553-4545
Web site: www.alcoa.com
Alcoa has produced aluminum products since 1888. They are also active in mining, refining, smelting, fabricating, and recycling—with 215 operating locations in 31 countries. Aluminum siding, including trim, fancy-cut shingles, clapboards, and many other patterns, is only one of Alcoa's many product lines.

Cedar Shake and Shingle Bureau

P.O. Box 1178, Sumas, WA 98295-1178
Fax: (604) 462-9386
Web site: www.cedarbureau.org
The bureau provides homeowners (and professionals) with information about cedar roofing and siding. You can contact them for help with installation specifications and care and maintenance guidelines for shingles and shakes. The Bureau provides free product literature and a list of manufacturers.

GAF Materials Corporation

1361 Alps Rd., Wayne, NJ 07470
Phone: (800) ROOF-411
Web site: www.gaf.com
Founded in 1886, GAF is one of the oldest manufacturers of commercial and residential roofing materials in the U.S. Their product line includes standard three-tab strip shingles, double- and triple-tiered architectural shingles, built-up roofing products, and the modern version of roll roofing—a rubbery, heat-sealed sheet material called modified bitumen.

24 WINDOWS & DOORS

Anderson Corporation

Phone: (800) 426-4261 / Fax: (651) 430-5589
Web site: www.andersoncorp.com
Anderson is a major manufacturer of windows. Visit their Web site to see the many types of windows they offer and find where to purchase them in your area. The site also has answers to common window maintenance questions.

Benchmark Door Systems

P.O. Box 7387, Fredericksburg, VA 22404
Phone: (800) 755-DOOR
Web site: www.benchmarkdoors.com
Three main lines of steel doors and frames offer a wide variety of styles, glazings, and trim details. Some of the products have a stainable vinyl coating made to simulate woodgrain over a 22-gauge steel construction that provides a 1½-hour fire rating. The insulated (foam-filled) doors are energy efficient.

Hy-Lite Products

101 California Ave., Beaumont, CA 92223
Phone: (800) 827-3691 / Fax: (800) 827-4920
Web site: www.hy-lite.com
Hy-Lite manufactures acrylic-block windows—windows that have the appearance of glass block that are completely prefabricated in standard frames. Hy-Lite's acrylic-block windows are available in aluminum and vinyl frames and as fixed, casement, and awning units.

L. E. Johnson Hardware

2100 Sterling Ave., Elkhart, IN 46516
Phone: (800) 837-5664
Web site: www.johnsonhardware.com
Johnson Hardware makes sliding- and folding-door hardware kits; universal repair kits for door hardware; pocket-door locks; pocket-door frame kits; closet rods and closet systems; architectural and commercial grade hardware; and folding, telescoping, and gaucho table legs.

Marvin Windows & Doors

P.O. Box 100, Warroad, MN 56763
Phone: (218) 386-1430
Web site: www.marvin.com
Marvin is one of the largest manufacturers of windows and doors, and offers a wide variety of glazing, framing, and cladding options. In addition to 11,000 stock windows and doors, the company also builds custom units to order. The Web site offers product information, catalogs, and the locations of local dealers.

Therma-Tru Doors

1687 Woodlands Dr., Maumee, OH 43537
Phone: (800) 537-8827
Web site: www.thermatru.com
With over 35 years experience, Therma-Tru Doors is a leading manufacturer of residential entry-door systems. They offer a complete door system, designed, engineered, and manufactured to work together. Their patented fiberglass door systems, backed by a lifetime-limited warranty, won't split, crack, warp, or dent. Call for a free catalog and dealer listings.

resource guide

25 DECKS & PORCHES

The Flood Company
Phone: (800) 321-3444
Web site: www.floodco.com
Flood is a 150-year-old, family-owned corporation that makes a variety of paint-related products, including penetrating stains, sealers, wood renewers, and cleaners. The company Web site offers a full rundown of products, information on application tools, and a store locator.

Pg. 518

Hickson Corporation
1955 Lake Park Dr., Suite 250,
Smyrna, GA 30080
Phone: (770) 801-6600
Web site: www.hickson.com
Hickson manufactures pressure-treated wood for decks, landscaping, walkways, gazebos, fences, and picnic tables. For information and building plans, such as "How to Build the Best Deck" and "How to Build Backyard Projects," call or visit their Web site.

Pg. 501

Kroy Building Products
P.O. Box 636, York, NE 68467
Phone: (800) 933-KROY / Fax: (402) 362-6797
Web site: www.kroybp.com
Kroy is a leading manufacturer of vinyl fencing, decks, railing, and related building products. Their nationwide network of licensed fabricators and dealers provides personal service and custom application of vinyl fence and related vinyl products anywhere, backed by a transferable limited lifetime warranty. Call the toll-free number listed above for catalogs and information about low-maintenance vinyl decking.

Pg. 508

26 WALKS, PATIOS & DRIVES

Asphalt Institute
Research Park Drive, P.O. Box 14052,
Lexington, KY 40512-4052
Phone: (606) 288-4960
Web site: www.asphaltinstitute.org
The Asphalt Institute is a U.S.-based association of international petroleum asphalt producers, manufacturers, and affiliated businesses. The Asphalt Institute's mission is to promote the use, benefits, and quality performance of petroleum asphalt, through engineering, research, and educational activities and through the resolution of issues affecting the industry.

Pg. 537

Co-Fair Corporation
4236 Commercial Way, Glenview, IL 60025
Phone: (800) 333-6700
Web site: www.co-fare.com

Co-Fair's products include Driveway Medic, a fast, effective driveway patching system. (The firm stresses that it is not associated with Doctor Driveway.) The company also makes Quick Roof, for repairs of flat and rubberized roofs (modified bitumen), and Bio-Green, a biodegradable ice-melting product that the firm says is more effective than regular salt.

Pg. 539

Unilock
Phone: (800) UNILOCK
Web site: www.unilock.com
Unilock introduced one of the first interlocking paving stone systems over 25 years ago. A series of flexible connectors fitted into slots molded into the blocks allow you to tie blocks together front to back and side to side.

Pg. 543

27 EXTERIOR STRUCTURES

Boundary Fence & Railing Systems
Phone: (800) 628-8928
Web site: www.boundary-fences.com
Boundary manufactures and distributes a variety of fences and railings. The firm does their own fence weaving and either vinyl- or powder-coating. They offer many types of chain-link mesh, hard-to-get fittings, ornamental wood gate hardware, over 150 professional fence tools, razor coil, and a line of 100% PVC fence.

Pg. 546

Cumberland Woodcraft Company
Carlisle, PA 17013
Phone: (800) 367-1884
Web site: www.cumberlandwoodcraft.com
This firm is one of the nation's largest and oldest manufacturers of period architectural millwork and reproduction artifacts. The generally Victorian designs in a line of over 350 products include mantlepieces, bars, sculptural figures, and complete gazebos. All products are made from premium grades of solid, kiln-dried woods for minimum shrinkage, mainly poplar and oak, that are sealed and finished on-site.

Pg. 554

Summerwood Products
733 Progress Ave., Toronto, Ontario M1H 2W7
Phone: (800) 663-5042
Web site: www.summerwood.com
Dozens of shed and gazebo designs are offered, each with many configuration options and extras. For example, you can specify a wall section with single or double doors, screening, or windows. Summerwood also sells their products as precut kits that might take a weekend to assemble, and as pre-assembled packages with siding and other materials already set on wall sections that might take two people only one day to erect.

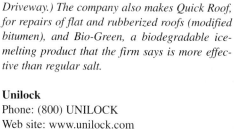
Pg. 554

Heritage Vinyl Products

661 Anderson Ave., Pittsburgh, PA 15220
Phone: (800) 473-3623
Web site: www.heritagevinyl.com
Heritage manufactures fencing and decking made from polyvinyl chloride. The products are covered by a lifetime transferable warranty against discoloring, peeling, blistering, warping, flaking, cracking, corrosion, and insect damage.

Pg. 545

Vixen Hill

Main Street, Elverson, PA 19520
Phone: (800) 423-2766
Web site: www.vixenhill.com
This firm manufactures prefabricated gazebos, custom cedar shutters, teak furniture, and other outdoor wood products. The line of gazebos and pavilions has full precut parts that bolt together. Roof panels have shingles already attached.

Pg. 555

28 YARDS

Ames Lawn and Garden Tools

P.O. Box 1774, Parkersburg, WV 26102
Phone: (800) 624-2654
Web site: www.ames.com
Ames–True Temper claims to be the world's largest manufacturer of non-power lawn and garden tools, including shovels, rakes, pruners and cutters, hose reels, and other equipment. This 225-year-old company reports that its tools have been used to help build many historic projects, such as Mt. Rushmore and the Statue of Liberty.

Pg. 562

Cooperative State Research, Education, and Extension Services (CSREES)

U.S. Dept. of Agriculture, CSREES, Rm. 3328, South Bldg., Washington, DC 20250-0907
Web site: www.reeusda.gov/news/statepartners/usa.htm
The Cooperative Extension Service offers educational outreach to people in a variety of areas, among them agriculture and natural resources. Through its extension agents, numerous publications, and Master Gardener phone information lines, Cooperative Extension Services offer many resources on lawn care. A national directory of services is available in many public libraries and at the Web site listed above.

Pg. 574

Peaceful Valley Farm Supply

P.O. Box 2209, Grass Valley CA 95945
Phone: (888) 784-1722 / Fax: (530) 272-4794
Web site: www.groworganic.com
Features a product line of over 2,000 items for the gardener and landscaper, including a wide variety of garden tools, organic fertilizers and sprays, soil amendments, and soil testing and monitoring instruments. Call for a free catalog.

Pg. 574

The Scotts Company

41 S. High St., Ste. 3500, Columbus, OH 43215
Phone: (800) 543-TURF
Web site: www.scottscompany.com
The Scotts Company, headquartered in Ohio since 1868, is the world's leading producer and marketer of products for do-it-yourself lawn and garden care, professional turf care, and professional horticulture. Scotts products are sold in the United States and throughout the world. Call their toll-free consumer help line listed above.

Pg. 575

Stihl

536 Viking Drive, Virginia Beach, VA 23452
Phone: (800) GO STIHL
Web site: www.stihlusa.com
Stihl manufactures a wide range of outdoor power equipment, including weed and hedge trimmers, blowers, sprayers, and earth augers. But they probably are best known for a complete line of bright-orange chain saws. It ranges from compact, homeowner models to very heavy-duty, long-bar professional tools. The firm has over 8,000 U.S. retail service centers. They provide product information and a dealer locator on their Web site.

Pg. 563

Special Thanks for Tools & Materials

Benjamin Obdyke Inc.	Wood roof underlayment
Carhartt Inc.	Work clothes
Carrier Corp.	Air conditioners
Clyde & Dale's L.L.C.	Sawhorses
Daly Slate Co.	Slate roof tiles
Englert	Metal roofing
Hamilton Manufacturing, Inc.	Insulation products
Hitachi Power Tools	Bench power tools
Innovative Insulation	Insulation products
Jade Industries Inc.	Carpet and rug pads
Kraftmaid Cabinetry	Kitchen cabinets
Makita U.S.A.	Power tools
Merillat Industries	Kitchen cabinets
Milwaukee Electric Tool Corp.	Power tools
Nutone	Fans, vents, lighting
Owens Corning	Insulation Products
Porter-Cable	Power tools
Ratech Industries, Inc.	Insulation products
Ryobi	Power tools
S-B Power Tool	Power tools
Shaker Workshops	Furniture kits
Sloss Industries	Insulation products
Stihl Inc.	Chain saws
Timberland	Work boots and clothes
Westile Roofing Products	Concrete roofing tiles
Williamson-Dickie Mfg. Co.	Work clothes

glossary

Actual dimensions The exact measurements of a piece of lumber, pipe, or masonry. See "Nominal dimensions."

Aerator The unit screwed onto the end of a faucet to control splashing.

Aggregate Crushed stone, gravel, or other material added to cement to make concrete or mortar.

Ampere (amp) A unit of measurement describing the rate of electrical flow.

Anchor bolt A bolt set in concrete that is used to fasten lumber, brackets, or hangers to concrete or masonry walls.

Apron Architectural trim beneath a window stool; also, the wider end of a drive that abuts the street.

Ashlar Stone cut at the quarry to produce smooth blocks that are easily stacked.

Auger Flexible metal cable used to clean out drains; also, a tool used for boring holes in the ground.

Backfill Soil or gravel used to fill in between a foundation or retaining wall and the ground excavated around it.

Baluster One of the vertical supports for a handrail.

Battens Narrow wood strips that typically cover vertical joints between siding boards.

Batter board A level board attached to stakes and used to position strings outlining foundations and footings.

Bay window A window that projects from a wall, creating a niche in the interior.

Beam A steel or wood framing member installed horizontally to support part of a structure's load.

Bearing wall A wall that provides support to the framing above.

Bevel An angled surface not at 90 degrees, typically cut into the edge of a piece of lumber.

Bird's mouth The notch cut near the tail end of a rafter where it fits on a top plate or horizontal framing member.

Blocking Lumber added between studs, joists, rafters, or other framing members to provide a nailing surface, additional strength, or as a fire stop to keep fire from spreading.

Board foot A measurement of wood by volume, equivalent to 1 foot square and 1 inch thick.

Bottom plate The horizontal framing member at the base of a wall.

Bridging Lumber or metal installed in an X-shape between floor joists to stabilize and position the joists.

Btu British thermal unit; the standard measurement of heat energy.

Cable Two or more insulated wires inside a sheathing of plastic or metal.

Cantilever Joists projecting from a wall to create a porch or balcony floor without external supports.

Carcass The basic case of a cabinet.

Casing The exposed trim around windows and doors.

Cement board Cement-based backer board used as an underlayment for tile.

Check valve A valve that allows water to flow in only one direction.

Chord The outer framing members of a roof truss. (See also "Web.")

Circuit breaker A protective device that opens a circuit automatically when a current overload occurs. They can be reset manually.

Cleanout A removable plug in a trap or drainpipe, which allows easier access for removing blockages.

Cleat A block used to support wood braces or other members.

Code The rules set down by local or country goverments that specify minimum building practices.

Collar tie A horizontal board installed rafter to rafter for extra support.

Column A vertical support in a building frame, made of wood, metal, or concrete.

Conduit Metal or plastic tubing designed to enclose electrical wires.

Control joints Joints tooled into the surface that make concrete crack in planned locations.

Cornice Ornamental trim at the meeting of roof and wall (exterior) or at the top of a wall (interior).

Coped joint A curved cut on a piece of trim that makes the reverse image of the piece it must butt against; made with a coping saw.

CPVC Chlorinated polyvinyl chloride; a plastic used to make hot-water pipe.

Cripple studs Short studs that stand vertically between a header and top plate or between a bottom plate and the underside of a rough sill.

Curing Providing proper moisture to a concrete slab to reduce cracking and shrinkage and develop strength.

Dado A wide, flat-bottomed groove cut at a right angle to the grain of the wood. Called a "rabbet" if cut at the edge of a board.

Dead load The weight of a building's components, including lumber, roofing, permanent fixtures, etc.

Deadman Also called a T-brace; a wooden cross brace at the end of a support used to hold a ceiling panel in place until it is fastened.

Deflection The bending of wood due to live and dead loads.

Dormer A shed- or doghouse-like structure that projects from a roof, built to add space to an attic.

Drip edge A metal piece bent to fit over the edge of roof sheathing, designed to channel rain off the roof.

Drywall Gypsum sandwiched between treated paper, used as an interior wall covering. Also called gypsum board or wallboard.

Dry well A hole in the ground filled with rocks or gravel, designed to catch water and help it filter into the soil.

D-W-V Drain-waste-vent; the system of pipes and fittings used to carry away wastewater.

Easement The legal right for one person to cross or use another person's land.

Eaves The lower part of a roof that projects beyond the supporting walls to create an overhang.

Efflorescence A deposit of soluble salts on the surface of masonry.

Elastomeric Made of a material that does not lose shape when subjected to heat or stress.

Escutcheon A metal plate that covers the hole in the wall around a pipe or faucet.

Façade The exterior face of a building.

Face brick A type of brick used when a consistent appearance is needed.

Face-nailing Nailing perpendicularly through the surface of lumber.

Fascia One-by or two-by trim piece nailed onto the end grain or tail end of a rafter to form part of a cornice or soffit.

Finial The decorative element on top of a post.

Fire blocking Horizontal blocking installed between studs to halt the upward progress of fire.

Fire brick A brick made of a special clay and baked at an extremely high temperature to make it resistant to heat.

Fish tape Flexible metal strip used to draw wires and cables through walls and conduits.

Flashing Thin sheets of aluminum, copper, rubber asphalt, or other material used to bridge or cover a space, such as between the roof and a chimney or cap blocks and wall.

Footing The part of a foundation that transmits loads to the soil; also, the base on which a stone wall is built.

Frieze board Trim board nailed horizontally on a building wall directly beneath rafters to provide a nailing surface for soffits and cornice trim.

Frost heave Shifting or upheaval of the ground resulting from alternate freezing and thawing of winter soil.

Frost line The maximum depth to which soil freezes in the winter.

Furring Narrow one-by or two-by wood strips used to create space—for example, between ceilings and joists or between insulated walls and masonry.

Fuse A safety device designed to protect circuits; they shut off the current in case of overload or short circuit.

Gasket Resilient material that seals joints against leaks, such as between door and jamb or pipe and fitting.

Gable roof A roof with two triangular ends.

Gable end The triangular wall section under each end of a gable roof.

Galvanized Coated with zinc to prevent rusting.

Gambrel roof A roof design common on barns and utility buildings that combines two gable roofs of differing slopes.

Girder A horizontal wood or steel member used to support some aspect of a framed structure. Also called a beam.

Ground The connection between electrical circuits or equipment and the earth.

Ground-fault circuit interrupter (GFCI) A device that detects a ground fault or electrical line leakage and immediately shuts down power to that circuit.

Grout A binder and filler applied to the joints between ceramic tile.

Gusset plates Metal or plywood plates used to hold the chords and webs of a truss together.

Gypsum board See "Drywall."

Hardwood Wood that comes from deciduous trees, such as oak and maple.

Header The thick horizontal member that runs above rough openings, like doors and windows, in a building's frame.

Hip jack rafter A rafter that runs from a top plate to a hip rafter.

Hip rafter A rafter that runs at a 45-degree angle from the end of a ridge to a corner of a building.

Hip roof A roof that has a central ridge and slopes in four directions.

HVAC Heating, ventilating, and air-conditioning.

glossary

Isolation joints Strips in concrete formwork separating it from adjacent materials or into discrete sections.

Jack rafters Short rafters that run between a rafter and a top plate or between two rafters in a rough opening.

Jack stud A stud that runs from the bottom plate to the underside of a header. Also called a trimmer.

Jamb The upright surface forming the side in an opening, as for a door, window, or fireplace.

Joist Horizontal framing lumber placed on edge to support subfloors or hold up ceilings.

Joist hanger Bracket used to strengthen the connection between a joist and a piece of lumber into which it butts.

Junction box Metal or plastic box inside which all standard wire splices and wiring connections must be made.

Kerf The narrow slot a saw blade cuts in a piece of lumber, usually about 1/8-inch thick.

Keyway A flat-bottomed notch or indentation created at the top of a footing to allow foundation walls to interlock.

Knockdown Having precut and prefit construction components; usually refers to unassembled furniture.

Lally column A steel pipe usually filled with concrete and used as a support column beneath girders and beams.

Lath Wood strips or metal mesh used as a foundation for plaster or stucco.

Lattice Thin strips of wood crossed to make a pattern for a trellis or arbor.

Leader The downspout in a gutter system; also, the duct that sends hot air to an outlet.

Ledger A horizontal board attached to a beam or other member and used as a shelf-like support for lumber that butts against the beam.

Live load All the loads in a building that are not a permanent part of the structure—such as furniture, people, and wind.

Mastic A thick, pasty adhesive.

Miter A joint in which two boards are joined at angles (usually 45 degrees) to form a corner.

Miter box An open-ended box with precut guides for angled or square saw cuts.

Mortar A mixture used to bind masonry or as a bedding for tile.

Mortise-and-tenon Wood joint where a protrusion (tenon) fits into a recess (mortise), usually at a right angle.

Mudsill Another name for "Sill."

Nominal dimensions In lumber, the premilling measurement for which a piece of lumber is named (i.e., 2x4); in masonry, the measured dimensions of a masonry unit plus one mortar joint.

Oriented-strand board (OSB) Panel material made of wood strands purposely aligned for strength and bonded by phenolic resin.

Particleboard Panel material made from wood flakes held together by resin.

Partition wall A non-load-bearing wall built to divide up interior space.

Paver A brick or other masonry unit designed for walkways and patios.

Penny (Abbreviation: d.) Unit of measurement for nail length, such as a 10d nail, which is 3 inches long.

Pier A concrete base used to support columns, posts, girders, or joists.

Pigtail A short piece of wire used to complete a circuit inside a box.

Pitch Loosely, the slope or angle of a roof; technically, the rise of a roof over its span.

Platform framing The framing method that builds walls, one story at a time, on top of platforms that are built on joists.

Plumb Vertically straight. A line 90 degrees to a level line.

Prehung door A door that's already set in a jamb, with hinges (and sometimes a lockset) preinstalled, ready to be installed in a rough opening.

Pressure treated Wood that has preservatives forced into it under pressure.

PVC Polyvinyl chloride; a plastic used to make drain and vent pipe.

R-value "R" is the measure of a substance's resistance to heat flow. An R-value is a number assigned to insulation. The higher the number, the better the insulation.

Rabbet A cut or groove at the edge of a piece of wood. Another piece fits into it to form a joint.

Raceway Surface wiring system that allows the addition of outlets, switches, and fixtures on top of a finished wall rather than inside.

Rebar Short for "reinforcement bar." Metal bars laid in a grid used to reinforce concrete.

Relief valve A safety device that automatically releases water due to excessive pressure or temperature.

Ridge The horizontal crest of a roof.

Ridgeboard The horizontal board that defines the roof frame's highest point, or ridge. Sometimes called a ridgepole.

Ridge cut The angled cut at the uphill end of a rafter which allows the rafter's end to rest flush against the ridgeboard.

Rim joists Joists that define the outside edges of a platform. Joists that run perpendicular to floor joists and are end-nailed to joist ends are also known as header joists.

Rip To cut wood in the same direction as the grain.

Riser In plumbing, a water-supply pipe that carries water vertically; in carpentry, the vertical part of a stair installed on edge, across the front of the step.

Scarf joint Joint formed when the ends of two pieces of lumber meet in the same plane at a 45-degree angle.

Screeding Using a straight 2x4 to strike off excess concrete poured into a form.

Seat cut (rafter) The horizontal cut in a bird's mouth that fits on a top panel or horizontal framing member.

Setback A local building code that requires structures to be built a certain distance from the street, sidewalk, or property line.

Sheathing Panel material, typically plywood, applied to the outside of a structure. Siding is installed over it.

Shed roof A roof that slopes in one direction only.

Shim A thin wedge of plastic or wood used as blocking to level or plumb doors, windows, and framing lumber.

Sill The horizontal two-by lumber attached directly to the masonry foundation. It supports the building's walls. Also, the piece of wood at the bottom of a window frame, typically angled to shed water.

Sillcock An outdoor water faucet.

Slab-on-grade Concrete foundation that serves as both the building's first floor and the structure's perimeter footings.

Sleepers Strips of wood installed to support a wood floor (as on a concrete slab).

Slope The rise of a roof over its run, expressed as the number of inches of rise per unit of run (usually 12 inches). For example: 6-in-12 means a roof rises 6 inches for every 12 inches of run.

Soffit The board that runs the length of a wall on the underside of the rafters, covering the space between the wall and the fascia.

Soleplate The bottom plate of a stud wall.

Spalling Surface flaking, as on brick or concrete.

Stool A narrow shelf that butts against a windowsill.

Story pole A piece of lumber (usually a 2x4) marked off in required dimensions to determine stair-height layouts and other elevations.

Stringer On stairs, the diagonal boards that support the treads and risers.

Stud Vertical two-by lumber that extends from the bottom plate to the top plate of a wall.

Subfloor The flooring underneath a finished floor, usually plywood or OSB decking installed on floor joists or sleepers.

Tail (rafter) The base or downhill end of a rafter.

Toenailing Driving a nail at an angle into the face of a board so that it penetrates another board beneath or above it.

Top plate The horizontal two-by board nailed to the top of wall studs.

Transformer A device designed to convert the voltage in a circuit to a different level.

Trap The water-filled curved pipe that prevents sewer gas from entering the house through the drainage network.

Trim One-by lumber used as siding corner boards or as finish materials around windows and doors, under eaves, or other architectural elements.

Trimmer See "Jack rafter"; "Jack stud."

Tripwaste Lever-controlled bathtub drain stopper.

Valley rafter A rafter that extends from a ridge to an intersecting corner of the building or another rafter.

Valve seat The part of the valve into which a washer or other piece fits, stopping the flow of water.

Veneer A thin piece or section of wood or masonry.

Volt The unit of measure of electrical force.

Water hammer A knocking in water pipes caused by a sudden change in pressure after a faucet or water valve shuts off.

Watt Unit of measurement of electrical power required or consumed by a fixture or appliance.

Web The inner members of a truss. (See also Chord.)

Weep hole A hole in a wall that allows water to seep through and relieve pressure.

Wythe The vertical section of a masonry wall, equal to the width of one masonry unit.

Zip tool A special tool used to remove courses of aluminum or vinyl siding.

index

index

index

index

index

photo credits

All photography by **John Parsekian**, principle photographer, except where noted.

Contributing photography by:

Merle Henkenius: 13 (bottom right), 66-67 (all), 80-81 (top row), 150-51 (bottom row), 156-57 (all), 160-161 (bottom row), 161 (middle right), 184-85 (all), 192 (all), 197 (all), 212-13 (bottom row), 216-17 (middle row, bottom row), 220 (all), 285 (bottom), 290-95 (all), 296 (bottom row), 297 (all), 298-99 (bottom row), 299 (top left, middle left), 302 (bottom left), 303 (bottom row), 304-5 (all), 306 (top right, middle right, bottom right), 307 (top left, middle row, bottom row), 308 (bottom right), 309 (top right, bottom left, bottom middle), 310 (bottom right), 311 (top right, middle, middle right, bottom row), 318-19 (bottom row), 334-35 (bottom row), 335 (top), 343 (bottom), 353 (all), 354-55 (bottom row), 356 (bottom left, bottom right), 357 (all), 358-59 (bottom row), 367 (top right), 384 (all), 385 (top row, middle row), 395 (all), 451 (middle left), 455 (all), 462 (left), 494-95 (all), 526 (all), 527 (top row, middle left, bottom row), 528 (top right, bottom row), 529 (all), 538 (all), 539 (top row), 546-47 (all), 552-53 (all), 562-63 (bottom row), 563 (top left), 566-67 (all), 569 (all), 572-73 (top row, bottom row), 577 (all)

Brian C. Nieves: 12 (all), 14 (all), 15 (bottom right), 18 (middle row, bottom left), 19 (middle left, middle, bottom left, bottom right), 20 (left column, middle right), 21 (middle left, middle right, bottom row), 22 (bottom left), 23 (middle left, middle, bottom row), 27 (middle column, right column), 29 (all), 30 (all), 31 (top row, upper middle row, lower middle row), 32 (all), 33 (top left, middle), 36-37 (all), 38 (all), 39 (top row, bottom half), 130 (top right) 148 (bottom right), 108 (all), 109 (top left, bottom right), 116-17 (bottom row), 118 (top), 122-23 (all), 154 (bottom), 155 (all), 159 (top left), 161 (top right), 163 (top right, middle left, middle right), 165 (top, middle), 170-71 (all), 178 (top row, middle row), 179 (top half), 186 (top), 187 (top row, middle row, bottom row), 188 (all), 189 (middle row), 190 (middle right), 194 (middle row, bottom right), 196 (all), 200-201 (bottom row), 202-3 (bottom row), 203 (middle row), 225 (top right, bottom right), 250-51 (all), 254 (all), 258 (all), 259 (top left, bottom half), 267 (all), 268 (bottom left), 269 (bottom half), 276 (middle column), 277 (middle & right column), 289 (top row, middle row), 296 (top), 303 (top right), 309 (top left), 311 (top left), 316-17 (all), 343 (top left, top middle, top right), 344 (top right, middle row, bottom middle, bottom right), 345 (top row, bottom row), 346-52 (all), 392-93 (bottom row), 398 (top), 399 (top), 401 (top left, bottom row), 402 (top row, bottom left), 403 (top, bottom), 437 (bottom right), 469 (middle left, middle right), 470 (all), 472-73 (all), 476 (top row, middle row), 477 (top row, middle row), 480 (top row, middle row), 490 (bottom right), 491 (bottom left, bottom middle), 530-33 (all), 534 (top row, middle row), 535 (top left, middle left), 548-49 (top row, bottom row), 557 (all), 559 (all)

CHAPTER 2: TOOLS
Page 19: Celotex (top left)
Page 22: Craftsman by Sears (bottom right)
Page 23: Black & Decker (top left)

CHAPTER 3: FASTENERS & ADHESIVES
Page 27: Paslode (bottom left)
Page 33: Makita, U.S.A. (bottom left)

CHAPTER 4: MASONRY
Page 50-51: Robert Anderson (top & bottom row)
Page 52: David K. Hand (sepia)
Page 52-53: Brick Industry Association (bottom)
Page 54: Prosoco (top)
Page 54-55: Brick Industry Association (bottom)
Page 57: Robert Anderson (all)

CHAPTER 5: FOUNDATIONS
Page 63: Portland Cement Association (all)
Page 65: Zircon Corporation (bottom)
Page 74: U.S. Department of the Interior, Bureau of Reclamation (sepia)
Page 74-75: Robert Anderson (bottom row)
Page 78-79: HouseGuard (bottom row)

CHAPTER 6: WOOD
Page 84: Bangor Convention & Visitors Bureau (sepia)
Page 85: Jorgenson Log Homes (all)
Page 86: Western Wood Products Association (top & middle row)
Page 86: Southern Pine Council (bottom row)
Page 87: APA—The Engineered Wood Association (top & bottom left), Trus Joist Macmillan (bottom right)
Page 88: Agricultural Research Service (top), Dr. James Jarrett, Mississippi State University, Dept. of Entomology (bottom)
Page 89: Agricultural Research Service (top, bottom), Dr. James Jarrett, Mississippi State University, Dept. of Entomology (lower middle)
Page 90: California Redwood Association (top left, top right, upper middle right)
Page 90: Stephen Munz, Oradell, NJ (lower middle right, bottom right)
Page 91: Southern Pine Council (all)
Page 92: Makita, U.S.A (all)
Page 94: APA—The Engineered Wood Association (top)
Page 95: Stephen Munz, Oradell, NJ (all)

CHAPTER 7: FRAMING
Page 105: Rocky Mountain Log Homes (top left), Lindal Cedar Homes (top middle), Haiku Houses (top right), Arkin Tilt Architects (bottom left), Earthwood (bottom right)
Page 109: California Redwood Association (middle left)
Page 114: Western Wood Products Association (top), Trus Joist MacMillian (middle)
Page 124: Ganondagen State Historic Park (Photographer: Frank E. Sadowski) (sepia)
Page 129: North American Steel Framing Alliance (top right)
Page 130: Southern Pine Council (middle row), Manufactured Housing Institute (bottom row)
Page 131: Manufactured Housing Institute (bottom left)

CHAPTER 9: FLOORS & STAIRS
Page 154: Otis Elevator Company (sepia)
Page 158-59: Custom Building Products (bottom row)
Page 159: Custom Building Products (top right, bottom right), Metropolitan Ceramics (upper middle), Dal-Tile (lower middle)
Page 166: Crain Cutter Company, Inc. (top)

CHAPTER 10: WALLS & CEILINGS
Page 174: Georgia-Pacific (top), Eisenhart Wallcoverings (bottom left), Crown Berger (bottom right)
Page 175: USG (top), Tasso (bottom left), York Wallcoverings (bottom right)
Page 177: New England Classic Interiors (top), Georgia-Pacific (middle)
Page 180: Celotex (bottom row)
Page 181: Celotex (top row, middle row, bottom left, bottom middle)
Page 182: Celotex (all)
Page 183: Celotex (top row, bottom left, bottom middle)
Page 187: Wagner Spray Tech Corp. (bottom right)
Page 190: USG (sepia)
Page 190-91: Don Wong (bottom row)

Page 193: Brewster Wallcoverings (all)
Page 194: Delta (top row, lower top middle), American Standard (lower top right)
Page 198: Hy-Lite Block Windows (top right), Pittsburgh Corning (middle row, bottom row)
Page 199: Corian (top), Pittsburgh Corning (bottom row)
Page 200: Elite (top left), Georgia-Pacific (middle left), White River Hardwoods/Woodworks (top right, middle right)
Page 201: Focal Point Architectural Products (top left), White River Hardwoods/Woodworks (middle left, top right)
Page 205: Chicago Metallic Corp. (top row, middle row)

CHAPTER 11: UNFINISHED SPACES
Page 208: Imperial Wallcoverings
Page 209: APA—The Engineered Wood Association (bottom)
Page 210: Certainteed (middle left, top, middle, and bottom right)
Page 212: Murphy Bed Co. (sepia)
Page 214: Celotex (all)
Page 218: Nutone (top left, bottom right), KraftMaid (bottom left)
Page 219: Murphy Bed Co. (top left), Robern (top middle), Pet Doors, U.S.A. (top right), CraftMaster (bottom left), Nutone (bottom middle, bottom right)
Page 221: Western Wood Products Association (top left), Paul M. Schumm/CH (top right), National Kitchen & Bath Association (middle left), KraftMaid (bottom left)

CHAPTER 12: CABINETS & COUNTERS
Page 225: Stephen Munz, Oradell, NJ (right column)
Page 229: International Kitchen & Bath Exchange (top), Amera-Dorchester (middle), AristoKraft (bottom)
Page 232: ILCO Unican Corporation (all)
Page 234: Merillat Industries (sepia)
Page 238: Corian (middle)
Page 240: Jim Roberson (bottom left, bottom right)
Page 242: Kitchen Solvers (top row)
Page 243: Dura-Oak (top half)
Page 247: Merillat Industries (left), National Kitchen & Bath Association (right)

CHAPTER 13: SHELVING & STORAGE
Page 252: Sears, Roebuck, & Co. (sepia)
Page 257: ClosetMaid (top row, middle right)
Page 260: Columbia Forests Products (bottom)

CHAPTER 14: FURNITURE
Page 265: H. Howard Hodgins Jr. (all)
Page 266: Sears, Roebuck & Co. (sepia)
Page 270: H. Howard Hodgins Jr. (middle row)
Page 271: H. Howard Hodgins Jr. (top & middle rows)
Page 272-73: H. Howard Hodgins Jr. (all)
Page 274: Joe Roberson (top & middle row), H. Howard Hodgins Jr. (bottom left)
Page 275: H. Howard Hodgins Jr. (all)
Page 278-79: H. Howard Hodgins Jr. (all)

CHAPTER 15: PLUMBING
Page 288: Sloan Flushmate (top)
Page 300: Sears, Roebuck & Co. (sepia)
Page 303: Moen (top left, middle left), Honeywell (middle)
Page 307: Re-Bath Corporation (top middle, top right)

CHAPTER 16: HEATING
Page 316: Linda L. Riley, Valley Forge Convention & Vistors Bureau (sepia)
Page 321: Honeywell (middle left, middle right) Holmes Products Corp. (middle center)

Metric Conversion

Length

1 inch	2.54 cm
1 foot	30.48 cm
1 yard	91.44 cm
1 mile	1.61 km

Area

1 square inch	6.45 cm²
1 square foot	92.90 cm²
1 square yard	0.84 m²
1 acre	4046.86 m²
1 square mile	2.59 km²

Volume

1 cubic inch	16.39 cm³
1 cubic foot	0.03 m³
1 cubic yard	0.77 m³

Common Lumber Equivalents

Sizes: Metric cross sections are so close to their nearest U.S. sizes, as noted below, that for most purposes they may be considered equivalents.

Dimensional	1 x 2	19 x 38 mm
lumber	1 x 4	19 x 89 mm
	2 x 2	38 x 38 mm
	2 x 4	38 x 89 mm
	2 x 6	38 x 140 mm
	2 x 8	38 x 184 mm
	2 x 10	38 x 235 mm
	2 x 12	38 x 286 mm
Sheet	4 x 8 ft.	1200 x 2400 mm
sizes	4 x 10 ft.	1200 x 3000 mm
Sheet	¼ in.	6 mm
thicknesses	⅜ in.	9 mm
	½ in.	12 mm
	¾ in.	19 mm
Stud/joist	16 in. o.c.	400 mm o.c.
spacing	24 in. o.c.	600 mm o.c.

Capacity

1 fluid ounce	29.57 mL
1 pint	473.18 mL
1 quart	1.14 liters
1 gallon	3.79 liters

Temperature

(Celsius = Fahrenheit − 32 x ⅝)

°F	°C
0	−18
10	−12.22
20	−6.67
30	−1.11
32	0
40	4.44
50	10.00
60	15.56
70	21.11
80	26.67
90	32.22
100	37.78

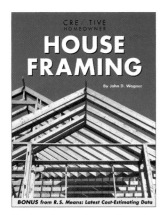

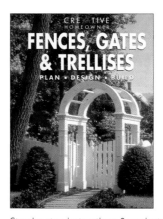
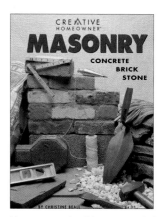
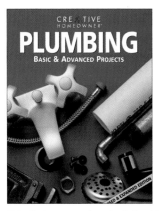

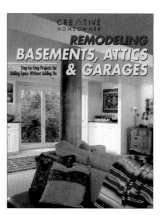
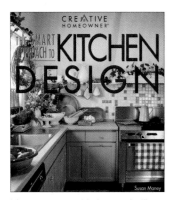

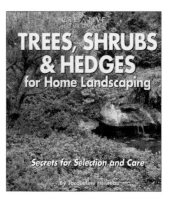